ISBN 978-1-331-98878-6
PIBN 10203225

This book is a reproduction of an important historical work. Forgotten Books uses
state-of-the-art technology to digitally reconstruct the work, preserving the original format
whilst repairing imperfections present in the aged copy. In rare cases, an imperfection in
the original, such as a blemish or missing page, may be replicated in our edition. We do,
however, repair the vast majority of imperfections successfully; any imperfections that
remain are intentionally left to preserve the state of such historical works.

1 MONTH OF
FREE
READING

at
www.ForgottenBooks.com

By purchasing this book you are eligible for one month membership to ForgottenBooks.com, giving you unlimited access to our entire collection of over 700,000 titles via our web site and mobile apps.

To claim your free month visit:
www.forgottenbooks.com/free203225

Similar Books Are Available from
www.forgottenbooks.com

HISTORY OF LONG ISLAND;

CONTAINING

AN ACCOUNT

OF THE

DISCOVERY AND SETTLEMENT;

WITH OTHER

IMPORTANT AND INTERESTING MATTERS

TO THE

PRESENT TIME.

BY BENJAMIN F. THOMPSON,
COUNSELLOR AT LAW.

"History presents *complete* examples. Experience is doubly *defective;* we are born too late to see the *beginning,* and we die too soon to see the *end* of many things. History supplies both of these defects: modern history shows the *causes,* when experience presents the *effects* alone: and ancient history enables us to guess at the *effects,* when experience presents the *causes* alone."
BOLINGBROKE.

NEW-YORK:

PUBLISHED BY E. FRENCH, 146 NASSAU STREET.

1839.

SCATCHERD AND ADAMS, PRINTERS.

To

THE HONORABLE SILAS WOOD,

LATE REPRESENTATIVE IN THE CONGRESS OF THE UNITED
STATES, FROM LONG ISLAND.

SIR:

The idea of dedicating this volume to you was co-
existent with the resolution to enter upon the compilation of it; and surely to no individual could it be
so justly or appropriately inscribed, as to one, to
whose talents, information, and indefatigable industry, the public are deeply indebted for the first attempt to perpetuate the civil and political history of
Long Island. That publication has received, as it deserved, universal approbation; and it is therefore
much to be regretted that your inclination for repose
should have prevented you from preparing a new and
enlarged edition of the " *Sketch of the first Settlement
of the several Towns upon Long Island*," in which event
the present compilation would not have been undertaken. The materials of your work have been so
fully incorporated into the present, as to give it a particular claim to your favor.

With sentiments of esteem and respect, I remain, Sir,

Your obt. Servant,

BENJ. F. THOMPSON.

January 1, 1839.

PREFACE.

In collecting materials for the History of Long Island, the compiler has sought to avail himself of every source of authentic and valuable information applicable to his design of making the work both interesting and useful. How far these endeavors may have been successful, must be submitted to the deliberate consideration of the reader. In justice to himself he can truly say he has avoided no reasonable labor or expense to make the publication worthy the approbation of the public, although he has fallen far short of satisfying himself, or of accomplishing all that he had anticipated on his first setting out. Ornament of style and eloquence of description have not been among the primary objects of the compiler; his principal aim having been throughout to present a brief, yet correct account of such matters in relation to Long Island, as he conceived best worth preserving, and most likely to prove a repository of valuable historical and statistical information. He is, however, constrained to acknowledge that had he, in the commencement, been able to realize in any considerable degree the labor and responsibility he was about to assume, and the obstacles to be encountered in his progress, he would have been most effectually deterred from the undertaking. The almost entire impracticability of describing, with any degree of minuteness, so many towns, villages, and other localities, without incurring the charge of tediousness or repetition, is one of the minor difficulties which the compiler has endeavored as much as possible to avoid. Another and more formidable embarrassment presented itself in the progress of his researches, which was in great measure unexpected, and had well nigh persuaded him to relinquish his further labor after a considerable mass of materials had been collected. This arose from the peculiar condition and deficiency of the records of many of the twenty-one towns which he examined. In general they are almost entirely wanting in matters of antiquity, and in others have been so negligently kept, as to be in great measure incapable of being understood. A few towns are comparatively of recent organization, having formerly been included in the territory of other towns, and of course can possess no records beyond the period of their formation; which is the fact in the towns of North Hempstead and Riverhead. In the town of Brooklyn there are no remaining records reaching beyond the revolution, they having been carried away about the close of the war by some evil-disposed individual. In all the other towns in King's County, excepting Gravesend, the ancient entries are uniformly in the Dutch language; and this practice was in some instances continued for half a century after the conquest in 1664.

The hand-writing in many cases is so peculiar, and so much defaced by time or otherwise injured, as to be in a great degree unintelligible; and those written in the Dutch language more particularly so, even to those who have some acquaintance with the language, now nearly obsolete; and, unless immediate measures are adopted in those towns to have their ancient records transcribed in English while any one can be found competent to the task, they will become not only a sealed book, but, so far as utility is concerned, a mere blank; and the compiler cannot but consider it matter of very sincere regret that so much indifference should prevail regarding the preservation of these venerable records of antiquity. When it is remembered that only two centuries have elapsed since this fair isle, now so far advanced in population and wealth, was the abode of a race of men scarcely elevated in the scale of intelligence above the wild beasts with which the country at that period abounded, it cannot but be matter of some importance, as well as of curiosity, to trace the progress of this strange eventful history, to mark the revolutions of time, and transmit its more important details to posterity. These considerations have been among the leading motives for this undertaking. A native of Long Island himself, and descended from an ancestry coeval with its settlement by Europeans, the compiler has been stimulated with the hope of being enabled to present to the attention of his fellow-citizens a series of valuable and interesting facts and incidents of the olden times. He has had the satisfaction, during the period devoted to this subject, to receive from the kindness of individuals many valuable communications, and for which he begs to express his grateful sense of obligation for favors thus gratuitously bestowed. His acknowledgments are especially due to the Hon. James Kent, Hon. Richard Riker, Joseph W. Moulton, Esq. William

Dunlap, Esq. Dr. Samuel Akerly, and John L. Law-
rence, Esq. of New-York; Hon. Jeremiah Johnson,
Hon. Gabriel Furman, and Benjamin D. Silliman, Esq.
of Brooklyn; Rev. Thomas M. Strong of Flatbush;
Hon. Singleton Mitchill and Robert W. Mott, Esq. of
North Hempstead; Hon. Silas Wood of Huntington;
Dr. James E. Dekay and John Nelson Lloyd, Esq. of
Oysterbay; Rev. Jonathan Hunting and Joseph H.
Goldsmith, Esq. of Southold; Rev. John D. Gardiner
and Luther D. Cook, Esq. of Sagg Harbor; Hon. John
A. King and the Rev. William L. Johnson of Jamaica;
Selah B. Strong, Esq. and General John R. Satterly
of Setauket. From the Hon. Secretary of State, and
the clerks of the several counties and towns upon
upon Long Island, the compiler has experienced the
utmost courtesy; all of whom have evinced their readiness to afford him every opportunity of examining the
records and documents in their possession. The compiler has been largely indebted to the contents of Mr.
Wood's able and comprehensive "Sketch of the First
Settlement of the several Towns upon Long Island,"
the most of which has been incorporated in the pages
of this work. Many valuable matters have also been
found in Mr. Furman's " Notes, Geographical and Historical, relating to the Town of Brooklyn;" and in the
article, Geology of Long Island, the compiler has availed himself of the very scientific and laborious reports
of Mr. Mather, being the most faithful and circumstan-
tial account ever published in relation to Long Island,
and which has been considered of too much importance to be omitted or abridged.

In this compilation, it is presumed something may
be found interesting to all classes of readers; and that

it may hereafter be referred to as a record of facts connected with the first settlement of the country, and with our colonial and revolutionary history. No apology, it is hoped, can be thought necessary for the occasional introduction of the names of individuals, and a few family details, which appeared to the compiler in some measure indispensable to the accomplishment of his object. Short biographical memoirs of some conspicuous characters have been introduced in connection with impartial narrative; and the compiler laments the want of proper materials for the history of others whose lives and actions are associated with the annals of our island. He is aware that much important matter might probably have been procured in time; but this is incident to the very nature of History, which is made up of isolated facts gleaned from an infinity of sources; so that if one should resolve not to publish till every thing was to be collected, his labor would never have an end; and what was already obtained, would in the meantime remain useless to others. Those (says a modern author) who are unacquainted with the nature of such an undertaking, may complain that we should publish before we had filled up all vacancies in our documents, and hence been able, not only to have been completely full upon every head, but at the same time to have given a more continuous narrative of the whole. This object, could it have been obtained, would have been as gratifying to the compiler as to the reader. But we can assure all such as are disposed to censure upon this score, that, had they been obliged to turn over, compare, examine, and collate, as many volumes and defaced records as the compiler has done, they would abandon

2

their censure by the time they had well entered upon their labors. Works of this character will always appear premature, as least to their author, for the reason that there is no end to the accumulation of materials ; and out of the mass of matter presented, he has but a choice of selection, and, after all, must necessarily reject much that is, in itself truly curious and valuable.

When it is considered that there are sufficient materials in the history of an individual town to make a respectable sized volume, the difficulty of comprising any thing like a complete account of twenty-one towns, with much other important matter, in a single volume of five or six hundred pages, will be perfectly apparent, and may constitute some apology for the imperfection of this work.

Finally, should his endeavors to be useful in this instance prove in any considerable degree satisfactory to the community, the compiler will conceive himself amply rewarded for a few months devoted to the accomplishment of an undertaking, which he believes to be of very great consequence both to the present and to future generations.

Hempstead, (L. I.) January 1, 1839.

HISTORY OF LONG ISLAND.

GENERAL DESCRIPTION.

Long Island may be described as the south-easterly portion of the State of New-York, and extending from about 40° 34' to 41° 10' North Latitude, and from 2° 58' to 5° 3' East Longitude from Washington City; being in length, from Fort Hamilton at the Narrows to Montauk Point, nearly one hundred and forty miles, with a mean range North 90° 44' East. Its breadth from the Narrows, as far east as the Peconic Bay, varies from twelve to twenty miles in a distance of ninety miles, widening in a space of forty miles from Brooklyn, and then gradually lessening in width to the head of Peconic Bay. This bay is an irregular sheet of water, into which the Peconic River discharges itself, expanding in width as it proceeds eastwardly from Suffolk Court House, and separating this part of Long Island into two distinct branches,—the northerly branch terminating at Oyster Pond Point, and the southerly branch at the extremity of Montauk; the latter branch being the longest of the two by about twenty miles.

Long Island is bounded on the West partly by the Narrows, partly by New-York Bay and the East River, and partly by Long Island Sound; on the North by the Sound; on the East by the Sound and Gardiner's Bay; and on the South by the Atlantic Ocean, together with the islands called the North and South Brother, and Riker's Island in the East River; Plumb Island, Great and Little Gull Island, Fisher's Island, and Gardiner's Island in the Sound; and Shelter Island, and Robin's Island in Peconic Bay. Probable area of the whole, fifteen hundred square miles, or nine hundred and sixty thousand acres. A ridge or chain of hills, more or less elevated, commences at New Utrecht in King's County, and extends, with occasional interruptions and depressions, to near Oyster Pond Point in the County of Suffolk. In some parts this ridge or spine (as it is sometimes called) is covered by forest, and in others entirely naked, having stones, and frequently rocks of considerable size, upon their very summits, presenting to the geologist and philosopher a curious subject of inquiry and speculation. The surface of the island north of the ridge is in general rough and broken, excepting some of the necks and points that stretch into the Sound, which are, for the most part, level ; while the surface south of the ridge is almost a perfect plain, destitute not only of rocks, but even of stones exceeding in weight a few ounces. On both sides of the island are numerous streams, discharging their contents into bays and harbors, affording convenient sites for various manufacturing establishments ; while the bays themselves are navigable for vessels of considerable size, where they are well protected from storms and heavy winds. On the south side of the island is that remarkable feature in the geography of the country, the great South Bay, extending from Hempstead in Queen's County, to the eastern boundary of Brookhaven—a distance of more than seventy miles of uninterrupted inland navigation. It is in width from two to five miles, and communicating with the sea by a few openings in the beach, the principal of which is opposite the town of Islip, called Fire Island Inlet, and through which most of the vessels enter the bay. In this bay are very extensive tracts of salt marsh, and islands of meadow, furnishing an immense quantity of grass annually to the inhabitants ; and its waters are equally prolific of almost every variety of shell and scale fish, which can never be exhausted. Wild fowl of many kinds, and in countless numbers, are found here, affording a pleasant recreation to the sportsman, and a source of profitable employment to many hundreds of individuals, who pursue it as matter of emolument. Indeed, the country generally, as well as the markets of New-York and Brooklyn, are mostly supplied by the produce of this bay, and is a mine of inexhaustible wealth. The bony fish that abound here are used extensively for fertilizing the soil, and is unsurpassed by any other manure. The beach which separates this bay from the ocean, is composed entirely of sand, which in many places is drifted by the winds into hills of the most fantastic forms, and in other parts is low and flat, scarcely rising a few feet above the level of the ocean. Very great and extraordinary changes are constantly taking place on this beach, exposed, as it is, to the continual action of the winds and the heavy waves of the wide and boisterous Atlantic. While in some parts much of the beach has been washed away, in others large accretions of alluvial matter have been made ; and at the same time the sand is carried onward so as that the guts or inlets are constantly progressing to the westward. In some instances these changes have been so rapid, that persons now living can remember when some of these inlets were miles farther to the eastward than they now are. Some persons have accounted for this progressive alteration from what they suppose to be the indirect effects of the Gulf Stream, which, moving in immense volume with a velocity of five miles the hour without diminution or interruption in an eastwardly direction, sweeping past the American coast from the Gulf of Mexico to Newfoundland, causes a current or eddy upon the shore in an opposite direction ; and its materials being composed of loose sand, is carried onward by the force of the current, and deposited in places to the westward. The existence of such a current upon the southern shore of Long Island is demonstrated by the fact of ordinary occurrence, that goods cast into the sea near the coast will soon be found floating to the west, without the agency of the wind or other cause, than the motion of the water in that direction. In the winter of 1814 and 1815, the bodies of those who were drowned in the wreck of the British Sloop of War, Sylph, as well as parts of the vessel and cabin furniture, were found, in a surprisingly short period after, along the beach to the eastward, even as far as Fire Island, more than fifty miles from the place where the accident occurred. That the existence of this current not being extensively known among mariners may account for some shipwrecks

upon this coast, is to be presumed, as some of them would seem
to be otherwise unaccountable, except from a wilful exposure
of property and life, by intentional casting of vessels upon
the coast. The southern shore of the island is everywhere
inaccessible to vessels of a large class, in consequence of the
flats and sand bars which stretch parallel with, and at a short
distance from, the beach. This is usually denominated the bar,
and in some places there are two, called the outer and the
inner bar.

The north, or Sound shore of Long Island is very irregular, being influenced in shape and form by the numerous bays
and headlands, and is fortified against the wasting effects of the
waves by masses of stones and rocks, projecting in some
places beyond the edge of the cliffs; and where these are not
found, the coast has evidently been worn away to a considerable extent by the sea in the course of centuries. The ridge or
spine of the island has some considerable high hills, and are
seen at a great distance at sea, serving as land-marks to the
sailor nearing the coast. One of these, called Harbor Hill in
the town of North Hempstead, has been ascertained to be 319
feet above tide water; and another in the West Hills, town of
Huntington, 339 feet elevation above the sea. There is, however, reason to believe that both are much higher than has
heretofore been supposed. Long Island Sound, a Mediterra-
nean Sea, separating the island from the main land of Connecticut, is connected with the ocean at each end of the island.
The Sound proper may be said to commence about Throg's
Point, near which place the tides by Sandy Hook and Montauk
generally meet each other. The course of the Sound is about
N. E. for eighteen miles between Stamford and Lloyd's Neck,
in which distance the shores are rugged and the channel
rocky, interrupted by small islands and projecting points. Beyond Lloyd's Neck, the Sound opens into a noble elliptical
expanse, from ten to twenty miles wide; presenting a fine view
of gently rising hills and sloping vallies, forests and cultivated
fields beautifully intermixed. The water of the Sound is in
general sufficient for vessels of the greatest draught, and free
from obstructions to its navigation. Its length is about one

hundred and fifty miles, reckoning from Sandy Hook to Montauk; and its average breadth may be about twelve miles. In some places it is more than twenty. The force of the current between Oyster Pond Point and Plumb Island is very great, but is exceeded by that called the Race in the vicinity of the Gull Islands, which, when increased by a north-east storm, is tremendous.

Proceeding eastwardly from the city of New-York, the East River, as it is generally denominated, has a tortuous course of sixteen miles. From the Battery to the mouth of Harlaem River, eight miles, the course is N. N. E.; and from thence to Throg's Point, east nearly eight miles more. At the bend opposite Harlaem River is the noted pass or strait, called Hell Gate, which is crooked; and from the numerous rocks, islands, eddies, and currents, is somewhat difficult and dangerous, particularly for vessels of large size; and many serious accidents have occurred at this place. The danger, however, is not so great as used to be supposed, or as much so as appears from the agitation of its waters at half tide to a stranger on his visit to the spot. At such times the water forms, by its course among the rocks, noisy whirlpools of terrific aspect, and capable of swallowing up or dashing in pieces the largest ships exposed to their influence. Besides the streams which empty into the Sound from the shore of Long Island, there are several considerable rivers of Connecticut that pour their contents into it from the north; among these may be mentioned the Saugatuc, the Housatonic, the Thames, and the Connecticut. The opinion has sometimes been advanced that the bed of the Sound was at some remote period covered by the waters of a lake; and there are many geological facts in corroboration of the opinion also entertained, that the shores of Long Island and the Island of Manhattan were once contiguous. A tradition is said to have prevailed among the Indians in that quarter that their ancestors could once cross from one side to the other upon the rocks. These shores strongly resemble each other in their character and structure, and the probability of their former union may be supposed as well established as the nature of the case admits.

SOIL AND CLIMATE.

The soil of Long Island is of a diversified character, and it is therefore difficult to give such a description as is applicable to any considerable part of it. Like the surface, it possesses a very great variety. It may be said, in general terms, of the soil upon the north side, the surface of which is undulating, that loam prevails; that upon the south is more sand than loam; while through the middle of the island it is composed chiefly of sand or gravel, covered by a thin stratum of mould formed by the decomposition of vegetable matters through a long series of years. The soil upon the high grounds is in most cases better than that upon the plains, yet that found upon the Points or Necks on both sides of the island are better than any other. The great Hempstead plain is principally composed of a coarse black sand, but possessing enough of inherent fertility to afford a sufficiency of pasture for many thousand cattle and sheep for more than half the year, and, when manured with ashes, is rendered quite productive. There is another extensive tract lying eastward from the Hempstead plains, and reaching to the head of Peconic Bay, composed so entirely of sand as to seem in a great measure incapable of any profitable cultivation by any process at present known. The soil of King's County possesses a greater natural fertility than almost any upon the island, except, perhaps, some parts of Newtown and Flushing. And the lands upon Great Neck, Little Neck, and Cow Neck, are also extremely fertile, and valuable for agricultural purposes. The extensive tracts of salt meadow and marshes, which abound in almost every part, particularly in the great south bay, furnish an immense quantity of healthy and nutritious food for large stocks of cattle, horses, &c. The shell banks, which heretofore existed upon the sites of ancient Indian villages, have been used as a manure with advantage. Upon the south side of the island, and in the towns of Riverhead and Southold, the bony fish has for several years past been the main article relied upon for fertilizing the soil; and the quantity of hay and grain which has been produced by it from a single acre, is extraordinary. The abundance of this kind of fish, and the comparative cheapness of the article, will probably always insure its use in those parts of the island where they are taken with the greatest facility and in the greatest quantity.

There is reason to believe that the farmers of Long Island furnish annually, for transportation to market, a surplus of beef, pork, hay, and grain, amounting to more than \$150,000 in value; and in all probability the produce of the South Bay falls very little short of that sum. The fire-wood sent annually to other places from the bays and harbors of this island must have amounted at least to \$60,000 for the last forty years. The value of a good part of which last article has been returned in ashes and other manure.

The climate of Long Island depends as much upon its insular situation as upon the latitude in which it is situated. The influence of the sea renders it more temperate than many other places in the same latitude in the interior. The humidity of our atmosphere and its variableness of temperature, renders it perhaps less conducive to health and longevity than if it were either colder or warmer, and less liable, at the same time, to great and sudden alterations. In the summer, and generally in the afternoon, the island is almost regularly fanned by a breeze from the ocean, which renders it a desirable place of residence at that enervating season of the year. The same cause melts the snow in winter, and often before it reaches the ground. The west and south-west winds predominate in more than half the months of the year; the thermometer seldom falling below zero in winter, or rising above ninety degrees in summer; the mean temperature being about fifty-one degrees, which is the ordinary temperature of springs and deep wells.

It is well known that the temperature of places in the same latitude is modified by the elevation of the land, the state of cultivation, proximity to the sea, or large bodies of water that do not freeze, and by the course of the prevailing winds. The temperature of the air is supposed to decrease in the same latitude one degree for every 590 feet of elevation above the level of the sea. The elevation of Mexico being 7217 feet above

3

the sea, in latitude 19° 18', reduces the temperature to that of places on a level of the sea in latitude 33° 30'.

The United States are less elevated above the sea than Europe, and the difference is in favor of a milder climate with us. The climate of this country has been estimated to be from 10 to 15 degrees colder than the corresponding latitudes in Europe. From the description of the climate of France and Italy by the Roman writers a few years before the Christian era, the temperature of those countries could not have been materially different from that of the United States at present. Their rivers were frozen solid, and the earth covered with snow more or less of the winter. Experience shows that rivers do not congeal with any degree of solidity until the thermometer is as low as 20, and in the United States in the latitude of Italy. The thermometer at present is seldom below 20 more than a few days during the winter. To produce the effects described, must have required quite as severe frost as now prevails in the same latitude in the United States, if not more so; and the same causes which have produced the change in the climate there, will have the same effect here, so far as they are common to both countries. The clearing up and cultivating the country is the most powerful cause that has contributed to this effect, and will have a great influence in meliorating the climate of the country. The trees which cover an uncultivated country, shield it from the rays of the sun, and deprive the earth of the heat derived usually from that source. It is proved by experiment that the temperature of improved land is ten degrees greater than wood land.

Evaporation and rain are sources of cold, and are more abundant in a country covered with timber; more moisture is supposed to evaporate from the leaves of a given quantity of green timber than from the same extent of water. The influence of these causes is lessened by cultivation; the earth becomes warmer and drier, and the temperature of the air is increased. The air from the sea has also a powerful effect on the climate; the sea being 8 or 10 degrees warmer in winter and colder in summer than the earth, and in proportion as the country is cleared, the air from the sea penetrates further into the country, moderates the heat in summer and the cold in winter ; and operates to render the temperature of the seasons more mild and uniform. The climate is also affected by the course of the winds. Formerly upon Long Island the north-west was the predominant wind in the winter months, and the north-east wind generally prevailed in the spring, and sometimes in the fall ; but at present, as before observed, the west and south-west are predominant in more than half the months in the year. These winds either come from the sea, or blow over a country less cold than that traversed by the north-west and north-east winds, and of course more mild and temperate.

The climate here is evidently undergoing a change, and becoming more uniform than heretofore ; the winters are less severely cold, and the summers not so scorching hot.

The extreme cold, and its long continuance in some seasons at intervals of eight or ten years, is probably attributable to the effect of large bodies of floating ice, which is formed at the Pole, and being detached from the great mass, is brought by the prevailing currents towards our coast, thereby disturbing the ordinary course of the seasons, and making the air, while passing our latitude, much colder and of longer continuance than it would otherwise be.

Thus, in the year 1816 there was frost upon Long Island in every month of the year, and the corn was killed almost universally by the fifth of September. The same cause occasioned the cold summers of 1836 and 1837, but not to the same extent, the floating ice being less extensive, or was carried by the winds further from the shores.

GEOLOGY OF LONG ISLAND.

Long Island does not present as much variety to the observation of the philosopher and geologist as some other parts of the state ; yet there is probably enough to warrant the belief of its gradual formation by natural causes, and that a greater part of the island, if not the whole, has been reclaimed from the ocean.

The discoveries made in excavating the earth to great depths in various places, seem to have left this point no longer a matter of uncertainty or doubt with those who carefully consider the subject. The reasonings and conclusions which these surprising developments have given rise to, are, to the scientific inquirer, most curious and interesting.

It is abundantly demonstrated that very extensive alterations have taken place, and are still in progress upon the shores, and within bays and harbors, by the inroads which the sea is incessantly making in some places, and the large accretions to the land in other locations.

The more extensive and extraordinary marine encroachments have been and are now in continual operation upon the south shore of the island, the materials of which it is generally constructed being incapable of opposing any considerable barrier to the violence of winds and waves, especially during the existence of heavy storms, driving, with inconceivable force and augmented energy, against the soft and yielding substance of the headlands and beaches.

Its effects and ravages are perceptible to the most common observation from one end of the island to the other; yet probably in no one place so palpable as about Gravesend, and particularly in the neighborhood of Coney Island. John Van Dyck, Esq. recollects when the beach at Coney Island was composed of high and extensive sand-hills, where it is now a flat and level beach, sometimes covered by the tides; and he has cut grass upon a part of the beach which is now at a considerable distance in the sea. At other places where the water was of sufficient depth to float vessels of 50 tons, it is now solid ground. Mr. Court Lake, of the same place, aged 79, states that his grandfather, about 110 years ago, cut a quantity of cedar posts upon a part of Coney Island which is now two miles in the ocean; and that he has himself cut fire-wood at a place now a mile and a half from the shore. There was also a house upon Pine Island, owned by one Brown, the site of which is now a great way at sea; and that Plumb Island was once covered by fine timber, where there is none now, the greatest part of the land having washed away.

The following interesting matter, contained in the learned

Reports made to the Legislature by W. W. Mather, Esq., relating to Long Island, is of too much consequence to be omitted.

The coast of Long Island on the south side, from Montauk Point to Nepeague beach, a distance of about 10 miles, is constantly washing away by the action of the heavy surf against the base of the cliffs, protected only by narrow shingle beaches of a few yards or rods in width. The pebbles and boulders of these beaches serve as a partial protection to the cliffs during ordinary tides in calm weather, but even then, by the bouldering action of the surf as it tumbles upon the shore, they are continually grinding into sand and finer materials, and swept far away by the tidal currents. During storms and high tides the surf breaks directly against the base of the cliffs, and as they are formed only of loose materials, as sand and clay with a substratum of boulders, pebbles, gravel, and loam, we can easily appreciate the destructive agency of the heavy waves, rolling in unbroken from the broad Atlantic. The destruction of land from this cause is less than one would be led to suppose, but still it is considerable. The road from Nepeague beach to Montauk Point, which was originally at some distance from the shore, has disappeared in several places by the falling of the cliffs. There are no data by which to estimate the inroads of the sea on this coast, as this part of the island is held in common by many associated individuals, who use it for pasturage, and it is inhabited by three herdsmen only, who are frequently changed, and who live several miles distant from each other.

From Nepeague beach to two miles west of Southampton, the south coast of Long Island is protected by a broad and slightly inclined sand beach, which breaks the force of the surf as it rolls in from the ocean. From Southampton, westward, the coast of the island is protected by long narrow islands, from one mile to five or six distant from the main island.

Some parts of the north shore of the south branch of the island, from Montauk Point towards Sagg Harbor, are washing away, but not so rapidly as on the south side of this branch of the island.

The eastern parts of Gardner's and Plum Islands, which are composed of loose materials, are washing away in consequence of the very strong tidal currents, and the heavy sea rolling in upon their shores from the open ocean. The action upon these coasts is so rapid as to attract the attention of the inhabitants, and calculations even have been made as to the time that will probably elapse before they will have disappeared. Rocks (boulders), that have formed a part of Plum Island, may now be observed at low water a mile or more from the present shore.

Little Gull Island, on which a light-house is located, was disappearing so rapidly a few years since, that it became necessary to protect it from the farther inroads of the ocean by encircling it with a strong sea wall.

Oyster Pond Point is wearing away rapidly, by the combined action of the waves during heavy north-east storms, and the strong tidal current, which flows with great velocity through Plum Gut. A small redoubt, about one quarter of a mile west of the Point, is nearly washed away; and Mr. Latham, the owner of the farm, says, that several rods in width have disappeared since his remembrance. During the heavy storm of the 12th Oct. 1836, the sea made a clear breach over about one quarter of a mile of the eastern part of the Point, washed away all the light materials, and cut a shallow channel through which the tide now flows. The effects of this storm were very marked at many localities on the north shore. The cliffs were undermined, and crumbled or slid down, exposing the geological structure, and presenting beautiful coast sections of the strata. The time subsequent to the storm until the winter set in, was devoted exclusively to meandering the coast on the north part of Suffolk County, in order to inspect in detail the geological structure and phenomena of the alluvial and tertiary deposites.

The destroying action of the sea upon the headlands and cliffs, where currents and a heavy surf beat against the coast, has been considered. Another effect of the sea is, the formation of marine alluvion. It results from the deposition of the materials transported coastwise by tidal and marine currents, and by the action of the waves in the direction of the prevailing winds and storms. The winds which produce the greatest transport of alluvial matter on the coast of Long Island, are from the north-east, during the heavy north-east storms. These storms bring in a heavy sea from the ocean, which, rolling obliquely along the shore, aided by the powerful tidal currents, sweeps the alluvia along in a westerly direction. The north-west winds are nearly as powerful as the north-east, and blow for a much longer period in the year; but do not bring an ocean swell, and the waves which they raise fall upon the shore in a line nearly perpendicular to the trend of the coast; so that their effect is to grind the pebbles and gravel to sand by the action of the surf, rather than to transport them coastwise. In this way, outlets of small bays are frequently more or less obstructed by bars, shoals, and spits, formed by the tidal currents sweeping past their mouths, and depositing the materials in the eddy formed by the meeting of the currents. If the strongest currents and prevailing winds be coincident in direction, the outlet of the harbor will of course be found upon the leeward side.

Almost every bay, inlet, and marsh on the north coast of Long Island, and also on the south coast, where they are not protected from the sea by the long sandy islands which have been mentioned in the preceding article, have their outlets blocked up entirely by the materials deposited, or so nearly as to leave only narrow entrances. Strong currents set along the shore, and these, aided by the oblique action of the surf, roll the pebbles and sand up the beach, which, on the retiring of the waves, are swept again into the surf, having described a semicircular line, and perhaps progressed several feet by the action of a single wave. This mode of transport is seen almost everywhere on these coasts. The cliffs are undermined, and the coarser parts of their wrecks are thus tumbled along from place to place by each succeeding storm. The particular local effects of such causes can only be fully understood by visiting the localities, or having accurate detailed topographical maps, like those now in progress under the supervision of the superintendent of the National Coast Survey. It is hoped that those maps of Long Island will be published before the geological survey of the State of New-York shall have been completed, in order that an accurate, detailed map of this part of the

State may be formed, so as to illustrate the numerous important geological details. The transporting action above alluded to, has been the most effective agent in the formation of the marine alluvians of Long Island. This island has been composed of one principal, and several small detached islands, which are now connected with each other and with the main island. The east end of the island, from Montauk Point to Nepeague beach, seems to have been, at some former time, two separate islands, which have since been connected with each other and with the main island by the westward currents sweeping along detrital matter, derived from the continual destruction of cliffs of loose materials. Nepeague beach is five miles long, a great part of which is loose, drifting sand, enclosing marshes and salt ponds. This beach is so low in some places that the tides frequently overflow it. The skeleton of a whale is said to be now imbedded in these sands. At Fort Pond Bay, a few miles east of Nepeague beach, a narrow strip of shingle, frequently overflowed by the tides, separates the Atlantic from this bay, which is separated from Long Island Sound by a beach sometimes open, but often blocked up with sand. Great Hog Neck and Little Hog Neck, near Sagg Harbor, were once islands, which have been united by a sand and shingle beach, and the latter with the main island. Farrington Neck, a few miles west of these, was an island which is now united with the main island by a low beach. That part of the township of Southold, which is situated on the main island, was originally three islands, now connected with each other and with the main island by beaches and marshes of alluvial formation. The effects of alluvial action can be distinctly seen on the map of Oyster Pond Point. It shows where two of the islands, which were once separated from the east end of the north branch of Long Island, have been connected by a beach and sand spit, enclosing a large pond, with an outlet only wide enough for a mill sluice. A tide mill is constructed at this outlet.

Those long points of alluvion, called sand spits, projecting from the land in the line of the eddy currents, and formed by them, are very common, and are, in fact, the unfinished beaches which will eventually obstruct the outlet of harbors and bays, and connect islands with each other. An interesting alluvial formation is now in progress on the north and north-west sides of Lloyd's Neck, in Huntington, and formed entirely by the deposite of the coarse detrital matter swept along by the current from the destruction of the high cliffs in the vicinity. This deposite is about one quarter of a mile broad, partly marsh and salt pond, protected by a high bank of shingle piled up and continued westward, so that the present outlet of the pond is half a mile further west than it was within a recent period; the shingle having been continually swept westward, while the flux and reflux of the tide through the narrow channel keeps its outlet open.

The ponds and small bays on the south side of Long Island, in the townships of South and East Hampton, frequently have their outlets closed by beaches formed by the detrital matter swept coastwise by the tidal currents and the waves. The long sandy islands on the south coast of Long Island, which protect it from the heavy waves of the Atlantic, are doubtless formed by the same cause. Long Beach is a sand-spit, extending from Ben's Point, near Oyster Pond Point, westward four and one-fourth miles; and has been formed by the detritus swept coastwise, and deposited in the eddy currents. This beach gives safety to Oyster Pond's harbor, by serving as a natural break-water. Two sand-spits were observed in Cold Spring harbor, resulting from causes similar to those above detailed.

The headlands and cliffs on this part of the island are continually wearing away by the action of the sea; and the materials of which they are composed, consisting principally of clay, sand, gravel, and pebbles, are transported by tidal currents, and deposited in other places. The tidal currents, in sweeping along the headlands and cliffs, undermine them, and, transporting the materials from which they are composed, form shoals, block up the mouths of small inlets and creeks, so as to form fresh-water ponds, by preventing the ingress of salt water, throw up sand beaches in front of marshes, form sand-spits across the mouths of harbors, and connect islands with each other and the main land.

4

Huntington Harbor, certainly one of the best on the island, is of alluvial origin.   By reference to the map of Long Island it will be seen that this harbor is formed by two necks of land, Lloyd's Neck on the west and north-west, and Eaton's Neck on the east and north-east.   Lloyd's Neck, which was originally an island, has been connected with the main island by a low sand beach, now overflowed at high water.   Eaton's Neck was formerly a cluster of four islands, which have in some way been connected with each other and with the main island.   A sand-spit, one and one-fourth mile in length, and from ten to twenty rods in width, makes out into the harbor from the south-west part of Eaton's Neck, and adds much to its safety ; as also a similar one from the south-east part of Lloyd's Neck.

There is abundant evidence that this harbor, and the safety of the smaller ones in the vicinity, are the result of alluvial action.   The materials composing the sand-beaches and spits which I have mentioned, are precisely like those now thrown up by the action of the surf ; they consist of pebbles, gravel, and fine siliceous sand, interspersed with water-worn shells belonging to genera and species now living on the coast ; and they are destitute of boulders, which characterise all those low places formed by the degradation of the superincumbent materials.

The beach, connecting Eaton's Neck with the main island, is three and a half miles in length, and ten to thirty rods in width.   Mr. Gardner, who "keeps the light" on Eaton's Neck, informed me, that some years since, a vessel, during a violent storm, having been driven upon this beach, and an excavation made to get her off, marsh mud was found beneath the sand near tide water level, precisely like that in a small marsh on the opposite side of the beach, clearly indicating the manner of formation at that place.

On the north-west part of Eaton's Neck, a sand-beach, one-half or three-fourths of a mile in length, has been thrown up in front of a marsh containing several acres.   It has formed rapidly since the remembrance of Mr. Gardner, who says he has seen sloops, loaded with wood, float in places now some feet above tide water level.

The long stretch of beach connecting Eaton's Neck with the main island, is continued three-fourths of a mile eastward, and is, a part of the way, formed in front of cliffs which it protects from the farther encroachment of the sea, and the remaining distance, before a small pond skirted with marsh, which formerly communicated with the sea by means of a creek, now filled with alluvial sand.

A sand-beach, one-fourth of a mile in length, has been formed between Long Island Sound and Crab Meadows, through which a creek, entering obliquely from the north-west, passes in a serpentine direction through the marsh. By the action of violent winds, the finer particles of sand are formed into hillocks, which are very slowly moving inland.

At Fresh Pond Creek is a similar sand-beach. The small pond at that place communicates with the sea by means of a small creek, which is often filled by alluvial sands, so as to prevent the ingress of the salt water. The obstruction has sometimes been removed by digging, and at others, the water, rising in the pond, bursts its barrier, and finds its way to the ocean, removing every obstacle, and making the channel deeper even than before.

At Sunken Meadows is a sand-beach one-half mile in length, through which a creek enters obliquely from the north-east. Mr. Abraham Smith says that this beach has extended thirty rods in an easterly direction since his remembrance.

On the north part of Crane's Neck is a shingle beach, about a mile in length, between Flax Pond and the Sound. The pond is skirted with marsh, and communicates with the sea by an opening called Flax Pond Gut. The tidal current is so strong on this part of the coast, that the finer materials have been carried onwards; while the coarser, consisting of pebbles, varying in size from a marble to two or three inches in diameter, have been left to form this beach. A large proportion of the finer materials appear to have been swept to the south-west part of the neck, where, having been deposited, they form shoals, and a long sand-beach between the sea and a marsh of several acres in extent.

By the action of water on the headlands, sand-spits have

been formed across the mouths of Old Man's, Drown Meadow, Setauket, Stony Brook, and Smithtown harbors.   They are rendered safer by these alluvial deposites, but they afford shelter only to vessels of small burthen, on account of sand-bars, which extend from the extreme points of the sand-spits across their entrances, which, I am informed, in some instances, are moving westward.

Land-slides, on a small scale, are a very common occurrence on the north coast of Long Island.   They are in some places caused by the sea undermining the cliffs, so that the superincumbent masses crack off at a short distance from their edges, and slide down to a lower level, carrying with them trees and shrubs, and sometimes without even changing their relative position.   Where the cliffs are high, they present the appearance of steps, in consequence of the successive slides.   A great number of examples of these slides may be seen a little west of Petty's Bight, between Hudson's and Roanoke Points, and between Eastbrook and Swezey's landing.   One of the most remarkable slides is at Fresh Pond Creek.   The land having thus slidden down within the reach of the surf, is carried away at high tides and during storms, thus allowing new slides to take place in succession.

Sand-dunes are low hills of loose sand, which have been piled up by the wind like drifting snow heaps, and, like them, are frequently changing their magnitude and position ; so that, in some places, productive lands are buried by the moving materials, while in others they are uncovered by their removal. An instance was mentioned to me of land in Southampton having been inundated by sand, and after a lapse of about fifty years, it was uncovered by its drifting off.   On sea-coasts, and in some other places in the interior of a country, the atmosphere is often clouded during high winds with the lighter particles of drifting sand, while the heavier are rolled along on the surface.   Every obstacle which creates an eddy current in the wind, as a rock, fence, bush or tree, causes a deposite of sand, which often serves as a nucleus of a hillock.   The sand-banks, when first formed, present almost as much variety of outline and form as snow-drifts after a snow-storm.   Examples were

own Meadow,
They are ren-
rd shelter only
ars, which ex-
cross their en-
:s, are moving

on occurrence
n some places
that the super-
ice from their

observed on the north shore of Long Island during the heavy winds of October, where heaps of drift sand, two or three feet deep, were formed in a few hours behind boulders and blocks of rock, which created eddy currents in the wind. Sand-banks, several feet deep, were observed in some of the ravines next the beach, that had been formed between the time of the storm of the 12th, and the time observed on the 17th of October. A small pond near Horton's Point has been converted into a meadow by the drifting sand filling it up, within the remembrance of Mr. Horton of Southold.

The sand-dunes along the shore are so prominent as to mark the line of coast in many places, when seen at the distance of several miles, presenting a very broken, undulating or serrated outline of white hillocks, from ten to forty feet high. On almost all the beaches are hillocks of drift sand, and in many places the high bluffs on the north coast are capped with them. Jacob's Hill, north-west of Mattituck, was once much higher than Cooper's Hill east of it; but the sand has blown off, so that it is now much lower at the former place. Some arable land has been covered over, and red cedar trees have been buried by the drift sand. The grounds occupied by the dunes are exceedingly irregular in form; in some places covered with small round-backed hills, with deep, irregular or bowl-shaped valleys, formed by the wind scooping the sand out where it is not confined by the roots of the scanty vegetation that gains a foothold in some places.

The south shore of Long Island, from Nepeague Beach to Southampton, is skirted with a line of sand-hills, presenting a very irregular, broken appearance in the distance. Nepeague beach is covered for a considerable breadth with loose, drifting sands, forming small hillocks of almost every variety of shape. The *South Beach* of Long Island is almost entirely a line of hillocks, and is composed of a chain of long narrow islands o land, from one to six miles from the main land.

Three kinds of sand are found on Long Island, viz. : siliceous sand, garnet sand, and iron sand. These sands are mixed with each other in variable proportions. They result, as has before been remarked, from the degradation of land, the disin-

le sand-banks,
iety of outline
xamples were

tegration of boulders, and the grinding up of pebbles by the action of the surf.

The siliceous sand is found everywhere along the coast, and constitutes most of the soil of the island. In some localities it contains grains of red and yellow feldspar; in others, grains of black hornblende. Much of it is of good quality for the manufacture of common glass, for sawing marble, and for making mortar.

Red garnet sand is not uncommon on the shore. In some operations this sand may perhaps be used as a substitute for emery.

Magnetic iron sand is found in small quantities along the whole coast of Long Island where the surf beats on the shore. It is so abundant in some localities after storms, that perhaps it may be collected for blotting sand and for iron ore. Layers of it, two or three inches thick, were seen in many places.

Garnet and iron sands both occur more abundantly after storms; and the reason is, that the surf, as it rolls upon the beach, carries the various kinds of sand along with it, and during the reflux of the wave the water washes back the lighter grains, leaving the heavy sands behind. Each wave repeats this process, and the garnet and iron sands thus accumulate in layers. The same principle is applied in the artificial separation of metals and ores from sand and pulverized rocks in metallurgic operations.

Salt marshes are very extensive on the coast of Long Island, and they are of much value for meadow lands. These alluvions result from a combination of several causes. The first step in their formation is, the deposite of a sand or a shingle beach, by marine currents sweeping along detrital matter, and depositing it in the eddy currents in front of shallow bays and re-enterings of the coast, so as to shelter these spaces from the action of the surf if they were before exposed to it; they are also made shallower by the sand and silt carried in bv the tide, the deposites from the surface waters of the adjacent country, and by sand drifted from the beach. Not only marine animals and plants, by their growth and decay, add new matter to the gradually shoaling pond or bay; but the accumulation of drifted sea-weed, trees, &c., serve to increase the alluvion at every successive storm. These various causes combined, gradually shoal the water with alluvial depositions, until marsh grass finally takes root upon the surface. In the formation of these marine alluvions, vegetable remains far exceed the other materials in volume, so that an imperfect marine peat results. The marine peat observed in most localities is of inferior quality : it is light and spongy, containing undecomposed vegetable matter.

Sand-stones, conglomerates and brown iron ore, are continually forming, in small quantities, in several localities, by the action of mineral springs, and by the decomposition of pyrites. At Broad Meadow Point, called also Iron Point, two or three miles east of Riverhead in Suffolk County, this recent sandstone may be seen, at low water, in thick, solid masses. It may also be seen in the sand cliffs between Roanoke Point and Mattituck Inlet.

Nodular masses of iron pyrites are not uncommon in the pebble beds of Suffolk County, and by their decomposition, form brown oxide of iron or haematite, enveloping the adjacent substances which serve as nuclei. When nodules of clay, or decomposable stones are thus enveloped, geodes of brown haemetite are the result. These are abundant at the high cliff on the north-east side of Lloyd's Neck, in Huntington. Where these geodes are numerous, a kind of ferruginous conglomerate is formed of gravel, pebbles, and geodes. At the above locality, the geodes and conglomerate were confined to a stratum of only a few inches in thickness. Two geodes were found filled with water.

The erratic blocks of Suffolk County are of some importance, as they furnish the only rocks for building and wall stones.

There is one circumstance connected with these boulders which we will mention, on account of the bearing it has upon some questions in the scientific part of geology. We will state only general facts, without entering at this time into the minute details, or the conclusions to be drawn from them. The boulders and blocks vary in size from a pebble to masses weighing several hundred tons, and are mostly found on the range of hills running through the island, and between them and the north shore. The boulders and blocks are contained in a stratum which is inter-stratified with deposites of sand, clay and gravel, and is often exposed along the coast. Some of the blocks, when first disinterred, exhibit scratches upon one or more of their sides. Rocks, like those occurring on Long Island, are found in Rhode Island, Connecticut, and along the Hudson river; and they are so similar in their mineralogical characters and associations, as to lead to the conclusion that they were originally derived from those places. Again, as we progress westward from Montauk Point to Brooklyn, along the north shore, there is a regular succession of the groups of boulders, pebbles and gravel, corresponding to the successive changes in the rocks on the north side of the Sound. For example, the boulders on the east end of Long Island are like the granite, gneiss, mica slate, green-stone, and sienite of Rhode Island and the east part of Connecticut; further westward, opposite New London and the mouth of Connecticut river, are boulders like the New London and Connecticut river granites, gneiss and hornblende rock; opposite New Haven are found the red sandstone and conglomerate, fissile and micaceous red sandstone, trap conglomerate, compact trap, amygdaloid and verd antique; opposite Black Rock are the granites, gneiss, hornblende, quartz and white limestone, like those in Fairfield County; and from Huntington to Brooklyn, the trap (compact, crystalline, &c.) red sandstone, gneiss, granite, hornblende rock, serpentine and crystalline limestone, are found identical in appearance with those of the country between New Jersey and Connecticut.

The clays of Suffolk County are so abundant and varied in their character, as to be adapted to various useful purposes. The beds are extensively wrought in some places, and the clays are mostly used for the manufacture of bricks; from four to five millions of which are annually made at West Neck in the town of Huntington alone.

White clays, which have the external characters of potter's clay, occur on West Neck, Lloyd's Neck, Eaton's Neck, East Neck, and Little Neck.

Brown clays, suitable for stone ware, and others for coarse

pottery, abound in many places in the west part of the county. Both the white and brown clays are carried to distant parts for these manufactures. Some of the clays have the external appearance of good fire clays, but actual experiment only can determine their fitness for this use. These clays contain no lime, and therefore are far less likely to melt in the fire than ordinary clays.

Some of the clay beds on West Neck and Lloyd's Neck are ochreous, and perhaps they may be profitably used in the manufacture of yellow ochre.

Fossil wood, or lignite, has been found in several places in the clays, and in their associated beds of sand and gravel, but in no instance in sufficient quantity for fuel. Sometimes it appears like charcoal, in others it is changed to iron ore, either hematite or pyrites. It was seen on Lloyd's Neck, Eaton's Neck, East Neck, Little Neck, and Mount Misery; and has been found in many places from 20 to 100 feet below the soil.

Peat, although not very abundant in Queen's, King's, and Richmond Counties, is very common. Many localities were observed. Those of the most importance are near Newtown. From a bog one mile westerly from Newtown, peat of a very superior quality has been dug for more than fifty years, and it is much used by some of the inhabitants. An extensive marsh of peat, which is probably deep and of fine quality, lies near the road from Williamsburgh to Jamaica, and is called the Cedar Swamp.

There may be about 30,000 cords of peat in this swamp. Small bodies of this combustible were seen in the ranges of hills in King's and Richmond counties. A meadow of two or three acres of ligneous peat was observed about one mile north of Jamaica. The owners of quagmires or quaking meadows will do well to examine them. Before many years shall have elapsed, these bogs will become valuable, where they are now regarded as nearly worthless. The inferior qualities of peat will, under judicious treatment in compost heaps, make a valuable manure.

The principal marshes of Long Island are, Nepeague Marsh; one between Sagg Pond and Mecock Bay, east part of Shinnecock Bay; between Moriches and Great West Bay; between

5

Ocombamack Neck and Fire-Place; between Ocombamack Neck and Patchogue; Patchogue and Nicolls's Neck; and the very extensive one from Nicolls's Neck to Rockaway; and those about Jamaica Bay and Coney Island.

There are also many on the north shore of Long Island, the principal of which are at Acabonnick, Oyster Ponds, Riverhead, Wading River, Smithtown Harbor, Crab Meadow, Lloyd's Neck, Oyster Bay Harbor; between Peacock and Oak Neck, Musquito Cove, north part of Cow Neck, Little Neck Bay, Flushing, Williamsburgh, Brooklyn, and Gowannus.

The salt marshes of Suffolk County are estimated to cover an area of 55 square miles; of Queen's County, 40 square miles; King's, 12 square miles; and Richmond 9 square miles; making an aggregate of 116 square miles, or 74,246 acres, of marsh alluvion of the south coast of New-York, exclusive of the extensive marshes on the south coast of Westchester County, which would probably swell the aggregate to 125 square miles, or 80,000 acres.

The headlands, generally, on the north shore of Queen's County are washing away. The blocks of rock, which were once imbedded in the loose soil of the island, are seen on the beach extending out far beyond low-water mark.

At Oak Neck, Fox Island, and Martinecock, as well as at Middle Island (commonly called Hog Island), the boulders extend far out at low water, and demonstrate the encroachment of the sea on the land. Middle Island and Oak Neck are parts of a peninsula which lies between Oyster Bay and Long Island Sound. They were once islands, but have been connected with each other, and with Long Island, by beaches formed of detrital matter swept from the headlands of Middle Island and Oak Neck. Extensive salt marshes are forming under the protection of these beaches, and are materially increased by the sand drifted from them. These beaches are observed to vary in form and magnitude, being sometimes increased or diminished in particular by the effects of a single storm. Fox Island (so called) was once an island, but is now connected with Oak Neck and Long Island on the east by a long beach. A long sand-spit, of a mile and a half in length, extends to near Peacock's, where it is cut off by an inlet, which communicates with the extensive marsh between Fox Island and Long Island. This beach and spit are derived from the materials washed from Fox Island and Oak Neck. Peacock's Point is also washing away. Stumps and logs of wood are seen below low-water mark. Martinecock Point, a mile or more west of Peacock's, must have washed away rapidly. A long point of boulders and blocks stretches far out into the Sound at ebb tide. This was once an island, which is also connected with Peacock's by a long sand beach. Another ancient island, now connected with Long Island on the south-west by a beach, is very near Martinecock on the west. These two islands and beaches enclose a large pond, the inlet of which is through a mill sluice between them. Mr Jacob Latting, who is an old and respectable inhabitant, and has been a resident in the vicinity more than half a century, informed us that these have been worn away many rods within his recollection. Mr. Latting pointed out to us the position of the beach between Peacock's and Fox Island during the revolution. The beach then dammed up the outlet of a marsh, through which a small stream ran, and a trunk was put in the beach in 1778, to allow the water to drain through, in order to prevent flooding the meadows. We saw the trunk in its original position. The beach has since made out about 200 yards in front of where it was at that time. He observed that these beaches are subject to considerable variations by storms, the materials being tumbled along either eastward or westward, according to the direction of the wind.

Sands's Point, on which a light-house has been long built, was washing away so rapidly some years since, that it became necessary to protect it by building a strong sea-wall along the shore. A reef of rocks, (the remains of ancient lands,) extends out some distance from the shore. The wall has afforded a protection against the encroachment of the sea, and about an acre of land has been added to that belonging to the United States, in consequence of the alluvial action of the surf depositing the sand and shingle in the eddy on the south side of the point. Mr. Mason, the keeper of the light-house, communicated these facts, and many others of much interest. The broad and extensive sand beach south of Sands's Point, a mile or more in length, was, since his remembrance, a salt marsh covered with grass. Mr. Mason is nearly 80 years of age. The materials swept from Sands's Point, and deposited on the edge of the marsh, have been drifted and washed over its surface.

At and near Kidd's Rock, three quarters of a mile eastward of Sands's Point, the wasting of the cliffs from the effects of the waves is very evident. The cliffs present mural escarpments towards the Sound, but the hills slope down gradually on the other side towards the salt marsh. This elevated land was formerly an island, but alluvial causes have formed a salt marsh where the water was sheltered from the sea. The wasting of the cliffs has caused the formation of long beaches--one connecting Kidd's Point with Sands's Point, and the other connecting with the high grounds south-east of the marsh on the west side of Hempstead Harbor. A small inlet through the north end of this beach allows the tide to communicate with the marsh. Boulders and blocks are seen imbedded in the strata forming the mural escarpments, and the shore below is also strewed with them. They also extend some distance from the coast, indicating that a considerable breadth of land has been washed away. The boulders protect the shore for a time, but the smaller ones and the shingle are gradually ground up by the action of the surf, and washed away; and during storms and high tides, fresh inroads are made. The beach between Kidd's Point and Sands's Point covers a part of the marsh, the ooze and marine peat of which may be seen at the foot of the beach at ebb tide. This indicates that high land, or else a beach, was once farther seaward, to afford protection for the formation of that part of the marsh. Only a few acres of high land remain at Kidd's Point, and if it should continue to be washed away as heretofore, (and much expense would be necessary to prevent it,) a century or two would be sufficient to effect its entire removal. Kidd's Rock as it is called, is a remarkable erratic block, which was imbedded in the loam of the tertiary formation. It has been undermined by the action of the sea, and has slid down to the shore, and cracked into many large fragments. These fragments probably weigh at least 2,000 tons; and several sloop loads of it have been shipped to New-York for building-stone.

A sand-spit has formed nearly across Hempstead Harbor, about three miles south of the mouth of the bay, and two miles north of the village of Montrose, at the head of the bay. It extends from the west shore, in an easterly direction, nearly across the harbor, leaving a deep inlet of one hundred to one hundred and fifty yards wide next to the eastern shore. It is owing to the same cause as the spit at Cold Spring. This spit is probably a thousand yards in length, but is not materially affected by storms. The detrital matter, *now* swept coastwise, is carried *through* the inlet and deposited in the inner harbor. Two large shoals have thus been formed, and it is said they are evidently becoming shallower every year, and at no distant time will form a considerable addition to the land. A small spit extends from the eastern shore a short distance north of the east end of the large one. Another spit, which extends on the west side of the bay, from the high bank on the west side of the harbor towards Kidd's Point, is separated from this point only by an inlet of thirty or forty yards, through which the tide flows into the marsh behind Kidd's Island. It is formed from the detrital matter both of this bank and of Kidd's Point.

A spit of some hundred yards in length extends from the north, partly across the mouth of Plandome Bay. It is derived from the detritus of some high banks in the bay, and Barker's Point on the north.

The beaches and spits we have been considering are trifling in extent and importance when compared with the Great South Beach of Long Island. This is a line of alluvial sand and shingle, extending from Nepeague, in East Hampton, to the mouth of New-York Bay, a distance of 104 miles; and having a direction of about west-south-west. It is not continuous, but is divided by inlets communicating with the bays which are situated between this and Long Island, and through these inlets the tide ebbs and flows. At Quogue, and several places east of this, Long Island communicates with the beach, either by marshes or by the upland; but westward, for about seventy miles, a continuous line of bays, from half a mile to six miles broad, extends uninterruptedly, and separates the beach entirely from Long Island.   This Great Beach is a line of spits and islands.   One of the islands is about twenty-five miles long, with a breadth of a few hundred yards.   They are all narrow and long; and when above the reach of the surf, they are covered by a labyrinth of hillocks of drifted sand, imitating almost all the variety of form which snow-drifts present after a storm.

Rockaway Neck is the only locality west of Southampton where the upland of Long Island approaches near the alluvial beach.   The land through this distance is increasing in area by constant depositions.   The beach at Far Rockaway, and for many miles east and west, is undergoing frequent local changes.   The surf frequently washes away several rods in width during a single storm, and perhaps the next storm adds more than had been removed by the preceding.   The sea frequently makes inlets through the beach to the bays and marshes, and as frequently fills up others.

The inlet at Rockaway Bay, called Hog Island Inlet, is continually progressing westward by the oblique action of the surf driving the sand, gravel, and shingle in that direction.   The deposite of these materials on the west end of the island beach tends to obstruct the inlet to the bay ; but the strong tidal current during the flow and ebb of the tide washes away the east end of Rockaway Beach as rapidly as the other forms.   The inlet is thus kept open.   Mr. Edmund Hicks, of Far Rockaway, has been long a resident here, and to him we are indebted for the fact just mentioned.   He knows Hog Island Inlet to have progressed more than a mile to the west within fifty years.

New Inlet is the main inlet from the ocean to the Great South Bay.   It was formed during a storm not many years ago.

Crow Inlet and Jones's Inlet are undergoing changes analogous to that of Hog Island Inlet.

Barren and Coney Islands are a part of the Great South Beach of Long Island.

Coney Island has already been referred to as washing away by the waves and marine currents.   It is alluvial, with the exception of a very small tract of tertiary, and is separated from Long Island by a small creek which winds through the salt marsh. Mr. Wyckoff, who has lived for many years on the island, remembers when this was a broad inlet; but it has been gradually filled up with silt, organic alluvions, and drift sand, until it is reduced to its present size.

The south part of Coney Island is a labyrinth of sand dunes, formed by the wind, which present almost every imaginable shape that such material can assume. These hillocks are from 5 to 30 feet high, with a few straggling tufts of beach-grass, and clumps of bushes half buried in the drifted sands. They owe their origin to a tuft of grass, a bush, or a drift log, serving as a nucleus. As the grass grows, the drifted sand settles among its leaves and partly buries it, and the process is renewed for years until a sand hill is formed. On the contrary, when there is nothing to bind the sand together or shelter it from the wind, it drifts away, leaving deep hollows. Drifted snow banks afford an apt illustration of the sand dunes of the south beach of Long Island, and in a high wind we can realize, in a small degree, the sand storms of the African and Arabian deserts.

The encroachments of the sea upon the east end of Long Island have before been mentioned. Vast masses of the cliffs of loam. sand, gravel, and loose rocks, of which Long Island is composed, are undermined and washed away by every storm. The water of the ocean coast is almost always found to have more or less earthy matter in suspension, much of which, except during storms, is derived from the grinding up of the pebbles, gravel, and sand by the action of the surf. It is estimated by Mr. Mather that at least one thousand tons of matter is thus transported daily from the coast of Long Island, and that probably that quantity, on an average, is daily removed from the south coast between Montauk and Nepeague Beach. This shore, of fifteen miles in length, probably averages sixty feet in height, and is rapidly washing away; and nearly one half the matter coming from the degradation of the land is supposed to be swept coastwise in a westerly direction.

There are many evidences that the east end of Long Island was once much larger than at present, and it is thought probable it may have been connected with Block Island, which lies in the direction of the prolongation of the island. But if these evidences were insufficient, the present rapid degradation of the coast in that vicinity, the constant transportation of matter westward upon the Great Beach, and the extent of this beach (more than one hundred miles long, with a breadth of one hundred to one thousand yards,) which is the result of this action, would, by most minds, be deemed conclusive.

The masses forming the erratic block group, and *terrain de transport*, are composed of blocks, boulders, pebbles, gravel, sand, loam, and clay, which are formed of the broken-up rocks reduced to various degrees of fineness, and transported a distance from their original situation.

The erratic blocks of Suffolk County, and the facts relative to their general distribution, were before alluded to. These blocks are the only wall stones and building stones on Long Island and the contiguous islands, with the exception of a small tract of gneiss in places near Hurlgate. The boulders and erratic blocks are found on the surface, and imbedded in a series of strata forming the range of hills which extend through Staten, Long, Plum, and Fisher's Islands. The boulders on Long Island are rarely found south of the hills, but on the north they are observed, both imbedded and on the surface, extending to the north shore. The varieties of rock forming the boulders in Suffolk County were mentioned before as being exactly similar, in all their characters, to rocks of granite, gneiss, mica, slate, hornblendic rocks, scienite, greenstone, serpentine rocks, verd antique, red and gray sandstones, &c. which occur in place in a northward direction from the localities where they are now found. It has also been observed that the general direction of these boulders form beds of similar rock in place, does not coincide with the line of bearing of the strata, or the direction of the hills. In Queen's and King's Counties the same general facts are observed. Granitic and gneissoid rocks predominate on the hills and shore from Oyster Bay to Little Neck Bay; and thence to Brooklyn, greenstone rocks are most abundant. The various rocks occurring on Long Island as erratic blocks, are much used for fences, wall-stones in wells, cellars, and basements of buildings. They are nearly indestructible by atmospheric agents, and will therefore be very durable. The sea-wall at Sands's Point is built of fragments of the boulders found in the immediate vicinity.

Some of the erratic blocks are of great magnitude. Hundreds of them have been seén that would weigh 50 tons each. Kidd's Rock has already been mentioned as a large erratic block, the fragments of which cover an area of 10 to 15 square rods, and weigh at least 2,000 tons. A large block was seen, half a mile to a mile south-south-east from the churches in Plandome, called Millstone Rock, and from an observation of its cubic contents, it was estimated to weigh 1,800 tons.

Some blocks of limestone, weighing from one to five tons each, were seen on the beach at Kidd's Island, half a mile from Sands's Point, which are precisely similar in mineralogical characters to the range of limestone extending from Barnegat to Pine Plains in Dutchess County.

Adjacent to these, were blocks of tremolite, of a yellowish grey color, and a species of grey amphibole, nearly like the Edenite of Orange County. On the north shore of Oak Neck, masses of granite, containing yellow feldspar, were observed. We have never seen granite in place similar to this. Red sandstone, and a few boulders of greenstone, also occur here.

A boulder weighing three or four tons, of dark green serpentine, containing radiated anthrophyllite, was found half a mile south-west of the head of Little Neck Bay. A large boulder of gray tremolite was found on the east shore of Cow Bay, in Plandome. Boulders of steatite and of talcose rock, containing anthrophyllite, were seen near the head of Little Neck Bay. Boulders of green, black, and sandy green serpentine, like those of Hoboken and York Island, are found at Brooklyn, Williamsburgh, and Jamaica. Boulders of a peculiar rock, composed of the materials of granite, with the feldspar in a state of decomposition, are found at Flushing, Williamburgh, Brooklyn, and on Staten Island. Boulders of granular white limestone, sometimes containing tremolite, occur at Hog Island, Lloyd's Neck, Oak Neck, Sands's Point, Hewlet's Point, Flushing, and Williamsburgh. They are similar to the limestones of Westchester

6

County.   Near Fort Hamilton, serpentine, greenstone, and red
sandstone, with some granite and gneiss, like those of York Island, form the mass of boulders.

Clays are not very abundant in Queen's, King's, and Richmond Counties.   White and blue clays, like those of West
Neck, Lloyd's Neck, Eaton's Neck, &c. are found on Middle
Island and the eastern shore of Hempstead Harbor ; but they
are so near the water level, where they were seen, that there
is little probability of their being extensively useful.   The
white clay on the western side of Middle Island is very pure,
lying in view at high-water mark, and perhaps extending higher in the bank, but covered with sand which has slidden from
above.   Reddish loamy clay was seen in the deep excavation
of the streets through the hill between Brooklyn and Gowannus.   An imperfect sandy brick earth occurs on the hills about
one mile north of Jamaica.   At this place from 300,000 to
350,000 bricks are made per annum.

On Hempstead Plains the wells are dug from 60 to 120 feet
deep, through beds of gravel and sand, before water is reached, which is a little above the level of the ocean.   The wells gradually decrease in depth thence to the shore.

The springs of Long Island are numerous, and present some
phenomena worthy of consideration.   Around the heads of the
bays and re-enterings of the coast along the north shore of
Long Island, copious springs break out very little above tide
water level.   In some instances they boil up through the sand
and gravel so as to form a brook at once ; in others, several
springs break out at the foot of the bank, and, uniting their waters, form a stream.   The numerous mills and manufactories
on the shores of many of the re-enterings of the northern coast
of Long Island, and which have no apparent streams communicating with their ponds to renew the supply of water, attract
the attention of most observers.   The water of these springs is
very pure, in consequence of its having been filtered through
beds of nearly pure siliceous sand and gravel.   It is thrown out
at the level of tide water, or at a higher level, where there are
strata impermeable to it.   Some of the most remarkable of these
springs, which are applied to manufacturing purposes, are about

Hempstead Harbor, at the head of Little Neck Bay, at the head of Cold Spring Harbor, and the south-west part of Oyster Bay Harbor.

In most parts of Long Island, water is not found in quantity, and is not permanent, except at about the level of the ocean, in consequence of the porous nature of the strata.

The soils of these counties are very variable, but at least four-fifths of the surface may be characterized by the terms sandy loam and loamy sand. There are many tracts of land where the soil is a heavy loam, and even a stiff clay; and others of a pure sand, which drifts, and is piled by the action of the wind. The variation of the soil is due to the different strata which form the country. Beds of sand and gravel are interstratified with those of loam and clay; and where irregularities occur in the contour of the ground, arising from denudation, a field of a few acres may exhibit almost every variety of soil, from a pure sand to a stiff clay. The art of the farmer is here put in requisition to modify the natural texture of the soils, and fit them to receive nutritive and stimulant manures with the greatest advantage. The heavy soils are dressed with sand, and the light soils with loam or clay, with a view to transform the whole into a loam of such texture as to make a pulverulent soil, and yet have it sufficiently argillaceous to retain a suitable quantity of water. The cultivated soils within twenty miles of New-York are so much modified by art, that their natural qualities could scarcely be determined without geological investigation. Many of the farmers expend from $50 to $70 per acre for street manure once in two or three years, and they are well repaid for their enlightened views and liberal expenditures. The soil is naturally very poor on the plains, but those parts which are well cultivated have become very productive. Street manure, yard manure, composts mixed with lime, rotted sea-weed, on which hogs and cattle are yarded, ashes, barilla, bone manure, and fish, are those in common use. Street manure probably exceeds all the others in quantity, and the bays and inlets on the coast, together with the Long Island rail-road, offer great facilities for its transport into the interior of the island. The marsh mud, and " muck " of the meadow, and the estuary mud, would make a valuable manure on the light soils. Lime answers well on the light soils of Long Island, and the farmers will find it to their advantage in using it on their lands, first putting it in heaps to slacken thoroughly, and spread with other manure upon the soil. On a considerable portion of Long Island the bony fish, called hard-heads or moss-bonkers, have become the principal article for fertilizing the soil; and the crops thereby produced are so abundant as to be almost matter of astonishment.

These fish weigh from one to two pounds each, and are either spread directly upon the land, or mixed with other substances to decompose. In some instances, at Southold, two or three hundred thousand, and it is even said that a million, have been caught at a time; and there are, probably, more than one hundred million used annually upon this island. The sandy land in Suffolk County could hardly be cultivated to advantage without the aid derived from these fish.

Mr. Mather is of opinion that they are not used by the farmers of Long Island in the most economical manner. From five thousand to fifteen thousand, he says, are spread over the ground, instead of being ploughed in. The soil is generally light, and the animal matter passes through it by the filtering action of water, so that its fertilizing effects are nearly exhausted by a single crop.

The object in using ashes, is, to keep the dry arid soils moist by the attraction of the potassa for water, and thus afford moisture, and a stimulating alkali to the growing plants. A great error in their use is to let them remain in heaps long exposed to the weather, an idea prevailing that ashes are improved by this means, and that if they were used in their raw state, would injure the crops. The fact is, that when used fresh, too many are used; as they contain a large proportion of potassa, and prove a too powerful stimulant to vegetation; but when exposed to the weather, the potassa deliquates by its attraction for moisture, and is removed by rains, leaving little except the inert earthy matter.

Silt, or creek mud, has been used with considerable advantage in some parts of Brookhaven; it is generally obtained from the bottom of bays, where there is very little action of the tide, and where the decomposition of vegetable and animal matter has been long accumulating. The long eel grass is pulled up with iron rakes, which bring up the decomposed matter with it.

On the subject of the Geology of Long Island, Dr. Mitchill has some remarks which are too valuable and interesting to be passed over. His examinations were principally confined to the north shore of the island, and to the islands in the East River.

" The Brothers," he observes, " are two small islands, lying upon the side of the ship channel in the East River, and called the North and South Brother. Their foundation is rocky, and has hitherto resisted the impetuosity of the waves and currents by reason of its hard structure. Both these, and the detached rocks and reefs around them, differ in no respect from the general character of the others."

Riker's Island lies in the middle of the Sound, nearly opposite the mouth of Flushing Bay; the banks of considerable height, but by no means so rocky as the last-mentioned. There is, however, a conspicuous mass of granite upon it, and several smaller rocks scattered about. From the loose and gravelly material of which it consists, its sides are gradually crumbling down and washing away, notwithstanding it is thickly spread with rocks and stones, the remains of former washings and encroachments of the water. Of Long Island, the Doctor observes, that the face of the country upon the north and south sides are very different from each other. On the north it is elevated, uneven, and much variegated with hill and dale; while on the south the traveller discovers little else than a flat surface, sloping gradually toward the ocean. Indeed, that part north of the ridge not only resembles the opposite shores of the main land in its general appearance, but also in its fossils and mineral productions. It appears to have been separated from the continent during the lapse of ages, by the encroachments of the salt water. The occurrence of no horizontal strata, and the frequency of vertical layers, lead to the conclusion that they are certainly in a state of primeval arrangement. The probable opinion, (says Dr. Mitchill,) is, that Long Island and the adjacent continent were once contiguous, or only separated by a small river; and that the strait which now divides them, was formed by successive inroads of the sea. This appears likely from the fossil bodies on both shores having a near resemblance; from the rocks and islands lying between them being found of similar materials; the distance being small; and that where the shore is not composed of solid rocks, there the water continues to make great encroachments, and to cause the high banks to tumble down, as may be seen in many places upon the north shore of the island, and as is more particularly the fact at Newtown, at Montauk and elsewhere, at this day.

To the eastward of Hellgate all the considerable rocks are solitary masses of granite. These are scattered over the upland and along the shore between high and low water. In the town of North Hempstead, not far from Manhasset, is one of the largest rocks of the kind. It is known in the records of the town by the name of Millstone Rock, and contains more than twenty thousand cubic feet. The appearance of the island on the south side of the hills induces the belief that the whole extent of level land between them and the sea is a dereliction of the waters. Its horizontal strata, its sandy and gravelly quality, and the rounded and water-worn surfaces of its quartzy pebbles, all lead to such a persuasion.

The land, besides, is very bare of vegetable mould, as well as rocks, and the timber generally of a smaller growth. The shells of marine animals are more frequently met with in digging wells; though it is said, that towards the west end of the island the remains of testacious creatures have been found at considerable depths on the north side of the ridge. Between Long Island and the continent there are several shoals, with rocks scattered over them, which are apparently sunken or wasted islands; and shows the extraordinary levelling power of the waves. One of these shallow places, whose rocks are bare at low water, lies off the extremity of Cow Neck, and occupies several acres almost in the middle of the Sound. From the injuries thereby sustained by vessels, they are called the " *Executioners.*" Another sandy spot, of many acres, with several large rocks appearing here and there above the little water that covers it, stretches far toward the main channel from the bottom of Great Neck. These rocks are called " *The Stepping Stones*," from a tradition of the Indians, that at some former distant period their ancestors could cross over here to the main. At Oldfield Point, Crane Neck, and Mount Misery, the land has been frittered away for a considerable extent, leaving a considerable area covered with rocks, visible at low water. Some facts remain to be mentioned to explain the rapid currents and dangerous navigation of Hellgate. This is a strait, one of whose sides is formed by Long Island and the other by Parsell's and Manhattan Islands. Between the two latter, Harlaem Creek empties itself. There is a small quantity of solid granite here, and the shores and intervening rocks and reefs almost entirely consist of it. Such a compact body impedes, on the Long Island side of it, the direct flow of the water of the Sound in a north-east and south-west direction so completely, that the current is forced to take a short and sudden turn around the point of Parsell's Island. This change of direction is nearly at a right angle with the ridges and strata of rocks which formerly connected the two islands ; and such has been its impetuous and irresistible force, that the dams of solid rock, which nature had constructed across, have been broken down and carried away, and nothing but their ruins are now perceptible. The foaming and agitation of the water over and among these rocks has given rise to the whimsical appellations of *Pot*, *Frying-Pan*, *Grid-Iron*, &c. The *Hog's-Back*, *Hallet's Point Reef*, *the Mill-Rock*, the *Middle Reef*, and the *South Rocks*, are plain and instructive monuments of the ancient arrangement. They are portions of strata remaining after all the rest has been swept away by the force of the current. On the shallows and flats of the South Bay, where there is little current except the swell and recession of the tides, certain vegetables delight to grow. The sand and mud, which had before been moveable, now becomes fixed. This process continues until the new island rises above common tide, and receives no more nutriment from the water. These are the islands and marshes of great extent, scattered almost the whole length of Long Island, and are of great value for the sedge which grows upon them. Hog Island in Hempstead Bay, and Coney Island, have been thus formed.

It is a universally conceded fact, that so much of Long Island
as lies southerly of the ridge of hills, is of secondary formation;
while it has been concluded that the remainder is of primeval
construction.   Yet there are many facts and circumstances
which, if they do not prove the contrary, are in such hostility
with it, as to be entirely irreconcilable to the idea that the north
side of the island has always existed as it now is.   Some of
these facts have been with considerable pains collected, and
are derived from such sources as to be entitled to our entire
belief.

Sand and gravel, mixed with marine shells, are found at
considerable distances below the surface in digging wells and
excavating the earth for other purposes.   These are found almost universally fifty feet and more below the soil in Brooklyn, New Utrecht, Flatbush, and Newtown.   The shell of a
periwinkle was found forty-three feet down at New Utrecht.
In Newtown, carbonated wood, sometimes alone and sometimes incrusted by pyrites, was raised from the bottom of a
shaft fifty feet deep.   In Bushwick, at forty-five feet, the body
of a tree was found by the workmen lying across the well, and
had to be cut away to allow them to proceed.   Wood has also
been found at great depths a little east of Westbury meeting-
house.   A well was dug by Messrs. William and John Mott in
1813, at Great Neck, three miles north of the ridge; at the
distance of thirty feet, on the upper surface of a stratum of
loose dark-red earth, lay shells of clams, oysters, and scollops;
at fifty feet a piece of wood was found, soft, rotten, and decayed.
Its ligneous character was, however, perfectly distinguishable.
On the land of Mr. Andrew Napier, three miles west of Jamaica
village, during the same year, several pieces of wood were
found twenty-five feet below the surface.   A well was dug
some years since near the Narrows at New Utrecht, and shells
of clams and oysters found at sixty-seven feet; the shell of the
large murex (*Periwinkle*) was discovered, very little damaged,
at two hundred and fifty feet.   President Dwight, who travelled
through Long Island in May 1804, mentions, that on the eastern border of Hempstead Plain, some workmen, who were digging a well, found a log of wood, three feet long and one in

diameter, at the depth of one hundred and eight feet; the exterior was decayed near an inch deep, the rest perfectly sound. In digging a well in the same neighborhood, a short time after, the greater part of a tree was discovered at the depth of one hundred feet. A part of the wood, says the Doctor, was put upon the fire, and burnt very well.

In the town of Huntington, about the middle of the island, the people, says he, were induced to believe there was a silver mine in a particular spot; with the inquisitive spirit usual in such cases, they dug to a considerable depth, and in their progress, found a tree, with its branches, buried in solid earth thirty feet below the surface: the branches were chiefly decayed. At Newtown, a deep pit was sunk in the side of a hill in 1804, for the purpose of forming an ice-house. The hill is about twenty rods from the shore of the East River at Hallet's Cove, and fifty feet above high-water mark. At the depth of twenty feet, the workman threw out a great many frogs, lodged in the coarse gravel. Their color was not so vivid as common, in other respects they resembled the common frog of this country. General Ebenezer Stephens, on whose land it was, observed them, and, although torpid at first, in a short time they recovered all the activity of their species. Mr. Henry Demilt, about thirty years ago dug a well upon the east side of Cow Neck, half a mile from the shore, and at the depth of thirty-four feet came to a stratum of creek mud and shells, the stench from which was such as induced him to abandon his design.

The late Mr. William Allen, in digging for water at Manhasset in 1824, found a quantity of oyster shells seventy-eight feet below the surface, and obtained water at one hundred and two feet. The earth at the bottom of the well being a clean white sand like that found upon the beach. intermixed with rounded pebbles.

Selah B. Strong, Esq., of Setauket, L. I., says that his grandfather, the late Judge Selah Strong, in digging a well near his mansion upon the Neck, where he then resided, shortly before the Revolution, found a large tree in a horizontal position, about forty feet below the soil, and in a good state of preservation.

7

Anthony Sherman, while digging a well in the year 1808, for Mr. Roderick Havens, upon Shelter Island, at the depth of fifty-seven feet found an Indian stone pestle, beautifully polished; also abundance of clam-shells mixed with beach sand and gravel.

Jeremiah Johnson, Esq. states that a well was dug about forty years ago by a Mr. Kolyer, at a place called Clam-Battery, in Newtown; and at the depth of seventy feet discovered a quantity of shells, mixed with what resembled shore sand; that Doctor Pater, in digging a well about thirty years since at New Utrecht, came, at one hundred and twenty feet below the soil, to a stratum of salt meadow resembling that in the neighborhood. And the same gentleman says, that, while commanding officer at Fort Green during the year 1814, a well was constructed there under his direction, for the use of the garrison, and at the depth of seventy feet clam-shells and sand were found, which had every appearance of having been at a former period washed by the sea.

Mr. Abraham Van Alst, at Bushwick, some years since, found a log of wood, well preserved, at forty feet below the soil; and several others in the same town, who dug wells, were compelled to abandon them on account of the filthy creek mud found at the bottom, which rendered the water unfit to be drank.

Dr. Dwight, in the account of his tour upon Long Island, observes as follows: " When we commenced our journey on this island, I proposed to my companions to examine, with a continual and minute attention, the stones of every size which should be visible to us throughout all the parts of our progress. This examination was made by us all with great care, and was extended to the stones on the general surface; to those washed out in hollow roads; to those uncovered on the summits and sides, and at the bottom of hills; to those found in the deepest vallies, and to those which were dug out of a considerable number of very deep wells.

" The result of this examination was, that all the stones which we saw, were, without any exception, destitute of angles, limited by an arched exterior, appearing as if worn by the long continued attrition of water, and in all respects exactly like those which in a multitude of places were found on the beach of the ocean.

"In ten or twelve instances, possibly a few more, we observed small rocks of granite on our road. Every one of these exhibited what I thought plain proofs of having been washed for a considerable length of time, and strongly resembled rocks of the same kind which have been long beaten by waves. I will not say that no other traveller would have considered these rocks as exceptions; but to my eye they exhibited manifest appearances of having been long worn by water. If this opinion be admitted, we did not find, in a progress of more than two hundred miles, a single stone which did not exhibit proofs of having been washed for a considerable time.

"On Montauk Point the stones have a different aspect, being angular, and having the common appearance of the granite rocks so generally found in New England.

"After we had passed Jamaica in our way to New-York, we found a similar change in the stones; most of them being angular, and presenting no evidence that they had ever been washed. Between these limits the stones are universally aquatic, if I may be allowed, for the sake of succinctness, to give them that name.

"From this extraordinary fact, it would seem a natural conclusion that the great body of this island, or perhaps more properly the materials of which it is composed, were at some former period covered by the ocean; and that by some cause, which cannot now be discovered, were thrown up into their present form.

"That Long Island was once united with the main, towards its western end, has been believed by a great multitude of persons from a bare inspection of the scenery. The narrowness and winding of the straits in many places, the multitude of intervening rocks and islands, the projection and course of the points between this island and the counties of New-York and Westchester, and the general aspect of both shores, have produced this opinion in minds which have been formed to very different modes of thinking."

From this train of accumulated facts, and the conclusions to which they necessarily lead the mind of the inquirer, it can hardly be denied that the alluvial character of the greater part of Long Island is placed beyond the pale of controversy, or even a rational doubt, in the opinion of those who have given the subject any considerable attention. We have been the more particular upon this interesting portion of geology, because it constitutes an important part of the natural history of Long Island, and is a subject of curiosity as well as utility.

DISCOVERY OF LONG ISLAND.

There are some traditions among the Spaniards and Dutch that probably this part of the world had been visited by Europeans long before the renowned Hudson sailed up the noble and majestic river that bears his name. Others have supposed that they had discovered sufficient proof, in the western part of our state, of its having been occupied at some very remote era by a race of men further advanced in the arts, and particularly in that of defensive warfare, than could be reasonably conceived of those who inhabited the country at the period of the discovery by Hudson.

No traces of a civilized people have ever been discovered upon this island, nor any evidence whatever to warrant the belief that any than savages ever possessed it, previous to the arrival of our European ancestors, in the early part of the seventeenth century.

We may therefore reasonably infer, in the absence of any proof to the contrary, that Hudson and his adventurous crew were the first white people that ever set foot upon the shores of Long Island.

In the work entitled, "History of New-York," by Joseph W. Moulton, Esq., which exhibits as much industrious research and studious accuracy as any historical work can claim, it is stated, that when Hudson first arrived within the waters of Sandy Hook, he observed them swarming with fish, and sent his men to obtain a supply. It may well be that they landed upon Coney Island, in the town of Gravesend, which was the nearest land; and if so, the Canarsee Indians were the first to

hail the approach of the long-to-be-remembered discoverer of
New-York.

Two hundred and twenty-nine years ago, being the 3d of
September, 1609, the chivalric Hudson first saw the shores of
this island.   On the 4th, it is related he sent his men on shore
in a boat, who, according to the words of his Journal, " *caught
ten great Mullet, a foot and a half long, and a Ray as great
as four men could haul into the ship.*"   Here, he says, they
found the soil of white sand, and a vast number of plumb trees
loaded with fruit, and many of them covered with grape-vines
of different kinds.   They saw, also, a great quantity of snipe and
other birds; and on the morning of the 12th they rode up into
the mouth of the great river.   Judge Benson says the name of
the river was Sha-te-muck.   The natives crowded to the
shores on beholding so strange a sight as a large ship, and men
so different in appearance and dress from themselves, and speaking a language also which it was impossible they could understand.   The emotions which they felt, and the opinions and
conjectures they must have formed on that most novel and interesting occasion, may be imagined, but can never be known.
Such a curious combination of circumstances was well calculated to excite fearful apprehensions in the minds of an ignorant and unsophisticated people.

The natives are described by *De Laet* as manifesting all
friendship when Hudson first landed among them.   They
were clothed, he says, in the skins of elks, foxes, and other
animals.   Their canoes were made out of the bodies of trees;
their arms, bows and arrows, with sharp points of stone fixed
to them, and fastened with hard pitch.   They had no houses,
he says, but slept under the blue heavens; some on mats made
of brush or bulrushes, and some upon leaves of trees.   They
had good tobacco, and copper tobacco-pipes.   After their first
acquaintance, they frequently visited Hudson's ship.   They
were the deadly enemies of the Manhattans, and a better people than they; who, says our author, have always conducted
toward the Dutch in a cruel and inimical manner.

Heckewelder relates, that from the best accounts he could
obtain, the Indians who inhabited Long Island were Delawares,

and early known by the name of Matauwakes according to
De Laet and Professor Ebeling.

Long Island at this time had various appellations, as Matou-
wake, Meitowax, *Matanwake*, and *Sewanhacky;* the last of
which means the " *Island of Shells ;*" and this appears to have
been the most current appellation. It is sometimes called Ma-
tanwax and Paumanake. Some of this variety are evidently
but different ways of spelling the same word, and others may
have been conferred by the neighboring nations, the Manbat-
tans, the Nehantic or Mohegan tribes. It is the better opinion
that the land was in most places destitute of timber ; and that
the population of the tribes had much diminished in conse-
quenco of incessant contests and bloody wars among them,
which threatened the extermination of the whole race. The
timely arrival of the white people, and the protection they afforded, may have been the means of saving them from destruction by their enemies.

THE LONG ISLAND INDIANS.

The origin of the American Indians is one of those curious
problems in the history of man that has given occasion to much
ingenious conjecture, and has been a standing subject of speculation and inquiry among antiquarians and philosophers in
every age, and among every civilized people, since the discovery
of the country. Thus far the investigation has not been attended by any very satisfactory results ; and from the peculiar intricacy of the subject itself there is little hope of entire success.
It seems to have been taken for granted that the race were originally from another country, and both Asia and Europe have
been assigned as the quarter from which they must have passed
to America; that they either came by the way of Behring's
Straits, or may have been driven by accident or misfortune
from some distant island, to which their ancestors may have arrived in the same way. If it be as necessary to account for the
existence of other animals found here, as for the native Indians,
a difficulty arises from the supposition that many of the tropi-
cal animals could never have existed for any length of time in

a region so intensely cold as Behring's Straits; and if these are admitted always to have been here, the argument is equally strong in favor of man. If the argument for emigration be of any force, it is just as strong in favor of the idea that Asia and Europe may have been peopled from America as the contrary. The Indians may have been equally indigenous as any other class of animals; and if they were originally planted here by the common parent of nature, they must necessarily have been endued by the same kind author with capacities and instincts graduated to the condition in which they were destined to live, and to subserve the great purposes of their creation.

With the exception of the Esquimaux, it has been conjectured that all the American tribes possess the same cardinal distinctions and the same physical characteristics: The differences which existed among various tribes in temperament, stature, or mental powers, may in great measure be accounted for upon grounds less improbable than the supposition of their having been a different order of men. The Indians of Long Island, whatever may have previously been their conduct toward one another or to distant tribes, were less troublesome to their white neighbors than the Indians north of the Sound. Nor does it appear that any formidable conspiracy ever existed with them to destroy the settlers, as was attempted, but too successfully, upon the main. The white people, by forming distinct settlements in different parts of the island, and separating the tribes, probably prevented any such combination being formed, if it were ever intended. The white population were distinguished for their prudence and vigilance; and the first dawning of hostility would create alarm, and the means of defence be instantly resorted to. That, difficulties sometimes occurred with a single tribe, and might have been provoked by the improper conduct of the whites themselves, it is reasonable to believe. The story of their griefs, or the wrongs they may have endured, can never be known; and they and their sufferings are equally buried in oblivion. Their written language, so far as they possessed any, was entirely of a symbolical character; and both deeds, contracts, and treaties were signed by a mark or symbol,—as the figure of a hatchet, pipe, bow, arrow, &c., each chief having his own appropriate

mark.   It was not uncommon, upon the death of a sachem leaving no son, or none but an infant, for the widow to assume and exercise most of the functions which her deceased husband had
done.   She was then called the sunk squa, or squa Sachem ; and
the records of the different towns present examples of deeds being
executed in such cases by female Sachems.   In some instances
the Sachem nominated a person to act as guardian for his son
during his minority.   Wyandance, the Long Island Sachem,
appointed Lyon Gardiner, and his son David Gardiner, as
guardians to his son Wyancombone ; and these persons actually
affixed their names to conveyances on behalf of their ward.
This singular appointment appears by the records of Easthampton to have been made in 1660, and continued till the young
Sachem came to the age which would authorise him to act for
himself.   Pending the Indian war in New England in 1675,
(designated as Philip's War,) which threatened the extermination
of the white people on the main, it was apprehended by the
eastern towns on Long Island that the Indians here might
be induced to unite with those hostile Indians to destroy
them also ; and thereupon such prudent and precautionary
measures were adopted as effectually prevented the consequences of such an union, if any such was in contemplation.   The
accounts of Philip's wars would be highly entertaining, but for
the unfeeling barbarities, and cold, calculating horrors of savage
warfare, which mark every stage of their progress.   For, not
contented with the destruction of cattle, grain, the plunder of
goods and conflagration of dwellings, they murdered all they
met without discrimination of age, sex, or condition ; beheading,
scalping, dismembering, and mangling their wretched and unfortunate victims, in a manner too revolting for recital.

The Algonquin or Chippeway race of Indians is one of the
most numerous in existence, and there is little doubt but that
all the tribes anciently in New-York and New England, were
of this race, if we may be allowed to consider identity of language as proof of the fact.   The vocabulary of the Narragansett tongue, recorded by Roger Williams, shows them to have
been of the same stock.   The Mohegans were progenitors of
the other tribes in New England who spoke the same tongue.

chem leav
me and ex-
,band had
hem; and
eeds being
e instances
for his son
d Sachem,
,ardiner, as
ons actually
their ward,
f Easthamp-
l the young
m to act for
id in 1675,

ided by the
here might
to destroy
ecautionary

ation. The
ning, but for
ors of savage
ss. For, not
ie plunder of
ered all they
; beheading,
hed and un-

is one of the

ngland, were
dentity of lan-
the Narragan
; them to have
progenitors of
e same tongue.

So were the tribes in Maine. The Delawares, or Lenni-Lenape, were of the same family; and their language has been pronounced by competent judges the most perfect Indian dialect in existence. The Iroquois, or Six Nations, once dreaded by all the other tribes from the Atlantic to the Mississippi, are Algonquins. This tribe extends from the mouth of the St. Lawrence to the Mississippi, and northward to the Great Slave Lake. On the western side of the Mississippi is another great Indian family, the Sioux. In the south of the United States we have four tribes,—the Chickasaws, Choctaws, Cherokees, and Creeks; of the latter the Seminoles are a part, whose towns were destroyed by General Jackson, their chiefs slain, and those who escaped death, effectually dispersed. The different and somewhat singular opinions which have existed upon this subject are amusing, although few of them are very satisfactory to the antiquary. The Rev. Thomas Thorowgood, in 1652, published a quarto volume to prove the American Indians to be the Jews, who had been lost to the world for more than two thousand years. Roger Williams seems to have entertained a similar opinion, as appears by his replies to questions propounded to him by an European correspondent. Cotton Mather, a curious and wonderfully prolific writer of the seventeenth century, affirms the same; and supposes that the Devil seduced these Jews from their own country, to get them (as he expresses it) out of the way of the "Silver Trumpets of the Gospel." Boudinot, in his book entitled "The Star in the West," conjectures the Indians of America to be the "long-lost tribes of Israel;" and last, though not least, may be mentioned our distinguished fellow-citizen, Mordecai M. Noah, Esq., who has composed a learned and ingenious dissertation to prove them to have been originally Jews, and a part of the lost tribes of his nation.

It is one of the peculiar traits of Indian character, and one which is apparently universal, that while the business of procuring food is the duty of the men, all other labor, however arduous or degrading, is devolved upon the women. The use of the axe and other domestic implements is considered by these self-created lords as beneath their savage dignity; while

8

to the weaker sex it belongs to plant corn, make and mend
garments, build wigwams, and attend to all the drudgery of
rearing children and other family affairs. Revenge is with
them a cardinal virtue, and to endure pain with heroic fortitude a quality worthy of high admiration. In short, to be
proof against suffering, however exquisite, and to be destitute
of all sympathy for that of others, is a characteristic of the savage in every part of the world.

WAMPUM AND TRIBUTE.

The frequent mention of the article wampum, in almost all
Indian conveyances, contracts, and treaties, and the circumstance of its being a part of the consideration, or price, in most
Indian deeds in former times, besides its use as a circulating
medium, as well among the natives as the white people at the
first settlement of the country, renders it not only proper, but
necessary, to give some account of so valuable a commodity.

Wampum (from wampi or wompi, signifying *white*,) shells,
or strings of shells, used by the Indians as an ornament of dress,
and as a badge of distinction among the chiefs, and particularly
among the women. They were sometimes worn as a belt or
girdle. It is sometimes called wampum-peague, wampeague,
or wompampeage; of which wampum is a contraction.

Seawan, was the name of Indian money, of which there
were two kinds : *wompam*, (which signifies *white*,) and *suckauhock*, (*sucki* signifying *black*.) Wompam or wompampeague,
or simply peague, was, though improperly, also understood
among the Dutch and English as expressive of the generic
denomination. Wompam, or white money, was made of the
stem or stock of the meteauhock or periwinkle : suckauhock,
or black money, was manufactured from the inside of the shell
of the quahaug, (*venus mercenaria*,) a round thick shell-fish,
that buried itself but a little way in the sand, and was generally found lying on it in deep water, and gathered by rakes or
by diving after it. The Indians broke off about half an inch
of a purple color of the inside, and converted it into beads.
These, before the introduction of awls and thread, were bored
with sharp stones, and strung upon sinews of beasts; and when

interwoven to the breadth of the hand, more or less, were called a belt of seawan or wompam. A black bead, the size of a straw, about one third of an inch long, bored longitudinally and well polished, was the gold of the Indians, and always esteemed of twice the value of the white; but either species was considered by them of much more value than European coin. An Indian chief, to whom the value of a rix-dollar was explained by the first clergyman of Renselaerwyck, laughed exceedingly to think the Dutch set so high a price upon a piece of iron, as he termed it. Three beads of black and six of white were equivalent, among the English, to a penny, and among the Dutch, to a stuyver. But with the latter, the equivalent number sometimes varied from three and six, to four and eight. One of Governor Minuit's successors fixed, by placard, the price of the "good splendid seawan of Manhattan" at four for a stuyver. A string of this money, one fathom long, varied in price from five shillings among the New Englanders, (after the Dutch gave them a knowledge of it,) to four guilders, ($1.66½,) among the Dutch. The process of trade was this: the Dutch and English sold for seawan, their knives, combs, scissors, needles, awls, looking-glasses, hatchets, hoes, guns, black cloth, and other articles of the Indian traffic; and with the seawan bought the furs, corn, and venison from the Indians on the seaboard; who also, with their shell money, bought such articles from Indians residing in the interior of the country. Thus, by this circulating medium, a brisk commerce was carried on, not only between the white people and the Indians, but between different tribes among the latter. For the seawan was not only their money, but it was an ornament to their persons. It distinguished the rich from the poor, the proud from the humble. It was the tribute paid by the vanquished to those, the Five Nations for instance, who had exacted contribution. In the form of a belt it was sent with all public messages, and preserved as a record of all public transactions between nations. If a message was sent without the belt, it was considered *an empty word*, unworthy of remembrance. If the belt was returned, it was a rejection of the offer or proffer accompanying it. If accepted, it was a confirmation, and strengthened friend-

ships or effaced injuries. The belt, with appropriate figures
worked in it, was also the record of domestic transactions.
The confederation of the Five Nations was thus recorded.
The cockle shells had, indeed, more virtue amongst Indians
than pearls, gold, and silver had among Europeans. Seawan was
the seal of a contract—the oath of fidelity. It satisfied murders and all other injuries; purchased peace, and entered into
the religious as well as civil ceremonies of the natives. A
string of seawan was delivered by the orator in public council
at the close of every distinct proposition made to others, as a
ratification of the truth and sincerity of what he said; and the
white and black strings of seawan were tied by the pagan priest
around the neck of the white dog suspended to a pole, and
offered as a sacrifice to *T'halonghyawaagon*, the upholder of
the skies, the God of the Five Nations.

The seawan was manufactured most abundantly upon Long
Island, which abounded in shells, and called, for this reason,
Seawan-hacky, or the " Island of Shells." The Poquanhock or
Quahang, and the Periwinkle were extremely plenty; and for
this reason, in all probability, it was that the Mohawks, the Pequods, and other powerful tribes, made frequent wars upon the
Long Island Indians, and compelled them to pay tribute in this
almost universal article of trade and commerce. The immense
quantity which was manufactured may account for the fact,
that in the most extensive shell-banks left by the Indians, it is
rare to find a whole shell; having all been broken in the process of making the wampum. And it is not unlikely that
many of the largest heaps of shells are the remains of a wampum manufactory.

The French at one period undertook the counterfeiting of
wampum by the substitution of a species of porcelain for shells,
and which, could it have succeeded, might have proved a profitable adventure; but the Indians at once discovered the trick,
and the manufacture of earthen money was given up. The
Dutch and English made great quantities from the genuine
material, and from the greater mechanical facilities they possessed, gave them a wonderful advantage in the manufacture.
But the consequence, as might be expected, was to diminish the

value of it in proportion to its abundance. In the commencement of the European settlements, and in all purchases
from the natives, wampum constituted a part of the price ; and
this, with a few articles of clothing of trifling value, were exchanged for large tracts of valuable land.

Hazard, in his collection of state papers, mentions that the
Narragansetts procured many shells from Long Island, out of
which they manufactured Indian money ; and that they likewise
frequently compelled the natives of the island to pay them large
tribute in wampum. Dr. Edwards supposes that all the tribes
upon Long Island, Staten Island, and Manhattan Island were
equally tributary to the Six Nations, of whom the Mohawks
were the most numerous and formidable. It is well known
they were the most dreaded of any of the northern tribes, so
much so, that even the name became associated with sensa-
tions of fear and alarm in the minds of children and young
people. The Pequots or Pequods, in the day of their power,
inhabited the country about Stonington, Groton, and New
London. To the north were the Mohegans, of whom Uncas
was the chief, as Saccacus was of the Pequots, at the time of the
first arrival of the white people. The Narragansetts occupied
a portion of country including Rhode Island, and gave name
to the beautiful bay between Point Judith and Point Seaconet
whose chief was Canonicus. All these tribes committed occa-
sioual hostilities upon the Long Island Indians, and particularly the Montauks, who were nearest to them, and who were
oftentimes obliged to purchase their safety by the payment of
tribute in corn and wampum.

In 1655 a large body of Indians, consisting of five hundred
from New Jersey and the North River, landed at New Amsterdam, where they were provoked into hostilities, and did much
injury. They then went to Staten Island, and committed
great havoc there. A part of them went over to Long Island
and threatened the settlement of Gravesend ; but as the Indians
there refused to join them, they retired without doing much
damage. In 1649 a murder wasp erpetrated at South Hampton, and the town was greatly alarmed at the hostile appearance of the Indians in that neighborhood for several days.

Many outrages, and even murders, were committed in the Dutch towns in 1652. In 1645 the town had ordered one half of the militia company to bring their arms to church with them upon the Lord's Day. And in 1651 the town of East Hampton ordered the inhabitants also to bring their arms to meeting with them, under the penalty of twelve pence for every neglect. In 1681 the Indians plundered a store in Huntington, and threatened the family.

The Montauks were doubtless superior in numbers and warlike skill to any other of the Long Island tribes, and this superiority was acknowledged by the payment of tribute; and it is evident from the early writers of New England, that the Pequots, the most powerful tribe in Connecticut, had at one time subdued the Montauks, and thereby the whole of the Long Island Indians were in subjection to the Pequots; and which they acknowledged by the payment of an annual tribute, for a time at least. But after 1637 they seem to have considered themselves in subjection to the English, and paid them, for their protection, the same amount of tribute which they had previously paid to the Pequots. In 1650, in consequence of their failure to pay, the New England commissioners sent Captain Mason to Long Island to require payment of the tribute due from the Indians, and to make arrangements for its more punctual discharge in future. In 1656 the Montauk chief visited the commissioners at Boston, and acquainted them that he had paid the tribute due from him at Hartford for the space of ten years, but that it was in arrear for the four last years, in consequence of the war in which they had been engaged with the Narragansetts. On which account the commissioners consented to release the payment of it. It is not easy at this day to perceive the justice of the imposition of this tribute by the white people. The Pequots, who had also been tributary to the English in 1650, remonstrated against the injustice of exacting tribute from them; in answer to which, the commissioners said it was imposed in 1635, for the murders they had committed. It was exacted from the Long Island Indians under the pretence that the whites afforded them protection from their red brethren, to whom they would otherwise have been forced to pay tribute

Governor Winthrop, in his Journal of 1637, says "The Indians sent in many Pequots' heads and hands from Long Island and other places, and Sachems from Long Island came voluntarily, and brought tribute to us of twenty fathoms of wampum each of them." From which it appears that the Long Island Indians were involved in wars, and dealt freely in the blood of their enemies when the opportunity offered. In 1636 Mr. Winthrop says that Mr. Withers, in a vessel of fifty tons, going to Virginia, was cast away upon Long Island; seven of his men were drowned in landing, some got in a boat to the Dutch plantations, two were killed by the Indians, who took all such goods as were left upon the shore. "In 1663," says the same author, "on the 2d of October, the barque Blessing, which was sent to the southward, returned; she had been at an island over against Connecticut; it is fifty leagues long, the east end about ten leagues from the main, but the west not one mile. The Indians there are very treacherous, and have many canoes so great as will carry eighty men." In Winthrop's History of New England, it is stated, that in 1638, Janemoh, the Sachem of Niantic, had gone to Long Island, and rifled some of those Indians which were tributary to that colony. "The Sachems complained to our friends of Connecticut, (says he,) who wrote us about it, and sent Captain Mason, with seven men, to require satisfaction; upon this Janemoh went to Connecticut, made his peace, and gave full satisfaction for all injuries." "In 1643, (he says) the Indians of Long Island took part with their neighbors on the main; and as the Dutch took away their corn, so they took to burning the Dutch houses; but these, by the mediation of Mr. Williams, were pacified, and peace re-established between them and the Dutch; at length they came to an accord with the rest of the Indians. Those Indians having cleared away all the English upon the main as far as Stamford, they passed on to Long Island, and there assaulted the lady Moody in her house divers times, for there were forty gathered there to defend it; they also set upon the Dutch with an implacable fury, and killed all they could come by, burnt their houses, and killed their cattle without restraint; so as the Governor, and such as escaped, betook themselves to their fort at Manhattan, and there lived and eat up their cattle." In Gookin's History, it is said, " The Pequots were a very warlike people about forty years since, (1624,) at which time they were in their meridian ; their chief Sachem held dominion over divers petty Sagamores, as over part of Long Island, over the Mohegans, and over the Sagamores of Quinipiac ; yea, over all the people that dwelt on Connecticut River, and over some of the most southerly inhabitants of the Nipmuck country about Quinebaug." Another writer observes, that when the Dutch began the settlement of New-York, all the Indians on Long Island and the northern shore of the Sound, on the banks of the Connecticut, Hudson, Delaware, and Susquehannah rivers, were in subjection to the Iroquois or Five Nations, and within the memory of persons now living, acknowledged it by the payment of tribute.   As a proof, it is mentioned that a small tribe near the Sugar-loaf Mountain, in 1756, made a payment of 20l. a-year to the Mohawks.

Tammany was an Indian chief of the Delaware or Lenni-Lenape tribe, and was living after the arrival of Penn ; his residence is said to have been where Germantown now stands. Societies named from this chief have been formed in New-York and other places, and the place of their meeting is called a wigwam ; Indian costume and phrases have also been adopted by these associations ; but they are now very much out of use. Some, however, have doubted the fact of the Long Island Indians being tributary, as has been stated by other writers.   The Dutch, (says the venerable Samuel Jones,) finding all the Indians within and adjoining their settlements on Long Island tributary to the Mohawks or Five Nations, probably concluded that all the Indians on the island were so.   On the contrary, says Mr. Jones, a tradition once prevailed among the Montauk Indians that their ancestors had wars with the Indians on the main, who conquered them, and compelled them to pay tribute. This confirms the assertion, so often made in history, that the Narragansetts once held dominion over a part of Long Island at least, and probably compelled the natives to assist them against their enemies.   When the English commissioners met at Hartford in 1650, Uncas came with a complaint that a Sachem of Long Island had killed some of his men, bewitched divers others, and himself also ; and desired of the commissioners that he might be righted therein.   About a year after the death of Miantonimoh, Ninigret undertook to organize a plan for extirpating the English, and sent a messenger to Wyandance, the Long Island Sachem, to engage him in it.   Instead of listening to his message, Wyandance seized upon Ninigret's messenger, bound him, and sent him to Captain Gardiner at Saybrook fort. From thence he was sent under a guard of ten men for Hartford.   But they were wind-bound in their passage, and obliged to put into Shelter Island, where an old Sachem lived, the eldest brother of Wyandance.   Here they let Ninigret's ambassador escape, and thus Ninigret was informed that his plan was discovered and defeated.   After the peace of 1654 between the Montauk Indians and those upon the main, the Long Islanders, pretending to visit Ninekunet at Block Island, slaughtered of his men near thirty persons at midnight, two of whom were of great note.   After which Ninigret surprised some of the Long Island Indians upon Gull Island, and killed many of them ; and for which massacre the general Court of Connecticut demanded several hundred fathoms of wampum as a satisfaction.

In 1761 the Indians had so diminished on Long Island, as in some places to have entirely disappeared, and in others greatly reduced ; and even the once powerful Montauks could only number thirty-eight families, and one hundred and ninety-two souls.   These were further reduced, in 1783, by the emigration of a considerable number to Oneida County with the Rev. Sampson Occom.

OF THE DIFFERENT TRIBES.

The Indians on Long Island, on the arrival of the white people, were found divided into distinct tribes, or collections of families, having different names, and exercising exclusive and independent authority or control over separate portions of the territory ; and these tribes had, moreover, each their chiefs and head men, called Sachems and Sagamores, with a sort of supreme power in the conduct of public affairs, questions of war, treaties, and the payment of tribute.   From the Sachems of the

different tribes, and sometimes from a few other head men associated with them, the lands were purchased by the white people, and from whom have descended the title to all the real estate upon the island.   Motives of honor, justice, and humanity,
as well as true policy, dictated the propriety of such a course
by strangers coming to settle in a country already occupied by
a people, the undisputed tenants of the soil.   The price was
was always fixed by the convention of the parties, and good
faith, it is believed, was always observed on the part of the
white people.

The principal tribes inhabiting the island at that distant period, and occupying distinct and well-defined portions of territory, were thirteen in number, and were the undisputed claimants of the lands, over which they exercised an independent
jurisdiction, as follows:

THE CANARSEE TRIBE claimed the whole of the lands now
included within the limits of King's County and a part of the
town of Jamaica.   The principal settlement was probably about
Flatlands, where there is a place which yet retains the name of
Canarsee, and was, perhaps, the residence of the Sachem.   The
last of the tribe is known to have died about 40 years ago.
The inhabitants, in the infancy of the settlement, had much difficulty with this tribe, and were compelled to erect places of
defence, to prevent the consequences of surprise.   The immense piles of shells at this place and upon Bergen Island, show
their number must at one time have been very considerable.

THE ROCKAWAY TRIBE were scattered over the southern
part of the town of Hempstead, which, with a part of Jamaica
and the whole of Newtown, were the bounds of their claim.
The greater part of the population was at Near Rockaway, and
as far west as the present site of the Marine Pavilion.   Those
Indians who resided at the head of Maspeth Creek in Newtown,
were a portion of this tribe, as deeds for land there were uniformly executed by the Rockaway Sachem, which could not
have been the case had the Maspeth Indians been a distinct
tribe.   This tribe had likewise a settlement upon Hog Island,
consisting of several hundred acres, situate in the waters of

Rockaway Bay. The banks of shells in different places are very large.

The MERRIC, MEROKE, or MERIKOKE TRIBE, as they have been differently denominated, claimed all the territory south of the middle of the island, from Near Rockaway to the west line of Oyster Bay; and were, in all probability, at some former period, a part of the Massapequa, or Marsapeague tribe. A part of the lands in the town of Hempstead were purchased of this tribe. They had a large settlement upon Hicks's Neck, and other Necks between that and the village of Merric.

The MASSAPEQUA, or MARSAPEAGUE TRIBE had their principal settlement at the place called Fort Neck; and from thence eastward to the bounds of Islip, and north to the middle of the island; being the usual boundary of all the tribes by a kind of common consent. The only remarkable battle between the whites and Indians was fought with this tribe, when their fort was taken and demolished by a force under the command of Captain John Underhill, about the year 1653.

The MATINECOCK TRIBE claimed jurisdiction of the lands east of Newtown as far as the west line of Smithtown, and probably to the west side of Nesaquake River. This was a numerous tribe, and had several large settlements at Flushing, Glen Cove, Cold Spring, Huntington, and Cow Harbor; and they possessed, from their local advantages, the means of subsistence very abundantly.

The NESAQUAKE TRIBE possessed the country east of the river of that name to Stony-Brook, and from the Sound to the middle of the island. The extensive shell-banks near the village of Nesaquake show that it was the site of a considerable settlement, and probably the residence of the Sachem.

The SEATALCOT, or SETAUKET TRIBE claimed from Stony-Brook to the Wading River, and was one of the most powerful tribes in the county. They inhabited the sides of the different creeks, coves, and harbors, and upon Little Neck, (now called Strong's Neck,) which is supposed to have been a royal residence.

The CORCHAUG TRIBE owned the remainder of the territory from the Wading River to Oyster Ponds, and were spread along the north shore of Peconic Bay, and upon the

Necks adjoining the Sound.   They probably claimed Robin's Island also.

THE MANHASSET TRIBE possessed Shelter Island, Ram Island, and probably Hog Island.   This tribe, although confined to about 10,000 acres, could, as tradition affirms, bring into the field more than 500 fighting-men.   The Sachem of this tribe was a brother of Wyandance, Sachem of Montauk.

THE SECATOGUE TRIBE adjoined the Masapequa Tribe on the west, and possessed the country as far east as Patchogue. The farm owned by the Willet's family at Islip is called Secatogue Neck, and was, it is supposed, the chief settlement, and residence of the Sachem.

THE PATCHOGUE TRIBE extended east from that place to Westhampton, and, as some think, as far as Canoe Place.   The principal settlements must have been Patchogue, Fireplace, Mastic, Moriches, and Westhampton.

THE SHINECOCK TRIBE claimed the territory from Canoe Place to Easthampton, including Sagg Harbor and the whole south shore of Peconic Bay.

THE MONTAUK TRIBE had jurisdiction over all the remaining lands to Montauk Point, and probably included Gardiner's Island.   The Sachem of this tribe was of so much consequence as to have been acknowledged the Grand Sachem of Paumanacke, as Long Island was sometimes called.

The lands in King's County were principally purchased by the governor of the New Netherlands from the natives, and by him disposed of to the settlers ; but in all the English towns, purchases were made by the planters directly from the Indians, and for which patents of confirmation were subsequently procured from the governor after the conquest.   It is presumed the Indian inhabitants paid little attention to the cultivation of the land, except the raising a small quantity of corn ; but depended, in great measure, upon the flesh of the deer and other wild game, and the great abundance of fish, clams, and oysters, which were found on every shore, and in every creek and harbor.   Except their canoes, some of which were very large, and their bows and arrows, the only materials of art among them, were some rude vessels of earth hardened in the fire, fragments of which are sometimes found. The manufacture of wampum, and its use as money, is an evidence that, however simple or limited the business of any people may be, some sort of circulating medium is indispensable. Governor Winthrop speaks of the superior elegance of the wampum made by the Long Islanders in the year 1634. The Dutch and English, both from necessity and convenience, resorted to this species of exchange, the value of which was adjusted by common consent and general usage.

The religious notions of the Long Island Indians are described in a communication from the Rev. Sampson Occom, an educated Indian minister, and published among the valuable collections of the Massachusetts Historical Society.

His words are, " *They believe in a plurality of Gods, and in one great and good Being, who controls all the rest. They likewise believe in an Evil Spirit, and have their conjurors or pawaws.*" This ceremony was of so odious a character in the opinion of the white people, that by the Duke's laws in 1665, it was enacted that " *no Indian should be suffered to pawaw, or perform worship to the devil, in any town within this government.*"

The language of the Montauk Indians is supposed to have been the same with that of all the Long Island Indians, and differing little from the Narragansetts and other New-England tribes.

It has been contended that no more than two original languages ever existed among the American Indians north of-the Roanoke, the Delaware and the Iroquois,—the languages of the different tribes from Mississippi to Nova Scotia being, at most, particular dialects of the Delaware language. The structure of the Indian tongue is admitted to be different in many respects from all other known languages, ancient or modern.

Sampson Occom, the Indian clergyman above named, was born at Mohegan, on the Thames, near Norwich, Connecticut, in the year 1723; and was the first Indian pupil educated by the Rev. Mr Wheelock, at Lebanon, in 1742, at the age of 19 years, were he remained four years. About the year 1755 he went to Montauk, where he opened a school, and officiated as public teacher of the Indian tribe there and preached also oc-

casionally to the Indians at Shinecock.   He continned at
Montauk Point about 10 years.   On the 29th of August, 1759,
he was ordained by the Suffolk Presbytery.   He next engaged
in a mission to the Oneidas, and continued with them till he
accompanied Mr Whittaker to Europe, and was the first Indian
preacher who visited England.   The houses in which he
preached were thronged.   Between February 16, 1766, and
July 22, 1767, he preached in various parts of the kingdom,
and between three and four hundred sermons.   On his return
from Europe, he remained a while at Mohegan, whence he removed, in 1786, to the Stockbridge Indians at Brothertown, Oneida
County.   Many of the Mohegans and several of the Montauk
tribe accompanied him to that place, where he died, in July,
1792.   While in England he preached in the crowded chapels
of London, and even occupied the pulpit of Whitfield with acceptance.   The house in which he formerly lived, and the
church in which he preached, are, or were lately, standing at
Montville, New London County, Connecticut.

PAUL CUFFEE, another Indian preacher, a man of singular
eloquence, and of very considerable powers of mind, formerly
labored among the Indians at Montauk and Shinecock; and
although not a person of much education, was a useful and respectable man.   He was buried nearly a mile west of Canoe
Place, where the Indian meeting-house then stood; and over
whose grave a neat marble slab has been placed, upon which
is the following inscription :—

Erected by the Missionary Society of New-York, in
    memory of the Rev. Paul Cuffee, an Indian of the
    Shinecock Tribe, who was employed by that Society
    for the last 13 years of his life on the eastern part of
    Long Island, where he labored with fidelity and suc-
    cess.

Humble, pious, and indefatigable in testifying the gos-
    pel of the grace of God, he finished his course with
    joy on the 7th day of March, 1812, aged 55 years
    and 3 days."

In Johnson's " *Wonder Working Providence,*" a book as rare
as it is singular, it is stated that when the English first com-

menced the settlement of Long Island, the Indians annoyed them much by the multitude of dogs they kept, which ordinarily were young wolves brought up tame, and continuing of a very ravenous nature.

In 1643, one year before the Dutch war with the Indians north of the Sound, the Governor made a treaty with Pennowits, Sachem of the Matinecock Indians; and in 1646 made a treaty also with Tackapausa, Sachem of the Marsapeague tribe, and with the representatives of five others.

Thus the Dutch on the west, and the English on the east end of the island, maintained a firm and constant friendship with the natives near them; the consequences of which were the most happy on both sides.

THE DUTCH GOVERNMENT.

The hope of discovering a north-west passage to India, which had long been a favorite project of the maritime powers of Europe, and as yet hardly abandoned, was the propelling motive of several voyages undertaken by Henry Hudson in the first part of the seventeenth century. Two of these voyages were made in the years 1607 and 1608, in the service of an English association, which, being at length discouraged by ill success, finally abandoned the enterprise. On his third voyage in the service of the Dutch East India Company, Hudson, with a picked crew of twenty men, partly English and partly Dutch, ran down the coast from Newfoundland to 35° 4' N. lat., to ascertain whether a passage to the Pacific might not be found through the continent of North America. Retracing his route, he entered Delaware Bay on the 28th of August, 1609, but declined to explore it on account of the intricacy of the channel. Following the eastern shore of New Jersey, he anchored his ship, the "Half-Moon," on the 3d of September, 1609, within the beach at Sandy Hook; and after exploring the river to Albany, again put to sea, and arrived in Europe the 7th of November, 1609.

Although disappointed in the main object of the voyage, the Dutch Company believed they might establish a profitable trade in furs with the natives upon the Hudson River; and repeated

voyages were afterwards made, that excited the ambition of
private adventurers, which the Company endeavored to prevent
by obtaining a decree of the States General in their favor,
thereby securing a monopoly to themselves. This took place
27th March, 1614.

In the service of this Company Adrian Block and Hendrick
Christiance sailed, in the year 1614, and arriving here, erected a
fort and a few dwellings upon Manhattan Island or its neighborhood by consent of the natives. The former of these navigators first sailed through Hell Gate, and passing the Sound
in his way to Boston, gave name to Block Island, and discovered Long Island to be entirely surrounded by water.

An alliance was immediately formed between the Dutch and
Indians as an indispensable pre-requisite to the safety of the infant settlement, and to ensure to themselves the full benefit of an
established trade. Yet, as the main object of the Company was
the commercial advantages to be derived from the fur trade,
little was done for some years in the way of colonization and
settlement of the country.

In 1621 the great West India Company was formed in Holland, sustained by the wealth and power of the " *States General*." The former licensed trading Company was merged in
this, which gave great additional means and facilities for
peopling the country with emigrants from Holland. And to
this circumstance may be ascribed the first successful attempts
of the Dutch to plant colonies in America.

In 1623 and 1624 the Company fitted out two ships for New
Amsterdam, as New-York was then called, in one of which came
Peter Minuit, the first director general or governor of the New
Netherlands.

Although the history of this interesting era is very defective,
in consequence of a want of documentary evidence, yet enough
has been preserved to exhibit the manner in which the settlement of the country gradually progressed from the first rude
beginnings to the establishment of regular government, and a
commerce of considerable extent and importance.

The West India Company had by their charter an exclusive
right to trade to America for twenty-four years, and the governor

held his commission by their appointment. The Dutch made a purchase of land upon the island called Manhattan in 1623, and gave to the settlement the name of New Amsterdam, and to the country generally New Netherlands; by which appellations they continued to be known till the conquest by the English.

King James, about the same time, granted a patent to the London Company, under which they laid claim to New-York. The Dutch and English both claimed Long Island upon the ground of prior discovery of the country, it having been a principle generally adopted by the European powers, or a part of the convential law of nations, that new discoveries should enure to the nation under whose authority, or by whose citizens they were made. And it was alleged by the English, that Sebastian Cabot had, while in their service, discovered the whole of North America from thirty to fifty-eight degrees of north latitude; that many voyages had been made to different parts of the coast by English navigators previous to the year 1606; and that King James had, by letters patent, in that year granted all that part of the continent between 34 and 45 degrees of north latitude to Sir Thomas Gates and others, with permission to divide themselves into two companies; the first to be called the London Company, and the other the Plymouth Company.

In consequence of these conflicting claims of territory, both powers endeavored to strengthen their authority by encouraging and extending their settlements upon this continent. The English, however, mostly confined their operations to New England, while the Dutch claimed New-York and New Jersey, and even the country as far east as Connecticut River.

Wonter Van Twiller, the first Dutch governor (so called) of the New Netherlands, assumed the administration in the year 1629, and continued in authority till 1638. Authentic history presents little account of the administration of this gentleman; but a work of exquisite humor, in which fiction builds upon the ground-work of truth, has fully amplified his renown; and the name of Diedrich Knickerbocker, his panegyrist, will for ever remind posterity of the imperturbable gravity and unutterable ponderings of " Walter the Doubter."

During his administration, settlements began to be made in

King's County, and near its close, or very soon after, in the
eastern part of Suffolk, particularly Southampton and Southold.   The respective settlements under the Dutch and English
in the several towns, were nearly cotemporaneous, and were
all considerably advanced within the period of forty years;
although there does not appear to have been any union or combination among them till the formation of Ridings at the conquest in 1664.   In the Dutch towns the lands were chiefly, if
not universally, purchased in the first instance from the natives
by the governor, and by him granted out to individuals or companies ; but in the English towns within the Dutch territory,
the lands were procured by the first settlers immediately from
the Sachems and head men of the several Indian tribes ; and
in the territory independent of the Dutch, the lands were bought
from the natives, (originally with the consent of the agent of
the Earl of Stirling,) and afterwards by their own free contract with the natives.   In the case of grants to companies
from the Dutch governor, the lands were subsequently divided
among the individual inhabitants by lot ; and in all other cases
of purchase, individuals were deemed entitled to a quantity of
land in proportion to the amount paid by each toward the
purchase thereof, or the expense of the patent by which it
was confirmed.   And long after the settlements of the several
English towns, in the distribution of the common lands of the
town, the number of acres apportioned to each individual was
in exact ratio with the sum contributed to the original purchase, or to the expenses incident to obtaining of patents, or
other charges of a public nature.   Thus, in the town of Hempstead the portions allotted to the individual inhabitants differed
from ten to two hundred acres.   In a few instances large and
valuable tracts were purchased by associations of individuals
for themselves, and have remained private property ever since.
Such is the case with the lands of Montauk and Shinecock.
A few towns have at the present time large quantities of common lands, which are only improved as a common pasturage,
or for cutting the grass.   The town of Jamaica possesses a
considerable tract of common meadows, which are rented out
for the benefit of the town, or cut by the inhabitants themselves ;

the same is the case in the town of Oyster Bay ; and the town of Hempstead has now more than twenty thousand acres of upland and meadow, used as public commons, and continuing in a state of nature. The English settlers, as well under the Dutch jurisdiction as otherwise, were originally united in their religious creeds and opinions, and were generally those contained in the confession of faith adopted by the Assembly of Divines at Westminster in 1642. Among them the Congregational form of church government prevailed till the year 1747, when the Presbyterian order was adopted as most likely to preserve purity of doctrine and a more efficient discipline. In some of the towns a minister was among the first settlers, and the organization of churches was deemed a matter of primary importance. In the Dutch towns the governor claimed the right of licensing ministers, by which he virtually assumed to be the head of the church, or the source of ecclesiastical authority. Many symptoms of superstition and a spirit of intolerance were early manifested, but not to the same extent as in some parts of New England. Those who were deemed heretics, were objected to by all, among whom the peaceable and unoffending Quaker was included. They seem to have been equally discountenanced by the Dutch and English ; and in some instances they were treated with no small severity. During the administration of Governor Stuyvesant, a very respectable member of the Society of Friends was even apprehended and transported a prisoner to Holland, for trial as a heretic ; and some years after that, a Quaker preacher was confined in the jail of Queen's County, for more than twelve months, for a similar offence. It may be said that this species of persecution, has existed to a greater or less extent in all ages : but the inconsistency seems the more apparent, and the incongruity greater, with those who for conscience sake had fled from tyranny and oppression in a foreign country, and sought an asylum in this, where they might enjoy entirely unmolested the most perfect freedom, civil and religious. Even these, with all their professed zeal for equality and justice, could persecute in their turn, and attempt to expel from the pale of society and fellowship the simple-hearted Quaker, who craved only the privilege of thinking for himself, and imparting his opinions freely to others.

The States General of the United Belgic Provinces, in their grant to the Dutch West India Company in 1621, reserved to themselves the power of commissioning the governor whom they should appoint.   The object was a politic one, and intended to connect the interest of the Company with that of the mother country, and by their influence and authority to secure a partial control at least over the colony ; and in 1623, when the Company fitted out two ships for the purpose of establishing trade here, Peter Minuit was sent out by them under the title of Director-general of New Netherlands, which was, in fact, but another name for governor ; and with him came a colony of Walloons, some of whom, it is supposed, settled on the west end of Long Island, and from whom the *Waal-bocht*, now called the *Wall-about*, received its name.   Slaves were introduced here as early as 1626, if not sooner ; and the Dutch carried on a traffic in slaves between Africa and Virginia.   Some were even carried there in 1620 in Dutch vessels.

William Kieft succeeded Wonter Van Twiller as governor of New Netherlands in 1638, and remained in office for the space of nine years.   During his administration he was beset with difficulties of every kind.   The Swedes, he conceived, encroached upon him at the south and the English on the east ; while in the years 1645 and 6 he was involved in extensive wars with the Indians, both upon Long Island and the Main.   Toward the close of his administration was fought the great battle of Strickland's Plain, with great slaughter on both sides.   In May, 1647, Peter Stuyvesant, a brave old officer, was commissioned governor, and speedily restored peace with the hostile Indians.   He also made such arrangements with the United Colonies of New England as to maintain a tolerable good understanding with them throughout his administration.   He remained in the office of governor till the conquest in 1664. All the powers of government—executive, legislative and judicial—were vested in him and his council.   He directly or indirectly appointed or commissioned all the public officers, framed he laws, and decided all important controversies.   He more-

over heard all appeals from subordinate magistrates, and required them to send such cases as were depending before them to
the council, to be decided as they saw fit.   In April, 1660, the
governor ordered the magistrates of Rusdorpe (Jamaica) to refer
a certain cause, then pending before them, to the council, to
be heard and determined ; and the magistrates of Middleburgh (Newtown) on another occasion were required to do
likewise.   He also ordered churches to be built, he installed
ministers, and even directed them when and where to preach.
He excluded those whose tenets he did not approve, and finally assumed and exercised the sole prerogative over the public
lands.   The Indian title was extinguished by him, and no purchase could be made of the natives without his leave and approbation.   He granted out at his pleasure, to individuals or
companies, parcels of land for settlement and cultivation, subject to such conditions and payments as he thought proper to
impose.   And from the frequent complaints made by the delegates of the different towns, it appears that he exercised the prerogative in a capricious and arbitrary manner ; refusing lands
to some, and making large and extravagant grants to others,
his favorites and political partisans.   The Dutch towns seem
to have been settled by degrees, and without any previous concert of individuals, or without any immediate organization of
courts for administering justice.   Nor does it seem that they
entered into any arrangement for self-government, but left every thing to the will and pleasure of the governor, who appointed officers of different kinds in the several villages, with more
or less power, and without any uniformity as to their number,
title, or duration of office.   As population increased, the people
were permitted to nominate magistrates, to be approved of by the
governor ; but their powers were not defined by any general law,
and therefore their acts frequently became matter of complaint.
In 1661 the governor established a new court, with greater and
more definite authority than before.   The magistrates subsequently chosen and approved, were authorized to decide controversies between master and servant, seller and buyer, landlord
and tenant; and to take cognizance of all breaches of the peace
and other misdemeanors; the Dutch courts generally pro-

ceeding according to the maxims and principles of the "civil law," which may properly be called the "common law" of the Dutch empire.

The English, who settled the towns of Gravesend, Newtown, Flushing, Jamaica, and Hempstead, became, from unavoidable necessity, though very reluctantly, Dutch subjects; but were allowed to hold lands, enjoy liberty of conscience, and employ their own ministers; yet in their choice of magistrates it was required that the approbation of the governor should be obtained, to authorize them to discharge the duties of their office. Hempstead and Gravesend were incorporated towns, yet the assent of the governor was equally required to sanction their election of magistrates, although it was alleged to be mere matter of form. They were also authorized by their charters to elect a scout (or constable), and a clerk or recorder, to take and preserve the minutes of town proceedings. The magistrates were vested with full power to try causes, civil and criminal, with a limited jurisdiction as to the amount in controversy and the nature of the crime; and to make ordinances or by-laws for the welfare and good government of the towns respectively. Flushing was also partially incorporated, but restricted by its charter from electing any other officer than a scout or constable, with power to preserve good order, heal differences between neighbors, and report all important cases to the governor for his consideration and decision. This town was afterwards endowed with the power of nominating magistrates, like the other towns; and such was the case with the towns of Newtown and Jamaica.

The general practice in those towns subject to the authority of the Dutch, was for the people to choose double the number of persons required, out of whom the governor selected and commissioned those who should serve as magistrates. In those towns which were independent of the Dutch, they elected annually a certain number of officers, whom they denominated townsmen; whose duty it was to superintend the public concerns of the town, and to take cognizance of all trespasses upon the town lands. They, moreover, were associated with the magistrates in making such prudential rules and regulations as they mutually considered the public good required, (except such as related to the admission of settlers and the disposition of lands), but which were to be submitted to the consideration of the people in town meeting, to be approved or disallowed by them. The authority of the townsmen, as well as of the justices, extended to such matters as concerned the police of the towns; and certain minor duties, such as related to the making and repairing of fences, prescribing the time and manner of feeding the common lands, planting the common fields, &c. The towns in Suffolk County were not subject to the control of any colony, nor had they any political connection with each other before the conquest, except certain conventional agreements for specific purposes. Being too remote from Europe to derive any protection from that quarter, and without political alliances here, the whole power of government was retained by and vested in the primary assemblies of the people; being an instance of a pure democracy, and which, apparently, answered all the ends of government in those days of ancient simplicity. They elected magistrates and other civil officers, and established courts, which decided causes with or without the intervention of a jury, according to the discretion of the court, subject to the ultimate decision of the town meeting, called the General Court, if either party was dissatisfied with the determination of the court below. The patents, or ground briefs, issued by the Dutch governors, were made by authority of the mother country, and usually commenced as follows: "We, director and council residing in New Netherlands, on the Island of Manhattan, under the government of their High Mightinesses the Lords, the States General of the United Netherlands, and the privileged West India Company," &c. The first patents enrolled bear date one year after the arrival of Governor Van Twiller; but there are no records remaining in the Secretary's office of the proceedings of the Dutch Government during his administration. In 1640, or a little before, a few English emigrants attempted a settlement at Oyster Bay; but the Dutch were so jealous of them, that Governor Keift sent a scout with a few soldiers, took some prisoners, and broke up the settlement. The character of his Excellency is represented as rash,

and disposed likewise to tyrannize over those whom he was
appointed to govern.   He is said sometimes to have sported
with the rights of the people, by rejecting, without reason, the
names of magistrates presented for his approbation from mere
wantonness and caprice, as was the case also with his successor.
The government was neither suited to the people, or calculated
to afford them adequate protection.   The laws were imperfect,
and many of them not at all adapted to the exigency of the
times ; and to aggravate the matter, the governor and council
were either indisposed or incompetent to remedy many important defects in the administration of civil and criminal justice.
The sense of public insecurity in time produced a spirit of
general discontent, and the people, with great unanimity, resolved to state their grievances to the governor, and to demand
redress.   Accordingly, the burgomasters of New Amsterdam
called upon the several Dutch towns to send delegates to a
convention in that city on the 26th of November, 1653.   They
met, and adjourned to the 11th of December following ; at which
time delegates from the city, from Brooklyn, Flatbush, Flatlands,
Gravesend, Newtown, Flushing, and Hempstead met ; and
after mutual consultation and discussion of various matters,
adopted a remonstrance, which was ably drawn up, and expressed in spirited but decent language.   The following extract from this ancient document contains the most material
parts of it, and shows sufficiently, that even in that day the people had not only intelligence enough to understand their rights,
but knew also the legitimate objects of civil government.
    " To the Honorable Director General and Council of New
Netherlands together, to the Council of the high and mighty
Lords, the States-General of the United Provinces :—
    " The humble remonstrance and petition of the colonies and
villages in the province of New Netherland, humbly show :
    " We acknowledge a paternal government, which God and
Nature has established in the world for the maintenance and
preservation of peace, and the welfare of men, not only principally in conformity to the laws of nature, but according to
the law and precepts of God, to which we consider ourselves
obliged by his word, and therefore submit to it.   The Lord

our God having invested their high Mightinesses the States-
General, as his ministers, with the power to promote the welfare
of their subjects, as well of those residing within the United
Provinces as of those at this side of the sea, which we grate-
fully acknowledge; and having commissioned in the same
view some subaltern magistrates, and clothed them with authority to promote the same end, as are the Lords Directors
of the privileged West India Company, whom we acknowledge
as lords and patroons of this place, next to your Lordships, as
being their representatives.

"We settled here on a mutual agreement and contract with
the lord patroons, with the consent of the natives, who were the
first proprietors of these lands; of whom we purchased the soil at
our own expense, and transformed a wilderness, with immense
labor, into a few small villages and many cultivated farms,
encouraged by the privileges which we obtained, and whose
preservation is dear to us

"The deep homage and profound respect which we feel for
the Government of the United Netherlands, consisting and co-
agulated from various nations of the world: That we, leaving
at our own expense, our country and countrymen, voluntarily
choose to submit to their protection, and being now immatricu-
lated in their body under our sovereign, the high and mighty
lords, the States-General whom we acknowledge:

"This being considered, we humbly solicit that this our remonstrance and petition may be received and well construed,
without being misinterpreted."

The remonstrance then sets forth their apprehensions of an
arbitrary government being established, rendering life and property unsafe. That injustice towards the natives might lead
them to commit outrages upon them. That officers are appointed contrary to law, and without the choice of the people.
That many obsolete laws are liable to be put in force, by
which many may be exposed to danger without knowing it.
That much delay hath occurred in the execution of grants to
those who had right to expect them. That large tracts of land
are conveyed to favored individuals, to the injury of others.
They then conclude as follows:

11

"As we exert ourselves to reduce all our griefs to six points, in the hope they will soon be redressed agreeable to the privileges of our country, when all discontents shall cease, a mutual harmony be restored and our anxiety relieved.

"We apply, therefore, to your wisdom to heal our sicknesses and pains. We shall remain thankful, and consider any further application needless, as we should otherwise be compelled to do.

"Upon which, humbly soliciting your Honors' answer on every point or article, in such a manner that we may remain satisfied, or proceed further, &c. as God shall direct our steps."

      "Your Honors' suppliant Servants,

"ARENT VAN HATTEN, MARTIN CREIGER, P. L. VANDER GIRST,	*New-York*.
FREDERICK LUBBERSON, PAULUS VANDER BEEK, WILLIAM BEEKMAN,	*Brooklyn*.
JOHN HICKS, TOBIAS FEEKS,	*Flushing*.
ROBERT COE, THOMAS HAZZARD,	*Newtown*.
WILLIAM WASHBORN, JOHN SOMERS,	*Hempstead*.
PETER WOLVERTON, JAN. STRYKER, THOMAS PENEWIT,	*Flatlands*.
ELBERT ELBERTSON, THOMAS SPICER,	*Flatbush*.
GEORGE BAXTER, JAMES HUBBARD,	*Gravesend*."

"Done Dec. 11, 1653."

To this remonstrance the governor and council gave no formal answer to the deputies, but entered a reply upon their minutes; denied the right of some of the towns to send deputies, particularly Brooklyn, Flatbush, and Flatlands; and protested against the meeting. In their observations, the gover-

nor and council reflect much on the English as the authors of
the public discontents, and especially upon George Baxter from
Gravesend, to whom they evidently impute the draft of the remonstrance.

Of Baxter and Hubbard it is ascertained that Baxter had
been an ensign, and James Hubbard a sergeant in the British
service, and are so named in the charter of Gravesend. They
seem both to have been men of talents and capacity, and were
generally entrusted with the management of the affairs of that
town. In 1642 Governor Kieft appointed the former his " English secretary to write his letters, with a salary of two hundred
and fifty guilders a year, in consideration of his talents and
knowledge of the English language, *and of the law.*" He was
appointed by Governor Stuyvesant himself one of the commissioners who negotiated the treaty of Hartford in 1650. He had
been educated in the principles of English liberty, and could
not therefore countenance the tyranny of the Dutch governor ;
his opposition to which made him the victim of Executive persecution, and it is supposed he was obliged to leave the country
to escape the resentment of the government. On the 13th of December, 1653, the deputies presented another remonstrance, in
which they declared that if they could not obtain redress or
protection from the governor and council, they must appeal to
their superiors in the Netherlands. This so irritated Stuyvesant, that with true Dutch resolution, he ordered them " to disperse, and not to assemble again upon such a business."

At this period the country was overrun with robbers, and
there appeared to the inhabitants, who suffered by their depredations, no mode of obtaining either relief or protection. As
the only alternative, the magistrates of Brooklyn, Flatbush and
Flatlands, united in forming a military company against "*robbers and pirates,*" and established a patrole in each village,
April 7, 1654. On the day following, the governor issued his
proclamation against certain robbers, whom he states " had
been banished from New England, and were wandering about
on Long Island."

In the same year the governor refused to confirm the election of Baxter and Hubbard, who had been chosen magistrates

for Gravesend; although they were among the original patentees of the town, had often previously been elected to the office of magistrate, and enjoyed the highest confidence of their fellow-citizens in every situation.

The rejection of these gentlemen excited so great a ferment in Gravesend, that the governor found it necessary to go there personally to appease it. It is stated in the records of November 23d, 1654, that the Governor went to Gravesend, and to effect his purpose was obliged to avail himself of the influence of Lady Moody, a connection of Sir Henry Moody, and one of the original patentees of that town. He conceded the nomination of the magistrates for that year to her; and her popularity reconciled the people to so extraordinary a measure, and produced submission to the arbitrary act of his Excellency.

Of Governor Stuyvesant, it is observed by Judge Benson, " That he was of the profession of arms, and had lost a leg in the service, which was supplied by one of wood. His skill and experience must have been very useful to him, as he was incessantly vexed with the marauding clans of the Mohegan family upon his New England possessions. He was in great difficulty with the Swedes on the Delaware; and his neighbors on the Connecticut River were also a great source of trouble and perplexity. In fine," says the Judge, " the whole of his duties and his character being considered, it may be questioned whether the chief magistracy among us has ever been confided to an individual of greater worth."

In consequence of disputes between the English and Dutch about the boundaries of their respective territories, commissioners from both, met at Hartford, September 19, 1650, and agreed, among other things, as follows :—" That upon Long Island a line run from the westernmost part of Oyster Bay, and so in a straight and direct line to the sea, shall be the bounds between the English and Dutch there; the easterly part to belong to the English, and the westernmost part to the Dutch." This instrument will be found at length in our Appendix. In pursuance of this determination, it was further ordered " At a session of the General Assembly at Hartford, March 10, 1663 :—

" This Court have voted Mr. Wyllys and Mr. Matthew Allyn to go over to Long Island, to settle government on the west end of the island, according to the agreement at Hempstead in February last; and those gentlemen are desired to issue the matter twixt J. Scott and Bloomer; and they are further desired to take in with them the assistance of the commissioners in those towns, for the regulating of any disturbances, as occasion is presented.

"A true copy from the public records of the Colony of Connecticut. Examined this 8th of August, 1664, by
"GEORGE WYLLYS, *Secretary*."

The government of Connecticut, after the receipt of their charter in 1662, asserted their right to the whole of Long Island, as appears by the proceedings, of which the following is a copy. ·

"At a General Assembly held at Hartford, May the 12th, 1664, for election,

"Whereas, his Majesty hath been graciously pleased to confirm unto this colony, by charter, all that part of his dominions in New England, bounded, as in the said charter is expressed, with the islands adjoining.

"This Court doth declare, that they claim Long Island for one of those adjoining islands, expressed in the charter, except a precedent right doth appear, approved by his Majesty.

"This Court doth desire and request the worshipful governor, Mr. Matthew Allyn, Mr. Wyllys, and Captain Youngs, to go over to Long Island, and to settle the English plantations on the island under this government, according to instructions given them.

"The aforesaid committee are hereby authorized to erect and constitute quarter Courts, or appoint other fit seasons for the keeping of court for the administration of justice, that all cases may be tried according to law, (life, limbs, and banishment excepted,) and to do their endeavors so to settle matters, that the people may be both civilly, peaceably, and religiously governed in the English plantations, so as they may win the heathen to the knowledge of our Lord and Saviour Jesus Christ by their sober and religious conversation, as his Majesty our Lord and King requires in his gracious letters patent, granted to his sub-

jects here, in this colony ; and in case of crimes of a capital nature, they are to have liberty to take the opportunity of the
Courts of Fairfield or Hartford ; the like liberty they have in
case of review.   They may also give oath to those who are accepted by this Court for freemen on the island, and to do what
else they judge may conduce for the good of the colony.

"A true copy from the public records of the colony of
Connecticut.   Examined this 8th day of August,
1664, by   GEORGE WYLLYS, *Secretary.*"

The commissioners accordingly came upon the island in
June, 1664, organized Courts in some of the towns, established
rules for the collection of rates, &c. ; but these arrangements
were frustrated almost immediately by the arrival of the English and the conquest of New-York, whereby Long Island
was annexed to the possessions of the Duke of York.   This
event was not altogether unexpected ; for on the 1st of November, 1663, the governor of New Netherlands, apprehending that
the English designed to invade the Dutch territories, convened a meeting of the magistrates of most of the towns at New
Amsterdam ; this meeting was composed of the magistrates of
New Amsterdam, Renselaerwyck, Beverwyck, Harlaem, Bergen, Staten Island, Flatlands, Flatbush, Brooklyn, Utrecht,
and Bushwick ; but they adjourned without effecting any
thing.   The Dutch government, by its oppressions, had become
generally unpopular ; even the Dutch inhabitants were disgusted with the administration, and the English were, of course,
extremely anxious for a change.

The English towns under the Dutch jurisdiction had long
determined on the first opportunity to withdraw themselves
from their authority.   They had held a meeting at Hempstead
during the winter, and agreed to put themselves under Connecticut, as some of the eastern towns had already done ; and
in consequence of these proceedings being made known to the
government of Connecticut, the General Assembly of that colony, on the 10th of March, 1663, appointed two commissioners
"to go to Long Island to settle the government on the west
end of the island, as above stated."   "The English," says
Smith, "were every day encroaching upon the Dutch."   The

following copy of a letter from Governor Stuyvesant to the West India Company, July 21, 1661, shows the state of things at that time :

" We have not, (says he) yet begun the fort on Long Island, near Oyster Bay, because our neighbors lay the boundaries a mile and a half more westerly than we do ; and the more as your Honors, by your advice of Dec. 24th, are not inclined to stand by the treaty of Hartford, and propose to sue for redress on Long Island and the fresh water river, by means of the States' ambassador.

" Lord Stirling is said to solicit a confirmation of his right to all Long Island, and importunes the present king to confirm the grant made by his royal father, which is affirmed to be already obtained. We have advice from England that there is an invasion intended against these parts, and the country solicited of the king, the duke, and the parliament, is to be annexed to their dominion. And for that purpose they desire three or four frigates, persuading the king that the Company possessed and held this country under an unlawful title, having only obtained of King James leave for a watering-place on Staten Island in 1623."

In November, 1663, the English inhabitants convened at Jamaica to concert measures of relief from the oppression of the governor and council. The number assembled on that interesting occasion was so great, that the government did not think it advisable to attempt either to interrupt their proceedings or to disperse the meeting by force.

CLAIMS OF THE ENGLISH TO LONG ISLAND, AND THE CONQUEST OF NEW-YORK.

King Charles the First, on the 22d day of April, 1636, made a request of the corporation for New England, called the Plymouth Company, to whom a charter had been granted by King James the First in 1620, to issue their patent to William Alexander, Earl of Stirling, for Long Island and the islands adjacent. This request of his Majesty was assented to by the Company, and a grant or patent issued accordingly. The Earl gave a power of attorney to James Farret on the 20th day of

April, 1637 ; thereby constituting and appointing him as his
agent to manage and dispose of the lands thus conveyed to him
by the Plymouth Company. The Earl of Stirling was a native of Scotland, where he was born in 1580, and was knighted
by James VI. of Scotland and 1st of England in 1614. He
obtained letters patent for Nova Scotia in 1620, and was created secretary of state for Scotland in 1626. He was made a peer
of Scotland in 1630, and Earl of Stirling in 1636. His death
took place in 1640. The title thus acquired to Long Island
was subsequently relinquished by his grandson, either to the
crown or to the Duke of York, previous to the grant of Charles
the Second in 1664, and in which the territory of Long Island
was included in express words, as will hereafter appear.
The power of attorney from the Earl of Stirling to his agent,
after reciting the issuing of the patent to him as aforesaid, and
stating that he was desirous of improving the lands granted to
him, and had, therefore, appointed the said James Farret to be his
attorney and agent, to take possession of the said islands, and to
plant and improve the same, proceeds as follows :—

" I, the said William, Earl of Stirling, do hereby empower
and authorise for me, my heirs, executors, and administrators,
and for every of us, to let, set, mortgage, sell, or by any other
way or means, for a present sum or sums of money, or for
yearly rent, to dispose of the said islands, or any of them, or
parts of them, for such time or times, term or terms of years, for
life or lives, or for ever in fee, as my said attorney or agent shall
judge most probably conducing to my profit and behalf, and to
the ends before specified. And after one or more plantations, or
colonies, or people, shall be there in any or all of the aforesaid
islands settled, to continue, erect, and establish such honest and
wholesome orders and ordinances amongst and for the benefit
of the said planters and colonies, as shall be judged, together
with and upon the advice of the right worshipful John Winthrop, Esquire, Governor of Boston Colony, in the said New
England, most tending to the preservation of the public peace,
the improvement of trade and commerce, and the due execution of justice in obedience to the laws of God, and as much
as may be agreeable to the laws of England." The said James

Farret was further authorized and permitted, by the said power of attorney, to take up and dispose of for his own use twelve thousand acres upon Long Island or the islands adjacent. In consequence of which he afterwards made choice of Shelter Island and Robin's Island in Peconic Bay, which, as will be seen, he sold to Stephen Goodyeare of New Haven on the 18th of May, 1641. The colony of Connecticut, after the reception of their charter in 1662, asserted a claim to Long Island under the clause of the charter which annexed to that colony the "islands adjacent." And the assembly at Hartford, on the 12th of May, 1664, formally resolved that it belonged to their jurisdiction, and appointed the governor and two other persons to "come upon the island in that behalf, to establish quarter courts and other courts for the administration of justice, provided their judgments should not extend to life, limb, or banishment;" and all capital cases were ordered to be tried at Fairfield or Hartford. The commissioners thus appointed came upon the island, and convened a meeting at Setauket in the summer of 1664, made a few decisions upon disputed claims among the inhabitants, and took some further measures in the execution of their delegated powers. The final arrangements were for some cause delayed, and were eventually frustrated by the arrival of Colonel Richard Nicolls in August, 1664, with a considerable naval force to take possession of New Amsterdam, in pursuance of an extensive grant of territory, made the 12th of March preceding, by King Charles II. to his brother James, Duke of York and Albany, and the consequent surrender of the city by the Dutch. The country included in this grant is thus described :

"All that part of the main land of New England, beginning at a certain place called or known by the name of St. Croix, adjoining to Nova Scotia in America, and thence extending along the sea-coast unto a certain place called Pemaquire or Pemaquid, and so up the river thereof to the furthest head of the same as it tendeth to the northward ; and extending from thence to the river Kenebeque, and so upwards by the shortest course to the river of Canada northward; and also all that island or islands commonly called by the several name or names

12

of Meitowacks, or Long Island, situate, lying, and being towards the west of Cape Cod and the Narrow-Higansetts, abutting upon the main land between the two rivers, there called or known by the several names of Connecticut and Hudson's river.   Together also with the said river called Hudson's, and all the land from the west side of Connecticut to the east side of Delaware Bay ; and also all those several islands called or known by the names of Martin's Vineyard and Nantuck's, otherwise Nantucket, together with all," &c.   " To be holden of us, our heirs and successors, as of our manor of East Greenwich in our county of Kent, in free and common soccage, and not in capite, nor by knight service yielding and rendering ; and the said James, Duke of York, doth for himself, his heirs and assigns, covenant and promise to yield and render unto us, our heirs and successors, of and for the same yearly, and every year *forty beaver skins* when they shall be demanded, or within ninety days thereafter. And we do further give and grant unto our dearest brother James, Duke of York, his heirs, &c., full and absolute power and authority to correct, punish, pardon, govern and rule, all such subjects of us, our heirs and successors, as shall from time to time adventure themselves into any of these parts or places aforesaid, or that shall or do at any time hereafter inhabit within the same ; as well in all cases or matters capital and criminal, as civil, both marine and others, so as the said proceedings be not contrary to, but as near as conveniently may be, agreeable to the laws, statutes, and government of this our realm of England ; and saving and reserving to us, our heirs and successors, the receiving, hearing, and determining of the appeal and appeals of all or any person or persons of, in, or belonging to the territories or islands aforesaid, in or touching any judgment or sentence to be there made or given ; and we do also for us, our heirs and successors, grant to our dearest brother James, Duke of York, his heirs and assigns, and to all and every such governor and governors, or any other officers or ministers, as by our said brother, his heirs or assigns, shall be appointed to have power and authority of government and command, in or over the inhabitants of the said territories or islands.

" Witness ourself at Westminster, the 12th day of March, in the sixteenth year of our reign.   By the King.

"HOWARD."

Immediately upon receiving this patent, the Duke of York constituted and commissioned Richard Nicolls, Esq. Deputy Governor of the colony ; and Robert Carr, George Cartwright, and Samuel Maverick, were joined with him as commissioners to demand and take possession of the country.

The Dutch inhabitants, by the vigilance of their governor, were not ignorant of the designs of the English court; for their records state, that on the 8th of July, 1664, intelligence was received from one Thomas Willet, an Englishman, that an expedition was preparing in England against the city of New Amsterdam, consisting of two frigates of forty and fifty guns, and a fly-boat of forty guns, having on board three hundred soldiers, and each frigate one hundred and fifty men ; and that they lay at Portsmouth waiting for a wind. News arrived also, from Boston, that they had already sailed.

The burgomasters were therefore called together, the fort ordered to be put in a posture of defence, and spies were sent to Milford and Westchester for intelligence. Boston was in the secret; for the court of Massachusetts had, in May preceding, ordered a supply of necessaries for the use of the ships on their arrival. The ships were four in number, one of which was called the Guerney. It was intended to rendezvous at Gardiner's Island in the Sound, but they parted in a fog about the 20th of July. The new governor and Sir George Cartwright were on board the Guerney, and fell in first with Cape Cod. The other ships, with Sir Robert Carr and Samuel Maverick, (commissioners,) were rightly concluded to be driven to the eastward. After dispatching a letter to Governor Winthrop of Connecticut, requesting his assistance, Colonel Nicolls proceeded to Boston. The other ships got into Piscataway. John Endicot was then governor of Boston, but old, and incapable of business. On the 27th of July the commissioners made a formal request in writing, " That the governor of Boston would pass an act to furnish them with armed men, who should begin their march to the Manhattans on the 20th of August ensuing ; and promised that if they could get other assistance, they would give them an account of it." This application was without success, and perhaps (as Smith says) from their disaffection to the Stuart family, by whose persecutions the inhabitants had been driven from Europe.

One of the ships entered the Bay of New-York several days before the others, and as soon as they were come up, Governor Stuyvesant sent a letter, dated August 19th, 1664, directed to the commanders of the English frigates, by John Declyer, one of the chief council, the Rev. John Megapolensis, minister, Paul Lunder Vander Grilft, and Mr. Samuel Megapolensis, Doctor in Physic, with the utmost civility, to desire the reason of their approach, and continuing in the harbor without giv-Sng notice, as they ought to have done. Colonel Nicolls answered the next day with a summons as follows :—

" To the Honorable the Governor and chief council at the Manhattans.

" Right worthy Sirs,

" I received a letter by some worthy persons intrusted by you, bearing date the 19th of August, desiring to know the intent of the approach of the English frigates ; in return of which, I think it fit to let you know that his Majesty of Great Britain, whose right and title to these parts of America is unquestionable, well knowing how much it derogates from his crown and dignity to suffer any foreigners, how near soever they be allied, to ursurp a dominion, and without his Majesty's royal consent to inherit in these, or any other of his Majesty's territories, hath commanded me, in his name, to require a surrender of all such forts, towns, or places of strength, which are now possessed by the Dutch under your command ; and in his Majesty's name I do demand the town, situate on the island, commonly known by the name of Manhattoes, with all the forts thereunto belonging, to be rendered unto his Majesty's obedience and protection, into my hands. I am further commanded to assure you, and every respective inhabitant of the Dutch nation, that his Majesty being tender of the effusion of Christian blood, doth by these presents confirm and secure to every man his estate, life, and liberty, who shall readily submit to his government. And all those who shall oppose his Majesty's gracious intention, must expect all the miseries of a war, which they bring upon themselves. I shall expect your answer by these gentlemen, George Cartwright, one of his Majesty's commissioners in America, Captain Robert Needham, Captain Edward Groves, and Mr. Thomas Delavall, whom you will entertain with such civility as is due to them, and yourselves and yours shall receive the same from,

"Worthy Sirs,

"Your very humble Servant,

"Dated on board his Majesty's   "RICHARD NICOLLS."
ship the Guerney, riding
before Nayack, the 20th of
Aug. 1664."

Governor Stuyvesant promised an answer to the summons the next morning, and in the meantime convened the council and burgomasters. The Dutch governor was a good soldier, (says Smith,) and had lost a leg in the service of the States. He would willingly have made a defence; and refused a sight of the summons both to the inhabitants and burgomasters, lest the easy terms offered might induce them to capitulate. The latter, however, insisted upon a copy, that they might com-communicate it to the late magistrates and principal burghers. They called together the inhabitants at the Stadt-house, and acquainted them with the governor's refusal. Governor Winthrop, at the same time, wrote to the governor and his council, strongly recommending a surrender. On the 22d of August the burgomasters came into the council, and desired to know the contents of the English message from Governor Winthrop, which Stuyvesant still refused. They continued their importunity; and he, in a fit of anger, tore it to pieces; upon which they protested against the act and all its consequences. Determined upon a defence of the country, Stuyvesant wrote a letter in answer to the summons; in which he fully denied the right of his Majesty, the King of England, to the territory; and setting forth the reasons why the title was in the Lords, the States-General. That by virtue of a grant and commission given by the said Lords and mighty States-General to the

West India Company, in the year 1621, with as much power, and as authentic, as his said Majesty of England hath given or can give to any colony in America, as more fully appears by the patent of the said Lords, the States-General, by them signed, registered, and sealed with their great seal, and shown to the deputies ; by which commission and patent together, and by divers letters, signed and sealed by the said Lords, the States-General, directed to several persons, both English and Dutch, inhabiting the towns and villages on Long Island, by which they are declared and acknowledged to be their subjects, which makes it appear more clear than the sun at noon-day, that the claim of England is absolutely to be denied.

" Moreover, (says the governor,) it is without dispute, and acknowledged by the world, that our predecessors, by virtue of the commission and patent of the said Lords, the States-General, have, and without control and peaceably (the contrary never coming to our knowledge), enjoyed Fort Orange about forty-eight or fifty years ; the Manhattans forty-one or forty-two years ; the South River forty years; and the Fresh-Water River about thirty-six years.   And that though the governors and commissioners of his Majesty had often quarrelled about the bounds of the Dutch possesssions, yet they never questioned their jurisdiction itself. On the contrary, in the year 1650, at Hartford, and the year before at Boston, they treated upon the subject; which is a sufficient proof, that had his Majesty been well informed, he never would have given a commission to molest and endamage the subjects of the Lords. the States-General ; and less that his subjects would attempt any acts of hostility against them.   Consequently, if his said Majesty were well informed of all that could be spoken upon this subject, he would not approve of what expressions were mentioned in your letter.   And in case that you will act by force of arms, we protest and declare, in the name of our said Lords, the States-General, before GOD and MEN, that you will act an unjust violence, and a breach of the articles of peace, so solemnly sworn, agreed upon, and ratified by his Majesty of England and my Lords the States-General ; and the rather, for that to prevent the shedding of blood in the mouth of February last we treated with Captain John Scott, (who reported he had a commission from his Majesty,) touching the limits of Long Island, and concluded for the space of a year. As touching the threats in your conclusion, we have nothing to answer, only that we fear nothing but what GOD (who is as just as merciful) shall lay upon us, all things being in his gracious disposal ; and we may as well be preserved by him with small forces as by a great army.

"My Lords, your thrice humble and affectionate Servant, and Friend,   PETER STUYVESANT."

"At the fort at Amsterdam, the ⎫
2d of September, new style, ⎬
1664." ⎭

While the Dutch governor and his council were contending with the burgomasters and people in the city, the English commissioners published a proclamation to the inhabitants of Long Island, encouraging them to submit, and promising them the king's protection and all the privileges of subjects. How far this flattering promise was fulfilled, will appear from the proceedings that afterwards took place at Hempstead, when a code of laws for the colony was published; by which it turned out that, so far from enjoying the privileges of British subjects, they were entirely excluded from the benefits of an assembly, or the right of choosing any one to represent them in the government. This proclamation was as follows :—

" By his Majesty's command. Forasmuch as his Majesty hath sent us by commission, under his great seal of England, amongst other things to expel or to receive to his Majesty's obedience all such foreigners as have, without his Majesty's leave and consent, seated themselves amongst any of his dominions in America, to the prejudice of his Majesty's subjects and the diminution of his royal dignity ; we, his Majesty's commissioners, declare and promise, that whoever, of what nation soever, will, upon knowledge of this proclamation, acknowledge and testify themselves to submit to this his Majesty's government, as his good subjects, shall be protected in his Majesty's laws and justice, and peaceably enjoy whatsoever God's blessing and their honest industry have furnished them with, and all other privileges with his Majesty's English subjects.

We have caused this to be published, that we might prevent all inconveniences to others, if it were possible ; however, to clear ourselves from the charge of all those miseries that may any way befall such as live here, and will not acknowledge his Majesty for their sovereign, whom God preserve.

"In his Majesty's frigate   }   RICHARD NICOLLS,
   the Guerney, August }   ROBERT CARR,
   20, 1664.   }   GEORGE CARTWRIGHT,
                                   SAMUEL MAVERICK."

As soon as it was ascertained by Stuyvesant's letter that he was averse to surrender, officers were sent to obtain volunteers in the western towns on Long Island as far as Jamaica and Hempstead. And preparations were also made by the shipping for an attack upon Fort Amsterdam. These movements, and probably urged likewise by those around him, induced Stuyvesant to write again to Col. Nicolls on the 25th of August, wherein, though he declares that he would stand the storm, yet, to prevent the spilling of blood, he had sent John De Decker, councillor of state ; Cornelius Van Ruyven, Secretary ; Cornelius Steenwyck, Major ; and James Cousseau, Sheriff ; to consult, if possible, of an accommodation. Nicolls, who by this time knew the dispositions and wishes of the people, answered immediately, from Gravesend, that he would treat about nothing but a surrender. The Dutch governor next day, the 26th, agreed to a treaty and surrender, on condition the English and Dutch limits were settled by the Crown and the States-General.

The English deputies were Sir Robert Carr, George Cartwright, John Winthrop, the governor of Connecticut, Samuel Wyllys, one of the assistants or council of that colony, and Thomas Clarke and John Pynchon, commissioners from the General Court of Massachusetts Bay. Whatever these persons should agree upon, Nicolls promised to ratify. At eight o'clock in the morning of the 27th of August, 1664, the commissioners on both sides met at the governor's farm (or Bowery,) where the articles of capitulation were signed. These articles were twenty-three in number, and were so framed as to protect the inhabitants in their rights, civil and religious, as citizens of the new government, to remove or remain at their pleasure, and to carry on trade and commerce as British subjects : the ports to be open to the Dutch vessels for six months ; public writings and documents to be carefully preserved. All persons in office to remain therein till the time of a new election ; previous differences and contracts to be determined according to the manner of the Dutch ; the officers, military, and soldiers, to march out with their arms, drums beating, colors flying, and with lighted matches ; and those disposed to continue in the country, to have fifty acres of land set out for them.

Favorable, however, as these articles were to the inhabitants, the Dutch governor refused to ratify them until two days after they were signed by the commissioners.

Governor Winthrop, on seeing the letters patent to the Duke of York, informed the English on Long Island that Connecticut had no longer any claims to the island ; that what they had done was for the welfare, peace, and quiet settlement of his Majesty's subjects, as they were the nearest organized government to them under his Majesty. But now that his Majesty's pleasure was fully signified by his letters patent, their jurisdiction ceased and became null.

The following is the conclusion of the commissioners on the subject of Long Island :—

The determination of his Majesty's commissioners relative to the boundaries of his Royal Highness the Duke of York's patent, and of the patent of Connecticut, November 30th, 1644.

By virtue of his Majesty's commission, we have heard the difference about the bounds of the patents granted to his Royal Highness the Duke of York, and his Majesty's colony of Connecticut ; and having deliberately considered all the reasons alleged by Mr. Allen, senior, Mr. Gould, Mr. Richards, and Captain Winthrop, appointed by the assembly held at Hartford the 13th day of October, 1664, to accompany John Winthrop, Esq., the governor of his Majesty's colony of Connecticut to New-York, and by Mr. Howell and Captain Youngs of Long Island, why the said Long Island should be under the government of Connecticut, which are too long to be recited. We do declare and order, that

the southern bounds of his Majesty's colony of Connecticut is the
sea, and that Long Island is to be under the government of his
Royal Highness the Duke of York, as is expressed by plain words
in the said patents respectively, and also by virtue of his Majesty's
commission, and by the consent of both the governor and the
gentlemen above named ; we also order and declare that the
creek or river called Mamoroneck, which is reputed to be about
twelve miles to the east of Westchester, and a line drawn from
the east point or side where the fresh water falls into the salt,
at high-water mark, N. N. W. to the line of the Massachusetts,
be the western bounds of the said colony of Connecticut, and
the plantations lying westward of that creek and line so drawn,
to be under his Royal Highness's government ; and all plantations lying eastward of that creek and line to be under the
government of Connecticut.

Given under our hands at Fort James, New-York, on Manhattan Island, this 30th day of Nov. 1664.

RICHARD NICOLLS,
GEORGE CARTWRIGHT,
SAMUEL MAVERICK.

We, underwritten, on behalf of the colony of Connecticut,
have assented unto this determination of his Majesty's commissioners in relation to the bounds and limits of his Royal Highness the Duke's patent, and the patent of Connecticut.

JOHN WINTHROP,
MATTHEW ALLEN,
NATHAN GOULD,
JAMES RICHARDS.

Governor Stuyvesant retained his large real estate upon the
Island of New-York. He made a visit to Holland the year following, but returned soon after, and finally died at New-York.
Judge Benson says that he came from Brazil, and that he lost
his leg in the attack upon the Island of Tobago.   That he
was an honest and brave man is certain ; and his posterity here
are among the most wealthy and respected of our fellow-citizens.

THE COLONIAL GOVERNMENT.

Governor Nicolls having thus peaceably obtained possession

of the country, and about to lay the foundations of his future government, it was determined to change the name of the colony; and in compliment to the Duke of York, to whom the country had been assigned, and to whom the governor was indebted for his office and authority, agreed to call it New-York; and the city of New-Amsterdam, the city of New-York. It also became a matter of great and indispensable necessity that a system of civil regulations should be matured and adopted, both to constitute general rules of action, and to produce a more perfect uniformity among the different towns, in some of which the English and in others the Dutch municipal law prevailed. Accordingly a meeting of delegates being convened at Hempstead, as will appear hereafter, for the purpose of adjusting any conflicting claims to lands, and settling the boundaries of the several towns, the deputies that attended were so highly gratified with the interview with the governor, and with the information imparted by him as to the liberal views and intentions of the Duke of York, that they drew up and signed an address full of gratitude and loyalty; but which, as soon as their constituents found they were to have no choice in the selection of magistrates, or a share in legislation, they manifested their disapprobation, and censured the deputies with so much severity, that the civil authorities thought it necessary to interfere; and accordingly, at a court of Assize, held in October, 1666, it was resolved that whoever thereafter should any way detract or speak against any of the deputies signing the address to his Royal Highness at the general meeting at Hempstead, should be presented to the next Court of Sessions; and if the justices should see cause, they should thence be bound over to the Assizes, there to answer for the slander upon plaint or information. This address, which excited so much uneasiness among the people, is well worthy of attention; a copy of which, with the names of those who signed it, is here presented :—

To His Royal Highness, the Duke of York.

March 1, 1665.

We, the deputies duly elected from the several towns upon Long Island, being assembled at Hempstead, in general meeting, by authority derived from your royal Highness under the Honorable Colonel Nicolls as deputy governor, do most humbly and thankfully acknowledge to your royal Highness the great honor and satisfaction we receive in our dependence upon your royal Highness according to the tenor of his sacred Majesty's patent, granted the 12th day of March, 1664; wherein we acknowledge ourselves, our heirs and successors for ever, to be comprised to all intents and purposes, as therein is more at large expressed. And we do publicly and unanimously declare our cheerful submission to all such laws, statutes, and ordinances, which are or shall be made by virtue of authority from your royal Highness, your heirs and successors for ever : As also, that we will maintain, uphold, and defend, to the utmost of our power, and peril of us, our heirs and successors for ever, all the rights, title, and interest, granted by his sacred Majesty to your royal Highness, against all pretensions or invasions, foreign and domestic ; we being already well assured, that in so doing we perform our duty of allegiance to his Majesty, as freeborn subjects of the kingdom of England inhabiting in these his Majesty's dominions. We do farther beseech your royal Highness to accept of this address, as the first fruits in this general meeting, for a memorial and record against us, our heirs and successors, when we, or any of them, shall fail in our duties. Lastly, we beseech your royal Highness to take our poverties and necessities, in this wilderness country, into speedy consideration ; that, by constant supplies of trade, and your royal Highness's more particular countenance of grace to us, and protection of us, we may daily more and more be encouraged to bestow our labors to the improvement of these his Majesty's western dominions, under your royal Highness; for whose health, long life, and eternal happiness, we shall ever pray, as in duty bound

For New-Utrecht,	Jaques Cortelleau,	Younger Hope.
" Gravesend,	James Hubbard,	John Bowne.
" Flatlands,	Elbert Elbertsen,	Roeloffe Martense.
" Flatbush,	John Striker,	Hendrick Gucksen.
" Bushwick,	John Stealman,	Gisbert Tunis.
" Brooklyn,	Hendrick Lubbertsen,	John Evertsen.

For Newtown,   Richard Betts,   John Coe.
" Flushing,   Elias Doughty,   Richard Cornhill.
" Jamaica,   Daniel Denton,   Thomas Benedict.
" Hempstead,   John Hicks,   Robert Jackson.
" Oyster Bay,   John Underhill,   Matthias Harvey.
" Huntington,   Jonas Wood,   John Ketcham.
" Brookhaven,   Daniel Lane,   Roger Barton.
" Southold,   William Wells, —   John Youngs.
" Southampton,   Thomas Topping,   John Howell.
" Easthampton,   Thomas Baker,   John Stratton.
" Westchester,   Edward Jessup,   John Quinby.

At this meeting was also promulgated a body of laws and ordinances for the future government of the province, commonly called, by way of distinction, the "Duke's Laws," a copy of which was furnished to the deputies, and filed in the clerks' offices of the different counties, where some of them remain to this time. Of this code we have prepared an analysis, which, it is presumed, embraces the principal features thereof in a condensed form.

All actions of debt, account, slander, and actions on the case concerning debts and accounts to be tried within the jurisdiction where the cause of action arose. Debts and trespasses under five pounds to be arbitrated, and if either party refuse, the justice to choose arbitrators, whose award to be final. All actions or cases from five to twenty pounds to be tried at the sessions, from whence there should be no appeal. Any person falsely pretending greater damages or debts than are due, to vex his adversary, to pay treble damages. If the action be entered, and the parties compromise it, yet the agreement to be entered by the clerk of the court. Upon the death of any person, the constable and two overseers to repair to the house of deceased to inquire after the manner of the death, and whether he left any last will or testament. But no administration to be granted, except to the widow or child until the third session after the party's death. The surplus of the personal estate to be divided as follows: one third to the widow, and the other two thirds among the children, except that the eldest son shall have a double portion. All amercements and fines, not expressly regulated by law, to be imposed at the discretion of the court. No justice of the peace, who hath set upon or voted in any cause, to have any voice in the court to which appeal is made. Parties appealing, to give security; and in criminal cases they shall also give security for good behavior until the matter is decided. No arrest to be made on the Sabbath, or day of humiliation for the death of Charles the First, of blessed memory, or the anniversary of the restoration of Charles the Second. And all arrests, writs, warrants, and proclamations to be in the name of his Majesty. All assessments to be made by the constable and eight overseers of the parish, and justices of the peace to be exempt from assessments during their continuance in office.

To rebuke an officer with foul words, so that he depart through fear without doing his duty, shall be taken for an assault, and punished accordingly. No Christian shall keep a slave, except persons adjudged thereto by authority, or such as have willingly sold or shall sell themselves. Every town to set out its bounds within twelve months after they are granted, and once in three years the ancientest town shall give notice to the neighboring towns to go the bounds betwixt their towns, and to renew their marks; the time for preambulation to be between the 20th and last of February, under the penalty of five pounds for neglect thereof; and owners of adjoining lands to go the bounds betwixt their lands once a year, under penalty of ten shillings. No person to follow the business of brewing beer for sale but those skilled in the art. The name and sirname of every inhabitant in the several parishes to be registered; and the minister or town clerk shall record all marriages, births, and burials in a book to be provided by the church-wardens. No body to be buried, except in public places, and in the presence of three or four of the neighbors, one of whom shall be an overseer of the parish. Persons punishable with death, are those who shall in any wise deny the true God or his attributes; those who commit any wilful or premeditated murder; he who slays another with a sword or dagger, that hath not any weapon to defend himself; those who lay in wait; poisoning, or any such wicked conspiracy; lying with any brute beast, (and the beast to be burned); man-stealing;

taking away life by false and malicious testimony ; denying his Majesty's right and title to his crown or dominion, or resisting his authority by arms ; conspiracy against the public ; children above the age of sixteen, and of sufficient understanding, smiting their natural father or mother, unless in self-defence from maiming or death.

Cattle and hogs to be marked with the public mark of the town and the private mark of the owner ; and horned cattle to be marked upon the horn. Every cause of five pounds or under to pay a tax of two shillings and sixpence ; if ten pounds, five shillings ; from ten to twenty pounds, ten shillings ; and for every ten pounds more, two and sixpence.

Whereas the public worship of God is much discredited for want of *painful* and able ministers to instruct the people in the true religion, it is ordered that a church shall be built in each parish capable of holding two hundred persons ; that ministers of every church shall preach every Sunday, and pray for the King, Queen, Duke of York, and the Royal Family ; and to marry persons after legal publication or license.

Sundays not to be profaned by travelling by laborers or vicious persons ; church-wardens to report twice a-year all misdemeanors,—such as swearing, profaneness, sabbath-breaking, drunkenness, fornication, adultery, and all such abominable sins. That no person employed about the bed of any man, woman, or child, as surgeon, midwife, physician, or other person, presume to exercise or put in practice any act contrary to the known approved rules of the art in each mystery or occupation. Courts of Sessions to begin in the east-riding first Tuesday of June ; the second Tuesday in the north-riding ; and the third Tuesday in the west-riding. The constable to whip or punish any one when no other officer is appointed to do it. All sales and alienations of property to be by deed, and under hand and seal. No condemned person to be executed within four days after sentence, and the person executed to be buried near the place of execution. If any woman shall causelessly absent herself from her husband, and upon complaint made to a magistrate shall refuse to return, she shall forfeit her dower, unless the husband afterwards affirm the same. Every minister within his parish is enjoined to pray and preach on the anniversary of the deliverance from the "Gun-powder Treason," the fifth of November, 1605 ; on the 30th day of January, to manifest detestation of the barbarous murder of Charles I. in 1649; and on the 29th of May, being the birth-day of Charles II. of blessed memory.

If any person commit fornication with any single woman, they shall both be punished, either by enjoining marriage or corporal punishment at the discretion of the court. Persons guilty of perjury to stand in the pillory three several court days, and render double damages to any party injured thereby. Apprentices and servants absenting themselves from their masters without leave, to serve double the time of such absence. Every town to have a marking or flesh-brand for horses. No ox, cow, or such like cattle, to be killed for sale or for private use without giving notice thereof to the town registrar. No person to be a common victualler, or keeper of a cook-shop or house of entertainment, without a certificate of his good behavior from the constable and two overseers of the parish ; nor suffer any one to drink excessively in their houses after nine o'clock at night under the penalty of two shillings and sixpence. No purchase of land from the Indians shall be valid without a license from the governor, and the purchaser shall bring the Sachem or right owner before him, to confess satisfaction. No one to sell, give, or barter, directly or indirectly, any gun, powder, bullet, shot, or any vessel of burden, or row-boat (canoes excepted,) with any Indian, without permision of the governor, under his hand and seal ; nor sell, truck, barter, give or deliver any strong liquor to an Indian, under penalty of forty shillings for one pint, and in proportion for any greater or lesser quantity; except in case of sudden extremity, and then, not exceeding *two drams*.

To be father, brother, uncle, nephew, or cousin-german to any party in a trial, shall exempt a juror from serving, if objection be made before he is sworn, but not afterwards. No person to reveal the dissenting vote of a juror on arbitration, under the penalty of ten shillings. Every town, at its own expense, shall provide a pair of stocks for offenders, and a pound 'for cattle, besides prisons and pillories in places where courts of sessions are held. The value of an Indian coat, to be given to any one who shall bring the head of a wolf to any constable upon Long Island, provided it be killed upon the island.

The court of sessions in each county shall take the proof of wills, which, with the wills, are to be transmitted to the " office of records " at New-York, when the executors shall receive a copy thereof, with a certificate of its being allowed, attested under their seal of office.

The town marks for horses upon Long Island shall be as follows : for Easthampton, A ; Southampton, B ; Southold, C ; Seatalcot, D ; Huntington, E ; Oyster Bay, F ; Hempstead, G ; Jamaica, H ; Flushing, I ; Newtown, L ; Bushwick, M ; Brooklyn, N ; Flatbush, O ; Flatlands, P ; New Utrecht, Q ; and Gravesend, R. At this period the present town of Riverhead was included in Southold, and the town of North Hempstead, in Hempstead.

These laws, with the alterations and additions made to them from time to time by the governor and council, continued to be the laws of the colony until October, 1683, when the first colonial legislature met, and the people were admitted, for a short time, to a share in the legislative power. The several towns were organized at the meeting at Hempstead, their bounds established, and the inhabitants required to take out new patents for the lands purchased within their limits. It was probably at the same time that the names of several towns were altered ; so that the town of Rustdorpe was to be called Jamaica ; Midwout was changed to Flatbush ; Amersfort to Flatlands ; Breuckelen to Brookland ; Middleburgh to Newtown ; and Vlissengen to Flushing. At the same time the towns of Long Island, Staten Island, and as some think Westchester, were erected into a shire, called Yorkshire. This shire was divided into three parts, denominated Ridings, as follows : the towns of King's County, Staten Island, and Newtown, constituted the West Riding ; the remaining towns of Queen's County, with perhaps Westchester, were called the North Riding ; while the towns in Suffolk County made up the East Riding of Yorkshire upon Long Island.

14

This remarkable code, of which the above is a mere general sketch or outline, is undoubtedly entitled to our sincere veneration, both on the account of the wisdom displayed by the framers of it, for the many valuable principles which are contained in it ; and also as a curious system of ancient legislation, to which our forefathers were compelled to yield obedience ; and as consisting also of many singular provisions, which were thought necessary at that time from the state of the country and the condition of its inhabitants. The system must be allowed to manifest more practical wisdom, and less of superstition and puerile absurdity than the famous code which is reported once to have prevailed in Connecticut, and known, from the color of the paper upon which it was first printed, as the " Blue Laws." The Duke's laws were to operate in a new-settled country with a mixed population, composed of emigrants from various nations, and holding a great variety of opinions upon the subject of government ; it could hardly therefore have been expected, even by the framers of them, that all their multiplied provisions and restrictions would be equally satisfactory to the whole population. It was probably the best which the then state of things admitted. Whether these laws were indeed compiled from the laws of the other English colonies which the governor had caused to be digested for the government of this province, or were drawn up in Great Britain by persons designated for the purpose ; certain it is that no set of men, however eminent for talents, or deeply versed in the science and practice of English jurisprudence, could be expected entirely to succeed in framing such a body of rules, and of adapting them to the opinions and necessities of a people with whom they were unacquainted, and of numberless circumstances of a purely local nature. It was accordingly soon found expedient to introduce many alterations and amendments, either to render them more acceptable to the people, or better suited to the peculiar exigencies of the times. The English towns which had been subject to the Dutch rejoiced at the change of affairs resulting from the conquest, as they were thereby absolved from obedience to a government which they despised ; and the other English towns equally exulted at the prospect of being relieved from the con-

stant jealousy and ambition of a foreign power in their neighborhood. The eastern towns on Long Island, notwithstanding,
would greatly have preferred to continue their former alliance
with Connecticut, and therefore they submitted, with very
general reluctance, to the separation. Some attempts were
made to retain their connection, and they were renewed on
more than one occasion thereafter.

The English towns, as well those which had been settled
under the Dutch as those associated with Connecticut, were au.
thorized, from the proclamation of the commissioners at the conquest, to expect that they should be admitted to the ordinary
privileges and immunities of British subjects, to participate in
the government, and have a voice in choosing representatives
to a General Assembly, with power to make laws for the government of the colony. How great then must have been their
astonishment as well as disappointment, when, on the promul-
gation of the Duke's laws at the convention held at Hempstead,
they found themselves deceived in their reasonable anticipa-
tions, and that by the very government which had inspired
them with hopes of enjoying very many civil and political
advantages, of which they had before been deprived. It cannot, therefore, excite much surprise that the people should feel
indignant at the servile submission of their deputies, contained
in their address to the Duke of York, drawn up and signed by
them at the meeting aforesaid. As the term "Riding" was
introduced at the conquest, and occurs so frequently in the history of the colony, some account of its origin and meaning
seems necessary for the general reader.

In Jacob's Law Dictionary it is mentioned that Riding is corrupted from the word Trithing, the name of a division of Yorkshire in England ; of which he says there are three, called the
East, West, and North Ridings. In the statute of 22d Henry VIII,
trithing, or trithing-reeve is defined the third part of a county,
or three or more hundreds or warpentakes; such are the
Laths in Kent, the Rapes in Sussex, and the Ridings in Yorkshire. And those who governed these trithings were called
Trithing-Reeves, before whom were brought all causes that
could not be determined in the hundred or warpentake. The

term is also used sometimes for the court held within the circuit of a trithing, of the nature of a Court Leet, but inferior to
the county court, to which causes might be removed from those
courts.

By an order of the governor and Court of Assize in 1675,
Staten Island was detached from Long Island, and permitted
to have a jurisdiction of itself as a town ; and in 1683 was
erected into a separate county. Newtown continued attached
to the west riding until the organization of the counties on
Long Island by the first General Assembly in the same year,
when it was made a part of the county of Queens.   Previous
to the convention at Hempstead in March, 1665, the following
circular was addressed by his Excellency, Governor Nicolls, to
the several towns on Long Island :—

"James-ffort in New-York, 8th February, 166$\frac{4}{5}$.

" Whereas the inhabitants of Long Island have for a long
time groan'd under many grievous inconveniences and dis-
couragem^{ts}, occasioned partly from their subjection, partly
from their opposition to a foreigne power, in which distracted
condition few or no lawes could be put in due execution, bounds
and titles to lands disputed, civil libertyes interrupted, and, from
this general confusion, private dissentions and animosityes have
too much prevailed against neighbourly love and Christian
charity.   To the preventing of the future growth of the like
evills, his Majesty, as a signall grace and honour to his subjects
upon Long Island, hath, at his own charge, reduc't the forraigne
power to his obedience, and by patent, hath invested His Royall
Highnesse the Duke of Yorke ; I am deputed to put in execution.   In discharge, therefore, of my trust and duty, to settle
good and known lawes within this government for the future,
and receive yor best advice and informacon in a genall meet
mg : I have thought fit to publish unto yo^u, that upon the last-
day of this present ffebruary, at Hempstead upon Long Island,
shall be a generall meeting, which is to consist of deputyes
chosen by the major part of the freemen only ; which is to be
understood of all persons rated according to their estates, whether English or Dutch, within your severall townes and precincts, whereof you are to make publication to the inhabitants

foure dayes before yo^u proceed to an election, appointing a certain day for that purpose.   You are further to impart to the
inhabitants from mee, that I do heartily recommend to them
the choice of the most sober, able, and discrete persons, without
partiality or faction, the fruite and benefitt whereof will return
to themselves, in a full and perfect composure of all controversies, and ye propagation of true religion amongst us.   They are
also required to bring wth them a draught of each towne limitts,
or such writings as are necessary to evidence the bounds and
limitts, as well as the right by which they challenge such
bounds and limitts, by grants or purchases, or both—As also
to give notice of their meeting to the Sachems of the Indians,
whose presence may in some cases be necessary.   Lastly, I do
require you to assemble your inhabitants and read this letter to
them, and then and there to nominate a day for the election of
two deputyes from your towne, who are to bring a certificate
of their ·election (wth full power to conclude any cause or matter relating to their severall townes) to me at Hempstead, upon
the last day of ffebruary, when (God willing) I shall expect
them.   Your assured friend,
"To the magistrates of the ⎫   " RICHARD NICOLLS."
   severall townes upon ⎬
   Long Island."   ⎭
   The laws thus prepared having been published, and the several towns recognized, with a few inconsiderable alterations
as to their boundaries, they were thereupon required to take
out new patents for the lands originally purchased from the natives.   This request of the governor appeared somewhat plausible, from the fact that a part of the county at least had passed
from the Dutch to the English, and some of the towns, particularly in Suffolk, had never obtained any patents whatever.
The governor appointed a high sheriff for the whole shire,
and a deputy sheriff for each riding ; together with a requisite
number of justices for the several towns. The high sheriff
and deputies were appointed annually, but the justices held for
an indefinite period at the governor's pleasure. In 1666 the
office of deputy was abolished, and in 1683 that of high sheriff

was discontinued, and a sheriff afterwards appointed for each county.

These laws authorized the several towns annually, on the first or second day of April, to elect a constable, at first eight, and by a subsequent amendment, four overseers; who were the assessors of the town, and with the constable were empowered to make regulations respecting matters which concerned the police, and good government of the town. The constable and overseers were required annually to appoint two of the overseers to make the rate for building and repairing the church, for the maintenance of the minister and for the support of the poor.

From the overseers, the constable selected the jurors who attended the courts of sessions and assize.

The principal courts established by these laws were the town court, the court of sessions, and the court of assize.

The town court was composed of the constable, and by an amendment of the original law, of two overseers; and had cognizance of all causes of debt and trespass under five pounds; and the justice of the peace was authorized, but not required, to preside in this court.

The court of sessions was established in each riding, and was to be held twice a year. It was composed of the justices of the peace of the several towns in the riding, each of whom was at first allowed £20 a year, which, in 1666, were altered into an allowance for their expenses.

This court had jurisdiction of all criminal causes, and of all civil causes over £5, arising in the riding. Causes were tried in this court in civil cases, and in criminal cases not capital, by a jury of seven men, and the verdict was determined by the voice of a majority; but in capital cases the jury consisted of twelve men, and they were required to be unanimous.

The judgments of this court for sums under £20, were final; from such as were for more than that sum, the parties might appeal to the court of assize.

The members of the council, the secretary of the colony, and the high sheriff, were respectively authorized to sit with the justices of the court of sessions; and when either of them was present, he was required to preside. The courts of sessions also took the proof of wills in the respective ridings.

The court of assize was composed of the governor, council, and magistrates of the several towns, and was held once a year in the city of New-York. It heard appeals from the sessions and other inferior courts.

Suits for demands above £20 might be commenced in this court on the warrant of the governor; so that it had original as well as appellate jurisdiction, and was a court of equity as well as common law.

The Duke's laws making no provision for a general assembly, the people had no voice in the government; but the governor had unlimited power, executive, legislative, and judicial. He was commander-in-chief; all public officers were appointed by him, and most of them held their offices at his pleasure. With the advice of his council he could make what laws he pleased, and repeal them in the same manner, even against the opinion or consent of the council.

Some of the amendments to the original code purport to have been made at the court of assize, of which the justices of the several towns formed a part. This was not a legislative but a judicial body; and the power of the justices with regard to legislation, was probably like that of the parliament of France before the revolution, merely to register the edicts made by the governor and council.

So far as they were permitted to interfere, the indulgence was calculated, if not intended, to lessen the responsibility of the governor without diminishing his power.

It is certain that their presence or concurrence was not necessary, and that the act imposing duties establishing an excise, and many other important acts, were adopted by the governor in council, and not at the court of assize. The people never considered the justices as their representatives, and censured the acts made at the court of assize as much as others. The governor presided in the court of assize, which, by appeal, had the control of all inferior tribunals. The judgments and decrees of this court were probably such as the governor dictated;

his assistants not being colleagues, but merely advisers, who held their authority under him, and were dependent on him.

In this court the governor united the character of both judge and legislator. He interpreted his own acts, and not only pronounced what the law was, but what it should be.

The charges of the several towns and counties under the Duke of York were defrayed by a direct tax on the persons and estates, real and personal, of the inhabitants, according to an estimate made by the constable and overseers of the several towns, in conformity with certain rules prescribed by law. The rate for the public or county charge in each riding was fixed by the governor and council, by the amount of its estimate. A penny in the pound was usually sufficient for the purpose. The tax was collected by the constables, and paid over to such persons in the several towns as were entitled to it on the warrant of the high sheriff. The town charges were fixed by the constable and overseers, and levied by the same estimate. Governor Lovelace in 1670, and Governor Dungan in 1686 or '87, both attempted to raise money for colony purposes, by their own authority ; but the attempt met with so much opposition, that it could not be carried into effect.

The colony charges were paid out of the monies arising from duties imposed by the governor and council on exports and imports. In the fall of 1664 Governor Nicolls established a tariff of duties on goods exported to the Netherlands ; and shortly after, on other goods, exported and imported

From the origin of the colony, each town was required to support its own poor ; the money to be raised by those who from time to time adjusted the contingent expenses of the different counties. By the Duke's laws the constable and overseers were required to take charge of the poor. In 1747 the several towns in Suffolk were authorized to choose overseers of the poor, and soon after some other counties were empowered to do the same. By the act of November 11th, 1692, the power of taking the proof of wills, and of granting letters testamentary and of administration, was vested in the governor, or a delegate to be appointed by him. In 1778, and not before, the legislature ordered surrogates to be appointed by the governor and council of appointment, in every county ; which is still continued, except that the power is now vested in the governor and senate. The courts of sessions, which by the Duke's law were to be held in each riding and afterwards in each county continued to be held with great regularity afterwards.

The records of this court, as originally constituted, and as re-organized by the act of 1683, are still to be found in the clerks' offices of Kings, Queens, and Suffolk. In King's there is a regular series of them, from 1669 to 1711. From these records it appears to have been a common practice for the secretary of the colony, a member of the council, or the high sheriff, to sit and act in court with the justices. In the record of the court held at Gravesend, December 13th, 1671, Mathias Nicoll, the secretary, is styled *president* of the court. This court was held at Gravesend from its origin till 1685, when it was removed to Flatbush by virtue of an act of the colonial legislature. There is also in the clerk's office of King's County, copies of most of the acts of the first assembly, passed in 1683 and in 1684, with one or more acts passed by the second assembly in 1685.

Smith, in his History of New-York, supposes that the court of assize had not been established till the time of Governor Lovelace. This is a great mistake. It was established by Nicolls in the code he had compiled for the government of the colony, and published in the assembly at Hempstead, March 1st, 1665. In the fall of the same year, the three last days in September, and the second, third, and fourth days in October, a general court of assize was holden at New-York, composed of Richard Nicolls, the governor, the members of the council, and the justices of the three ridings of Yorkshire, on Long Island and Staten Island.

The number of justices who attended this court rendered it a grievance. In the act of 1684, passed for its repeal, it is alleged that it had " become a great charge and expense to the province ; and by reason of the great number, not so fit and capable to hear and determine matters and causes of a civil na ture, usually brought to the said court;" and it was for that reason abolished.

15

The last court of assize held under Sir Edmund Andross, October 6th, 1680, was composed of the governor, five councillors, the mayor of New-York, five aldermen, and seventeen justices of the peace.

THE PUBLIC DISCONTENT.

The people on Long Island considered some of the laws established by the original code as arbitrary and oppressive; and they deemed some that were made by Col. Lovelace, who commenced his administration in May, 1667, as still more exceptionable.

They at length resolved to represent their grievances to the governor and council, and to pray for redress.

October 9th, 1669, the towns of Hempstead, Jamaica, Oyster Bay, Flushing, Newtown, Gravesend, Westchester, and East Chester, severally petitioned for redress.

They enumerated the defects in the existing laws which they wished to be remedied, stated the provisions which they wished to be adopted, remonstrated against the restrictions which the governor had imposed on trade; and reprobated, as the greatest of their grievances, the exclusion of the people from any share in legislation.

In their petitions they refer to the proclamation issued to the people of Long Island and others, by the commissioners, on their first landing at Gravesend, before the surrender of the colony, promising that they " should enjoy all such privileges as his Majesty's other subjects in America enjoyed ;" the most important of which they allege is a participation in the power of making the laws by which they are to be governed, " by such deputies as shall be yearly chosen by the freeholders of every town and parish :" and they claimed a fulfilment of that promise.

They also complain of it as a grievance, that any acts should be made by the governor under pretence of his secret instructions ; and pray " to be informed what is required of them by virtue of the commission granted by his Royal Highness the Duke of York."

The governor and council received the petitions, granted some of their minor requests, but in the most important cases refused any redress.

The town of Southampton was purchased and settled under the authority of the Earl of Stirling while he held the island, which circumstance the people of that town supposed exempted them from the necessity of taking out a patent for their lands from the governor, as was required of other towns by the laws of 1665, and neglected to do it; in consequence of which the governor and council, at the court of assize, October 8th, 1670, declared the titles to lands in that town invalid, unless a patent was obtained for them within a limited time

By another act passed at the same time, a levy or contribution was ordered to be made in the several towns on Long Island, to repair the fort at New-York.

The governor had also imposed duties on goods imported and exported according to his pleasure for the support of government, and was now attempting to raise money by a direct tax for other purposes without the consent of the people.

Several of the towns were alarmed at the precedent about to be established as dangerous to their liberties, and determined to resist it.

The want of a general assembly was felt as a great grievance from the first establishment of the Duke's government; the inhabitants considered themselves in great measure disfranchised, and themselves little better than slaves, liable at all times to suffer by the arbitrary exactions of the government; in short, that the whole system was only a tyranny in disguise, which, under the color of prerogative, might at any time trample upon the most sacred rights of the people under the plausible pretence of upholding the authority of government and supporting the dignity of the crown; against all which alarming encroachments the people possessed no constitutional security or any mode of redress, should petition and remonstrance fail, short of open and direct opposition to the government itself. The governor, it has been seen, possessed the sole appointing power; and united in himself all the attributes of despotic authority, which he might any time, and frequently did, exercise in

the most arbitrary manner. This concentration of power in
the hands of a single individual might well alarm the timid,
and awaken the most serious jealousies and discontents among
the entire population of the colony, which was, in fact, the case.
Difficulties continued to exist even after the establishment of
the assembly, by the influence which the governors possessed,
and their sometimes refusing their sanction to laws the most
salutary and indispensable for the public security.

It was evidently the object of many governors to control, as
far as possible, the public revenues, and to fill their own pockets
at the expense of the people ; and there are not wanting instances of their having accumulated large fortunes in a surprisingly
short period by acts of oppression and peculation.

The governor could suspend the members of the council and
appoint others, subject to the King's approbation ; he had a
negative on the acts passed by the assembly and council ; he
had power to summon, prorogue, or dissolve the assembly ; and
with consent of the council, who were in general sufficiently
submissive, could dispose of the public lands, and disburse the
public money raised for the support of government.

For some years the public revenue went into the hands of a
receiver general, who was appointed by the crown, and was not
accountable to the assembly. The acts for raising revenue for
the support of government were continued for a series of years
without appropriation ; and the council exercised a concurrent
power over revenue bills, as in other cases.

This mode of managing the revenue was liable to great
abuse. An indefinite support enabled the governor to dispense
with the assembly, and rendered him in a great measure independent of them during that period ; and the omission of specific appropriations enabled the governor to fix the salaries of
all public officers, to dispose of the public monies as he pleased,
gave him the entire power over the civil list, and led to misap-
plication and embezzlement.

The English colonists on Long Island brought with them
the doctrine that taxation and representation were inseparable
—that the power of disposing of his own money was the birth-
right of every British subject, and one of the elementary prin-

ciples of British liberty,—and that taxes could only be imposed with the consent of the people, by their representatives in a general assembly.

They had for some years paid a direct tax of a penny in the pound to defray the public charges of the several towns and counties, of which they had not complained.

The towns of Southold, Southampton, and Easthampton, in a joint meeting by their delegates at Southold, agreed to contribute to the repairing of the fort, " if they might have the privileges that other of his Majesty's subjects in these parts have and do enjoy," alluding to the governments of New England.

June 24th, 1672.—The town of Easthampton, to whom the proceedings of the delegates were communicated, approved of the decision of the deputies, and agreed to comply with the order, "if the privileges may be obtained, but not otherwise." The towns of Huntington, Flushing, Hempstead, and Jamaica, by the votes of their respective town meetings, refused to comply with the order, and communicated the reasons of their refusal in writing to their respective constables and overseers, to whom the order was sent.

The people of Huntington assigned this among other reasons for their refusal, viz : " because they were deprived of the liberties of Englishmen ;" intimating that they deemed it a violation of their constitutional rights that their money should be taken from them without their consent by their representatives in a general assembly.

The people of Jamaica, in justification of their refusal, stated that they considered themselves already sufficiently burdened by the enhanced price which they paid for their goods, in consequence of the duties which the governor had imposed on them, in addition to a penny in the pound, which they paid towards the public charges. That a compliance with the order would be contrary to the King's instructions, which forbid any law to be enforced on the country that was contrary to the laws of the nation ; meaning, that no law for taking their money out of their pockets without their consent by their representatives, was consistent with the British constitution. " That on the same principle that this order was imposed, they might be required to maintain the garrison, and whatever else we know not, till there be no end; but if it may appear to us that it is the King's absolute order to impose the said burdens and disprivilege us, contrary to his former good intentions and instructions, and contrary to the liberties his Majesty's subjects enjoy in his territories and dominions, we shall, with patience, rest under the said burdens until address be made to the king for relief."

The votes of Flushing and Hempstead have not been discovered, but there is no doubt they were to the like effect. The constables of Flushing, Hempstead, and Jamaica, laid the resolutions of their respective towns before the ensuing court. of sessions of the north-riding held at Jamaica; but it seems that the court did not act on them. They then laid them before the court of sessions of the west-riding, which met the next week, December 21st, 1670, at Gravesend. That court, under the influence of the secretary of the colony, who presided, and a member of the council, after examining the writings containing the proceedings of the said towns, adjudged " That the said papers were in themselves scandalous, illegal, and seditious ; tending only to disaffect all the peaceable and well-meaning subjects of his Majesty in these his royal Highness's territories and dominions." And the court further ordered " That the said papers should be presented to the governor in council, for them to proceed on as they shall conceive will best tend to the suppression of false suggestions and jealousies in the minds of peaceable and well-meaning subjects in alienating them from their duty and obedience to the laws."

Agreeably to this illegal order, the papers were presented to Governor Lovelace, and were by him and his council adjudged to the flames, and ordered to be publicly burnt before the town-house of the city, at the next mayor's court to be held there.

It was this sage and humane Governor Lovelace, who, as Smith in his History of New Jersey informs us, in 1668 wrote to Sir Robert Carr, who was then in authority there, that the best method to keep the people in order was "to lay such taxes upon them as may not give them liberty to entertain any other thoughts but how they shall discharge them."

THE RE-CONQUEST BY THE DUTCH.

There is a chasm in our history from 1672 to 1674, which English writers have not seemed very anxious to supply; for it was during this period that the colony of New-York came into the possession and under the government of its former masters, the Dutch. In the war of Charles II. and Louis XIV. against Holland in the year 1773, the Dutch attempted to recover their authority in America. In that year two small Dutch squadrons, commanded by Captain Cornelius Evertsen and Captain Jacob Benkes, were despatched to the West Indies to destroy, as far as possible, the English and French West India trade. In the course of this expedition they captured one hundred and twenty sail of English and French merchant vessels, which they despatched to Europe, and which arrived safe at Cadiz. The captains of the Dutch squadrons, highly elated with their great success, concluded to extend their operations to New-York. They accordingly united their forces, and sailed for their port of destination. Meeting with no obstacle, they arrived at Sandy Hook on the 30th of July, and in a few hours were in full possession of the city of New-York. The garrison, with forty pieces of ordnance, was taken without opposition or a gun being fired. Captain Manning, the commandant of the fort, most cowardly surrendered it to them without making any defence whatever. He was afterwards tried for treachery and cowardice by a court-martial, and sentenced to have his sword broken over his head.

The commanders of the squadron appointed Captain Anthony Colve to be governor of the colony, who immediately set about reinstating the Dutch government.

August 14, 1673, he issued a proclamation to the several towns on Long Island, requiring each of them to send two deputies to New-York, with full powers to make their submission to the states general and the prince of Orange on behalf of the town.

The Dutch towns, and the English towns that were settled under the Dutch, submitted to the new government. The En-

glish towns seem at first to have paid some attention to the proposals of the governor, but soon declined them.

October 1st, 1673, the Dutch governor sent William Knyff
and Anthony Malypart to the English towns, requiring them
to take the oath of allegiance. Oyster Bay complied; Huntington and Brookhaven offered to sign an agreement to be faithful
to the Dutch government, but refused to take any oath that
would bind them to take up arms against the crown of Great
Britain

The three eastern towns declined any compromise, and sent
deputies to Connecticut, to solicit that colony to take them under
her jurisdiction, and to furnish them with aid against the Dutch
if they should attempt to enforce their demands.

October 9th, 1673, the general court referred their application to a committee, consisting of the governor, assistants, and
two others; and authorized them, with the concurrence of Massachusetts and Plymouth, to grant their request, and to do what
should be most advantageous for the mutual benefit of the parties.

The committee agreed to take them under their jurisdiction,
erected the three towns into a county, established a county
court, appointed judges and such other civil and military officers
as they deemed necessary, and sent a military force to their
aid.

October 25th, the governor sent William Knyff and Nicholas
Voss to the towns of Huntington and Brookhaven; and, to induce them to comply with his wishes, promised them liberty of
conscience, security of property, the choice of their officers, in
the same manner as the like privilege had been enjoyed by the
Dutch; and also consented that the oath of allegiance should be
so modified as to accommodate their scruples.

Huntington and Brookhaven consented to yield to the wishes
of the governor on condition that none but the magistrates
should take the oath required of them. This was conceded, and
these two towns submitted on those terms.

October 30th, the Dutch governor sent Cornelius Steenwyck,
first councillor, and two others, to the eastern towns, to persuade
them to comply with the same terms.

They sailed down the Sound, and called at Shelter Island, where they fell in with Samuel Wyllis and Captain Winthrop, who had been sent to the island, by Connecticut, to carry their resolutions into effect. The Dutch commissioners visited South-old, and found the people assembled and in arms. They offered to take their submission in writing, and to accept of the oath of allegiance from the magistrates. The people of that town, however, refused all manner of submission, and the commissioners returned without effecting the object of their mission.

In the mean time the governor of Connecticut wrote to the Dutch governor, and remonstrated against his attempting to extend his jurisdiction over the English towns that never had been subject to the Dutch government. This produced a captious correspondence between the two governors.

The Dutch governor undertook to reduce the eastern towns by force, and Connecticut assisted them to repel his attempts. The Dutch forces sailed down the Sound towards the east end of the island, and attempted several descents ; but effected nothing, except the collection of a sum of money of Nathaniel Sylvester of Shelter Island for the property of his brother Constant Sylvester, and Thomas Middleton, which the Dutch governor had illegally confiscated and sold to him.

Trumbull, in his history of Connecticut, states that the Dutch threatened the eastern towns with destruction by fire and sword, unless they would submit and swear allegiance to the states general ; that they sent ships and an armed force towards the east end of the island, and made several descents; but that, by assistance of the troops which had been sent by Connecticut, they were in all instances repulsed and driven from the island.

October 14th, 1675, the general court of Connecticut returned Major Treat public thanks for his good conduct in defending the colony and the towns on Long Island against the Dutch, and for his subsequent services.

November 26th, 1673, Connecticut, in conjunction with her confederates, declared war against the Dutch, and made preparations to commence hostile operations in the spring.

The Dutch governor seems to have been alarmed at these preparations. March 27th, 1674, he ordered all vessels to be

16

removed to a particular place, lest they should hinder the defence of the city ; and made provision for the transportation of
the inhabitants of the neighboring villages " in case of an attack."

Peace was concluded in Europe, February 9th, 1674, and the
news of it suspended hostilities, although no official account of
it was received till several months afterwards.

By the treaty, all conquests were to be restored to their former owners ; but no person being sent to receive the surrender
of the colony, the British government was not reinstated until
the ensuing fall.

The people of Southold, Southampton, and Easthampton,
dreaded the prospect of a return to the Duke's government, and
determined to use their utmost efforts to resist it.   They accordingly chose delegates, and sent them to Connecticut to solicit
their continuance under the protection and government of that
colony.

May 14th, 1674, the general court took their application
into consideration, and consented that they should continue in
association with that colony, with the same privileges as other
towns, as far as was in their power to make the grant.

The general court also appointed or re-appointed Captain
John Youngs, Captain John Howel, and Mr. John Mulford,
judges of the county court, and appointed Samuel Wyllis, John
Talcott, and the secretary, or any two of them, to go over to
the island to order and settle the affairs of the people there, and
to establish such military officers among them as they should
judge necessary.

June 13th, 1674, the town of Easthampton appointed a committee, who were ordered, in conjunction with Southampton
and Southold, to petition the king to suffer them to continue
under the jurisdiction of Connecticut.

These towns continued attached to Connecticut when the
colony was restored to the Duke of York.

THE RESTORATION OF THE DUKE'S GOVERNMENT.

After the conclusion of peace, June 29th, 1674, the Duke of

York, to remove all doubt respecting his title, obtained a new patent for the territories which had been granted to him by the patent of March 12th, 1664; and shortly after appointed Major, afterwards Sir Edmund Andros, governor of his territories in America.

October 31st, 1674, Sir Edmund arrived at New-York, received the surrender of the colony from the Dutch authorities, and reinstated the Duke's former system of government. Sir Edmund immediately sent to the three eastern towns, requiring them to return to the government of the Duke of York.

The deputies of the three towns sent a memorial to the governor, in which they state " That, by the aid furnished them by the kindness of Connecticut, they had repelled the Dutch; that they had joined them, and come under that government; that that government had appointed both their civil and military officers; that they had become bound by oath to that colony, and could not dissolve the connexion without their approbation."

November 17th, the people of Southold, by a vote of their town meeting, declared themselves "to be under the government of his Majesty's colony of Connecticut, and that they would use all lawful means so to continue."

The town of Easthampton instructed their deputies, who were appointed to consult with those of the other towns, what course they should take " to see that all lawful endeavors be put forth to the utmost for our continuance under that government."

November 18th, 1674, the governor and council ordered that a messenger be again sent to the three towns, requiring them to restore the former overseers and constables to their places, " under the penalty of being declared rebels;" and ordered the three deputies who signed the memorial on behalf of the respective towns, to wit: John Mulford, John Howell, and John Youngs. to appear and answer before the council on the like penalty

Thus the endeavors of the eastern towns to continue under the jurisdiction of Connecticut were unavailing, and they were obliged, however reluctantly, to return to the government of the Duke of York.

Sir Edmund pursued the same arbitrary course that his predecessor had done.

November 26th, 1674, he suspended a term of the court of sessions in the east-riding of Yorkshire, and ordered the towns of Huntington and Brookhaven to have their business for the term transacted at the ensuing court of sessions at Jamaica in the north-riding, because the three eastern towns had not returned the accounts of the constables and overseers of those towns according to his orders.

In April, 1681, the same governor arbitrarily summoned Isaac Platt, Epenetus Platt, Samuel Titus, Jonas Wood, and Thomas Wicks, inhabitants of Huntington, to New-York; and caused them to be imprisoned without trial, and without being chargeable with any legal offence, but, as is supposed, merely for having attended a meeting of delegates of the several towns for the purpose of contriving the means of procuring a redress of grievances. Sir Edmund seems shortly after to have left the colony. June 29th, 1681, Anthony Brockholst presided in the court of assize as commander-in-chief.

THE FIRST COLONIAL ASSEMBLY.

June 29th, 1681, the grand jury, at a special court of assize, in which Anthony Brockholst presided, presented the want of a general assembly as a grievance; and the court appointed Captain John Youngs, the high sheriff of Yorkshire, to draw a petition to be sent to the Duke of York for the privilege; which he did, and it was signed by the clerk, by order of the court, and forwarded to his Royal Highness, who seems to have listened to the prayer of the petition, and instructed the new governor to summon a general assembly as soon as he arrived in the colony.

Col. Thomas Dongan, the new governor, arrived August 27th, 1683, and soon after issued orders to the high sheriff to convene the freeholders of the several ridings, to choose representatives to meet him in assembly the 17th of October ensuing.

This first assembly met according to the summons, in New-York, October 17th, 1683, and elected Matthias Nichols, one of the representatives from New-York, their speaker.

The assembly, at their first session, adopted a bill of rights, established courts of justice, repealed some of the most obnoxious of the Duke's laws, altered and amended others, and passed such new laws as they judged the circumstances of the colony required.

By the act of October 29th, 1683, a court was established in every town, for the trial of causes of debt and trespass under forty shillings, to be holden the first Wednesday of every month, by three persons commissioned for that purpose, without a jury, unless demanded by one of the parties, and then to be granted at the expense of the party demanding it. A court, called a court of sessions, was established, to be held yearly in every county by the justices of the peace of the said county, or any three or more of them, for the trial of all causes, civil and criminal, arising in the county, by the verdict of twelve men; the court to continue only three days. A court of general jurisdiction was established, called a court of Oyer and Terminer and general gaol delivery, with power to remove all causes and judgments over five pounds from inferior courts; and to examine, correct, or reverse the same; to be holden by a judge and four justices of the peace, to be commissioned for that purpose in each respective county once in every year. Either by a law or an ordinance in 1684, two judges were appointed to hold this court.

This assembly had another session in October, 1684. At that session they abolished the court of assize, made further alterations in the Duke's laws, and enacted several new ones.

A new assembly was summoned in September, 1685, and met at New-York the ensuing October, and chose William Pinhorne their speaker. This assembly passed several acts, among which were the two following, to wit: An act, passed November 4th, 1685, for regulating the proceedings of monthly courts throughout the province, by which the jurisdiction of the court was extended to five pounds; and an act, passed November 7th, 1685, for removing the court of sessions of King's County from Gravesend to Flatbush.

There is no evidence that this assembly ever met again, or that any other was summoned, except one by Leisler during his exercise of supreme power, until the arrival of a governor under William and Mary in 1691.

Charles II. died February 6th, 1685, and the Duke of York succeeded him by the title of James II.; and as he determined to have as little to do with parliaments as possible, so it is probable that he revoked the power which he had given to his governors to call assemblies, and determined that they should rule the colony by his instructions alone, without admitting the people to any participation in the public councils.

By the act of November 29th, 1683, the governor and council were constituted a court of chancery, with an appeal to the king. The governor was authorized to appoint a deputy and other officers.

On the 2d of November, 1683, an act was passed to divide the province into shires and counties ; in which it is enacted as follows :

" QUEEN'S COUNTY, to conteyne the severall towns of New-town, Jamaica, Flushing, Hempstead, and Oyster Bay ; with the severall out-farms, settlements, and plantacons adjacent.

" KING'S COUNTY, to conteyne the severall towns of Bosh-wyck, Bedford, Brucklyn, Fflatbush, Fflatlands, New Utreht, and Gravesend ; with the severall settlements and plantacons adjacent.

" SUFFOLK COUNTY, to conteyne the severall towns of Huntington, Smithfield, Brookhaven, Southampton, Southold, Easthampton to Montauk Point, Shelter Island, the Island of Wight, Fisher's Island, and Plumb Island ; with the several out-farms and plantacons adjacent."

Andross having been appointed governor of New England, New-York was added to his government; and an order of the king was read in council at New-York, July 28th, 1688, directing Colonel Dongan to deliver the seal of the province to Sir Edmund, who shortly after re-visited the province and assumed the government.

August 25th, he issued new commissions to the civil officers of King's and Queen's counties.

On his return to Boston, the affairs of New-York were conducted by Nicholson the lieutenant governor, and council.

It is supposed that Col. Dongan immediately retired to his farm as a private citizen, where he remained until the spring of 1691, or longer, before he left the country.

The news of the accession of William and Mary to the throne reached Boston in April, 1689; and the people immediately rose, seized the governor, whose tyranny had become intolerable, and imprisoned him, where they determined to detain him till they could hear from England.

The news of the proceedings in Boston prompted certain persons in New-York, whose zeal or ambition was too impatient of delay to await the changes which would necessarily have succeeded the revolution in England, to wrest the government out of the hands of Nicholson the lieutenant governor.

May 31st, Captain Jacob Leisler put himself at the head of the party, seized the fort and kept possession of it. June 3d, he was joined by the other captains of the militia, with their companies. They immediately issued a proclamation, stating that their intention in seizing the fort was to keep it for King William; and that they would surrender it to the governor who should be appointed by him. Nicholson immediately retired aboard a vessel, and returned to England. June 12th, Leisler and his friends wrote to the several towns on Long Island, inviting them to send two men from each county to meet the deputies of the other counties at New-York, on the 26th instant, to form a committee of safety; and also to send two men from each town to assist in guarding the fort.

It is supposed that King's and Queen's counties complied with the request, although there was a powerful opposition in Queen's county to the measure.

The several towns in Suffolk met by their deputies at Southampton, June 20th, where a majority of them refused to send deputies to New-York; and immediately opened a negotiation with Connecticut, and made another unsuccessful effort to put themselves under the jurisdiction of that colony, the laws and institutions of which were more congenial with their ideas of good government than those of any royal province.

Most or all of the other counties, it is supposed, sent their deputies to New-York.

The committee of safety, which met at New-York June 26th, 1689, gave Leisler the superintendance of things ; and he managed the public affairs according to their advice till the ensuing fall.

In December, letters were received from England, directed to "Francis Nicholson, or in his absence to such as for the time being take care for preserving the peace and administering the laws in their Majesty's province of New-York in America;" and authorizing Nicholson "to take upon him the chief command, and to appoint, for his assistance, as many of the principal freeholders and inhabitants as he should think fit."

Leisler chose to consider these letters, in the absence of Nicholson, as addressed to himself, and immediately assumed the title and power of lieutenant governor. He selected a council, appointed public officers in the several counties, and commissioned them in his own name, and demanded an entire submission to his authority.

He summoned a general assembly in the spring of 1690, (probably to procure supplies for the protection of the frontiers ;) which met in New-York the 24th of April. and chose John Spratt their speaker. It is not known that any thing was done at this meeting.

They were soon prorogued to the 1st of September. No members attended from Suffolk, Albany, and Ulster ; and one from New-York, and one from Queen's County, refused to serve ; so that it could not have consisted of more than eight or nine members.

During this period the towns in Suffolk County had several meetings to consult about the course which it would be proper for them to pursue, without coming to any agreement. The summons to choose assembly-men was received March 15th, 1690, which they refused to obey.

The people of Huntington, in April, 1690, signified their willingness to recognize the authority of Leisler.

The people of Easthampton came to a resolution, the 3d of May, that they would not submit to Leisler, but would continue as they were. This town consented, however, September 9th,

1690, that certain monies which they had formerly raised for public use, and which had not been paid to the government, should be paid to Leisler, or to his order.

The county sent no members to the assembly, and does not seem to have been reconciled to Leisler's authority; but continued in a divided and neutral condition during his administration.

January 1st, 1690, Leisler issued a warrant to have Andrew Gibb, the clerk of Queen's County, brought before him, to answer for not delivering the papers belonging to the office to Mr. Denton, the new clerk, whom he had appointed.

February 15th, he issued orders to the sheriff, and to the civil and military officers of that county, to secure Col. Thomas Dongan, the late governor, in his own house, and to bring Col. Thomas Willett, Capt. Thomas Hicks, Daniel Whitehead, and Edward Antill, Esquires, before the council.

February 21st, he gave orders to have Col. Dongan, Stephen Van Cortland, Anthony Brockholst, and Matthew Plowman, Esquires, seized and brought before him.

August 9th, 1690, Leisler issued a proclamation, requiring the members of assembly to meet at New-York the first day of September ensuing, to which day they were prorogued.

August 11th, after reciting that Nathaniel Pierson, one of the deputies elected to the assembly for Queen's County, and Wilhelmus Beekman, one of the deputies from New-York, had refused to serve at the meeting in April, he ordered those counties respectively to choose others in their room, to meet with the deputies of the other counties at their ensuing session in September.

It seems that the opposition in Queens was not suppressed by the measures before taken for that purpose.

October 18th, 1690, Leisler ordered Major Milbourn "to take what force he could raise, to suppress the opposition in Queen's County."

October 26th, he suspended the court of oyer and terminer, about to sit in King's County, "until the counties on Long Island should be reduced to obedience."

October 30th, Leisler, after stating that a rebellion existed in Queen's County, issued orders to Samuel Staats and Capt.

Thomas Williams "to suppress it." He also ordered Thomas Williams and Samuel Edsdall to go to Flushing Bay to examine the vessels there, to see that none were employed in a way prejudicial to his interest. Capt. Richard Ingolsby arrived at New-York with his company the last of January, 1691, and demanded possession of the fort, which Leisler refused ; which added a new subject to the public contentions.

The colony seems to have continued in this convulsed condition to the end of Leisler's administration.

Leisler's authority was terminated by the arrival of Henry Slaughter, the new governor, March 19th, 1691.

He refused to deliver up the fort to the new governor ; and thus violated all his former professions of zeal for King William, forfeited all claim to any merit for his services, and incurred the reproach as well as the penalty of usurpation.

Leisler, and Milbourn his son-in-law, were tried and convicted of high treason ; and the warrant for their execution was issued by the advice of both the council and assembly.

Leisler's son preferred a complaint against the governor, which was referred to the lords of trade ; who reported, March 11th, 1692, "that they were humbly of opinion that Jacob Leisler and Jacob Milbourn, deceased, were condemned, and had suffered according to law."

November 12th, 1694, the parliament, on the application of Leisler's son, reversed their attainder ; and, in compassion to their families, restored them their estates.

In the journals of the colonial assembly, April 18th, 1691, much credit is allowed by them to be due to Captain William Kidd for his many good services done for the province in attending, as they say, with his vessels ; and expressing an opinion that he should be suitably rewarded ; and accordingly we find that the same assembly, upon the 14th of May next ensuing, made an order that the sum " of one hundred and fifty pounds should be paid to Captain Kidd as a suitable acknowledgment for the important benefits which the colony had derived from his services." The commission of Governor Slaughter, of January 9th, 1589, constituted the foundation of the Colonial government here, after the revolution in England,

and continued as it was then settled, with few innovations, until the American revolution. The executive power was vested
in the governor; and the legislative power in the governor,
council, and assembly, subject to the revision of the king, to
whom all laws were to be sent within three months after their
passage. The council at first consisted of seven members,
which number was afterwards increased to twelve, and were
appointed by the king. The assembly was composed of -dele-
gates from each county, chosen by the freeholders. The number was regulated by law. The term of service was indefinite
till 1743, when it was limited to seven years. Among the first
acts of the administration of Governor Slaughter, was that of
May 6th, 1691, for quieting and settling the public disorders,
which had long prevailed to the destruction of public confidence
and regard for private right. Another act was passed at the
same time for confirming all previous charters, patents and
grants, under the seal of the province, both which acts gave
very general satisfaction. Governor Slaughter died suddenly,
and was buried in old Governor Stuyvesant's vault. The government for the remainder of the year 1691 was administered
by Richard Ingolsby, the lieutenant governor, and continued
till the arrival of Benjamin Fletcher in 1692. He soon got at
variance with the assembly, and became of course unpopular.
He consulted his own mercenary views more than the interest
of the people he was sent to rule over. One of the acts of
Governor Fletcher was the establishment of a public fair or
market at Jamaica every Thursday, for the sale of all kinds of
cattle, grain, &c.; and for holding two fairs yearly in the counties of Suffolk and Queens, and one in the county of Kings.
The one for Kings to be held at Flatbush, those for Queens at
Jamaica, and those for Suffolk, one at Southampton and the
other at Southold. An act was also passed April 10th, 1693, for
calling Long Island the "Island of Nassau," which was never popular, and became obsolete in a few years thereafter. It was during the administration of Governor Fletcher that the first printing
press was established in the city of New-York, by William Bradford, an important era in its history, and an event worthy of long
remembrance. By the act of May 6th, 1691, the courts of com-

mon pleas and sessions were distinctly organized. The court
of common pleas was to be holden by a judge and three justices,
to be assigned for that purpose ; three of whom to form a quo-
rum, with power to hear and determine all causes arising in the
county, triable at the common law ; and whose decision should
be final in all cases under twenty pounds, except where the title to land came in question.

The court of sessions was to be holden by the justices of
the peace in Kings the second Tuesday of May and September,
at Flatbush ; in Queens, the third Tuesday of May and September, at Jamaica ; and in Suffolk, the last Tuesday in March
at Southampton, and the last Tuesday in September at Southold ; to continue only two days. The court of common pleas
was to be opened immediately after the termination of the sessions, and to continue only two days.

The act which was passed for settling a ministry and raising
a maintenance for them was extremely unpopular, except
among Episcopalians, for whose benefit it was perhaps covertly
intended, and excited very general discontent. From the language of the act itself, and the character of many who were in
favor of it, it seemed that there could have been no intention
of confining its benefits exclusively to the church of England
party ; and accordingly the assembly, to make the matter more
clear and satisfactory, in 1695 resolved that the benefits of the
act extended to the dissenting protestant clergy equally with
others ; but the governor rejected that interpretation, and applied it solely to the Episcopal clergymen, and they continued
to engross its advantages till the period of the American revolution. By this act, among other things, Queen's County was
divided into two precincts, namely, Hempstead and Jamaica.
The precinct of Hempstead included the township of Oyster
Bay, and the precinct of Jamaica also included the town of Flushing. There were at this time a very few families of Episcopalians in the country ; and the application of the act, according to his Excellency's exposition of it, was deemed an imposition, and a grievance of no ordinary magnitude. The result
was of course that the great mass of inhabitants were most un-
justly obliged to contribute to the support of ministers of ano-

ther church, whose ceremonies and doctrines they believed to be both erroneous and ridiculous.

Governor Fletcher continued in the administration of the government till the close of the year 1698, and was succeeded by Richard, Earl of Bellamont, who retained the office till 1701. One of the most important and popular acts of his administration was that passed the 12th of May, 1679, for "vacating, breaking and annulling," several very extravagant grants of his immediate predecessor to some of his party favorites, and to the vestry and wardens of Trinity Church. In 1701, John Nanfan, Esq., was appointed lieutenant governor. He held the office but a single year, and was superseded by the appointment of Edward, Lord Cornbury. The real name of his Excellency was Edward Hyde, and he was the son of the celebrated Earl of Clarendon ; and having been among the first to desert from the army of King James, his Majesty King William chose to make him some return for his loyalty to him, by appointing him governor of New-York. It would appear, however, that his sense of justice was as weak as his bigotry was uncontrollable, as the following among other instances may serve to illustrate.

During a great sickness in New-York, the governor and council decided upon removing into the country, and the village of Jamaica was deemed the most convenient on many accounts. The Presbyterian minister, Mr. Hubbard, happening to live in one of the best houses in the place, his Excellency requested to be allowed the use of it, which was politely tendered by the occupant, and Mr. Hubbard put himself to a considerable trouble and inconvenience for the governor's accommodation. The consequences were different from what he could have expected, even from a gentleman. In return for his generosity, the governor, instead of surrendering the house to its original possessor, when about to leave the place most perfidiously delivered it into the hands of the Episcopal party, and even encouraged the sheriff to seize upon the parsonage lands also, and appropriate them for the benefit of that denomination. This illegal and wanton act of the governor was followed by a series of difficulties in the churches of Jamaica, which continued to disturb their harmony for more than twenty years. In addition to this act of baseness, the same governor, in 1707, actually caused two Presbyterian ministers to be imprisoned for presuming to preach without his particular license. This miserable tool of royalty was a bankrupt in reputation and fortune at home, and had been sent here to fatten upon the people. Queen Anne, who succeeded to the throne in 1702, continued his appointment. He finally left the country in 1708, and returned to Europe. He died at Chelsea on the 1st of April, 1723.

He was succeeded in the office of governor of New-York by Lord Lovelace, Baron of Hurley, who dying a few months after, left Mr. Ingolsby, who was governor once before, to administer the government; and he being displaced, Gerardus Beekman, president of the council, in the absence of the commander-in-chief, filled the office till April, 1710.

General Robert Hunter assumed the administration as governor in 1710, which he retained till 1719. About three thousand persons, who were called Palatines, accompanied him to America for the purposes of settlement. These people had shortly before fled to England from the rage of religious persecution in Germany. Many of them settled in the city of New-York, where they erected a Lutheran church; while others located on a tract of some thousand acres in the manor of Livingston. It was during the administration of Governor Hunter, that an expedition was undertaken against Canada, and which failed entirely, after a very considerable waste of time and money. On the 2nd of November, 1717, an act was passed for destroying foxes and wild cats upon Long Island, they having become both numerous and mischievous. The reward for killing a wild cat was nine shillings, and for a fox, five shillings.

Colonel Peter Schuyler, as president of the council, directed the affairs of the province from the time of Governor Hunter's departure till the 17th of September, 1720, when William Burnet, Esq. assumed the government. He was the eldest son of the celebrated Bishop Burnet, and was born at the Hague, in March, 1663. He was named William in honor of the Prince of Orange, who was his godfather. His means had been dissipated in the great South-Sea scheme, and the office of governor of New-York was intended to repair in some measure his broken fortunes. In the assembly of the year 1721, and mainly, as is supposed, through the influence of the governor, a very singular bill was introduced, with the more singular title of " An act against denying the divinity of our Saviour Jesus Christ; the doctrine of the blessed Trinity; the truth of the Holy Scriptures, and spreading atheistical books ;" but the good sense of the assembly immediately rejected the bill. On the 17th of June, 1726, an act was passed, entitled "An act to prevent the setting on fire or burning the old grass on Hempstead Plains, which," says the preamble of the act, " is frequently set on fire by several of the inhabitants, through folly and the gratification of their own wanton tempers and humors." And persons were also appointed in the act to assist in extinguishing such fires ; the persons named were Captain John Tredwell, Mr. James Jackson, Mr. William Cornwell, Nathaniel Seaman, Benjamin Seaman, Obediah Valentine, Thomas Williams, Peter Titus, Henry Willis, John Pratt, Nathaniel Townsend, Jeremiah Robbins, Thomas Powell, Samuel Jackson, Thomas Seaman, John Mott, John Mott, jr., John Whitson, John Birdsall, John Tredwell, jr., James Burtis, and Caleb Carman ; all of whom were residents of the town of Hempstead. Burnet was afterwards appointed governor of Massachusetts and New Hampshire. He died the 7th of September, 1729.

John Montgomerie, Esq. was the next governor of the colony, and entered upon his duties the 14th of April, 1728. He was a Scotchman, had been bred a soldier, and latterly had held the office of groom of the bed-chamber to his Majesty George II. He was a gentleman of mild temper, and fond of retirement. No extraordinary acts of a public nature characterized his short administration, and he died, greatly lamented, on the 1st of July, 1731. On his decease the chief command of the province devolved upon Rip Van Dam, Esq., the oldest of the council, and an eminent merchant of New-York ; which he relinquished on the arrival of Governor William Cosby, August 1, 1732. This gentleman was as much distinguished

for his folly and imprudence as his predecessor was for prudence and good sense. It was, however, during his administration that an act was passed on the 14th of October, 1732,
to regulate the ferry between New-York and Brooklyn, and to
establish, for the first time, the rates of ferriage. Some of these
rates were as follows :—For a horse or beast, one shilling; a
calf or hog, four pence; a sheep or lamb, three pence; a wagon or cart, five shillings; and for every person ten grains of
sevil pillar or Mexican plate, or two pence in bills of credit.
" Always provided that a sucking-child, or some remnants of
goods or other small goods which a woman carries in her apron,
or a man or a boy under his arm, shall be free."

" In the administration of Governor Cosby," says the historian Smith, " there was something to admire, and much to condemn." No governor commenced his administration with better prospects and greater popularity, yet none endeavored less
to retain the confidence and respect of the people. With high
opinions of prerogative, and being decidedly hostile to free and
equal legislation, he became at length odious to the colony, and
was finally deserted and opposed by many who had been his
best friends. He died the 7th of March, 1736, and the direction of public affairs devolved upon George Clarke, Esq., as
lieutenant governor, although violently opposed by the personal friends of Rip Van Dam, who, they thought, as the oldest of
the council, was best entitled to supply the vacancy. But Mr.
Clarke was afterwards confirmed in the office by the commission of the king. It was during the administration of Governor Clarke that the act was passed, on the 16th of December,
1737, for lowering the interest of money upon loans to seven
per cent., as the high and excessive usury before taken, it was
said, had been found by experience to be a very great discour-
agement of trade. It was also in his time that the memorable
conspiracy was discovered called the " Negro Plot," which, it
was supposed, had for its object the destruction of the whole
city of New-York by fire. This was in the year 1741. The
first fire broke out at his Majesty's house at Fort George, near
the chapel, and some other adjacent buildings. Fires continued to happen daily, and were at first supposed to be accident-

al, but at length such disclosures and confessions were made, that prosecutions were set on foot. A number of people of color were committed to jail as incendiaries, kept in dungeons for some months, and finally condemned to be hanged. Mr. Horsemanden, the recorder of the city, says, " many people had such terrible apprehensions on the subject, that several negroes, some of whom had assisted to put out the fires, were met and imprisoned ; and when once *there*, were continued in confinement, because the magistrates could not spare time to examine them." During this dreadful consternation, more than one hundred and fifty negroes were imprisoned, of whom fourteen were burned at the stake, eighteen were hanged, seventy-one transported, and the remainder pardoned, or discharged for want of proof. At this gloomy period the population of the city was twelve thousand, of whom one-sixth part were slaves ; a strange comment upon the professions of those who had left Europe for the sole purpose of enjoying perfect freedom in America. Governor Clarke, it must be admitted, studied his own interest ; for he retired from office with a fortune of a hundred thousand pounds sterling, surely no mean sum in that day. His Excellency George Clinton, who had been commissioned as governor of New-York, arrived on the 23d of November, 1743, which put an end to the administration of Governor Clarke. At this time the finances of the colony were any thing but prosperous. He was descended from an ancient and respectable family in Somersetshire, England, and was bred to the law. His wife was an heiress of the elder branch of the house of Hyde, in the county palatine of Chester, and where he afterwards died in 1763. He was the son of Francis Clinton, Earl of Lincoln. His administration of ten years was turbulent and unhappy. He was involved in a violent controversy with the assembly, instigated, as is believed, by Chief-Justice De Lancey, the ruling demagogue of that period. Yet, notwithstanding the public discontents, more laws were passed, and more valuable improvements took place in the internal police of the province, than during any preceding reign. This gentleman was received with great joy by the people, because they wanted a change, but were quite as well pleased to be rid of him a few

years after. He was a man of indolence, fond of wine, and
therefore unfit to discharge the duties of his office. He, like
his predecessor, managed to amass a fortune of eighty thousand
pounds sterling, which he carried with him to Europe. He
was succeeded, in 1753, by Sir Danvers Osborne. He arrived
in October, and was received with great rejoicings ; but in consequence of the loss of his wife, which produced great depres-
sion and melancholy, he was found, on the fifth day after his
arrival, suspended by a handkerchief to the fence of Mr. Murry,
one of the council. This unhappy gentleman had the reputation of great personal worth ; he had been a member of parliament, and was the brother-in-law of the Earl of Halifax. On
the death of Mr. Osborne, the administration fell upon the Hon.
James De Lancey, who had been a distinguished leader of the
government under Mr. Clinton. He was now both chief-justice and lieutenant governor, commencing with the latter office in 1753. He was but little acquainted with jurisprudence
when made a judge, yet by great industry and perseverance
he became in the end a learned and profound lawyer. He remained at the head of the government until the arrival of Sir
Charles Hardy in 1755, and again as successor to Hardy from
1757 to 1760; and died August 2d of the latter year. His
daughter was the wife of the celebrated William Draper, whose
fame will be as lasting as the letters of Junius.

Sir Charles Hardy was a distinguished officer of the British
navy, but his arrival as governor scarcely diminished the power of Mr. De Lancey, since the governor, being ignorant of civil
affairs, and entirely unacquainted with the colony, put himself
into his hands, and was guided mainly by his counsels. It
was during this year that preparations were made for a war in
America between the English and French. The governor
was promoted to the rank of rear admiral of the blue, with a command in the projected expedition against Louisburgh, and therefore left the administration in the hands of Mr. De Lancey. In July, 1758, the British under Colonel Bradstreet captured Fort Frontinac, and several armed vessels on the St. Lawrence. The
New-York troops consisted of two detachments ; one commanded by Lieut. Col. Charles Clinton, consisting of 440 men, un-

der Captains Ogden of Westchester, Dubois of New-York, Bladgley of Dutchess, and Daniel Wright of Queens; the second was commanded by Lieut. Col. Isaac Corse of Queens, and Major Nathaniel Woodhull of Suffolk, with six hundred and sixty-eight men, under Captain Elias Hand of Suffolk and Richard Hewlett of Queens.

On the death of Chief-Justice De Lancey in 1660, the administration devolved upon Cadwallader Colden, Esq., being the senior member and president of the council. He soon after received the commission of lieutenant governor at the age of seventy-three years. This gentleman, a celebrated physician, botanist, and astronomer, was a native of Scotland, and graduated at Edinburgh in 1705. Allured by the fame of Penn's colony, he came to America in 1708. Governor Hunter was so well pleased with him that he became his warm friend, and offered him his patronage if he would come to New-York. He consequently settled here in 1718, and was the first person that filled the office of surveyor-general in this colony. On the arrival of Governor Burnet he was made one of the council, and rose afterwards to the head of the board, thus succeeding to the administration of the government in the absence of the governor. He owned a large tract of land in Orange County, but afterwards purchased a farm at Flushing in Queen's County, which he named "Spring Hill," to which he retired from the cares and perplexities of office, and where he died on the 21st day of September in the year 1776.

Mr. Colden was relieved from the duties of his office for one year, commencing October 26th, 1762, by the arrival of Robert Monkton, Esquire, who had been appointed governor of the province; but being afterwards placed at the head of an expedition against Martinique, he left the government again to Mr. Colden, with an agreement, it is said, to divide equally between them the salary and perquisites of the office of governor.

Sir Henry Moore was commissioned as Governor of New-York in 1765, at the time when the attempt was made to impose stamp paper upon the people, and gave rise to a spirit of opposition and jealousy of their rulers that was never afterwards allayed, and which ended in revolution and the establish-

ment of independence. He, however, managed with so much
discretion, as to avoid any very considerable difficulties till his
death, which happened September 11th, 1769. His communications to the assembly were characterized by good sense and
brevity; and in enforcing the odious requirements of the parent country, he did not suffer his zeal for the crown to urge
him into indiscreet controversies with the people among whom
he lived, and whose respect and esteem he appeared anxious
to preserve. At the termination of his administration, the supreme court of the colony consisted of the following named
judges,—Daniel Horsemander, chief-justice, and David Jones,
William Smith, and Robert R. Livingston, judges. The salary
of the first was three hundred pounds, and that of the others
two hundred each. On the death of Sir Henry Moore the
duties of lieutenant governor again fell upon Mr. Colden, and
continued so till the 18th of November, 1770; when John, Lord
Dunmore, the new governor, arrived. He was less avaricious
than some of his predecessors; for when the assembly, on the
17th of January, 1771, voted him two thousand pounds as a
salary for the ensuing year, he refused it, and returned a message, saying, " that the king had appointed him a salary out of
his treasury, and he wished this allowance omitted." The object of this refusal was not so very disinterested as it might at
first appear, as it was intended to keep the governor independent of the people, and to raise monies for the support of the
government by the imposition of taxes upon the colonists. His
Lordship finally removed to Virginia, where he was made governor, and his place was supplied by the arrival of William
Tryon, Esquire, as governor, the 8th of July, 1771. Governor
Dunmore was, in 1775, obliged to abdicate the government of
Virginia, and take refuge on board of a man-of-war. He manifested his resentment and the badness of his heart by acting the
part of a corsair and plunderer. He also caused the conflagration
of Norfolk, January 1, 1776. In 1786 he was appointed governor of Burmuda, and died in England in 1809. His wife was
Lady Charlotte Stewart, daughter of the Earl of Galloway.

Governor Tryon commenced his administration at a time of
great excitement, and it required the utmost prudence to stear

clear of the most serious difficulties with the people. Yet he managed with so much discretion as to preserve the good will of the inhabitants till the period when all regular government was dissolved in the elements of revolution. On the 2nd of September, 1773, he laid the first stone of the New-York Hospital. He left the colony in April, 1774, and returned again in 1775, at the instance of the ministry ; but did not again meet the assembly, that body having adjourned the 3d of April, 1775, and never convened any more. Addresses of friendship were presented to him from many public and corporate bodies ; and King's College (now Columbia), in which he had founded a professorship, conferred upon him the honorary degree of Doctor of Laws. It is much to be lamented that a person possessing so many amiable qualities, and a reputation for kindness and humanity, should, from his zeal for monarchy or resentment toward his opponents, have forfeited so entirely the good opinion of all his American friends. and incur all the odium due to the most consummate villany, by conduct so atrocious and disgraceful as he afterwards exhibited. For he seemed to have changed his nature, and to enjoy a sort of demoniac pleasure in burning and plundering villages and towns as a means of distressing the inhabitants.

With Governor Tryon terminated the list of colonial governors, and with him expired also the name of colony and subjects of a foreign power. The territory was organized into a state, and its citizens joined heart and hand with their political brethren in the other provinces, in every measure calculated to free them from oppression, and to establish a free and independent government. And on the 4th of July, 1776, was published, by the representatives of a free people, that Declaration which has been emphatically denominated the Charter of American Liberty.

The whole history of the colonial government sufficiently demonstrates, that it is in vain to expect a patriotic devotion to the public welfare, and the happiness of the people, from rulers not connected with the country they govern by ties of personal feeling, and a kindred interest in the prosperity of its citizens ; and that a subserviency to the crown and disregard of the wel-

fare of the community, are vices inherent in the very nature
of colonial governments.

SUFFOLK COUNTY.

This county includes all that part of Long Island which lies
eastward of the township of Oyster Bay, excepting Lloyd's
Neck, which is attached by law to the county of Queens. It
is about one hundred and ten miles in length, and in some parts
twenty in breadth. It is bounded northwardly by the Sound,
eastwardly and southwardly by the Ocean, and westwardly by
Lloyd's Neck, Cold Spring Harbor, and the east bounds of
Queen's County; including Gardiner's Island, Plumb Island,
the Great and Little Gull Islands, Fisher's Island, Shelter Island,
and Robin's Island.

This county was organized on the 1st of November, 1683,
at which time the ridings were abolished, and Long Island was
divided into three counties, as they have remained ever since.
It is subdivided into nine distinct municipalities or towns, to
wit: Huntington, Smithtown, Islip, Brookhaven, Riverhead,
Shelter Island, Southampton, and Easthampton.

The first court of sessions in this county, of which any record
remains, was held under the authority of the Duke's laws, on
the 6th day of March, 1677; and at which the presiding officers
were as follows:

MATHIAS NICOLLS, President,
THOMAS WILLET, Councillor,
THOMAS BAKER,   ⎫
ISAAC ARNOLD,   ⎬ Justices.
RICHARD WOODHULL.   ⎭

The act of 1683 required two courts of general sessions to be
held in each county, annually, and those for this county to be
holden at the town of Southampton; at which place they continued to be held, together with the court of oyer and termi-

ner, for about forty years, when they were held occasionally at Southold, where the prison was established.

The oldest minute which has been discovered relative to the court of common pleas in this county, is as follows :

" At a court of common pleas held at Southampton the next day after the court of general sessions terminated, being the 28th day of March, in the ninth year of his Majesty's reign, anno domini, 1723.

> Present, HENRY SMITH and BENJAMIN YOUNGS, Esquires, Judges.
>
> ROBERT HUDSON and JOSEPH WICKHAM, Esquires, Justices.
>
> WILLIAM SMITH, Clerk.
>
> Attornies, HOPKINS, CLOWES, and VERNON."

This court was held under the act of the 6th of May, 1691.

At a court of general sessions, held the last Tuesday of March, 1723, the presiding justices were Timothy Brewster, Jeremiah Scott, Joseph Wickham, Selah Strong, William Smith, and Brinley Sylvester. The court of common pleas, October 1, 1724, was held by Benjamin Youngs and Richard Floyd, judges, and Joseph Wickham, Thomas Chatfield, and John Foster, justices.

About this time a court house, or county hall, was built at Riverhead, then a part of Southold, where the court was held for the first time, on the 27th of March, 1729.

Under the ordinance of 1699, the names of judges of the court of common pleas, were as follows, from 1723 to 1775.

1723, Henry Smith, Benjamin Youngs, and Richard Floyd.

1729, Henry Smith, Benjamin Youngs, and Samuel Hutchinson.

1738, Henry Smith, Joshua Youngs, and Thomas Chatfield.

1752, Richard Floyd, Elijah Hutchinson, and Hugh Gelston.

1764, Richard Floyd, Samuel Landon, and Hugh Gelston.

1771, William Smith, Samuel Landon, and Isaac Post.

1775, William Smith, Samuel Landon, and Isaac Post.

The names of the clerks of the county, from 1669 to 1776, are as follows :

Henry Pierson, from	1669 to 1681.	C. Congreve, from	1716 to 1722.
John Howell,	1681 to 1692.	Samuel Hudson,	1722 to 1730.
Thomas Helme,	1692 to 1709.	William Smith,	1730 to 1750.
Henry Smith,	1709 to 1716.	William Nicolls,	1750 to 1775.

The members of the general assembly of the colony from this county, from its establishment in 1691 to 1775, and for the respective periods mentioned, were as follows:

Henry Pierson,	1691 to 1695.	Epenetus Platt,	1723 to 1739.
Matthew Howell,	1691 to 1693.	Samuel Hutchinson,	1726 to 1748.
John Tuthill,	1693 to 1694.	Daniel Pierson,	1737 to 1748.
Matthew Howell,	1694 to 1705.	Eleazer Miller,	1748 to 1768.
John Tuthill,	1695 to 1698.	William Nicolls, 2d,	1739 to 1769.
Henry Pierson,	1693 to 1701.	Eleazar Miller,	1768 to 1769.
William Nicolls,	1702 to 1723.	William Nicolls, 3d,	1768 to 1769.
Samuel Mulford,	1705 to 1726.	Nathaniel Woodhull,	1769 to 1775.

William Nicolls, 3d, 1769 to 1775.

The following persons were members of the council from 1683 to 1704. Colonel John Youngs, from 1683 to 1698; Colonel William Smith, from 1691 to 1698; and Mr. William Nicolls, from 1691 to 1704. The justices of the peace for the county, in 1763, were as follows:

Richard Floyd,	Isaac Post,	Daniel Wells,
Hugh Gelston,	Thomas Youngs,	Parker Wickham,
Samuel Landon,	Robert Hempstead,	Thomas Cooper,
John Chatfield,	Isaac Hubbard,	Benajah Strong,
Richard Woodhull,	Nathaniel Woodhull,	Jonathan Thompson,
George Phillips,	Jonas Williams,	Joseph Lewis,
Richard Miller,	Thomas Jarvis,	William Phillips,
Nathaniel Baker,	Burnet Miller,	Charles Floyd,
Isaac Barnes,	John Still Winthrop,	Samuel Allen,
John Pierson,	Thomas Helme,	Obediah Platt,
Benjamin Conkling,	James Reeve, jun.	Ebenezer White,
Richard Woodhull, jun.	Selah Strong,	Samuel Hunting,
Maltby Gelston,	Thomas Sandford,	Barnabas Terril,
William Hubbard,	Phineas Fanning,	Benjamin Brown.
John Woodhull,	Thomas Osborn,	

Deputies to the convention which met the 10th of April, 1775, for the purpose of electing delegates to the first continental congress: William Floyd, Nathaniel Woodhull, Phineas Fanning, Thomas Tredwell, and John Sloss Hobart.

Members of the provincial convention which met the 27th of May, 1775: Nathaniel Woodhull, John Sloss Hobart, Ezra L'Hommedieu, William Smith, Thomas Wickham, Thomas

Tredwell, David Gelston, John Foster, James Havens, Selah Strong, and Thomas Deering.

Members of the convention to form the constitution of this state, in 1777, were as follows : William Smith, Thomas Tredwell, John S'oss Hobart, Mathias B. Miller, Ezra L'Hommedieu, Nathaniel Woodhull, Thomas Deering, and David Gelston.

The following were members of the convention which met at Poughkeepsie, June 17th, 1788, and adopted the constitution of the United States : Henry Scudder, John Smith, Jonathan N. Havens, Thomas Tredwell, and David Hedges.

The population of this county at different periods have been as follows : In 1731, 7675 ; in 1771, 13128 ; in 1786, 13793 ; in 1790, 16440 ; in 1800, 19444 ; in 1810, 21113 ; in 1820, 24272 ; in 1825, 23695 ; in 1830, 26780 ; in 1835, 28724.

In 1810, there were in this county 1062 looms ; and during that year were manufactured, chiefly in families, 51220 yards of woolen, 158390 of linen, and 4087 of cotton cloth.

There have been three capital executions in this county since the revolution, as follows : William Erskine, (black) of Brookhaven, convicted of rape, September 14th, 1791, and executed October 5, 1791. William Enoch, of Huntington, convicted of the murder of his wife in June, 1834, and executed January 12th, 1835. John Hallock, of Brookhaven, convicted of the murder of a colored woman, May 10th, 1836, and executed July 2d, 1836.

The delegates to the convention of 1821, for amending the constitution of this state ; Ebenezer Sage, Usher H. Moore, and Joshua Smith.

By the act of March 8th, 1773, William Smith, Samuel Landon, and Maltby Gelston, were appointed commissioners of excise for the county.

The first judges of this county since the revolution have been Selah Strong, appointed in 1783 ; Ebenezer Platt, in 1794 ; Abraham Woodhull, in 1799 ; Thomas S. Strong, in 1810 ; Joshua Smith, in 1823 ; Jonathan S. Conkling, in 1828 ; and Hugh Halsey, in 1833.

Surrogates. Thomas Tredwell, from 1787 to 1791. Nicoll

Floyd, from 1791 to 1823.   Ebenezer W. Case, from 1823 to 1827 ; and Hugh Halsey from 1827 to the present time.

The clerks of the county, since 1776, have been as follows : William B. Bevans, appointed in 1783 ; Ezra L'Hommedieu, in 1784 ; Hull Osborn, in 1810 ; Charles H. Havens, in 1812 ; Charles A. Floyd, in 1820; Charles H. Havens, elected in 1822 ; Joseph R. Hunting, 1829 ; and George S. Phillips, the present clerk, in 1838.

The district attornies, since the act requiring one in each county, have been as follows: Silas Wood, appointed in 1818. Selah B. Strong, in 1821.   Charles A. Floyd, in 1830, and Selah B. Strong again in 1834.   The following extracts from court records and other sources are sufficiently curious and interesting to be preserved, and present a diverting representation of the olden times, both in the language and subject matter of most of them.ʾ

" At a court of sessions held at Southampton on the 4th of March, 1669, a complaint is prosecuted to the court against Mr. John Laughton, for his misdemeanour in saying to Mr. John Howell that hee was a traytor to ye State, and hee would prove him soe.   Mr. Laughton being called, appears, and being questioned by ye cort about itt, hee owned yᵗ he called Mr. Howell soe, and confessed yᵗ hee had noe just cause soe to call him. The Cort adjudg Mr. Laughton to pay a fine of £3 to ye county, and costs of cort, in current pay without further trouble.

" Edward Avery ye Smith at Easthampton, being brought before ye cort to answer for his committing of fornication with her hee now calls his wife ; hee acknowleged injeniously the fact or offence, and undertaking for his wife therein also.   The cort give sentence that he shall pay £3 as a fine to the county, and costs of cort, all which he promiseth to satisfie," &c.

" Mrs. Alice Stanborough entereth complaint against Mr. Edwards of their town of Easthampton, for his turning a water course upon her land and housing to her great damage and inconvenience, to the value of £5 10s.   The complaint being prosecuted at this court, and the witnesses on both sides duly considered, the cort doth give their judgmᵗ and order as followeth :—that the plf. sueing for £5 10s. damage but not proving it, this cort doth judg and determine according to law in that case provided, that ye plf. shall lose her suite or plainte, and pay unto ye deft. costs of suite. And for prevention of any further trouble betweene the plf. and ye deft. concerning the turning of a flux of water into ye plf's grounds, this cort doth order that ye constable of Easthampton, and 3 of theire overseers, namely, Stephen Hand, Nathaniel Bishop, and Steeven Hedges, shall view the ground belonging to the plf. and deft. and set down, order, and dispose of that occasion as may be most convenient for both ye parties, with the assistance of Mr. Mulford—and what those 4 men doe determine, as to where the water shall run, shall be a finall conclusion betweene the plf. and deft., they being to satisfie the s^d 4 men for what pains they shall bee at."

"John Cooper, as Attorney for Mr. James Mills of Virginia, enters an action of debt against Hackaliah Bridges, on which accompt some of his goods were attached; the jurymen were Joshua Barnes, Joseph Raymer, Richard Howell, Thomas Topping, Thomas Goldsmith, Robert Dayton, and Ensigne Bayly of Huntington. The plf. produced his letter of atty. from Mr. Mills. Also the plf. produced several writings knowne to bee signed by ye s^d Hackaliah, which was compared with ye s^d bill, to confirme to the cort the reality thereof. The jury finde for ye plf. and 30s. costs of suite. The cort give judgm^t accordinge."

"At a cort of sessions held March 6, 177½. The constable and overseers of Easthampton enter complaint against Reneck Garison and his wife, for being guilty of fornication before they were marryed. It being sufficiently proved, ye cort give sentence that they both shall have corporall punishment publickly, viz: with five stripes a-piece. But John Denison and Cornelius Vonk, engaging to the justices to pay forty shillings to the country for ye s^d Reneck and his wife, as a fine, the said sentence is reversed." "A complaint against Peeter Whittere, March 7, 167½, for his abusive carriage toward Justice Mulford. The cort doth order and sentence, that ye s^d Peeter shall make acknowlegment of his evil and abusive carriage, next Lord's day come seven-night, at ye publique meeting in Easthampton,

to the satisfaction of Mr. Mulford; and hee is to pay ye costs
of ye complainte, as also his former fine imposed."

"January ye 14, 1672, Mr. John Tomson of Seatauk, plf.
enters an action of slander or deffamation against Richard Mintorne, deft. to be tryed at ye next cort of sessions.

" The plf. and dft. are agreed as follows :

" Be it known to all, that I, Richard Mintorne of Southampton,
doe acknowlege that I have spoken ffoolishly and inadvisedly
to the dissparagement of Mr. John Tomson of Seatauk, and
that of my knowledge I know nothing of it.   And this I give
for a publique satisfaction—as witness my hand.

"RICHARD MINTORNE."

The proof of last wills and testaments were anciently taken
before the courts of sessions, by virtue of a commission or authority from the governor and council, under the Duke of York,
and when approved, were recorded in the minutes of the court;
and the records of the court, as well as of the several towns,
abound with copies of wills and inventories of the personal estates of deceased persons.   As a specimen of ancient wills, the
following is considered worthy of preservation ; it is supposed
to be in favor of a young lady whom the testator had engaged to
marry should he live to return from the voyage he was about
to take, and as a proof of his attachment.

" I, Lattimer Sampson, of Oyster Bay, Long Island, being intended (God permitting) to travell to the Barbados, and well
knowing the casualty of man's life and certainty of death, do
make, constitute, and appoint this to bee my last will and testament, in manner and form following ; that is to say : I give,
will and bequeath all my estate, both real and personal, on Long
Island, Shelter Island, and elsewhere in New England ; and
the gains and advance (the principal being repaid in England,
within two years after my decease) of all such goods as shall
bee sent to mee (within one year after the date hereof,) upon
my proper accompt, unto Grizzle Sylvester, daughter of Nathaniel Sylvester of Shelter Island ; and to her heyres and assigns
for ever.   And I doe hereby constitute and appoint the said Nathaniel Sylvester, and the said Grizzle Sylvester, to bee my
executor and executrix of this my will.   In testimony where-

of, I have hereto set my hand and seal. Dated, Shelter Island,
the 16th day of the month called ffebruary, 1668.

"LAT. SAMPSON. [L. S.]"

It should be remarked that the testator died abroad, and the
young lady afterwards became the wife of James Lloyd, Esq.,
of Boston ; and in consequence of which he became entitled to
a part of Lloyd's Neck, then called Horse Neck.

Extracted from the New-York Mercury, June 29th, 1772.
" We hear from Brookhaven, that on the night of the 18th instant, about midnight, a barn belonging to Mr. Samuel Davis, of
that place, was discovered to be all in flames, so that the fire
could not be extinguished till the barn was burnt to the ground.
The people who assembled on this occasion perceived another
barn hard by to be on fire at both ends, but as the fire had been but
lately kindled, it was soon suppressed ; and while they were
about it, they perceived a third barn at a little further distance
to be also on fire, which they likewise suppressed. These fires
were supposed to be designedly kindled by a runaway negro
who had belonged to Mr. Davis."

From the same. " We learn from South-haven in Suffolk
County, on Long Island, that about four o'clock last Monday afternoon, Nathaniel Brewster, Esq., of that place, being in the
woods with one of his negroes, attempted to correct him
for some misdemeanor, which the negro resented, and wounded his master, by giving him several such heavy blows
on his head with a billet of wood that he expired the next
morning. The negro was tried the next day, and being found
guilty of the murder of Mr. Brewster, was to be executed last
Friday."

From Rivington's New-York Gazette, January 16, 1774.
" From Huntington, on Long Island, we are informed that last
Christmas-day, Mr. Ebenezer Platt being hunting deer with
some other young men near that village, they surrounded
a swamp where the game were, and agreed with each other
not to enter any part of it. Mr. Platt seeing a buck at some distance, rushed forward, and one of his companions hearing a
noise in the bushes, immediately fired and lodged five swan-

shot in Mr. Platt, three of which entered his arm, and two his body, which render his life despaired of."

New-York Mercury, March 10, 1778. "Moses Sawyer, who formerly lived at Shelter Island, came over from the main a few days since and robbed the farm of William Nicolls, Esq., at said island, of one hundred and ten bushels of wheat; and carried off grain belonging to Thomas Deering."

New-York Gazette, February 16, 1778. "At two o'clock last Thursday morning, a party of twelve rebels seized at Coram, in Suffolk County, two wagons loaded with dry-goods, the property of Obediah Wright of Southampton. These marauders had been several days on the island, visited most parts, and committed many robberies; especially at the house of Colonel Floyd, Setauket, which they robbed of goods and cash to a considerable amount; and took some property of Mr. Dunbar, who rides down the island occasionally, and happened to lodge in the house that night."

From the same, June 19, 1780. "Last Wednesday three boats going from New-York to Huntington, were attacked near Butler's Point by two rebel boats from Connecticut, which they beat off, after exchanging several shots; but one of the boats not sailing so well as the others, was run on shore and burnt."

From the same, August 13, 1781 "Last Thursday night eight rebel whale-boats made their appearance at Flushing Bay, and landed a few men; but as they did not like the appearance of things, they speedily embarked."

From the New-York Journal, September 29, 1782. "On Saturday last two men were detected in transporting some forces to Long Island near Flushing; they were sent to Killingworth and committed to gaol, and about the same time thirty sail of shipping were seen under Long Island taking in wood."

From the Long Island Star, September 10, 1813. "On the evening of Friday the 5th instant, eleven men belonging to Fire Place, went to the south shore with a seine for fish, viz.: William Rose, Isaac Woodruff, Lewis Parshall, Benjamin Brown, Nehemiah Hand, James Homan, Charles Ellison, James Prior, Daniel Parshall, Henry Homan, and John Hulse.

On Saturday morning the afflicting discovery was made that they were all drowned. The boat came on shore in pieces, and also eight of the bodies. The first six named persons had families."

It is, perhaps, not generally known, even to the reading portion of the community, that any solemn judicial investigation of a charge of witchcraft ever took place in this State while a colony ; although cases of this sort were common in some of the New England colonies in the early part of their settlement, and the most horrible consequences, not to say murders, ensued upon the most ridiculous charges and suspicions of a correspondence between a most unfortunate class of human beings and the author of evil. The following narration is extracted from the records in the Secretary of State's office, Book A, relating to the Courts of Assizes, beginning in the year after the English conquest, in 1665.

" At a Court of Assizes held in New-York on the 2d day of October, 1665, the triall of Ralph Hall and Mary his wife, upon suspicion of witchcraft ; the names of the persons who served on the Grand Jury, were Thomas Baker, of Easthampton, fforeman of the Jury ; Captain John Symonds, of Hempstead ; Mr. Hallett, of Jamaica ; Anthony Waters, Thomas Wandall, of Marshpathkill ; Mr. Nicolls, of Stamford ; Balthazer de Haart, John Garland, Jacob Leister, Anthonio de Mill, Alexander Munro, Thomas Searle, of New-York.

" The prisoner being brought to the barr by Allard Anthony, sheriff of New-York : this following indictment was read, first against Ralph Hall, and then against Mary his wife, viz :—

" The constable and overseers of the towne of Seatalcott, in the east riding of Yorkshire, upon Long Island, do present, for our soveraigne lord the king, that Ralph Hall, of Seatalcott aforesaid, upon the 25th day of December, being Christmas day last was twelve months, in the fifteenth year of the raigne of our soveraigne lord Charles the Second, by the grace of God, king of England, Scotland, ffrance and Ireland, defender of the faith, &c., and severall other days and times since that day, by some detestable and wicked arts, commonly called witchcraft and sorcery, did (as is suspected) maliciously and feloniously practise and exercise, at the said town of Seatalcott, in the east riding of Yorkshire, on Long Island aforesaid, on the person of George Wood, late of the same place, by which wicked and detestable arts the said George Wood, (as is suspected) most dangerously and mortally sickened and languished, and not long after, by the aforesaid wicked and detestable arts, the said George Wood (as is likewise suspected) died.

"Moreover, the constable and overseers of the said towne of Seatalcott, in the east riding of Yorkshire, upon Long Island aforesaid, do further present, for our soveraign lord the king, that some while after the death of the aforesaid George Wood, the said Ralph Hall, did (as is suspected) divers times, by the like wicked and detestable arts, commonly called witchcraft and sorcery, maliciously and feloniously practise and exercise, at the said town of Seatalcott, in the east riding of Yorkshire, upon Long Island aforesaid, on the person of an infant child of Ann Rogers, widow of the aforesaid George Wood, deceased, by which wicked and detestable arts, the said infant (as is suspected) most dangerously and mortally sickened and languished, and not long after, by the same wicked and detestable arts, (as is likewise suspected) died : and so the said constable and overseers do present, that the said George Wood, and the said infant childe, by the ways and means aforesaid, most wickedly, maliciously, and feloniously were (as is suspected) murdered, by the said Ralph Hall, at the times and places aforesaid, against the peace of our soveraign lord the king, and against the laws of this government in such cases provided. The like indictment was read against Mary, the wife of Ralph Hall : Thereupon several depositions accusing the prisoners of the fact for which they were indicted, were read ; but no witnesses appeared to give testimony in court, *viva voce*, then the clerk calling upon Ralph Hall, bade him hold up his hand, and read as follows : Ralph Hall, thou standest here indicted for that, having not the fear of God before thine eyes, thou didst, upon the 25th day of December, being Christmas day last was twelve months, and at several other times since (as is suspected) by some wicked and detestable arts, commonly called withcraft and sorcery, maliciously and feloniously practise and exercise upon the bodies of George Wood and an infant child of Ann Rogers; by which said arts the said George Wood, and the infant child (as is suspected) most dangerously and mortally fell sick, and languished unto death. Ralph Hall, what dost thou say for thyself—art thou guilty or not guilty? Mary, the wife of Ralph Hall, was called upon in like manner. They both pleaded not guilty, and threw themselves to be tried by God and the country. Whereupon their case was referred to the jury, who brought into the court the following verdict, viz :—

" We having severally considered the case committed to our charge, against the prisoners at the bar, and having well weighed the evidence, we find that there are some suspicions by the evidence of what the woman is charged with, but nothing considerable of value to take away her life ; but in reference to the man, we find nothing considerable to charge him with.

" The court, therefore, gave this sentence: That the man should be bound, body and goods, for his wife's appearance at the next sessions, and so on from sessions to sessions, as long as they stay within this government. In the meanwhile to be of good behavior. So they were returned to the sheriff's custody ; and upon entering into a recognizance according to the sentence of the court, they were released.´

" Appeals, actions, presentments, &c. entered for hearing and tryall, at the generall court of assizes, to be held in New-York, beginning on the first Wednesday of October, 1670 :

" In the case of Katharine Harryson, widow, who was bound to the good behavior upon complaint of some of the inhabitants of Westchester, until the holding of this court. It ordered, that in regard there is nothing appears against her deserving the continuation of that obligation, she is to be released from it, and hath liberty to remain in the towne of Westchester, where she now resides, or any where else in the government, during her pleasure.

" A release to Ralph Hall, and Mary, his wife, from the recognizances they entered into at the assizes :—

" These are to certify to all whom it may concerne, that Ralph Hall, and Mary, his wife, (at present living upon the great Minifords island) are hereby released and acquitted from

any and all recognizances, bonds of appearance or other obligations entered into by them or either of them, for the peace or
good behavior, upon account of any accusation or indictment
upon suspicion of witchcraft, brought into the court of assizes
against them, in the year 1665; there having been no direct
proofs nor further prosecution of them since. Given under my
hand at Fort James, in New-York, this 21st day of August,
1668.   R. NICOLLS."

*Names of those who have represented the County of Suffolk, in the House of
Assembly of the State of New-York, from 1776 to the present time.*

1777. Burnet Miller, David Gelston, Ezra L'Hommedieu, Thomas Tredwell,
      Thomas Wicks.
1778. The same.
1779. The same.
1780. The same.
1781. The same.
1782. The same.
1783. The same.
1784. David Gelston, Thomas Youngs, Ebenezer Platt, John Smith, Jeffrey
      Smith.
1785. The same.
1786. Jonathan N. Havens, David Hedges, Thomas Youngs, Jeffrey Smith,
      Nathaniel Gardiner.
1787. Jonathan N. Havens, David Hedges, Daniel Osborn, John Smith, Caleb
      Smith.
1788. Jonathan N. Havens, John Smith, Daniel Hedges, Daniel Osborn.
1789. Jonathan N. Havens, David Hedges, Nathaniel Gardiner, John Smith,
      Henry Scudder.
1790. Nathaniel Gardiner, Henry Scudder, John Smith, Jonathan N. Havens.
1791. Jonathan N. Havens, John Gelston, John Smith, Philetus Smith, Thomas
      Wickham.
1792. Jonathan N. Havens, John Smith, John Gelston, Henry Scudder.
1793. Jonathan N. Havens, John Smith, Ebenezer Platt, John Gelston.
1794. Jonathan N. Havens, John Smith, John Gelston, Joshua Smith, Jr.
1795. Jonathan N. Havens, John Gelston, Isaac Thompson, Joshua Smith, Jr.
1796. Abraham Miller, Silas Wood, Jared Landon, Joshua Smith, Jr.
1797. The same.
1798. Abraham Miller, Silas Wood, Josiah Reeve, John Howard.
1799. John Smith, Jared Landon, Nicoll Floyd.
1800. Silas Wood, John Smith, Jared Landon, Nicoll Floyd.
1801. Nicoll Floyd, Mills Phillips, Abraham Miller, Jared Landon.
1802. Israel Carll, Jared Landon, Abraham Miller, Tredwell Scudder.
1803. Israel Carll, Josiah Reeve, Jonathan Dayton.
1804. David Hedges, Israel Carll, Sylvester Dering.
1805. Jared Landon, Israel Carll, Jonathan Dayton.
1806. The same.

1807. Israel Carll, David Hedges, David Warner.
1808. Israel Carll, Jonathan Dayton, Thomas S. Lester.
1809. Mills Phillips, Abraham Rose, Daniel T. Terry.
1810. Abraham Rose, John Rose, Tredwell Scudder.
1811. Tredwell Scudder, Thomas S. Lester, Jonathan S. Conklin.
1812. Abraham Rose, Usher H. Moore, Nathaniel Potter.
1813. Benjamin F. Thompson, Henry Rhodes, Caleb Smith.
1814. Thomas S. Lester, Nathaniel Potter, Jonathan S. Conklin.
1815. Tredwell Scudder, John P. Osborn, John Wells.
1816. Abraham Rose, Benjamin F. Thompson, Phineas Carll.
1817. Israel Carll, Thomas S. Lester, Abraham Parsons.
1818. Charles H. Havens, John P. Osborn, Nathaniel Miller.
1819. John P. Osborn, Isaac Conklin, Daniel Youngs.
1820. Charles H. Havens, Abraham Parsons, Ebenezer W. Case.
1821. John M. Williamson, Isaac Conklin, John P. Osborn.
1822. Tredwell Scudder, Hugh Halsey, John M. Williamson.
1823. Samuel Strong, Joshua Fleet.
1824. Hugh Halsey, Josiah Smith.
1825. Joshua Smith, David Hedges, Jr.
1826. John M. Williamson, Usher H. Moore.
1827. Samuel Strong, George L. Conklin.
1828. Tredwell Scudder, Abraham H. Gardiner.
1829. John M. Williamson, David Hedges, Jr.
1830. Samuel Strong, Noah Youngs.
1831. George S. Phillips, George L. Conklin.
1832. John M. Williamson, Samuel L'Hommedieu.
1833. David Hedges, Jr., William Wickes.
1834. William Sidney Smith, John Terry.
1835. George S. Phillips, George L. Conklin.
1836. Charles A. Floyd, Nathaniel Topping.
1837. John M. Williamson, Josiah Dayton.
1838. Charles A. Floyd, Sidney E. Griffin.
1839. Joshua B. Smith, Joseph Wickham Case.

From Bradford's New-York Gazette, May 18, 1737.
" These are to give notice, that on Monday the 16th instant,
there dyed at the house of Plat Smith, in Smithtown, in Suffolk
county, on Long Island, alias Nassau Island, one Hugh Reny,
a pedlar ; and the said Plat Smith, not knowing certainly where
the said Hugh Reny's relations live, he therefore gives this public notice when and where he dyed, and that what money
he had and his pack of goods are in the hands of the said
Plat Smith, where his friends and relations may come and
receive the same."

From the same, July 17, 1780. " We heard from Setauket
that last *F*riday night a party of rebels surrounded the house

of Doctor Punderson, took him prisoner, and carried him to Connecticut; and on that night the same party took Mr. William Jayne, jun. The rebels told Mrs. Punderson that they had taken the Doctor to exchange for John Smith, and Mr. Jayne for William Phillips, who were taken at Smithtown, at the widow Blydenburgh's, on a trading party."

From the Long Island Star, January 24, 1815. "On the evening of the 16th instant, during a snow-storm, the British sloop of war *Sylph*, rating eighteen guns and three hundred and ninety tons, commanded by Capt. Dickens, with a crew of officers and men, in number one hundred and seventeen, went ashore on the south side of Long Island, near Shinecock. She drove over the bar, head onwards, within a few rods of the shore. The inhabitants attempted to give relief, but the height of the surf and the violence of the wind made it impossible to reach the vessel. Sixty of the crew were safe in the main-top and rigging until eight o'clock, when a tremendous sea capsized the vessel, and broke her in two, fore and aft. Only *five* of the crew were saved, and *one hundred and eleven* drowned. The captain was a young man, and had been lately married. Some of the bodies were found near the wreck, others floated as far west as Fire Place, and even to Fire Island Inlet. The humanity and kindness of the people of Southampton, were handsomely acknowledged in the account given to Commodore Hotham, and nobly responded to by him."

EXTRACT FROM THE STATE CENSUS OF 1835.

Towns.	Males.	Females.	Total persons.	Paupers.	Number of acres of improved land.	Grist Mills.	Number of yards of domestic fulled cloth.	Yards of linen, cotton, and other thin cloths.	Yards of flannel and other woollen cloth not fulled.	Militia.	Electors.	Persons of color.	Neat cattle.	Horses.	Sheep.	Hogs.
Brookhaven.	3162	3404	6·66	10	35141		5556	4675	4850	579	1410	513	4590	1294	8451	3846
Easthampton	893	926	1819	12	17827	6	1785	2365	1528	187	405	168	2487	473	4903	1013
Huntington.	2765	2733	5498	16	32532	9	3272	771	359	591	1220	312	3530	1387	11044	3833
Islip.	784	744	1528	5	8016	1	711	712	577	110	329	207	1634	289	1307	1108
Riverhead.	1074	1064	2138	16	12302	3	1909	1514	1202	278	473	57	2234	522	1930	1328
Smithtown.	199	781	1580	4	10937	3	947	969	485	122	363	238	1581	443	3896	1552
Southold.	1600	1336	2936	21	23351	7	2954	4912	1698	265	722	58	3751	689	3786	2684
Southampton.	2652	262	5275	15	23105	10	2093	5410	2431	543	1050	494	4738	828	5416	2131
Shelter Island	152	181	333	2	4836	1	80	50	53	16	62	21	426	63	2837	266
Total.	14581	13793	30673	101	168047	50	20207	21378	13382	2691	6034	2068	24971	5988	43570	17768

EXTRACT FROM THE COMMON SCHOOL RETURNS,
JANUARY 5, 1838.

Towns.	Number of School Districts.	Number from which returns are received	Average number of months in the year.	Amount of public money received and expended.	Amount paid for wages.	Number of children taught during the year.	Number of children in town between 5 and 15 years of age.	Amount of public money distributed to districts.
Brookhaven.	33	33	9	$633,10	$2435,18	1885	1859	$662,39
Easthampton.	6	6	9	178.00	491,09	355	450	178,04
Huntington.	26	23	8	586,25	2064,90	1434	1706	566,29
Islip.	8	8	10	170,43	520,53	433	524	162,68
Riverhead.]	13	12	10	202,95	719,47	549	578	212,12
Shelter Island.	1	1	11	33,80	230,00	95	90	33,80
Smithtown.	11	10	8	175,35	554,95	410	472	167,00
Southampton.	19	18	9	474,18	1343,46	1185	1342	503,79
Southold.	14	14	10	300,67	1477,73	953	867	311,71
Total	133	125	9	$2754,73	$9837,31	7299	7884	$2797,82

QUEEN'S COUNTY

This county was organized March 1, 1683, and now contains
all that part of Long Island which is bounded easterly by Suffolk County ; southerly by the Atlantic Ocean ; northerly by
Long Island Sound ; and westerly by King's County, including
Lloyd's Neck or Queen's Village, the islands called the North
and South Brother, Riker's Island formerly called Hallet's Island, and all the other islands lying in the Sound opposite the
said bounds and southerly of the main channel.   It is sub-di-
vided into six townships, namely : Jamaica, Newtown, Flushing, North Hempstead, Hempstead, and Oyster Bay.   It appears, from several public documents which have been preserved, that the courts of the county were originally held for the
most part at Hempstead, and where the governor ordered meetings of delegates from the different towns on various occasions.
By the act of assembly passed 1683, by which the counties
and towns upon Long Island were organized and established,
the county courts were required thereafter to be held at the village of Jamaica.   They were held there for about seven years
in the old stone church, which stood in the middle of the pre-

sent Fulton Street opposite Union Hall Street.   In the year 1690
a court-house and jail were erected upon the site now occupied
by the Female Academy, and continued to be used for the
purpose of holding the courts of the county until the present court-house was built upon the north side of Hempstead
Plains, in the town of North Hempstead, in the year 1778.
Why this location was chosen, it is difficult to determine, except from the circumstance of its being near the geographical
centre of the county.   The records of this county commence
with its organization, and the first entry is a release from one
James Feeke, dated Feb. 1, 1683.   At this time John Bowne
was treasurer of the county.   His dwelling-house in Flushing,
which was erected in 1661, is still standing, and bids fair to
last another half century.

At a court of sessions held at Jamaica on the 8th of June,
1675, the following officers were present : Mathias Nicolls,
(secretary,) president ; Chidley Brooke, councillor ; and Sylvester Salisbury, high sheriff.   Thomas Hicks was appointed
judge under the commission of Governor Andross, and in pursuance of the act of assembly, in the year 1691, and held the office till 1699 ; at which time an ordinance was passed in relation to the office of judges of the common pleas, and by authority of which the following named persons were appointed,
and held their offices for the periods mentioned respectively.

From 1699 to 1703, John Coe.
     1703 to 1710, Thomas Willet.
     1710 to 1723, Thomas Willet and John Jackson.
     1723 to 1730, Thomas Willet and Isaac Hicks.
     1730 to 1734, Isaac Hicks, David Jones, and John Tallman.
     1734 to 1738, David Jones, John Messenger, and James Hazzard.
     1738 to 1740, David Jones, James Hazzard, and Thomas Hicks.
     1740 to 1749, James Hazzard, Thomas Hicks, and John Willet.
     1749 to 1756, Thomas Hicks, David Seaman, and Joseph Sacket.
     1756 to 1757, Thomas Hicks, Jacob Smith, and Penn Townsend.
     1757 to 1771, Thomas Hicks, Valentine H. Peters, and Penn Townsend.
     1771 to 1774, Thomas Hicks, Valentine H. Peters, and Daniel Kissam.

The several clerks of the county, from its formation to the
revolution, were as follows :

From 1683 to 1688, William Nicolls.   1710 to 1722, Joseph Smith.
     1688 to 1702, Andrew Gibb.   1722 to 1757, Andrew Clark.

1702 to 1710, Samuel Clowes,   1757 to 1770, Whitehead Hicks.
From 1770 to 1775, Thomas Jones.

The following persons were elected to the assembly at different periods, from its origin in 1691 to the revolution:

Daniel Whitehead, from 1691 to 1705.
John Robinson,   1691 to 1693.
John Jackson,   1693 to 1709.
Jonathan Whitehead,   1705 to 1709.
John Tallman,   1709 to 1710.
John Townsend,   1709 to 1710.
John Jackson,   1710 to 1716.
Thomas Willet,   1710 to 1726.

Isaac Hicks, from 1716 to 1739.
Benjamin Hicks,   1726 to 1737.
David Jones,   1737 to 1757.
Thomas Cornell,   1739 to 1759.
Thomas Hicks,   1759 to 1761.
Thomas Cornell,   1761 to 1764.
Zebulan Seamen,   1759 to 1774.
Daniel Kissam,   1764 to 1775.

Thomas Willet was a member of the council from 1677 to 1692. Jacob Blackwell and John Tallman were appointed deputies from this county to the convention at New-York, April 10, 1775, to choose delegates to the continental congress. The members of the provincial convention, which assembled in May, 1775, were Jacob Blackwell, Captain Jonathan Lawrence, Daniel Rapelje, Zebulan Williams, Joseph French, Joseph Robinson, Nathaniel Tom, Thomas Hicks, and Richard Thorn. The persons elected to form the constitution of this state in 1777, were Jonathan Lawrence, Rev. Abraham Kettletas, Samuel Townsend, James Townsend, Jacob Blackwell, and Mr. Van Wyck. The members of the convention which met at Poughkeepsie, June 17, 1778, and adopted the constitution of the United States, were Samuel Jones, John Schenck, Nathaniel Lawrence, and Stephen Carman.

The population of this county at different periods has been as follows: In 1731, 7895; in 1771, 10980; in 1786, 13084; in 1790, 16014; in 1800, 16983; in 1810, 19336; in 1820, 20519; in 1825, 20331; in 1830, 22460; and in 1835, 25130.

The surrogates of this county, since the institution of the office, have been appointed as follows: Joseph Robinson, 1787; David Lamberson, 1815; John D. Ditmas, 1820; John W. Seaman, 1821; Nicholas Wyckoff, 1826; and Henry I. Hagner, 1834.

The office of first judge of the county courts has been held successively by Benjamin Coe, Cary Dunn, Effingham Lawrence, James Lent, Singleton Mitchell, and Benjamin W. Strong.

The office of county clerk has been held as follows : Abraham Skinner, from 1778 to 1796. Daniel Kissam, from 1796 to 1812. Walter Burling, from 1812 to 1820. Edward Parker, from 1820 to 1821. Samuel Sherman, from 1821 to 1836; from which time it has been held by John Simonson.

Eliphalet Wickes was appointed district attorney for the county in 1818; William T. McCoun in 1821; Benjamin F. Thompson in 1826; and William H. Barroll in 1836.

Delegates to the convention in 1821 for amending the constitution of this state, Rufus King, Elbert H. Jones, and Nathaniel Seaman.

The following list contains the names of those who have represented the county in the house of assembly since the year 1776 :

1777. Philip Edsall, Daniel Lawrence, Benjamin Coe, Benjamin Birdsall.
1778. The same.
1779. Benjamin Birdsall, Daniel Lawrence, Benjamin Coe.
1780. Philip Edsall, Daniel Lawrence, Benjamin Coe, Benjamin Birdsall.
1781. Benjamin Coe, Daniel Lawrence, Benjamin Birdsall.
1782. Philip Edsall, Daniel Lawrence, Benjamin Coe, Benjamin Birdsall.
1783. Benjamin Coe, Daniel Lawrence, Benjamin Birdsall, Nathaniel Tom.
1784. Hendrick Onderdonk, James Townsend, Samuel Riker, Benjamin Coe.
1785. James Townsend, John Sands, Joseph Lawrence, Abraham Skinner.
1786. Samuel Jones, Daniel Whitehead, James Townsend, Daniel Duryea.
1787. John Townsend, Samuel Jones, Richard Thorn, John Schenck.
1788. Samuel Jones, Stephen Carman, Whitehead Cornell, Francis Lewis.
1789. Samuel Jones, Stephen Carman, Whitehead Cornell, John Schenck.
1790. Samuel Jones, Stephen Carman, Samuel Clowes, Benjamin Coe.
1791. Samuel Clowes, John Schenck, Samuel L. Mitchill, Nathaniel Lawrence.
1792. Samuel Clowes, Whitehead Cornell, Nathaniel Lawrence.
1793. Jacob Hicks, Samuel Clowes, Whitehead Cornell.
1794. Harry Peters, Samuel Youngs, Samuel Clowes.
1795. Nathaniel Lawrence, Samuel Clowes, Stephen Carman.
1796. The same.
1797. Lewis Cornell, Daniel Kissam, John M. Smith, William Pearsall,
1798. William Pearsall, John I. Skidmore, Stephen Carman, Whitehead Cornell.
1799. John J. Skidmore, John M. Smith, Stephen Carman, Whitehead Cornell.
1800. Abraham Monfort, Isaac Denton, Jonah Hallet, John I. Skidmore.
1801. Jonah Hallet, Joseph Pettit, Abraham Monfort, John I. Skidmore.
1802. John D. Ditmas, Joseph Pettit, William Mott, Abraham Monfort.
1803. Stephen Carman, Henry O. Seamen, Abraham Monfort.
1804. Stephen Carman, John D. Ditmas, William Mott.
1805. Henry O. Seaman, Stephen Carman, Benjamin Coe.

1806. Henry O. Seaman, Benjamin Coe, John W. Seaman.
1807. Henry O. Seaman, William Mott, Stephen Carman.
1808. Henry O. Seaman, John W. Seaman, Jacobus Monfort.
1809. Stephen Carman, William Townsend, Daniel Kissam.
1810. The same.
1811. The same.
1812. The same.
1813. Stephen Carman, Daniel Kissam, John Fleet.
1814. Daniel Kissam, Stephen Carman, Solomon Wooden.
1815. The same.
1816. Stephen Carman, Daniel Kissam, William Jones.
1817. The same.
1818. The same.
1819. John A. King, Stephen Carman, Daniel Kissam.
1820. John A. King, Thomas Tredwell, William Jones.
1821. John A. King, John D. Hicks, Benjamin T. Kissam.
1822. William Jones, Timothy Nostrand, Thomas Tredwell.
1823. Benjamin T. Kissam, John D. Hicks.
1824. William Jones, Thomas Tredwell.
1825. The same.
1826. The same.
1827. The same.
1828. The same.
1829. Henry F. Jones.
1830. The same.
1831. Thomas Tredwell.
1832. John A. King.
1833. Thomas B. Jackson.
1834. The same.
1835. The same.
1836. Jarvis Jackson.
1837. The same.
1838. John A. King.
1839. Elias Hicks.

Although prosecutions for the supposed crime of witchcraft were not uncommon in some of the New England colonies at an early period of the settlements, and many hapless victims were sacrificed to this unaccountable delusion, yet it is believed that charges of this kind were very rare in this part of the country, and no person was ever executed in this colony on that account. It is, however, ascertained that at least one individual in this county was suspected of a secret correspondence with the author of evil, and measures were taken to bring the supposed culprit to trial. In the year 1660, suspicions of this nature fell upon one Mary Wright, a very

poor but ignorant woman of the town of Oyster Bay ; and it became a matter of grave necessity, that an offence of such enormous depravity should be fully and satisfactorily investigated.
But as there existed at that time no domestic tribunal, which the
people considered competent to hear and determine a matter of
such magnitude, or none to which they thought proper to submit the case, it was finally concluded to transport the accused
party to the general court of Massachusetts, where charges of
this sort were more common, and the proofs necessary to support them better understood.   She was accordingly arraigned
there, and the matter inquired into with all the formality usual
on such occasions.   The evidence of her guilt failed, and she
was acquitted of the crime of witchcraft.   She was, nevertheless, convicted of being a Quaker, a crime, in the estimation of
the court, of almost equal enormity ; and was sentenced to be
banished out of the jurisdiction.   In the general assembly of
this province, on the 22d day of September, 1701, Thomas
Willet, John Tallman, and John Willet, members from this
county, were expelled from the house, and declared guilty of a
contempt, for contumaciously refusing to take their seats in the
assembly, and also for sending a paper to the house, written,
as the committee reported, *in barbarous English, and shewing
their ignorance and unacquaintedness with the English language.*   This curious paper is so peculiar in its style and matter, as to be an object of some curiosity at this day, and therefore worthy of preservation.   The following is a literal copy
from the journals of the assembly of that period :

   " On the 20th day of Ougost last, the house, consisting of 2
Persons, wheareof the Speeker was one, Tenn of the number
did in the House chalings the Specker to be unquallified, for his
being an aliane, and afterwardes did repetit the same to the Gov-
ner, which they have all so giv in under theare hands ; upon
which heed the House being equally divided, could giv noe decision.   Till you giv us fader satisfacktion, and the Speeker
clere him self from being an aliane, we cannot acte with you,
to sit and spend ower Tyme, and the country's money, to mak
actes that will be voyd in themselves."   The following is from
the New-York Gazette of September, 1777 : " Whereas, I, Ben-

jamin Carpenter, of Jamaica, butcher, did, on the 22d day of
August last, violently assault and beat Joseph French, Esq.,
one of his Majesty's justices for Queen's County, at a time when
his hands were held, and did otherwise greatly abuse him in
the execution of his office; I do therefore in this public manner
declare that I am sorry for what has happened, and most humbly beg forgiveness. I do further declare, that I will of my
own accord cause this my acknowlegement to be inserted for
two weeks successively in the public newspapers of the city
of New-York; that I will, at the head of each company of militia of said county, at their next muster, read this my acknowlegement; and I will immediately pay into the hands of the
churchwardens of the town of Jamaica the sum of five pounds
currency, for the use of the poor of said town.

"BENJAMIN CARPENTER."

From the New-York Journal of February 10, 1774: "We
hear from Long Island, that on Saturday, the 29th ult., as Dr.
William Lawrence, of Musquito Cove, was returning from the
city in a sleigh, wherein with him were Mr. Jordan Coles, and
Mrs. Carpenter, widow of Mr. Thorn Carpenter, deceased,
when they were got near home, in descending a long steep hill,
where a large rock projected into the road, the horses, taking
fright, ran violently down the hill, when one of them running
against the rock, was killed dead on the spot, and the people
thrown out of the sleigh. Dr. Lawrence escaped with little
hurt, Mr. Coles was considerably injured, and Mrs. Carpenter
much more."

EXTRACTS FROM OLD RECORDS, NEWSPAPERS, &c.

*Court of Sessions, held at Jamaica, for the North-riding,
April 2d, 1667.* "Cause tried between Thomas Ochel, plaintiff, and John Bale, defendant. George Cummings, witness,
heard John Bale's wife tell her husband that he and Ochel
made exchange about two hats, and that he was to give ten
shillings to boot if her husband was willing, and at the hearing of it grumbled, but could not tell what *he* said, but *she* said
she hoped her husband had more wit than that. The court has

seriously considered the business about the two hats, and seeing that John Bale wore the hat, and did not return Thomas Ochel's hat again ; Ordered that John Bale pay Thomas Ochel ten shillings for the hat, and what he owes him besides, and costs."

" Ordered at the same court, that Richard Ogden and John Ludlum shall take order of every man's arms and ammunition within *fower* days after the end of this weeke, and for neglect herein shall pay five shillings a man, and what palpable and aparant defects they shall find, shall return to the authority at the plase."

" Also it was agreed that every man of our inhabitants having sufficient warning to a town meeting, that every man shall come to the plase at the hour appointed, and for neglect, shall pay as followeth : for not coming at the hour, sixpence ; for not comeing at all, two shillings ; and for departing away without license, twelve pence."

Court of Sessions, held at Jamaica, April 10, 1671. " Samuel Davis having by his own confession taken away divers particulars, and also a jug, from a private place where an old squaw had hid them, and the said squaw making her complaint against him, he hath three days allowed to make the said squaw satisfaction. And the magistrates do further award that the said Samuel Davis, upon penalty of ten pounds, shall appear at the next sessions in September, to answer this said fact, and in the mean time to be of the good behavior."

From the New-York Gazette, March 12th, 1726. " On Friday last, died at Jamaica, Queen's County, Samuel Mills, yeoman, (who was born in America,) aged ninety-five years. He was always a very laborious, honest man, of a very temperate life, and was able to do a good day's work but a few days before he died. He lived sixty-eight years with one wife, who is still alive, by whom he had sixteen children. He hath left behind him nine children, eighty grand-children, and fifty-four great-grand-children, and several of his great-grand-children are marriageable. His wife was delivered of a child when she was one and fifty years of age."

From the Constitutional Gazette, January 27, 1776. " On Tuesday last, seven hundred Jersey militia, and three hundred

Jersey regulars, entered Queen's County to disarm those who opposed American liberty; and although they have repeatedly declared their resolution of defending their arms at the risk of their lives, yet such is the badness of their cause, (which no doubt rendered them cowards,) that they were disarmed without opposition; and the generality of them have sworn to abide by the measures of the congress. Two young men brought seventeen prisoners into Hempstead with their arms; and a boy of twelve years of age demanded a pair of pistols of a man who had threatened to shoot the first person that attempted to disarm him, but with fear and trembling delivered his pistols to the boy, who brought them away in triumph."

In Provincial Congress, New-York, February 19, 1776.
"The petition of William Cock and Thomas Cock of Oyster Bay in Queen's County, was read and filed, in the words following, to wit:—'The petition of *William and Thomas Cock* humbly sheweth, that we your petitioners are inhabitants of said county, and that at the last election of deputies for the provincial congress we opposed the election of deputies for said county; since which we are convinced of our error, and think it was absolutely necessary that there should be a representation of said county. And your petitioners did not oppose the choice of said deputies from any desire or inclination of injuring this country, but was owing entirely to error of judgment. And that your petitioners are ready to obey all orders and recommendations of the continental and provincial congresses. Your petitioners therefore desire that your honorable body will take our case into consideration, and grant us such relief in the premises as to you shall seem meet. (Signed)

'WILLIAM COCK,
'THOMAS COCK.'

"On hearing the said petition read, and upon due consideration thereof, and considering that any former resolves of this congress against the delinquents of Queen's County were only intended to convince them of their error, and bring them to a just sense of their duty to the public.—*Ordered*, that the said petitioners be restored to the state and condition in which they were before the passing of the said resolves, during their good behavior.   A true copy from the minutes.

" ROBERT BENSON, Secretary."

Address of the people of Queen's County to Governor Try-on, October 21, 1776.   " To his Excellency William Tryon, governor of the province of New-York.   We, the freeholders and inhabitants of Queen's County, are happy once again to address your Excellency in the capital of the province.   Anxiously do we look forward to the period when the disobedient shall return to their duty, and the ravages of war cease to desolate this once flourishing country.   That we may be restored to the king's most gracious protection.   We entreat your Excellency to present our petition, and rely on your known humanity and benevolence for the exertion of your influence in behalf of the *well-affected* county of Queens, that it may again, in the bosom of peace, enjoy the royal favor, under your Excellency's paternal care and attention.   Signed, by desire, and in behalf of the freeholders and inhabitants of Queen's County,

" DAVID COLDEN."

Extract of a letter from *Governor Tryon* to *Lord George Germaine*, December 24, 1776 :

" On the 10th instant I reviewed the militia of Queen's County, at Hempstead, when eight hundred and twenty men were mustered ; and on Thursday following I saw the Suffolk militia at Brookhaven, where eight hundred men appeared ; to all of whom, as well as to the militia of Queen's County, I had in my presence an oath of allegiance and fidelity administered.   A very large majority of the inhabitants of Queen's County have indeed steadfastly maintained their loyal principles, as have small districts in Suffolk County.   Three companies, I learned, had been raised out of Suffolk County for the rebel army, most of whom, I was made to understand, would quit the service if they could get home.   While on Long Island, I gave certificates to near three thousand men, who signed the declaration presented by the king's commissioner's proclamation of the 30th of November last.   Large bodies of the people have already taken the benefit of the grace therein offered them."

From Hugh Gaine's New-York Gazette, July 27, 1780.
" Mr. Gaine: Sir— As the account of the capture of the crew
belonging to the rebel privateer sloop *Revenue,* published in
your paper of the 10th instant, is wrong in several particulars,
you will please insert the following :—Thirteen of the militia of
loyal Queen's County, commanded by Ensign *Elijah Wood,*
namely, *Joseph Mott, John Mott, Joseph Raynor, Elijah Raynor, Ezekiel Raynor, Rheuben Pine, Benjamin Palmer,
Abel Southard, (who was wounded,) Richard Green, Amos
Shaw, Isaac Smith, Joseph Smith, William R. Smith,* assembled, and after a skirmish of six hours, took ten of the rebels
prisoners, together with their boat. Ensign Wood was then
reinforced by twenty-six more, namely Lieutenant McKain,
an officer on half-pay, Israel Smith, Stephen Powell, William
Johnson, Samuel Johnson, Abraham Simonson, Joshua Pettit,
William Pettit, James Pettit, Morris Green, William Pearsall,
James Denton, James Southard, Elijah Cornell, Rheuben Jackson, Benjamin Cornell, Elijah Handly, Uriah Seaman, Barnabas Smith, David Pine, Michael Demott, (a trooper,) Joseph
Dorlon and Alexander Dunlap."

From the New-York Mercury, September 1, 1760. "Lately
died, at Jamaica on Long Island, after a few days' illness, Samuel Clowes, Esq., in his eighty-seventh year. He was for
many years a noted lawyer, and was skilled in mathematics, in
which he was instructed by the famous Dr. Flamstead. He
has left a numerous posterity and an unblemished character."

New-York Gazette, September 10, 1780. "Last Sunday
night died, at Jamaica on Long Island, of a very painful illness,
Doctor Jacob Ogden, in the 59th year of his age. Through a
long course of successful practice he acquired an extensive
and respectable acquaintance, who valued him for his great
kindness of heart, which marks the honest and benevolent man.
To the community in general his death must prove a loss ; but
when applied to the private feelings of a family, who tenderly
loved him, it becomes the heaviest of calamities."

Independent Gazette, Dec. 13, 1783. "On Monday, the
glorious event of peace was celebrated by the Whig inhabitants
of Queen's County at Jamaica. At sunrise, a volley was fired

by the continental troops stationed in town, and the thirteen
stripes were displayed on a liberty-pole, which had been erected for the purpose.   At four o'clock a number of gentlemen of
the county and officers of the army who were in the neighborhood, sat down to an elegant dinner, attended by the music of
a most excellent band, formerly belonging to the line of this state.
After drinking thirteen toasts, the gentlemen marched in column,
thirteen abreast, in procession through the village, preceded by the
music, and saluting the colors as they passed.   In the evening
every house in the village, and several miles around, was most
brilliantly illuminated, and a ball given to the ladies concluded
the whole.   It was pleasing to view the different expressions of joy
and gratitude apparent in every countenance on the occasion.   In
short, the whole was conducted with the greatest harmony, and
gave universal satisfaction.   An address was likewise agreed
upon, to his Excellency George Clinton, governor of the state,
and signed by Francis Lewis, John Sands, Richard Thorn,
Joseph Robinson, Prior Townsend, Abraham Skinner, Benjamin Coe, Robert Furman, and James Burling.

   " The governor returned a very polite answer on the 12th,
in which he thanked them for their respectful address, and concluded by saying, ' You have now abundant opportunities,
which I have the highest confidence you will cheerfully embrace, of manifesting your patriotism by a firm attachment to
our excellent constitution, and a steady support of good government, domestic tranquillity, and the national justice and honor.'
                                                    " GEORGE CLINTON."

   The following is a list of justices of the peace for Queen's
County, in the year 1783 :

Thomas Hicks,	Thomas Betts,	Samuel Smith, jun.
Jacob Smith,	Benjamin Woolsey,	John Jackson,
Penn Townsend,	John Wyckoff,	Samuel Townsend,
Josiah Martin,	James Denton,	Christopher Robert,
James Hazzard,	Isaac Smith,	Tallman Waters,
Daniel Rapelyea, jun.	Thomas Smith,	Philip Edsall,
Abraham Polhemus,	John Betts,	Henderick Brinkerhoff.
Daniel Kissam,	Benjamin Whitehead,	Samuel Moore, jun.
William Jones,	Benjamin Hewlett,	Hendrick Eldert,
Joseph Kissam,	John Van Wyck,	Joseph Skidmore,
Samuel Smith,	Peter Tallman,	Samuel Clowes.
Direck Elbertson,	Richard Alsop,	

EXTRACT FROM THE STATE CENSUS OF 1835 FOR THE COUNTY OF QUEENS.

Towns.	Males.	Females.	Total persons.	Paupers.	Acres of improved land.	Grist Mills.	Yards of domestic fulled cloth.	Yards of linen, cotton, and other thin cloths.	Yards of flannel and other wollen cloth not fulled.	Militia.	Electors.	Persons of color.	Neat cattle.	Horses.	Sheep.	Hogs.
Hempstead.	3306	3348	6654	30	29501	13	2605	718	137	711	1400	375	3800	1691	2820	2938
Oyster Bay.	2536	2547	5083	9	34261	5	1756	2696	1356	874	1145	295	4727	1866	15147	5622
North Hempstead	1715	1645	3360	10	29738	9	548	1245	912	322	646	693	2655	1132	8177	4430
Flushing.	1904	1739	3643	9	13090	5	291	293	216	220	537	672	1852	816	3605	2718
Jamaica.	1488	1397	2885	4	12264	5	12	330	78	269	557	328	1558	799	115	1178
Newtown.	1901	1604	3505	9	10683	3	302	270	176	253	502	364	1716	861	225	1572
Total.	12850	12280	25130	71	129537	40	5514	5552	2875	2649	4797	2727	16308	7165	30089	18458

EXTRACT FROM THE RETURNS OF COMMON SCHOOLS TO THE LEGISLATURE, JANUARY 5, 1838.

Towns.	School districts.	Districts from which returns are received.	Average No. of months in the year.	Amount of public money received and expended.	Amount paid for wages.	Number of children taught during the year.	Number of children between 5 and 16.	Amount of public money distributed.
Flushing.	8	6	7	$333,03	$251,36	219	787	$ 333,03
Hempstead.	17	17	9	638,77	1478,05	1054	1928	653,77
Jamaica.	8	7	9	221,66	970,96	395	735	274,85
Newtown.	8	6	11	279,66	1833,47	444	676	318,73
N. Hempstead.	10	6	9	259,15	788,96	241	578	337,58
Oyster Bay.	20	16	9	759,54	1758,68	882	1398	1149,24
Total.	77	58	9	$2491,81	$7081,49	3235	6102	$3067,20

KING'S COUNTY.

This county was organized the 1st of November, 1683, by an act dividing the province into counties, and abolishing the ridings which previously existed. It is bounded easterly by Queen's County, northerly by the county of New-York, westerly by the middle of the main channel of the Hudson River,

22

from the southern boundary of the county of New-York, to the ocean, and southerly by the Atlantic Ocean ; including Plum Island, Barren Island, Coney Island, and other islands south of the town of Gravesend.

It is divided into six towns ; namely, Bushwick, Brooklyn, Flatbush, Flatlands, New Utrecht, and Gravesend. The courts of this county were originally held in the village of Gravesend, and the court house was erected upon one of the squares of the village plot, near the place now occupied by the Reformed Dutch Church. The courts were removed, in 1686, to the village of Flatbush, in pursuance of an act of the colonial assembly, which had been passed the preceding year. One of the most ancient entries that has been discovered upon the records of this county is contained in the following words:—" At a court of sessions held at Gravesend the 16th day of June, by his Majesty's authority, in the twenty-first year of the reign of our Sovereign Lord, Charles the Second, by the grace of God, of Great Brittaine, ffrance, and Ireland, King, Defender of the ffaith, &c., in the year of our Lord 1669.

" Present, MATHIAS NICOLLS, Esquire, Secretary, President.

"Mr. CORNELIUS VAN RUYVEN, Captain
JOHN MANNING, Mr. JAMES HUBBARD, } Justices.
and Mr. RICHARD BETTS,

" Whereas, during this court of sessions, there hath been several misdemeanors committed in contempt of authority in this town of Gravesend, by one throwing down the stocks, pulling down of ffences, and such like crimes ; the court also find that there was no watch in the town which might have prevented it ; and being the offenders cannot be discovered, it is ordered that the town stand fined in five pounds till they have made discovery of the offenders." Many other acts of the like kind are noticed in the records, which exhibit the mischievous disposition of some portion of the people at an early period. Among others, is the following

" Sept. 14, 1696, about eight o'clock in the evening, John Rapale, Isaac Remsen, Joras Yannester, Joras Danielse Rapale, Jacob Reyersen, Aert Aersen, Tunis Buys, Garret Cowenhoven, Gabriel Sprong, Urian Andriese, John Williamse

Bennet, Jacob Bennet, and John Meserole, jr,. met armed at the court-house of Kings, where they destroyed and defaced the king's arms which were hanging up there."

The first court-house at Flatbush was erected in 1685, and remained till a larger one was built there in 1758, the expenses of which, amounting to four hundred and forty-eight pounds, were raised by an assessment upon the inhabitants of the county. It became so much out of repair, and was found in many respects so inconvenient, that a new court and jail were erected in 1792, and stood till destroyed by fire on the 30th of November, 1832. Since which time the county courts have been holden in the town of Brooklyn. It is reported that the prisoners, with one exception, exerted themselves during the conflagration to extinguish the flames, and immediately voluntarily submitted to be re-imprisoned in another place selected for the purpose. This building had been erected at the expense of two thousand nine hundred and forty-four dollars, under the superintendence of John Vanderbilt, Johannes E. Lott, and Charles Doughty, Esquires.

The following list contains the names of the judges of this county anterior to the American revolution :

Cornelius Sebring,	1715 to 1718.	John Lefferts,	
Cornelius Vanbrunt,	1718 to 1720.	Abraham Schenck,	} 1761 to 1766.
Peter Stryker,	1720 to 1722.	Samuel Garretson,	
Daniel Polhemus,	1722 to 1724.	Cornelius Vanbrunt,	
Peter Cortileau,	1724 to 1729.	Samuel Garretson,	} 1766 to 1770.
Samuel Garretson,	1729 to 1732.	John Lefferts,	
Ryck Suydam,	1732 to 1739.	John Lefferts,	
Christopher Codwise,	1739 to 1742.	Jeremiah Remsen,	} 1770 to 1777.
Johannes Lott,	1742 to 1745.	Peter Nagel,	
Abraham Lott,	1745 to 1749.	Englebest Lott,	
Isaac Sebring,	1749 to 1752.	Theodones Polhemus,	} 1777 to 1780.
Samuel Garretson,		Jeremiah Vanderbilt,	
Barnabas Ryder,	} 1752 to 1761.		
Charles De Bevoice,			

List of County Clerks before the Revolution :

1671 to 1682,	John West.	1704 to 1715,	Henry Filkin.
1682 to 1684,	Peter Smith.	1715 to 1726,	John M. Sperling.
1684 to 1687,	John Knight.	1726 to 1750,	Adrian Hegeman.
1687 to 1704,	Jacobus Vandewater.	1750 to 1775,	Simon Boerum.

1775 to 1783, John Rapelje.

Names of first Judges. when appointed.	*Clerks since the Revolution. when appointed.*	*District Attornies. when appointed.*
1808, William Furman.	1784, Jacob Sharp.	1819, James B Clarke.
1823, Leffert Lefferts.	1800, Leffert Lefferts.	1829, Nathan B. Morse.
1827, Peter W. Radcliff.	1816, Abraham Vandeveer.	1833, William Rockwell.
1830, John Dikeman.	1821, Joseph Dean.	
1833, Nathan B. Morse.	1822, Abraham Vandeveer.	
1838, John A Lott.	1837, Charles E. Bulkeley.	

The following are the names of those who represented this county in the colonial assembly, between the respective periods mentioned from 1691 to 1775 inclusive :

Nicholas Stillwell, from 1691 to 1693.	Cornelius Van Brunt, from 1699 to 1716.
John Poland, 1691 to 1693.	Samuel Garretson, 1716 to 1737.
Coert Stuyvesant, 1693 to 1694.	Richard Stillwell, 1726 to 1727.
Johannis Van Ecklen, 1693 to 1698.	Johannis Lott, 1727 to 1761.
Henry ffilkin, 1694 to 1695.	Abraham Lott, 1737 to 1750.
Cornelius Sebring, 1695 to 1698.	Dominicus Vandeveer, 1750 to 1759.
Myndert Coerten, 1698 to 1699.	Abraham Schenck, 1759 to 1767.
Gerardus Beekman, 1698 to 1699.	Simon Boerum, 1761 to 1775.
Cornelius Sebring, 1699 to 1726.	John Rapelje, 1767 to 1775.

Cornelius Van Ruyven, member of the council.

The *deputies* who met in convention at New-York, April 10, 1775, to choose delegates to the continental congress, were Simon Boerum, Richard Stillwell, Theodorus Polhemus, Denyse Denyse, and John Vanderbilt. The *delegates* selected by the convention were Johannis Lott, Henry Williams, J. Remsen, Richard Stillwell, Theodorus Polhemus, John Lefferts, Nicholas Cowenhoven, and John Vanderbilt. These delegates convened at New-York on the 22d of May, 1775, and continued to meet at different places from time to time till the adoption of the constitution of the state in April, 1777.

The *members* of the *provincial congress* from this county were Henry Williams, Jeremiah Remsen, Theodorus Polhemus, and John Lefferts ; but it does not appear that, after the first meeting of Congress, any one of them attended subsequent to the 30th of June, 1776. The delegates from this county to the convention which met at Poughkeepsie on the 27th of June, 1778, to adopt the constitution of the United States, were Peter Lefferts and Peter Vandervoort.

The *population* of this county at different periods has been as follows: In 1731, 2150 ; in 1756, 2707 ; in 1771, 3623 ;

in 1786, 3986; in 1790, 4495; in 1800, 5740; in 1810, 8303; in 1820, 11187; in 1825, 14679; in 1830, 20535; in 1835, 32057. The last capital execution in this county was of a man by the name of Wessels, who was hanged in 1786 for the crime of forgery.

John Lefferts, Esq., of Flatbush, now deceased, was the delegate from this county to the convention of 1821, for amending the constitution of this state.

The following list contains the names of those who have represented this county in the assembly since the revolution:

1777 to 1783. William Boerum, Henry Williams.
1784. Johannes E. Lott, Rutger Van Brunt.
1785 & 1786. John Vanderbilt, Charles Doughty.
1787 & 1788. Cornelius Wyckoff, Charles Doughty.
1789 to 1791. Peter Vandervoort, Aquilla Giles.
1792. Charles Doughty.
1793. Aquilla Giles.
1794 to 1799. Peter Vandervoort.
1800 & 1801. Jacob Sharpe, jun.
1802. John C. Vandeveer.
1803 to 1808. John Hicks.
1809 & 1810. Jeremiah Johnson.
1811 to 1813. John C. Vandeveer.
1814. Jeremiah Lott,
1815. Tunis Schenck.
1816 and 1817. Richard Fish.
1818. Cornelius Van Cleef.
1819 & 1820. Tunis Schenck.
1821 & 1822. Jeremiah Lott.
1823. William Conselyea, jun.
1824 to 1826. William Furman.
1827 & 1728. Clarence D. Sacket.
1829. John Wyckoff.
1830 to 1833. Coe S. Downing.
1834 & 1835. Philip Brasher.
1836. John Dikman.
1837. Richard V. W. Thorne, Joseph Conselyea.
1838. Benjamin D. Silliman, Cornelius Bergen.
1839. Jeremiah Lott, Cornelius Bergen.

The surrogates of this county since the establishment of the office, have been as follows:

From 1787 to 1793, Johannes E. Lott.
1793 to 1799, Jacobus L. Lefferts.
1799 to 1814, William Livington.
1814 to 1833, Jeremiah Lott.
And from 1833 to the present time, Richard Cornell.

" At a court of general sessions, held at Gravesend Dec. 1, 1669:

"John ffirman, plf. *vs.* Abm. ffrost, deft. } The plaintiff declared in an action of defamation, how that the defendant reported him to be a perjured person and common lyer; which was sufficiently proved, and also confessed by the defendant. The jury brought in the verdict for the plaintiff, with five pounds damages, and costs."

" This court having taken into consideration the miscarriages of Samuel Scudder and Thomas Case, *Quakers*, by disturbing and seducing the people and inhabitants of this government, contrary to the peace of our sovereign lord the king, doe therefore order that they forthwith give security to the value of forty shillings sterling, before Mr. Justice Betts, for their good behavior and appearance at the sessions."

" Upon the complaint of the constable of Flatbush that there are several persons in the town who doe refuse to pay their minister,—The court doe order that such persons who shall refuse to pay their minister, it shall be taken from them by distress."

" October 11, 1693. At a meeting of the justices of King's County, at the county hall. Present, Roeleff Martense, Nicholas Stillwell, Joseph Hegeman, and Henry ffilkin, Esqs., justices; John Bibout of Broockland, in the county aforesaid, we aver being committed by the said justices to the common jail of King's County, for divers scandalous and abusive words spoken by the said John against their majesties of the peace for the county aforesaid, to the contempt of their Majesty's authority and breach of the peace; the said John having now humbly submitted himself, and craves pardon and mercy of the said justices for his misdemeanor, is discharged, paying the officers' fees, and being on his good behavior till next court of sessions, in November next ensuing the date hereof."

During the same year in the town of Bushwyck, a man named Urian Hagell was imprisoned for having said, on a training day, (speaking jestingly of the soldiers,) " *Let us knock them down; we are three to their one.*" The justices called these *mutinous, factious,* and *seditious words,* and threatened to imprison the offender.

May 8, 1694, two women of the town of Bushwick were indicted at the sessions in this county, for having *beat* and *pulled the hair* of Captain Peter Praa while at the head of his company of soldiers on parade. One of them was fined £3, and the costs £1 19s. 9d; and the other 40s. and the costs £1 19s. 9d. During the same year Volkert Brier, constable of Brooklyn, was fined £5, and the costs, amounting to £1, by the court of sessions, *for tearing and burning an execution directed to him as constable ;* on account of which he made the following application to the governor for relief:

The Petition of Volkert Brier.

" To his Excellency. The humble peticon of Volkert Brier, inhabitant of the towne of Broockland, on the Island of Nassau.

" May it please your Excellency, your peticoner being fined five pounds last court of sessions, in King's County, for tearing an execucon directed to him as constable. Your peticoner being ignorant of the crime, and not thinking it was of force when he was out of his office, or that he should have made returne of it as the lawe directs, he being an illiterate man could not read said execucon nor understand any thing of lawe: humbly prays yr Excellency yt you would be pleased to remit said fine of five pounds, yr peticoner being a poor man, and not capaciated to pay said fine without great damage to himself and family. And for yr Excellency yr peticoner will ever pray, &c.

" VOLKERT BRIER."

November 12, 1695, the court ordered that the constables of the towns shall, on Sunday or Sabbath day, *take law* for the apprehending of all Sabbath-breakers, and search all houses, taverns, and other suspected places, for all profaners and breakers of the Sabbath day, and bring them before a justice of the peace to be dealt with according to law; and for any neglect of the constable, he should pay a fine of six shillings. The court also made an order requiring each of the towns to cause to be immediately erected a good pair of *stocks* and a good *pound,* by which, it seems, they were resolved to keep both man and beast in proper subjection.

By an act of assembly, July 27th, 1721, it was declared that the road, or *King's Highway,* from the ferry upwards to the town of Breuckland, as far as the swinging-gate of John Rapelje just above the house and land of James Harding, should be and remain the common road, or *King's Highway,* from the said ferry, to the said swinging-gate for ever.

It appears, that in 1654 this county was so infested by *robbers*, who committed violence and outrage upon the property of the inhabitants, that the magistrates of the several towns united in forming a company to act *against robbers and pirates*, and created for this special purpose an officer in each town, called a *Sergeant*, with a suitable guard.

During the administration of the Dutch government, the poor, in the several towns under their jurisdiction, were maintained by fines imposed for the commission of different offences, and by voluntary contributions taken up in the churches, as was the custom upon the Sabbath and on other public occasions.

"*At a Court of Sessions, held at Gravesend, June* 21, 1671. —Present, Mathias Nicholls, president ; Mr. Cornelius Van Ruyven, Captain John Manning, Mr. Thomas Lovelace, Mr. James Hubbard and Thomas Betts, justices ; Robert Coe, high sheriffe ; constables ' sworn, John Ramsden for Newtown ; John Hanch, fflatbush ; Wessell Garrett, Bushwicke ; Simon Johnson, fflatlands ; John Thomas, New Utrecht ; Ralph Cardell, Gravesend ; and Lambert Johnson, Brookeland. The following resolution was adopted :—

" We, his majestie's justices, being assembled at a court of sessions at Gravesend, for the West-riding of Yorkshire upon Long Island, being assisted by some of the governor's council, and likewise of our brethren of the North-riding, and having had the perusal of three papers presented at the court of sessions at Jamaica the week before, from and in the names of the towns of Flushing, Hempstead, and Jamaica, upon mature deliberacon and consideracon had thereupon ; we have unanimously concluded and adjudged that the said papers are in themselves scandalous, illegal, and seditious ; tending only to disaffect all the peaceable and well-meaning subjects of his majesty's territories and dominions ; and do declare this to bee our sentiments and opinions, the which we humbly present to his Honor the Governor' and his councell to proceed upon itt as they shall conceive will tend to the suppression of such mischiefs as may arise by the impression of ffalse suggestions and jealousies in the minds of peaceable and well-meaning subjects from their duty and obedience to the laws."

"Thomas Lambertson and his wife, Plaintiffs, ⎫
           vs.   ⎬
John Low, Defendant.   ⎭

"Action for deffemacon. Cause left to the court.

"The defendant *confest* that he was *drunke*, and was very sorry for defaming of the plaintiff's wife, and begg'd his pardon in open court. The court order that he pay the costs of the plaintiff's attendance, and keep a civil tongue in his head."

There is reason for supposing that tobacco was an article much cultivated in some portions of this county in the early part of the settlement, as well for exportation as for domestic consumption among the Dutch, with whom tobacco was considered almost a necessary of life. To guard against frauds in the manufacture of this commodity, and to preserve its reputation, the following act was passed in 1638, commonly called the *Tobacco Statute.*

"Whereas the Hon. Director and council of New Netherlands have deemed it advisable to make some regulations about the cultivation of the Tobacco, as many Planters' chief aim and employ is, to obtain a large crop, and thereby the high name which our Tobacco has obtained in foreign countries is injured —to obviate which, every Planter is seriously warned to pay due attention that the Tobacco appear in good condition ; that the superfluous leaves are carefully cut away ; and further, that the Tobacco which is spunged is not more wetted than is required. That what is intended to be exported from New Netherlands be first carried to the public store-house, to be there examined, weighed and marked, and to be paid there the duties which are due to the company ; to wit, five of every hundred pounds, in conformity to the grant of the company. And for all which we appointed two inspectors under oath. Those who transgress this ordinance shall lose all his Tobacco by confiscation, and besides arbitrarily ᐟcorrected and punished. And further, that no contracts, engagements, bargains or sales, shall be deemed valid, except those written by the secretary, while all are warned to conform themselves to this statute at their peril. Done at Fort Amsterdam, August 19, 1638."

The following persons were justices of the peace for this county in 1763 :

Abraham Schenck.
Samuel Garritson, Jun.
John Lefferts.
Jacobus Debevois, Jun.
Thomas Polhemus.
Garret Cowenhoven.
Jeremiah Remsen.

Aury Remsen.
Englebert Lott.
Johannis Beigen.
Phillip Nagel, Jun.
Bareut Johnson.
John Suydam.
Derric Remsen.

Jeremiah Vanderbilt.
Peter Cortelyou.
Albert Van Biunt.
Cornelius Wyckoff.
Christopher Codwise.
Leffert Lefferts.
Abraham Voorhis.

Agreement made with Johannis Van Eckkellen, schoolmaster of Flatbush, in 1682.

" *Art.* 1.—The school shall begin at 8 o'clock, and go out at 11; shall begin again at 1 o'clock and end at 4. The bell shall be rung before the school begins.

Art. 2.—When school opens, one of the children shall read the morning prayer as it stands in the catechism, and close with the prayer before dinner; and in the afternoon, the same. The evening school shall begin with the Lord's prayer, and close by singing a psalm.

Art. 3.—He shall instruct the children in the common prayers; and the questions and answers of the catechism on Wednesdays and Saturdays, to enable them to say them better on Sunday in the church.

Art. 4.—He shall be bound to keep his school nine months in succession, from September to June, one year with another; and shall always be present himself.

Art. 5.—He shall be chorister of the church; ring the bell three times before service, and read a chapter of the Bible in the church between the second and third ringing of the bell; after the third ringing, he shall read the ten commandments and the twelve articles of faith, and then set the psalm. In the afternoon, after the third ringing of the bell, he shall read a short chapter or one of the psalms of David, as the congregation are assembling; afterwards he shall again set the psalm.

Art. 6.—When the minister shall preach at Brooklyn or Utrecht, he shall be bound to read twice before the congregation from the book used for the purpose. He shall hear the children recite the questions and answers of the catechism on Sunday, and instruct them.

Art. 7.—He shall provide a basin of water for the baptism, for which he shall receive twelve styvers in Wampom for every baptism, from the parents or sponsors. He shall furnish bread and wine for the communion, at the charge of the church. He shall also serve as messenger for the consistories.

Art. 8.—He shall give the funeral invitations, and toll the bell; and for which he shall receive, for persons of fifteen years of age and upwards twelve guilders; and for persons under fifteen, eight guilders; and if he shall cross the river to New-York, he shall have four guilders more.

The school money.

1st. He shall receive, for a speller or reader, three guilders a quarter; and for a writer, 4 guilders, for the day-school. In the evening, four guilders for a speller or reader, and five guilders for a writer, per quarter.

2d. The residue of his salary shall be four hundred guilders in wheat (of Wampom value,) deliverable at Brooklyn Ferry, with the dwelling, pasturage and meadow, appertaining to the school.

Done and agreed on in consistory, in the presence of the constable and trustees, this 8th day of October, 1682. Signed by Casper Van Zuren and the consistory."

" I agree to the above articles, and promise to observe them.

" *Johannis Van Eckkellen.*"

EXTRACT FROM THE STATE CENSUS OF 1835, FOR THE COUNTY OF KINGS.

Towns.	Males.	Females.	Total persons.	Paupers.	Acres of improved land.	Grist Mills.	Yards of domestic fulled cloth.	Yards of cotton, linen, and other thin cloths.	Aliens not naturalized.	Electors.	Militia.	Persons of color.	Neat cattle.	Horses.	Sheep.	Hogs.
Gravesend.	371	324	695		2587	2		255	31	134	62	105	326	237	80	157
New Utrecht.	733	554	1287		4009			135	59	197	99	165	394	338	12	415
Flatlands.	363	321	684		2881	1		158	20	114	70	116	381	239	81	406
Flatbush.	847	690	1537	231	5777	3			34	211	66	260	662	490	81	894
Bushwick.	1889	1436	3325		2655	2			394	575	449	176	1179	396	8	866
Brooklyn—1st Ward	680	843	1523						141	227	91	105	19	91		3
2d.	2419	2255	4674		2		8000		615	811	381	147	76	282	26	205
3d.	1204	1560	2764		7				86	401	169	116	34	98	2	35
4th.	2731	2993	5724		3				582	919	413	360	33	192		185
5th.	2391	2119	4510						427	690	326	46	46	106		129
6th.	1120	1019	2139		463			30	265	283	109	53	444	279		213
7th.	1078	964	2042		1260				400	344	212	136	918	252		485
8th.	286	201	487		1545			40	82	102	53	51	346	163		313
9th.	438	228	666		1343			74	205	99	31	62	302	192	1	310
Total.	16550	15507	32057	231	22532	8	8000	702	3431	5007	2532	1897	5160	3355	291	4616

(Note in Paupers column, spanning the Brooklyn wards: "In Flatbush is the County poor-house.")

EXTRACT FROM THE RETURNS OF COMMON SCHOOLS MADE
TO THE LEGISLATURE, JAN. 5, 1838.

Towns.	School districts.	Districts making returns.	Average number of months in the year.	Public money received and expended.	Amount paid for wages.	Number of children taught	Children between 5 and 16.	Amount of money distributed.
Brooklyn.	7	7	12	$1893,86	$2076,02	1580	5645	$2013 56
Bushwick.	3	1	12	150,25		148	612	150,25
Flatbush.	2	2	12	56,54	300,00	60	344	144,87
Flatlands.	2	2	12	62,10	658,00	83	164	62,10
Gravesend.	2	2	12	58,88	341,00	76	194	58,88
New Utrecht.	3	3	9	126,80	687,51	145	284	126,80
Total	19	17	11	$2348,43	$4062,53	2092	7243	$2586,46

TOWN OF EASTHAMPTON.

This is the most easterly town on Long Island. It is situated upon the southern branch thereof, and includes the peninsula of Montauk and Gardiner's Island. It is bounded on
the east by the confluence of the Ocean with the Sound ; on the
south by the Atlantic Ocean; on the west by Southampton ;
and on the north by Gardiner's Bay and the Sound. The
south shore is in some places a low sandy beach, in others formed into hills of every variety of shape ; but upon Montauk
there are high and rugged cliffs, against whose base the waves
dash with almost continued violence—any thing like a perfect
calm here, being a rare occurrence. The northern shore is
much less exposed to the action of the sea, for the most part
level, and is indented with numerous coves and small ponds or
bays, which abound with fish, and are, in some instances, navigable for vessels of small burthen. The greatest length of
this town, from the west line to Montauk Point, is about twenty-five miles ; and centrally distant from the city of New-York
one hundred and ten miles; from Albany two hundred and sixty ; and from the court-house at Riverhead, thirty miles. The
town was settled in 1649 by about thirty families from Lynn
and the adjacent towns of Massachusetts, where they had tar-

ried awhile after their arrival from England. Previous to the
settlement, arrangements were made with the governors of
New Haven and Connecticut to obtain a title to the lands from
the native Indian proprietors. This undertaking was soon accomplished by these gentlemen, and the conveyance which they
procured from the natives is as follows :—" April the 29th, 1648.
This present wrighting testyfieth an agreement betwixt the
Worshipful Theophilus Eaton, Esq., Governor of the Colony of
New Haven, the Worshipful Edward Hopkins, Esq., Governor
of the Colony of Connecticut, their associates on the one parte ;
Poygratasuck, Sachem of Manhassett ; Wayandanch, Sachem
of Mountacutt ; Momometou, Sachem of Chorchake ; and Nowe-
donah, Sachem of Shinecock, and their associates, the other party. The said Sachems having sould unto the aforesaid Th :
Eaton and Ed : Hopkins, with their associates, all the land
lying from the bounds of the inhabitants of Southampton
unto the east side of Mountacutt high-land, with the whole
breadth from sea to sea, not intrenching uppon any in length or
breadth which the inhabitants of Southampton have and doe
possess, as they by lawful right shall make appeare ; for a consideration of twenty *coates*, twenty-four *hatchets*, twenty-four
knives, twenty *looking-glasses*, one hundred *muxes* already received by us the forenamed sachems, for ourselves and associates ; and in consideration thereof we give upp unto the said
purchasers all our right and interest in said land, to them and
their heirs, whether our or other nation whatsoever, that doe
or may hereafter challenge interest therein. Alsoe we, the sayd
Sachems, have covenanted to have libertie ffor ourselves to *ffish*
in any or all the *cricks* and *ponds*, and hunting *upp and downe*
in the woods, without molestation ; they giving to the English
inhabytants noe just offence, or injurie to their goods and chattels.
Alsoe, they are to have the *ffynnes* and *tayles* of all such whales
as shall be cast upp, to their proper right, and desire they may be
friendly dealt with in the other parte. Alsoe they reserve libertie to *ffish* in convenient places ffor *shells* to make *wampum*.
Alsoe Indyns hunting any *deare* they should chase into the
water, and the English should kill them, the English shall
have the *body* and the Sachems the *skin*. And in testymony

of our well performance hereof, we have set our hands the day
and yeare above written.   (Signed.)

"In presence of Richard Wood-⎫   " POYGRATASUCK, ×
    hull, Thomas Stanton, Rob-⎬   WAYANDANCH, ×
    ert Bond, and Job Sayre.   ⎭   MOMOMETOU, ×
                                                    NOWEDONAH. × "

The precaution shown by the purchasers in procuring a conveyance from the sachems of the four eastern tribes was wisely
intended to protect the inhabitants from any pretence or claim
on the part of the Indians, and prevent all controversies with
their descendants, which might disturb the peace or endanger
the future safety of the plantation.   The title which had thus
been acquired by Eaton and Hopkins was, in the succeeding
year, duly transferred to the settlers, whose names, and those
who were associated with them soon after, are as follows :

John Hand, sen.,	John Miller,	Samuel Beltnapp,
John Stretton, sen.,	Luke Lilles,	Charles Barnes,
Thomas Tallmage, jun.,	Benjamin Price,	Samuel Parsons,
Robert Bond,	Thomas Osborn, sen.,	Joshua Garlick,
John Mulford,	William Hedges,	ffulke David,
Thomas Tomson,	Ralph Dayton,	Nathaniel Bishop,
Daniel How,	Thomas Chatfield,	William Barnes,
Joshua Barnes,	Thomas Osborn, jun.,	Lyon Gardiner,
Robert Rose,	William Edwards,	John Osborne,
Thomas James,	William ffithian,	Jeremiah Neale,
William Mulford,	Richard Brookes,	Stephen Hand,
Richard Stretton,	William Symonds,	Thomas Baker.

The town was at first called *Maidstone*, probably by reason
that Lyon Gardiner and some others of the first planters came
from a town of that name in the county of Kent, England.
But it was shortly after changed by general consent to that of
Easthampton, which appellation it has ever since retained,
and which seemed appropriate from its relative situation in regard to the town of Southampton, which had been settled about
ten years before.   The division line of these two towns was a
matter of considerable uncertainty, and occasioned a disagree-
able controversy between their inhabitants, which lasted till the
year 1664, when all disputes were terminated by commissioners appointed for that purpose by the governor, and by whom
the boundaries were permanently established as they now are.

A gift of the remaining lands of Montauk was made by the natives, some years after the settlement, as an acknowledgment and consideration of the protection which had been extended to the individuals of that tribe, threatened, as they were, with invasion and extermination by their enemies, and which obliged them to take refuge among their white neighbors of Easthampton. The following is the most material part of the conveyance given on the occasion, and setting forth, likewise, the reasons which had induced them to make it:

"Whereas, of late years there has been sore distresses and calamities befallen us, by reason of the cruel opposition and violence of our deadly enemy, Ninnecraft, Sachem of Narragansett, whose cruelty hath proceeded so far as to take away the lives of many of our dear friends and relations, so that we were forced to fly from Montaukett for shelter to our beloved friends and neighbors of Easthampton, whom we found to be friendly in our distresses, and whom we must ever own and acknowledge as instruments, under God, for the preservation of our lives, and the lives of our wives and children to this day, and of the land of Montaukett from the hands of our enemies; and since our comeing among them, the relieving us in our extremities from time to time. And now, at last, we find the said inhabitants of Easthampton our deliverers, cordial and faithful in our former covenants, leaving us freely at liberty to go or stay, being ready to perform all the conditions of our aforesaid agreement. After serious debate and deliberation, in consideration of the love which we have and do bear unto these our trusty and beloved friends of Easthampton, upon our own free and voluntary motion, have given, granted unto them and their heirs, all the lands," &c. This instrument then proceeds to describe and convey all the remaining lands of Montauk eastward of the original or first purchase, reserving to themselves the right and privilege of living there again, and of using such portions of the land as their necessities might require—which right and privilege they and their posterity have ever since continued to enjoy. In the preamble of this conveyance, allusion is made to the cruel and perfidious massacre of the Sachem and many of his best warriors, a few years before, at Block Is-

land; for, being there on some important occasion, they were
surprised in the night by a party of the Narragansett Indians;
but were promised their lives should be spared upon laying
down their arms, which they had no sooner done, than they
were set upon and murdered in the most barbarous manner,
only one of the whole number escaping to relate the horrid
deed.   The Sachem himself was reserved for further cruelty,
and being conveyed to the Narragansett country, was there tor-
tured to death by being compelled to walk naked over flat rocks,
heated to the utmost by fires built upon them.   Ninigret, the
chief of that powerful tribe, (called also by the different names
of *Janemo, Ninicraft,* and Nenekunet,) had a violent hatred of
the Montauks, for not only refusing on a former occasion
to unite with him in destroying the white people, but for
having discovered the plot to the English, by which his design was frustrated, and the inhabitants saved from destruction.   The words of Captain Gardiner are, " Waiandance,
the Long Island Sachem, told me, that as all the plots of the
Narragansetts had been discovered, they now concluded to let
the English alone until they had destroyed Uncas, the Mohegan chief, and himself; then, with the assistance of the Mohawks
and Indians beyond the Dutch, they would easily destroy us,
every man and mother's son."   Indeed, it seems suspicions
were generally entertained that the Dutch not only countenanced the Indians in their hostility to the English, but had also
secretly supplied them with arms.   Several Indian Sagamores
residing near the Dutch, reported that the Dutch governor had
urged them to cut off the English, and it was well known that
Ninigret had spent the winter of 1652 and 3 among the Dutch.
In consequence, a special meeting of the commissioners was
convened at Boston, in April, 1653, but several Indian sachems,
who were examined denied any agreement with the Dutch to
make war upon the English.   Ninigret declared that he went
to New Amsterdam to be cured of some disease by a French
physician; that he carried thirty fathoms of wampum with
him, of which he gave the doctor ten and to the governor fifteen, in exchange for which the governor gave him some *coats
with sleeves, but not one gun.*

On the first day of August, 1660, and after the death of the Sachem Wyandanch, his widow, called the *Squa-Sachem,* and her son, united in a deed of confirmation to the original purchasers for the lands of Montauk ; and described by them *as extending from sea to sea, and from the easternmost parts thereof to the bounds of Easthampton,* for the consideration of one hundred pounds, to be paid in ten equal annual payments, *in Indian corn* or *good wampum* at six to a penny. The names inserted in the original conveyance are as follows :

Thomas Baker,	Thomas Osborn, sen.	William Barnes,
Robert Bond,	William Hedges,	Samnel Parsons,
Thomas James,	Thomas Osborn, jun.	Nathan Burdsill,
Lion Gardiner,	Richard Stretton,	Robert Daiton,
John Mulford,	Roger Smith,	William Edwards,
John Hand,	Jeremiah Meacham,	George Miller,
Benjamin Prior,	John Osborn,	Steven Osborn,
Thomas Tomson,	William Simons,	John Miller,
Thomas Tallmage, jun.	William ffithian,	Steven Hand,
Thomas Chatfield,	Richard Brookes,	William Mulford,
John Stretton,	Joshua Garlick,	Nathaniel Bishop.

A patent, confirming and assuring to the inhabitants of the town the lands formerly purchased from the native Indians, was obtained from Governor Nicolls on the 13th of March, 1666. The names of the patentees are, John Mulford, justice of the peace, Mr. Thomas Baker, Thomas Chatfield, Jeremiah Conklin, Thomas Hedges, Thomas Osborn, sen., and John Osborn ; for themselves and their associates the freeholders and inhabitants of the town of Easthampton ; together with all havens, harbors, creeks. quarries, woodlands, meadows, &c. ; and, what is somewhat peculiar, this patent contains no reservation of any quit-rent, as was usual in most charters granted by the colonial governors. It may gratify curiosity to be informed, that the names of thirteen of the original settlers of this town are extinct, while there are descendants of the remainder in the fifth, sixth, seventh, and eighth degrees, residing here ; and in many cases the posterity of the first inhabitants are in possession of the identical lands of their ancestors. At the beginning of the settlement, a house lot, consisting of ten or

24

twelve acres of ground, was laid out to each proprietor at the south end of the town, and upon each side of the town pond (so called), for the greater convenience of water for themselves and their cattle. The woodlands and meadows were next laid out, and allotted to individuals by town vote. All public measures were adopted in town meetings, called in the records the general court; at which it was made the duty of every male inhabitant to attend. And to this court were brought all appeals from magistrates and other public officers. But these meetings were liable to disorder and tumult from the number of those who attended, and the want of a more efficient judicial system was become too obvious to be longer dispensed with; in which emergency the people very naturally looked to their brethren of New England for assistance. Accordingly, on the 7th of March, 1658, it was ordered and determined by the general court, upon due consideration, that Ralph Dayton, one of their most discreet men, should go to Connecticut to procure the evidence for their lands, and a code of laws. Whether the commissioner brought over, among other things, a copy of the famous "Blue Laws," we are not informed. The probability is, that most of the provisions of that singular code had by this time become in a good measure obsolete even with the Yankees themselves. The town of Southampton had erected one or two grist-mills in the early part of the settlement, and the people of this town were under the necessity of carrying their grain there to be ground. The first mill is said to have been worked by oxen; and in the absence of horses, bulls were used for transporting the grain. This town continued an independent plantation or community until the year 1657, when, by mutual consent, and for more perfect protection, they put themselves under the jurisdiction of the colony of Connecticut. The magistrates having frequently, in difficult cases, found it necessary to consult with their neighbors of Southampton and Southold, and sometimes also " *the gentlemen at Hartford.*"

On the 9th of December, 1658, it was voted in the general court, and decided, " that the capital laws, and the laws and orders that are noted in the bodie of laws that came from Connecticut, shall stand in force among us." In the municipal arrangement of public officers, they consisted of three magistrates, a recorder or clerk, and constable; the latter was considered an important office, being a conservator of the peace and a moderator of the general court, and was, as matter of course, always a person of mature years and of established character and respectability. The duty of the recorder was not only to enter the proceedings of the town meetings, but the decisions of the magistrates, and even the depositions and testimony of witnesses upon trials. Trials were either with or without juries, at the discretion of the magistrate. From the year 1650 to 1664, about sixty cases tried before the courts are found recorded in the town books, mostly for small debts and actions of slander; which latter action seems to have been extremely frequent in most of the towns. The recovery in such cases was limited to five pounds, while in other actions the jurisdiction was unlimited. An extraordinary instance occurred in the case of Lion Gardiner of the Isle of Wight, who was prosecuted in this court for a claim of five hundred pounds sterling. The case was this: A Southampton man had hired a Dutchman to bring him a freight from the Manhadoes to Easthampton. The vessel was taken by the English, and brought to that island, when Captain Gardiner retook her in behalf of the Dutch owners. Being prosecuted by the original captors to recover from him the value of the vessel and cargo, as well as damages which had been sustained, and the subject matter being not only of great importance, but involving principles of law beyond the learning of the town magistrates, it was very properly determined to refer the case to the court at Hartford. The plaintiff having probably little confidence in the justice of his cause, failed to appear, and the matter was dropped. The general town court possessed of course unlimited authority in all respects, and every matter of a public nature, or concerning the interest and safety of individuals, was heard and determined in this primary assembly of the people. It was usual, if not required, that all important contracts and agreements, and particularly those entered into between the English and Indians relating to the killing of whales, should be entered upon the town books, and signed by the parties in presence of the clerk and certified by him.   Boat whaling was so generally practised, and was considered of so much importance by the whole community, that every man of sufficient ability in the town was obliged to take his turn in watching for whales from some elevated position on the beach, and to sound the alarm on one being seen near the coast.   For the want of other materials, at the commencement of the settlement the first houses and other buildings were covered with straw ; and for the greater safety from fires, it was required, under a penalty, that the owner of every dwelling should furnish himself with a ladder that should reach as high as the ridge ; and a person was likewise appointed to see that chimnies were kept well plastered upon the inside and swept frequently.   Laws were also passed rendering it highly penal to dispose of any guns, swords, lead or powder, to the Indians ; or selling to any Indian more than *two drams* of *strong water* at any time.   These people were occasionally troublesome to the settlers, and in 1653 became so dangerous that the inhabitants took measures to obtain a large supply of ammunition from the fort at Saybrook, and a patrole was almost constantly on duty to guard against the consequences of a sudden attack.   The general court passed an order authorizing the guard to shoot any Indian that should refuse to surrender when hailed the third time.   And it was usual, at this perilous crisis, for the people, or some portion of them, to carry their arms with them to the church on Sunday.

The government under Oliver Cromwell having resolved on a war against the Dutch settlements in America, circulars were addressed on the subject to the different towns to request their assistance.   Accordingly the people of this town, on the 29th of June, 1654, determined as follows : " Having duly considered the letters that came from Connecticut, wherein men are required to assist the power of England against the Dutch, we do think ourselves called to assist the said power accordingly."   In the year 1655 the inhabitants entered into an agreement or civil combination in the words following :

" Forasmuch as it has pleased the Almighty God, by the wise dispensation of his providence, so to order and dispose of things, that we, the inhabitants of East-Hampton, are now dwelling together ; the word of God requires that to maintain the peace and union of such a people, there should be an orderly and decent government established, according to God, to order and dispose as occasion shall require ; we do therefore sociate and conjoin ourselves and successors to be one town or corporation, and do for ourselves and successors, and such as shall be adjoined to us at any time hereafter, enter into combination and confederation together, to maintain and preserve the purity of the Gospel of our Lord Jesus Christ, which we now possess ; as also the discipline of the church, which, according to the truth of said gospel, is now practised among us ; as also in our civil affairs to be guided and governed by such laws and orders as shall be made according to God, and which by the vote of the major part shall be in force among us. Furthermore we do engage ourselves, that in all votes for choosing officers or making orders, that it be according to conscience and our best light. And also we do engage ourselves by this combination to stand to and maintain the authority of the several officers of the town in their determinations and actions, according to their orders and laws, that either are or shall be made, not swerving therefrom. In witness whereof," &c.

The first settlers of the several towns in Connecticut seem to have entered into formal contracts of this nature. The preceding is said to have been taken from that of Windsor, and it is probable that the English towns on Long Island, in their origin, adopted compacts of a similar kind.

"March 19, 1657, it is ordered that Thomas Baker and John Hand is to go to Connecticut for to bring us under their goverment, according unto the terms as Southampton is, and also to carry up Good wife Garlick, that she may be delivered up unto the authorities there, for her tryal of the cause of Witchcraft, which she is suspected for." The town was received into the jurisdiction of Connecticut, but the fate of good wife Garlick is not known. On the arrival of Governor Nicolls in 1664, and his assuming jurisdiction over the whole of Long Island, and requiring the several towns to submit to his authority, this town passed the following resolve: " The inhabitants of this town, understanding that we are off from Connecticut, and

the magistrates not willing to act further upon that account ;
that we may not be without law and goverment, it is agreed
the former laws and magistrates shall stand in force till we have
further order from York." The cautious vigilance and systematic prudence of the people of this puritan town may be
seen from the following extracts from the town records: " May
10, 1651, it ordered that no man shall sell his accommodation
to another without consent of the town, and if any purchase
without consent, he shall not enjoy the same."

" No man shall sell any liquor, but such as are deputed
thereto by the town, and no more than half a pint shall be
drank at a time among four men ; and it is further ordered
that good man Megg's lot shall not be laid out for James to go
to work on, and that he shall not stay here."— "February
12, 1656, it is ordered that whoever shall raise up a false
witness against any man, to testify that which is wrong, it
shall be *done* unto him *as* he had thought to have done unto
his neighbor, whatever it be, even unto the taking away of life,
limb, or member."—" And whosoever shall rise up in anger
against his neighbor, and strike him, he shall forthwith pay
ten shillings to the town, and stand to the censure of the court ;
and if, in smiting, he shall hurt or wound another, he shall pay
for the same, and also for the time the person is thereby hin-
dered."—" And whosoever shall slander another, shall be liable
to pay a fine of five pounds."—" April 11th, 1664, it appearing
that Nathaniel York did strike Obediah the Indian, several
stripes, he is satisfied from him by *half a bushel of corn*, and
his fine is left to the town's determination."—" January 19th,
1695, it is resolved that the Rev. Mr. James shall have preference in the grinding of his corn at the mill on the second day
of every week, and shall be preferred to any other person, unless his grain shall be in the hopper."

" *March 7th*, 1650.   At a general court it is ordered that any
man may set guns to kill wolves, provided they be not set
within half a mile of the town, and also to take up the guns by
sunrise ; and further, that it shall not be lawful to sell any dog
or bitch, young or old, to any Indian, upon penalty of thirty
shillings."   " June 3d, 1653.   It is ordered that one half of the

town shall carry arms to meeting upon the Lord's Day, with
four sufficient charges of powder and shot." May 8th, 1655.
It is ordered, that for the prevention of abuse among the Indians,
by selling them *strong waters*, no man shall carry any to them
to sell, nor yet send any, nor employ any to sell for them ; nor
sell any liquor in said town to any Indian for their present
drinking, *above two drams* at a time." It seems that the practice
of boat whaling along-shore was practised here at an early period, and was probably pursued to some extent on the whole
south shore of the island. Contracts were frequently entered
into between the white people and the Indians, to engage in
whaling, many of which are recorded. The following are copied from the town books :

" Easthampton, Aprill 2d, 1668. Know all men by these
presents, y^t wee whose names are signed hereunto, being Indians of Montauket, do engage ourselves in a bond of ten
pounds sterling for to goe to sea uppon ye account of killing
of whales, this next ensuing season, beginning at the 1st day
of November next, ending by ye first of Aprill ensuing ; and
that for ye proper account of Jacobus Skallenger and his partners of Easthampton ; and engage to attend dilligently with all
opportunitie for ye killing of whales or other fish, for ye sum
of three shillings a day for every Indian ; ye sayd Jacobus
Skallenger and partners to furnish all necessarie craft and tack-
ling convenient for ye designe." " Agreement made the 4th
of January, 1669, between ye whale companies of East and
Southampton. If any companie shall finde a dead whale uppon the shore, killed by ye other, a person shall bee immediately sent to give notice ; and the person bringing the news to bee
well rewarded. And if one companie shall finde any whale so
killed at sea, they shall endeavor to secure them, and have one
half for their pains, and any irons found in them to bee returned to' ye owners."

In 1654, the magistrates of the town ordered the rates to be
paid in wheat at four shillings and sixpence a bushel, and Indian corn at three shillings and sixpence. The first meeting-
house was erected in the year 1652, which was twenty-six feet
square and covered with thatch, as most, if not all, the houses

were at that time.   Previous to which, meetings were held at
the ordinary kept by Thomas Baker, and for which he was allowed eighteen pence for each Lord's Day.   A second meeting-
house was built in 1673, and to which the following entry re-
fers: " Whereas there was an agreement made between the
town and Joshua Garlick about building a meeting-house,
know therefore all men by these presents, that he hath finished
his work according to the town's expectation:—September 10
1674.   Benjamin Conkling, Richard Shaw, John Parsons,
John Mulford, Thomas Talmage."   The present church was
built in 1717, and is of course at this time more than one hundred and twenty years old.   It had formerly a second or upper
gallery, which has been taken down, and the interior so far
modernized as to lose its ancient appearance in a great measure.

The Rev. Thomas James was the first minister in this town,
and an early settler in the year 1650.   His ancestry is not
known.   It is conjectured, however, that he was a son of the
Rev. Thomas James, who preached at Charlestown, in Massachusetts, in 1633, who went to Virginia as a missionary in
1642, and, as is supposed, afterwards returned to England.
It is the tradition that he came from England before he had
finished his studies, and that he completed his education with
some of the ministers who at that time adorned the churches
of New England.   He was a man of strong natural powers,
had a good education, understood public business, and was often employed by the town to act for them on difficult emergen-
cies.   He was recorder of the town, and much of the first records are in his hand-writing.   In 1651 the inhabitants agreed
to give him fifty pounds a-year for his labors in the ministry
among them.   Mr. James seems to have been the first person
employed to instruct the Indians on the island.   In the accounts of the society for propagating the gospel in New England for 1661, there is an allowance of ten pounds to Mr.
James of Easthampton, for preparing himself for that difficult
employment; and in the accounts for the succeeding three
years, there is an allowance of twenty pounds a-year for each
of those years to Mr. James, for his salary for instructing
" the Indians at Long Island."   He continued here till his death,

in 1696. The people employed a Mr. Jones to assist him during the three last years of his life, in consequence of his age
and infirmities, he having relinquished forty pounds of his
salary to enable them to do it. Mr. James ordered his body to
be laid in a position contrary to that of his people, and he was
buried in that manner. On the 20th of November, 1695, he
sold and conveyed his real estate to John Gardiner, of Gardiner's Island, for five hundred pounds, one half of which was
paid immediately, and Mr. Gardiner obligated himself to pay
the other half to the *assigns* of Mr. James within one month
next after his decease. From his selling his estate, and especially from the omission of any terms of relationship in the description of the persons to whom Mr. Gardiner was to pay the
residue of the purchase money, it has been inferred that Mr.
James did not leave any posterity ; yet it is ascertained that he
left two daughters, one of whom was the wife of a Mr. Stretton,
and the other of Mr. Dimont, both of this town.

Mr. James seems to have been very zealous for the preservation of civil liberty and the protestant religion, which he saw
endangered by the arbitrary measures and bigoted principles of
James II. and his catholic governors, and probably freely and
boldly expressed his apprehensions in the pulpit. In the minutes of the council for November 18th, 1686, it is stated, that
on the reception of two depositions charging the Rev. Thomas
James, of Easthampton with having preached a certain seditious sermon on the 17th of October preceding, an order was
passed for a warrant to be issued to have Mr. James before the
council that day fortnight to answer the premises. The result
cannot be ascertained from the records. There is little known
also of his character, but sufficient indications in the records of
the town evince that he was a faithful preacher and prudent
man.

The Rev. Nathaniel Hunting was the successor of Mr. James.
He was born at Dedham, Massachusetts, November 15, 1675.
His grandfather was John Hunting, who came from England
in September, 1638, and settled at Dedham, where he died,
April 12, 1682. He is said to have been a near relative of the
memorable John Rogers, who for his religion was burned at the

25

stake in the reign of Queen Mary.   Mr. Hunting, of Dedham,
had three sons, of whom one was John, the father of the minister of this town.   His wife was Elizabeth Payne, by whom he
had seven sons and three daughters.   His son, the Rev. Mr.
Hunting, graduated at Harvard College in 1693, and came to
this town in 1696, where he was finally settled, September 13,
1699, at a salary of sixty pounds a-year ; in addition to which,
the town gave him the use of all the parsonage lands, built him
a house, and gave it to him, with the lot it stood upon, in fee.
He continued to preach till 1746, a period of fifty years, and
having become infirm, was at his own request dismissed.   His
death took place in 1753.   His wife was Mary Green, by whom
he had ten children, four of whom died young.   His only
daughter married Mr. Coit of New-London.   Six sons attained
maturity ; two were farmers, and the rest liberally educated.
Nathaniel and Jonathan were ministers, but were compelled to
desist from preaching on account of their health.   The latter died
here in 1750 ; Edward was a physician, and died here in 1745 ;
Nathaniel died in 1770 ; Samuel was a merchant, and lived at
Southampton.   *His* son, Samuel, graduated at Yale College in
1767, and died in the West Indies, where he had been sent upon
public business during the revolution.   Benjamin, another son,
was the late Colonel Hunting, one of the principal founders of
the whaling business at Sagg Harbor, and who died, greatly respected, on the 17th of August, 1807, at the age of fifty-three.
The Rev. Jonathan Hunting, of Southold, is a grandson of the
last-named Nathaniel Hunting.

The third minister of this town was the Rev. Samuel Buell,
born at Coventry, Connecticut, September 1, 1716, and graduated at Yale College in 1741.   He studied theology with the
Rev. Doctor Edwards of Northampton, afterwards president of
Princeton College.   He was ordained as an itinerant preacher
in 1743, and on the 19th of September, 1746, was installed
pastor of this church.   When Long Island fell into the hands
of the British in 1776, he remained with his people, while
many of the inhabitants removed, and did much to relieve their
distresses.   He was attached to literature and science, and was
the father and patron of Clinton Academy.   His house was the

mansion of hospitality. Possessing a large fund of instructive and entertaining anecdote, his company was pleasing to persons of every age. He followed two wives and eight children to the grave. His only surviving child is the widow of the late Rev. Aaron Woolworth of Bridgehampton. His first wife was Jerusha, daughter of the Rev. Joseph Meacham of Coventry; the second was Mary, daughter of Elisha Mulford of this town ; and the third, Mary, daughter of Jeremiah Miller, and who still survives. Mr. Buell died July 19th, 1798, and, with his two predecessors, completed a ministerial period in this place of one hundred and fifty-four years. His daughter Jerusha was the wife of David Gardiner, and mother of the late John Lyon Gardiner, of Gardiner's Island.

The fourth minister of this town was the Rev. Lyman Beecher, who was born at Guilford, Connecticut, in 1773, and graduated at Yale College in 1797. His settlement took place September 5, 1799, and remained till 1810, when he removed to Litchfield. He shortly after went to Boston, where he was greatly distinguished for his superior talents, his theological acquirements, and pulpit eloquence. These qualifications, united with long experience, have established his fame, and caused him to be promoted to the presidency of Lane Seminary in Ohio, where his abilities have full scope for exercise, and his sphere of usefulness is greatly extended. His person and character have been thus briefly described by a writer who seems to have been well acquainted with him :—"Doctor Beecher (says this writer) is in size below the usual stature; spare and rigid, with bones of brass and nerves of steel-like elasticity. His walk and gesticulation are characteristically rapid and vehement ; his grey eye kindles incessantly with the action of his mind, and the whole of his face indicates an energy unsubdued and unsubduable, with a moral fearlessness before which stern men will involuntarily feel their spirits quailing." He has within a few years been subjected to strong opposition, and no little censure from his theological brethren; and his publications have been criticized with great severity, whether properly or not, must be left to the decision of those better skilled than we profess to be, in those metaphysical subtleties which make no inconsiderable part of most of religious systems. It is probable, however, that the difficulties he has encountered have had a tendency to elevate the character and enhance the popularity of Dr. Beecher. His immediate successor here was the Rev. Ebenezer Phillips, a descendant of the Rev. George Phillips, former minister of Brookhaven. He was settled in 1811, and removed, a few years after, on account of his health, and was succeeded by the Rev. Mr. Condict. The present clergyman is the Rev. Samuel R. Ely.

Clinton Academy was erected here in 1785, being the first institution of the kind upon Long Island, and is much indebted, for its origin and success, to the Rev. Dr. Buell, and Mr. William Payne, father of John Howard Payne, formerly known as the "American Roscius." Mr. Payne had a high reputation as an instructor, and the school under his management obtained much celebrity. He removed, some years after, to New-York, and finally to Boston, where he conducted a seminary with great credit and usefulness. This academy has always maintained a reputable rank among similar institutions, and has done much to elevate the standard of education in this part of the island. The Rev. Henry Davis, late president of Hamilton College, the Hon. Alfred Conkling, one of the judges of the District Court of the United States, and Silvanus Miller, Esq., an eminent counsellor of the city of New-York, and former surrogate, are natives of this town, and received their early education at this seminary. President Dwight, in his travels, speaking of this place, says, "A general air of equality, simplicity, and quiet, is visible here, in a degree perhaps singular. Sequestered, in a great measure, from the busy world, the people exhibit not the same activity and haste which meet the eye in some other places. There is, however, no want of the social character, but it is regulated rather by the long-continued customs of this single spot, than by the mutable fashions of a great city." The village of Easthampton is confined to a single street, of about a mile long and eight or ten rods wide. The dwellings are about one hundred, mostly of antiquated appearance, and rarely painted. The village of Amagansett is situated three miles further east, is of similar appearance, and of nearly equal antiquity, if we may judge from the number of graves, and the early date of many of the inscriptions. The houses are about fifty ; and the inhabitants, like those of the town, generally are farmers and mechanics.

The peninsula of *Montauk* contains nine thousand acres, a part of which was formerly covered with wood, which has of late years much depreciated. There are several ponds of fresh water, and some considerable bays, which communicate with the Sound. The land is owned by about forty individuals, as tenants in common. The original shares are divided into eighths, worth at this time three hundred dollars each, and entitles the owner thereof to the pasture of seven cattle or forty-nine sheep. The Indians have a usu-fructuary interest in a portion of the land ; but as the race is nearly extinct, this incumbrance must be of short duration. The soil of this tract is generally of a good quality, and affords a great deal of pasture, for which it is used entirely. The surface is rough, and in some places so precipitous as to render the travelling somewhat alarming. There is a sublimity and wildness, as well as solitariness here, which leave a powerful impression on the heart. In a storm, the scene which the ocean presents is awfully grand and terrific. On the extreme point stands the tall white column erected by the government for a light-house in 1795, at an expense of twenty-two thousand, three hundred dollars. It is constructed of stone in the most substantial manner, and would seem almost to bid defiance to time and the elements. There is a public-house near by, much resorted to by strangers in the warm season from every quarter of the country. The following beautiful and descriptive lines, written on the spot by Mrs. Sigourney in 1837, are well worthy of preservation ·

> " *Ultima Thule!* of this ancient isle,
> Against whose breast the everlasting surge
> Long travelling on, and ominous of wrath,
> For ever beats. Thou lift'st an eye of light
> Unto the vex'd and storm-toss'd mariner,
> Guiding him safely to his home again.
> So teach us, 'mid our own sore ills, to wear
> The crown of mercy, and with changeless
> Eye, look up to Heaven."

A singular event took place in this town about half a century ago, the circumstances of which seem worth relating., An itinerant pedlar, with the usual assortment of *notions*, arrived in the village late upon a Saturday evening, and apparently afflicted with the measles. As the most expeditious mode of notifying the people of his arrival, he resolved to attend church next morning, against the remonstrances of his host, who thought it highly improper. He, however, persisted, and accordingly placed himself in the midst of the worshipping assembly. After meeting, the facts transpiring, excited great alarm and indignation, and the wrath of the people was kindled against the pedlar. He saw, but too plainly, indications of the rising storm, and very prudently shouldered his pack early in the morning, and made the best of his way to the next town. But the incensed populace were not disposed to let him off so easily; a few young men pursued and brought him back to the village, where they vented their wrath upon their victim by parading him through the street upon a rail, and ever and anon plunging him over head and ears into one or other of the town ponds, of which there happened, very conveniently for their purpose, to be one at each end of the village. Having finally escaped from his enemies, he made no delay in finding a lawyer, and who happened to be the late Aaron Burr. The terrors of the law were fully visited upon the delinquents, and resulted in a verdict for the plaintiff of one thousand dollars. The defendants were of course dissatisfied, and the people of the town could not perceive the justice of the verdict, seeing that more than ninety of them caught the measles, of which several are said to have died.

Gardiner's Island was called by the Indians *Manchonock*, and by the English *Isle of Wight*. It lies upon the north-east side of Gardiner's Bay, and contains about three thousand three hundred acres, including the beaches and fish-ponds. The shape is irregular, the soil of a good quality, and there is a sufficiency of woodland and salt meadow. From its first settlement in 1639 to the year 1780, it remained an independent plantation; but in the latter year it was annexed by law to the town of Easthampton, and of which it constitutes a very important part, being generally assessed for about one sixth of the public expenses of the town. Its distance from the nearest shore of Long Island is three miles, six from Oyster-Pond Point, and ten from the village of Easthampton.

By virtue of his authority from the Earl of Stirling, James Farret conveyed this island to Lyon Gardiner on the 10th of March, 1639, he having previously agreed with the native Indian proprietors for their right. The consideration paid to the Indians, according to well-established tradition, was one large black dog, one gun and ammunition, some rum, and a few Dutch blankets. He was also to pay to the Earl of Stirling and his heirs the yearly sum of five pounds, if demanded.

" Of Lyon Gardiner, Governor Winthrop in his journal says, that on the 29th of November, 1635, there arrived a small barque of twenty-five tons, sent by the Lords Say and Brook, with one *Gardiner,* an expert *engineer* or work-base, and provisions of all sorts, to begin a fort at the mouth of Connecticut River." In Trumble's History, it is said " that Lyon Gardiner, who had been procured to superintend the fort at Saybrook, and who afterwards commanded the garrison, was a gentleman of respectability and worth." He was a native of Scotland, and had served as a lieutenant in the British army in the Low Countries. He belonged to the republican party, with the illustrious Hamden, Oliver Cromwell, and others of the same spirit. He continued in the command at Saybrook till the fall of 1639, when he removed to, and took possession of, the island which he had purchased in the spring. On the settlement of Easthampton, ten years thereafter, he removed there, where he continued to reside. He was chosen a magistrate, and transacted various public business till his decease in 1663. His son David, born at Saybrook April 29, 1636, is generally believed to have been the first white child born in Connecticut, as his daughter Elizabeth, born September 14, 1641, was the first child born of European parents within the limits of Suffolk County.

The family Bible of Mr. Gardiner is now in possession of his descendants upon the island, in which is written, in his own hand, as follows : " In the year 1635, the 10th day of July,

came I, Lyon Gardiner, and Mary my wife, from Woden, a
town of Holland, where my wife was born, being the daughter
of one Diricke Willemson ; her mother's name was Hachir,
and her aunt, sister of her mother, was the wife of Wouter Le-
anderson, Old Burger Muster, dwelling in the Hostade, over
against the Bruser, in the Unicorne's Head ; her brother's name
was Punce Garretson, also old Burger Muster.   We came from
Woden to London, and from thence to New England, and
dwelt at Saybrook fort four years ; it is at the mouth of Connecticut River, of which I was commander ; and there was
born to me a son, named David, the first born in that place ;
and in 1638 a daughter was born, named Mary, 30th of August,
and then I went to an island of my own, which I had bought
of the Indians, called by them Manchonock, by us Isle of
Wight, and there was born another daughter the 14th of September, 1641, she being the first child of English parents born
there."   While he lived upon the island, he was instrumental
in performing an important service to Wyandance, the Long
Island Sachem, in return for which the Sachem presented
him a deed in 1659 for the land which now composes the town
of Smithtown, and which Mr. Gardiner, in 1663, sold to Richard
Smith, the first settler of that town.   The service performed by
Gardiner was the redeeming from his Indian enemies the
Sachem's daughter, who, with others, had been captured at
Block Island.

His son Daniel went to England, where he married in 1657,
and came into possession of the island on the death of his
father in 1663.   In 1689 he was chosen by the eastern towns
to represent them on some matters of importance before the general assembly at Hartford, where he died suddenly, and was
buried at that place.   The following is a copy of the inscription upon his tomb in the city of Hartford,

    " Here lyeth the body of Mr. David Gardiner, of Gar-
    diner's Island, deceased July 10, 1689, in the fifty '
    fovrth year of his age, *well, sick, dead* in *one hovr's
    space.*"

He left two sons, John and Lyon.   The former possessed
the island, and the latter settled in Easthampton, and was ac-

cidentally shot by one Samuel Bennet, while hunting deer together near *three-mile-harbor*. He left two sons, Lyon and Giles. The latter died young, leaving no son. Lyon remained in the town, where he died in 1781, at the age of ninety-three. He was a wealthy farmer, and was highly esteemed and respected. His sons were John, Lyon, and Jeremiah. Lyon died without issue. John lived in the town of Easthampton, where he died in 1780, aged fifty-nine. He was a man of more than ordinary talents, much devoted to philosophy and the mathematics, for which he was distinguished. He had a son, John, who hired the estate of his father, and followed the business of a farmer till a short time previous to his death. In 1795 he purchased a farm at Moriches, where he died, at the age of forty-eight, in the year 1800. He left three sons, the Rev. John D. Gardiner, Abraham H. Gardiner, and Dr. Aaron F. Gardiner. John Gardiner, the eldest son of David, died in possession of the island in 1764. His sons were David and John. The latter became the owner of Eaton's Neck about the year 1786, where he died, a few years since, leaving three sons, Jonathan, John, and Matthew. David became the owner of the island, and married the daughter of the Rev. Mr. Buell, by whom he had two sons, John Lyon, and David. The latter settled at Flushing, where he died, leaving sons. John Lyon married the daughter of the Hon. Roger Griswold, and died upon the island, November 22, 1816. His son, John G. Gardiner, is now the owner, and in possession of the island, having purchased the interest of his surviving brother and sister. The staple produce of this island are beef, wheat, and cheese ; and the average stock consists of twenty-five hundred sheep, one hundred horses, sixty-five cows, and four hundred other neat cattle.

The notorious pirate Kidd, having visited, and buried a valuable treasure upon this island, it may seem not improper to give a brief account of that individual.

WILLIAM KIDD, the famous freebooter and pirate, was the commander of a merchant vessel which sailed between New-York and London, and celebrated for his nautical skill and enterprise : on which account he was strongly recommended

by Mr. Livingston of New-York, then in London, as a proper
person to take charge of a vessel which Lord Romney and
others had purchased, and were then fitting out against the
hordes of marauders which infested the Indian seas, and prey-
ed upon the commerce of all nations. The expense of this expedition was £6000 sterling.   It was a joint fund, to which the
King, Lord Somers, the Earl of Rumsey, the Duke of Shrewsbury, the Earl of Oxford, Lord Bellamont, and Mr. Livingston
were contributors.   Kidd agreed to be concerned to the amount
of one-fifth of the whole, and Mr. Livingston became his surety for the sum of £600.   He soon set sail, and arrived on the
American coast, where he continued for some time, and was
useful in protecting our commerce, for which he received much
public applause ; and the assembly of this state voted him the
sum of £250 as an acknowledgment of his services.   He soon
after established himself at the Island of Madagascar, where
he lay like a shark, darting out at pleasure, and robbing with
impunity the vessels of every country.   Having captured
a larger and better vessel than his own, he burnt the one in
which he had sailed, and took command of the other ; in
which he ranged over the Indian coast from the Red Sea to
Malabar, and his depredations extended from the Eastern
Ocean, back along the Atlantic coast of South America,
through the Bahamas, the whole West Indies, and the
shores of Long Island.   The last of which were selected as the
fittest for depositing his ill-gotten treasures.   He is supposed
to have returned from the east with more valuable spoil than
ever fell to the lot of any other individual.   On his home-
ward passage from the West Indies to Boston, where he
was finally apprehended, he anchored in Gardiner's Bay, and
in the presence of the owner of the island, Mr. Gardiner, and
under the most solemn injunctions of secrecy, buried a chest
of gold, silver, and precious stones.   On the 3d of July, 1699,
he was summoned before Lord Bellamont at Boston, and ordered to report his proceedings while in the service of the company ; which, refusing to do, he was immediately arrested and
transported to England, where he was tried, convicted, and
executed at "Execution Dock" on the 12th of May, 1701.

He was found guilty of the murder of William Moore, gunner of the ship, and was hung in chains. Mr. John G. Gardiner has a small piece of gold cloth, which his father received from Mrs. Wetmore, who gave also the following account of Kidd's visit to the island. " I remember, (she says,) when very young, hearing my mother say that her grand-mother was wife to Lord Gardiner when the pirate came to that island. He wanted Mrs. Gardiner to roast him a pig; she being afraid to refuse him, roasted it very nice, and he was much pleased with it. He then made her a present of this cloth, which she gave to her two daughters ; what became of the other, know I not ; but this was handed down to me, and is, I believe, as nice as when first given, which must be upwards of a hundred years."

It having been ascertained that he had buried treasures upon this island, commissioners were sent by Governor Bellamont, who obtained the same, and for which they gave the following receipt :

" A true account of all such gold, silver, jewels, and mer-chandize, late in the possession of Captain William Kidd, which have been seized and secured by us pursuant to an order from his Excellency, Richard Earl of Bellamont, bearing date July 7, 1699.

Received, the 17th instant, of Mr. John Gardiner, viz: ounces.

No. 1. One bag of dust-gold,   -   -   -   -   - $63\frac{3}{4}$

   2. One bag of coined gold,   -   -   •   -   - 11

      and one in silver, -   -   -   -   -   - 124

   3. One bag dust-gold,   •   -   -   .   - $24\frac{3}{4}$

   4. One bag of silver rings, and sundry precious stones, $4\frac{7}{8}$

   5. One bag of unpolished stones, -   -   - $12\frac{1}{2}$

   6. One piece of crystal, cornelian rings, two agates, two amythists.

   7. One bag silver buttons and lamps,   -   -   -   -

   8. One bag of broken silver, -   -   -   -   - $173\frac{1}{2}$

   9. One bag of gold bars, -   -   -   -   - $353\frac{1}{2}$

 10. One do.   -   -   -   -   -   - $238\frac{1}{2}$

 11. One bag of dust-gold, -   -   -   -   -   - $59\frac{1}{2}$

 12. One bag silver bars.   •   •   -   -   - 309

       Samuel Sewall, Nathaniel Byfield,

       Jeremiah Dummer, Andrew Belcher,

                   Commissioners.

TOWN OF SOUTHAMPTON.

This town, called by the natives Agawam, is bounded south by the ocean, west by Brookhaven, north, partly by Riverhead and partly by Peconic Bay, separating it from Southold, and east by Easthampton.   Length, from east to west, about twenty miles ; and breadth, in the widest place, six miles. The name was given in remembrance of Southampton in England, from which port the settlers took their departure from Europe, The surface is generally level, and the soil a light sandy loam, except the western part, which is mostly sand, and the roads heavy and tedious.   About the villages of Southampton, Bridgehampton, and Sagg, the soil is naturally fertile, and is well cultivated.   This town was settled in 1640, being cotemporary with the settlement of Southold, nine years previous to Easthampton and fifteen anterior to Brookhaven.   In Ogilby's America, it is mentioned that about the year 1640, by a fresh supply of people that settled Long Island, there was erected a town called Southampton, and severed (he says) from the continent of Newhaven, they not finding a place in any other of the colonies.   In Winthrop's Journal, he states that about forty families, finding themselves straitened, left the town of Lynn with the design of settling a new plantation.   They invited Mr. Abraham Pierson, of Boston, to become their minister, who, with seven of the emigrants, entered into a church covenant before they departed.   By an agreement, bearing date the 17th of April, 1640, James Farret, agent of the Earl of Stirling, authorized Captain Daniel How, Job Sayre, and others their associates, to purchase lands, and form a settlement on Long Island ; " with as full and free liberty, both in church order and civil government, as the plantations in Massachusetts enjoyed." In consequence of this agreement, Captain How and his associates sailed from Lynn in a vessel belonging to him, and arrived at Cow Bay, in the western part of Long Island, sometimes called Scout's Bay.   On their arrival they made a purchase of the natives, which extended from the eastern part of Oyster Bay to the western part of Cow Bay, (afterwards named How's

Bay,) to the middle of the plains, being half the breadth of the island; and immediately commenced a settlement in the western part of their purchase. "On receiving information of this, Governor Kieft sent men to take possession, who set up the arms of the Prince of Orange on a tree. The Lynn people cut down the tree, and began to build. Captain How likewise took away the Prince's arms, and in stead thereof an Indian drew a very ugly face. This so incensed the governor, that he sent Cornelius Van Tienhoven, the secretary, the under-sheriff, a sergeant and twenty-five soldiers, to break up the settlement. The party set out on the 14th, and returned the 15th of May. They found the company, consisting of eight men and a woman with an infant, who had erected one house, and were engaged in erecting another. The party brought six of the men with them to the governor, to wit, Job Sayre, George Wells, John Farrington, Philip Cartland, Nathaniel Cartland, and William Harcher, whom he confined, and examined on oath. On examination it appeared that they came from Lynn, near Boston, and were brought to the island by James Farret, in a vessel commanded by Daniel How, both of whom had returned to New-Haven. On the 19th, these men, on signing an agreement to leave the place, were dismissed." After their settlement at Cow Bay was broken up, Captain How and his associates came to this town, bargained with the natives for a tract of land, and advanced them a part of the consideration to secure the purhase. On the 13th of December, 1640, they arranged the payment of the balance, obtained a deed for the land, and commenced their settlement. They held their first town meeting on the 6th of April, 1641, and their proceedings are regularly recorded from that period. The acknowledgment to the Earl of Stirling, or his heirs, was fixed by Governor Winthrop of Boston in 1641, according to an agreement with James Farret, at four bushels of Indian corn, payable the last day of September annually, at Southampton. Soon after their arrival, they were joined by other families, according to agreement previously made at Lynn; for while there, they formed a civil contract, and entered into articles of confederation for their future government. Of one of these instruments the following is a copy:

"Know all men whome these presents may concerne, yt whereas it is expressed in our agreement that the power of disposinge of lands and admission of inhabitants into our plantacon, shall at all tymes remaine in the hands of us, the said undertakers, to us and our heyres forever; and our intent and meaning is, that when our plantacon is layd out by those appoynted accordinge to our artikle; and that there shall be a church gathered and constituted accordinge to the mynde of Christ, that then wee doe ffreely lay downe our power both of orderinge and disposinge of the plantacon, and receivinge of inhabitants, or any other thinge, provided that they shall not doe any thing contrary to the true meaninge of the fformer artikles. ffurthermore, whereas it is expressed in a fformer artikle, that the lands of the undertakers should at all tymes remaine ffree, affordinge any help to build meetinge-houses, or makinge a bridge, or mendinge of highways or the like, duringe the tyme of their discontinuance ffrom the plantacon; it is thought meete that it shall take place and stande in fforce but two yeares, unless there be some good reason given for it; and then those shall have land only for the third yeare, provided that within the third yeare they come back again." Previous to leaving the town of Lynn, Captain How purchased of Edward Howell, Edward ffarrington, Josiah Stanborough, George Wells, Job Sayre, Edward Needham, Henry Walton, and Thomas Sayre, their parts of the vessel in which they were to embark for Long Island. On which account he agreed to transport as many goods as the undertakers should desire, at a certain sum per ton in payment of the price of the vessel, which was sixty-five pounds. And it was further stipulated, that the vessel should be wholly employed in the service of the plantation, and not be sold away without consent of the company; and also that the said vessel should be ready at the town of Lynn, to transport the persons and goods of the company, three times in the year, if required. This contract bears date the 10th of March, 1639, and still remains, although much mutilated, in the clerk's office of the town. The names of the settlers who had arrived during the first twelve months, were as follows :

Daniel How,
Thomas Goldsmith,
John Oldfields,
Samuel Dayton,
Thomas Burnet,
John Howell,
Thomas Sayre,
Edward Howell,
William Odell,
Thomas Topping,
John Woodruff,
Allen Breed,
Edmnnd ffarrington,
Isaac Hillman,
John Cooper,
George Woods,

Henry Pierson,
Richard Post,
Obediah Rogers,
John Fordham,
John Lum,
Samuel Osman.
John Rose,
James Herrick,
Chris\topher Foster,
Joseph Raynor,
Ellis Cook,
John Jagger,
Richard Smith,
Thomas Hildreth,
John Hampton,
Joshua Barnes,

Abraham Pierson,
Edward Needham,
Samuel James,
John Gosman,
John Bishop,
John White,
William Payne,
John Jessup,
Josiah Howe,
Henry Walton,
William Harker,
John Jennings,
Benjamin Haynes,
George Wells,
Job Sayre.

The conveyance for eight miles square of land from James Farret, the agent of Lord Stirling, to the above-named persons, is recorded on the town books as follows

"MEMORANDUM ; It is agreed upon between James Farret, agent, and Edward Howell, John Gosmer, Edmund ffarrington, Daniel How, Thomas Halsey, Edward Needham, Allen Breed, Thomas Sayre, Henry Walton, George Wells, William Harker, and Job Sayre ; that whereupon it is agreed upon in a covenant passed between us touching the extente of a plantacon in Long Island, that the aforesaid Mr. Edward Howell and his co-partners shall enjoy eight miles square of land, or so much as the said eight miles shall containe, and that now lie in said bounds, being layd out and agreed uppon : It is to begin at a place westward from Shinnecock, entitled the name of the place where the Indians drawe over their cannoes out of the north bay, over to the south side of the island, and from there to run along that neck of land eastward the whole breadth between the bay aforesaid, to the easterly end of an island or neck of land lying over against the island commonly known by the name of Mr. Farret's Island. To enjoy all and every parte thereof, according as yt is expressed in our agreement elsewhere, with that island or neck, lying over against Mr. Farret's Island, formerly expressed. JAMES FARRET."

" Thomas Dexter, } Witnesses.
Richard Walker." {

A deed for the same lands from the Indians to John Gosmer, Edward Howell, Edmund ffarrington, George Wells, Edward Needham, Thomas Sayre, Job Sayre, Edmund Halsey, Thomas Halsey, Henry Walton, Daniel Howell, John Cooper, Allen Breed, and William Harker, bears date December 13, 1640, for the consideration of sixteen coats already received, and also fourscore bushels of Indian corn, to be paid upon lawful demand by the last of September, 1641 ; and upon further consideration *" that the said English shall defend us the sayd Indians from the unjust violence of any Indians that shall illegally assaile us."*

In 1652, " the town meeting agreed to allow their neighbors of Easthampton liberty to grind their corn at their mill, provided they helped to open the sepoose."

The inhabitants, at their settlement, had entered into a contract with each other, to be governed by such laws and orders as should be made by the major vote, and to support the authority of the magistrates in executing such ordinances as should be in force among them.   In most of the towns the decisions of the magistrates were conclusive upon the parties ; but in this town an appeal was allowed from the magistrates to the town meeting, called the general court, which heard the appeal, and gave such judgment as the majority approved.   The town courts were vigilant in repressing and punishing all kinds of vice and profanity ; and in 1653 they ordered that if any person over fourteen years of age should be convicted of *wilful lying* by the testimony of two witnesses, he should be fined five shillings, or set in the stocks five hours ; and if any person should be convicted of *drunkenness,* he should be fined ten shillings for the first offence, twenty for the second, and thirty for the third.   By a resolution of town meeting in 1645, it was ordered, " that if any man shall take away any part of any man's *working tools,* or *irons, harrows, yoakes, chaynes,* or *plowes,* from any part of the common field without license from the owners, they shall pay to the owner ten shillings toward making restitution."

In Allen's American Biography, it is said that " Allen Breed was one of the first settlers of Lynn ; that he was born in England in 1601, and arrived in this country in 1630.   He was a farmer, and lived in the western part of Summer-street, Lynn, possessing two hundred acres of land.   He is one, of the grantees named in the Indian deed of Southampton, Long Island, and died March 17, 1692, aged ninety-one.   His descendants in Lynn and other towns in Massachusetts are numerous ; from one of whom was derived the name of Breed's Hill, celebrated for the battle of 1775, called by mistake the battle of Bunker's Hill."   It is probable that he returned again to Lynn, as did Edmund Farrington also ; for it appears from the history of that town that he built a mill there in 1655, where a pond was dug, and a new brook opened for half a mile, called Farrington's Brook. He died in 1680, at the age of eighty-eight years.   Captain Daniel How, another of the original settlers of this town, in the year 1645 transferred his possessions to John Gosmer, for four pounds, payable in wampum, two cows, and ten bushels of barley.   He went to Easthampton, and was one of the first settlers of that town.   He had been admitted a freeman of Lynn in 1634, was a representative in the general court of Massachusetts in 1636, and was several times re-elected.   He was also lieutenant of an artillery company in 1638, in which year he removed to Newhaven, and from thence to Long Island.

"At a town meeting, October 6th, 1652, it is ordered that whoever makes it appear that he killeth any wolf within the bounds of this town, shall have paid unto him by ye town the sum of twenty shillings ; and he yt killeth a wolf at Quaquaout shall have ten shillings in like manner ; and it is further ordered, that if any goats are found without a keeper, and any person so finding them, bring them home unto the owners, they, the owners of the said goats, shall pay a penny the goat for them unto those who so bring them home, and also pay for the harm which it shall appear is done by them."   The following extracts show the manner in which testimony was taken and recorded in the general court of Southampton, the style and abbreviations being scrupulously preserved as a matter of curiosity to the reader.

"*Southampton, April* 24, 1655.   The deposition of Mr.
27

Richard Smith :—This deponent sayth, when he was uppon the jury concerning ye tryall of an action depending in cort betweene John Cooper and Jonas Wood, wee received divers testimonies in cort, which were broght in by ye said Jonas Wood, whereby wee of ye jury found for Jonas Wood, amongst wh testimony's was the deposition of Goody Bishop, Goody Garlick, and Samuel Parsons.—*May* 1, 1655. The deposition of Christopher ffoster, who affirmeth upon his oath, yt being at Hempstead a little before the last winter, when and where he heard a bargaine contracted betweene Jonas Halsted and Jonas Wood, Hallifax, viz: Jonas Wood did buy of ye foresaid Jonas four hoggs, which hoggs this depont. doth affirme that hee saw delivered at Southampton.—*March* 9, 1655. The deposition of Ann White. This depont. sayth yt shee heard Thomas Dale tell Sara Cooper that Mark Meggs did come to him once when hee was almost fuddled, and asked him if hee did not remember hee heard Henry Pierson say at Goodman Coy's, that Jonas should bee cast out of church and commonwealth shortly ; whereunto Thomas Dale answereth noe, I did not hear him say noe such thinge. Taken before me, Thomas Topping, Justice.

" *At a town meeting, November* 14, 1665. It is concluded that John Jessup is to call forth thirty men to goe to the west sepoose, and if any refuse to goe, being warned, shall pay unto ye town five shillings. Also, whoever hath any convenient toole fitt for the worke, and refuseth to lend the same, shall also pay five shillings, and the said John Jessup shall have power to levy the fine by way of execution, and returne account thereof to ye towne.

" *At a general court, held March* 6, 1654. It is ordered that noe Indian shall digg for ground-nuts in the plain, or digg in any ground, uppon penalty of sitting in the stocks for ye first fault, and for the second to be whipped. And if any of ye English see any Indian howing or digging as aforesaid, they may peaceably bring them to the magistrates, if they can ; if not, to take the hoes or digging instruments away from them ; and this to take effect as soon as the Sachem or Indians have warning hereof.

"*February* 7, 1655. An action of defamation of Thomas Rogers against James Gill. Verdict of the jury—wee finde for ye Plaintive, first our charges, and the said James to bee sharply whipped, and then banished out of this jurisdiction ; with this proviso, yt his creditors will bee bound to keep him to his good behaviour, or else to sell him out of our jurisdiction for two years' service, and the towne be noe more troubled with him. Judgment is granted accordingly by the cort.

"*May* 10, 1656. At a towne meetinge it is concluded and agreed uppon, that Mr. Edward Howell shall have power to nominate and appoint two neighbours of this towne to goe to the Connecticut, to treat of matters that may concerne this towne, and to put us under their jurisdiction for future goverment.

"*April* 10, 1653. It is ordered by the general court, that henceforth the Indians shall not any of them come to this towne, or into the plaines, or any nearer the towne than the head of the Long Creek at the west end of the plaines; neither shall any of them come to the Mill with any gun, or bow and arrows, uppon penalty of forfeiting any such instrument to any Englishman who shall take them away from any such Indian.

"*At a towne meeting, held ye 16th day of June,* 1653, it is ordered and concluded by the major vote of the inhabitants that Jonas Wood shall goe wt ye vessell at North Sea, wh is shortly to goe to the River's mouth, as a messenger from this towne unto Captaine Mason, to obtaine for ye towne a store of ammunition, accordinge to order of the collony in that behalf; and the towne doe promise to pay him what in reason is meet for his tyme and expenses.—*August* 18, 1653. At a towne meetinge it is ordered that there shall be another attempt to let goe Shinnecock water." From this entry, it is probable that Shinnecock Bay was not then connected with the ocean, or that the entrance had become closed by sand, as is the case with several ponds in this town at the present day. In the year 1675 there were in this town seventy-five men who bore arms in the militia, and they were required to meet for inspection six times a-year. In 1659 the town voted to send to Connecticut for a copy of their laws, and selected from them such

as they deemed applicable to their condition; and the uniformity which prevailed in most of the English towns may be
attributed to the fact of their having extracted most of their
laws from the same code. The salary, both of the minister
and the schoolmaster, was raised by an assessment upon the
inhabitants, and was generally apportioned according to the
number of acres of improved land which each one possessed.
In order to secure the influence and protection of the people of
New England, as well from the Dutch as the Indians, this town
early sought an alliance with Connecticut, and was received
into that jurisdiction in the year 1644. They were consequently represented by deputies in the general court at Hartford ;
but no attempt appears to have been made by Connecticut to
levy taxes upon the town until the reception of the charter of
the colony in 1662. The following persons were deputies from
this town to the general court of Connecticut at the periods
mentioned :

From 1655 to 1658, Thomas Topping.   From 1659 to 1663, Thomas Topping.
          1658 to 1659, Alexander Knowles.   1633 to 1664, Edward Howell.

The Rev. Abraham Pierson was the first minister of this
town. He had been a preacher in Yorkshire, England. He
came to Boston in 1639, and joined the church there. Those
English emigrants who had made a stand at Lynn, having
agreed to form a settlement upon Long Island, Mr. Pierson
consented to accompany them, and he assisted materially in
organizing the settlement. He continued with them till they
put themselves under Connecticut in 1644. He preferred being
connected with New-Haven, because in that colony the right of
voting was confined alone to church members. He, therefore,
with a few of his adherents, removed to Branford near New-
Haven, which had begun to be settled in 1638, and there put
themselves under the colony of New-Haven. When this colony renounced her independence, and became consolidated with
Connecticut in 1662, Mr. Pierson, adhering to his former opinions, again removed with some of his congregation to a part of
New Jersey which they called Newark, where they made a
settlement, whereby Mr. Pierson became the first pastor of a *third*
settlement. In 1668 the people there, voted to pay the expen-

ses of his removal, contributed to the digging him a well, and allowed him £80 salary a-year. He died there in the year 1680. His son, Abraham, who graduated at Harvard College in 1669, became the first president of Yale College, at Killingworth, in 1701, and continued there till his death in 1707. The Rev. Dr. Ashbel Greene, of Philadelphia, is his grandson.

The next minister of this town was the Rev. Robert Fordham, settled in 1649. He also came from England. Johnson, in his *Wonder-Working Providence*, says, "Mr. Fordam first went to the west part of Long Island," and it is probable that he accompanied the Rev. Mr. Denton to Hempstead in 1644, as he is the first person named in the Dutch patent of that town from Governor Kieft, and he resided at Hempstead when he received the invitation to remove to this town. He remained the minister here till his death in 1674. He was a man of learning, and the owner of a large estate. His library was valued after his death at fifty-three pounds, and his property at two thousand. The Rev. Josiah Fordham, who was his grandson, preached awhile at Setauket after the death of Mr. Brewster in 1690. The next clergyman of this town was the Rev. Joseph Taylor, who arrived in 1680. He came from New-Haven. But little information has been obtained concerning him, except that he died, April 4, 1682, at the age of thirty-one, having preached about two years. He was followed by the Rev. Joseph Whiting in 1682. He was the youngest son of the Rev. Samuel Whiting, a distinguished preacher at Norfolk, England, and the first minister of Lynn, Massachusetts. Mr. Whiting graduated at Harvard College in 1661. His daughter married the Rev. Jeremiah Hobart, afterwards minister of Hempstead. Cotton Mather, speaking of him, says, "Joseph is at this day a worthy and painful minister of the gospel at Southampton." He left a son, who graduated at Harvard in 1700, settled as the minister of Concord, New Hampshire, in 1712, where he died in 1752. As the records of this church are extremely defective, little can be learned respecting the subsequent clergymen beyond their names. It is ascertained that the Rev. Samuel Gelston settled here in 1727, and remained till his death, October 22d, 1782, having preached about

fifty-four years. It was during his time that the Suffolk presbytery was formed, and the government of several of the
churches in the county was changed from the congregational
to the presbyterian form. He was educated at Harvard University, where he graduated in 1722. His successor in the
ministery here was the Rev. Herman Dagget, who graduated at
Brown University in 1783. His settlement took place in 1791,
and after several years he removed to the parish of Middletown,
in the town of Brookhaven, officiating a part of the time in the
church at Fireplace. He finally removed to Connecticut.
The next clergyman was the Rev. David S. Bogart, a native
of Queen's County, and who graduated at Columbia College
in 1790. He was settled in 1796, removed to North-Hempstead in 1812, and from thence to the city of New-York, where
he now resides. The Rev. John M. Babbit was settled here
in 1813, but removed in 1818; and was succeeded by the Rev.
Peter Shaw in 1820. The present clergyman is the Rev.
Henry N. Wilson.

The first church here, was built in 1641, the year succeeding
the settlement of the town, and remained for sixty-five years.
A second church was erected in 1707, and which, having stood
one hundred and thirteen years, was succeeded by the present
stately edifice in 1820. The academy near the church was
completed in 1831, and has been thus far well supported. It
is a handsome and convenient structure, and is creditable
to the spirit and intelligence of the people concerned in
its erection. By an act of Assembly, passed May 16th,
1669, the *precinct* of Bridgehampton and Mecoxe was declared to be a distinct parish, *for the building and erecting a meeting-house ;* and the first church was finished in
a year or two thereafter. It was taken down in 1737, and the
present edifice erected in its stead. This place was called by the
Indians *Segaboneck.* The village was contemplated to have
been built a little south of the present site, and the place intended is still designated as the *old town.* The first pastor of
this church was the Rev. Ebenezer White, who graduated at
Harvard College in 1692, and was settled here in 1695. His
health failing, he resigned in 1748, and died in 1756. He was

succeeded by the Rev. James Brown, son of the Rev. Chadd Brown, of Providence, Rhode Island ; and related to those worthy individuals, the liberal founders of Brown University in that state. He graduated at Yale College in 1747, and was settled here in 1756. His removal took place in 1775, and the parish had no regularly stated preacher till the 30th of August, 1787, when the Rev. Aaron Woolworth was installed here. He was born at Long Meadow in Massachusetts, October 25, 1763, and graduated at Yale College in 1784. His wife was the daughter of the Rev. Dr. Buell of Easthampton, whose memoirs he published. His death occurred the 2d of April, 1821. He was a man of much classical learning, an eloquent divine, and extensively acquainted with ecclesiastical history. His immediate successor was the present clergyman, the Rev. Amzi Francis.

The Methodists have erected a very handsome church in the centre of the village of Bridgehampton, which is an ornament to the place. The Hon. Nathan Sandford, late chancellor of this state, and a senator in the congress of the United States, was a native of this part of the town. Mr. Foster Rhodes, who accompanied the late Henry Eckford to Constantinople, and who has since been engaged as ship-builder to the Sultan, was born in the village of Southampton, and is a son of Mr. Henry Rhodes, merchant of that place. On a late occasion of launching one of the largest ships in the world, (in Turkey,) the Sultan was so elated at his success, that he embraced Mr. Rhodes in the most enthusiastic manner, and presented him at the same time a gold medal set in diamonds, of great value and of exquisite beauty. Southerly of this village is a splendid sheet of water, known as Mocoxe Bay, communicating with the ocean by a narrow inlet, and abounding with oysters of a superior quality. It is about four miles long, and less than one in breadth. Sagg Pond is also of considerable size, but is liable to have its inlet obstructed by sand carried into it by the current, and requiring to be cleared out occasionally. The village of Sagg was settled at an early period. The inhabitants are farmers, and the land here, as well as about Bridgehampton, is well cultivated. Sagg-Harbor derived its name from having been originally the port or landing-place of Sagg. Shinnecock Bay, (sometimes called Southampton Bay,) is a very charming piece of water. It is more than ten miles long, and from three to four wide. It is separated from the ocean by a narrow sand-beach, which has doubtless been entirely formed by the sea. This beautiful expanse of water has long been celebrated for the excellence and variety of its marine productions. The clams found here are of a superior quality, and so abundant as to afford almost constant employment for about fifty persons, who probably take more than ten thousand dollars worth an-nually, which are properly prepared, put up in casks, and trans-ported up the western and northern canals to the utmost limits of the state. The territory of Shinnecock, containing some thousand acres, is little else than a series of sand hills, in-terspersed with intervals of level ground, which yield sufficient pasture for a considerable number of cattle and sheep, for at least half the year. The northern portion, adjoining Peconic Bay, is the best soil, and is indented with a few coves, which yield a quantity of salt grass about their edges. The western part, where it is connected with the main island, was called by the natives *Merosuck*, or Canoe-Place, and where they used to transport their canoes across from the north to the south bay. There is a tradition that a small ditch or canal once existed here between the two bays, which was constructed under the direction of *Mongotucksee* or *Long-knife*, who once reigned lord of the Montauks and other neighboring tribes. A small remnant of the Shinnecock race still lingers on the south-eastern part of this tract, where they have a small church and a few comfort-able dwellings; but their ancient language and customs are no longer preserved.

Sagg-Harbor is the most populous, wealthy, and commercial place in the county, and may therefore not improperly be con-sidered the emporium of Suffolk. The capital employed in trade here probably exceeds that of the whole county besides, there being nearly a million of dollars invested in the whale-fishery alone, employing a tonnage of more than six thousand, exclusive of several fine packets and other vessels engaged in the coasting business. It is supposed that no permanent settlement was attempted here previous to 1730, and then only a few small cottages were erected near the head of the present wharf, for the convenience of those engaged in fishing. Most of the land in the vicinity was then covered with timber and forest, and it is probable also that no inconsiderable number of Indians dwelt in the vicinity. In 1760 several respectable families established themselves here, perceiving that it possessed many local advantages, and built for themselves comfortable houses. In 1767 the number of inhabitants had so increased, that it was resolved to erect a house for public worship, and without the advantage of regular preaching, the people were accustomed to assemble on the Sabbath at the *beat of drum,* and hear a sermon read by one of the congregation. They began soon after more largely to appreciate the commercial facilities offered by the adjacent waters, and fresh efforts were made to improve upon the old practice of *boat-whaling.* For this end small sloops were fitted out, and ranged the ocean at some distance from the coast ; but when a whale was caught, it became necessary to return to port for the purpose of boiling out the oil upon the shore.   The business had made but little progress when hostilities commenced between the mother country and her colonies in 1775 ; and this island being the next year abandoned to the enemy, commerce of every kind was of course suspended till the close of the contest in 1783.   Several British ships took their stations in the bay, and this village was made not only a depot for military stores, but the garrison for a considerable body of soldiers.   During the war it became the theatre of one of the most extraordinary feats that was accomplished during the revolution.   It has generally been denominated *Meig's Expedition,* and the circumstances are thus related by the historians of that period :

"In retaliation for the burning of Ridgefield in Connecticut, by General Arnold and the wretches under his command, in April, 1777, a few soldiers from Newhaven went on a predatory excursion to Long Island.   A quantity of provisions had been collected at Sagg Harbor, and to destroy these was the object of the expedition.   The enterprize was one of the most spirited and successful of that eventful period.   General Par-

28

sons conceived it possible to surprise the place, and confided
the execution of it to Lieutenant-colonel Meigs, who embarked
from Newhaven, May 21, 1777, with two hundred and thirty-
four men, in thirteen whale-boats. He proceeded to Guilford,
but on account of the roughness of the sea, could not pass the
Sound till the twenty-third.   On that day, at one o'clock in the
afternoon, he left Guilford with one hundred and seventy men,
under convoy of two armed sloops, and crossed the Sound to
Southold, where he arrived at six o'clock.   The enemy's troops
on this part of the island had marched for New-York two or
three days before, but it was reported that there was a party at
Sagg Harbor on the south branch of the island about fifteen
miles distant.   Colonel Meigs ordered the whale-boats to be
transported over the land to the bay between the north and south
branches of the island, where one hundred and thirty men embarked, and at twelve o'clock at night arrived safely on the other
side of the bay within four miles of Sagg Harbor.   Here the
boats were secured in a wood, under a guard, and the remainder of the detachment marched quickly to the harbor, where
they arrived at two o'clock in the morning, in the greatest order, attacking the outpost with fixed bayonets, and proceeding
directly to the shipping at the wharf, which they found unpre-
pared for defence.   The alarm was given, and an armed
schooner with twelve guns and seventy men began to fire upon
them at the distance of one hundred and fifty yards, which continued three quarters of an hour, but did not prevent the troops
from executing their design with the greatest intrepidity and
effect.   Twelve brigs and sloops, one of which was an armed
vessel of twelve guns and one hundred and twenty tons of hay,
corn, oats, ten hogsheads of rum, and a large quantity of mer-
chandize, were entirely destroyed.   Six of the enemy were killed and ninety taken prisoners.   Not one of Colonel Meig's
men was either killed or wounded.   He returned to Guilford
at two o'clock in the afternoon, having been absent only twenty-
five hours ; and in that time had transported his troops by land
and water full ninety miles, and completed his undertaking
with the most entire success.   On the report of this matter to

the commander-in-chief, he addressed the following letter to General Parsons:

"Head-quarters, Middlebrook, May 29th, 1777.   Dear Sir.— I am just now favored with your letter of the 25th by Major Humphrey. The intelligence communicated by it is truly interesting and agreeable. And now I shall take occasion not only to give you my hearty approbation of your conduct in planning the expedition to Long Island, but to return my sincere thanks to Lieutenant Col. Meigs, and all the officers and men engaged in it. This enterprise, so fortunate in the execution, will greatly distress the enemy in the important and essential article of forage, and reflects much honor upon those who performed it. I shall ever be happy to reward merit when in my power, and therefore wish you to inquire for a vacant ensigncy in some of the regiments for Sergeant Gennings, to which you will promote him, advising me of the same and the time.   I am, Sir, &c.   G. WASHINGTON."

The result of this expedition was considered of so much consequence, and so highly deserving of public approbation, that congress voted a sword to be presented to Colonel Meigs as a token of their sense of the *prudence, activity, enterprise* and *valor*, with which it had been conducted; and the commander-in-chief published the affair with expressions, of great applause in general orders. In the year 1783 the inhabitants of this place, who had been for a period of seven years exiled from their homes, again returned, and united their energy and skill to revive commerce and other branches of business, which had been prostrated by the war. Their exertions were attended with tolerable success, and they were enabled in a short time to witness a limited but prosperous trade, both foreign and domestic.

Although, as has been seen, a Presbyterian church had been erected here in 1767, and different preachers had been engaged to officiate for stated periods, yet no clergyman was regularly settled here previous to 1797 in which year the Rev. Daniel Hall from Connecticut was installed as the minister of the parish. He continued here till the year 1806, when he removed to the church at Shelter Island, where he died in 1812. He was a man of plain and unaffected manners, of a kind and amiable disposition, and charitable toward those who chanced to differ from him in their opinions. In the month of October, 1812, the Rev. John D. Gardiner, a native of the county, and son of John Gardiner of Moriches, was installed the minister of this church. He was educated at Yale College, where he graduated in 1804. He was settled several years as a clergyman in New Jersey before his removal here. He continued in the discharge of his parochial duties with zeal and ability, and with the approbation of his people, till the month of June, 1832, when, anxious for retirement from his arduous labors, he withdrew from the ministry, and has since enjoyed, in the bosom of his family and the private circle of his friends, all the endearments of domestic and social life, respected and esteemed by the community around him. In the year 1817 preparations had been made for the erection of a new church, and most of the materials had been procured when they were consumed in the awful conflagration that involved the destruction of the most valuable portion of the village. But by the renewed energies of the people, and the individual exertions of Mr. Gardiner, means were procured; and the present large and handsome edifice was completed on the 18th of June, 1818. The Methodists erected a small church here in 1809, which they have since disposed of to the Catholics, and erected a new church a few years since, which, from its elevated situation and architectural finish, is an ornament to the village.

This port was formerly included in the collection district of New London; and in 1771 a commission was given to Nicoll Havens of Shelter Island "to inspect the trade and navigation of Southold, and the harbors, bays, creeks, and other places in the neighborhood thereof, and for the preventing of illicit trade within the district of the port of New London." After his death, the office was held by Thomas Deering, and which he retained until Sagg Harbor became a port of entry, and a new collection district was established by congress, subject to the regulations of the treasury department of the United States. Since which time the collectors have been John Gelston, Henry P. Dering, Thomas H. Dering, and John P. Osborn. Henry P. Dering received his appointment from General Washington in May, 1790, and held the office till his death, April 30th, 1832.

The whaling business upon this part of the island has existed, in some form or other, for a great length of time, and may be said to be almost coeval with the settlement of the country by the white people. Both individuals and companies at an early period were engaged in the pursuit of whales along the south shore, in boats built expressly for the purpose, and kept ready at convenient stations upon the beach. In the year 1760, three sloops, owned by Joseph Conkling, John Foster, and a few others, called the *Goodluck*, *Dolphin*, and *Success*, cruised for whales in latitude 36° north. Whales at that period were more abundant along-shore than at present, although some are yet taken by boats at East and Southampton almost every year. The whales, when secured, were drawn upon the shore, cut in pieces, and conveyed a distance to be boiled out. This process was so offensive, that the town meeting of Easthampton, in 1690, prohibited the practice within a certain distance of any habitation. In 1785, a vessel owned by Col. Benjamin Hunting and Captain Silas Howell, was sent as an experiment to a more southern latitude, and by her success laid the foundation of a more extensive prosecution of the business. In a short time thereafter, the *Brig Lucy*, owned by Col. Hunting, made the first voyage from this port to the coast of Brazil; this vessel was owned by him as late as 1797. The attempt was crowned with success, and served as a stimulus to others. Something has also been done in the cod-fishery from this place. In the Suffolk Gazette of January 18, 1808, it is stated that six thousand six hundred quintals of cod-fish were brought in here during the preceding year. But all commercial operations were of course suspended during the war of 1812, 1813, and 1814. In 1815 the business of whaling was again revived, and has continued to increase gradually in amount and importance to the present time. The sperm fishery around Cape Horn in the Pacific, and around the Cape of Good Hope in the Indian Ocean, was not commenced till 1817. In September of that year the *Argonaut*, owned by Silas and Lewis Howell, commanded by Eliphalet Halsey, sailed for the Pacific, and returned in June, 1819, with seventeen hundred barrels of sperm oil. This business is not only attended with heavy expense, but also with no little risk of property and life. One or two melancholy instances deserve to be mentioned. The ship *Governor Clinton* sailed from here in August, 1833, and is supposed to have been lost in a typhon, or hurricane, on the coast of Japan, in September, 1834. The whole crew, consisting of twenty-nine persons, among whom was Samuel Ludlow, *captain*, Daniel E. Brown, *mate*, Daniel Leek, *second mate*, William D. Schellinger, *third mate*, Erastus E. Halsey, Charles Howell, Sylvester Stanbrough, and Henry Miller, *boat steerers*, Benjamin Payne, *cooper*, Edward P. Jennings, *carpenter*, were drowned. Again, the ship Telegraph, belonging to S. and N. Howell, commanded by John E. Howell, left here for the coast of Chili, in October, 1834; and on the 20th of May, 1836, entered Resolution Bay in the island Ohitahoo for wood and water. On the succeeding night, the wind from the mountain blew with such violence as to sever the ship's cable, and drive her out to sea, where she struck upon a reef of rocks, and was entirely lost, with twenty-two hundred barrels of oil and sperm. The people on board were fortunately saved by another vessel.

Mr. Luther D. Cook of this port, a gentleman of well-known intelligence, and extensively connected with this branch of commerce, has obligingly furnished us with some statistical information, which is deemed of too much importance to be omitted. From the statement of this gentleman it appears, that in the year 1837 there were twenty-three arrivals and twenty-nine departures of whaling-ships from this place; the number of men and boys employed on board exceeding eight hundred. In order to appreciate the extraordinary progress which has been made in this business, it is only necessary to remark that, in 1815 there were only three ships owned here, and that in 1838 the number amounted to twenty-nine; exhibiting an increase of twenty-six ships in twenty-three years. This shows also how much may be accomplished by the ever-restless spirit of enterprise and industry so characteristic of the American people; and is nowhere so extensively displayed as in this department of navigation. While many other places possess local advantages not enjoyed here, yet the ship owners of this port have accomplished more in this expensive and hazardous business than the whole State of New-York besides. What may be the experience of the future, can only be conjectured. On account of the number of vessels, both at home and abroad, engaged in this species of commerce, it is very doubtful whether the business will be found as profitable as heretofore. The whales are unceasingly pursued from one point to another over every part of the ocean, rendering them more shy, and are consequently taken with far more difficulty than formerly. From the immense number which are now annually captured compared with previous years, upon the various whaling stations, they will probably become scarce ; and from being constantly harassed, more formidable. Indeed, it now requires all the skill of the most practised individuals in managing the boats and in throwing the harpoon. These difficulties, together with the low price of oil, have rendered some late voyages not only profitless, but actually attended with loss. It is calculated by Mr. Cook, from the most correct data, that on the 1st of January, 1838, there were not less than five hundred and fifty-three vessels of different descriptions in the sperm and right whale fishery from the several ports of the United States. It also appears, that from the year 1804 to 1837 there have been one hundred and ninety-eight arrivals of whaling vessels at this port, producing three hundred and thirty-eight thousand six hundred and ninety barrels of oil ; forty thousand five hundred and four barrels of sperm ; and one million five hundred and ninety-six thousand seven hundred and sixty-five pounds of whalebone. That in the years 1834 and '35 there were seventeen arrivals, amounting in the aggregate to six thousand three hundred and sixty-one tons, being an average of three hundred and eighteen tons to each vessel. That in 1837 the arrivals were twenty-three, producing eight thousand six hundred and thirty-four barrels of sperm, thirty-one thousand seven hundred and eighty-four barrels of oil, and two hundred and thirty-six thousand seven hundred and fifty-seven pounds of bone. That during the same year the departures were

twenty-nine, including one from James-Port, one from Cutchogue, and two from Green Port, all bound for the south Atlantic Ocean. In the year 1838 the tonnage employed in whaling from this port amounted to eleven thousand seven hundred, to which, if we add five thousand four hundred and
thirty-seven of enrolled and licensed tonnage employed in the
coasting trade, will increase the sum total to seventeen thousand
one hundred and thirty-seven tons of shipping belonging to
Sagg Harbor. The growth and prosperity of this village has been
the necessary consequence of the extensive capital employed
in commerce, and the various occupations to which it gives
rise. The wealth and trade of the place may with propriety
be said to be founded upon the whaling business, and will
doubtless keep pace with its increase. The population is now
about three thousand; and it contains four hundred dwellings,
twenty-five dry-good and grocery stores, two drug-stores, two
watchmakers' shops, two lumber-yards, two sail-makers' shops,
three fire engines with regularly organized companies, four
butchers' stalls, a bakery, several hotels and boarding-houses,
two printing-offices, fourteen coopers'-shops, which manufacture to the amount of twenty-five thousand barrels of oil casks
annually, a book-store and circulating library, and a public
library of more than eight hundred volumes. The manufacture of marine salt by solar evaporation was formerly carried
on to a considerable extent near this village, and in other
places in the vicinity, but it has not been found recently to yield
a sufficient profit to warrant its continuance.

There are sometimes to be found in a country village individuals living in comparative obscurity, and making no preten-
ces to any kind of superiority, who nevertheless manifest some
extraordinary talent, and possess, in reality, accomplishments
parallel with some whose reputation has been widely diffused
in the scientific world. Such an individual may be found
here in the person of EPHRAIM N. BYRAM, a native of this
village, and a self taught mechanic and astronomer. Indeed,
his attainments may almost be said to be universal, as there are
few subjects of science which he has not explored, and in which
he has not made a very creditable proficiency. He has scarcely

ever travelled beyond the limits of the village, and for many
years has not been a mile from his own shop; his time and attention being constantly devoted to mechanical and scientific
pursuits. He not only invents and executes the most ingenious
and complicated machines, as clocks, telescopes, and musical
organs, but even fabricates the implements with which his
other works are constructed. This gentleman, without any of
the advantages of family, education, or wealth, and struggling
with a constitution naturally delicate, has obtained a most extraordinary knowledge of many branches of art and science,
which might be thought, with a person in his situation, impossible. Among a variety of other mechanical contrivances,
planned and executed by himself alone, is a *Planetarium*,
which exhibits the relative situation and movements of the solar
system more perfectly than has perhaps ever been done before.
By the most curious and intricate combination of mechanical
appliances, it is made to represent the position and revolutions
of the celestial bodies in the most beautiful and harmonious
order; and evinces that the mind which could conceive and
accomplish such an undertaking, must be deeply imbued with
the elementary principles of astronomy and the physical sciences. The extreme delicacy and neatness of every part of
this wonderful production of art are only equalled by the sublime conceptions with which its author must have been inspired.

The Hon. EBENEZER SAGE, long a resident of this village,
was born at Chatham, Connecticut, August 16, 1755, and graduated at Yale College in 1778. Having qualified himself as
a physician, he settled, about the year 1790, at Easthampton,
and soon after married Ruth, daughter of Dr. William Smith
of Southampton. In 1798 he returned to Connecticut, but
came back and settled at Sagg Harbor in a short time after,
where he spent the remainder of his life with great usefulness
and respectability. He was a cautious and skilful practitioner,
and a man of much science and literature. He possessed great
equanimity of temper, and this, with a talent for humor, rendered
his company and conversation at all times agreeable. He
was elected to the eleventh, twelfth, and thirteenth congresses, in
which he satisfied his political friends. In 1821 he was a delegate
29

in the convention for amending the constitution of this state. He survived his wife several years, and died, esteemed and lamented, January 20, 1834.

The first newspaper printed upon Long Island was issued in this village by David Frothingham on the 10th of May, 1791. It was entitled *Long Island Herald*, and was transferred, on the 2d of June, 1802, to Selleck Osborn, and the title was changed to the Suffolk County Herald. On the 20th of February, 1804, he relinquished the paper to Alden Spooner, and removed to Litchfield, where he also published a paper called the *Witness*, and was soon after convicted and imprisoned for a political libel, under circumstances which excited much sympathy among his republican friends. He afterwards published a paper in Boston, and in 1823 a volume of original poems. He went, a year or two after, to Wilmington, Delaware, where he published a paper entitled the *American Watchman*. His death took place at Philadelphia, October 1, 1826. He was a person of considerable talents; as a writer, respectable, and as a poet, holds a conspicuous rank among the list of American bards.

Mr. Spooner again altered the title of the paper to that of the *Suffolk Gazette*, and which he continued to publish till the 23d of April, 1811, when he relinquished it for the *Long Island Star*, at Brooklyn.

The next newspaper was the *Suffolk County Recorder*, commenced in 1816 by Samuel A. Seabury; the name of which was changed to that of the *American Eagle*, and was discontinued in about two years thereafter. On the 3d of August, 1822, the *Corrector* was established by Henry W. Hunt; and on the 16th of September, 1826, the *Republican Watchman*, by Samuel Phillips; which two last-named papers continue yet to be published weekly.

On the declaration of war against Great Britain in 1812, preparations were made to protect this place against the enemy, and a small detachment of militia was stationed here, who employed themselves in erecting a fortification upon the high ground overlooking the harbor. No regular garrison was established, however, till the summer of 1813, when the British ships, taking their station in Gardiner's Bay, threatened to land at several points in the vicinity of this port. At that time three or four hundred men were placed here, and were continued til the end of the war. Some part of the time a company of artillery, and another of regular troops, were stationed here; and in 1814 one or more companies of sea fencibles. But at no time was the number of soldiers sufficient to have effectually defended the place against the enemy, had the capture of it been considered by them an object of sufficient importance to have warranted the attempt. It was wholly impossible to have prevented their landing at various places bordering upon the bay, and they accordingly visited at pleasure Gardiner's Island, Montauk, and Oyster Ponds; taking such provisions as their necessities required, and for which, it is believed, they generally paid an equivalent. In June, 1813, a launch and two barges, with about one hundred men from the squadron of Commodore Hardy, attempted to land at the wharf in the night; but being timely discovered, the alarm was sounded, and the guns of the fort brought to bear in the direction of the boats; so successful was the means used, that the designs of the enemy were effectually frustrated. They had only time to set fire to a sloop which they took from the wharf, when a shot from the fort raked her fore and aft, and obliged them to abandon her. The Americans going on board, extinguished the flames, when they found a quantity of guns, swords, pistols, and other instruments, which the invaders, (deeming discretion to be the better part of valor,) had left in their hurry to escape.

On the 26th of May, 1817, the village was visited by a desolating fire, that in a brief space laid the most valuable portion of it in ruins. It originated in the dense part of the village, and the wind blowing a gale, such was the rapidity of the flames, that, notwithstanding the utmost exertions of the firemen and citizens, many of the best houses and stores, with a great quantity of merchandize, were consumed. Even goods that had been rescued from the buildings on fire, were subsequently, by the changing of the wind, burnt in the streets. This was, indeed, a terrible calamity, as the inhabitants had but just begun to revive from the total prostration of trade by the war.

Ships nearly ready for sea were delayed by the destruction of the stores destined for their use.   The public sympathy was manifested on the occasion, and donations to a considerable extent were obtained for the more suffering portion of the population.   The event, however, proved that the ambition of the people was equal to the emergency ; and the ground swept over by the fire, was in a short time covered with buildings more convenient and substantial than before, and by which the appearance of the village was materially improved.   The wharf was formerly the property of the state, at whose expense it was constructed ; but is now owned by an association of individuals, who share the profits arising from the use of it. It remedies, in some degree, the want of a sufficient depth of water, by being extended several hundred feet into the bay.   On the western part of the village, and within the limits of the corporation, is Otter Pond, covering several acres of ground, on which was formerly a mill ; and, having a communication with the cove at the upper part of the bay, is stocked with fish, and furnishes fine sport for the angler.

Hog-Neck is situated in the bay, and within a few hundred yards of the village, with which it has lately been connected by a handsome bridge, constituting an important link in the route across Shelter Island to Green Port.   This neck contains several hundred acres of indifferent soil, but which its insular situation affords facilities for improving, and is thereby rendered quite productive.

Between Canoe-Place and Quogue is a small hamlet, denominated *Good Ground,* a sort of *oasis* in the desert of sand which surrounds it.   It has a Methodist church and post-office. *Quogue* is a more considerable settlement, about fourteen miles from the village of Southampton, and near the western limits of the town.   It is much resorted to in the summer for its pure air, and the abundance and excellence of the game that is found here.   It has two good public-houses, and the inhabitants are generally farmers.

STEPHEN SAYRE was born in this town in 1745, where he spent a portion of his early life.   Few persons were ever more conspicuous for personal beauty and accomplishments.   He was a staunch Whig in the revolution, and it is believed that his visit to England, in 1775, was as confidental agent of government. Such was his prepossessing manners and appearance that he soon gained admission into the best society, and was upon intimate terms with many leading men in the administration there. He connected himself in marriage with an English lady of rank, by whom he acquired a handsome fortune. Having entered into financial and commercial business, his acquaintance became extensive, and this, added to his very popular manners, caused him to be chosen high sheriff of the city of London. By his advocacy of the American cause, and his open opposition to the arbitrary measures of the administration, he drew down upon himself the displeasure of government, which led to his arrest upon a charge of *treason*, and for which he was most unceremoniously thrown into the Tower. The following particulars of this affair are found in the *London Public Ledger* of October 25, 1776:—" Between the hours of nine and ten on Monday morning, Mr. Slavely, of Half Moon Street, Piccadilly, and Mr. Mann of Queen Ann Street, Westminster, (king's messengers,) attended by a constable, repaired to the house of Stephen Sayre, Esquire, in Oxford Street. As an excuse to obtain an interview with him, they pretended a forged draft for £200 had been issued by the bank, of which Mr. Sayre is a proprietor. He no sooner appeared, than they acquainted him that they had an order, signed by Lord Rochford, one of the secretaries of state, to take him into custody on a charge of high treason; and to search for, take and carry with them, such of his papers as they might deem effectual for their purposes. Mr. Sayre heard the summons with composure, and obeyed its dictates with manly dignity; conscious of his innocence, he smiled at the malignity of the charge, and in perfect reliance upon his own integrity, permitted the officers to search his tables and rifle his bureau. They conducted him to Lord Rochford, where they also found Sir John Fielding. The charge in the information was, *that Mr. Sayre had expressed an intention of seizing the king's person as he went to the parliament house, and of taking possession of the Tower*, &c. The advice of Mr. Sayre's counsel was, that he should not answer any interrogations which Lord Rochford or Sir John Fielding might put, nor sign any paper whatever.   Mr. Sayre was then ordered into an adjoining apartment, and afterwards committed a close prisoner to the Tower.   On the 14th of December, 1776, he appeared at the Old Bailey, and his counsel, Mr. Arthur Lee, moved to discharge the recognizance entered into on the 28th of October last, on Mr. Sayre's being brought before Lord Mansfield upon a writ of habeas corpus.   Mr. Baron Burland, who, with the Lord Mayor, presided at the court, accordingly discharged the recognizance ; and Mr. Sayre immediately gave orders to commence actions against Lord Rochford, the under secretaries of state, and the king's messengers." In Gorden's History of the Revolution, it is stated that " in 1775 many suspicions were entertained of combinations in favor of America, and upon certain hints thrown out, Mr. Sayre, an American, and a banker in London, was secured; and being examined before the secretary of state, Lord Rochford, and confronted by his accuser, was committed to the Tower for high treason, on the ridiculous charge of designing to seize his Majesty at noon-day in his passage to the house of peers, of conveying him a prisoner to the Tower, and afterwards out of the kingdom, and of overturning the whole form of government, *by bribing a few sergeants of the guards*." Mr. Sayre remained may years after in London, engaged in speculation and commerce ; and on his return to America, settled upon a plantation which he had purchased upon the Delaware, near Bordentown, New Jersey, and where he spent the remainder of his days.   The estate of Mr. Sayre is said to be now owned by Joseph Bonaparte, ex-Emperor of Spain ; and upon which he has erected a splendid and expensive private establishment.

In the History of the Arts of Design in the United States, lately published by William Dunlap, Esquire, honorable mention is made of another gentleman, also a native of this town ; and which, with a few trifling corrections that our acquaintance with this person enables us to make, we take the liberty to introduce in this place.

NATHANIEL ROGERS was born at Bridgehampton in 1778.

His father, John T. Rogers, was a respectable farmer of that place; and the subject of this notice has the honor of springing from the same class of citizens that gave birth to West, Wright, Vanderlyn, Fisher, Mount, and a long list of American artists, the yeomanry of the country. His mother was a daughter of the Rev. James Brown, minister of the parish for near fifty years, and grand-daughter of the Rev. Mr. Prime, former minister of Huntington. The father of Mr. Rogers, although the owner of a good farm, well knew it would not answer to divide it into four parts; and therefore, after giving his sons a good education, two of them chose a mercantile, and the other a mechanical employment. Nathaniel was put apprentice to a ship-builder at Hudson, where he served his master as clerk also; for he says of himself, that his business was " *to keep the accounts, pay off the workmen, and serve out the grog.*" Much of the time he was employed in drafting and making models, at which he exhibited very considerable ingenuity and skill. In about a year after he was wounded by a severe cut in the knee, which disabled him from labor, and rendered him no longer serviceable to his employer. He was accordingly dismissed from his indentures, and returned to his parents' house, where he received, of course, every attention that his unfortunate condition required. This accident has sometimes been playfully mentioned by his friends as the most *fortunate cut* he ever made. But it may with propriety be supposed, that a due exercise of the same energies in the business originally intended, might have procured results equally advantageous, although of less consequence in public estimation.

Having a taste for drawing, he had now sufficient leisure and opportunity of indulging in the perusal of such books as were calculated to impart information in his favorite department. He began also to copy prints, and even made some slight essays at designing. His physician, Dr. Samuel H. Rose, possessed a mind, education, and taste, that might in some situations have gained him high praise, and was, as all who knew him can testify, a person of much goodness of heart. And seeing and sympathizing with the suffering boy, he sought to amuse him, and at the same time to encourage his wishes, by presenting him a few pencils and a box of colors. The young invalid felt fresh inspiration at this unexpected good fortune, and soon set about attempting the portraits of some of his more intimate acquaintance. Although, as might be expected, they were very imperfect performances, yet to them they appeared as wonderful likenesses. Going, soon after, to New-York, he procured an introduction to Mr. Howell, an artist, and a native of Long Island, by whom he was encouraged and instructed. Mr. Howell, however, died not long after, of consumption. Rogers now determined within himself to be a painter, but his more prudent father considered it a precarious undertaking, and one in which to obtain mediocrity only, would be equal to a failure. He therefore urged his son to fit himself for one of the learned professions, frankly offering to furnish the means. To this urgent request he agreed, and was accordingly placed at school preparatory to entering upon the study of a profession. But his strong passion for the fine arts still haunted his imagination, and portraits and pictures flitted occasionally across his fancy, disturbing the regular course of thought. On a visit which he made about this time to some friends at Saybrook, he fairly commenced the business of a portrait painter, and drew some tolerable likenesses of several of his acquaintance. His kind-hearted parent now believing that he saw more solid evidences of his son's ability to distinguish himself in the art, gave consent for him to begin a course of study ; and immediate arrangements were made with Mr. Wood (at this period successfully prosecuting the business of a painter in New-York). For this kind instructor Rogers has ever entertained feelings of gratitude and personal kindness ; and when he fell into adversity, was both able and willing to administer to his relief, and to the sincere gratification of both. The young aspirant now set up for himself, and soon found employment; so that he was shortly after able to transmit a few *bank notes* to his father, with a special request that he would invest them for him to the best advantage. The old gentleman's doubts of his son's ultimate success, if any he had at this time, were completely dispelled, and his former anxiety on his account most agreeably relieved. Wood soon after removed to Philadelphia, and left the field open to Rogers.   His business increased, and his reputation as a painter continued to advance until he obtained the first rank in miniature painting.   His incessant application to business at one time threatened his health, but by timely relaxation and proper care he has been restored.   He married in 1818 Caroline Matilda, daughter of Captain Samuel Denison of Sagg Harbor, and has several children whom he has educated, having saved a competent independence from his profession. He is a member of the National Academy, and no longer pursues his business, except as an occasional amusement.   His character and conduct through life are worthy the imitation of the generation of young artists who aspire either to fame or fortune.

TOWN OF SHELTER ISLAND,

Is situated between the north and south branches of Long Island, at the eastern extremity of Peconic Bay, bounded by its waters on the north, west, and south, and by Gardiner's Bay on the east.   The island is about six miles long, and four broad in the widest part; containing about eight thousand acres, divided into several farms.   The number of families is seventy, and the inhabitants about three hundred.   The surface is in general undulating, and covered in part by oak and other timber.   The soil is of a good quality, and in general well cultivated.   There are some ponds of fresh water, and one upon the southerly side of the island covering about thirty acres of ground.   Peat is found in considerable quantity, but has hitherto been little used.   The shores are indented by coves and small bays, and their edges abound with salt grass.   There are many beautiful sites for building, and the prospect from many points is various and picturesque.   The Indian name of this island is *Manhansack-aha-qushu-wamock*, meaning, *an island sheltered by islands.*   It was the residence of the Manhasset tribe, and the place where the sachem lived is still called "Sachem's Neck."   In the power of attorney executed by William Alexander, earl of Stirling, to James Farret, authorizing him to dispose of Long Island, he was at liberty to select

30

for his own use twelve thousand acres, in consequence of which he made choice of this and Robins' Island in Peconic Bay, both of which, on the 18th of May, 1641, he sold to Stephen Good-year of New-Haven, who, on the 9th of June, 1651, conveyed the same to Thomas Middleton, Thomas Rouse, Constant Sylvester, and Nathaniel Sylvester, for *sixteen hundred weight of good merchantable Muscovado sugar.* The grantees procured an immediate confirmation of the title from Yokee, the Manhasset Sachem, and his chief men, and who covenanted and agreed at the same time to *put away all their dogs ;* and in case any damage was done to the purchasers by them, to make a proper satisfaction for the same forthwith.

Rouse conveyed his quarter part of the island to John Booth, who, on the 8th of May, 1656, transferred his interest to Nathaniel Sylvester. The latter, on the 12th of September, 1662, sold a portion to his brother, Constant Sylvester. The English having, two years after, made the conquest of New-York, this island came of course under the jurisdiction of the colonial government; and on the 31st of May, 1666, a patent of confirmation of the purchase from the agent of Lord Stirling, was granted by Governor Nicolls to the then owners, Constant and Nathaniel Sylvester, their heirs and assigns; they yielding and paying annually thereafter, on the 1st day of May, *one lamb,* as an acknowledgment to the Duke of York. On the re-capture of New-York by the Dutch in 1673, Governor Colve, by a formal act of the 28th of April, 1674, confiscated the rights, whatever they might be, of Thomas Middleton and Constant Sylvester as public enemies ; and sold the same, on the 28th of August following, to the said Nathaniel Sylvester for five hundred pounds, taking his bond for the same, in consequence of which he became sole owner of the island. When the country was about to be restored to the English by treaty, and the governor expected soon to leave New-York, he concluded to secure the money due upon the bond ; and accordingly despatched a vessel and about fifty soldiers to the island, and by means of threats and intimidation compelled Mr. Sylvester to pay it, which they carried off.

Nathaniel Sylvester had five sons, *Giles, Nathaniel, Con-*

stant, Peter, and *Benjamin ;* all of whom succeeded to the ownership of the island, as tenants in common in equal parts. Nathaniel afterwards sold his interest to the Havens' family, and settled at Rhode Island, where he died, leaving a son by the name of Brinley Sylvester.   Peter and Benjamin conveyed to their brother Giles, and who, dying without issue, devised his estate to William Nicolls of Islip, and the same is now possessed by the children of the late Samuel B. Nicolls.   Brinley Sylvester having acquired title to a portion of the island, partly by purchase, and partly by devise from his relations, removed here in 1737, and erected the large mansion-house of the late General Dering, now the property of Samuel S. Gardiner, Esq. Brinley Sylvester died here, December 24th, 1752; and the property descended to his daughter, who intermarried with Thomas Dering, an eminent merchant of Boston, who consequently removed to this island, where he died, leaving the property to his two sons, Sylvester and Henry P. Dering. The firstnamed, better known as General Dering, married a daughter of Nicoll Havens, and who still survives her husband. The following is a copy of the inscription upon the tomb of General Dering :

" Sacred to the memory of General Sylvester Dering, who departed this life, October 8th, 1820, aged sixty-one. He united a sound and active mind with ardent and exemplary piety. He lived not for himself, but for the community around him. He was a kind councillor and faithful friend. The prevailing disposition of his heart was sympathy for the distressed, and corresponding efforts for their relief. For a long course of years he held various offices in church and state, and died lamented and beloved."

Henry P. Dering married Miss Fosdick of New London, and died April 30th, 1832, leaving a widow and several children. He was born here July 3d, 1763, and removed to Sagg Harbor, where he held, for a great number of years, the offices of postmaster and collector of the customs for that port, and until the time of his death. Few men had a more extensive acquaintance, or obtained and enjoyed through life a more enviable share of public confidence and esteem.

The Hon. Jonathan N. Havens was the son of Nicoll Havens, and born here in 1758. He graduated at Yale College in 1777. In 1786 he was elected to the assembly of this state, and continued in that body many years. He was a member of the convention that adopted the constitution of the United States in 1778. He was a representative in the fifth congress, and remained in that body till his death in 1799. The character of this distinguished man is briefly summed up in the following inscription upon his tomb:

> "Erected to the memory of Jonathan Nicoll Havens, Esq., representative in the Congress of the United States. He was esteemed by a numerous acquaintance, as a man of superior talents and erudition; a philosopher, statesman, and patriot; and died, greatly lamented, October 25, 1799, in the forty-second year of his age."

The following epitaphs are copied from head-stones in the Shelter Island burial-ground, and are remarkable for the singular contrast they exhibit, in the last solemn act of the deceased:

> "*In Memory of*
> Benjamin Conkling, who died February 21, 1826, aged eighty-two. It is but justice to the character of Mr. Conkling to say that he was an obliging neighbor; in his habits industrious, in his dealings honest. He liberally aided the cause of virtue and religion, and in his last moments bequeathed a large proportion of his property to the Presbyterian church and congregation of Shelter Island, for the support of the gospel."

> "*In Memory of*
> Shadrach Conkling, who died January 23d, 1827, aged eighty-eight. Mr. Conkling possessed a sound mind and excellent understanding, and was a firm patriot, a good neighbor, charitable and strictly moral. He owned, at the time of his decease, a large estate, which he bequeathed to his relations, who were all very poor, and among whom were seven orphan children. Posterity will decide upon the wisdom manifested in the disposition of the estates of these two brothers."

By some conventional agreement in former times between the proprietors of this island and the people of Southold, the concerns of the island, so far as they were of a public nature, were transacted in the town-meetings held at Southold. This sufficiently appears from inspecting the records of that town, and accounts for the circumstance of there being no town records previous to the year 1730, when the first town-meeting was held, and an entry made thereof in the following words:

"Precinct of Shelter Island, April 7, 1730.

At a town meeting held this day,—William Nicolls was chosen supervisor; John Havens and Samuel Hudson, assessors; Edward Havens, collector; and Edward Gilman, clerk."

The male inhabitants of the town at this time, of full age, were as follows:

William Nicolls,	Edward Havens,	Noah Tuthill,
John Havens,	Samuel Vail,	Sylvester L'Hommedieu,
Samuel Hudson,	Thomas Conkling,	Henry Havens,
George Havens,	Edward Gilman,	Samuel Hopkins,
Elisha Payne,	Brinley Sylvester,	John Bowditch,
Joel Bowditch,	Jonathan Havens,	Daniel Brown.
Abraham Parker,	Joseph Havens,	

The first church was erected by the Presbyterians in 1733, the funds for defraying the expense of which, were collected upon the island and the adjacent towns. It was taken down in 1816, when the present church was erected upon the same spot. They have had a settled clergyman here for short periods only, and at long intervals.

During the revolution this island was stripped of its wood for the use of the British army and navy; and great injury was committed upon the property of the inhabitants, most of whom, if not all, were decided and active Whigs, and of course had no reason to expect any favor or indulgence from the public enemy. The growth of timber is, however, very rapid, and vast quantities have since been disposed of by the owners. Few tracts of land are better adapted for farming purposes, and especially for the raising of stock and grain. Ram Island (so called) lies upon the north-east side of Shelter Island, and is now connected with it by a narrow strand of alluvial formation. It is owned by Mr. Thomas Tuthill, and contains about four hundred acres of moderately good land. The surface is rough, and has generally been appropriated for the pasturing of sheep, a business heretofore found very profitable. An act for the establishment of a ferry between this town and Southold has been passed, and, when carried into effect, will facilitate and increase the travel from one branch of Long Island to the other.

TOWN OF SOUTHOLD.

This town occupies the north branch of Long Island, and includes the peninsula of Oyster Ponds, Plumb Island, the two Gull Islands, and Fisher's Island in the Sound, and Robin's

Island in Peconic Bay. It is bounded west by Riverhead, north and east by the Sound, and south by the bay which separates this town from Southampton and Shelter Island. Its length, from the west bounds to Oyster Ponds Point, is about twenty-three miles, and its greatest breadth four miles. The Indian name of this town is *Yennecock*, and was purchased from the Corchougs, a tribe that possessed this part of the island, in the summer of 1640. Most of the first planters were originally from Hingham, in Norfolk, England : and came here by the way of New-Haven. The Rev. John Youngs, who had been a preacher in England, was their leader. He organized a church at New-Haven, and they, with others willing to accompany them, commenced the settlement of this town. The principal men among them besides Mr. Youngs, were William Wells, Barnabas Horton, Thomas Mapes, John Tuthill, and Matthias Corwin. The governor of New-Haven, Theophilus Eaton, and the authorities there, had not only aided the first settlers in their negotiations about the purchase of the soil, but actually took the conveyance in their own names, and exercised a limited control over the territory for several years, which eventually occasioned some dissatisfaction among the inhabitants. The civil and ecclesiastical concerns of the settlement were conducted in a similar manner with the other plantations under the jurisdiction of New-Haven. All government was reputed to be in the church, and none were admitted to the entire privileges of freedom, or free burgesses as they were called, except church members ; a court was in like manner instituted, which was authorized to hear and determine all causes, civil and criminal, and whose decisions were to be according to the laws of God as contained in the holy scriptures. In the general court (or town meeting), consisting also of church members, was transacted the ordinary business of the plantation. In these, orders were made in relation to the division of lands, the enclosure or cultivation of common fields, the regulation of fences, highways, and the time and manner of permitting cattle and sheep to go at large upon the common lands ; and such further measures as were required for the mutual defence of the settlement from hostile attacks on every side. One of the first ordinances required every man to provide himself with arms and ammunition, and to assemble at an appointed place, whenever warned so to do, under a certain penalty for neglect in any of these respects. The plantation made early provision for the education of children, the preservation of good morals, and the support of religion. A committee was appointed to regulate the admission of new settlers, and no one could become an inhabitant without their approbation ; and no planter could sell or let his house or land to a stranger, but only to such as were approved by the said committee, under a heavy penalty. The plantation found it not only difficult, but attended with great and serious embarrassment, to enforce rigidly the rule of the jurisdiction excluding all but church members from voting at elections ; and having in this respect infringed upon its severity, the jurisdiction of New-Haven, in 1648, sent over a delegation of their principal men to consult upon the necessity and importance of keeping the government in the hands of " *God's Elect*." The consequence was, that the town agreed, in future, to conform faithfully to the laws of the jurisdiction in this respect. The law here referred to, was that adopted in the year 1643, which, being somewhat curious, is here presented to the reader :

" At a General Court, held at New-Haven for the Jurisdiction, the 27th of October, 1643.

PRESENT.

Magistrates.		*Deputies.*	
Theophilus Eaton, Governor.		George Lamberton	pr New-Haven.
Stephen Goodyear, Deputy.	H. H.	Nathaniel Turner	
Thomas Gregson.		John Astwood	pr Milford.
William Fowler.	M.	John Sherman	
Edmund Tapp.		William Leete	pr Guilford.
Thurston Raynor, S.		Samuel Disbrough	
Thomas Fugill, Sec.	N. H.	Richard Gildersleve	pr Stamford.
Tho. Kimberly, Marshall.		John Whitmore.	

I. It was agreed and concluded, as a fundamental order not to be disputed or questioned hereafter, thatt none shall be admitted to be free Burgesses in any of the Plantations within this Jurisdiction for the future, but such Planters as are members of some or other of the approved Churches in New England; nor shall any but such free Burgesses have any vote in any Election (the six present freemen att Milforde enjoying the Liberty with the Cautions agreed.) Nor shall any power or trust in the ordering of any Civill Affayres be att any time put into the hands of any other than such Church members; though as free Planters all have right to their Inheritance and to commerce, according to such Grants, Orders, and Lawes as shall be made concerning the same.

II. All such free Burgesses shall have power in each Town ande Plantation within this Jurisdiction to chuse fitt and able men from amongst themselves (being Church members as expressed before) to be the Ordinary Judges to heare and determine all inferiour Causes, wthér. Civill or Criminal; provided thatt no Civill Cause to be tryed in any of the Plantation Courts in value exceed 20s. ande that the punishment of such Criminals according to the minde of God revealed in his' word touching such offences doe not exceed Stocking and Whipping, or if the fine be pecuniary thatt it exceed not five pounds, in wch. Court the magistrate or magistrates, if any be chosen by the free Burgesses of the Jurisdiction for thatt Plantation, shall sitt and assist with due respect to their place, ande sentence shall pass according to the vote of the major parte of each such Courte, onely if the partyes or any of them be nott satisfyed wth. the Justice of such sentences or Executions, appeals or complaynts may be made from ande agaynst these Courts to the Courts of Magistrates for the whole Jurisdiction.

III. All free Burgesses in the Jurisdiction shall have a vote in the Election of Magistrates, whether Governour, Deputy Governour or other Magistrates, with a vote for Treasurer, Secretary and Marshall, &c. for the Jurisdiction, and for the case of such Burgesses, ande especially in remote plantations they may vote by proxi by sending in their votes, which votes shall be sealed in the presence of the free Burgesses, and the free Burgesses may chuse for each plantation as many Magistrates as the situation of Affayres may require, and no plantation shall be left destitute of Magistrates if they desire one chosen out of those in church fellowship with them.

IV. All the Magistrates for the whole Jurisdiction shall meete twice a yeare att New-Haven on the Monday immediately before the sitting of the two fixed General Courts hereafter mentioned, to keep a court called a court of Magistracy for the tryall of weighty ande capitall causes, whether civill or criminall, above those submitted to the ordinary judges in the particular plantations, and to receive and try appeals brought to them from the Plantation courts, and to call the inhabitants, whether free Burgesses, free Planters or others, to account for the breach of any laws established, and for other misdemeanours, and to censure them according to their offence. Less than four Magistrates shall nott compose a court; but it is required and expected all the Magistrates to attende of the Jurisdiction. If not present, they shall be liable to a fine of 20s. unless excused on account of God's Providence preventing. Appeals and complaints can be made from this to the General Court as the last resort. Besides the Plantation Courts ande the Court of Magistrates, there shall be a general court for the jurisdiction, which shall consist of the Governour and all the Magistrates within the Jurisdiction, and two deputies for every plantation in the Jurisdiction to be chosen previously. This court shall sit at New-Haven twice every year, viz. on the first Wednesday of April and the last Wednesday in October, at the last of which the officers for the ensuing year shall be chosen. The Governour, or in his absence, the Deputy Governour, shall have power to summon a General Court at any other time, and no one belonging to the court shall be absent on penalty of 20s. fine.

V. The court shall, with all care and dilligence, provide for the maintainance of the purity of Religion, and suppress the contrary, according to their best light from the word of God, and by the advice of the Elders and churches in the jurisdiction so far as it might concern the civill power. 2d. This court shall have power to make and repeal lawes, and to require their execution while in force in all the several plantations. 3d. To impose an oath upon all the Magistrates, to call them to account for breach of Lawes, and to censure them according to offence; to settle and levie rates and contribution of the Plantations for the public service, and to heare and determine causes, whether civill or criminall; they to proceed according to the Scriptures, which is the rule of all righteous lawes and sentences. Nothing shall pass as an act without the consent of the majority of the magistrates and of the majority of the Deputies. In the Generall Court shall be and reside the supreme power of the Jurisdiction."

The difficulties and discontents that arose from the control which the colony of New-Haven claimed to exercise over the lands of this town, made it necessary, at a subsequent period, to send over agents from time to time to negotiate upon the subject; and, in consequence of which, the following proceeding took place at New-Haven in 1649:

"At a General Court held at New-Haven for the Jurisdiction, the 30th May, 1649. The ffreemen of Southold desired that the purchase of their plantation might be made over to them. The court told them that they are ffree to make over to them what right they have, either by a deed or by an act in court, that it might stand upon, to ffree them from all future claymes from themselves, or any under them, as themselves upon due consideration shall propound or desire. Mr. Wells being questioned about some land he had received of some Indians in Long Island by way of gift, in which Mr. Odell of Southampton hath a part, and himself did draw a deed, wherein the land was passed over from the Indians to them, which is contrary to an order made in this Jurisdiction. Against which carriage the court shewed their dislike. But Mr. Wells doth now before the court fully resign up all his interest in that land to the jurisdiction, and will be ready to give a deed to declare it when it shall be demanded of him. Mr. Youngs informed the court that they at Southold had, according to order, purchased a plantation westward from the Southold, about eight miles, of the Indians, which, by the best information they can get, are known to be the right owners of that land, called by the name of *Mattatuck* and *Aquabouke,* and this for the jurisdiction of New-Haven and Connecticut; which purchase comes to in the whole six pounds six shillings; the particulars how it arises, being expressed in the deed, which they desired might be repayd; and accordingly the Treasurer had an order from the court, and did pay it to them. Likewise Lieutenant Budd spoke of another purchase that was made, but did not give full information nor a perfect account thereof."

"At a general court held at New-Haven for the jurisdiction, the 2d of May, 1658, the deputies of Southold propounded the desire of their town to re purchase of the jurisdiction a parcel of land called *Mattatuck* and *Aquabouke,* which the court considering, by vote declared that the paying seven pounds, *in good pay,* the said land is *their's,* which was accepted by the

deputies." And again : " At a general court of the same jurisdiction, held the 25th of May, 1659, Mr. Wakeman acknowledged seven pounds received from the deputies of Southold for
the land re-purchased by them, called Mattatuck and Aquabouke,
but being paid in wampum, Mr. Wells undertook to answer
the damage that he should sustain by it."

Immediately after the reception of the charter granted by
Charles II. to Connecticut, in 1662, and with which New-Haven was now associated, they claimed a complete civil jurisdiction over the English towns upon this island ; and the general court at Hartford took upon themselves the appointing of
all officers in the said towns, not permitted by the charter to be
chosen by the people ; and to make this exercise of authority
the more acceptable, the towns were empowered to elect deputies to represent them in the general court.   This union
with that colony continued till the conquest in 1664, when it
was reluctantly abandoned, but was hastily renewed on the re-
capture of New-York by the Dutch in 1673.   The Dutch governor undertook to reduce them to obedience, but by the interference of Connecticut it was prevented ; and at the restoration of New-York in 1674, several towns were found attached
to Connecticut, and which they were most anxious to continue.
They sent deputies over to solicit their co-operation, and on
the 13th of June, 1674, this town, in conjunction with South
and Easthampton, agreed to petition the king for permission to
remain under the jurisdiction of Connecticut.   But Sir Edmund Andross, the new governor, took effective measures to
oblige them to submit to his authority.

In the year 1649 the Indians in the vicinity, who had been
heretofore friendly, exhibited a hostile disposition, committed
many outrages against this town and Southampton, and even
perpetrated one or more murders.   It was therefore resolved to
keep *watch and ward*, and to apply to New-Haven for assistance and protection.   They were again troublesome in 1657;
but no considerable combination seems to have been entered
into, to interrupt the peace of the settlement.

The individual commissioned by the Governor in 1674 to
demand the return of the town to his authority, was Silvester

Salisbury, afterwards high sheriff of Yorkshire. On his arrival here, he addressed the following notice to the inhabitants of the town, whom he caused to be assembled for the purpose :

"December 10, 1674. Gentlemen—Know yee, that I am empowered by ye Honoured Governor of New-York, to receive the return of this place into the collony of New-Yorke, and the government thereof, pursuant to his Majesty's royall graints to his Royall Highnesse ye Duke of Yorke. Whreupon I doe declare to all, that I doe receive and accept of ye return and surrender of this place from under ye collony of Connecticut, by whose protection they have been secured from ye Dutch invasion, unto the obedience of his Royall Highnesse. As witness my hand at Southold the day and year above sayd.

"SILVESTER SALISBURY."

The charter of Connecticut before mentioned was similar in many of its provisions to the constitution which the people of the province had previously formed for themselves in 1639, before their arrival in the town ; and was therefore little more than a development of the same general principles.

It was the liberal spirit of this charter, and the protection it afforded to civil and religious liberty, which increased the anxiety of the eastern towns to preserve their union with Connecticut. And although Long Island was not expressly named in the charter as a part of the territory included within the jurisdiction of that province, yet the names of some of the magistrates of Southold were inserted among those appointed to administer the government. This circumstance, in addition to a clause in the charter annexing the "islands adjacent" to Connecticut, furnished a very plausible pretext for claiming the jurisdiction over Long Island. It was probably by the consent, if not at the instance of Southold and of South and Easthampton, that Connecticut set up a construction of her charter, which, if it could have been maintained, would have embraced all the English towns, and consequently all the other towns after the conquest, The following proceedings at Hartford relate to this matter :

"At a general court held at Hartford, the 12th of May, 1664, it is declared that they claim Long Island as one of the '*adjacent islands*' expressed in the charter, except a precedent right doth appear, approved by his Majesty." And afterwards again, on the 17th of November, 1674, the inhabitants of Southold being legally convened in town meeting, they resolved as fol-

lows: " We doe unanimously declare and owne that we are at
this present time under the government of his Majesty's colony
of Connecticut, and are desirous so to continue." And on the
arrival of Governor Andross, and after being reluctantly obliged
to submit to his authority, they refused for some time to apply
for or accept a patent of confirmation for their lands. Nor did
they in fact acquiesce until his Excellency threatened to dis-
franchise them, and to treat them as enemies, contumaciously
refusing to acknowledge the authority of their lawful sovereign.
Upon this they consented to receive a patent, and one was accordingly issued on the 31st day of October, 1676, in which
the following persons were named as patentees, to wit: Isaac
Arnold, justice of the peace; Captain John Youngs, Joshua Horton, constable, and Barnabas Horton, Benjamin Youngs, Samuel
Glover, and Jacob Corey, overseers of the poor, for and on behalf
of themselves and their associates, the freeholders and inhabitants
of said town. The lands included in the patent are described as
" bounded on the west to a certain river or creek called the
Wading Creek, in the Indian tongue *Pauquacumsuck,* and to
the eastward by Plum-Gut, together with the islands thereto
belonging; on the north side with the Sound or North Sea;
and on the south with an arm of the sea or river which runneth
up between Southampton land unto a certain creek which
fresh water runneth into, called in English the Red-Creek, by
the Indians *To- Yongs ;* together with the said creek and meadows belonging therewith, so running on a straight line from the
head of the afore-mentioned fresh water, to the head of the small
brook that runneth into the creek called *Pauquacumsuck,* including all the necks of land and islands within the aforesaid
described bounds and limits." On the 27th of December next
following, the patentees by deed, which is duly recorded, released to the town the interest acquired by the patent.

Robin's Island, is situated in Peconic Bay, nearly opposite
the village of Mattetuck; and contains four hundred acres of
land, much of which is covered with timber, and the remainder used for pasture and cultivation. This island was a part
of the lands made choice of by the agent of Lord Stirling for
his own use, and was conveyed, with Shelter Island, to Thomas

Goodyeare, in the year 1641. In the American revolution it was a part of the estate of Major Parker Wickham, which by his attainder was confiscated, and was afterwards purchased of the commissioners of forfeitures by the late Mr. L'Hommedieu, by whose executors it was conveyed to the present owners. More than twenty thousand dollars' worth of wood has been sold off within a few years.

The peninsula of *Oyster-Ponds* is the eastern extremity of the main island, upon the north branch thereof; and connected with it by a narrow sand beach, evidently formed by the action of the sea. Oyster-Ponds is about five miles long and one broad, and is perfectly level, with the exception of a chain of small hills adjoining the Sound. The soil is not surpassed by any upon Long Island, and is equally well cultivated. It is divided into several fine farms, upon which are raised very superior crops of hay and grain. A very considerable quantity of excellent beef, pork, butter and cheese, is annually made here for exportation. This fine tract of land was originally purchased of the natives by Mr. Hallock in 1646, and who subsequently took in with him, as part owners, three others, by the names of Tuthill, Youngs, and Brown. There are rocks here of immense size, some of which have been used for fencing. Indeed, the stones are sufficiently abundant to enclose a great part of the land with wall, divided into fields of convenient size. The principal article which is here relied upon for fertilizing the soil, is the bony fish, of which almost any desirable quantity is easily obtained upon the shores at the proper season. The population of Oyster-Ponds is between five and six hundred, more than half of which is located at the west end, formerly called *Oyster-Pond's Village*, now distinguished by the more classical name of *Orient*. Here are two churches, a post-office, some stores, mechanic shops, and two docks or wharves. Fifteen vessels are owned, principally sloops and small schooners; which are mostly employed in conveying paving stone to New-York, and in the fishing business. It is, on the whole, a very pleasant village, and presents an extensive prospect over the adjoining waters. A little northwest of the village, and between two considerable elevations near the Sound, is an ancient cemetery, filled with graves almost to the very summit of the hills. The stones are mostly of blue slate, common in former times, but now so worn and defaced by time and the elements, that very few of the older epitaphs can be read. The singular and very secluded situation of this place of sepulture, gives to it an appearance which cannot fail to excite the most intense interest in the visiter. Many of the inscriptions are more than one hundred and seventy years old, and so peculiar for their quaintness and a sort of saintly humor, as to be almost ludicrous. The two following, of a more recent period, are given as fair samples of many others; one of which having no date, is of itself a singular circumstance :

" In memory of
Michal, wife of Nath'l. Tuthill,
  who died Feb. 15, 1756.
Beneath this little stone
Does my beloved lie, '
O pity, pity me, whoever passeth by ;
And spend a tear at least,
Or else a tear let fall, on my
Sweet blooming rose, whom
God so soon did call."

" Here lyes Elizabeth, once
  Samuel Beebee's wife,
who once was made a living soul,
But now's deprived of life.
Yet firmly did believe, that at
the Lord's return; she should be
Made a living soul, in his own
shape and form—Liv'd 4 and thirty
years a wife, Died in her 57,
Has now lay'd down her mortal
soul, in hopes to live in Heaven."

Upon the eastern part of Oyster-Ponds, is the large and splendid hotel and boarding establishment of Jonathan F. Latham, which, for the beauty of its location and extent of accommodations, will not suffer materially by comparison with those at Coney Island and Rockaway. This retreat is much resorted to by strangers during the warm season, for the benefit of pure air and sea-bathing. Near the hotel are still visible the remains of a fort, erected during the revolution by a party of American soldiers, under the command of Col. Henry B. Livingston, for the purpose of preventing the landing of the British troops upon this part of the island.

Nearly a mile easterly of Oyster-Pond Point is Plumb Island, about three miles in length, and containing eight hundred acres of land, between which and the Point is Plumb-Gut, uniting the waters of the Sound and Gardiner's Bay. The population is about seventy-five, and most of the island is

owned by Mr. Jerome, who resides upon it. It was purchased
from the Corchoug tribe in 1667 by Samuel Wyllys of Hartford,
for one barrel of biscuit, one hundred muxes, and a few fish-
hooks; and afterwards became the property of Joseph Beebee of
Plymouth. The surface is rocky and uneven, the soil of a moderate quality, and its shores abounding with fish. It was once
called the *Isle of Patmos*. On the west side, the United
States have erected a light-house. Here was formerly a large
rock, so exactly poised upon another still larger, as to present
quite a natural curiosity. During the revolution some British
soldiers attempted to dislodge it, for the mere pleasure of
seeing it roll into the abyss below, but were unsucessful. In
1814 a few of Commodore Hardy's sailors were more fortunate, and moved from its ancient resting-place this huge
mass of granite, which had hitherto rested undisturbed since
the creation. A few miles north-east from Plumb Island, in that
part of the Sound which, on account of the swiftness of the current, is called the *Race*, are situated the Great and Little Gull
Islands. These must long since have disappeared but from
their being composed of solid rock. The larger island contains
about fifteen acres, and the other only one. Upon the latter
a light-house was erected some years since, more important to
mariners than almost any other upon the coast, this being the
principal entrance from the ocean into the Sound. The wasting effects of the waves have made it necessary to protect the
works by a sea-wall, which consumed in its construction more
than twenty-five thousand tons of stone, brought from the Connecticut shore. The scene presented here during an easterly
storm is not only sublime, but terrific; and the heavy surf
breaking upon the shore, shakes the very foundations of the
buildings, and threatens to overwhelm the whole island with
its mountain waves. To the north-east of these islands,
and between them and the main land of New England, lies
another island belonging to this town, called Fisher's Island,
which is larger than either of those before mentioned, and of
greater value.

Fisher's Island lies about six miles north-east of the Gull
Islands, is four from Stonington, and nine from New London. It

was originally called Vissher's Island, and was so named by Captain Adrian Block, who, as De Lact says, "in the year 1614 built a yatch (at New Amsterdam), with which he sailed through the Hellegat into the Great Bay (the Sound), and visited all the places thereabout, and went as far as Cape Cod." He named Block Island after himself, and probably this island after the name of some one of his companions. It is nearly nine miles long, and of a medial width of one mile ; containing about four thousand acres. The surface is undulating, and sometimes hilly ; the shores irregular, with two convenient harbors, called east and west harbors, the latter of which is of the most importance. *Mount Prospect*, near the west end of the island, is a high sand-bluff; and near the middle of the island is another, still higher, which overlooks the adjacent country, and may be seen a good distance beyond Montauk Point. Some parts of the island are rocky, and there are many large single rocks upon the surface. The salt meadows are extensive, and a few of the swamps afford an excellent peat, which is much used for fuel. There are some tracts of level land, and the pasture fields are both large and well watered by never-failing ponds ; one of which, near the centre of the island, occupies between forty and fifty acres of ground. A greater portion of the soil is appropriated for grazing, and is capable of sustaining three thousand sheep, three hundred neat cattle, and other kinds of stock in proportion. A smaller amount of stock is now kept ; the raising of English hay being considered more profitable. The staple articles raised here are wool, (of the Saxony and merino breeds,) butter and cheese. The beef and mutton made here are of superior quality and flavor. The base of one of the hills is a fine clay, of which great quantities of bricks have been burned. There are forty-five persons of all ages upon the island employed in the business of the farms, dairy, &c. This island has been in the Winthrop family from the first purchase by John Winthrop, governor of Connecticut, son of John Winthrop first governor of Massachusetts. The purchase was made in 1644. The wife of Mr. Winthrop was the daughter of the celebrated Hugh Peters, who was executed in London, on the 16th of October, 1660. Mr. Winthrop was a man of fine natural genius, and greatly improved by education and study. He was chosen governor of Connecticut in 1657, and again in 1659, which office he retained till his death, April 5th, 1676. A patent of confirmation was granted to him by Governor Nichols, on the 28th of March, 1668, by the terms of which the island was declared "to be reputed, taken and held an entire enfranchised township, manor and place of itself; and to have, hold, and enjoy equal privileges and immunities with any town, enfranchised place or manor, within the government of New-York; and to be in no wise subordinate or belonging unto or dependent upon, any riding, township, place, or jurisdiction whatever." In the year 1680 the government of Connecticut laid claim to this island as being within their jurisdiction; in consequence whereof his excellency, Governor Andross, addressed the following spirited and laconic epistle to the Hon. William Leet, Governor of Connecticut:

"Honble Sr.—Being advised by an order or warrant from yourself and some assistants sent to ffisher's Island, I am much surprised att your Intrenching upon his Maties Letters Patents to his Royal Highness, as well as the Grant by Govenour Nicolls to the Honoble. John Winthrop, Esq. (late Governor of Connecticut) for sd Island; which Island and Grant it is my Duty to Assert, as much as this or any other part of the Govermt; And therefore desire that you will, without delay, recall sd warrant or order, and forbear any the like proceedings for the future, to prevent great Inconveniencys; and remaine your Effectionate neighbour and Humble Servant,   E. ANDROSS."

"To the Honble William Leet, Esqr. Gover-
r.our of his Maties colony of Connecticut."

On the death of Mr. Winthrop in 1676, the island descended to his son, John Fitz Winthrop, who was likewise governor of Connecticut from 1698 to his death, November 27, 1707. At his decease, without issue, the island passed to his nephew John Winthrop, son of his brother Wait Still Winthrop, and thence to *his* son, Francis Bayard Winthrop, whose death took place in 1817. He devised the island to his four sons, John Still Winthrop, Francis Bayard Winthrop, William H. Winthrop, and Thomas C. Winthrop. William H. Winthrop having purchased the interest of his co-tenants, is now sole owner of this valuable estate. From papers in the possession of this gentleman, it appears that an attempt was made by one of his ancestors, in the year 1712, to transport a pair of *moose deer*

32

from this island to England, as a present to Queen Anne, which failed by the death of one, and the other breaking its leg ; and her majesty was finally presented with the *horns* only.

There are twelve churches, Presbyterian, Baptist, Methodist, and Universalist, within the limits of this town, the most of which have been recently erected. The first church, and of the Presbyterian order, was built in 1642, and was succeeded by another in 1684, which remained till 1803, when the present church was erected in its place.

The *first* minister was the Rev. John Youngs, who was also one of the first settlers of the town. He had been a preacher at Hingham, England ; and came to New-Haven in 1638, from whence he removed with a part of the members of his church to this town in 1640, where he continued till his death in 1672. His posterity are numerous, and many of them are now residents of this and the neighboring towns. His eldest son, Col. John Youngs, was appointed under the authority of Connecticut (after the reception of their charter in 1662) a judge, for the towns of Long Island subject to their jurisdiction. And in 1681 he was created high sheriff of Yorkshire, (including the whole of Long Island ;) which office he held for several years. He was in all respects a highly intelligent and respectable individual. His death occurred in 1698. His son Benjamin, and grandson Joshua, were successively judges of the county. The Rev. Daniel Youngs, another descendant of the Rev. John Youngs, was the third minister of Brookhaven, where he died in 1753.

The *second* minister of this town was the Rev. Joshua Hobart, son to the Rev. Peter Hobart, who died at Hingham, Massachusetts, January 20, 1679. Three of his brothers were likewise clergymen. One of them, the Rev. Nehemiah Hobart, was father of the Rev. Noah Hobart of Fairfield, Connecticut, and grandfather of the Hon. John Sloss Hobart, forme rjudge of the supreme court of this state. The Rev. Joshua Hobart was born at Hingham in 1628, and graduated at Harvard College in 1650. His settlement took place in 1674, and his death in 1717. His brother, Jeremiah Hobart, was the second minister of Hempstead.

The *third* minister of the town was the Rev. Benjamin Woolsey, born in 1687, and graduated at Yale College in 1709. He settled here in 1720, and in 1736 removed to Dor-oris in Queen's County, where he died in 1750. His sons were Melancton and Benjamin, of whom more particular notice will be taken hereafter.

The *fourth* minister was the Rev. James Davenport, son of the Rev. John Davenport of Stamford, and grandson of the celebrated John Davenport who came from England with Governor Eaton in 1637, and was the first minister of New-Haven. Mr. Davenport was born at Stamford in 1710, and graduated at Yale College in 1732. He settled in this town in 1738. A few years after he began to entertain new views of religion, and became a wild and visionary enthusiast. He travelled much about the country, and his extraordinary discourses were listened to by thousands. He finally became so troublesome, that in 1742 the general assembly of Connecticut, requested the governor and council to have him transported out of that colony. He eventually recovered from this state of mental delusion, and published to the world a confession of his errors. He removed from this town in 1746, and died at Freehold, New Jersey, in August, 1755. His brother, Abraham Davenport, was a colonel and judge in Connecticut, and died at Stamford in 1789. His son John, born at Freehold in 1752, became the minister of Deerfield, New Jersey, and died July 13, 1821, at Lysander in this state.

The *fifth* minister of this town was the Rev. William Throop, who graduated at Yale College in 1743, settled here in 1748, where he died in 1756; and was succeeded by the Rev. John Storrs. Mr. Storrs graduated at Yale College in 1756, was settled here in 1763, and again removed in 1787. The next minister was the Rev. Joseph Hazard. His settlement took place in 1797. He removed in 1808, and subsequently died at Brooklyn, where he left an only daughter. The Rev. Zachariah Greene was settled in the parish of Cutchogue in 1786, and removed to Brookhaven in 1797, where he still resides. The Rev. Jonathan Huntington, one of the present ministers of this town, is a great-grandson of the Rev. Nathaniel

Hunting, second minister of Easthampton. He graduated at Yale College at 1804, was settled here in 1807, and is much esteemed for his many amiable qualities.

For some years after the conquest, the county courts were held occasionally in this town, and a prison for the county was ordered by the court of sessions to be prepared here *for the punishment and safe keeping of prisoners.* The following, from the town records, relates to this subject : " Southold, December 15, 1684, there was chosen by vote at town meeting, Samuel Youngs and Thomas Clarke, both carpenters, to view and appraise the old meeting-house in order to make a county prison of said house, and upon their return they give in, they valued the body of the house at thirty-five pounds·" On the sixth of April, 1725, a new jail having been erected at Riverhead, it was resolved at town meeting that the prison-house should be sold by the overseers *if they could get what it was worth.*

The village of Greenport, which was commenced by a few spirited individuals in 1827, is already the largest and most prosperous village in the town, and bids fair to become a place of much commercial importance. It is very conveniently as well as advantageously situated at the head of what is called Southold Harbor, a part of the great Peconic Bay, twenty-three miles east of the court-house. It was at first laid out into streets and building lots in a regular manner, and now contains about one hundred dwellings and six hundred inhabitants. A large and convenient hotel has been erected, two churches, and a school-house ; besides wharves and railways for the accommodation of vessels, the water being of sufficient depth for the largest ships, well sheltered from storms, and rarely, if ever, obstructed with ice. Several brigs, schooners, and smaller vessels are owned here, employed in the coasting trade, besides five other vessels, amounting in the aggregate to two thousand tons, successfully engaged in the South Atlantic whaling business. That this highly privileged spot is destined to make still more extraordinary advances in population and trade there can be no reason to doubt ; and should the Long Island rail-road reach its intended destination at this place, it will

become, in many respects, an important out-port of the commercial metropolis of the Union. Cutchogue and Mattatuc are
thinly settled vicinages ; and the people, as is the case of the inhabitants of this town in general, are agriculturists, and among
the most prosperous in the county. Fish is very commonly
used as manure, and has produced most extraordinary results
to the farming interest of the town.

The Presbyterian church at Mattatuc was built in 1697, and
rebuilt in 1830. The one in Southold parish was erected in
1805, and that at Franklinville in 1830. At the latter place
is a neat academy, completed in 1832. The Methodist church
at Cutchogue was built in 1829 ; and the Universalist church
in Southold parish, in 1835. There are several fine necks of
land upon the south side of the town, the most important of
which are Great and Little Hog-Neck. The former contains
some hundreds of acres divided into a number of farms. The
soil of the town may be denominated a sandy loam ; the surface level, except on the north, which is stony, rough, and hilly.
The shore on this side is irregular, and there are some considerable necks or points which project into the Sound, particularly Horton's, Rocky, and Duck Pond Points, and constitute
separate farms.

On a grave-stone of one of the first emigrants to this town
is the following inscription :

> " Here Lyeth Buried HE Body of Mr. Barnabas Horton.
> Born at Mousley, in Lestershire, in Old England ; and died
> at Southold HE 13th day of July, 1680, aged 80 years."
> " Here sleeps my body, tombed in the dust,
> " Till Christ shall come and raise it with the just."

> *Another.*

> " HERE LYETH THE BODY OF CAPTAIN JOHN CONKELYNE, BORN
> IN NOTTINGHAMSHIRE IN ENGLAND, WHO DEPARTED THIS LIFE
> THE SIXTH DAY OF APRIL, AT SOUTHOLD, ON LONG ISLAND, IN
> THE SIXTY-FOURTH YEAR OF HIS AGE." ANNO DOMINI. 1694."

The names of Horton, Youngs, and Conkling, which were
among the first settlers of the town, are still the most numerous.
In the year 1670 Jasper Griffing, a native of Wales, settled
here, where he died, April 17, 1718, leaving three sons, Jasper,
John and Robert. The first settled at Lyme, the second at

Riverhead, and the third remained here.   The late Rev. Edward Griffing, of Newark, and George Griffing, Esq. of New-York, are descendants of the last-named Jasper Griffing.

The Hon. Ezra L'Hommedieu, was a native of this town. His grandfather Benjamin was born at La Rochelle, in France, and was one of the persecuted Hugonots, who, on the repeal of the edict of Nantz, fled to Holland, from whence he came to America in 1686.   In 1690 he settled in this town, and soon after married a daughter of Nathaniel Sylvester of Shelter Island, by whom he had two sons, *Benjamin* and *Sylvester*. The latter was the father of the late Samuel L'Hommedieu, Esq. of Sagg Harbor.   Benjamin married Martha, daughter of Ezra Bourne of Sandwich, Massachusetts, June 4th, 1731, and died September 17, 1755.   Their son, Ezra L'Hommedieu, was born here August 30, 1734, and graduated at Yale College in 1654.   His first wife was Charity, daughter of Nicoll Floyd of Brookhaven, and sister of General William Floyd, whom he married December 24, 1756.   She died July 31, 1785, and on the 15th of June, 1803, he married for his second wife, Catharine, daughter of Nicoll Havens of Shelter Island, by whom he had a daughter, afterwards the wife of Samuel S. Gardiner, a respectable member of the New-York bar.   Mr. L'Hommedieu was educated a lawyer, and became eminent in his profession. He was early called into the public councils of the state, and for a period of forty years without intermission his name is found associated with the prominent patriots and legislators of the state and Union.   He was elected to congress in 1779, and was a member of several succeeding congresses previous to the adoption of the federal constitution in 1788.   From this time till a short period before his death, he was almost constantly in the senate of this state.   He was appointed clerk of the county of Suffolk in 1784, and retained the office for twenty-six years. He was fond of agricultural pursuits, and both by his example and writings did much to advance the science and practice among his fellow-citizens.   His death took place the 27th of September, 1811, in the 78th year of his age, leaving behind him an exalted reputation for intelligence and private worth.

Thomas S. Lester was born in this town in 1781, and after receiving a good common education, commenced the study of the law under the direction of Mr. L'Hommedieu, by whom he was patronized and assisted, and to whose professional practice he succeeded in 1805. He held for some time the office of district attorney, and was several times elected to represent the county of Suffolk in the assembly. In short, he was an active and highly useful man; and his premature death, at the age of thirty-six, on the 13th of September, 1817, was universally regretted by his friends and the public.

JOHN WICKHAM, an eminent lawyer of Virginia, whose death took place at Richmond on the 17th of January, 1839, was also a native of this town, a son of John Wickham, a respectable farmer. He left here in early life, and established himself in the practice of the law at Richmond, where he acquired a high reputation and amassed a large fortune.

ZACHEUS GOLDSMITH was born here on the 8th of May, 1766. He very early manifested a strong disposition for the acquisition of knowledge, and was enabled, by his application and industry, to supply in a great measure, the want of a liberal education. He read with avidity every thing that came in his way, and by dint of a retentive memory became possessed of a large fund of general information. His acquaintance with history, for which he had a peculiar relish, was extensive and accurate; and a desire to become familiar with the geography of his own country, and to witness her extent and resources, led him, while a young man, to travel over the western territory of the United States, when it was for the most part a wilderness, and attended by dangers sufficient to intimidate the most resolute adventurer. He traversed much of the same country again at an after-period, when it had become the theatre of civilization and improvement; and had the satisfaction, as he expressed it, of seeing the wilderness blossom like the rose, and the desert rejoicing in the existence of towns, villages, and cities, with all the animated accompaniments of trade and commerce. Mr. Goldsmith was the advocate of liberty and equal rights, and wished for the gradual abolition of slavery in all the states. His temper was mild and conciliatory; and it was rare that any thing was able to disturb his equanimity or provoke his resentment. His conduct was most exemplary, and worthy the imitation of others. He died in the seventieth year of his age, on the 8th of April, 1835.

TOWN OF RIVERHEAD.

This town is bounded easterly by Southold, southerly by Southampton, westerly by Brookhaven, and northerly by Long Island Sound. It was formerly embraced within the limits of Southold, which originally extended from the eastern boundary of Brookhaven to Oyster-Pond Point, and remained so till the passage of the act of the 13th of March, 1792, by which it was set off from Southold, and organized as a separate town, deriving its name from that of the principal settlement at the head of Peconic Bay or River, where the same is navigable for very small vessels only. The first town meeting was held here the 7th of April, 1792, when the following named persons were elected town officers, to wit: David Wells, supervisor: Josiah Reeve, town-clerk; John C. Terry, Joseph Wells, and Benjamin Petty, assessors; Jeremiah Wells, and Spencer Dayton, commissioners of highways; Daniel Terry, Zachariah Hallock, and David Edwards, overseers of the poor; and Syranus Brown, collector. Only a comparatively small portion of the lands of this town is under improvement, and much of the remainder, from the natural sterility of the soil, is incapable of profitable cultivation. Much of the territory is covered with wood, and this article has long been a staple for transportation. In the southern section of the town the surface is level, the soil light and sandy, and the timber chiefly pine: while toward the Sound the surface is rough and hilly, the soil loamy, and oak timber more generally prevails. The hills on the north are a part of the spine or ridge of the island, and the cliffs near the shore are high and precipitous.

There are two considerable streams in the town, one upon its western border, called the Wading River, or Brook, and by the Indians Pauquacumsuck, which, commencing in the south part of the town, discharges itself into a salt creek setting up from the Sound; and the other called the Peconic River, which has its origin in the eastern part of Brookhaven, runs easterly to, and terminates in Peconic Bay. Upon the latter stream are several mills and manufactories, which have been in active operation for many years, and the quantity of water is supposed sufficient to propel double the machinery yet erected upon it. Many plans have been in agitation to improve the navigation of this stream. and among other measures for the accomplishment of the purpose, a company was incorporated on the 10th of March, 1835, with a capital of ten thousand dollars, to make a sloop channel from the head of navigation in Peconic River. up to the dam or bridge at the village of Riverhead ; and which, if carried into effect, as is confidently expected, the value of property in the neighborhood will be greatly enhanced, population essentially increased, and business of every description experience fresh inspiration. Capital and enterprize only, are required, in addition to the advantages afforded by nature, to make this place the theatre of a variety of useful manufacturing establishments. The recent improvements in the village of Riverhead, as well as those of James-Port, two miles east, are satisfactory indications of what may, in a surprisingly short period, be accomplished by the union of energy and industry.

The county buildings are located in this village, and the courts have been held here, uninterruptedly, for more than a century. Instead of a few mean and scattered dwellings as formerly, it now contains a handsome collection of well-built houses, stores, and mechanic shops. The court-house, standing in the midst as a faithful sentinel, to watch over the peace and welfare of the inhabitants, while the cross-barred windows of the jail frown indignant upon all violations of the laws. Here is a Congregational. a Methodist, and a New Jerusalem church, several stores, two hotels, a drug-shop, grist-mill, saw-mill, fulling-mill, and a due proportion of mechanics and artisans. A handsome female academy was erected in 1835, and has been thus far well patronized. The following observations, in relation to this part of the country, are contained in the late President Dwight's journal of his travels through Long Island in the year 1804:—"Riverhead (says he) is the shire town of this county. The court-house, a poor decayed building, and a mi-

serable hamlet, containing about ten or twelve houses, stand near
the efflux of the river. From this account of the court-house,
it will naturally be expected that the business of lawyers and
sheriffs is not here in very great demand, nor in very high reputation. The suspicion is certainly well-founded. The county court, or court of common pleas, sits here twice a-year ; as-
sembles on Tuesday, and, after having finished its whole business, adjourns almost always on the succeeding day. No
lawyer, if I am not misinformed, has hitherto ever been able to
get a living in the county of Suffolk. I entertain a very respectful opinion of the gentlemen of the bar, but all will agree
with me in saying, that this exemption from litigation, while it
is a peculiar, is also a very honorable characteristic of this
county. Not far from this hamlet is a spot of ground, about
three miles in diameter, which, as I was informed by good authority, is covered with shrub oaks and pines not more than
five or six feet in height. In the whole tract there is not a single tree of the usual size, although it is surrounded by a forest
of such trees. The cause of this phenomenon, in a place where
the soil is substantially the same with that of the neighboring
country, is not easy to assign." Were the venerable president
now alive, and to travel over the same ground, he would have
the satisfaction of seeing a pretty decent-looking court-house,
something more than *a miserable hamlet*, and a very respectable population of steady, industrious citizens. He would find,
too, that even in the county of Suffolk the annual crop of litigation is considerable ; that there are about one dozen lawyers
living in the county, two of whom are located in this village,
and most of them at least getting a tolerable living by their
professions alone. But times are materially changed in thirty
years, and improvement is now the order of the day.

The villages of Aquabogue and Upper Aquabogue, Fresh
Ponds, Baiting-Hollows, and Wading-River, are considerable
vicinages, with churches and school-houses in each. A few
miles west of the village of Riverhead, and upon the Peconic
stream, there was some years since a manufactory of bar-iron,
conducted by Solomon Townsend, now deceased, which was
discontinued at his death. During the late war with Great

Britain, a number of vessels, owned here, and employed in carrying wood to different places, were captured by the enemy, and either burned, or suffered to be redeemed by their owners at exorbitant prices. The people, finally, determined, should a fit opportunity offer, to retaliate upon these marauders of their property; and accordingly, in the summer of 1814, an occurrence took place, that reflects much credit upon the courage and activity of the inhabitants, the facts and circumstances of which are thus related in the newspapers of that period, as contained in a communication from Capt. John Wells to Col. Jeremiah Moore:

"Riverhead, June 1, 1814. Sir,—I have the honor to inform you that a battle was fought here yesterday, about eleven o'clock in the forenoon, between a few of the militia of your regiment and double their number of the enemy, which terminated in the total defeat of the latter. About ten o'clock in the forenoon, an alarm was given that two large barges were standing for our shore from the British squadron, then lying six or seven miles out in 'the Sound. About thirty militia of Captain Terry's, Reeve's, and my company, collected before they reached the shore. The enemy advanced with two large barges, containing about twenty-five or thirty men each, within musket-shot of the shore; when they saluted us with their cannon and a volley of musquetry, and then gave three cheers, and proceeded to the sloop *Nancy*, lying on the beach. As they were on the eve of boarding her, we opened a destructive and well-directed fire upon both the barges, which silenced their fire, and stopped their oars in an instant. They were so slow in wearing the barges and rowing off, that we had several fires into them before they could get out of musket shot. I am happy to say that the men fought well, without a symptom of fear; neither was a man wounded among us. But from what we saw, we have reason to believe that many of the enemy were killed and wounded. We made immediate preparations for another engagement, thinking they might send a large reinforcement, which we should have been happy to have met, as *we* received a reinforcement shortly after the engagement, who found they were too late to take part in the affair. The officers present were Captain John Terry, myself, Usher H. Moore, and Ensign James Fanning. Your's respectfully,
"To Lieutenant-Colonel Jeremiah Moore. JOHN WELLS, Captain."

JOHN CLEVES SYMMES was born in this town in 1740, and removed, early in life, to New Jersey, where he was allied in marriage with Susannah, daughter of William Livingston, afterwards governor of that state. She was sister to the late Hon. Brockholst Livingston, and to Sarah, wife of Governor Jay. Mr. Symmes was well known for his enterprising spirit, the flattering prospects he once had in view, and for his extraordinary reverse of fortune. In February, 1777, he was made an associate judge of the supreme court of New Jersey, and in the year 1787 he made a successful application to the general government to purchase a tract of land, immediately north of the Ohio, and between the Miami rivers. A bargain was concluded with the commissioners of the board of treasury, for a tract which it was expected would contain a million of acres, but was found to embrace less than six hundred thousand. Of this he made payment for no more than two hundred and forty-eight thousand. In 1794 he received a patent from President Washington for three hundred and eleven thousand six hundred acres, the residue being reserved in pursuance of sundry acts of congress. Judge Symmes removed to the North-west Territory in 1789, and was appointed one of the district judges of the United States, having previously been a representative in congress. Under his direction, Major Stites and twenty-five emigrants from New Jersey made a settlement at Columbia, six miles from Cincinnati, at which latter place he died in February, 1814. A large and respectable procession attended his remains from the residence of his son-in-law, General William H. Harrison, to a principal landing-place on the Ohio river, where military honors were performed by the infantry company commanded by Capt. M'Farland. The body was then taken in a barge to North-Bend, and interred on the spot which Judge Symmes had previously selected. His daughter, Mrs. Harrison, was educated at Easthampton ; and by many who knew her, is esteemed a lady of great personal and mental accomplishments.

JOHN CLEVES SYMMES, jr., son of Daniel Symmes of this town, and nephew of the judge, was also born here. He was adopted as well as educated by his uncle, and accompanied him to the west. During the late war he was a captain in the army, and distinguished himself by his intrepidity upon the Niagara frontier. His death took place at Hamilton, Butler county, Ohio, June 19, 1829. He was an amiable man, and had a mind much imbued with science. He was also projector of a new theory of the earth, upon which he delivered lectures in many places, and gained some disciples among scientific men. He believed this earth to be a hollow

sphere, open at the poles ; that it had within it several other con
centric hollow spheres, open also at their poles; and that it was
possible to pass from one pole to the other through the centre
of the earth. This novel conjecture met with so little success,
that the author became dejected : a morbid melancholy took
possession of his mind, and hastened his death in the meridian
of life.

HULL OSBORN, an attorney and counsellor at law, a gentleman highly esteemed for his strict integrity and inoffensive
manners, was a native of Southold, where he was born in 1771,
and was for many years a resident of this town. He died at
Westhampton, December 25, 1834. He possessed little talent
as a public speaker, but was well read in the science of jurisprudence, and was greatly useful in the community by his professional acquirements. He retired in a great measure from
the practice of the law, and assumed the vocation of a farmer
for several years before his death.

TOWN OF BROOKHAVEN.

This town embraces the whole width of the island, and
includes more territory than any other in the county. It is
bounded—north by the Sound, east by the towns of Riverhead
and Southampton, south by the Atlantic Ocean, and west by
the towns of Islip and Smithtown ; containing an area of more
than one hundred and three thousand acres, of which only
about thirty-five thousand are improved. The south beach,
opposite the town of Islip, also belongs to this town. The territory upon the south side of the town was purchased from the
Sachem and chief men of the Patchogue tribe ; and that upon
the north side, from those of the Seatalcot tribe. The first
settlement in the town was commenced at Setauket in the
year 1655, which occasioned the town to be so denominated.
How it acquired the name of Brookhaven, is conjectured from
the fact of its having within its limits a number of considerable streams, the most of which afford at present sufficient
water-power for propelling machinery for grinding grain, and
for other purposes. The original planters were Presbyterians

and well-educated men, who possessed a competent knowledge
of the laws and constitution of England, and brought with them
the true spirit of freedom and independence.   The persecuting
temper of Charles I., aided by the infamous proceedings of the
Star-Chamber and the High-Commission Court, were the
means of driving many from their native country, to seek an
asylum in some distant quarter of the world.   Hence the immense immigrations to every part of the United States in the
seventeenth century.   The number of persons who first came
to Setauket in 1655 is not exactly known, but the names of
those who composed the settlement in the course of two years
thereafter, are as follows:

Richard Wooodhull	Edward Avery	Richard Waring
Zachariah Hawkins	John Smith	Thomas Thorp
Peter Whitehaire	Samuel Dayton	Richard Bryant
John Jenners	John Davis	Samuel Eburne
Henry Perring	William Frost	Timothy Brewster
Andrew Gibb	John Thomas	John Brewster
William Satterly	Elias Baylis	Daniel Brewster
Thomas Biggs	John Thomson	William Poole
John Tooker	Thomas Ward	Thomas Sharpe
Henry Rogers	John Roe	George Phillips
William Fancy	John Budd	Thomas Smith
Jacob Longbotham	Henry Brooks	Moses Burnet
Daniel Lane	William Williams	Richard Smith
Richard Floyd	Robert Woolley	Thomas Helme
Francis Muncy	Samuel Akerly	Joshua Garlick
Obed Seward	Arthur Smith	John Moger
John Wade	Joseph Combs	Robert Akerly.
William Salyer	Richard Waring	
Robert Smith	Joseph Mapes	

Most of these persons, if not the whole, came directly from
Boston and its neighborhood, and agreed to form an independent settlement or community upon this part of the island.   The
lands were purchased at different times as the number of inhabitants increased and their necessities seemed to require.
Purchases were sometimes made by individuals for their own
use, with the consent of the proprietors of the town, whose number never exceeded fifty-five.   The civil affairs of the settlement were conducted by magistrates elected from among themselves, and by rules and ordinances adopted in the primary
assemblies of the people.   After the conquest of New-York,

and on the 7th of March, 1666, a patent of confirmation for their purchases of the natives, was obtained from Governor Nicholls, by which he fully ratified, confirmed, and granted to Captain John Tucker, Mr. Daniel Lane, Mr. Richard Woodhull, Henry Perring, and John Jenner, for themselves and their associates, " all that tract of land, which, (says the patent,) hath already been, or that hereafter shall be, purchased for and in behalf of the said town, whether from native Indian proprietors or others, within the bounds and limits hereafter set forth and expressed, (viz.) that is to say, the west bounds to begin at the line run by the inhabitants of said town between them and Mr. Smith's land of Nissequake, as in his patent is set forth, and to go east to the head of the Wading River or Red Creek ; from whence, as also from their west bounds, to stretch north to the Sound and south to the sea or main ocean ; all which said tract of land within the bounds and limits aforefaid, and all or any plantations thereupon, from henceforth are to belong and appertain to the said town ; together with all havens, harbors, creeks, quarries, woodlands, meadows, pastures, marshes, waters, rivers, lakes, fishing, hunting, hawking, and fowling, and all other profits, commodities, emolument, and hereditaments, to the said land and premises within the limits and bounds aforementioned described, belonging, or in any wise appertaining."

The first most important entry upon the town books, is a copy of the conveyance from Wyandanch, the Montauk Sachem, (and sometimes styled the Grand Sachem of Paumanake, or Long Island,) to Richard Woodhull and *the rest of his neighbors,* for two necks of meadow land upon the south side of the island ; the consideration for which is stated to be twenty coats, twenty hoes, twenty hatchets, forty needles, forty muxes, ten pounds of powder, ten pounds of lead, six pair of stockings, six shirts, one trooper's coat, made of good cloth, twenty knives, and one gun.

"*At a town meeting, February 2d,* 1671, it was voted and agreed that the constable and overseers is to send a letter to Captain Nicolls, for his coming down about the purchasing of the south meadows, and to give him encouragement by granting him an allotment at the south, as others have, for a gratification." This is supposed to refer to Mathias Nicolls, who was secretary to the first English governor, and a lawyer of much consideration; as was the case with his son, William Nicholls, who, many years after, settled at Islip.

"*At a town meeting, November* 17, 1671, it was voted and agreed upon, that there shall be a village at the Wading River, or thereabouts, of eight families, or eight men, to have accommodation as the place will afford."

On the nineteenth day of November, 1675, a conveyance was procured from the Setauket Sachem, and signed by him, together with a few other Indian chiefs of that tribe, for the purpose of confirming former grants, and for other lands within the limits therein mentioned not before fully described. This instrument is not only a very curious document, but is otherwise of sufficient importance to be preserved in the history of the town. It is in the words following:

" Know all men by these presents, that I, Gie of Setauket, Sachem, now living in Setauket in the east-riding of Yorkshire, with all my associates that have been the native proprietors of all the lands of Setauket, doth fully and absolutely ratify and confirm unto the patentees and their associates of Brookhaven, else Setauket, all those parcels of land that have been bought of any of us or our ancestors, that is to say, from the west line that runs from Stoney Brook to the North Sea, and south to the middle of the island, and so to extend to the Wading River or Red Brook, and to the middle of the island south, and so to the North Sea or Sound. I say, I Gie doth for myself and my associates, or any that have any thing to do with any part or parcel of land within the line above-mentioned, of all that the inhabitants have purchased, doth for ourselves, our heirs and assigns, ratify and confirm unto the inhabitants of Setauket, to them, their heirs, executors, administrators, and assigns, with all the uplands, meadows, timber-trees, with all harbors, creeks, ponds, and fishing, fowling, hunting. with all and singular privileges, appurtenances, profits, that any way do or shall belong unto the said tract of land above-mentioned, to have and to hold. And what part or parcels of land that is within the aforesaid bounds, that is to say, from the west line of Stoney Brook to the east line of Wading River, and from thence to the middle of the island south, and to the Sound north, that is yet unpurchased, I Gie, Setauket Sachem, myself and my co-partners and associates, doth fully give unto Mr. Richard Woodhull whatsoever uplands or meadows that we apprehend is unbought by the inhabitants of Setauket, I say for some causes and considerations us moving, doth fully and absolutely give unto Mr. Richard Woodhull, sen., all the uplands and meadows, timber-trees, with all and singular privileges and appurtenances, profits whatsoever, from us, our heirs, or any that shall come after us, to him the said Richard Woodhull, to whom he shall dispose it, to him, them, and their heirs for ever, to have and to hold without let or molestation, and to the full and absolute confirmation of all the above-said premises, and every part of them we do hereunto set our hands and seal, this 19th day of November, 1675.

"Signed, sealed, and delivered   Gie Sachem, L. S.
in the presence of us,   Martuse, L. S.
        Robert Phillipson,   John Mahue, L. S.
        Richard Mann.   Massecarge, L. S.
                          Ochedouse, L. S."

Mr. Woodhull, in a few days thereafter, released to the inhabitants of Brookhaven the interest acquired by the said purchase, as follows:

" To all Christian people whom this may concern. Know Ye, That I, Richard Woodhull, living in Brookhaven else Setauket, in the east riding of Yorkshire, for some valuable causes and considerations, doth assign, freely give, and make over to the inhabitants of Brookhaven, all my right and interest that is given me by Setauket Indians, that is to say, both land and meadows, timber trees, or whatsoever is expressed in the above said confirmation and bill of Gie, I say I, Richard Woodhull, for myself, my heirs, executors, administrators and assigns, have freely given and make over all that right and title given to me by the Indians, to the inhabitants of Brookhaven, else Setauket, to them, their heirs, executors, administrators, and assigns, to have and to hold, and to the true confirmation of the same, I do hereunto set my hand this 23d of November, 1675.

" RICHARD WOODHULL, L. S."

" Signed, sealed, and delivered
in the presence of us,
     Robert Phillipson,
     Richard Howell."

" *At a town meeting, December* 18, 1685, it was voted and agreed that Mr. Samuel Eburne shall go to Yorke, to confer with the governor about our lands within our patent; and to get a new patent, and that the town is willing to find the governor twenty sheep for a present forthwith; and that Mr. Samuel Eburne shall follow his private instruction, and not go beyond it, and that Mr. Thomas Helme shall write a petition for the town to the governor."

In pursuance of this application, a patent was issued, including all former grants, on the 27th of December, 1686, by Governor Dongan, to John Palmer, Richard Woodhull, Samuel Eburne, Andrew Gibb, William Satterly, Thomas Jenner, and Thomas Helme, trustees of the freeholders and commonalty of the town of Brookhaven, and their successors, to the use and behoof of the freeholders or inhabitants respectively, their several and respective heirs and assigns for ever. " To be holden

34

of his said Majesty, his heirs and successors in lineage, according to the manner of East Greenwich, in the county of Kent, within his Majesty's realms of England, yielding, rendering, and paying yearly therefor, and every year henceforth, unto our sovereign lord the king, his heirs and successors, or to such officer or officers as shall be appointed to receive the same, the sum of one lamb, or two shillings current money of this province, upon the 25th day of March, at New-York, in full of all rents, or former reserved rents, services, acknowledgments, and demands whatsoever. And from henceforward and for ever, the said trustees of the freeholders and commonalty of the town of Brookhaven do and may have, and use, a common seal, which shall serve to execute the causes and affairs, or whatsoever, of them and their successors." And the said John Palmer, Richard Woodhull, Samuel Eburne, Andrew Gibb, William Satterly, Thomas Jenner, and Thomas Helme, were appointed by the said patent the first trustees, to remain in office until others should be chosen in their stead. By this patent the town was incorporated, and unusually large powers and privileges were conferred. Seven trustees, a clerk, constable, and two assessors, were authorized to be annually elected by the majority of the freeholders and freemen of the town. Under and by virtue of the authority of this extensive patent, (which has since been confirmed by an act of the legislature,) the trustees have ever since exercised complete authority over the corporate property of the town.

Town records, August 1, 1686, *memorandum* that Richard Floyd, sen., hath exchanged a share of meadow and upland at *Occumbomack,* with William Satterly, for a share of meadow at *Patersquash,* with half the amendment of meadow belonging to the said William Satterly.

On the 9th of October, 1693, Governor Fletcher granted a patent to Colonel William Smith, one of the members of the council and chief-justice of the province, for a large tract of land upon the south side of Brookhaven, known since by the name of *Smith's Patent,* "bounded west by a river called East Connecticut, north by the country road, near the middle of the island, east by Mastic River, and south by the Main Sea; with all the islands in the bay between the main land and the beach, from a certain gut or inlet called Huntington East-Gut, to a place called *Cuptwauge,* being Southampton west bounds." In this patent was likewise included a certain neck or peninsula, called Little Neck, lying in Setauket, the Indian name of which was *Minasseroke.* These tracts of land were, by the said patent, erected into a lordship or manor, called *St. George's Manor.* The greater part of this property is still in the possession of the posterity of Col. Smith, and is owned by William Smith, William Sidney Smith, and Selah B. Strong, Esquires.

"*At a legal town meeting, July ye* 13*th,* 1687, warned by Mr. Justice Woodhull, it was voted and agreed that ten pounds a-year shall be payd to the maintenance of a School-Master for the future, and that the trustees agree with Mr. Francis Williamson to officiate as School-Master, for thirty pounds a-year, twenty pounds whereof is to be payd by the children."

"*May* 7, 1687, *at a town meeting,* it was voted and agreed that the Indians should be disarmed, and to surrender themselves upon demand, otherwise to be looked upon as enemies. Ten men were chosen to go to ye South to disarm ym, and their arms to be left at Capt. Woodhull's."

"*At a town meeting, held the* 18*th day of May,* 1687, it was unanimously agreed that a house should be built upon the land that was Goodman Moger's, the same dimensions of Jonathan Smith's, to remain a Parsonage-house to perpetuity. And the town also agreed that sixty-five pounds should be given for the land, and the trustees were ordered to take a bill of sale for the same ; and were further ordered to agree with a workman to build the said house, and that whatever the trustees did therein, should be *obliging to the whole town.*" This arrangement for a parsonage was made several years subsequent to the employment of a minister, for the Rev. Nathaniel Brewster was settled here in 1665, being ten years from the commencement of the plantation. He was a nephew of Elder William Brewster, one of those bold and independent adventurers that arrived in the famous *Mayflower* in 1620, and laid the foundations of the Plymouth colony. The *Rev. Nathaniel Brewster* was a graduate of the first class of Harvard College in 1642, most of

whom returned to England in consequence of the liberty then
allowed to all denominations of Christians.   He was settled as
a minister at Norfolk; but at the restoration, Episcopacy being
encouraged by the government, at the expense of the Independents, he came back to America, and was settled in this town
in 1665 as above mentioned, his three sons having preceded
him by several years.   " *At a town meeting, held October* 24,
1665, it was voted and agreed to purchase the house and lot of
Matthew Prior for the accommodation of Mr. Brewster."   He
continued here till his death, in 1690.   His wife was Sarah,
daughter of Roger Ludlow, Esq. one of the most eminent men
of New England.   He was a member of the council, and deputy governor of Massachusetts and Connecticut; and was the
compiler of the first Connecticut code of laws.   For some
reasons he became displeased with public affairs in the colony, and removed, in April, 1654, to Virginia, where he died.
His daughter is represented as a person eminently distinguished
for her genius and literary acquirements.   Mr. Brewster and his
wife were interred in the Presbyterian burying-ground of
Setauket, but the inscriptions upon their tomb-stones are too
much defaced to be read.   He left three sons, John, Timothy,
and Daniel; all men of excellent character, and highly useful
during their lives.   Their posterity are still numerous and
respectable.   It would seem, that either from age or other infirmity, Mr. Brewster was incapable of discharging his pastoral
duties for some years before his death; for at a town meeting
held October 31, 1685, by the warrant of Mr. Justice Woodhull,
Samuel Eburne was chosen by vote to be minister of the town;
" and it being proposed unto him, that in regard of some *tender
consciences*, he would omit the *ceremony* in the book of Common Prayer, the said Samuel promised, that according to their
desire, in regard of their *tender consciences*, to omit and not
use the aforesaid *ceremonies* in the public worship, *except to
such as should desire the same.*"   " *At a training-day, September* 26, 1687, it was ordered by a major part of the town,
that Mr. Jonah ffordham of Southampton, be sent unto, desiring
him to officiate in the work of the ministry in this town."   He
appears to have declined the invitation; and in the same year

of Mr. Brewster's death, April 15, 1690, "it was voted by a majority of the people present, that Mr. Dugald Simson should be desired to continue with them as their minister; and it was ordered that his salary for the year 1689 should be paid according to the rate made the year before; and that Richard Floyd and Peter Whitehaire should collect the same."

" *At a town meeting, April ye 10th,* 1697, it was fully agreed that Mr. Justice Woodhull and Justice Smith shall treat in behalf of this town and Smithtown, with Mr. Phillips, in order to his settling among us, in case he will engage to perform faithfully the duty of a minister of the gospel among us during the time of his natural life. That they shall offer to his acceptance, fourty pounds in money, to be raised and levied upon this town and Smithtown, and Colonel Smith's manor; and likewise the house and lot that was sould by Thomas Jenner to Capt. Clark; and also a farm of outland toward Nasakeges' Swamp; and likewise that Mr. Phillips be desired to remain with us upon mutual tryall of each other for ye space of one whole yeare." The *Rev. George Phillips* was the son of the Rev. Samuel Phillips, of Rowley, Massachusetts, and grandson of the Rev. George Phillips, of Boxford, England, afterwards first minister of Watertown, Massachusetts, (having arrived with Governor Winthrop in 1630.) Mr. Phillips was born at Rowly in 1664, and graduated at Harvard College in 1686. He came from Boston to Jamaica, Long Island, in 1693, where he preached till his removal to Setauket in 1697. He continued here till his death, April 3d, 1739. That he was a man of solid talents is generally believed, and possessed a happy vein of wit and humor, that rendered his company and conversation always agreeable. He was interred in the Presbyterian buryingground of Setauket, where a handsome stone was erected to his memory a few years since, by Phillip Roe, Esq. one of his descendants. Many of the Phillips' family have been eminent in New England; and the Rev. Doctor Miller has observed, that few families in this country have been more distinguished for liberal donations to religious and literary institutions. One of them founded Andover Academy; another, that of Exeter; two have been governors of Massachusetts, and one mayor of Boston.

At a meeting of the trustees of this town, October 13th, 1702, the following proceeding took place in relation to the ordination of the Rev. Mr. Phillips, which was some years after his settlement here : " Whereas preparation is made for Mr. Phillips' ordination, and he having made application that some person be appointed in the town's behalf, to present him to the persons who are to ordain him, it is *ordered* that Daniel Brewster, Samuel Thompson, and Timothy Brewster be a committee to present Mr. Phillips in the town's behalf to be ordained, and that they accept him in the town's behalf, to be their minister." The town was extremely liberal of their gifts to Mr. Phillips ; for at a town meeting, November 12th, 1695, it was ordered that *one hundred acres* of land near *Nasakeage Swamp* be laid out for the Rev. George Phillips at the *ordinary* of the town, by Richard Woodhull, surveyor ; and again, on the 12th of June, 1701, *one hundred acres* more were voted to him for his use ; and if he continued here for his life, *then* to be to him and his heirs for ever.

" *At a town meeting, August* 28, 1710, it was agreed that a meeting-house be built upon the meeting-house green, to be improved in such a manner as the majority of contributors shall agree, and according to the tenor of an instrument in writing bearing date ye 29th of July, 1710 ; also, Col. Henry Smith, Col. Richard Floyd, Justice Adam Smith, Selah Strong, Samuel Thompson, and Jonathan Owen, were chosen to order the building, to proportion the same and the place of setting up, where it shall stand and remain for the public use." The building was soon after erected, and continued to be occupied till 1766, when, being somewhat decayed, and insufficient also to accommodate the increased number of the congregation, it was taken down, and a new church erected in that year. The town records contain the following entry in relation to this new building : " *Memorandum of the Meeting-house ;* on the 10th of February we began to get timber, and on the 19th of the same month we raised the house, in the year of our Lord 1766." This edifice, although greatly injured by the British during the revolution, was subsequently repaired, and stood till 1811, when it was taken down to make way for the present handsome and commodious structure, which was completed in that year. The pulpit was a present from the Presbyterian church in Cedar-street, New-York. One of the regulations of the town in rela-tion to the old meeting-house, is so curious and singular as to be thought well worthy of preservation as a relic of the age in which so novel a measure was adopted. It is recorded upon the town books as follows:

"At a meeting of the trustees of Brookhaven, August 6th, 1703. Whereas there hath been several rude actions of late happened in our church by reason of the people not being seated, which is much to the dishonor of God and the dis-couragement of virtue. For preventing of the like again, it is *ordered* that the inhabitants be seated after the manner and form following: All freeholders that have or shall subscribe within a month to pay 40 shillings to Mr. Phillips to-ward his sallary shall be seated at the table, and that no *women* are permitted to sit there, except *Col. Smith's Lady*, nor any *woman-kind*; And that the Presi-dent for the time being shall sit in the right-hand seat under the pulpit, and the clerk on the left; the trustees in the front seat, and the Justices that are inhabit-ants of the town are to be seated at the table, whether they pay 40 shillings or less. And the pew, No. 1, all such persons as have or shall subscribe 20 shillings; and the pew, No. 2, such as subscribe to pay 15 shillings; in pew, No. 3, such as subscribe to pay 10 shillings; No. 4, 8 shillings; No. 5, 12 shillings; No. 6, 9 shillings; No. 7, for the young men; No. 8, for the boys; No. 9, for ministers' widows and wives; and for those women whose husbands pay 40 shillings, to sit according to their age; No. 11, for those men's wives that pay from 20 to 15 shillings. The alley fronting the pews to be for such maids whose parents or selves shall subscribe for two, 6 shillings; No. 12, for those men's wives who pay from 10 to 15 shillings; No. 13, for maids; No. 14, for girls; and No 15, free for any. Captain Clark and Joseph Tooker to settle the inhabitants according to the above order.".

The next minister of this church was the *Rev. David Youngs*, son of the Rev. John Youngs of Southold. He was born in 1719, and graduated at Yale College in 1741. His set-tlement took place in 1745, and he remained till his death in 1753. In this brief period he was so fortunate as to obtain and secure the respect and confidence of his people. On his de-cease the congregation were happy to procure the services of the Rev. Benjamin Tallmadge, a gentleman of fine talents and a first-rate classical scholar. He was born at New-Haven, Janu-ary 1, 1725, graduated at Yale College in 1747, and settled here in 1754. His first wife was a daughter of the Rev. John Smith of White Plains, whom he married May 16, 1750, and by whom he had several sons. She died April 21, 1768; and on the 3d of January, 1770, he married a daughter of Thomas Strong of this town. He died February 5th, 1786, greatly beloved and respected by the whole community : his widow survived him more than fifty years. Mr. Tallmadge was succeeded in the ministry by the *Rev. Noah Wetmore.* He was descended from Thomas Wetmore, one of the first settlers of Middletown in 1670. He was born there in 1731, and graduated at Yale College in 1757. His wife was a daughter of Ithuel Russel of Branford. He settled as a minister at Danbury in 1760, from whence he removed to this place, April 17, 1786, where he died, March 9, 1796. He left three sons, Noah, Apollos, and Samuel, and one daughter, who married Dr. David Woodhull. The *Rev. Zachariah Greene* was the successor of Mr. Wetmore. He is the son of Samuel Greene, of Hanover, New Hampshire, and his mother was Jane White, a near relative of Hugh White, who was among the first that had the courage to overleap the German settlements on the Mohawk. Mr. Greene is one of thirteen children, and was born at Stafford, Connecticut, January 11th, 1760. At an early age he volunteered in the American army, and aided in erecting the fortifications upon Dorchester Heights, which compelled the enemy to evacuate Boston ; and was on guard during the night of the houses being burnt on Dorchester Neck. He was afterwards among the forces that opposed the landing of the British at Throg's Point in October, 1776, and was in the battle at the White Plains. In November, 1777, he marched with the army into Pennsylvania ; and at the battle of White Marsh received a bullet through the shoulder, which disabled him from further service. He soon after entered Darthmouth College, where he graduated in 1780. Having chosen the profession of a clergyman, and being in due time licensed to preach, he was settled as the minister of Cutchogue in the town of Southold, June 28, 1787, from whence he removed to Setauket, September 27, 1797.

The history of the Episcopal Church in this town is very obscure, few records of its proceedings having been preserved. It is not probable that there was a single Episcopal church, or even minister, in the whole colony at the time of the conquest in 1664. But after the revolution in England and the accession of Queen Mary to the throne, the governors and most other officers of state were of the Episcopal order, and therefore very naturally confined the patronage of government to those of that denomination. This circumstance furnished a strong inducement for persons of that order to immigrate to this province, and large and sometimes extravagant grants were made by the colonial governor to the church of England. Although the statutes of uniformity were never intended to affect the colonies, and the government had heretofore professed to encoucourage a perfect equality among Protestants of different sects, yet it soon became apparent that official influence was almost exclusively exerted in favor of Episcopacy, which, in the end, produced bad consequences, and, in some instances, hostility to the government itself. Lord Cornbury had committed outrage upom the Presbyterian church of Jamaica in 1702, and as his bigotry could not well be satiated by a single act, he prohibited the Dutch ministers and teachers from the exercise of their spiritual functions without his special license. In 1707 he again interfered with the Dissenters, forbidding the Dutch congregation in New-York to open their church to Mr. Mr. McKemie, a Presbyterian preacher, whom he imprisoned, and Mr. Hampton also, another minister of the same sect, for preaching at Newtown. It is, however, but charitable to believe, that few of the Episcopal church approved or even countenanced such acts of intolerance and persecution.

Caroline Church, in Setauket, was erected in 1730, and was the first Episcopal church on Long Island, built expressly for the use of that denomination. In 1734 the town gave them a piece of land around it, *for a yard and burial-ground.* This building, after having been repeatedly altered and repaired, is still standing, being nearly one hundred and ten years old. The society itself had been previously organized in 1725, under the ministration of the Rev. Mr. Standard, but prospered more abundantly under his successor, the Rev. Alexander Campbell, who arrived here from England in 1729, and during whose time the church edifice was completed. He removed in 1732, and was followed by the Rev. Isaac Brown in 1733. He

35

was a gentleman of education and talents, having graduated at
Yale College in 1729, and continued to officiate here several
years.   In 1747 he removed to New Jersey, and was succeeded the same year by the Rev. James Lyon from Ireland.   He
was a gentleman of good abilities and great energy of character, but at the same time very eccentric.   His death took place
in 1786, from which time, till 1814, the congregation had no
permanent clergyman.   In the latter year the Rev. Charles
Seabury was engaged, and has thus far zealously devoted himself to promote and sustain the best interests of the church.
This worthy pastor is the son of the Rev. Samuel Seabury,
late bishop of Connecticut and Rhode Island, and grandson of
the Rev. Samuel Seabury, former rector of the church at Hempstead.   Mr. Seabury succeeded his father as the minister of
New London, where his grandfather had also preached for thirteen years previous to his removal to Hempstead.

Besides the churches already mentioned, there is a Congregational church at Old-Mans, first erected in 1720, and rebuilt
in 1805, of which the Rev. Noah Hallock was for many
years pastor.   The Presbyterian church at Middletown was
built in the year 1800, and the Rev. Herman Daggett was installed there in 1801, but removed to Connecticut in 1807,
where he died.   He was succeeded by the present minister, the
Rev. Ezra King.   The Presbyterian church at Fire-place was
erected in 1740, and rebuilt in 1828.   The Congregational
church of Patchogue was built in 1767, for which the present church was substituted in 1822.   The Methodists also
built a church here in 1830.   The Baptist church at Corum
has now stood about ninety years.   A Methodist church was
erected at Stoney Brook in 1817, and another has lately been
commenced at Port Jefferson.

This town, like most others, presents a diversity of surface
and soil ; but in general it is sufficient to say, that on the north
it is broken and somewhat hilly, the soil a sandy loam ; while
the rest of the territory is a level and sandy plain, with occasional tracts, well fitted for cultivation.   The land in the vicinity of the Sound, and especially about the bays and harbors,
is of the best quality, and the timber abundant and thrifty.

Crane Neck, Old-Field, Strong's Neck, Dyer's Neck, and
Mount Misery, are respectively fine tracts of land, and have
more or less salt meadows attached to them. The two former
project some distance into the Sound, and are separated from
each other by Flax-Pond Bay, formerly fresh water, which was
used for rotting flax, submerged in it. About the year 1803
the water was let out by a channel dug across the beach;
the pond now abounds with fish, and its shores with salt grass.
Old-Field extends still further to the north, and has a light-
house upon the extreme point, erected in 1823 at a cost of three
thousand, five hundred and eighty dollars. It contains about
five hundred acres, divided into several farms, and lies between
Flax Pond and Oldfield, or Conscience Bay. Strong's Neck,
formerly called Little Neck, is the property of Selah B. Strong,
Esq., lying between Oldfield Bay and Setauket Harbor, and is
almost an island, being attached by a narrow isthmus of meadow to the main island. It contains about four hundred and
sixty acres, the most of which is under high improvement.
The soil is a strong loam, and the surface moderately undulating in some parts, in others nearly level. The stones are sufficiently numerous to put the greater part of the fields into stone
wall. This neck is deficient in forest trees, which is the only
circumstance impairing its value. The prospect from many
points is extensive, and highly picturesque, presenting to the admirer of natural scenery a varied and beautiful landscape.
From the local advantages of this charming place, it may well
be ranked with the most pleasant and agreeable residences
upon the island. There is a peculiarity in regard to the numerous springs with which the shores of this neck abound, that
while those near low water mark are perfectly fresh, others
more distant are impregnated with saline particles. This neck
was called by the Indians Minasseroke, and is believed to have
been the residence of the Sachem and a portion of the Scatal-
cot tribe. It was sold by the town proprietors to Colonel
Smith, and was included in his patent of St. George's Manor,
in 1693. It belonged to the late Judge Selah Strong at the
time of his death, of whom the following particulars may be
interesting to many. He was descended from John Strong, a

native of Taunton, in Somersetshire, England, whose father was Richard Strong. John Strong sailed from Plymouth, March 30, 1630, and arriving in America in May following, settled at Dorchester, Massachusetts; from whence, in 1636, he removed to Windsor, Connecticut, and with Roger Ludlow and others, aided in the settlement of that town. In 1659 he removed to Northampton, where he died, April 4, 1699, at the age of ninety-four. His son Thomas lived there also, and died February, 20, 1690. *He* had sixteen children, of whom the eldest was Selah, born December 22, 1688, and while a young man, came to Brookhaven, where he died April 15, 1732. His first son was Thomas, who married Susannah, daughter of Samuel Thompson, great-grandfather of the compiler of this work. Mr. Strong died May 14, 1760, leaving an only son, the subject of this notice. Judge Strong was born December 25, 1737, and died July 4, 1815. His wife was a daughter of William Smith, grand-daughter of Henry, and great-grand-daughter of Col. Wm. Smith above named. Judge Strong was several times elected to the legislature of this state, and held the office of first judge of the county courts from 1783 to 1794. He was an extensive practical farmer, and was esteemed a man of excellent understanding and much intelligence. His children were eight in number, the most of whom are now living. He conveyed his large estate of *Mount Misery* to his son Thomas S. Strong, Esq., who has also held the office of first judge for a period of thirteen years. This valuable tract of land lies upon the east side of the harbor of Port Jefferson, and has the harbor of Old Mans on the east. It contains many hundred acres of land, and much fine timber. The surface is uneven, but the soil is of good quality, and produces abundance of grass, hay, and grain.

The *Harbor of Port Jefferson, Setauket Harbor, and Old-Field Bay*, have one common inlet from the Sound; and the two former afford excellent accommodations for vessels of a middling class. The village of *Port Jefferson* (formerly Drown Meadow) has lately become a place of some commercial importance; it is pleasantly situated at the head of the bay, and may contain a population of three hundred, principally en-

gaged in ship-building and navigation. Here are several ship-
yards, railways, stores, hotels, and a considerable number of
mechanics. It is much indebted for its commencement and
present prosperity to the enterprise of the late Captain John
Wilsie, who began to build vessels here about forty years ago.
About three miles eastward of this place is the settlement of
Old Mans, consisting mostly of farmers. The surface is broken and stony, and the soil of rather an indifferent quality;
there is, however, a considerable tract of salt meadow between
the upland and the Sound, which is highly valuable. Two
miles further east is the village of *Miller's Place*, situated on a
handsome plain, considerably elevated, and overlooking the
Sound to a great distance. It was first settled by Andrew Miller in 1671, and the most ancient grave found here is that of
his daughter, who died a young woman in 1690. This is a
quiet and handsome village, containing about twenty-five dwellings and one hundred and thirty inhabitants. The soil is
excellent and well cultivated. A small but neat academy was
built in 1834, and has proved thus far a useful institution.

Setauket receives its name from being the principal residence of the Seatalcot tribe of Indians. It is the oldest and most
populous settlement in the town, is situated upon both sides
of the harbor, and occupies about two square miles, being nearly
equidistant from Port Jefferson on the east, and Stoney Brook on
the west. For many years after the first arrival of the white people, and before the erection of mills, their grain was conveyed to
Milford and other places in Connecticut, to be made into flour.
A grist mill was, in 1690, built upon the east side of the village,
which has been discontinued for more than seventy years;
one having been erected upon the stream on the west side,
which has been succeeded by one more valuable, a few years
since. Setauket was the scene of many revolutionary events,
and no small number of robberies and murders were committed by the British and their Tory allies. In 1777 a body
of the enemy, commanded by Col. Richard Hewlett, had taken
possession of the Presbyterian church, and surrounded it with
a picket and other means of defence. On the 14th of August,
about one hundred and fifty men, under the command of Col.

Parsons, embarked from Black Rock in a sloop and six whale-boats, with muskets and a brass six-pounder, for the purpose of capturing the force encamped here.   They landed before day-break the next morning at Crane-Neck-Bend, where, leaving their boats with a sufficient guard, marched as quick as possible to the village.   A flag of truce was sent to the church de-manding a surrender, which being refused, the firing commenc-ed on both sides.   In a short time word was brought from the boats, that some British ships were proceeding down the Sound, and fearing that their return might be intercepted, Col. Parsons ordered a retreat to the boats, and the party arrived again at Black Rock the same evening, with a few of the enemy's horses and some military stores.   The soldiers engaged in this ex-pedition were volunteers from Col Webb's regiment, among whom were the Rev. Mr. Greene and the late Captain Brew-ster.   Twenty years and one month thereafter the former was installed minister of the same church, than which a more im-probable event could hardly have been conjectured.

The village of *Stoney-Brook* is on the western side of the town, adjoining the Sound, and has one of the best and most accessible harbors upon this part of the island.   The number of dwellings is about sixty, and the population between three and four hundred.   Ship-building has been advantageously conducted here for many years, the place being much indebt-ed for its present prosperity to the energy and industry of the late Captain George Hallock.   There are one brig, eight schoon-ers, and fifteen sloops now owned here, all engaged in the coasting trade.   More than four thousand cords of oak and walnut wood are annually sent from this port; and there are returned about twenty thousand bushels of ashes, one thousand of bone, and three thousand loads of street manure.   It is, on the whole, a place of considerable activity, and well located for business.   Many hundred loads of Indian shells found here, have been used for fertilizing the soil in the neighborhood, some of which shells were covered by a stratum of sand of more than five feet in depth.

Corum is situated near the centre of the town, and has been the seat of town business for more than sixty years, ; town meetings having previously been held at Setauket. The dwellings are not numerous, and the population only one hundred and fifty. It has a level surface and a sandy soil, with little natural fertility. Here is the town poor-house, with a small farm attached, which is well cultivated, mostly by the inmates of the house; and the poor are not only decently but comfortably maintained, at a small expense to the town. In or near this village the British had accumnlated a large quantity of forage in the winter of 1780, which was entirely destroyed by a few troops under Col. Tallmadge on the 23d of November, while on their return from a successful expedition to Mastic.

It is with no small gratification we are enabled to mention that Dr. Isaac Hulse, now a distinguished surgeon of the navy, was born here, August 31, 1796, being the youngest son of the late Caleb Hulse, Esq., of this place. While a youth, he left his paternal roof, and set out to seek or make his own fortune. In a short time he was found engaged in teaching a small school in the county of Westchester, where, by his amiable conduct and desire for improvement, he attracted the attention of some respectable and intelligent individuals, who gave him free access to their libraries. This rare opportunity he did not fail to improve, and his thirst for knowledge kept pace with his advancement. His first earnings were employed in procuring instruction from others, and at the Jamaica academy commenced an acquaintance with the Latin, Greek, and French languages, in which he so far improved himself by his own unremitted exertions, as in a short space to be able to instruct others. In a few years he was engaged in superintending a classical school in the city of Baltimore, and by his genius and application was in a short time sufficiently advanced to enter upon the study of medicine in the university of Maryland, and about the year 1820 was honored with a diploma and a gold medal as the reward of merit.

In 1821 he received the commission of assistant surgeon in the Navy of the United States, and made several cruises in national vessels to the coast of Africa, the West Indies, and the Gulf of Mexico. In 1824 he was appointed surgeon to the Navy Hospital at Gosport, Virginia; and soon after was transferred, at his own request, to the hospital at Pensacola, where he continued with increasing reputation, till September, 1838, when he received from President Van Buren the appointment of Fleet Surgeon of the West India squadron, to which he is still attached. His medical reports to the secretary of the navy exhibit talents and acquirements of a high order; indeed, it is rare to find an individual, who, with so few advantages, and by his own unassisted endeavors, has acquired such distinction, or secured so prominent a reputation in his profession, as Dr. Hulse. While his private character and scientific accomplishments do honor to his birth-place, his wonderful success may well serve as a stimulus to all ambitious youth, who aspire to fame and usefulness in any profession.

Patchogue, so called from the name of the Indian tribe that once possessed the territory around it, is the most compact and populous village on the south side of the island. It contains seventy-five dwellings and between four and five hundred inhabitants. It has a Congregational and a Methodist church, two hotels, several stores, a grist mill, paper mill, two cotton factories, one of woollen cloth, two tanneries, and other mechanical branches. It is, upon the whole, a pleasant village, and much resorted to by strangers, on account of its vicinity to the bay and ocean, and the numerous game which they afford. It is distant sixty miles from the city of New-York, and upon the great thoroughfare from Brooklyn to Sagg Harbor. Four miles east, and adjoining the margin of the bay, is the recently-built village of *Bell-Port,* which owes its origin to the spirit and enterprise of Thomas and John Bell and a few others. It already contains more than thirty dwellings and two hundred inhabitants, an academy, three stores, two ship-yards, railways, and wharves extending several hundred feet into the bay. From the progress already made, it is but reasonable to anticipate a considerable advancement in its business and population. Five miles east of this place is another, called Fire-Place, where is a mill, public-house, a church, and some half a dozen dwellings. It is chiefly important as a rendezvous for sportsmen. The stream called *East-Connecticut* commences in the middle of the island, and terminates in the bay a distance of twelve miles. It abounds with trout, and some other fish of the finest kind. Crossing this stream to the east, we come to that part of Col. Smith's original purchase called by the Indians *Mastic*, and divided into several farms, one of which formerly belonged to General William Floyd, and another to the lamented General Woodhull. The general beauties and delights of this romantic spot have been so happily depicted by the poet *Hearne*, that we shall gratify the reader by the insertion of his verses :

THE GROVES OF MASTIC.

Far in a sunny cool retreat,
　　From folly and from noise remote,
I shun the scorching, noon-day heat,
　　Contented in my peaceful cot;
Thro' towns and glades I often stray;
　　Of turn somewhat monastic,
And spend the solitary day
　　Amongst the groves at Mastic.

Dame Nature, in a kinder mood,
　　When things were first created,
Decreed this spot near ocean's flood,
　　An Eden when completed; .
Here all the luxuries of life,
　　She spread with hand all plastic,
Beyond the reach of noise and strife,
　　Among the Groves at Mastic.

When Spring her annual visit pays,
　　Sol puts a brighter face on.
And Zephyr fills our creeks and bays,
　　With brant and geese in season ;
Here, on Smith's Point, we take our stand ;
　　When free from toils gymnastic,
Where Death and *lead* go hand in hand,
　　Among the fowl at Mastic.

Sometimes the tim'rous trout we wait
　　Along the streamlet's border,
With well-dissembled fly or bait,
　　And tackle in good order.
Or catch the huge enormous bass,
　　Be his course e'er so drastic,
While sitting on the verdant grass,
　　Close by the Groves at Mastic.

36

The grouse, the pheasant, and the quail,
  In turn we take by changes,
Or hunt the buck with flippant tail,
  As through the wood he ranges;
This strings our nerves! oh, pleasant toil,
  We want no epispastic,
Nor Doctor, with his castor oil,
  Among the Groves at Mastic.

There rosy health, of blooming hue,
  That wholesome child of morn,
Is seen on faces not a few,
  Their features to adorn:
Here length of life makes wisdom sage,
  Life's active spring elastic,
And lets none die, except with age,
  Among the groves at Mastic.

Moriches is that part of the town lying easterly from Mastic, and extends from Mastic River to the eastern limits of Brook-haven. The country is thinly settled, and the people mostly farmers. The soil is sandy, with a slight mixture of loam ; but from the facility of manuring with sea-weed and fish, is made tolerably productive. The name of Long-Wood has lately been conferred upon a part of Col. Smith's purchase between the north and south country roads, owned by one of his descendants, William Sidney Smith. The following account of the loss of human life near this place is recorded in the New-York Journal of February 10, 1774 :

" On Monday, the 24th ult. the house of Mr. Jesse Raynor, in St. George's Manor, was destroyed by fire. His wife had sent their five smaller children to bed in a loft, to which they ascended by a ladder, and had with them a piece of pine-knot lighted. The straw-bed took fire. She went up, and threw the burn-ing bed down the hole of the loft, which, falling on the floor, burst into a flame. Her husband came with some of the neighbors, and saved a part of the goods. But when he perceived not his wife and children, his anguish was inconsolable. The eldest daughter, who went for her father, could tell nothing after the throwing down of the bed from the loft. As there is no person surviving who was present at the conclusion of this awful tragedy, nothing more is known than that his wife and five children were destroyed, some of their bones being discovered among the burning ruins."

It has been seen, that among the first European settlers of this town was Richard Floyd. He was a native of Wales, from whence he emigrated in 1654. By the frequent divisions of land among the proprietors of the town, as well as by individual purchase, he became in time the owner of a considerable real estate, some of which is still possessed by his posterity. He was a magistrate in the town and a colonel of militia. From the frequent recurrence of his name in the records of that period, it is evident that he was not only a person of distinction, but a highly intelligent and useful man. The inscription upon his tomb is illegible; but upon that of his wife enough remains to show that she died at eighty years of age in 1706. His son Richard was born in 1661, and married a daughter of Col. William Nicolls of Islip. The inscription upon his tomb declares him to have been colonel of the county, and judge of the common pleas. His death took place February 28, 1737. One of his daughters married her cousin, William Nicolls, and another was the wife of Col. Thomas Dongan, governor of the province. Mrs. Nicolls survived her husband, and married Dr. Samuel Johnson, of Stratford, Connecticut, afterwards president of the college of New-York. The third Richard Floyd was like his father, a man of wealth and reputation. He was also a colonel of the county and judge of the common pleas. His death took place April 21, 1771. His children were Richard, Elizabeth, John, Margaret, Benjamin, Gilbert, William, Mary, and Anne. Richard, the eldest, married Arrabella, daughter of Judge David Jones, of Queen's County, and settled upon a farm at Mastic, which was afterwards forfeited by his adherence to the enemy in the revolution : he died at the city of St. John's. His children were Elizabeth, Anne, and David Richard. The latter, in pursuance of the will of Judge Jones, and by legal authority, adopted the name of Jones. He married Sarah, daughter of Hendrick Onderdonk, and died February 10, 1826, leaving two sons, to wit: Brigadier General Thomas Floyd Jones, and Major General Henry Floyd Jones, the last of whom is now a senator in the state legislature.

GENERAL WILLIAM FLOYD was the son of Nicoll Floyd, and great-grandson of the first Richard, who settled at Setauket in 1655. His father had besides, seven children, *Ruth, Tabitha, Nicoll, Charles, Charity, Mary,* and *Catherine.* He died in 1752. General Floyd was born at Mastic, December 17th, 1734. His early education was not such, as from the wealth and ability of his father, might have been expected. His natural intelligence was great, and his moral character elevated. His first wife was a daughter of William Jones of South-ampton, by whom he had three children, Nicoll, Mary, and Catherine. The former has long possessed the estate at Mastic, and enjoyed in an eminent degree the public respect and confidence. Mary married Col. Benjamin Tallmadge of Litchfield; and Catherine became the wife of Dr. Samuel Clarkson of Philadel-phia. The second wife of Gen. Floyd was a daughter of Benajah Strong of Setauket, by whom he had two daughters, Ann and Eliza. The first married George Clinton, son of the late Vice-President of the United States; and the other became the wife of James Platt of Utica. Mrs. Clinton, after the death of her husband, married Abraham Varick of New-York. Gen. Floyd was early chosen an officer in the militia of Suffolk County, and rose eventually to the rank of Major General. He was soon after elected a member of the provincial assem-bly, and in 1774 was sent a delegate from this province to the first continental congress. In 1777 he was elected a senator; and on the 9th of September of that year took his seat in the first constitutional legislature of this state. On the 15th of October, 1778, he was appointed by the legislature a member of con-gress, and was re-appointed, on the 14th of October, 1779, in conjunction with Ezra L'Hommedieu and John Sloss Hobart. He was also one of that immortal band of patriots, who, on the 4th of July, 1776, signed and published to the world the great charter of American Independence. When the British took pos-session of Long Island, his family fled for safety to Connecticut; his house was occupied by the enemy, and he remained an exile from his estate for nearly seven years. The devastations committed upon his property in his absence, were very great. In 1784 he purchased a valuable tract of land in Oneida County, and to which he removed with his family in 1803. There he continued to reside with the good opinion of his fellow-citizens, and in comparative independence, till his death, which occurred at Weston, August 4th, 1821.

At an early period of the controversy between Great Britain and her colonies, the feelings of Gen. Floyd were strongly enlisted on the side of the people, and he entered with zeal into every measure calculated to ensure their rights and liberties. These feelings on his part excited a correspondent sympathy on the part of the people, and led to his subsequent appointment to the first continental congress, which met at Philadelphia the 5th of September, 1774; and he most heartily con-curred in all measures adopted by that body. He served on numerous important committees, and by his ardor and fidelity rendered essential service to the patriotic cause. He enjoyed unusual health till near the close of life, and the faculties of his mind remained unimpaired to the last. In his person, he was of a middle stature, and possessed a natural dignity, which seldom failed to impress those with whom he associated. He was eminently a practical man, without ostentation or vanity. When his plans were once formed, he found no reason to alter them; and his firmness and resolution were seldom equalled. In his political character there was much to admire. Uniform and independent, his views were his own, and his opinions the result of reason and reflection. If the public estimation of a man be a just criterion by which to judge, General Floyd was excelled by few of his cotemporaries; since, for more than fifty years, he was honored by his fellow-citizens with offices of trust and responsibility.

NATHANIEL NORTON. Among the number of native-born citizens of Long Island, who contributed by their talents and exertions to assert and establish the freedom and independence of their country, and whose best days were devoted to her service ; it is to be lamented that many worthy individuals have passed into oblivion, while scarcely any thing is remembered of their particular services ; however much their efforts may have contributed to success in that dark and trying period of American history.   In the rank of this class of patriots may be reckoned the subject of this notice, yet it is evident that he performed much in the sacred cause of liberty and his country. Mr. Norton was born in Brookhaven, in the year 1742. What were the particular circumstances and employment of his juvenile days are not exactly known: At an early age he volunteered as a private in the provincial corps in the French war, (which commenced in 1756,) in the force commanded by Major General Bradstreet; and in the year 1760 was stationed at Oswego. Mr. Norton displayed on all occasions the characteristics of a brave and prudent soldier. In the beginning of 1776 he was appointed and commissioned as lieutenant in the fourth New-York Continental Regiment, commanded by Col. Henry B. Livingston ; and continued attached to that body till toward the end of the year 1781, when the five New-York regiments were consolidated ; and although he was not appointed to a command in those regiments, yet such was the estimate of his services and usefulness, that his pay and appointments were continued to him during the remainder of the war ; and by a resolution of Congress became entitled to his due succession of rank.   In the same year he was secretly commissioned by Governor Clinton to obtain loans of money from the wealthy Whig inhabitants of Long Island for the use of the government ; and thereupon the better to conceal this object and fulfil its duties, he was appointed to the command of a small national vessel called the "Suffolk," in which he cruised in the Sound, between Sand's Point and Newhaven. In this business he was very successful, and obtained large sums on the faith of the government, which he regularly delivered to the governor.   Captain Norton had previously done duty in the corps de reserve at the battle of Monmouth, on the 28th of June, 1778, and was engaged with the artillery in that action. He afterwards accompanied General Sullivan in the expedition against the Six Nations, then occupying the western part of this state, but was prevented by sickness from taking an active part in the actions of Bemus' Heights and Stillwater, which led to the capture of the British army under Burgoyne.   After the war, Captain Norton retired to his farm in this town, and remained till 1790, when he became an elder, and subsequently a minister in the Baptist church. He was settled for some time in Connecticut, and afterwards at Herkimer in this state. In 1805, age and bodily infirmity made it necessary to relinquish his pastoral duties, and he spent the remainder of his days in retirement ; which a pension from the government enabled him to do in a comfortable manner. His mental powers were active and vigorous, his memory retentive, and his conversation at all times interesting and agreeable. He died suddenly, while on a visit to New-York, the 7th of October, 1837 ; and his funeral solemnities were attended by his surviving brethren of the Cincinnati, of which he was, at the time of his death, the oldest member. By his own previous desire his body was conveyed to Brookhaven, and interred in the burial-ground of the Baptist church at Corum on the 10th of October, 1837.

CALEB BREWSTER, was born at Setauket, in the town of Brookhaven, in 1747. He was the son of Benjamin Brewster, grandson of Daniel Brewster, and great-grandson of the Rev. Nathaniel Brewster of that place, who is supposed to have been a nephew of Elder William Brewster, who arrived with the pilgrims at

Plymouth in 1620.   The father of Mr. Brewster was a farmer, and the education of his son was restricted to the ordinary branches taught in a country school, which at that period comprehended only reading, writing, and arithmetic. Being naturally of an ardent and enterprising disposition, and anxious to explore beyond the confines of his native town, he chose the life of a sailor ; and at the age of nineteen engaged himself on board a whaling vessel, commanded by Captain Jonathan Worth, bound to the coast of Greenland.   His next voyage was to London in a merchant ship, and upon his return found his country involved in the revolutionary contest.   His enthusiasm in the cause of liberty did not allow him to hesitate for a moment the course which his duty called him to pursue, and he immediately volunteered his services in securing American independence. He was honored in a short time with the commission of lieutenant of artillery, and from that time forward was eminently distinguished for zeal and intrepidity, possessing to the fullest extent the confidence of the officers of the army and that of the commander-in-chief.   In short, such was the exalted opinion entertained of his integrity, courage, patriotism, and prudence, that in 1778 he was employed as a confidential and secret agent of Congress ; and he devoted himself through the remainder of the struggle in procuring and transmitting the most minute, accurate, and important intelligence relative to the movements and intentions of the enemy at different points, and particularly in New-York and on Long Island for which he was uncommonly well qualified, as well by his intimate topographical knowledge of the country, as his acquaintance with the people on both sides the great political question, and therefore knew in whom, of either party, he could venture to confide   He was among those who, under Col. Parsons, crossed the Sound to Long Island in August, 1777, for the purpose of capturing a body of British and Tories, who, under Col. Hewlett, had taken possession and garrisoned the Presbyterian church at Setauket.   On the 23d of June, 1780, he was appointed captain of artillery, and was frequently engaged with separate gangs of marauders, who sometimes extended their predatory excursions upon the main.   In November, 1780, he was a volunteer in the expedition under Major Tallmadge to the south side of Long Island, where they surprised and took prisoners a party of British troops encamped upon Smith's Point at Mastic, and on their return destroyed a large quantity of hay and military stores at Corum.   In 1781 he engaged with and captured an armed boat with her whole crew, in the Sound, which he carried safely into Black Rock Harbor. Upon reporting the result of this enterprise to the commander-in-chief, he received from him the following, in reply to his application to be allowed a more considerable force :

" Head-Quarters, New-Windsor, Feb. 23, 1781.

   " Sir —It is not in my power at present to spare any further number of men for your detachment, as I am obliged to call in many guards, and weaken other necessary ones, to support the garrison of West Point. You will dispose of the boat, and what you took in her, for the benefit of the captors. I am, sir,
" Your obedient servant,
" G. Washington."

   On the 7th of December, 1782, Captain Brewster, with the whale-boats under his command, gave chase to several armed boats of the enemy in the Sound, and after a desperate encounter, in which most of the men on both sides were either killed or wounded, he succeeded in capturing two of the enemy's boats.   This action has generally been denominated, by way of distinction, the *boat fight ;* and at the time was justly considered, in connection with its attendant circumstances, one of the most valorous and extraordinary engagements of that portentous period. It was indeed a truly perilous adventure; yet the contest lasted only twenty minutes, and some of his boats refusing to come up, he was compelled, from his peculiar situation, to engage with the enemy almost single-handed. During this short but terrible conflict, his shoulder was pierced by a rifle ball, which passed out at his back. His prudence and resolution enabled him to keep this occurrence a profound secret till the enemy surrendered, when he found himself exhausted from the effusion of blood. After reaching the shore, he was confined, under the hands of a surgeon, for some time ; for the injury thus received he was placed upon the pension-roll of the army, and continued to receive a gratuity from his country for the remainder of his life. He participated in several other important and hazardous engagements, while attached to the line of the army, the interesting particulars of which it is now impossible to ascertain, as none of his compatriots on those occasions are now living. On the 9th of March, 1783, he took command of a sloop at Fairfield, for the purpose of attacking the *Fox,* a British armed vessel in the Sound ; and as soon as he came near, he ordered his men to board her with fixed bayonets, himself leading the way. In less than two minutes she became their prize. Captain Johnson of the Fox, and two men, were killed, and several others wounded ; while Captain Brewster had not a person injured. This extraordinary exertion on his part was more than his then state of health could endure, and in consequence of which he was confined to his bed for several months. When he recovered, the preliminaries of peace had been exchanged, and his beloved country had assumed her appropriate station among the free nations of the earth. In 1784 he married Anne. daughter of Jonathan Lewis, of Fairfield, Connecticut ; where he continued afterwards to reside, when not in public service, to the close of life. In 1793 he was commissioned as lieutenant of the revenue cutter for the district of New-York ; and such was his well-known skill and prudence, that on the death of Captain Dennis, soon after, he was appointed her commander, which he retained till 1816, with the exception of three years of Mr. Adams's administration, to which he was opposed. In that year he retired to his farm at Black Rock, where he departed this life at the age of seventy-nine years, February 13, 1827. In stature, Captain Brewster was above the common size, of fine proportions, a commanding countenance, a constitution athletic and vigorous, and of extraordinary activity. His talent for wit and humor was almost unrivalled, and for relating anecdotes few men could be found more entertaining.

His Excellency Governor Tompkins, Dr. Mitchill, James Fairlie, Esq. and several other gentlemen, accompanied Captain Brewster in a voyage around Long Island, in September, 1809 ; and so highly gratified were they all with his polite attention to their comfort, that it was resolved to present him a silver cup as a token of their obligation and regard. The fort at Staten Island, where most of the gentlemen were present, was the spot chosen for delivering the cup, on which occasion Dr. Mitchill made an address in his usual able manner, which was happily responded to by Captain Brewster. On the subject of his military services, Mr. Knox, former secretary at war, on the petition of Captain Brewster, reported to the house of representatives, the 21st of June, 1790, that " he was a lieutenant of artillery during the war, and was confidentially employed in an armed boat by the commander-in-chief, to keep open the communication between Connecticut and Long Island, for the purpose of obtaining intelligence. That he performed this hazardous service with fidelity, judgment, and bravery; and the approbation of Washington, appears by his certificate, dated June 10, 1784. And that, by the execution of the trust reposed in him, he became peculiarly obnoxious to the enemy, who made many attempts to take or destroy him. That in the month of December, 1782, he and those under his command behaved with the highest gallantry in an engagement with three of the enemy's armed boats, the largest of which, with the commanding officer, he captured, after an obstinate resistance; and in which action he was dangerously wounded, and carried into Connecticut, at a distance from any hospital, where he languished a long time under the pain of his wound."

BENJAMIN TALLMADGE. This able soldier, statesman, and patriot, has been honorably mentioned in the histories of his time as an active and enterprising officer of the revolution. He was the son of the Rev. Benjamin Tallmadge of Setauket, where he was born, Feb. 25, 1754. His mother died while he was at the age of fourteen years, but his father survived till the year 1786. He very early exhibited a fondness of learning, and under the tuition of his father, who was an excellent classical scholar, made such progress, that at twelve years of age he was examined by President Dagget of Yale College, then on a visit to Brookhaven, and found well qualified to enter that institution. He, however, did not enter till some years after, and graduated in 1773. Soon after, he was invited to take charge of the high school at Weathersfield, which station he held until his entrance into the army. The legislature of Connecticut having resolved to raise their quota of troops for the campaign of 1776, he accepted a commission of lieutenant, and soon after received the appointment of adjutant in the regiment of Colonel Chester. He joined his regiment in New-York in June, from which time to the end of the war he was in constant and active service. He was engaged in the battle of Long Island on the 27th of August, 1776, and was one of the rear-guard when the army retired to New-York from their lines at Brooklyn. Before the regiment to which he belonged was discharged, he received the appointment of captain of the first troop in the second regiment of dragoons. The regiment was ordered to rendezvous at Weathersfield, where the winter was occupied in preparing for the campaign of 1777. In the course of this year he received the commission of major, and was honored with the confidence of the commander-in-chief and principal officers of the army. He was in most of the general battles that took place with the main army in the northern states, at Long Island, White Plains, Brandywine, Monmouth, Germantown, and White Marsh. He opened, this year, a secret correspondence (for General Washington) with some persons in New-York, and particularly with the late Abraham Woodhull, of Setauket, which lasted through the war. He kept one or more boats constantly employed in crossing the Sound on this business. On Lloyd's Neck, an elevated promontory between Huntington and Oyster-Bay, the enemy had established a strongly fortified post, with a garrison of about five hundred men. In the rear of this fort a band of marauders had encamped themselves, who, having boats at command, were constantly plundering the inhabitants along the main shore, and robbing the small vessels in the Sound. This horde of banditti Major Tallmadge had a great desire to break up; and on the 5th of September, 1777, embarked with one hundred and thirty men of his detachment, at Shippan Point, near Stamford, at eight o'clock in the evening. In about two hours they landed on Lloyd's Neck, and proceeded to the attack, which was so sudden and unexpected, that nearly the whole party was captured, and landed in Connecticut before morning. Not a man was lost in the enterprise. For the purpose of breaking up the whole system of intercourse between the enemy and the disaffected on the main, he was appointed to a separate command, consisting of the dismounted dragoons of the regiment and a body of horse. While stationed near North-Castle, a prisoner was brought in, calling himself *John Anderson*, but who turned out to be *Major Andre*, on his way to New-York after his interview, near West Point, with the infamous *General Arnold*. Of this prisoner Major Tallmadge had the custody up to the day of his execution, and walked with him to the gallows at Tappan, October 2d, 1780. In November of the same year he resumed his favorite scheme of annoying the enemy on Long Island, and having obtained the most accurate information of Fort St. George, erected on a point projecting into the South Bay at Mastic, he communicated his project to the commander-in-chief, who, considering the attempt as too hazardous, desired him to abandon it. Having crossed the Sound and examined the particular condition of the post, he was finally authorized to risk the enterprise, by the following letter from Washington.

" Head-Quarters, Nov. 11th, 1780.

" Sir.—I have received your letter of the 7th instant. The destruction of the forage collected for the use of the British army at Corum upon Long Island, is of so much consequence, that I should advise the attempt to be made. I have written to Col. Shelden to furnish you a detachment of dismounted dragoons, and will commit the execution to you. If the party at Smith's house can be attempted without frustrating the other design, or running too great a hazard, I have no objection. But you must remember that this is only a secondary object, and, in all cases, you will take the most prudent means to secure a retreat. Confiding entirely in your prudence as well as enterprize, and wishing you success,

I am your's, &c.,

" G. Washington."

In pursuance of this communication Major Tallmadge ordered the detachment to repair to Fairfield. Here being met by other troops, the party embarked, the 21st of November, 1780, at four o'clock, P. M., in eight whale-boats. The whole number, including the crews of the boats, amounted to eighty men. They crossed the Sound in four hours, and landed at *Old-Mans* at nine o'clock. The troops had marched about five miles, when it beginning to rain, they returned, and took shelter under their boats, and lay concealed in the bushes all that night and the next day. At evening the rain abating, the troops were again put in motion, and at three o'clock in the morning were within two miles of the fort. Here he divided his men into three parties, ordering each to attack the fort at the same time at different points. The order was so well executed, that the three divisions arrived nearly at the same moment. It was a triangular enclosure of several acres, strongly stockaded, well barricaded houses at two of the angles, and at the third a fort, with a deep ditch and wall, encircled by an abattis of sharpened pickets, projecting at an angle of forty-five degrees. The stockade was cut down, the column led through the grand-parade, and in ten minutes the main fort was carried by the bayonet. The vessels near the fort, laden with stores, attempted to escape, but the guns of the fort being brought to bear upon them, they were se-

37

cured and burnt, as were the works and stores.   The number of prisoners was
fifty-four, of whom seven were wounded. While they were marched to the boats
under an escort, Major Tallmadge proceeded with the remainder of his detachment, destroyed about three hundred tons of hay collected at Corum, and returned to the place of debarkation just as the party with the prisoners had arrived, and reached Fairfield by eleven o'clock the same evening; having accomplished the enterprise, including a march of forty miles by land and as much by
water, without the loss of a man.   Congress passed a resolve complimentary to
the commander and troops engaged in this expedition, which was said by them
to have been planned and conducted with wisdom and great gallantry by Major
Tallmadge, and executed with intrepidity and complete success by the officers
and soldiers of his detachment. The following was addressed to him by the commander-in-chief:

" Morristown, Nov. 28, 1788.

" Dear Sir.—I have received with much pleasure the report of your successful
enterprise upon Fort George, and the vessels with stores in the bay, and was
particularly well pleased with the destruction of the hay at Corum, which must,
I conceive, be severely felt by the enemy at this time.   I beg you to accept my
thanks for your judicious planning and spirited execution of this business, and
that you will offer them to the officers and men who shared the honors of the enterprise with you.   The gallant behavior of Mr. Muirson gives him a fair claim
to an appointment in the second regiment of dragoons, when there is a vacancy.
And I have no doubt of his meeting with it accordingly, if you will make known
his merit, with these sentiments in his favor.   You have my free consent to reward your gallant party, with the little booty they were able to bring from the
enemy's works.   Your's, &c.,

" G. WASHINGTON."

During that part of the campaign of 1781 in which the main army was in
Virginia, Major Tallmadge was left with the forces under General Heath in the
Highlands on the Hudson ; still, however, holding a separate command, he moved wherever duty or a spirit of enterprise dictated.   In continuation of his former design of annoying the enemy upon Long Island, he marched his detachment
to Norwalk ; and as Fort Slongo, at Tredwell's Bank, near Smithtown, was possessed by a British force, he determined to destroy it.   On the night of the 9th of
October, 1781, he embarked a part of his troops under the command of Major
Prescott, with orders to assail the fort at a particular point.   At the dawn of
day the attack was made, the fortress subdued, the block-house and other combustible materials burnt, and the detachment returned in safety with their prisoners, and a handsome piece of brass artillery.   On the 11th of April preceding,
Major Tallmadge had written to General Washington, wherein he says :—" At
Lloyd's Neck it is supposed are assembled about eight hundred men, chiefly refugees or deserters from our army.   Of this number there may be about four hundred and fifty or five hundred properly armed.   Their naval squadron consists
of one vessel of sixteen guns, two small privateers, and a galley.   About eight
miles east of Lloyd's Neck, they have a post at Tredwell's Bank, of about one
hundred and forty men, chiefly wood-cutters, armed.   I have seen an accurate
draft of this post and works." He believed that if two frigates should enter the
Sound in the absence of the British fleet, and at the same time a suitable body of
troops were embarked in boats, the posts might be cut off ; and he offered to aid

or direct an enterprise for such an object. To this proposition the commander-in-chief replied as follows:

"New-Windsor, April 8, 1781.

"Sir.—The success of the supposed enterprise must depend on the absence of the British fleet, the secrecy of the attempt, and a knowledge of the exact situation of the enemy. If, after you have been at the westward, the circumstances from your intelligence shall still appear favorable, you will be at liberty to be the bearer of a letter to the Count de Rochambeau, to whose determination I have referred the matter.   Your's, &c.,

"G. WASHINGTON."

Nothing more is heard of this matter till the July following, when the Count de Barras, having no employment for his squadron at Newport, detached for this service three frigates, with two hundred and fifty land troops, the whole under the command of the Baron d'Angely. The detachment sailed on the 10th of July, and was joined in the Sound by several boats, with a few volunteers and pilots from Fairfield. But it was soon evident that the fort on Lloyd's Neck was much stronger than had been supposed, and not to be carried without the help of cannon, which had not been provided. The party, after a few shots from the fort, re-embarked, having two or three killed and wounded. Among those mortally wounded was Heathcote Muirson, the individual so favorably mentioned by General Washington in his letter to Major Tallmadge inserted above. He was a son of Dr. Muirson of Setauket, and had graduated at Yale College in 1776. His death, as may well be supposed, was a source of grief to all who were acquainted with his many amiable qualities.

After the affair of Fort Slongo, Major Tallmadge returned to the neighborhood of White Plains, where he found full employment, in guarding the inhabitants against the refugee corps under Col. De Lancey, and the cow-boys and skinners who infested the lines. In the course of the ensuing winter he took his station on the Sound, and arranged another plan to beat up the enemy's quarters on Long Island; but a violent storm prevented its being carried into effect; he succeeded however, in capturing many of the enemy's vessels engaged in illicit trade between the opposite shores, and several cargoes of valuable goods were taken and condemned. The secret correspondence conducted by Major Tallmadge, during several years, within the British lines, has been before alluded to. And when the American army was about to enter the city of New-York after the peace, he entered before it was evacuated by the British, that he might afford protection to those who were the secret friends of their country, and who otherwise would have been exposed to ill-treatment, as refugees or tories. He retired from the army with the rank of colonel. He was for several years treasurer, and afterwards president, of the Cincinnati Society. In March, 1784, he married Mary, daughter of General William Floyd of Mastic; and by her had several children, one of whom is the Hon. Frederick A. Tallmadge, a senator of the State of New-York. In 1800 Col. Tallmadge was chosen a representative in congress from Connecticut, having previously established himself in extensive mercantile business at Litchfield. He was, while in congress, during eight successive elections, a firm and judicious member of that body, and watchful over the political interest of a country, whose independence he had so nobly contributed to achieve. After sixteen years of service in the national legislature, he declined a re-election, and retired to private life. To public objects of benevolence he gave largely and freely. He died, beloved and venerated for his services and worth, March 7th, 1835.

We cannot conclude our account of this town without mentioning three other individuals, natives of Brookhaven, who, by their virtues and talents, do credit to the place of their birth, and therefore deserve honorable notice in the history of Long Island.

Henry S. Mount, Shepherd A. Mount, William S. Mount, three brothers, artists, are sons of the late Thomas S. Mount of Setauket; their mother, a daughter of the late Major Jonas Hawkins of Stony-Brook. These ingenious young gentlemen have been respectfully mentioned by Mr. Dunlap in his *History of the Arts of Design,* and from which the following particulars are principally extracted:

HENRY S. MOUNT, the eldest, served an apprenticeship at the business of sign-painting with the late Lewis Child of New-York, and has long been acknowledged equal to any individual in that branch of the arts, which he still pursues as his main occupation. He has besides exhibited very considerable talent in portrait painting, and more especially in pictures of *still-life.* He is a student of the National Academy of Design, and has frequently produced pictures in the gallery of Clinton Hall which have elicited high praise from the most eminent judges, and been the subject of general admiration.

SHEPHERD A. MOUNT, the next brother, was brought up to the coach-making business in the city of New-Haven, and immediately on completing his apprenticeship, turned his attention to portrait-painting, which he has pursued with such brilliant success, as to make it his principal pursuit; indulging, however, occasionally in *landscape* and *design,* in which his fine taste for coloring has enabled him to produce very handsome specimens. Many of his late portraits possess great excellence, not only as correct and faithful delineations of personal features, but also as highly finished pictures. He is likewise a student of the National Academy, and does equal credit to himself and the institution with which he is associated.

WILLIAM S. MOUNT, the junior of these brothers, was born at Setauket, November 26, 1807, and put at an early age, with his brother, at sign-painting, which he soon relinquished for a higher department of the arts. He has displayed, (says Mr. Dunlap,) uncommon talent, both in fancy pictures (or composition of figures,) generally rustic and comic, and at the same time in portrait-painting. At an early period of his career he eagerly sought for and examined pictures by different masters; and West's *Madness of Lear* and *Ophelia* led him to study composition. His selecting these, from among many other pictures exhibited in the same place, is a proof of his discriminating eye and correct taste. In 1826 he entered a student of the National Academy, and at the annual exhibition he produced for inspection his first composition figure, *The Daughter of Jairus,* which attracted much attention. His next was a *Rustic Dance,* still better, which evinced that he had discovered the path in which he was destined to excel. A constant attention to drawing, a profound study of such specimens of *coloring* as fell in his way, with great devotion to the practice and study of *design,* has already been rewarded by a skill of uncommon grade; and he now occupies, by the unanimous consent of those best able to appreciate his merits, the first rank in the class of humorous and domestic scenes. Besides the two admirable performances above-named, this gentleman has produced, among other charming pictures, the *Last Visit*, the *Raffle*, the *Courtship*, the *Tough-Story*, the *Fortune-Teller*, the portrait of Jeremiah Johnson, Esq., in the common council-room of the city of Brooklyn, that of the Rev. Mr. Carmichael of Hempstead, and the splendid full-length of Bishop Onderdonk in the chapel of Columbia College.

TOWN OF ISLIP.

This town is situated upon the south side of the island, and centrally about forty-five miles from the city of New-York. Bounded on the east by Brookhaven; on the south by the bay; on the west by Huntington; and on the north by Smithtown and Brookhaven. It extends east and west about sixteen miles and has a medial width of eight miles. Most of the territory lies between the south and middle country roads as formerly travelled, including Ronkonkoma Pond and a part of the settlement of Hoppogues. More than half the lands of the town is embraced by the boundaries of Nicolls' Patent. The town received its name from the first European settlers, many of whom came from Islip, in Oxfordshire, England. The country was at that time thickly populated by Indians, from whom the lands were purchased. The *Secatogue* tribe claimed the lands west of the *Connetquot River*, and from whom purchases were made; while the soil on the east was bought from *Winnequaheagh*, Sachem of Cannetquot, a semi-tribe or family inhabiting the sides of that stream in 1683. Judging from the great abundance of the necessaries of life, and other local advantages enjoyed by these people, it is reasonable to infer, that at some period their numbers must have been very great; yet they seem to have been of a pacific character, and at the settlement of the white inhabitants, manifested a friendly disposition, and instances of hostility were very rare. They have now disappeared entirely, leaving nothing but extensive shell banks, here and there, to acquaint us of their previous existence. In consequence of the number of swamps and streams which intersect the town, and thereby impeding the travel on the south side from east to west, there were few inducements for settlers; accordingly we find that the increase of population was very gradual, and no town meeting was held previous to the year 1700, although the town began to be

settled as early as 1666, being several years later than any
other town upon Long Island. The very valuable neck of
land, now owned by Dr. Udall and the Willett family, is still
called by the name of *Secatogue,* and was probably the residence
of the Sachem and a considerable portion of the Indian tribe.
Before the construction of bridges over the larger streams, the
travel was necessarily confined to the interior of the island,
and occasioned a great number of roads to be marked out,
which were afterwards abandoned, and no traces of many of
them are now to be discovered; thereby, in some instances
producing confusion and uncertainty in relation to boundaries,
which were frequently very loosely expressed, and almost impossible to be satisfactorily ascertained. It has been conjectured, and not without reason, that the separation of the oak
and pine timber was assented to by the Indian tribes inhabiting
the north and south sides of the island, as the dividing line
between their respective territories; this was considered to be
about the middle of the island, consequently many roads near
this imaginary boundary would acquire the common designation of middle or country roads, although one or more miles
from each other, in particular places. If any patent was ever
issued for lands in this town, exclusive of that to Mr. Nicolls in
1684 and others confirmatory thereof, it has not been discovered. The records now existing in the clerk's office of the
town commence with the year 1720, and the first town meeting was held in April of that year. The want of any previous
documents may be accounted for by the fact of a great part
being the property of a single individual, and the population of
the remaining portion of the town very thinly settled, consequently no necessity existed for town meetings. The minutes of the first meeting for town purposes are as follows:

" Precinct } At a meeting of the said Precinct the first tuesday of April,
of } being the sixth year of the reign of our sovreign Lord George
Islip. } the first over Great Britain, Anno. Dom. 1720, it was by a major vote, then and there declared and agreed as followeth:

Benjamin Nicolls, Supervisor.
Thomas Willets and John Moubray, Assessors.
Isaac Willetts, Collector; and James Saxton, Constable."

The names of the freeholders of the town at that time were as follows :

Benjamin Nicolls
Thomas Willets
John Moubray
Isaac Willets
Daniel Akerly
Josepeh Dow
John Moger
James Saxton
William Gibb
George Phillips, Jun.

John Arthur
Amos Powell
John Smith
Samuel Muncy
William Green
Richard Willets
William Nicolls
Anning Moubray
Joseph Saxton
James Morris

Israel Howell
John Scudder
Annanias Carll
Stephen White
Amos Willets
Daniel Phillips
Joseph Udall
Samuel Tillotson.

The extensive domain known as Nicolls' Patent, includes more than sixty square miles of land, and has, since its first purchase from the natives, by successive entailment, been preserved as one estate. It was obtained from the Indians in 1683 by William Nicolls, and is described in the conveyance therefor, as " all that neck, tract, piece, or parcel of land on the south side of Long Island, bounded on the east by a certain river, called *Conetquot ;* on the south by the Sound, (bay;) on the west by a certain river called *Cantasquntah ;* and on the north by a right line from the head of the said river called *Conetquot,* to the head of the said river called *Cantasquntah ;* to have and to hold the said neck, piece, or parcel of land and premises, with all and singular the appurtenances, unto the said William Nicolls, his heirs and assigns for ever ;" and for which a patent of confirmation was granted by Governor Dongan on the 5th of December, 1684. Letters patent were likewise issued on the 1st of November, 1686, corroborating the former, and including, moreover, "a certain other piece or parcel of land and meadow ground unimproved, and not as yet granted to any person whatsoever, being bounded on the east by the lands of the said William Nicolls, on the south by the Sound or bay, on the west by a certain creek or river called or known by the name of *Wingatthappagh,* and on the north by a right line from the head of the said creek or river, called *Conetquot.*" And on the 20th of February, 1697, another patent was issued to the said William Nicholls, by Governor Fletcher, for land as follows, to wit:

" A certain parcel of vacant unimproved land, in part adjoining the land of
said Nicolls and of Andrew Gibb, bounded easterly by a brook or river to the
westward of a point called Blue-Point, known by the Indian name of *Manow-
tassquott*, and a north and by east line from the head of said river to the country
road ; thence along the old road westerly until it bears north and by east, to the
head of *Ovawake* river; and thence by a south and west line to the head of the
said river, and so running easterly along by the land of said Nicolls and Gibb, to
the head of *Conetquot*, and down said river to the Sound ; and from thence along
the sound easterly to the mouth of the Manowtassquot aforesaid ; together with
a certain fresh pond called *Raconckomy Pond*."

Ronkonkoma Pond, in the north-west part of the town, is a
beautiful and picturesque sheet of water, which from its location
is an object of much curiosity, and in magnitude almost deserving
to be called a lake. It is more than three miles in circumference,
and situated near the geographical centre of Long Island. Its
shape is nearly circular, the water perfectly clear and of great
depth. Those who have lived long in the neighborhood assert, that there is an undeviating septennial rise and fall of the
water in this pond, which, if true, is a phenomenon well worthy
the investigation of the geologist and philosopher. It is enclosed
by a narrow beach of the purest white sand, which circumstance, it is said, gave occasion for its Indian appellation, the
translation of which into English is *sand-pond.* It abounds
with fish of various kinds, of which the most prevalent is the
yellow perch. Some of these were in 1790 transferred by Dr.
Mitchill to the waters of Success-Pond in Queen's County.
It is difficult to conceive an object more gratifying to the lover
of nature, the admirer of beautiful scenery, than this pond,
which being in the midst of an extensive forest, the stranger,
on first beholding its placid and silvery surface, is inspired
with rapture and delight. The extensive forests which border
upon this pond, are stocked with herds of deer, who, when
hard pressed by the sportsman and his dogs, often, as a last resort, betake themselves to the water in the hope of escape ; but
this resource avails them not ; boats are procured, and the poor
terror-stricken animals are soon overtaken and destroyed.
Notwithstanding a great many. of these interesting creatures
are every year sacrificed for the enjoyment of the hunter, their
numbers are not sensibly diminished ; the great range afforded
them, and the almost impenetrable morasses in which they may
be in a measure secure from attack, allows opportunity for in-

crease ; and however much persons of refined sensibilities may deprecate the seeming cruelty of this fashionable amusement, there will always be found individuals not merely to justify the practice, but even ready to join in it with an ardor and enthusiasm known only to sportsmen.

The surface of this town is level and destitute of stone, the soil light and sandy, with a slight mixture of loam in different places. The meadows are very abundant, and yield an immense quantity of the best sedge and salt grass. The bay on the south is four or five mile wide, containing an inexhaustible variety of fish, and is visited by a countless number of wild-fowl, such as geeese, ducks, brant, &c., at almost all seasons of the year. The sea-weed and fish procured from the bay, and manure made by stock, constitute the main articles used for fertilizing the soil ; and many farms by this means are rendered highly productive and profitable. The population of the town is chiefly confined to the south country road, and in the western part of the town forms an almost continuous village. Mills have been erected on the principal streams, and the water-power is sufficient for more, should interest or necessity require their erection. The different necks of land, as well as the brooks and small rivers, had formerly distinct and appropriate Indian names, which are preserved in ancient deeds, and well known to some of the older inhabitants. Till within a few years there was but one house for public worship in the town. This is a grotesque looking edifice, of small dimensions and singular shape, standing upon the country road near the middle of Nicolls' Patent. It was erected in the year 1766, principally, if not entirely, at the expense of the (then) opulent proprietor of that immense estate. In the cemetery adjoining the church, which is called *St. John's Episcopal Church*, is a monumental tablet, upon which is the following inscription, commemorative of the amiable qualities of the late owner of Nicolls' Patent :

" Sacred to the memory of William Nicolls. Hospitality, charity, and good-will toward his fellow-man, were the marked characters of his life ; and a perfectly resigned submission to the will of his Creator distinguished the sincere Christian at the hour of death, which took place, Nov. 20, 1823,

" Æ. 24."

38

There are numerous islands situate in the bay, belonging to this town, the most important of which are the Fire Islands, and give name to the principal inlet by which vessels enter the bay.   Upon the main beach near this inlet, a substantial light-house was erected in 1825, at an expense of eight thousand dollars, and is what is called an eclipsed light.   The beach opposite this town, which belongs to Brookhaven, has, since the settlement of the white people, experienced many and extraordinary changes, exposed as it is to the never-ceasing action of the winds and waves of the ocean.   In the trial of an important cause some years since, one Jacob Seaman, an aged inhabitant, testified that about the year 1764 the ocean made a breach through the beach between *Fire Island Inlet* and *Gilgo Gut*, and formed the island now called *Cedar Island*, by the mass of sand washed into the bay.   Isaac Thompson, Esq., one of the judges of the county, spoke also of a gut formerly existing, called Huntington Gut, between *Cedar Island* and *Oak Island*, which has entirely disappeared, and the place become solid beach.   John Arthur, an old man, had been told, when a boy, that *Fire Island* Inlet broke through after the purchase made by Mr. Nicolls in 1683, and was at that time called the *New Gut*.   Col. Floyd stated, that about sixty years before 1814, there were *seven inlets* east of Fire Island Inlet, which were from a quarter to half a mile wide.   Dr. Udall, an aged and respectable physician, stated that he had heard David Willets, an old man, then deceased, declare that *Fire Island* Inlet was formerly called the *Great Gut*, and sometimes *Nine-mile Gut*, because when it first broke through, it was *nine miles wide*.   This is supposed to have occurred in the year 1691.   In the year 1773 the Fire Islands were not as they now are, but a mere sand-spit, producing only a few patches of salt grass, and were called *Seal Islands*.

From the New-York Gazette, June 4, 1781.   "A number of whale-boats got into the South Bay, near Islip, from Connecticut, and took off one vessel and plundered some others.   They also robbed several people on shore.   This induced a royal party of militia to follow the crews of the boats down to Canoe-Place, where they surprised them, killed one, wounded another, and made the whole party prisoners, with four boats and thirty stand of arms; a part of the pirates were subsequently confined in a sugar-house in New-York."

New-York Magazine, July, 1802. " On the 28th of September, 1801, a serpent, of a species unknown to the people there, was killed in a swamp at Islip. Its length was seven feet, and of proportional thickness.'' It was on the belly and sides of a straw color; on the back were thirty-six black spots, reaching from the head to the tail, and on each side of this row were other dark brown spots. It had no fangs or biting-teeth, and was therefore not venomous. In the lower part of the mouth was a considerable fleshy portion like a tongue, which terminated in a long bicuspidated projection. It had scuta both on the belly and tail, which amounted to about three hundred. From these characters it is evident that it belonged to the genus *Boa ;* the number of the scuta so exactly corresponding to the species termed constrictor, and is said in India to grow to the length of thirty feet, and to be capable of destroying the largest animals by entwining itself about the body of its victims."

From the same. " The glow-worm is a native of Long Island, and made its appearance at Islip in October, 1802, in moist places, beside fences and under locust trees. Their light is on the tail or posterior portion of the body, like that of the fire-fly or lightning-bug (lampyrus). At times, seemingly optional with the animal, it was kindled to a remarkable brightness. On some of the fine evenings of October, the appearance of these glow-worms (cicindela,) lying thick among the grass, was like that of burning coals, and made a brilliant exhibition, as they bespangled the ground. This animal neither stings nor bites, is nearly an inch long, and resembles the millipedes in shape."

In connection with the history of this town; it may not be unacceptable to the reader to have a brief account of the first proprietor of the extensive domain known by the general designation of *Nicolls' Patent.* '

WILLIAM NICOLLS was the son of Mathias Nicolls, descended from an ancient and honorable family at Islip, in Oxfordshire, England ; and came to America with his uncle, Richard Nicolls, commander of the expedition sent to reduce New-York from the possession of the Dutch government, in 1664, and was the first governor of the colony under the Duke of York. Mathias Nicolls was immediately appointed secretary of the colony and a member of the council. He was likewise authorized, *ex officio,* to preside with the justices in the courts of Sessions of the several ridings organized after the conquest. In 1672 he was chosen mayor of New-York, and after the act of 1683, remodelling the courts of justice, he was appointed one of the judges of the colony. In this capacity he officiated for the last time in Queen's County, Sept. 12, 1687, a short time before his death. He made several purchases of land on Little Neck and Great Neck in Queen's County, which, in 1687, he conveyed or devised to his son William, the subject of this notice, and which he disposed of afterwards to different persons. In 1718 he conveyed twelve hundred acres upon that part of Cow Neck called Plandome, to Joseph Latham, for two thousand two hundred and fifty pounds, in the deed for which there is a special reservation of sixty square feet, where he states his father, Mathias Nicolls, lies buried.

It is presumed that William Nicolls was born in England, and came over, when a boy, with his father, in 1664. He was well educated, and having chosen the profession of the law, acquired a high standing at the New-York bar. He was appointed the first clerk of Queen's County in 1683, which he held till his removal to the city in 1688. In 1683 he made his first purchase of land at Islip, which, with others subsequently acquired, were confirmed in 1697 by a patent of Col. Fletcher, who was distinguished for his extravagant grants of the public lands.

In 1704 Mr. Nicolls became the proprietor of a tract of land on Shelter Island, by virtue of a devise in the will of Giles Sylvester, comprehending a large proportion of that island. He was a warm friend of liberty, and friendly to the revolution in favor of William and Mary, but was opposed to the arbitrary and impolitic measures which were adopted by Leisler, rather, it would seem, to secure his authority than to advance the interests of the revolution. In consequence of his disapprobation of the course pursued by Leisler, he was imprisoned, as well as others who had courage and honesty enough to avow their sentiments in relation to public affairs. In March, 1691, Governor Slaughter having arrived, called Leisler to account, liberated Nicolls and other state prisoners, and settled the foundations of the future government of the colony. March 23d, he appointed Mr. Nicolls a member of the council; and in 1695 he was sent to England by the assembly, as the agent of the colony to solicit the interference of the crown for enforcing the contributions which had been allotted to the other colonies in defence of the country against the encroachments of the French, (which fell with unequal weight upon the colony of New-York;) and for which service the assembly allowed him $1000. In 1698 he was suspended from the council by the new governor, the Earl of Bellamont, who, on his arrival, seems to have embraced the views and adopted the feelings of the Leislerian party, and exerted his official influence to crush their opponents. In 1701 he was elected a member of assembly for the county of Suffolk; but not being a resident of the county as required by law, he was not suffered to retain his seat. To avoid a similar result, it is supposed he fixed his residence permanently on Great Neck, in Islip, which afterwards became the principal seat of the family. In 1702 he was again elected a member of assembly for Suffolk, and was by the house elected their speaker. He was from that time regularly elected a member of every succeeding assembly till his death, and was also re-elected speaker. In 1718 he resigned the speaker's chair on account of his health, which seems to have prevented his attendance for the few last years of his life.

He was a member of assembly twenty-one years in succession, and speaker sixteen years of the time. On the 30th of March, 1691, he was employed with James Emmot and George Farrawell, as king's council, to conduct the prosecution against Leisler and his associates; and he was also one of the council employed by Nicholas Bayard in March, 1702, in his defence against a political prosecution instituted by Nanfan, the lieutenant-governor, and pursued with all the violence and bitterness of party rancor, for circulating and signing petitions to the king and parliament, in which the abuses of power by his Honor and his friends were enumerated: a report of which case is published in the state trials of that year. He was also one of the council employed in the defence of Francis McKemie, a Presbyterian clergyman, in June, 1707, who was indicted for preaching; which was brought about by the bigotry of the governor, Lord Cornbury: a narrative of which is contained in a pamphlet published in New-York in 1755. He was twice married. One of his wives was Anna Van Rensselaer, daughter of Jeremiah Van Rensselaer, Esq., and widow of Killian Van Rensselaer, who was the heir of the original proprietor of the manor of Rensselaerwick.

Mr. Nicholls served in the assembly at a period when the colony was divided into bitter parties, and when a variety of interesting questions occurred between the governors and assembly, which affected the rights and independence of the assembly. On all these questions he was on the side of the assembly, and appears to have been uniformly friendly to the principles of freedom; both in his professional and political employments he was a firm and decided friend to the rights of the people and to the best interests of the colony. He died in 1723 or '24, and left a number of children. Several of his descendants have been distinguished by public stations. His eldest son Benjamin settled at Islip, and married Charity, daughter of Richard Floyd, by whom he had two sons, William and Benjamin. He died young; and his widow married the Rev. Doctor Johnson of Stratford, who was afterwards president of the college at New-York, under whose care her two sons received a liberal education. William inherited the estate of his father, and remained at Islip; Benjamin settled in New-York, and acquired a distinguished rank at the bar. William Nicolls the second, the second son of Mr. Nicolls, (to whom he devised his estate on Shelter Island,) was also educated a lawyer, and was a man of talents. He was a member of assembly for the county of Suffolk for twenty-nine years in succession; and during the last nine years was speaker of the house. He was first elected in 1739, and was re-elected a member of every succeeding assembly till his death. It is supposed that he died in the spring of 1768. The governor, Sir Henry Moore, dissolved the assembly February 6th, 1768; and the tradition is, that he was taken sick on his journey home, and died at a house on Hempstead Plains. He much resembled his father in his political sentiments, and was also a decided friend to the rights of the colonies. He is supposed to have concurred in the addresses to the king, lords, and commons, which were adopted by the assembly in 1764 and 1765, and which he signed as their speaker. These addresses abound with patriotic sentiments. In that of 1764 they say that "It would be the basest vassalage to be taxed at the pleasure of a fellow-subject." In that of 1765 they assert that "An assumption of power by the British parliament to tax the colonies, if acquiesced in or admitted, would make them mere tenants at will of his Majesty's subjects in Britain." This gentleman died a bachelor, and his estate descended to William Nicolls the third, the eldest son of his brother Benjamin. William Nicolls the third, (commonly called Lawyer Nicolls,) was appointed clerk of the county of Suffolk in 1750, and continued to hold that office till his death, March 29, 1780. During the last four years of his life the administration of justice was suspended by the war, and the office was of course without profit. It is said that some time before his death he labored under a partial paralysis, which disqualified him for business. His last entry upon the records was made November 8, 1776. In March, 1768, he was elected a member of assembly for the county of Suffolk, with Eleazer Miller, to supply the vacancy occasioned by the death of his uncle. That assembly being dissolved January 2d, 1769, he was again elected in March, 1769, with Col. Woodhull, a member for Suffolk. This was the last assembly under the colonial government, and continued till it was superseded by the provincial congress or convention, which met in May, 1775. During the period of this assembly, the disputes between the mother country and the colonies arrived at a crisis. The time for action had arrived; and the question, whether the colonists were to be vassals of the British parliament or enjoy the rights of freemen, was to be decided by force. The prospect of a conflict so unequal, in which the result was so doubtful, staggered many who were friendly to the colonies. The occasion required all the zeal and energy of the most ardent patriotism.   Col. Woodhull was qualified for the crisis, and met it without dismay; Mr. Nicolls was less energetic and decisive.

Admitting that he was decided in his opposition to the measures of parliament, yet it must be conceded that he wanted the energy and boldness of his grandfather and uncle, either of whom, judging from the course they took on other occasions involving similar principles, would have been at the head of the opposition.   This gentleman left two sons, William and Benjamin.   He devised his estate on Shelter Island to his son Benjamin, and his large estate at Islip to his son William; which, with the exception of a few farms which the legislature of the state of New-York thought proper to take out of the course of the law, by limitations in his will, after passing three descents, continues undiminished in the family.   The last-named William Nicolls remained upon the estate at Islip, and died at an early age in the year 1799.   His son, the late William Nicolls, was born after the decease of his father, and at the age of twenty-one came into possession of the estate in fee.   Upon his death intestate in 1823, it descended to his three children as tenants in common.

TOWN OF SMITHTOWN.

This town, at first called Smithfield, was originally conveyed to Lyon Gardiner, of Gardiner's Island, in 1659, by Wyandanch, chief Sachem of Long Island, in grateful remembrance for kindness shown to the Sachem in the redemption of his daughter from her captivity among the hostile Indians across the Sound.   It is bounded north by the Sound, east by Brookhaven, south by Islip, and west by Huntington; and lies upon both sides of Nesaquake River.   In 1663 it was sold by Mr. Gardiner to Richard Smith, the common ancestor of the numerous families of the name of Smith, in this town and elsewhere, by which he became proprietor of most of the lands now constituting the town of Smithtown; the title being confirmed to him by the Nesaquake Indians in 1662; and for which a patent of confirmation or assurance was obtained from Governor Nicolls the same year.   In the succeeding year Mr. Smith procured a further grant from the Nesaquake Sachem, for a tract of land upon the west side of that river, for which, including his former purchase, a second patent was issued by the Governor on the 25th day of March, 1667, in which the boundaries are recited as follows: "Easterly by a certain run of water called Stony Brook, stretching north to the Sound, and southerly bearing to a certain fresh-water pond called Ronkonkoma, being Seatalcott's west bounds ; which said parcel of land was heretofore granted by patent to Richard Smith by the said Richard Nicolls." The omission of a western boundary in this patent may have in part induced a controversy which ensued between the town of Huntington and Mr. Smith, concerning the title to lands upon the west side of Nesaquake River. This controversy, after being protracted for some time, was eventually decided before the court of assize held at New-York in 1675, and resulted in favor of Mr. Smith ; and in order to establish his claim beyond dispute, a new patent was granted, according to his desire, a year or two after, by his Excellency, Governor Andross, as follows :

" Edmund Andross, Esquire, Seigneur of Sausmares, Lieutenant and Governor-General under his Royall Highness, James, Duke of York and Albany, and of all his territories in America.

" To all to whom these presents shall come, sendeth greeting. Whereas there is a certain parcell of land scituate, lying, and being, in the east-riding of York-shire upon Long Island, commonly called or known by the name of Nesaquake lands, bounded eastward by a certain runn of water called Stony Brook, stretching north to the Sound, and southward bearing to a certain fresh-water pond called Raconkamuck, being Seatalcott west bounds, from thence south-westward to the head of Nesaquake River, and so along the said river as it runns unto the Sound. Also another parcell or tract of land on the west side of the said river, extending to the westernmost part of Joseph Whitman's Hollow, as also to the west side of Leading-Hollow to the fresh pond Unshemamuck, and the west of that pond att high-water mark, and so to the Sound, being Huntington east bounds ; which said parcell or tract of land, on the east side of Nesaquake River, was heretofore granted by patent unto Richard Smith, the present possessor, by Coll. Richard Nicolls, and to his heyres and assigns forever ; as also that on the west side of said river ; with some provisoes and restrictions, the which has since, by due course of law att the General Court of Assizes, held in the year 1675, been recovered by the said Richard Smith from the town of Huntington. Know yee, that by virtue of his Maties letters patent, and the commission and authority unto me given by his Royall Highness, havè rattifyed, confirmed and granted, and by these presents do rattify, confirm, and grant unto the said Richard Smith, his heyres and assigns, the aforesaid parcells or tracts of land on both sides the Nesaquake River. Together with all the lands, soyles, woods, meadows, pastures, marshes, lakes, waters, fishing, hawking, hunting, and fowling; and all other profits, commodities, and emoluments to the said parcells of land and premises belonging, with their and every of their appurtenances ; and every part and parcell thereof. To have and to hold the sayd parcells or tracts of land and premises, with all and singular the appurtenances, unto the said Richard Smith, his heyres and assigns. to the proper use and behoof of him, the said Richard

Smith, his heyres and assigns for ever. The tenure of the said land and premises to bee accoiding to the custom of the manor of East Greenwich, in the county
of Kent, in England, in free and common soccage and by fealty only. As also
that the said place bee as a township, and bee called and known by the name of
Smithfield or Smithtown, by which name to be distinguished in all bargains and
sales, deeds, records, and writings. The said Richard Smith, his heyres and
assigns, making due improvement on the land afore-mentioned, and continuing
in obedience and conforming himself according to the laws of this government;
and yielding and paying therefor, yearly and every year, unto his Royall Highness's use, as an acknowlegement or quit-rent, one good *fatt lamb*, unto such officer or officers as shall be empowered to receive the same. Given under my hand,
and sealed with the seal of the province in New-York, this 25th day of March,
in the twenty-ninth year of his Ma^tles reign, Anno Dom , 1677.

" E. ANDROSS. "

Richard Smith, the patentee above named, arrived at Boston
from England in the year 1650, where he married, and remained till 1655, when he came with a number of emigrants to
Long Island, and was one of the first proprietors of Brookhaven. He lived at Setauket several years. The records of the
town sufficiently indicate that he was not only an active, intelligent individual, but was a leading character and a magistrate.
After his removal to Smithtown, he sold most of his lands there,
the conveyances for which are recorded in a book now in the
office of the county clerk. His death took place at an advane-
ed age, about the close of the seventeenth century. Only a
small part of his great real estate was disposed of during his
life. Some time after his decease, in the year 1707, his children, whose names were Richard, Jonathan, Job, Adam, Samuel, Daniel, and Deborah, made application to the court of assizes held at New-York, for the appointment of commissioners
to make a division of the remaining lands among them ; whereupon the court appointed Richaid Woodhull of Brookhaven,
John Hallock of Southold, and George Townsend of Oyster-Bay, to make the partition required. This commission
was duly executed, and the division made was subsequently
confirmed by the court in the same year. It is probable that
horses were very rare during the first settlement of this town,
or that they had not as yet been introduced ; which accounts for
Mr. Smith's having made use of a large bull for many purposes
for which horses were afterwards used, which occasioned him

to be designated as the bull-rider, and his posterity to this day as the *Bull Smiths,* while the descendants of Col. William Smith of Brookhaven are as familiarly known as the *Tangier Smiths,* he having once filled the office of governor of Tangier. There are also upon the island two other distinct races or families by the name of Smith, the one called *Rock Smiths* and the other *Blue Smiths,* the origin of which is matter of conjecture. Many singular traits of character, and not a few strange stories, are related concerning this famous progenitor of the Smiths of Smithtown, the records of which have too much the semblance of fiction to be worth perpetuating.

The area of this town is nearly ten miles square. The surface on the north is a good deal broken and hilly, while on the south it is nearly a level plain. The soil is generally good, and well cultivated. The timber is abundant, and has long been a staple article of exportation. The Nesaquake River is the only considerable stream in the town ; commencing in the southern part of it, and running a northerly course to the harbor adjoining the Sound. The population is much scattered over the surface, but there are, nevertheless, several pleasant vicinages in different parts, which deserve particular mention. The most considerable village is that called the *Branch,* which is centrally situated upon the middle country road, and where the public business of the town is usually transacted. Here is a tavern, post-office, store, and about a dozen dwellings, owned principally by farmers. The Presbyterian church was originally built in 1750, and the present more modern edifice in 1823. It is probable that a church existed in some part of the town previous to 1750, as the records thereof mention that on the 13th day of February, 1717, Richard Smith and his four brothers gave a tract of land upon the west side of Nesaquaké River to *Daniel Taylor,* in consideration of his having agreed to labor among the people in the work of the ministry for four years.

Between the Branch and Stony-Brook is a small, but neat hamlet, called *Mills' Pond,* consisting of a few houses arranged about the borders of a pond, used as a common watering for cattle. At the head of Stony-Brook harbor is another considerable settlement, and one other upon either side of Nesaquake river, a few miles from the Sound.   On the east side of this river, and near the residence of the late Richard Smith, was the dwelling-place of his ancestor, the patentee of the town ; and this was probably the site of the principal settlement of the Nesaquake tribe, as well as of the Sachem.   At the head of boat navigation upon this river, is the village called the *Head of the River*, which has long been a place of considerable business, having several valuable mills and machinery, employed for various mechanical purposes.   In the north-west part of the town is another settlement, called *Fresh-Ponds*, where there is a Presbyterian church, in which the Rev. Joshua Hart officiated pastor from the year 1792, till his death a few years since. On the southern limit of the town is the neighborhood of Hoppogues, where a Methodist church has been erected for several years.   Here is the residence of the Hon. Joshua Smith, who has frequently represented the county in the legislature, and held the office of first judge of the common pleas from 1823 to 1828.

The first minister of this town of whom any record has been preserved, was the *Rev. Abner Reeve.*   He was a native of Southold, and graduated at Yale College in 1731.   He was employed in this town in the year 1735, but whether settled or not, is not certainly known.   He subsequently preached at Westhampton, Fire-Place, and Huntington, without being regularly settled in either.   He removed, in 1750, to Blooming-Grove in Orange County, and from thence to Brattleborough in Vermont, where he died.   He was an amiable man and a good scholar, but wavering in his disposition and somewhat eccentric.

His son, the late Hon. TAPPEN REEVE, was born at *Fire-Place* in the town of Brookhaven, October, 1744, and graduated at Princeton College in 1763. He here formed an agreeable intimacy with the daughter of president Burr and sister of the late Col. Burr, whom he afterwards married.   He studied law in one of the eastern states, and entered upon his professional course at Litchfield, Connecticut, in 1772.   He was a firm patriot in the revolution.   In 1798 he was appointed a judge of the superior court of that state, and afterwards chief justice, which office he held till 1814.   He was in the practice of the law about twenty-six years, and was the founder of a Law Academy at Litchfield, which was the most useful, successful, and distinguished in this country, until the one instituted at Harvard College under the auspices of Judge Story. He presided over the Litchfield Law School for nearly forty years, and sent forth pupils to every part of the United States, richly endowed with the principles and practice of the law. Judge Reeve was distinguished for simplicity of manners and for purity of principle and conduct. At his decease, December 13, 1823, his pupils in every part of the country met, and passed resolutions highly favorable to his character. Among these meetings was that of the Baltimore bar, at which the Hon. Robert Goodloe Harper presided. The resolutions contained the warmest effusions of gratitude and veneration. Dr. Beecher, in his funeral oration, said of him : " I have never known a man who loved so many persons, and was himself beloved by so many."

The *Rev. Napthali Dagget* was settled here in 1751. He was a native of Attleborough, Vermont, and graduated at Yale college in 1748. His wife was Sarah, daughter of Richard Smith of this town. In 1756 he removed to New-Haven, and accepted the professorship of divinity in Yale College ; and after the death of President Clapp, in 1666, he officiated as president till the accession of President Stiles in 1777. In 1779 he distinguished himself by his courage and patriotism when the city of New-Haven was attacked by the British troops in their incendiary expedition against the maritime towns of Connecticut. They took him prisoner, most shamefully beat and insulted him, and compelled him to walk several miles in extreme hot weather. This savage treatment in all probability accelerated his death, which occurred November 25, 1780.

The next minister of this town was the Rev. Thomas Lewis, of whom little is known, except that he graduated at Yale College in 1741, came here in 1763, and again removed in 1769. The *Rev. Joshua Hart* was a native of the island, graduated at Princeton in 1770, settled here in 1773, in 1792 left the church in the Branch, and settled in the parish of Fresh Ponds, where he continued till his death a few years since. He was a man of considerable powers of mind, assisted by a good education ; and his convivial talents were such as to make his conversation at all times interesting and agreeable.

The *Rev. Luther Gleason*, from Stillwater, Saratoga county, was settled here in 1797, and remained until dismissed for alleged misconduct in 1806 ; since when a number of clergymen have been successively engaged, whose continuance has been for short periods.

THOMAS TREDWELL, ESQ , late of Plattsburgh, was a native of this town, and one of the most useful men of his day. He was well educated, and was distinguished for firmness and prudence during the difficult and trying period of the revolution. He was almost constantly engaged in public business; was chosen a member of the provincial convention in 1775, and elected afterwards to the provincial congress from Long Island. He was also a member of the first senate of this state under the constitution, and seems to have been, in all respects, fitted to the perilous times in which he lived. He received, as he merited, the highest testimonials of respect and confidence from his fellow-citizens on all occasions where judgment and perseverance were required to be exercised. He was the first surrogate of this county, appointed in 1787, and retained the office till 1791; soon after which he removed to Plattsburgh, and was appointed also the first surrogate of Clinton county, which he held till his death in 1826.

The late President Dwight, in the journal of his travels through this island in 1804, has the following remarks: " The best land, (says he,) which we saw on this day's journey, is in and about Smithtown. Here we dined, or rather wished to dine , the inn at which we stopped, and the only one on the road, not having the means of enabling us to satisfy our wishes. In this humble mansion, however, we found a *young lady*, about eighteen, of a fine form and complexion, a beautiful countenance, with brilliant eyes, animated with intelligence, possessing manners which were a charming mixture of simplicity and grace, and conversing in language which would not have discredited a drawing-room or a court. Her own declarations compelled us to believe, against every preconception, that she was a child of this very humble uneducated family. But nothing we saw in the house could account for the appearance of her person, mind, or manners. I was ready to believe, as all my companions were, when we left the spot, that some

' Flowers are born to blush unseen,
And waste their *sweetness* on the desert air.''

It may gratify the curiosity of the reader to know, that the house referred to was kept at that time in the Branch by Derick McCoun ; and that the young lady, (so highly extolled by the venerable Doctor,) was his daughter, now the widow of the late Major Smith of Patchogue.

" At a town meeting, held in Smithtown, August 9th, 1774, it was resolved, and we do fully declare ourselves ready to enter into any public measures that shall be agreed upon by a general congress; and that Solomon Smith, Daniel Smith, and Thomas Tredwell be a committee for said town, to act in conjunction with committees of the other towns in this county, to correspond with the committee of New-York; and the said committee is fully empowered to choose a delegate to represent this county at the general congress; and that said committee do all that shall be necessary in defence of our just rights and liberties against the unconstitutional acts of the British ministry and parliament, until another committee be appointed."

In a note to Moulton's History of New-York, it is stated, that an obituary appeared in a newspaper, printed in 1739, of the death of a negro at Smithtown, Long Island, reputed to have been *one hundred and forty years old*, who declared that he well remembered when there were but *three houses* in New-York. The memory, therefore, of this remarkable individual must have extended back to the first settlement of New Amsterdam, (as New-York was then called,) in 1626.

TOWN OF HUNTINGTON.

This is the most westerly town in Suffolk County; bounded on the north by the Sound, on the east by a line running from Fresh Ponds to the north-west angle of Winnacomac Patent, from thence to the creek east of Sunquam's Neck, then down said creek to the South Bay, and from thence south to the Ocean; on the south by the Ocean; on the west by Cold Spring Harbor, and by a line running from the head of the said harbor to the creek west of West-Neck; then down the said creek to the South Bay, and from thence southerly to a monument upon the beach, fixed by commissioners in 1797. Its extent on the Sound being about ten miles, upon the South Bay six, and from north to south twenty miles; containing nearly one hundred and sixty square miles. In 1691 Horse-Neck, now called Lloyd's Neck, which lies within the bounds of Huntington Patent, was annexed to Queen's County by an act of the legislature, and has remained so ever since. The earliest deed for land, within the bounds of this town, was given by the Indians to Theophilus Eaton, Governor of Newhaven, for Eaton's Neck, in 1646. The first Indian deed to the original settlers of Huntington, was obtained in 1653, and comprised six square miles, being all the lands between Cold Spring and East Cow Harbor, and extending from the Sound to the old country road, including Horse-Neck, which, it seems, was not intended to be conveyed by the Indians, but was sold, in 1654, to three men living in Oyster-Bay. The consideration paid for the purchase of 1653, was six coats, six bottles, six hatchets, six shovels, ten knives, six fathoms of wampum, thirty muxes, and thirty needles; which was no doubt considered by the grantors an adequate compensation. In 1656 the people of Huntington obtained a deed for the land extending from Cow Harbor to Nesaquake River, and from the Sound to the country road. A part of the South-Necks was purchased in 1657, and other parts in 1658 and at subsequent periods, together with the lands lying south of the middle country road. The lands in the town were claimed by three different tribes, the Matinecocks, the Massapequas, and the Secataugs. Both Wy-

andanch, Sachem of Montauk, and the Sachem of Nesaquake,
denied the right of the Matinecock Indians to the land between
Cow Harbor and Nesaquake River, which they had sold to the
people of Huntington.   The conflicting claims of these differ-
-ent tribes produced a long controversy between Huntington
and the proprietor of Smithtown, which, after an arbitration
and several lawsuits, terminated in 1675, in a division of the
disputed territory ; and the boundary between the towns was
determined to be a line running from Fresh Pond to Whitman's Hollow ; the north-west corner of Winnecomac Patent.
The first settlers in all cases purchased their lands from the Indians who claimed them ; the price paid was very inconsiderable, and usually consisted of blankets, clothing, fishing implements, and sometimes of guns and ammunition, with a small
quantity of wampum.   The settlers at first only took up a
house-lot in the village, and this is supposed to be all the land
taken up before the first patent.   Immediately after the conquest of New-York in 1664, the governor ordered the purchasers of Indian lands to take out a patent for the confirmation of their contracts, and forbade any further purchases
to be made from the natives without a license from the government.   The governor, with the advice of the council,
had the disposition of the public lands.   No purchase could be
made without his license, and none was of any avail unless
confirmed by patent, for which such sums were demanded as
avarice dictated.   The fees charged for patents constituted a
perquisite of the governor, and quit-rents charged on them produced no inconsiderable revenue to the crown.   In 1666 the
inhabitants of Huntington obtained a patent, by which the
whole territory between Cold-Spring and Nesaquake River,
and between the Sound and the Sea, was erected into a town,
with town privileges ; but the patent gave no power to the inhabitants to purchase the lands still held by the Indians within
the limits of the town.   In 1685 the governor issued a patent
for lands in the town, which in 1675 had been adjudged by
the court of assize to be within the limits of the original patent,
and in 1686 he required the inhabitants to purchase the
lands within the town which had not been obtained of the

Indians, in order that they might be compelled to take out new patents for them. The original patent was made subject to such quit-rent as should be afterwards fixed, and became, eventually, a subject of difficulty between the governor and the people of the town. To compel them to consent to its being fixed according to his wishes, Governor Dongan, in 1686, seized their patent, and obliged them to raise £29 4s 7d, in satisfaction of quit-rent and the expense of a new patent, which passed the council August 2d, 1688, and was one of the last acts of his administration. This last patent was similar to the former, and which, after 'confirming the titles to lands already purchased, granted all the remainder thereof within the limits of the patent (except the necks on the south side and the land to the north of them) absolutely to the inhabitants, according to their rights or shares in the original purchases, and also incorporated the town. The patentees named in the original patent, in 1666, were Jonas Wood, Robert Seely, John Ketcham, Thomas Scidmore, Isaac Post, Thomas Jones, and Thomas Wicks. In 1694 another patent was granted by Governor Fletcher, by which the eastern limit of the town was altered, their former purchases confirmed, and the right of pre-emption to all the lands within the boundaries of the patent, not then purchased, secured to them. The expense of this patent was £56 18s 3d, of which sum £50 was paid to the governor and public officers. The names inserted in the last patent are Thomas Wicks, Joseph Bayley, Jonas Wood, John Wood, John Wicks, Thomas Brush, and John Adams; and they are called trustees of the freeholders and commonalty of the town, with the usual powers of a civil corporation.

In an early period of the settlement, in this town as well as in others, almost all domestic trade was carried on by means of exchange. Contracts were made to be satisfied in produce, and even the judgments given in the courts, were made payable in grain, at fixed prices, or in *merchantable pay at the current price*. The prices were established by the governor and court of assize; and in 1665 the assessors were ordered to fix an estimate for stock. Accordingly, a horse or mare four years old and upward, was to be taken in pay at twelve pounds; a

cow four years old and upward, at five pounds ; an ox or bull
of the same age, at six pounds ; and other articles, as pork,
wheat, corn, &c., at proportionate prices.   In the draft of a contract between the town and a schoolmaster in 1657, the salary
was to be paid in *current pay ;* and in 1686 the town contracted
with a carpenter to make an addition to the meeting-house, to
be paid in produce.   Even executions issued by the magistrates,
were satisfied in the same way.   " At a town meeting, April 4,
1661, it was agreed that a *firkin of butter* should be paid in, at
Steven Jarvis's house by the middle of June, for the satisfaction
of a debt due from ye town to Ensigne Briant."   The more effectually to preserve the public morals, the people excluded
from society those whom they thought likely to injure them.
In 1662 they appointed by a vote at town meeting, a committee,
consisting of the minister and six of their most respectable citizens, to examine the characters of those, coming to settle among
them ; with power to admit or reject, as they judged most likely
to benefit or injure society, with a proviso, that they should not
exclude any " that were honest, and well approved by honest
and judicious men ;" and forbid any inhabitant to sell or let house
or land to any one not approved by the committee, under the
penalty of ten pounds, to be paid to the town.   In 1653 the
town forbade any inhabitant to entertain a certain obnoxious
individual longer than the space of a week, either gratuitously
or for pay, under the penalty of forty shillings.

"At a town meeting, held May 14, 1658, it was agreed by a
major vote, that tow men beeing chose to goe to Newhaven
about joining in goverment with them ; and also to a tend the
bisnis of the ships that was caste away on the south side ; and
that they that belonge to the ships bisnis, shall bear tow-third
of the charges in sendin of the tow men, and one-third the
towne in generall shall paye."   And 27th December, 1658, it
was " ordered that the Indians have ten shillings for as many
wolves as they kill within our bounds, that is, ten shillings a
year, if they make it evident they were so killed."   March 5,
1665, the town court gave judgment, " that defendant pay the
debt in wheat or peas, at merchant prices."

" At a towne meating, Nov. ye 10th, 1686, it was agreed upon by ye generalitie of ye inhabitants, that too men should be sent to Yourke in order to ye Govenor's letter ; the men chosen by ye towne for yt purpose was Tho. Powell and Isaac Platt."

July 29, 1682, the town court ordered a person to pay a fine of twenty shillings, or make such acknowledgment as the court would accept, for having brought a bag of meal from Oyster-Bay on the Sabbath ; and on the 3d of June, 1683, required a written confession from three men, who had travelled on the Sabbath from Huntington to Hempstead.

In order to secure the due administration of justice in this town and to punish crimes, a court was early established by the people, composed of three magistrates, a clerk, and constable, chosen annually at town meeting. The parties were entitled to a jury of seven men, a majority of whom were competent to render a verdict. In cases of slander and defamation, (which were by far the most common,) the judgment was frequently in the alternative, that defendant make confession in open court, or pay a pecuniary satisfaction. In one instance of gross slander the defendant was adjudged to be placed in the stocks, which appears to be the only instance on record of corporal punishment in the town. Nor does it appear that a single criminal prosecution took place in the town previous to 1664, slander and trespass being the most aggravated cases on record.

In 1660 the town resolved to put themselves under the jurisdiction of Connecticut, and were received accordingly. In 1662 they elected two deputies to attend the next general court of election at Hartford, in May, 1663. This connection was dissolved, of course, on the conquest of New-York in 1664. On the 18th of October, 1660, the town established a house of entertainment, and made its continuance to depend upon the correctness with which the keeper discharged the trust ; and January 2d, 1682, the town court ordered the estate of an intemperate person to be attached, that it might be "secured, preserved, and improved for his livelihood and maintenance, and that the town might not be damified."

The first minister of this town was the Rev. William Leveridge or Leverich. He came from England with Captain Wiggin and company, arriving at Salem, October 10, 1633. He preached at Dover, Massachusetts, till 1635. In 1638 he removed to Sandwich, and in 1647 was employed by the commissioners of the United Colonies as a missionary, and resided for the most of the time at Plymouth. He is mentioned by Morton, in his history of Plymouth, as among the ablest ministers in the colony of Massachusetts in 1642. In April, 1653, he visited Long Island, and made a purchase, with others, at Oyster-Bay. It is probable that he devoted some part of his time, after his removal to Oyster-Bay, in instructing the natives, either on Long Island or elsewhere. From the accounts of the commissioners presented to the society for propagating the gospel in New England, it appears they allowed Mr. Leveridge small sums, from time to time, between 1653 and 1658, for his services among the Indians. In 1657 they desired him to instruct the Corehaug and Montauk tribes, at the east end of the island, if his situation would admit of it. In 1658 he was established as the minister of this town, and on the 10th of February, 1662, the people, by a vote at town meeting, appointed two men to purchase a house and land for a parsonage ; and by a similar vote, the 7th of June following, granted to Mr. Leveridge the use of all the meadow about Cow-Harbor, on both sides of the creek, as long as he should continue their minister. In 1670 he removed to Newtown, and was the first minister of that place.

In April, 1673, the people, by a vote at town meeting, authorized the magistrates, with certain other persons named for the purpose, to endeavor to procure a minister for the town ; and in January, 1676, by a similar vote they agreed to invite the Rev. Eliphalet Jones, to continue with them as their minister, and that he should have twenty acres of land *where he chose to take it up.* He deferred his acceptance of the invitation till the 10th of June, 1677, when, at a public training, the choice of the people was expressed in his favor with one dissenting voice. Mr. Jones was the son of the Rev. John Jones, (who came to Boston in 1635, and settled at Concord in 1637.) He was born Nov. 6, 1640, and died in this town in 1731, at the age of ninety-three. He appears to have been a man of great purity and simplicity of manners, and a faithful and successful preacher. In consequence of his increasing age and infirmity, the town, on the 19th of June, 1719, engaged the Rev. Ebenezer Prime to assist him, which he did till June 5, 1723, when he was ordained as his colleague. After the death of Mr. Jones, the Rev. Mr. Prime continued the minister of Huntington till October 30, 1766, when the Rev. John Close was settled as his colleague. After the departure of Mr. Close in 1773, Mr. Prime continued without a colleague till his death. Mr. Prime was born at Milford, Connecticut, in 1700, and graduated at Yale College in 1718. His first wife was a daughter of Nathaniel Sylvester of Shelter Island, by whom he had a son that died while a student in Yale College; and two daughters, one of whom married the Rev. James Brown of Bridgehampton, and the other Mr. Israel Wood of this town. His second wife was a daughter of Judge Youngs of Southold, by whom he had a son by the name of Benjamin, who afterwards became an eminent physician. His third wife was a Miss Carle of this town, whom he left a widow at his death in 1779.

The next minister was the Rev. Nathan Woodhull, son of Captain Nathan Woodhull of Setauket. He was born in 1752, graduated at Yale College in 1775, and settled in this town in 1785; from whence he removed to Newtown in 1789, where he died in 1810. He was succeeded by the Rev. William Schenck, a native of New Jersey, graduated at Nassau Hall in 1767, and settled here in 1794. He continued here till 1817, when he removed with his family to Ohio. His wife was a daughter of Robert Cumming, Esq. of Freehold, New Jersey. He was succeeded by the Rev. Samuel Robinson, who settled in 1817, and removed in 1823; after which the Rev. Nehemiah Brown and the Rev. Mr. Halliday were successively engaged for short periods.

The first Presbyterian church was erected in the village of Huntington in 1665, enlarged in 1686, and succeeded by another on the site of the present church in 1715. This stood till the revolutionary war. The British troops, stationed here during the winter of 1777, took possession of it, tore up the seats,

and made a store-house of it. It remained in this condition
till the fall of 1782, when it was torn down by order of Colonel Thompson, and the materials were employed in the construction of barracks in the fort upon the burying-hill.

The Episcopal church, called St. John's, was erected in 1764 ;
and the only settled clergyman in this church was the Rev.
James Greaton. He graduated in 1754 at Yale College, and
came to reside here in 1767, where he died in 1773. His wife
was Mary Wheelright of Boston, by whom he had two sons,
John and James. After his death she became the wife of Dr.
Benjamin Y. Prime. A Presbyterian church was erected between Crab-Meadow and Fresh-Pond, in the eastern part of the
town, shortly before the revolutionary war, and was supplied a
part of the time by the Rev. Joshua Hart, minister of Smithtown. Another has lately been built at Red-Hook. A Methodist church was erected at Comac in 1786, and a second
in 1831. A handsome Universalist church was completed in
the village of Huntington in 1837. Huntington Academy was
erected in 1794, and has proved one of the most useful schools
in the country. The village of Huntington is the most ancient
and populous in the town, and has a fine harbor. The other
navigable waters on the north side of the town are Cold-Spring,
Lloyd's Harbor, and Great and Little Cow-Harbor. The bay
formed by Eaton's Neck and Lloyd's Neck affords a depth of
water for vessels of the largest class, and was used as a station
for ships during the revolution. The South-Bay, which bounds
the town on the south, is evidently decreasing in width, and
the depth of water constantly lessening by the sand washed
and blown into it from the beach. The village of Little Cow-
Harbor is now called Centre-Port, and the name of Great-Cow-
Harbor changed to North-Port ; each having a considerable population, and easy communication with the Sound. Comac
and Dix-Hills also contain a number of houses; but the most
active and thriving village is Babylon, upon the south side of
the island, in full view of the bay and ocean. It is situated upon
Sunquams Neck, and has a fine stream of water on either
side, upon which mills have long been erected. The population is about two hundred and fifty, with two good hotels, some

half a dozen stores, and several mechanic shops. Few places are more pleasantly and eligibly situated for business, and for the resort of those who delight in sea air and the amusements of fishing and fowling. It is about forty miles from the city of New-York. The first Presbyterian church was built in 1730, which was demolished by the British during the revolution, and its materials conveyed to Hempstead to aid in the erection of barracks at that place. A new church was finished soon after the peace, which has lately been converted into a dwelling-house, and a larger and more elegant edifice erected in its place, with a bell presented by David Thompson, Esq. of New-York. The society of Universalists are also preparing to erect a house for public worship in the village, which, when not occupied by them, is to be *free* to all denominations of Christians.

The surface of this town along the Sound, and for two or three miles from it, is rough and hilly, sometimes stony. It then becomes level, and so continues from two to four miles in different places, when there occur three separate ridges or groups of hills, the *West Hills*, the *Hills around the Long-Swamp, and Dix-Hills*. These are irregular, and extend two or three miles each way. South-westerly of Dix-Hills, after a small interval of level land, is another group, called the *Half-Way-Hollow-Hills*. From which the descent to the South-Bay is an inclined plane, and so gradual as to be imperceptible. The South-Bay has upon its northern shore a continuous strip of salt-meadow, nearly a mile wide. The soil near the Sound, and particularly upon the necks, is the best in the town. The high grounds are the most valuable and productive. The pine plains in the middle of the island are a mass of sand, with occasional spots having a thin covering of loam. The whole of the town is evidently alluvial, for in no part can the earth be excavated to any considerable distance without meeting with sand and gravel, bearing evident marks of long attrition by water. On a slope at the west end of the Half-Way-Hollow-Hills, coarse sand-stones, of a dark yellow color, intermixed with mineral substances, have been found. Also the sulphuret of iron ; and at the depth of eighteen feet, limbs of trees and the outer bark of the pitch-pine have been discovered, their inter-

stices filled with a mineral.   At the first settlement of the town,
wolves, wild-cats, wild-turkies, swans, and pelicans were found
in abundance ; and the wolves were so mischievous, that boun-
ties were freely given for their destruction.

Eaton's Neck, which lies upon the north, and extends some
distance into the Sound, is a valuable tract of about fifteen
hundred acres.   There is a due proportion of arable land, woodland, and meadow.   On the extreme point a light-house was
erected in 1798, at an expense of $9,750.   This neck takes its
name from Governor Eaton of New-Haven, who obtained it
from the Indians in 1646.   It was sold to Richard Bryan of
Milford, in 1684, whose descendants conveyed it to John Sloss
of Fairfield.   His daughter became the wife of the Rev. Noah
Hobart of that place, and eventually it became the property of
her son, the late Hon. John Sloss Hobart, former judge of
the supreme court of this state ; who, at the close of the revolution, conveyed it to John Watts of New-York, and sold by
him to John Gardiner, the ancestor of the present owners.

West Neck is likewise a highly valuable and fertile tract of
land, of many hundred acres, between Cold-Spring and Huntington Harbors, to which Lloyd's Neck is attached by a
low flat sand-beach or strand.   In addition to its other local advantages, it contains very extensive beds of choice clay, from
which millions of brick have been manufactured.   On the east
side of Huntington Harbor is *East Neck*, which is neither so
large or fertile as the former.   It is, however, more elevated,
and affords from many spots very sublime and romantic views
of the distant scenery.   A splendid mansion has lately been
erected in an elevated position by Professor Rhinelander of
New-York as a country residence, which is seen to great advantage from all parts of the adjoining country.

A newspaper was established in this town by Samuel A. Seabury in 1821, called the " *American Eagle*," which was continued till about the year 1825 ; and on the first of May of that
year a monthly magazine, entitled the " *Long Island Journal
of Philosophy*," was commenced by Samuel Fleet, which, for
want of sufficient patronage, was relinquished in a year or two
after.

JOHN SLOSS HOBART, mentioned above as a former owner of Eaton's Neck and an inhabitant of this town, was born at Fairfield in 1635. He graduated at Yale College in 1757, and although not bred a lawyer, was a man of a sound education and excellent understanding. His deportment was grave and his countenance austere; yet he was a warm-hearted man, and universally respected for his good sense, his integrity, his pure moral character, and patriotic devotion to the best interests of his country. He possessed the entire confidence of the public councils of the state, and on all fitting occasions this confidence was largely and freely manifested. He was appointed to the bench of the supreme court of this state in 1777, and continued in the office for about twenty years. He was (says Chancellor Kent) a faithful, diligent, and discerning judge during the time he remained upon the bench. He was selected as a member from this state of a partial and preliminary convention that met at Anapolis in September, 1786, and was afterwards elected by the citizens of New-York a member of the state convention in 1788, which ratified the present constitution of the United States. When he retired from the Supreme Court in 1798, he was chosen by the legislature of this state a senator in Congress. His friend, the late Hon. Egbert Benson, caused a plain marble slab to be affixed in the wall of the chamber of the supreme court in the City-Hall of the city of New-York, to the memory of Judge Hobart, with the following inscription upon it, which, though bordering on that quaint and sententious style so peculiar to Judge Benson, contains a just and high eulogy on the distinguished virtues of the deceased:

> "John Sloss Hobart, was born at Fairfield, Connecticut. His father, a minister of that place. He was appointed a Judge of the Supreme Court in 1777, and left it in 1798, having attained sixty years of age. The same year he was appointed a Judge of the United States District Court for New-York, and held it till his death in 1805. As a *man*, firm—as a *citizen*, zealous—as a *Judge*, distinguishing—as a Christian, sincere. This tablet is erected to his memory by one, to whom, as a friend—close as a brother."

BENJAMIN YOUNGS PRIME. This eminent physician was the son of the Rev. Ebenezer Prime, minister of Huntington, where he was born about the year 1746. He received his classical education at Princeton College, where, after graduating, he remained awhile as tutor, and afterwards commenced the study of medicine with Doctor Jacob Ogden, who was, for nearly forty years, a respectable physician at Jamaica, and who published an ingenious and valuable treatise upon scarlet fever, a disease at that time little known in this country. After completing his course of studies, Dr. Prime sailed for Europe, and while there attended some of the more celebrated medical schools of London, Edinburgh, and Paris; after which he made an excursion to the city of Moscow. He was honored with a degree at most of the institutions which he visited, and was much noticed and respected for his amiable manners and extraordinary attainments. Returning to America, he commenced practice in the city of New-York, where he obtained much distinction; and on the city being entered by the British troops in Semptember, 1776, he was compelled to abandon his business and prospects; for, being a staunch Whig, and accustomed to lash the enemy with the satire of his pen, to remain among them at such a time might expose him to inconvenience and danger. About this time he contracted a matrimonial alliance with the widow of the Rev. James Greaton, by whom he had two sons and three daughters; the youngest of whom is the Rev. Nathaniel S. Prime of Newburgh, a scholar and man of talents. Doctor Prime continued to use his pen and to indulge his poetic vein in lampoons upon the British officers and soldiers, and to encourage by every means the hopes and exertions of his countrymen. Having finally become suspected as the author of some severe publications, in which the enemy and their Tory allies were held up to public scorn and ridicule, attempts were made to take him prisoner; but being acquainted with their designs, he took refuge with his family in Connecticut, where he remained till the restoration of peace. He next settled as a physician in his native place, where he had constant employ- ment, extending his practice to a considerable distance in all directions, till the close of his valuable life on the 31st of October, 1791. He was a man of great natural abilities, possessed much genius for poetry; and his learning, both pro- fessional and miscellaneous, was various and extensive. He died in the vigor of life and in the midst of usefulness, universally respected and lamented. His widow survived him for a period of nearly fifty years.

TOWN OF OYSTER-BAY.

This town embraces a larger extent of territory than any other in the county of Queens; and is bounded north by the Sound, east by Suffolk County, south by the Atlantic Ocean, and west by the towns of Hempstead and North Hempstead, together with Lloyd's Neck lying opposite the town of Hun- tington. The name is, doubtless, derived from the beautiful bay on its northern border, which anciently is said to have abounded in oysters of the finest quality. In the spring of 1640 an attempt was made to form a settlement upon the pre- sent site of the village of Oyster-Bay by Captain Edward Tom- lyns, his brother Timothy Tomlyns, and a few other persons from the town of Lynn, without having obtained permission from the Dutch or consent of the agent of the Earl of Stirling, who at that time resided in Boston. They met with such opposition from the Dutch, who remonstrated against their proceedings, that they abandoned the place and returned again to Massachusetts. James Farret, the authorized agent of the Earl, was so much displeased with the conduct of these adventurers, that he forth. with drew up a formal protest against them, which is thus recorded in Winthrop's History of Massachusetts :

"Know all men by these presents, that whereas Edward Tomlyns and Timo- thy Tomlyns, together with one Housard Knowles and others, have lately entered and taken possession of some part of the Long Island in New-England, which was formerly granted by Letters Patent of our Sovereign Lord, King Charles, to the Right Hon. William Earl of Stirling and his heirs: I, James Farret, by virtue of a commission under the hand and seal of the said Earl to me made for the disposing and ordering of the said Island, do hereby protest and intimate, as well to the said Edward Tomlyns and others, the said intruders, as to all others whom it may concern, that neither they, nor any of them, nor any other person or persons, (not claiming by or from the said Earl,) have or shall have, or enjoy any lawful right, title, or possession of, in, or to the said island, or any part thereof; but that the said Earl, his heirs and assigns, may and will at all times, when they please, implead or eject, either by course of law or lawful force, if need be, all the said intruders, their servants, tenants, or assigns; and may and will recover against them and every of them, all damages and costs in this behalf sustained, or any color of title, or pretence of right, by grant from the governor of New England, or any other notwithstanding. In testimony whereof I have made and published this protest and intimation before *John Winthrop*, one of the magistrates and council of the Massachusetts, in New England aforesaid, and have desired that the same be recorded there, and in other jurisdictions in these parts, and have published and showed the same to the said Edward Tomlyns in presence of the witnesses. Dated at Boston, the 28th of 7th month, An. Dom. 1641, in anno Regis Domini Nostri Caroli Angliæ, decimo septimo.

" James Farret."

In the history of Lynn, it is mentioned that the said Edward and Timothy Tomlyns were men of distinction in the early settlement of Massachusetts, who, as well as Daniel Howe, were frequently chosen representatives to the general court between the years 1634 and 1640. In 1642 some of the English again advanced as far as Oyster-Bay, within the tract which had been previously purchased from the Indians by Captain Howe, and were again repulsed by Governor Kieft, and some of the persons taken and imprisoned in New-York. The line of separation between the respective territories of the two powers was a constant source of difficulty, and the public harmony was disturbed by mutual complaints of encroachments both on Long Island and the Main; and it was at length attempted to put an end to the controversy by definitely settling the boundaries of the respective territory.

On the 19th of May, 1643, the colonies of Plymouth, Massachusetts, Hartford, and New-Haven, united for their mutual security and the protection of the settlements connected with them; and the public affairs were transacted by two commissioners from each, by whom all controversies between the English and Dutch were from that period managed on the part of

41

the English. A treaty for the adjustment of differences and the establishment of boundaries between the two powers, was negotiated by Simon Bradstreet and Thomas Prince on the part of the commissioners; and by Thomas Willet and George Baxter on the part of the Dutch, at Hartford, the 19th of September, 1650. By that treaty, as has been seen, it was agreed " that a line run from the westernmost part of Oyster-Bay, and so a straight and direct line to the sea, should be the bounds betwixt the English and Dutch; the easterly part to belong to the English, and the westernmost to the Dutch. When this town came to be settled by the English, a dispute arose between them and the Dutch governor, respecting the western limits of the bay, and this, with the delay of the States-General to ratify the treaty, furnished the Dutch governor with a pretext for not fulfilling it.

The first permanent settlement in this town was upon or near the site of the village of Oyster-Bay, in the year 1653; and the Indian deed for the first purchase was given by the Matinecock Sachem, as follows:

"Anno Domini, 1653—This writing witnesseth that I, Assiapum, alias Moheness, have sold unto Peter Wright, Samuel Mayo, and William Leveridge, their heyres, exets, administr, and assigns, all the land lying and scituate upon Oyster-Bay, and bounded by Oyster-Bay River to the east side, and *Papequtunck* on the west side, with all ye woods, rivers, marshes, uplands, ponds, and all other the appertainances lying between ye bounds afore-named, with all the islands to the seaward. excepting one island, commonly called Hogg-Island, and bounded near southerly by a point of trees called *Cantiaque;* in consideration of which bargain and sale he is to receive as full satisfaction, six Indian coats, six kettles, six fathom of wampum, six hoes, six hatchets, three pair of stockings, thirty awl-blades or muxes, twenty knives, three shirts, and as much Peague as will amount to four pounds sterling. In witness whereof he hath set his mark, in the presence of   his

" William Washborne, Anthony }   Assiapum or Moheness, *f* mark."
  Wright, Robert Williams.   }

Upon the above instrument is an endorsement, as follows ·

"The within-named Peter Wright and William Leveridge, do accept of, as joynt purchasers with ourselves, William Washborne, Thomas Armitage, Daniel Whitehead, Anthony Wright, Robert Williams, John Washboine, and Richard Holdbrook, to the like right as we have ourselves in ye land purchased of Assiapum, and particularly mentioned in ye writing made and subscribed by himself, with the consent of other Indians respectively interested, and in ye names of such as were absent, acted by him and them. As witness our hands. *Peter Wright, Samuel Mayo, William Leverich.*"

In Hazard's collection of state papers, it is mentioned that the vessel which brought Mr. Leveridge here belonged to Captain Thomas Willet, Samuel Mayo, William Paddy, and John Barnes of Barnstable; and as war then prevailed between the English and Dutch in Europe, she was taken while within the Dutch limits, having gone to Hempstead-Harbor, and landed their cattle and goods, because there was no house erected at Oyster-Bay in which they could be received. The capture was made by Thomas Baxter of Rhode Island, who was cruising against the Dutch commerce, under authority of Rhode Island, and took sides with the mother country; upon, which the commissioners of the United Colonies were obliged to interfere, to procure a restoration of the vessel.

One of the most ancient records of the town is a grant of land to Henry Townsend, dated the 16th of September, 1661, with permission to build a mill at Mill-River upon the west end of the town; meaning, probably, the west side of the settlement as then existing; which is probably the same as has been owned by the Townsend family ever since.

It would seem that much trouble was experienced by the first settlers, in consequence of the conflicting claims of the English and Dutch to this part of the town; and in June, 1656, the commissioners of the United Colonies, in answer to a communication from the Dutch governor, reproveth him for still continuing to claim Oyster-Bay, contrary to the treaty made at Hartford. These disputes involved the inhabitants in much perplexity, for, in order to avoid giving offence to either power, they were under the necessity of observing a sort of neutrality between the contending parties; and on the 13th of Dec. 1660, the town meeting resolved that no person should intermeddle, to put the town either under the Dutch or English, until the difference between them be ended, under the penalty of fifty pounds sterling. In 1659 the directors of the West India Company ordered the Dutch governor to erect a fort, or to build a block-house, on their East-Bay, in order more effectually to resist the encroachments of the English. Although the treaty of Hartford was ratified by the States-General on the 22d of February, 1656, the Dutch governor was reluctant to give up his claim of jurisdiction over this town, or a part of it.   But on the 8th of January, 1662, the people of the town took a more decided stand, avowing their allegiance to the king of England, and resolved to defend any who should be molested for exercising authority among them, at their joint expense; and it is presumed that the town, about this period, united with other English towns upon the island in putting themselves under Connecticut.   The exact boundaries between this town and Huntington were a subject of dispute, which occasioned the following letter, dated the 5th of July, 1669 :

" Friends and neighbors of the town of Huntington.   We once more desire you in a *loving*, friendly way, to forbear mowing our neck of meadow, which you have presumptuously mowed these several years; and if, after so many *friendly warnings*, you will not forbear, you will force us, *friends and neighbors*, to seek our remedy in law, not else; but resting your *friends and neighbors*.   By me, in behalf of the town of Oyster-Bay.   MATEIAS HARVEY, Town Clerk."

On the 29th of Sept., 1677, a patent of confirmation for the lands already purchased from the natives was obtained of Governor Andross, in which the boundaries are thus described :

" Beginning on the east, at the head of Cold-Spring Harbor, and running a southward course across the Island to a certain river called by the Indians Warrasketuck; then along the sea-coast westerly to another certain river called Arrasquaung; then northerly to the easternmost extent of the Great Plains, where the line divides Hempstead and Robert Williams' bounds; from thence westerly along the middle of said plains till it bears south from the said Robert Williams' marked tree, at the point of trees called Cantiaque; then on a north line, somewhat westerly, to the head of Hempstead Harbor on the east side of the Sound; and from thence easterly along the Sound to the afore-mentioned north and south line, which runs across the island by the Cold-Spring aforesaid; to Henry Townsend, sen, Nicholas Wright, Gideon Wright, Richard Harrison, Joseph Carpenter, and Josias Latting, for themselves, their associates, the freeholders and inhabitants of the said town, their heyres, successors, and assigns, for ever."

On the 26th of May, 1663, the Indians sold a part of Matinecock to Capt. John Underhill, John Frost, and William Frost; another part on the 20th of April, 1669, to Richard Latting; another part on the 1st of Dec. 1683, to Thomas Townsend; and upon the 9th of January, 1685, the chiefs, namely, *Sucanemen* alias *Runasuck*, *Chechagen* alias *Quaropin*, *Samose* (son of *Tackapausha*), being empowered by the rest of the Indians, conveyed the residue of Matinecock, together with some other lands, for the price of sixty pounds of *current mer-chantable pay,* to James Cock, Joseph Dickerson, Robert Townsend, Samuel.Dickerson, Stephen Birdsall, James Town-send, Daniel Weeks, Isaac Doughty, John Wood, Edmund Wright, Caleb Wright, John Wright, William Frost, and John Newman ; and thereupon the said grantees agreed to accept, as joint purchasers with them, the following-named persons, being then the acknowledged inhabitants and freeholders of the town, comprising the most complete list of names at that time, which the records present :

John Townsend, Sen.	John Pratt,	Hope Williams, of Lusum.
Daniel Townsend,	Thomas Willets	
John Dewsbury,	Samuel Weeks,	Lawrence Mott,
William Crooker,	Joseph Weeks,	William Buckler,
John Applegate,	Peter Wright,	Josias Latting,
Thomas Youngs,	George Downing,	Thomas Cock,
John Rogers,	Richard Harcutt,	William Hauxhurst,
Hannah fforman, for her son Moses.	Daniel Coles, jun.	Elizabeth Dickson,
	John Cock,	James Bleven,
John Robbins,	John Weeks,	Daniel Whitehead,
Thomas Townsend,	Henry Franklin,	Samuel Tiller,
Samuel Birdsall,	John Townsend, sen. of Lusum,	Robert Coles,
Josias Carpenter,		Richard Kirby,
Sampson Hauxhurst.	Henry Bell,	William Thorncraft,
Adam Wright,	Richard Willett,	Robert Godfrey,
Thomas Weeks,	Meriam Harker,	Ephraim Carpenter,
Nathan Birdsall,	John Williams, of Lusum.	Joseph Sutton.
Mathew Prior,		

A separate patent was obtained from the governor for the purchase of Musquito Cove, cotemporaneously with that for the other part of the town, and purports to be for seventeen hundred acres, the quit-rent for which was fixed at one bushel of good winter wheat annually. The records of the town during the last years of the 17th century, are filled with numerous conveyances for land from the natives, both to the town and to individuals, divisions and allotments among the proprietors of the town, wills, and contracts of different descriptions. "At a town meeting held March 21, 1689, Richard Harcut and John Townsend were deputed to go to Jamaica to appoint two men from the county to be at York on the tenth of April next, to consult of the affairs of the country." On the 19th of Feb.

1693, the town met to consider the late act of assembly for settling two ministers in the county, and decided that it was against their judgment, and reported to the governor that they could do nothing about it. In 1693 a purchase was made from the Masapequa Indians for a tract at Fort Neck on the south side of the Island, by Thomas Townsend, for fifteen pounds *current silver money,* which, on the 29th of June, 1695, he gave to his son-in-law Thomas Jones and daughter Freelove.

By the act of 1691 Horse Neck, (now Lloyd's Neck,) which had heretofore been an independent plantation, and the only manorial estate in the county, was annexed to the town of Oyster-Bay.

Lloyd's Neck, called by the Indians Caumsett, contains about three thousand acres of land, projecting into the Sound between Cold-Spring and Huntington Harbor. The soil is of an excellent quality, one half of which is appropriated to cultivation, and the other to the growing of timber. It was erected into a manor called Queen's Village in 1685, during the administration of Governor Dongan ; and an application for a renewal of the like privileges was made by the owners to the legislature the 27th March, 1790, which was refused. The British troops took possession of it during the revolution, erected a fort, and committed depredations to a great extent; having, during the course of the war, cut down and disposed of between fifty and a hundred thousand cords of wood. The reproduction was so rapid, that for the last fifty years more than a thousand cords have been annually sold.   Independent of its fine soil and many local advantages, there is an inexhaustible mine of fine white clay, suitable for pottery, and a bed of yellow ochre, of unknown extent, which may be employed as a substitute for paint. The purchase of this Neck was made the 20th Sept. 1654, from Ratiocan Sagamore of Cow-Harbor, by Samuel Mayo, Daniel Whitehead, and Peter Wright, three of the first settlers of Oyster-Bay, for the price of three coats, three shirts, two cuttoes, three hatchets, three hoes, two fathom of wampum, six knives, two pair of stockings, and two pair of shoes. They sold to Samuel Andrews, on the 6th of May, 1658, for £100, and the sale was confirmed by *Wyandanch,* the Long Island Sachem, on the 14th of the same month. On the death of Andrews, the Neck was conveyed to John Richhill the 5th of Sept. 1660, who, on the 18th of Oct. 1666, sold it to Nathaniel Sylvester, Thomas Hart, and Latimer Sampson, for £450 Sylvester released to his co-tenants, Oct. 17, 1668, a patent having been obtained from Governor Nicolls on the 20th Nov. 1667. The executors of Hart sold his moiety to James Lloyd of Boston for £200, Oct. 17th 1679, he having married Grizzle Sylvester, who had become entitled by devise from Sampson to his portion of the Neck. Mr. Lloyd now became proprietor of the whole estate. He died, Oct. 16, 1693, having devised the property to his children, one of whom, Henry Lloyd, came here to reside in 1711. Having acquired the interest of his co tenants, he became in time the sole owner of the Neck, which, in consequence of being included in the general boundaries of Huntington purchase, was claimed by that town. On appeal to the court of assise, the claim of the town was disallowed, and, to prevent a renewal of any such pretence in future, Mr. Lloyd procured a release from a greater part, if not from all, the freeholders of the town of Huntington. The division line between him and the town was definitely fixed by David Jones of Oyster-Bay, Richard Woodhull of Brookhaven, and William Willis of Hempstead, arbitrators mutually chosen for the purpose in 1734.

Henry Lloyd was born Nov. 23, 1685, and died March 10, 1763. His wife, Rebecca, was the daughter of John Nelson of Boston, whom he married Nov. 23, 1708, and by whom he had ten children. He devised the Neck to his four surviving sons, Henry, John, James and Joseph. Henry was born Aug. 6, 1709, and having espoused the royal cause in the revolution, his part of the estate became forfeited by his attainder, and was subsequently purchased of the commissioners of forfeitures by his brother John. James was born March 14, 1728, and was an eminent physician in Boston, where he died in 1809. His son, the Hon. James Lloyd, a distinguished senator in congress from Massachusetts, died suddenly while on a visit to New-York, a few years since, leaving to his children a spotless reputation and a princely fortune. Joseph was born Dec 19, 1716, and died at Hartford June 20, 1780. John, the other brother, was born Feb. 19, 1711, and married Sarah, daughter of the Rev. Benjamin Woolsey of Dos-Oris ; and had children Henry, John, Rebecca, Abigail and Sarah. Of these, Henry died, a few years since, unmarried. Abigail became the wife of Dr. James Cogswell of New-York, one of the most excellent men of his day, and greatly distinguished not only for his professional eminence, but for his noble philanthropy and public spirit. Sarah intermarried with the late Hon. James Hillhouse, senator in congress from Connecticut, eminent for his intelligence, and his entire devotion to every measure calculated to advance the public interest of the state and Union. James Hillhouse, Esq. of New-Haven, so favorably distinguished for his extensive literary attainments and fine poetical genius, is his son. The last-named John Lloyd was about thirty years old at the commencement of the revolutionary war ; and when the enemy took possession of Long Island, he was compelled to leave his large possessions to the free plunder of those who were influenced by no rule of law or justice, and great was the injury sustained. ‑He received an appointment in the commissariat, the very responsible duties of which he discharged with a fidelity which met the approbation of the commander-in-chief. On his return to his farm in 1783, he married Amelia, daughter of the Rev. Ebenezer White, of Danbury, Connecticut. The office of judge of Queen's County was tendered him by Governor Jay, which, from his love of retirement, he declined. His death, which was sincerely regretted by those who knew him, took place at the age of forty-seven, in the year 1792. His widow survived till 1818.

His only son, John Nelson Lloyd, a gentleman of great respectability and worth, resides upon the Neck, being the owner of more than one-third part of it ; while another portion belongs to the children of his deceased sister, Angelina, who intermarried with George W. Strong. Esq., a distinguished counsellor of the city of New-York.

The remains of the fort erected upon the western side of the Neck near the Sound, are still visible. An attempt was made to capture this garrison in July, 1781, by a force under the command of the Baron de Angely, but which proved unsuccessful, partly from the want of cannon, and partly from mistaking the true point of approach to the fort. This place was visited during the war by Prince William Henry, since King William IV. of England. The mansion of Mr. Lloyd is on the south side of the Neck, a beautifully romantic situation, the charms of which are intended to be portrayed by the late Governor Livingston in his delightful poem entitled " Philosophic Solitude."

Dos-Oris is likewise an interesting place, situated on the Sound a short distance north of Glen-Cove. The name is alleged to be a contraction of the words *Dos Uxoris*, and intended to imply that the property had been derived to some of its former owners through the female line. The location is not only beautiful and picturesque, but well calculated for business. Several extensive milling establishments have long been erected here, and proved a source of considerable pecuniary emolument. The soil in the vicinity is of excellent quality, and the facilities for improvement are rarely exceeded. This valuable property was originally obtained of the Matinecock Indians by Lewis Morris, a merchant of the island of Barbados, (uncle of Richard Morris, first proprietor of Morrisiana,) for which a patent of confirmation was granted by Governor Dongan in 1685. The whole, or a great part of it, was subsequently conveyed by Morris to Daniel Whitehead of Jamaica, Long Island ; and was devised by him to his daughter, wife of John Taylor, whereby it descended to her only daughter, Abigail, who intermarried with the Rev. Benjamin Woolsey, minister of Southold. After his marriage, Mr. Woolsey removed to Dos-Oris, where he continued till his death. One of his daughters became the wife of Dr. George Muirson of Setauket, a distinguished physician, and celebrated for his successful treatment of the small-pox ; more than two thousand having been inoculated by him, of whom only five died. Of this number was his grandson, George Muirson Woolsey. Heathcote Muirson, son of Dr. Muirson, an amiable youth and ardent patriot, was mortally wounded during the attack upon Lloyd's Neck in July, 1781, as above mentioned. Another daughter of Mr. Woolsey married the Rev. Noah Wells of Stamford, a theologian of much acuteness, and distinguished for his controversial writings on the subject of American Episcopacy. . He died in 1776. A third daughter was the wife of John Lloyd, as above stated. Mr. Woolsey had also two sons, Me-

lancton and Benjamin. The former, better known as Col.
Woolsey, father of the late Gen. Melancton Woolsey of Cumberland Head, near Plattsburgh, and grandfather of Commodore Melancton T. Woolsey of the United States navy.
General Woolsey was created a field-officer at the age of
twenty-two, and rendered very important services upon the
northern frontier. After the revolution, he took up his residence near Plattsburgh, and died at Trenton, June 29th, 1819,
while on a journey to visit his son, then commanding at Sacket's
Harbor. One of Col. Woolsey's daughters was the second wife
of the Hon. James Hillhouse of New-Haven.

Benjamin Woolsey, second son of the Rev. Mr. Woolsey, graduated at Yale
College in 1744, and resided at Dos-Oris, in the commission of the peace, till his
death in 1770. His estate was sold to Nathaniel Coles; the other portion having
been conveyed by the executors of Col. Woolsey to John Butler in 1660, came
also into the possession of Mr. Coles, who married the daughter of Mr. Butler,
and thus descended to the late John B. Coles and Gen. Nathaniel Coles. The
said Benjamin Woolsey married Miss Isaacs of New Rochelle, by whom he
had two daughters, one of whom married Moses Rogers, an eminent merchant
of New-York; and the other the Rev. Timothy Dwight, afterwards president of
Yale College, and one of the most learned men of the age. His death took
place January 11th, 1817, but his widow still survives at an advanced age, in the
full possession of her mental faculties. After the death of his wife, Mr.
Woolsey married Ann, daughter of Dr. Muirson, (who had married his sister,)
and by whom he had several children. William W. Woolsey and George M.
Woolsey of New-York, are sons of Mr. Woolsey. Another of his daughters
married Captain Palmer of the British army, and emigrated to Ireland. His
daughter Elizabeth married William Dunlap, well known for his eminence in
the fine arts, and as the author of many valuable publications.

Oyster-Bay Village, including the Cove, (so called,) contains about sixty dwellings, and three hundred and fifty inhabitants. From its position, fronting on the Bay and Sound, it may
be considered one of the most desirable places of residence in
this part of the island, and some gentlemen of wealth and taste
have made choice of it accordingly. The view from many
points is charmingly picturesque, presenting, in common with a
few other locations in this quarter of the country, a variegated
prospect of land and water, of forest and cultivated fields. Between the water of the Bay and Sound is *Middle* or *Centre
Island,* formerly called *Hog-Island,* once probably encircled
by water, but now connected with the main land of Matinecock

by a long sandy beach of alluvial formation. It contains about six hundred acres of the most valuable land, divided into three farms, and highly improved. On the west of the village is the country-seat of the Hon. William T. McCoun, vice-chancellor of the first circuit, a gentleman of high judicial acquirements and acknowledged ability in his official station. In front of his mansion is a rock of considerable size, from which the celebrated George Fox addressed a large assemblage in 1672, while on a tour through Long Island. On the high ground near the Baptist church, are the remains of a fortification erected by Col. Simcoe, in the revolution, to prevent any hostile American force from entering the Bay ; and while here, was visited by the unfortunate Major Andre a short time previous to his arrest and execution. On the east side of the village, which is called the Cove, in a romantic spot shaded with trees, and having a luxuriant view of the Bay and surrounding scenery, is the private residence of Dr. James E. Dekay, an individual favorably known for his amiable character, and his proficiency in science and literature. His "*Sketches of Turkey*" alone have elevated him far above the majority of travellers ; to this excellent performance the reading world are deeply indebted for a more correct delineation of Turkish character and manners than has before been published.

The first Baptist church in this village was erected in 1724, and still remains, a curious relic of that age. It is about twenty feet square, with a quadrangular pointed roof, and no longer used for "*lodging folk disposed to sleep ;*" having lately been converted into a stable. The present church was built in 1801. The first minister of this congregation was the Rev. William Rhodes, a native of Chichester, England, who was engaged here in 1700, before the erection of the church. His successor was the Rev. Robert Feeks, the son of a Quaker, who was both prudent in his behavior and of liberal sentiments. He continued to preach till 1740, and died at the age of eighty-nine. The Rev. Thomas Davis, from Pennsylvania, was settled here in 1745, and, after several years, returned to his native state. The Rev. Caleb Wright, a grandson of Mr. Rhodes, had accepted an invitation to settle ; but having died suddenly after his arrival in November, 1752, his installation sermon was changed to a funeral oration. In 1789 the Rev. Benjamin Coles was settled, and continued till within a few years of his death in 1811. The Rev. Marmaduke Earle was associated in the ministry with Mr. Coles in 1800, in which year the Oyster-Bay academy was completed, and of which Mr Earle was the superintendent for nearly thirty years. He is still pastor of the church, and devotes a portion of his time to the business of instruction, although far advanced in years.

Glen-Cove, formerly called *Musquito Cove,* is a considerable village, conveniently situated upon the east side of Hempstead Harbor near its confluence with the Sound. It has long been a place of much activity, and has a good deal increased within a few years. There is a stream passing through it sufficient for mills and other machinery. There are two good hotels, several stores and mechanic shops. It possesses also a small academy, and an Episcopal church called St. Paul's, erected in 1834, which stands upon an eminence overlooking the neighboring country to a considerable extent. The Dutch church at Wolver-Hollow was originally built in 1732, and having stood just one hundred years, was followed by the present church in 1832. At *Matinecock, Buckram, Cedar-Swamp, Wheatly,* and *Wolver-Hollow,* are a good number of inhabitants, mostly farmers, who possess abundantly the necessaries and most of the luxuries of life. *Jericho,* anciently called *Lusum,* is a pleasant village near the centre of the town, eight miles east of Queen's County court-house. It is a part of the original purchase of Robert Williams in 1650, and from whom the title to the land has been derived. The dwellings are about forty, and the inhabitants two hundred and fifty. It is supplied with pure water issuing from the base of a hill near the village. The Friend's meeting-house was first erected in 1689, at which time several Quaker families took up their residence here, and soon after on the neighboring lands about *Westbury,* so called from its situation west of Jericho. This place is memorable as being the residence of Elias Hicks, the celebrated Quaker preacher, who settled here in 1771, and died in 1830. *Norwich* is situated about midway between the villages of Jericho and Oyster-

Bay, and at the present eastern termination of the turnpike leading to Flushing. It contains about twenty-five houses, one or
two stores, a fine hotel, and nearly two hundred inhabitants,
principally agriculturists. The Methodist church was built
about four years since. *Westbury* is a rich agricultural district, between Jericho and the court-house, level and fertile ; a
majority of the inhabitants are Friends, and have two places for
religious worship; the one of ancient date, the other erected within a few years, occasioned by the unhappy divisions now existing
among this respectable fraternity of Christians. *Hicks-ville*,
two miles south of Jericho, is located upon the eastern part of
the great plains, at the present termination of the Long Island
railroad. The car-house, and other necessary erections of
the company, a hotel, and a few private houses, constitute the
village ; there are, however, good reasons for supposing it may
hereafter become the site of some considerable manufacturing
establishments, especially from the facility afforded for expeditious and cheap communication with the cities of Brooklyn
and New-York. *Bethpage* is a considerable though scattered
settlement at the east of the great plains, where there is a
Friends' meeting-house, and about two hundred inhabitants,
who are farmers. The south side of the town has a level surface, and a light sandy soil, covered by a thin stratum of vegetable mould. The most interesting portion of this part of the
town is that known by the name of *Fort Neck*, so called on
account of two old Indian forts, the remains of which are still
very conspicuous. One of these is situated on the most southerly point of land adjoining the salt meadow, and is nearly, if
not exactly, a square, being about thirty yards on each side.
The breast-work or parapet is of earth, and there is a ditch or
moat on the outside, which appears to have been about six feet
wide. The other fort was on the southernmost point of the
salt meadow adjoining the bay, and consisted of palisadoes set
in the meadow. The tide has worn away the meadow where
the fort stood, and the place is now a part of the bay, and covered with water. In the bay between the meadow and the
beach are two islands, called *Squaw Islands ;* and the uniform
tradition of the Indians was, that the forts were erected by their

ancestors a great while ago, for defence against their enemies ; and that upon their approach, the women and children were sent to these islands, which occasioned them to be so called. The first and most substantial dwelling erected here by the white people was the *Old Brick House,* said to have been built by Captain Thomas Jones in 1695. It was doubtless considered a more than ordinary specimen of architecture in that day, and finished in a superior style. Many improbable fictions in relation to the owner of the mansion have been preserved, and more strange, not to say marvellous legends, have been cherished and circulated in regard to the edifice itself, which ignorance and superstition have not failed to magnify, and sufficient to fill the lonely and benighted traveller with fear and anxiety. A correspondent of the New-York Mirror, a few years since, speaking of the *Brick House,* says : "*This venerable edifice is still standing, though much dilapidated, and is an object of awe to all the people in the neighborhood. The traveller cannot fail to be struck with its reverend and crumbling ruins as his eye first falls upon it from the turnpike ; and if he has heard the story, he will experience a chilly sensation, and draw a hard breath while he looks at the circular sashless window in the gable end. That window has been left open ever since the old man's death. His sons and grandsons used to try all manner of means in their power to close it up. They put in sashes, and they boarded it up, and they bricked it up, but all would not do ; so soon as night came their work would be destroyed, and strange sights would be seen and awful voices heard.*" This curious and venerable relic of bye gone ages stood for a period of more than one hundred and forty years, unscathed, except by the hand of time ; and until 1837, when it was removed to make way for the extensive improvements of David S. Jones, Esq., near which he has erected one of the most costly and magnificent mansions in the state. The appendages to this splendid establishment are in keeping with the principal edifice, and do credit to the liberality and taste of their opulent proprietor. Although there is a large proportion of uncultivated land in the town, yet its agriculture has long been respectable. On the 21st of Dec.

1767, a society, formed in New-York for the encouragement of the arts, awarded a premium of ten pounds to Thomas Youngs of this town, for having raised, the year before, twenty-two thousand young apple-trees.

The village of *Cold-Spring* is situated at the head and upon both sides of Cold-Spring Harbor, consequently it is partly in the town of Huntington. The Indian name of this harbor is *Wawepex*. The village collectively contains about seventy dwellings, and nearly five hundred inhabitants, including those employed in the several factories. A large flouring mill was erected here in 1792, at an expense of twelve thousand five hundred dollars, and is capable of manufacturing into flour more than one thousand bushels of grain a-week. There are likewise two extensive woollen factories. The first built in 1816, by William M. Hewlett and John H. Jones, cost ten thousand dollars; and the second in 1820, by William H. Jones, John H. Jones, and Walter R. Jones, at an expense of twelve thousand five hundred dollars. Both are now owned by the three last-named gentlemen, in which are manufactured daily, into flannels and broad-cloths, more than one hundred and twenty pounds of wool. This place has likewise three stores, a lumber-yard, two wharves, fourteen coasting sloops, and two schooners; besides two ships, of three hundred and fifty tons each, belonging to the Cold-Spring Whaling Company, incorporated in 1836, which has thus far been successful. St. Thomas's Episcopal church was erected here in 1836, and is a handsome edifice. The situation is pleasant and the prospect extensive. The present rector is the Rev. Isaac Sherwood. This town has been the recipient of two considerable legacies; one of three hundred pounds was given in 1798 by David Jones, the interest to be annually appropriated for the education of poor children belonging to the town; and the other of thirty thousand dollars, bequeathed by the late Samuel Jones in 1836, to the towns of Oyster-Bay and North Hempstead, to be called the *Jones' Fund;* the income whereof is directed by the testator to be applied exclusively for the support of the poor of the said towns.

The following revolutionary anecdote is too interesting to be omitted. In 1779

Major-general Silliman was appointed by the Governor and council of Connecticut, superintendant of the coast of Fairfield. In the month of May, Sir Henry Clinton directed a small company of refugees to cross the Sound in a whale-boat from Lloyd-Neck, and, if possible, to take him prisoner. One of them was an inhabitant of Newtown, named Glover, a carpenter who had previously been in the employ of the general, and having been some time at the house, was perfectly acquainted with the safest and easiest modes of access to it. The crew consisted of nine—one was left in the boat, and eight came to the house about midnight. The family were awakened by a violent assault upon the door. The General sprang from bed, raised a musket and approached the door. As he passed by the window, he saw the men, and at once comprehended their design. He attempted to fire, but his musket only flashed. At that instant the assailants broke through the window and seized him, exclaiming that he was their prisoner, and that he must go with them. At his request they permitted him to dress, and having plundered him of a fusee, a pair of pistols, a sword, and a few other articles of small value, proceeded with expedition to the shore, which they reached about two o'clock, and immediately embarked for Long Island. As they approached the shore of Lloyd's Neck, Colonel Simcoe, the commanding officer, who was waiting for them, exclaimed, "Have you got him?" They answered, Yes. "Have you lost any men?" No. "That is well, your Sillimans are not worth a man, nor your Washingtons." General Silliman's eldest son was taken with him. The prisoners were ordered to the guard-house. The General asked whether this was the manner they treated prisoners of his rank. The adjutant replied, "We do not consider you in the same light as we should a continental General." How, then, said the General, will you view me when an exchange shall be proposed? "I understand you," said the officer, and withdrew. These questions, probably, saved the General from the indignity of being confined in a guard-house. Soon after, he and his son were conducted in a carriage to New-York under an escort of dragoons, and on his arrival a large body of people assembled to see him. A friend advised him to withdraw to avoid insult, and very kindly conducted him to good lodgings. Here he remained for some time, when he was ordered to Flatbush. At that time there was no prisoner in the possession of the Americans whom the British would accept for the General, and after some consideration it was determined to procure one. The person selected was the Hon. Thomas Jones of Fort Neck, Long Island, a justice of the supreme court of the province of New-York; and Captain Daniel Hawley of Newfield, (now Bridgeport,) undertook to accomplish the design. On the 4th of November, 1779, about twenty-five volunteers, under the command of Captains Hawley, Lockwood, and Jones, and Lieutenants Jackson and Bishop, set off from Newfield Harbor. They crossed the Sound that evening, arrived at Stoney-Brook near Smithtown, and marched to Mr. Jones' residence, where they arrived on the 6th about nine o'clock in the evening, the whole distance fifty-two miles. There was a ball in the house, and the noise of music and dancing prevented the approach of the adventurers being heard. Captain Hawley knocked at the door, and perceiving that nobody heard him, forced it, and found Judge Jones standing in the entry. He instantly told him he was his prisoner, and immediately conducted him off, together with a young gentleman whose name was Hewlett. A guard of soldiers was posted at a small distance from their road. When they came near the spot, Judge Jones hemmed very loud, and was forbidden by

Captain Hawley to repeat the sound. He, however, did repeat it; but being told by his conductor that another repetition would be followed by fatal consequences, he desisted. On their way they were obliged to lodge in a forest through the day. The third night they reached their boat, having taken two prisoners more, crossed the Sound, and arrived safe at Black-Rock on the 8th, except six men, who being in the rear, were overtaken and captured by the light horse. As soon as Mrs. Silliman heard of the Judge's arrival, she sent him an invitation to breakfast, which he accepted And during several days that he remained at her house, she used every means in her power to make his situation agreeable. But although few ladies could contribute more effectually to such a purpose, the Judge was distant, reserved, and sullen. From this place he was ordered to Middletown. It was a long time before the British would consent to an exchange ; but in May, 1780, they agreed that if one Washburn, a refugee of a notoriously bad character, could be included in the exchange as a kind of make-weight, they would release General Silliman for Judge Jones, and his son for Mr. Hewlett. The vessel which conveyed him met another employed to transport General Silliman to his own house on the Sound. The two gentlemen having dined together, proceeded immediately to their respective places of destination. The General's return was welcomed with demonstrations of joy by all the surrounding country ; but Judge Jones was doomed to further suffering, for, having taken a very decided stand in favor of royalty, his estate at Fort Neck was forfeited by his attainder, and on the approach of peace he departed for England, where he ended his days—an exile from his friends and countrymen.

JOHN UNDERHILL. On the farm of one of his descendants in this town is the grave of this wonderful man, of whose singular career so much is said in the histories of Massachusetts, Rhode Island, Conneticut, and New-York. Few individuals were more conspicuous, or rendered more important services to the colonists, than Captain Underhill, and especially in their wars and controversies with the various Indian tribes. He was a man of the most untiring energy, activity, and courage ; and such was the rapidity of his movements, that his enemies were generally taken by surprise, and consequently defeated. He had served as an officer in the British forces in the low countries, in Ireland, and at Cadiz. He came from England to Massachusetts soon after the settlement of that colony, and was generally employed in such expeditions as required extraordinary courage and energy. He had an important command in the war of the Pequots in the years 1636 and 7. After which he removed to Connecticut, and settled at Stamford ; and was a delegate from that town to the general court at New-Haven in 1643, and was appointed an assistant justice there. He was the personal and political friend of Sir Henry Vane, who, at the age of twenty-six years, was appointed governor of Massachusetts in 1637. Underhill was made, the same year, commander of the troops at Saybrook. He was engaged with Captain Mason in the attack upon the Indian fort at Mystic, where the fierce spirit of that tribe was broken down by the loss of so many men as were then destroyed ; even Saccacus was discouraged and fled to the Mohawks, and very soon those Indians, as a tribe, were extinguished. In 1641 he was chosen governor of Exeter and Dover, but was soon in great difficulty with the church, of which he was a member. He was an enthusiast in religion, so far as outward appearances were concerned, but a debauchee in practice. Yet, strange as it may seem, the church did not censure him so much for the irregularity of his conduct, as for saying that he dated his conversion from the time he was *smoking tobacco*; from whence they conjectured it could not be sincere. His character was somewhat eccentric in many respects, and in every thing he did was prone to run into extremes. So early as 1634 he was one of the deputies or representatives from Boston to the general court of Massachusetts, and was known in the country about the year 1632, according to the accounts of the treasurer of the colony at that time; by which it appears he was paid a pension of thirty pounds a-year for services rendered the colony, probably in the wars with the Indians, for which on every account he was peculiarly fitted. "He was," says Hutchison, "one of the most forward of the Boston enthusiasts." Hubbard says, that in 1636 he was in high favor with the governor, or, as he calls him in his book, *right worthy Master Vane.* He made a voyage to England in 1638, where he was interrogated and banished on account of his adherence to Mr. Weelwright and the seduction of a female. Indeed, the latter was a crime of which he was often accused, and doubtless not without good reason. While in England this year, he published a curious little book, which he entitled, *News from America, or a New and Experimental Discorerie of New England; containing a true relation of warlike proceedings these two years past, with a figure of the Indian fort or palisado; by John Underhill, a commander of the Warran there. London printed,* 1638. This singular production has lately been republished by the Historical Society of Massachusetts, and is in all respects characteristic of the author. In Hutchinson, it is said, that in 1638, upon the Lord's day, Captain Underhill having been privately dealt with upon suspicion of incontinency with a neighbor's wife, and not hearkening to it, was publicly questioned and put under admonition. The matter was, according to his explanation, "*for that the woman being very young and beautiful, and withal of a jovial spirit and behavior, he did daily frequent her house, and was divers times found there alone with her, the door being locked on the inside, and confessed it was ill, because it had the appearance of evil in it; but that the woman was in great trouble of mind and sore temptation, and that he resorted to her, to comfort her; and that when the door was found locked upon them, they were in private prayer together.*" But his conduct, says the historian, was *clearly* condemned by the elders. "He afterwards confessed his adultery, and in the year 1640, before a great assembly at Boston, on a lecture day and in the courthouse, he sat upon a *stool of repentance,* with a white cap on his head; and with many *deep sighs,* a *rueful countenance,* and *abundance of tears,* owned his wicked way of life, his adultery and hypocrisy, with many expressions of sincere remorse, and besought the church to have compassion on him, and deliver him out of the *hands of Satan*" Yet the church considered his confession insincere, and cast him out of their communion. In 1639 he solicited to be received with a few families upon Long Island, and to enjoy the privileges of an inhabitant of the Dutch government; which request was granted by the governor upon condition he and his adherents should subscribe the oath of allegiance to the States-general and the Prince of Orange. He was afterwards employed by the Dutch to take command in the war against the Indians north of the Sound and west of the Connecticut settlements. This contest lasted till 1646. In Trumble's history of Connecticut, it is stated that Underhill destroyed three hundred Indians north of the Sound, and one hundred and twenty upon Long Island, who had crossed the Sound to ravage and destroy the Dutch plantations there. At the conclusion of this war he settled at Flushing. On the refusal of the commissioners of the

United Colonies to embark in the war between England and Holland, he applied to Rhode Island, and on the 17th of May, 1653, they resolved to appoint a committee from each town for the *ripening matters that concern the Dutch*, whom they style the enemies of the commonwealth, to defend the English plantations from them, or for *offending* them, as should be thought necessary ; and agreed to lend two great guns, twenty men, and other aid. They also granted a commission to Captain Underhill and Mr. William Dyre, and another to Edward Hull, *to go against the Dutch, or any enemies of the Commonwealth of England*. Under this commission he made an attack upon some of the Long Island Indians at Fort Neck, in which he was successful, took their fort, and destroyed great numbers of the people. He afterwards removed to his farm at Oyster-Bay (on which his great-grandson now resides) ; and was, in 1665, a delegate from that town to the meeting assembled at Hempstead by order of Governor Nicolls, and by whom he was appointed sheriff for the north-riding of Yorkshire upon Long Island. The Dutch government had, it seems, been detected by Captain Underhill, at a former period, in carrying on intrigue with some of the Indian tribes for the destruction of the English ; and, in consequence of his disclosures, such offence was given to the former, that a guard of soldiers was sent to take him. He was carried to the city, and for a time confined in prison ; but engaging to be faithful to the Dutch in future, he was suffered to depart without either punishment or reproof. He died upon his farm in Oyster Bay in 1672.

Hon. Samuel Jones. This eminent citizen and patriot was the son of William Jones, and grandson of Captain Thomas Jones who emigrated from Strabane in Ireland in 1692. He first came to Rhode Island, and was, in a year or two after, married to Freelove, daughter of Thomas Townsend ; and received from him in 1695 a deed of gift for a valuable tract of land on the south side of this island, called Fort-Neck, from the existence of two Indian forts near the Bay. Here he erected a substantial dwelling, made from bricks burned upon the land, which stood for more than one hundred and forty years, and familiarly known for the last fifty years as the " *Old Brick House.*" Amid much traditional history of this extraordinary individual, a small proportion only can be received as matter of fact. It is ascertained pretty satisfactorily, that he was engaged in the famous battle of the Boyne, fought in 1690 between the English under William III., and the Irish under James II., in which the former were victorious ; and, coming to America, he brought with him a commission from the king to cruise against Spanish property, the two nations then being at war ; which he doubtless did not fail to employ to his advantage as opportunity offered. After his settlement here, he engaged largely in boat-whaling along-shore, which, at that period and before, was practised extensively upon the whole south coast of the island. For this purpose he gave employment to a great number of natives, whose services were procured at a cheap rate. He died in 1713, and was interred, agreeably to his own previous desire, within one of the above-mentioned Indian forts, near the bottom of the upland, upon his own farm, where his monument may still be seen, bearing the following inscription composed by himself :

> " From distant lands to this wild waste he came,
> This spot he chose, and here he fixed his name ;
> Long may his sons this peaceful spot enjoy,
> And no ill fate their offspring ere annoy."

Captain Jones left three sons and four daughters—David, Thomas, William, Margaret, Sarah, Elizabeth, and Freelove. Thomas died unmarried Margaret married Ezekiel Smith ;. Sarah, Gerardus Clowes ; Elizabeth, Jacob Mitchill ; and Freelove, Jacob Smith. David, to whom and his posterity was devised in tail a greater part of the paternal estate, was born in Sept. 1699. He was educated a lawyer, became highly distinguished in his profession, and was justly esteemed a man of very superior mental attainments. In 1737 he was chosen a member of the provincial assembly, and continued in that body till 1758. For thirteen years he filled the office of speaker ; and on one occasion had the firmness to order the doors of the assembly closed against the governor, until a bill, then under discussion, could be passed, and which his Excellency had determined to prevent by an immediate prorogation. In 1758 he was appointed a judge of the supreme court of the colony, which he resigned in 1773, and died October 11, 1775. During his whole life, and in every situation, he was the unyielding advocate of the rights of the people against every species of royal encroachment; and no man participated more largely of the public confidence and respect. By suffering a *common recovery*, the *life estate*, devised to him by the will of his father, was changed into a *fee*, which he devised to his son Thomas for his life, with remainder, on failure of issue, to the testator's daughter Arrabella and her issue in tail. The said Thomas Jones, (more commonly called Judge Jones,) married a daughter of Lieut. Governor James De Lancey, and, espousing the royal cause in the revolution, was, on the restoration of peace, compelled to leave the country ; upon which he retired to England, where he died. The large and substantial mansion now possessed by General Thomas Floyd Jones, was erected by Judge Jones shortly anterior to the war, and was doubtless much superior to any private residence at that period upon Long Island. William Jones, the third son of Captain Jones, and father of the subject of this notice, was born April 25, 1708, and married a daughter of Captain John Jackson of Hempstead, and by whom he had sixteen children, fourteen of whom lived to have families. He was a highly respected and intelligent farmer, and resided at West-Neck in the town of Oyster-Bay, where he built the dwelling-house now occupied by his grandson, Thomas Jones. He died August 29, 1779. His son, Samuel Jones, the object of this memoir, was born July 26, 1734. His early education was limited ; and while young, he chose the occupation of a sailor, in which capacity he made several voyages to Europe in the merchant service. He was ultimately deterred from prosecuting the business further by the impressions made upon his imagination in a dream, in which he fancied the loss of the vessel in which he was about to embark upon another voyage. He was next placed in the office of William Smith, an eminent lawyer of New-York, who was subsequently chief-justice of the colony, and afterwards of Lower Canada. Mr. Jones was in due time admitted to the bar, and in a surprisingly short period found himself surrounded by friends and honored with an extensive and lucrative practice. For his exemplary industry, high attainments, and great purity of character, he presented a model for the imitation of all who aimed at distinction in jurisprudence. His office was sought by students, and, besides the late De Witt Clinton, he instructed many who afterwards rose to much distinction. At the dawn of the revolutionary contest he was called into the public councils, and continued to fill important and responsible offices till age admonished him to retire to private life. He spent the remainder of his days upon his farm at West-Neck, indulging his taste for reading and observation, the fruits of which were communicated to the world through the medium of the press. He died November 21, 1819. Such was the estimation in which he was held by the legal profession, that his opinions were generally acquiesced in for their accuracy and justice. He was often in the assembly ; and in 1778 was a member of the convention that adopted the constitution of the United States, of which body his intimate friend, George Clinton, was president. It is well known that much contrariety of opinion prevailed in that body, and that the result was a matter of expediency and compromise among the members. He drew most of the amendments proposed, and which were subsequently adopted as a part of that instrument. He was, in short, indefatigable in every situation ; and nothing was ever permitted to interrupt the performance of any public duty. In 1789 he was associated with the late Richard Varick in revising the statutes of this state, which was executed principally by Mr. Jones, with uncommon accuracy and expedition. He was the same year appointed recorder of New-York, the duties of which were discharged with ability and integrity, till he was succeeded, in 1797, by the Hon. James Kent. In 1796 he was requested by Governor Jay to draft a law for establishing and regulating the office of comptroller, to which he was appointed, and which he retained for several years. "I rely, (says the late Dr. Hosack,) on the testimony of others, when I speak of the legal talents of the late Samuel Jones: common consent has indeed assigned him the highest attainments in jurisprudence, and the appellation of the *father of the New-York bar*. He justly ranked among the most profound and enlightened jurists of this or any other country, and acted a useful and conspicuous part in organizing our courts and judiciary system after the revolution. He was a liberal and enlightened Whig, and advocated the cause of independence with zeal and success." "No one, (says Chancellor Kent,) surpassed him in clearness of intellect, and in moderation and extreme simplicity of character; no one equalled him in his accurate knowledge of the technical rules and doctrines of real property, and in familiarity with the skilful and elaborate, but now obsolete and mysterious, black-letter-learning of the common law." He was distinguished for coolness, candor, and deliberation in debate, and sought the substantial rather than the showy part of an orator. He left five sons—Samuel, William, Elbert, Thomas, and David. The first-named has held the office of chancellor of this state, and is now chief-justice of the superior court of the city of New-York.

ELIAS HICKS. This distinguished individual among the Society of Friends, was born in the town of North Hempstead on the 19th of March, 1748. His education was extremely limited, and at the age of seventeen he was placed an apprentice to the trade of a carpenter, which he pursued with diligence for several years, and was laborious and industrious in a high degree. On the 2d of January, 1771, he married Jemima, daughter of Jonathan Seaman of Jericho, and went to reside in the house of his father-in-law, where he spent the remainder of his life. He left several daughters, but none of his sons lived to maturity. His connection with the Friends probably led him at an early period to embrace their sentiments, which he advocated and enforced with zeal and ability ever after. He began his public labors in the Society in 1795, and travelled, at different periods, over a great portion of the United States, from Maine to Ohio, and in the province of Canada. In 1771 he visited every town upon Long Island, and held one or more meetings in each. In 1793 he travelled in New En-

gland, and went as far as Portland in Maine ; being absent five months, and passing over a distance of more than two thousand miles. In 1798 he traversed the
States of New-York, Pennsylvania, Delaware, Maryland, and Virginia, a distance of sixteen hundred miles, and held one hundred and forty-three meetings.
In 1803 he entered the province of Upper Canada, and returned through western
New-York to Saratoga, a distance of more than fifteen hundred miles. In 1806
he again explored New England, travelling more than a thousand miles, and held
sixty meetings. In 1810 he went to Ohio, and returned through Pennsylvania
and New-York ; performing a journey of two thousand miles. These are only
a part of the immense labors of this indefatigable man; and it is reasonable to
believe that, during his public ministry, he must have travelled, at different times,
more than ten thousand miles, and that he pronounced on those occasions at
least one thousand public discourses.

He likewise found time to write and publish much upon religious subjects,
upon war, and the practice of negro slavery. He was the friend and advocate of
civil and religious liberty ; and through a long life, it is believed that he acted up
to the sentiment which he publicly proclaimed. Of his character and qualifications as a religious teacher, as well as the utility of his preaching, different opinions have been, and will probably continue to be entertained. It has been alleged that he was the occasion of all the controversies and dissensions which have
of late years so unhappily distracted the Society of Friends; while it is denied by
some, that he is chargeable therewith,`and disclaim altogether the name of *Hicks-
ite*, by which one party is designated. The attempt has rarely been made to im-
pugn his moral character or inculpate the sincerity of his conduct. If he was
wrong in any of his opinions, we are compelled to admit the honesty of his motives ; and if he was a deluded man, none who knew him best can believe he
was either an impostor or hypocrite. Whatever may be thought of his religious
creed, it must be confessed that through a long, laborious, and active life, few
men have borne a more conspicuous part, or wielded a more powerful and endur-
ing influence among those who were accustomed to attend upon his public discourses. He was a person of a rough exterior, but of vigorous intellect ; and
making no pretensions to elegance of style, he reasoned with much force, and addressed himself to the every-day, common-sense, rather than the imagination of
his auditors. That he was no ordinary individual, must be acceded by all who
are capable of appreciating the extent of his exertions, and the unwavering confidence with which he maintained, through a long course of years, the opinions
and doctrines which he adopted in early life.

TOWN OF HEMPSTEAD.

This town is bounded north by North Hempstead, east by
Oyster-Bay, south by the ocean, and west by Jamaica.   It originally included the territory now comprising the town of North-
Hempstead, of which a partition took place in 1784.   In our
account of Southampton, it has been seen that an unsuccessful
attempt was made by some of the settlers of that town, in 1640,
to form a settlement independent of the Dutch, in the vicinity

of Cow-Bay, and which was frustrated by the interference of the governor. The first permanent settlement in this town is supposed to have been commenced on the site of the present village of Hempstead in 1643, by a few emigrants from New England, who came originally from a place commonly called *Hemel*-Hempstead, twenty-three miles from the city of London. These persons found it indispensable to their safety to submit to the jurisdiction of the Dutch government, and accordingly took the necessary measures to obtain its permission and sanction in furtherance of their wishes. On the 16th of Nov. 1644, a patent or ground-brief was granted by Governor Kieft, of which the most material part is as follows :

" Know all men whom these presents may in any wise concern, that I, William Kieft, (or Kierst), Esq. governor of the province called New Netherlands, with the council of state there established, by virtue of a commission under the hand and seal of the high and mighty lords, the States-General of the United Belgic Provinces, and from his Highness, Frederick Hendrick, Prince of Orange, and the right honorable the Lords Bewint Hibbers of the West India Company, have given and granted, and by virtue of these we do give and grant, unto Robert Fordham, John Sticklan, John Ogden, John Karman, John Lawrence, and Jonas Wood, with their heirs, executors, administrators, successors or associates, or any they shall join in association with them, a certain quantity of land, with all the havens, harbors, rivers, creeks, woodland, marshes, and all other appurtenances thereunto belonging, lying and being upon and about a certain place called the Great Plains, on Long Island, from the East River to the South Sea, and from a certain harbor now commonly called and known by the name of Hempsted Bay, and westward as far as Matthew Garritson's Bay ; to begin at the head of the said two bays, and for to run in direct lines that they may be the same latitude in breadth on the south side as on the north, for them, the said patentees, actually, really, and perpetually to enjoy in as large and ample manner as their own free land of inheritance, and as far eastward, in case the said patentees and their associates shall procure one hundred families to settle down within the said limit of five years after the date hereof: giving and granting, and by virtue of these presents we do give and grant unto the said patentees and their associates, with their heirs and successors, full power and authority upon the said land, to build a town or towns, with such fortifications as to them shall seem expedient, with a temple or temples to use and exercise the reformed religion, which they profess, with the ecclesiastical discipline thereunto be'onging ; likewise giving and granting, and by virtue of these presents we do give and grant to the said patentees, their associates. heirs, and successors, full power and authority to erect a body politic or civil combination among themselves, and to nominate certain magistrates, one or more under the number of eight, of the ablest, discreetest, approved honest men, and him or them annually to present to the Governor of this Province, for the time being, for the said Governor-general for the time being, to elect and establish them for the execution of government among them, as well civil, political, as judicial." Which said ground-brief or instrument also contains various other grants of power, privileges, and franchises to the said grantees, their associates, heirs, and successors, touching their government, the execution of the laws, and the exercise of rights and authority; such as the holding of courts to decide causes, civil and criminal; and to give the first sentence for the deprivation of life, limb, stigmatizing, or burn-marking of any malefactor, if they in their conscience should deem them worthy; and to cause the execution of the sentence, if the party condemned made not his appeal to the chief-court, holden weekly in the Fort Amsterdam; and from the expiration of ten years from the first general peace with the Indians, one tenth part of all the revenue derived from the ground *manured with the plow or hoc*, should belong to the governor, if the same shall be demanded before it is housed.

The first division of land, of which any record remains, took place in the year 1647; which shows the following persons to have already become residents in the town

John Karman,	Thomas Armitage,	Thomas Sherman,
Jeremy Wood,	Simon Sering,	Francis Yates,
Richard Gildersleeve,	Terry Wood,	John Ellison,
William Raynor,	Thomas Willet,	Abraham Smith,
Benjamin Coe,	Henry Pierson,	William Shadding,
John Ogden,	Joseph Scott,	Thomas ffoster,
Samuel Strickland,	Henry Whitson,	Roger Lines,
John Toppin,	Richard Lewis,	John Lewis,
Jonas Wood,	Thomas Stephenson,	Christopher ffoster,
John Fordham,	John Coe,	Samuel Clark,
William Lawrence,	William Scott,	John Hudd,
Henry Hudson,	John Storge,	Thomas Pope,
Thomas Ireland,	William Williams,	Daniel Whitehead,
Richard Valentine,	James Smith,	Robert Williams,
William Thickstone,	William Rogers,	Edward Raynor,
Nicholas Tanner,	Richard Ogden,	John Sewall,
William Smith,	Robert Jackson,	John Smith, sen,
Edmond Wood,	John Foucks,	Samuel Baccus,
John Smith, jr.,	John Lawrence,	John Stricklan.

In consequence of frequent disturbances between the English settlers and their Indian neighbors, and particularly with the Masapequa tribe, a meeting was convened at Hempstead on the 12th of March, 1656, and a treaty happily concluded between the governor and Tackapausha, Sachem of Masapequa, with other Sachems and head-men of divers petty tribes; in which, among other things, it was agreed that the people of Hempstead, according to the lines expressed in their patent, and what they had purchased, should thereafter enjoy the same without molestation from the Sachems or their people. In pursuance of the stipulations in this treaty, the following document was executed by the Indians on the 4th of July, 1657 :

" Know all men by these presents, that we, the Indians of Massapege, Mericocke, and Rockaway, whose names be hereunder written, for ourselves and all the rest of the Indians that do claim any right or interest in the purchase that Hempstead bought in the year 1643, and within the bounds and limits of the whole tract of land concluded upon with the governor of Manhattans, as it is in this paper specified, do, by these presents, ratify and confirm, to them and their heirs for ever, freely, firmly, quietly, and peaceably, for them, and their heirs and successors forever, to enjoy, without any molestation or trouble from us, or any that shall pretend any claim or title unto it, the Mentoake Sachem being present at the confirmation.   In witness whereof, we, whose names be here-under written have hereunto subscribed.

" The mark (*vrr*) of Takapasha, the Sachem of Massapeage.

The mark (*Cɩu*) of Wantagh, the Mantaoke Sachem.

The mark (*B*) of Chegonoe.

The mark (*Cɩɩ*) of Romege.

The mark (Ew'*c*) of Mangwanh.

The mark (ᴆ) of Waakeatis.

The mark (N*ᵉ*) of Rumasuekaman.

The mark (4) of Ocraking.

The mark (M) of Worotum.

" In the presence of Richard Gildersleeve, John Seaman, John Hicks.

Scripsit per me,
JOHN JAMES, Clerk."

In the treaty above mentioned, made in March, 1656, three specific articles were agreed upon as follows: 1. That all injuries formerly passed in the time of the governor's predecessors should be forgiven and forgotten since the year 1645, and never to be remembered.   2. That Tackapausha being chosen the chief Sachem by all the Indian Sachems from Masapequa, Secatogue, Mericoke, Rockaway and Canarse, with the names of the rest, both Sachems and natives ; he hath agreed to put him and themselves, and their lands, under the protection of the Dutch, according to the agreement made at Hartford; and agree to give no countenance to their or the governor's enemies.   And 3d. That the inhabitants of Hempstead, according to the lines expressed in the patent, and what they have purchased, shall enjoy it without trouble from the Sachem or his people, either of person or estate.

On payment of the price agreed upon by the inhabitants of

the town for their lands previously purchased, the following instrument of satisfaction was executed by the Sachems and head-men :

"We, the Indians above written, do hereby acknowledge to have received of the magistrates and inhabitants of Hempstead all our pay in full satisfaction, for the tract of land sold unto them, according to the above and within written agreement, and according to patent and purchase. The general bounds is as followeth : beginning at a place called Mattagarretts Bay, and so running upon a direct line north and south, from north to south, and from sea to sea ; the bounds running from Hempstead Harbor, due east to a point of trees adjoining to the land of Robert Williams, where we left marked trees, the same line running from sea to sea, the other line beginning at a marked tree standing at the east end of the great plains, and from that tree running upon a due south line, and at the south sea by a marked tree made in a neck called Mashatchoung, and from thence upon the same line to the south sea. And we, whose names are hereunto subscribed, do further engage ourselves and our successors to uphold and maintain this our present act, and all our former agreement, to be just and lawful ; that the aforesaid inhabitants of Hempstead shall enjoy the said lands according to the marked bounds, with all privileges thereunto any way belonging or appertaining, for them, their heirs and successors for ever. And we do bind ourselves to save and defend them harmless from any manner of claim or pretence that shall be made to disturb them in their right, or in any part thereof, hereby binding us and our successors to cause them to enjoy the same peaceably, without any molestation or interruption, for them, their heirs and successors for ever. Whereunto we have subscribed this the eleventh day of May, anno 1658, Stilo Novo.

Wantuck,	*Tachapausha,*
Cheeknaw,	*Martom,*
Sayasstock,	*Peese Roma.*

"A true copy, compared with the original, and both of them being written by me,   JOHN JAMES, Clerk."

At a town meeting, held July 10, 1658, the town deputed Richard Gildersleeve to go down to the Manhattans to agree with the governor concerning the tythes, which are not to exceed one hundred sheeples of wheat, and to be delivered at the town harbor. At the same time they agreed to pay the herdsman that attended their cattle twelve shillings sterling a week in butter, corn, and oats, at fixed prices. Six bushels of corn was allowed by the town for the killing of a wolf; and the price of corn was two shillings and sixpence a bushel, wheat four shillings, pork three pence a pound, butter sixpence, lodging two pence a night, beer two pence a mug, board five shillings a week, victuals sixpence a meal, and labor two and sixpence

44

a day.   It was further agreed by the town, that the inhabitants should be ready at the sounding of the horn to turn out their cows, and the keeper was required to be ready at the time the sun was half an hour high, to drive them to the pasture, and about half an hour before sun-down, to bring them home again, and to drive them one day in each week to Cow-Neck.

At this time Cow-Neck was enclosed by a fence, extending from the head of Little-Neck Bay to the head of Hempstead Harbor, each person being entitled to put in a number of cows to fatten, in proportion to the number of *standing-gates*, or pannels of fence made by them; and afterwards in the distribution of the land, the share allowed was adjusted by the same rule, in consequence of which it was divided among a few persons only.   Except the great plains, much of the common lands of the town was anciently enclosed in large fields, for pasturing of different kinds of stock, and denominated according to the use intended, as the ox-pasture, the cow-pasture, calf-pasture, &c.

" At a town meeting, March 14, 1659, there was granted unto John Roads of Rusdorp, one great hollow, containing about two acres, the which he is to secure in a sufficient fence, and possess it for seven years, paying yearly eighteen pence the acre, with the tythe, the which he is to pay at Hempstead."

" At the aforesaid town meeting it was granted unto Thomas Jacobs, one hollow, containing one and a half acre, upon the terms above specified, likewise unto Thomas Ellison one and a half acre lying by the Island of Trees.   And there is granted unto Robert Williams, by general vote of town meeting, six acres of meadow land formerly in possession of Roger Lines, that, paying all rates and duties belonging thereunto, he shall enjoy the said meadow for him, his heirs and assigns for ever.   Also, the same day was let to Robert Williams the town *barn* for this ensuing year, for the sum of fifty-three shillings, to be paid in corn at the usual prices, and the *yard* is to be common both to the house and barn."   In 1659 the town licensed John Smith to keep an *ordinary*, and to sell therein meat and drink, and to lodge strangers in such a manner as not to be offensive to the laws of *God or man*.   " It was voted and agreed at the same town meeting, that any person absenting himself or herself from public worship on the Lord's day, or other public days, should, for the first offence pay *five shillings*, for the second *ten*, for the third *twenty*, and after that be subjected to *corporal punishment* or *banishment*."   " At a town meeting, held November 26, 1684, it was concluded by a major vote, that Left. John Jackson, Justice Searing, and Jonathan Smith, sen., should go to New-York to meet the Indians, and there to *agitate* concerning their lands, and also to endeavor at the purchasing of a patent for the town; and also the ending the difference concerning the bounds between our neighboring town, Jamaica, and us, with full power to make a final end. There is also granted unto Robert Williams three acres of the town land, lying in the bevil, for the sum of three pounds, to be paid in such corn, as, by the blessing of God, the land shall produce."

This town continued for more than forty years to enjoy undisturbed the rights and privileges, and to exercise the powers and duties authorized by the patent of Governor Kieft, and by which the town was also incorporated. But in the year 1683 his Excellency Governor Dongan, who was an occasional resident of this town, gave the people thereof, as well as others, to be informed of his determination to compel them to purchase from him new patents for their lands. the price of which he claimed as a perquisite of his office, but to which the people were reluctant to submit; and when it was found no longer avoidable. they seemed particularly anxious to procure a new patent as cheap as possible, which caused much delay, and produced no little difficulty between the governor and the inhabitants. The following extracts from the town records relate to this matter:

" At a town meeting, held the 16th of February, 1683, Mr. Seaman, Mr. John Jackson, and John Tredwell, were chosen to go down to New-York, in order to the getting a patent for the whole bounds of the town according to the first purchase and the draft drawn." The object not being accomplished, it was again voted, March 31, 1684, " That those who go down to New-York in respect of getting a patent for our own town bounds, that they get it as reasonable as they can, for the good of themselves and the rest of the inhabitants, and also upon as good terms." Nothing yet being effected, again, " At a town meeting, April 4, 1684, Mr. John Jackson, Mr. Symon Searing, and Mr. John Tredwell are appointed to go down to New-York by the governor's order sent to the town, and to see the getting of a patent for the town, giving these, our deputies, full power to act for us and in our behalf as fully as if we were personally present, provided that our lands shall be assured to us, our heyres and successors for ever, to be our free lands of inheritance, we rendering and paying such acknowledgments as shall be agreed upon between the governor and our deputys." The purposes of the deputies not being accomplished, again, "At a town meeting, December 12, 1684, there was chosen by the major vote, Justice Searing and Nathaniel Pearsall to go and request the governor for a patent, and to get it on as reasonable terms as they can ; and what these our deputies do, shall be as authentic as if we were personally present ourselves." Still we find them unsuccessful; and, "At a town meeting, April 3, 1685, there was chosen by a major vote, John Jackson, John Tredwell, and Jonathan Smith, sen., to go to York to get a patent for our town upon good terms as possible, and what our deputies do we shall feel ourselves obliged."

After all these exertions on behalf of the town, a patent was finally obtained, of which the following is a copy, and furnishes a familiar example of the numerous patents issued by Governor Dongan, out of which he and his officers contrived to raise no inconsiderable revenue from the pockets of the people.

" Thomas Dongan, Lieutenant-governor and Vice-admiral under his Royal Highness James Duke of York, of New-York and its dependencies in America, to all whom these presents shall come, sendeth greeting: whereas there is a certain town in Queen's County, called and known by the name of Hempsted, upon Long Island, situate, lying and being on the south side of the Great Plains, having a certain tract of land thereunto belonging, the bounds whereof begin at a marked tree standing at the head of Matthew Garrison's Bay, and so running from thence upon a direct south line due south to the main sea, and from the said tree a direct north line to the Sound or East River, and so round the points of the necks till it comes to Hempsted Harbor, and so up the harbor to a certain barren sand-beach, and from thence up a direct line till it comes to a marked tree on the east side of Cantiagge Point, and from thence a south line to the middle of the Plains, and from thence a due east line to the utmost extent of the Great Plains, and from thence upon a straight line to a certain tree marked in a neck called Maskachoung, and so from thence up a due south line to the south sea, and the said south sea is to be the south bounds from the east line to the west line, and the Sound or East River to be the northerly bounds, as according to several deeds or purchases from the India owners, and the patent from the Dutch governor, William Kieft, relation thereto being had doth more fully and at large appear

"Now Know Ye, that by virtue of the commission and authority unto me given by his Royal Highness, James, Duke of York and Albany, Lord Proprietor of this Province, in consideration of the premises and the quit rents hereinafter reserved, I have given, granted, ratified, and confirmed, and by these presents do give, grant, ratify, and confirm unto Captain John Seaman, Simon Searing, John Jackson, James Pine, senior, Richard Gildersleave, senior, and Nathaniel Pearsall, as Patentees for and on the behalf of themselves and their associates, the freeholders and inhabitants of the said town of Hempsted, their heirs, successors, and assigns for ever ; all the before-recited tract and tracts, parcel and parcels of land and islands, within the said bounds and limits, together with all and singular the woods, underwoods, plains, meadows, pastures, quarries, marshes, waters, lakes, causeways, rivers, beaches, fishing, hawking, hunting and fowling, with all liberties, privileges, hereditaments and appurtenances, to the said tract of land and premises belonging or in any wise appertaining, to have and to hold the said tract of land and premises, with all and singular the appurtenances before mentioned and intended to be given, granted, ratified, and confirmed unto the said Captain John Seaman, Simon Searing, John Jackson, James Pine, senior, Richard Gildersleave, senior, and Nathaniel Pearsall, the said patentees and their associates, their heirs, successors and assigns, to the proper use, benefit and behoof of them, the said patentees and their associates, their heirs, successors and assigns for ever; to be holden of his said Royal Highness, his heirs and assigns, in free and common soccage, according to the tenor of East Greenwich in the county of Kent, in his Majesty's kingdom of England. Provided always, that neither this patent, nor any thing herein contained, shall be construed or intended to the prejudice or infringement of any right, claim or pretence, which his Royal Highness, James Duke of York, his heirs and successors now hath or hereafter may have, to a certain tract of land within the bounds of this said patent, commonly called or known by the name of Hempstead Little Plains, and all the woodland and plains between the said Little Plains and the bay, which lies betwixt Rockaway Meadows and the said meadows, bounded on the east with Foster's Meadow River, and on the west with Hempsted west line, and likewise one entire piece of land containing seven hundred acres, lying and being on Cow-Neck. And I do hereby likewise confirm and grant unto the said patentees and their associates, their heirs, successors and assigns, all the privileges and immunities belonging to a town within this government. Yielding, rendering and paying yearly and every year at the city of New-York, under his Royal Highness, or to such office or offices as by him shall be appointed, to receive the same, twenty bushels of good winter wheat, or four pounds in good current money of New-York, on or before the twenty-fifth day of March. In testimony wherof, I have caused these presents to be entered upon record in the secretary's office of the said Province, and the public seal thereof have hereunto affixed and signed with my hand, this seventeenth day of April, in the thirty-seventh year of his Majesty's reign, and in the year of our Lord one thousand six hundred and eighty-five."

" THOMAS DONGAN."

" J. SPRAGG, Secretary "

Immediately after the patent was procured it was resolved in town meeting, that a tax of two and a half pence per acre should be assessed upon the freeholders of the town, for defraying the price of the patent, the expenses of those employed in obtaining it, and for other purposes. The tax list made on this occasion is presumed to include all the owners of land at that time in the town, and is therefore worthy of preservation as exhibiting the names of the principal inhabitants of Hempstead in the year 1685.

Names.	Acres.	Names.	Acres.	Names.	Acres.
Robert Dinge	22	Elias Burland	25	Jer. Wood, jr.	68
Edmund Titus	150	William Wetherle	30	William Valentine	40
Samuel Titus	50	John Pine	101	Robert Bedell	3½
Hannah Hudson	22	Joshua Jacocks	88	Samuel Pine	60
William Gripman	25	Jonathan Seaman	65	Thomas Oakly	70
John Buck	27	George Baldwin	37	Jonathan Burg	20
Sam. Raynor	43	Richard Minthorne	100	Joseph Ginnin	80
John Serion	100	Thomas Gildersheve	10	Joseph Williams	100
Simon Serion	171	Jonathan Smith	180	Richard Valentine	71
James Pine, sen.	500	Thos. Southerds, sen.	214	John Bates	5
Nathaniel Pine	9	Thomas Rushmore	277	John Bates, jr.	53
Solomon Simmons	163	John Champion	187	John Elison	125
William Smith	100	Goodm Smith, sen.	200	William Beachman	130
Richard Denton	50	John Carl	208	Col. Thos. Dongan	200
Joseph Langdon	110	John Mott	70	Mr. Sprag	288
William Jecoks	80	Thos. Elison, sen.	270	Edward Avery	70
Thomas Seaman	108	John Elison, sen.	60	Richard Combs	26
John Smith, jr. Rock.	230	Rich. Gilderslieve,	100	Elias Bailey	54
Daniel Bedell	130	Rich. Gildersheve, jr.	280	John Wolly	139
John Williams	240	Richard Totten	65	Thos. Daniels	24
James Pine	249	Arthur Albertus	52	William Thorne	150
Elias Dorlan	100	John Johnson	25	Robert Hobs	24
Aaron Underdunk	100	James Beates	59	Robert Hobs, jr.	25
Widow Valentine	40	William Lee	40	Thomas Hutchings	18
Benj Simmons	154	Thomas Ireland	70	Nathaniel Pearsal	236
John Morrell	137	Peter Johnson	50	Thomas Pearsal	190
Richard Elison	60	Henry Maniford	75	Henry Willis	75
Edward Hare	70	Henry Liminton	352	Cornelius Barnes	100
Christopher Dean	100	Richard Osborn	183	John Foster	55
William Jones	66	Obediah Valentine	44	Captain Seaman	400
Samuel Embree	100	Widow Willis	172	Sam. Seaman	3
Tim. Halstead, jr.	78	Hope Willis	120	John Coe	150
Captain Jackson	430	Harman Johnson	25	John Smith, Rock.	50
Samuel Denton	240	Barnes Egleson	53	Peter Totten	21
Isaac Smith	22	Jacob Peterson	25	John Seaman, jr.	58
John Cornwell	50	John Bedell	46	William Thickstone	83
Edward Cornwell	50	Thomas Cheesman	22	Daniel Pearsal	190
Joseph Balden	50	John Smith, Rock.	50	George Pearsal	190
Jona. Smith, sen.	220	Abraham Smith	150	Henry Willis	140
John Smith.	260	Edward Sprag	92	Benj. Burtsal	50
Joseph Smith	156	Jeremiah Smith	100	William Davis	50
Joseph Wood	10	John Smith, blue	368	Joseph Mott	66
Jer. Wood, sen.	300	John Carman	180	John Tiedwell	350
Josias Starr	14	Caleb Carman	180	Tim. Halsted, sen.	300
Richard Stiles	152	Benj. Carman	70	James Rily	50
John Townsend	46	Moses Embree	70	Adam Mott	64
John Dozenboro	100	Henry Johnson	25	Harman Flower	59
John Burland	25	Abraham Frost	50	Joseph Petit	34

Names.	Acres.	Names.	Acres.	Names.	Acres.
William Heger	55	Thomas Willis	30	Sam. Smith	11
John Hawkins	64	Robert Miller	36	Peter Smith	11
Sam. Allen	41	William Johnson	. 25	Thomas Southard, jr.	69
William Ware	83	Ephraim Valentine	40	John Southard	3
John Hubs	56	Robert Bedell	3	John Robinson	100
Christr. Yeomans	150				

From the above list of inhabitants, it will be seen that Col. Thomas Dongan, governor of the province, was the owner of two hundred acres of land in the town. He had a farm and country residence at that period on the north side of the plains, and is supposed to be the same now in possession of the heirs of the late Tuthill Reeve, a little west of the place called Hyde-Park.

On the 6th of April, 1784, an act was passed, entitled " *An act to divide the township of Hempstead into two towns,*" by which it was enacted that all that part of the said township south of the country road that leads from Jamaica, nearly through the middle of Hempstead Plains, to the east part thereof, should be included in one township, and be thereafter called and known by the name of *South-Hempstead ;* and all the residue of the said township of Hempstead should be included in one township, and be thereafter called and known by the name of *North-Hempstead.* That the inhabitants of either town should continue to enjoy the right of oystering, fishing, and clamming in the waters of the other. The name of *South-Hempstead* was changed to *Hempsted* by a subsequent act passed the 7th of April, 1801.

It is believed that no house for religious worship was erected in this town beyond the limits of the present village of Hempstead, (except at Near-Rockaway,) till within seven years last past. The first Presbyterian church was erected in the northwest part of the village in the year 1648, being four years after the settlement of the town, and the charter or patent from the Dutch governor. It stood near the present Burly-Pond. This building was twenty-four feet square, and continued to be occupied till 1673, when, " *At a town meeting,* held the first day of April, 1673, Mr. Seaman and John Smith [Blue] were chosen to agree with Joseph Carpenter to build a new meeting-house, *thirty feet long, twenty-two wide,* and *twelve feet stud,* with a *leanto* on each side." This house was erected near the spot now occupied by the Episcopal church, and came, as well as the church lands, into the possession of the Episcopalians, by whom they have since been held.

The Rev. Richard Denton, a Presbyterian or Independent, was the first minister settled in this town. He had been a preacher at Halifax in England, from whence he came to Watertown, Massachusetts, in 1634. In 1635 he removed with a few associates to Connecticut, and commenced the settlement of Weathersfield. In 1641 he went to Stamford, and in 1644, with a part of his congregation, came to Hempstead, who, with a few others already here, assisted in organizing the settlement of the town. He remained here till his death in 1663, the year preceding the conquest of New-York. Cotton Mather, in his Magnalia, represents Mr. Denton as an excellent man and able preacher, and that he left behind him a manuscript *system* of *divinity,* entitled "*Soliloquia Sacra,*" which was spoken of, by those who had seen it, in high terms. Although many of his posterity still remain in this town, no trace of the work spoken of has been discovered among them. It has not been satisfactorily ascertained that any clergyman was settled here from the decease of Mr. Denton, till the 6th of May, 1682, when the town agreed to invite the Rev. Jeremiah Hobart to be their minister, and agreed to give him a three acre lot, *where it was most convenient,* also fifty acres of woodland, to be taken up *where he pleased;* his cattle to have liberty of commons, and himself to have the use of all the parsonage lands and meadows. It was likewise agreed that a house should be built for him upon the town lot, (where the Episcopal parsonage now stands), thirty-eight feet long, eighteen feet wide, and ten feet between the joists, and to be a *comfortable house to dwell in.* Then follow the names of seventy-nine subscribers to his salary of seventy pounds a-year, with fire-wood *free cost.* The salary was to be paid in corn and cattle at the current price. Mr. Hobart was the son of the Rev. Peter Hobart, of Hingham, Massachusetts, and brother to the Rev. Joshua Hobart of Southold. He was born in England in 1630, and came

over with his father while a child, in 1635. He graduated at
Harvard College in 1650, and preached first at Topsfield, Massachusetts. He came here in 1682, and soon after married a
daughter of the Rev. Joseph Whiting of Southampton. From
hence he removed, in 1696, to Haddam, Connecticut ; where he
died in 1717, at the age of eighty-seven, on the Sabbath, between meetings, having preached in the forenoon of that day.
He was grandfather of the celebrated David Brainard, one of
the most admired preachers of his time. For more than one
hundred years from the removal of Mr. Hobart, the Presbyterian church here had no settled clergyman, depending
upon the casual preaching of missionaries, or upon ministers
hired for short periods ; and the congregation became, in couse-
quence, much diminished by the union of many of its members with the Episcopal church. The Rev. Charles Webster
was installed the pastor of this church in 1818. He is the son
of the late Charles R. Webster, of Albany, and graduated at
Union College in 1813. He continued here respectable and
useful in a high degree, till he was dismissed at his own request in 1837. By his industry, zeal, and perseverance, the
church edifice was enlarged, and the congregation much
strengthened and increased. He is now comfortably settled at
Middletown, New Jersey. His successor is the Rev. Sylvester Woodbridge, Jr. son of the Rev. Sylvester Woodbridge of
New-York. He was born at Sharon, Connecticut, June 15,
1813 ; graduated at Union College in 1830 ; and was settled as
the minister of Westhampton, Suffolk County, in 1734; from
whence he removed to this place in 1737.

A new Presbyterian church was erected in the village of
Hempstead in 1762, which was much injured by the British
troops, who had possession of it during the revolution, and was
finally destroyed by fire in April, 1803. The present edifice
was erected on the same spot a few years after, and was enlarged and improved in 1825. In the year 1701, the town, being entirely destitute of a minister, made application to the
society in England for propagating the gospel in foreign
parts. In pursuance of which the Rev. John Thomas, an Epis-
copalian minister, arrived in 1704. By his prudence and amia-

45

ble conduct, the people were in general satisfied ; and he continued to live upon terms of mutual respect and confidence
till his death in 1724. He was succeeded, in 1725, by the Rev.
Thomas Jenny, with whom the records of the Episcopal church
commence.   This gentleman officiated in the church which had
been erected by the Presbyterians in 1673, without any complaint
or opposition, a greater part of whom became in the end reconciled to the ceremonies, rites, and discipline of the Episcopal
church.   In 1734 this edifice was taken down, and another
erected on the same spot, or very near it, for which a royal
charter was obtained in 1735, whereby the freeholders and inhabitants of the town, in communion with the church of Eu-
gland, were incorporated, by the "*name and style of St.
George's Church, Hempstead ;*" and by which the house then
built, with half an acre of common land on which it stood, were
granted them.   This church was occupied from that period
until 1822, when the present large and handsome edifice was
erected.   The ceremony of dedication being performed by
Bishop Hobart, Sept. 19, 1823.

The Rev. Mr. Jenny removed from this church in 1742, and
was succeeded the same year by the Rev. Samuel Seabury.
He was the first minister of the Episcopal church at New-London, where he was settled in 1728, and remained till his removal to this parish, where he continued till his decease, June 15
1764.   He left behind him a character that is held in high esteem, and an example worthy of all imitation.   His son, Samuel, born at New-London in 1728, graduated at Yale College
in 1751, succeeded his father as minister at New-London ;
and in 1784 was created bishop of Connecticut and Rhode Isl-
and, which he held till his death, Feb. 25, 1796.   The next
minister of this church was the Rev. Leonard Cutting, graduated in 1754 at Pembroke College, Oxford, and whom an attachment to the principles of liberty had induced to visit our
shores.   In him were happily blended the polished habits
of a gentleman with an extensive and profound erudition.
His settlement here took place in 1766, and his resignation in
1784.   He had been a tutor in King's College, New-York, in
1756, and was likewise professor of classical literature.   Af-

ter his settlement in this town, he opened and maintained a classical school of a high order, at which many young men were educated, some of whom subsequently acquired great eminence in different pursuits; among this number may be mentioned the late Dr. Samuel L. Mitchill and Edward Griswold. Mr. Cutting was succeeded, in March, 1785, by the Rev. Thomas Lambert Moore. He was born in the city of New-York in 1754, and received his education at King's (now Columbia) College. He was one of the best and most amiable of men, and labored zealously and successfully for the interests of his church and people till his death, April 20, 1799. The Right Reverend Richard C. Moore, Bishop of Virginia, is his brother; and esteemed one of the most able and eloquent men of the age. After the death of Mr. Moore the congregation were so fortunate as to procure the services of the Rev. John Henry Hobart. He was the son of Enoch Hobart of Philadelphia, where he was born, September 14, 1775. He was educated at Princeton College, where he graduated in 1793. Undetermined as to a profession, he entered upon the business of a merchant, but relinquished it for the study of theology, which he pursued under the direction of the late Bishop White of Pennsylvania. In 1795 he was employed as a tutor in his alma mater. His ordination took place in 1798. The next year he was settled as minister of Christ Church, New Brunswick; from whence he removed to Hempstead in June, 1800. Here, according to his own subsequent declaration, he passed some of his happiest days. His wife was a daughter of the Rev. Thomas Bradbury Chandler of Elizabethtown, a man of eminent talents, and distinguished for his able controversy with Dr. Chauncey, and a memoir of the Rev. Dr. Johnson, former president of Columbia College. In Dec. 1800, Mr. Hobart was invited to be assistant minister of Trinity Church, New-York, which he accepted, as a sphere of greater usefulness, and better suited to the display of his extraordinary abilities. In 1811 he was elected bishop of the diocese upon the resignation of Bishop Moore. In 1823 he visited Europe, in which he made the tour of England, Scotland, and Switzerland; also Rome, Venice, and Geneva; and returned again to New-

York in 1824. While on a journey to the western part of this state, he was overtaken by disease at Auburn, where he died, Sept. 12, 1830. His remains were brought to the city of New-York, and interred under the chancel of Trinity Church, where an appropriate monument has been erected to his memory. The Rev. Seth Hart was the successor of Mr. Hobart in this town. He was born at Berlin, Connecticut, June 21, 1763, and graduated at Yale College in 1784. He was first settled as a minister at Wallingford, where he continued about six years, and removed here in the beginning of 1801. He was a good classical scholar, possessing a mild and amiable temper, with a disposition social and benevolent. Much of his leisure time was devoted to the instruction of youth, and he acquired a high reputation as a teacher. A paralytic attack, in 1828, disabled him from the performance of the more active duties of his profession, and occasioned his resignation in 1829. He died lamented, the 16th of March, 1832, leaving a widow and several children. His eldest son, William Henry Hart, is an Episcopal clergyman at Richmond, Virginia, and a man of excellent character. The Rev. Richard D. Hall was born in Philadelphia in 1789, and, after officiating in several churches in his native state, settled here in 1829, where he was faithful and assiduous in the discharge of his parochial duties till 1834, when he voluntarily resigned, and returned again to Pennsylvania. He was succeeded the same year by the Rev. William M. Carmichael. He is the son of Mr. James Carmichael of Albany, where he was born, June 28, 1804, and graduated at Hamilton College in 1826. In 1832 he was settled at Rye in the county of Westchester, from whence he removed to this town in Aug. 1834; and has hitherto labored with fidelity and success to advance the interest and prosperity of the church and congregation. A beautiful organ has also been procured; and Trinity Chapel, at Far Rockaway, is mainly indebted for its existence to his zeal and perseverance. This chapel has been furnished with a bell through the liberality of Joseph and Oliver T. Hewlett of New-York.

Hempstead Village, the largest and most populous in the town, is pleasantly situated on the southern margin of the great

plains, twenty-one miles from New-York, and three from Queens County court-house. It contains ten streets, mostly built upon, has within a square mile two hundred dwellings and sixteen hundred inhabitants. The public buildings are the Presbyterian and Episcopal churches above-mentioned, a large Methodist Episcopal church, erected in 1822, and the Hempstead seminary, incorporated May 2d, 1836, and completed in 1838. The site of the seminary is well-chosen, and the building a specimen of modern architecture, combining .... with utility and convenience. It is .... three stories high, besides basement .... surmounted by a balustrade and cupola. .... its .... painting and general appearance of the .... may be considered the crowning ornament of the village, and creditable alike to the character and intelligence of the stockholders. Under the superintendence of its present efficient instructor, it cannot fail to .... a distinguished rank among the kind of institutions of the state. In the village there are four places of entertainment, twelve dry goods, grocery, and provision stores, a printing office, fire-engine company, two drug stores, two cabinet makers, ... saddle and harness-makers, ... and .... meat .... walls, three blacksmiths, a baker, ... carries one .... The streets of .... and others have been since .... here by William Hutchinson .... in .... 8th of May, 1830, when was .... "Long Island Telegraph and .... which title was, on the 11th of November, 1831 changed to the "Hempstead Inquirer." The establishment was transferred to James G. Watts in April, 1842, and at his death, June 30, 1843, the publication devolved upon his son, James G. Watts, who conducted it till May, 1853, when it .... to John W. Smith, the present editor and proprietor. In this village is also located the office of the "Long Island Farmer's Fire Insurance Company," incorporated April 28, 1834, with a capital of

plains, twenty-one miles from New-York, and three from
Queen's County court-house. It contains ten streets, mostly
built upon; has within a square mile two hundred dwellings
and fourteen hundred inhabitants. The public buildings are
the Presbyterian and Episcopal churches above-mentioned,
a large Methodist Episcopal church, erected in 1822, and the
Hempstead seminary, incorporated May 2d, 1836, and completed in 1838. The situation of the seminary is well-chosen,
and the building a handsome specimen of modern architecture,
combining chasteness and elegance with utility and convenience. It is sixty by forty feet, two stories high, besides basement and attic; the whole surmounted by a balustrade and
cupola. From the commanding position and general appearance of this noble structure, it may be considered the crowning
ornament of the village, and creditable alike to the character
and intelligence of the stockholders. Under the superintendence of its present efficient instructor, it cannot fail to attain
a distinguished rank among the kindred institutions of this
state. In the village there are four houses of entertainment,
twelve dry goods, grocery, and provision stores, a printing-
office, fire-engine company, two drug stores, two carriage-
makers, two saddle and harness-makers, a sash and blind-
maker, two butchers' stalls, three blacksmiths, a baker, a stone-
cutter, a tanner and currier, two cabinet-makers, two gun-
smiths, two watch-makers, and various other mechanics and
artisans. The streets of the village were first named in 1834,
and others have been since laid out. A press was established
here by William Hutchinson and Clement F. Le Fevre on the
8th of May, 1830, when was published the first number of the
"*Long Island Telegraph and General Advertiser*," which
title was, on the 11th of November, 1831, altered to the "*Hempstead Inquirer*." The establishment was transferred to James
G. Watts in April, 1832; and at his death, June 23, 1834, the
publication devolved upon his son, James G. Watts, who conducted it till May, 1838, when it was assigned to John W.
Smith, the present editor and proprietor. In this village is also
located the office of the "*Long Island Farmer's Fire Insurance Company*," incorporated April 29, 1833, with a capital of

$50.000, and has been thus far a profitable institution. The Long Island rail-road is two miles north of the village, to connect it with which a branch rail-road is now constructing.

In the Episcopal cemetery are the graves of the late Henry Eckford and three of his children; one of whom was the widow of the lamented Dr. Drake, a gentleman highly esteemed as a man, a scholar, and a poet. Mr. Eckford was for many years one of our most valuable and active citizens. A native of Scotland, he came to New-York when a young man, and engaged extensively in ship-building. By his great industry and enterprise he acquired a fortune, and at the same time the respect and confidence of the community. His wife was Miss Marion Bedell, of Hempstead. As an able and skilful shipwright, he had few equals and no superior; in the full tide of success and in the zenith of prosperity, he was suddenly subjected to heavy pecuniary embarrassment, which resulted in the sacrifice of a large portion of his property, and induced him to seek elsewhere the means of repairing his broken fortunes. In 1830 we find him at Constantinople, patronized and employed by the Sultan of Turkey, in the construction of a navy, upon terms which evinced the high confidence reposed in him by the government. In the latter part of the year 1832 he was attacked by an acute disease, which in a few days terminated his valuable life. His body was brought to the United States in one of his own vessels, and interred in this village on the 22d of February, 1833.

The Village of Jerusalem is upon the eastern boundary of the town, and was settled in 1666 by Captain John Seaman and his six sons, to whom a special patent was granted by Governor Nicolls for a considerable tract of land there previously purchased by them from the *Meroke* tribe of Indians. Its location is pleasant, and the population about one hundred and fifty. The Friends have a meeting-house here, erected in 1827, a large portion of the inhabitants being of that denomination.

The Village of Near Rockaway is about five miles southwesterly of the village of Hempstead, and is conveniently situated at the head of Rockaway Bay, which can be approached by vessels of sixty or eighty tons. Here are several stores, a lumber-yard, ship-yard, grist-mill; which, with a few coasting sloops and schooners owned here, make it a place of much activity and business. In the Bay, nearly opposite, is Hog-Island, containing about six hundred acres of upland and meadow, and which has given name to the principal inlet from the ocean. In the Bay are extensive tracts of salt-meadow, as is the case upon the whole south shore of the town. A Methodist church was erected in the vicinity in 1790, and the first belonging to that denomination in the bounds of Hempstead.

One of the most remarkable features in the geography of this town is Far-Rockaway, which has long been celebrated as a fashionable watering-place, having been annually visited by thousands in pursuit of pure air and the luxury of sea-bathing. The waves of the ocean break upon the beach, which unites at this place with the upland. The house most frequently resorted to in former times has been removed, and its place supplied by an establishment more befitting the unrivalled beauty and sublimity of the situation. The corner-stone of the MARINE PAVILION was laid the first day of June, 1833, with appropriate ceremonies. It is a large and splendid edifice, standing upon the margin of the Atlantic; and has hitherto been kept in a style not excelled by any hotel in the Union. The main building is two hundred and thirty feet front, with wings, one of which is seventy-five and the other forty-five feet long. The peristyles are of the Ionic order, the piazza being two hundred and thirty-five feet in length by twenty in width. The sleeping apartments number one hundred and sixty. The dining-room is eighty feet long, and the drawing-room fifty. It was erected by an association of gentlemen of the city of New-York, the cost, including the land and standing furniture, $43.000, and was sold to the present owners, Stephen Whitney and Charles A. Davis, Esquires, for $30.000, in May, 1836. The atmosphere here is fresh, cool, and delightful; invalids soon find themselves benefitted, and all experience fresh inspiration and increased vigor by repeated plunges in the ocean. One of the best private boarding-houses near this place is *Rock-Hall*, originally built for a family residence by the late Dr. Martin.

Over one of the fire-places in this house is a beautiful painting of a *child* and *dog*, said to have been executed on the spot by the great American artist, *John Singleton Copley*, father of Ld. Lyndhurst, late chancellor of England.

COL. BENJAMIN BIRDSALL. It is unfortunately the case with many of the distinguished actors in the revolution, and in relation to the subject of this notice in particular, that few events in their history have been preserved. The truth is, that many men of exalted patriotism, who filled their respective parts, both in public and private life, with honor and usefulness, were naturally unobtrusive, pursuing the even tenor of their way without parade or ostentation. Among those who, in the crisis that *tried men's souls*, devoted their best years to the service of their country, was Benjamin Birdsall. He was descended from an ancestor of the same name among the early inhabitants of Hempstead, and who emigrated from England in 1657. He was the son of Thomas Birdsall, and born in this town September 17, 1736. Being intended by his father for the occupation of a farmer, he enjoyed no other advantages for education than such as an ordinary country school at that day afforded. Blest with a good natural understanding, and having a fondness for reading, he was enabled in a few years to acquire a valuable stock of general and useful information, which subsequent observation did not fail materially to improve. He married Freelove, daughter of Major William Jones of Oyster-Bay, by whom he had several children. The revolutionary contest having commenced, presenting to the consideration of every patriot matters of high interest, Mr. Birdsall did not hesitate as to the course he ought to pursue. Apprehensions were entertained that it was the intention of the enemy to invade Long Island, and it became indispensable that measures should be adopted to prevent or repel the attempt. Having obtained a captain's commission, Mr. Birdsall was enabled to procure about sixty volunteers, with whom he marched to the west end of the island in the summer of 1776, and aided the forces under General Putnam in throwing up entrenchments upon the heights of Brooklyn. He was actively engaged in the battle of the 27th of August, 1776, which resulted so disastrously for the Americans, and in which great numbers were killed and wounded. He retreated with the army to New-York, marched with them when they left the city, and encamped at Harlaem Heights. Soon after this event, a circumstance occurred which exhibited in bold relief the intrepidity and patriotism of Captain Birdsall. An American vessel, laden with flour for the army, had been captured by the British in the Sound; and Captain Birdsall, believing she might be retaken, offered, if the undertaking were approved by his superior officer, to superintend the enterprise in person. The proposal met the approbation of the commanding officer, when the captain, with a few select men, made the experiment, and succeeded in sending the vessel to her original destination. But it so happened that himself and one of his men were taken prisoners by the enemy. It was his fate to be imprisoned in the jail, then called the Provost, under the surveilance of that monster in human shape, the infamous Cunningham He requested the use of pen, ink, and paper, for the purpose of acquainting his family of his situation. On being *refused*, he made a reply, which drew from the keeper some opprobrious epithets, accompanied by a thrust of his sword, which penetrated the shoulder of his victim, and caused the blood to flow freely. Being locked up alone in a filthy apartment, and denied any assistance whatever, he was obliged to dress the wound with his own linen; and there to endure, in solitude and misery, every indignity which the malice of the Provost-marshal urged him to inflict upon a *damned rebel*, who, he declared, "*ought to be hanged.*" General Washington, when made acquainted with his situation, took measures to have his wife and children conveyed from Long Island to Dover in Dutchess County, where they remained during the war. During his incarceration, Captain Birdsall was honored with the commission of colonel, and after a few miserable months of confinement and starvation, an exchange took place, by which he was again set at liberty.

So great was the sympathy of the public for his sufferings, and confidence in his patriotism and intelligence, that in 1777 he was chosen a member of the assembly by the people of his native county, in which body he continued till the establishment of peace in 1783. He soon after returned with his family to his farm, which he found had suffered much devastation by those who had possessed it in his absence. In 1794 he disposed of it, and removed to the mills which he owned near the village of Jerusalem, where he died, highly beloved and regretted, July 30, 1798.

Benjamin Birdsall, Esq. of the city of New-York, a gentleman equally distinguished for his energy and perseverance, as for his intelligence, patriotism, and moral worth, is the only surviving son of Colonel Birdsall.

TOWN OF NORTH-HEMPSTEAD,

Is bounded north by the Sound, east by Oyster-Bay, south by Hempstead, and west by Flushing. This town was originally included within the limits of Hempstead, but by an act passed the 6th of April, 1784, entitled "*An act to divide the township of Hempstead into two towns,*" it was declared that "all that part of the said township of Hempstead north of the country road that leads from Jamaica nearly through the middle of Hempstead Plains to the east part thereof, shall be included in one township, and be hereafter called and known by the name of North-Hempstead." The town, therefore, having had no separate existence previous to the year 1784, can possess no public records extending beyond that period; and the early history of its settlement being blended with that of the original town, little remains to be said upon this branch of the subject. The improvements which have taken place in the town since its separation and its present appearance is all that can be expected, and amounts to a mere descriptive account of things as they at present exist. The surface of this town is in many

46

respects different from that of Hempstead, having a ridge of
hills, a portion of the spine of Long Island, passing through
it from east to west; the land south of this elevated tract,
partaking in some degree the nature of the plains, while that
on the north is rough and often stony.   Indeed, all that portion
of the island lying between the villages of Flushing on the
west and Huntington on the east, bounded north by the Sound
and south by the hills, deserves particular notice, for the peculiarity of its general features.   This tract is indented for half its
width between the ridge and Sound by seven large bays or harbors, called by the several names of Flushing-Bay, Little-Neck-
Bay, Manhassett-Bay, (formerly Cow-Bay,) Hempstead-Harbor,
Oyster-Bay, Cold-Spring, and Huntington-Harbor.   These sheets
of water occur in regular succession, being from four to six
miles in length, and having in their general form a wedge-like
shape, with mouths or entrances from one to three miles wide ;
and is in almost every case defended by a sand-beach, a sort of
natural break-water, formed by the continual action of the
tidal currents, and leaving in some instances only a passage-
way or channel for vessels.   The distance from the west side
of Flushing-Bay to the east side of Huntington-Harbor, in a
direct line is about twenty-eight miles ; while, following the in-
dentations of the coast produced by these bays, will make the
distance upwards of eighty miles ; forming an extensive water-
front, presenting a great variety of surface, abounding in fine
scenery, in which the cultivated field, the forests, the waters of
the bays, the broad expanse of the Sound, whitened with the sails
of commerce, the mill, the farm-house, and the country residence,
alternately attract the attention and delight the eye of the admirer of the beautiful and picturesque.   The soil in general,
especially upon the necks, is fertile and productive.   Its undulating surface presents a greater varieties of soil, and is adapted,
of course, to different kinds of cultivation.   The timber is
abundant, and of the most valuable kinds, as well for building
as for fuel.   The locust-tree flourishes in this region, particularly upon Manhassett and Great Neck.   The tradition exists,
that the first of this kind of tree ever known here was brought
from Virginia a century and a half ago, by a Mr. Sands, who,

with his two brothers, came from Block-Island, and purchased the land in the vicinity of what is now called Sands's Point, in the year 1686. From a few trees planted here by this person, all the locust trees now upon this part of Long Island are supposed to have been derived. Almost every farm in the town has its forest of locust, and in some instances extends to fifty and a hundred acres. Agriculture is the principal pursuit of the people of this town, yet a considerable number are engaged in navigation, in mercantile, and mechanical employments. The average size of the farms being from seventy-five to three hundred acres. Fine crops of Indian corn, wheat, rye, oats, and grass are annually grown ; the system in general pursued is a rotation of different crops ; and the great facilities for obtaining manure from the city of New-York have induced the extensive use of ashes, street manure, bone, &c.

The country between Flushing and Huntington consists of a succession of promontories formed by the bays before mentioned, containing from two to forty square miles each. The villages at the head of the bays are connected together by the North-Hempstead turnpike, which ranges across the north part of the necks ; and from which, to the head-lands formed by these promontories into the Sound, the distance varies from two to six miles. Over this surface are to be found residences of a superior order, and inhabited by a class of men who are among the most valuable citizens, independent farmers, living upon their own estates, whose attention is devoted to their improvement, and to the encouragement of arts and industry with those around them. So long as this class of men are prosperous, with the influence that justly belongs to them, all that is valuable in our public institutions will be preserved, liberty be secure, industry rewarded, sound morals prevail, and just conceptions of our social, political, and moral duties will preserve the character of the people from degradation.

This is the county town of Queen's County ; the court-house and jail are located upon the northern side of the Great Plains, having been erected in 1788. One of the greatest natural curiosities in this town is the beautiful pond at *Lakeville,* formerly called *Success Pond.* It is situated in a deep basin upon the highest part of the ridge of hills extending through Long Island, perfectly clear and of great depth.   It is about five hundred rods in circumference, surrounded by a high bank, and is altogether a romantic and beautiful object.   It was stocked with the yellow perch many years since by the late Dr. Samuel L. Mitchill, who, in the third vol. of the Medical Repository, says ; " *In 1790 my Uncle Uriah Mitchill, sheriff of Queen's County, and myself, went to Ronkonkoma Pond in Suffolk County, a distance of forty miles, in a wagon, for the purpose of transporting alive some of the yellow perch from thence to Success Pond.   We took about three dozen of those least injured by the hook, and put all but two into Success Pond in good condition ; and in two years thereafter, they had so multiplied as to be caught by the hook in every part of the Pond.*"

Lakeville has long been a place much resorted to, and always greatly admired by the lovers of natural scenery ; and now that a large and convenient hotel has been erected, and other improvements made by the taste and liberality of its owner, cannot fail of becoming a still more interesting spot to those who appreciate the pleasures of a country life, and who delight to revel in all its luxuriance of landscape, here so beautifully displayed.   *Great-Neck*, formerly called *Madnan's Neck*, comprises many hundred acres of fertile and well-cultivated land.   It contains several handsome private residences ; and among others, that of Robert W. Mott, Esquire, is a rural paradise, possessing every charm which can delight the eye and gratify the man of taste.   Between this neck and Manhasset, is the bay formerly called *How's-Bay*, and sometimes *Scout's-Bay*.   One Daniel How, and a few associates, having attempted a settlement here in 1640, but were driven off by Governor Kieft, who sent a scout (or constable) with a guard of soldiers for that purpose.   *Manhasset* is the name lately substituted for *Cow-Neck*, and designates a rich and fertile tract lying between the last-mentioned bay and *Hempstead-Harbor*.   It contains between four and five thousand acres of first-rate land, and is cultivated in the best manner by skilful and experienced farmers.   At the head of this neck, and situated on the North-Hempstead turnpike, is a small cluster of buildings, consisting of three

houses for public worship, a tavern, academy, and two or three
private dwellings. . The Dutch church was erected in 1817 ;
the Episcopal, called Christ Church, in 1803; the Friends' meeting house, many years before ; and the academy attached to
Christ-Church, in 1818; in which there is a public library
of five or six hundred volumes. *Plandome*, the residence of
Singleton Mitchill, Esq., was originally purchased by Mathias
Nicolls, secretary of the colony during the administration of
Richard Nicolls, first English governor of New-York, a patent
for which was issued in 1670. This purchase contained
six hundred acres. Mr. Nicolls died here in 1690, having
devised the estate to his son William, who, in 1718, conveyed
the same to Joseph Latham for £2,250. At the most northerly
part of Manhasset is *Sands's Point*, so called from the name of
the first purchaser. It is one of the most delightful situations
that can be imagined. A light-house was erected here in
1809, at an expense of $8,500. It is of stone, of an octagonal
shape, and eighty feet in height. Near this place there was
formerly a rock of immense size, called *Kidd's Rock*, from a
belief, generally entertained, that the notorious freebooter had
made valuable deposites in the vicinity ; and parties of infatuat-
ed adventurers used occasionally to resort here for the purpose
of enriching themselves with portions of the pirate's treasures ;
but which had been so artfully concealed, that all attempts
proved abortive. During the revolution, bands of marauders
were accustomed to land upon these shores, under the cover of
night, and by attacking detached farm-houses, rifle the inhabitants of their money and other valuables, which they compelled them to give up at the peril of their lives ; and availing themselves of the speed of their whale-boats, would reach their
lurking places among the small islands in the Sound or the
main shore before an alarm could be given. Indeed, so great
was the apprehension of these sudden attacks, that many of
the inhabitants had the windows and doors of their houses secured by bars of iron, to prevent surprises ; and it became
usual for numbers to pass the night in the woods or other secret places, from an apprehension of personal violence, which
in various instances was wantonly and cruelly inflicted. In

some cases life was taken without any provocation, or in revenge for their disappointment at not finding money.   In one
instance, which is worthy of being recorded, a Mr. Jarvis, who
resided at Manhasset, aided by an old lady living in the same
house, succeeded in beating off one of these gangs with the loss
of several killed and wounded on the part of the assailants.
The night not being dark, they were seen and fired upon by
the man from the windows, who was furnished with loaded
muskets by the brave old lady as fast as he could discharge
them effectually.   Three miles easterly of the churches at
Manhasset, is the village of *Hempstead-Harbor*, pleasantly lo-
.cated at the head of the bay ; and possessing a water-power
which has contributed to make it a place of considerable manufacturing importance.   The dwellings are about forty, and the
population two hundred and fifty.   The first paper-mill ever
built in this state was erected here, nearly a century ago, by
Andrew Onderdonk, ancestor of the present head of the Episcopal church of the state of New-York.   There are now here
a grist-mill, paper-mill, saw-mill, a factory for cutting glass-ware,
a Methodist church, a hotel, and two or three stores, besides a
number of mechanics and artizans.   Harbor-Hill, in the immediate neighborhood, is one of the most elevated upon the island,
being three hundred and nineteen feet, and as some think, more,
above tide water.   The view from this eminence is not only very
extensive, but sublime and beautiful beyond description ; it is certainly not surpassed by any other upon Long Island.   On the east
side of the habor, about a mile north of the village, is *Montrose*,
where it is calculated to found a series of manufacturing establishment and connected with the city of New-York by steam
navigation for a greater part of the year.   Along the shores in
the vicinity of this place are numerous and never-failing springs
gushing out at the base of the hills, affording water-power for
any quantity of machinery which may be required.   The
prospect of the harbor and surrounding country is very beautiful.   The minute grouping of landscape and water, hill and
dale, foliage and flower, with an infinite variety of light and
shade, present to the lover of natural scenery a picture truly
.delightful.   The corner-stone of an Episcopal church was

laid at Hempstead-Harbor in 1835 by the bishop of the diocess, but nothing farther has been done towards the erection of
the building. The average number of paupers maintained in
this town is from fifteen to twenty, at an annual expense of
eight hundred dollars. These unfortunate persons, who, as in
other towns, are for the most part the victims of intemperance,
are annually hired out to the lowest bidder, and kept in a way
that must render the poor-house an object of disgust, except to
the most degraded. In this respect the county of Queens is
behind most of the counties in the state; and it is much to be
hoped that those who have the direction in this matter will
in a short period adopt the same benevolent and enlightened
policy, that so creditably distinguishes all but three counties in
the state of New-York.

In the south-western part of the town is *Hyde-Park*, the former residence of George Duncan Ludlow, Esq., one of the judges
of the supreme court of the colony; whose estate, as well as that
of his brother, Col. Gabriel Ludlow, were forfeited to the state,
in consequence of their adherence to the royal cause during
the revolution. The celebrated English radical, William
Cobbet, resided here in 1817, when the dwelling was accident-
ally destroyed by fire. This extraordinary and eccentric individual was born at Farnham, in Surrey, England, in 1762;
and was not only a man of great abilities, but one of the most
voluminous political writers of the age. He was believed to
have performed such valuable services for the cause of liberty,
that Sir William Windham declared in parliament, " *a statue
of gold* ought to be erected to his memory." He was a representative in the house of commons at the time of his decease,
June 25, 1833. The great power of this man lay in wielding,
more effectually than they were ever before, those weapons of
controversy which tell upon the *common sense* of mankind.
When he had a subject that suited him, he handled it, not so
much with the artificial skill of an accomplished writer, as with
the perfect and inimitable natural art with which a *dog picks
a bone.*

Among the number of eminent individuals born in this town,
may be mentioned the names of the late SAMUEL L. MITCHILL,

Professor of Natural History, &c. in Columbia College; BENJA-
MIN KISSAM, Professor of the Institutes of Medicine; and
WRIGHT POST, Professor of Surgery; also DR. RICHARD S.
KISSAM, an eminent physician; and DR. VALENTINE MOTT,
who ranks among the first surgeons of the age.

In the vicinity of Hyde-Park was the residence of the late EDWARD GRISWOLD.
He was born on the 11th of August, 1766, and was the son of Joseph Griswold,
a wealthy distiller of New-York His classical education was acquired under the
instruction of the Rev. Leonard Cutting, of Hempstead. At the age of seventeen
he commenced the study of the law, and was admitted to the bar before the age
of twenty years.   His uncommon industry and assiduous attention to business
secured him in a short time a profitable practice, and his office was filled with
students desirous of deriving advantage from his uncommon stores of legal
knowledge.   One of these was the late John Wells, whose death took place at
Brooklyn, on the 6th of September, 1823. As a commercial lawyer, Mr. Wells
was acknowledged to stand unrivalled at our bar. He was an orator of the first
order. He had, (says his biographer,) a masterly manner of clothing a long
chain of connected ideas in the choicest language; and perhaps no individual in
this country ever reached the same elevation, and occupied so large a share in the
public eye upon the mere footing of professional eminence and worth. Mr.
Griswold was distinguished for his good sense, his great analytical powers, a
clear discrimination of legal principles, and their application to facts in any particular case.   His retirement from the active duties of his profession took place
many years since, yet his advice and assistance continued to be anxiously sought
after, even by the most eminent of the profession; and such was the deference
shown to his opinions, that his authority was generally considered quite satisfactory. More than forty years ago he visited Paris, where he married a lady of
fortune, by whom he had an only child, now the wife of General Berthemy,
possessing an important, military station in the kingdom of France. Mr.
Griswold again visited Paris in 1810, where he found the late Col. Burr, and
to whom he loaned the sum of two thousand franks at one time, to relieve him
from penury and distress.   It was Mr. Griswold's intention to have remained in France, and was negotiating for a country-seat about twenty miles from
Paris, but which was for some cause broken off, and he returned to his farm in
North Hempstead, where he spent the remainder of his life, and where he died
suddenly by an attack of apoplexy, Feb. 26, 1836.   Col. Burr entertained the
most profound respect for the talents and legal acquirements of Mr. Griswold,
and said he was the only person he ever saw who loved the black-letter lore of
the common law, for its own sake.   Mr. Wells too, in the full zenith of his reputation, spoke of the professional habits and acquirements of his early tutor and
friend in terms of the highest respect.   The example alone of such a man must
have been of very great advantage to his pupil, and in one respect at least
there was a remarkable similarity between them. This was a most powerful and
singular habit of mental abstraction, which enabled them to sit down in the
midst of their families or a crowd of company, separate themselves from the
sports, the business, or the noise around them, and, insulated and deaf to every
thing that was passing, pursue their studies, equally unconscious of any thing
like interruption, as if in the deepest retirement of the closet.

DR. SAMUEL L. MITCHILL. This amiable man and eminent philosopher was born at Plandome, in North Hempstead, August 20, 1764. He was the third son of Robert Mitchill, an industrious farmer of this town, who was descended from Sir Humphrey Mitchill of Old Widson, in the county of Berks, England. Robert and his wife were in good standing with the society of Friends, and brought up their children in the habits and strict morality of that sect. He died in 1789, leaving six sons and two daughters. On the maternal side Dr. Mitchill was descended from the family of Latham. Joseph Latham was born in Bristol, England, in 1674, and married Jane Singleton. He came to New-York in 1700, and commenced ship-building, which he followed with such success as to be able in 1718 to purchase a farm of six hundred acres upon Cow-Neck of William Nicolls for £2.250. Two hundred and thirty acres of this land are now owned by his great-grandson, Singleton Mitchill, the gift of his uncle Dr. Samuel Latham. Joseph Latham deceased in 1748, and the property descended to his son William, who died in 1763, whose daughter was the wife of the said Robert Mitchill. Dr. Mitchill was particularly assisted and patronized by his uncle, Dr. Latham, who was a skilful and intelligent medical practitioner in his native place. The resources of this gentleman happily enabled him to enter upon and complete that system of education which the limited income of his father of necessity denied. Of his uncle he always spoke with becoming gratitude and ardent affection. At an early age he was placed under the direction of the Rev. Leonard Cutting, the minister of Hempstead and a graduate of the University of Oxford. With this excellent instructor he continued for several years, and acquired an intimate acquaintance with classical literature, which constituted one of the favorite amusements of his leisure hours through life. It is due to this kind preceptor to state, that he early predicted the future eminence of his pupil, and contributed by his praise and encouragement to its fulfilment. While at Hempstead he obtained a partial knowledge of the French language from Mr John H. Hentz, which he further perfected on his subsequent visit to France. After acquiring some of the elementary principles of medicine with Dr. Latham, he, in 1780, became a pupil of Dr. Samuel Bard of New-York, with whom he continued about three years. Dr. Latham died in 1781; after which young Mitchill had little further opportunity for education. In 1784 he went to Europe, and was at the medical school of Edinburgh, then adorned by the talents of Cullen, Black, and Monro. He there had for his friends and compeers the late Thomas Addis Emmet and Sir James Mackintosh; and we have the testimony of the former that no student of the University exhibited greater tokens of promise. On the death of this gentleman at New-York in 1828, Dr. Mitchill performed the melancholy duty of pronouncing his eulogium. On his return from Europe in 1786, he devoted a portion of his time to acquire a knowledge of the laws and constitution of his country, under the direction of Robert Yates of Albany, at that time chief-justice of the state of New-York. By the influence of this gentleman he was employed in the commission for holding a treaty with the Iroquois Indians, and was present at the adjustment made at Fort Stanwix, 1788, in which the right to a large portion of the western district became the property of the state. In 1790 he was chosen a member of the legislature from Queen's County, and in 1792 was appointed Professor of Natural History, Chemistry, and Agriculture, in Columbia College; at this school he first made known to his countrymen the new theory of chemistry recently matured by the genius of Lavoisier and his associates, in opposition to the theory of his former master, Dr. Black. In 1796 he made his able

47

mineralogical report of a survey of the state of New-York; and in 1797 commenced the publication of the Medical Repository in connection with Drs Miller
and Smith, of which he was chief editor for more than sixteen years. In 1799
he was united in marriage with Mis. Catharine Cock, daughter of Samuel
Akerly of the city of New-York. He was a member of numerous scientific institutions. Of the Lyceum of Natural History of New-York he was the founder,
and for many years president. He enriched its annals with many contributions,
and still further displayed his zeal and liberality by a donation of a large portion
of his valuable cabinet. For about twenty years he acted as one of the physicians of the New-York Hospital. Notwithstanding his immense literary labors
and publications on almost every subject of science, he found time to mingle in
the bustle of politics. He was elected from the city of New-York a member of
the seventh, eighth, and ninth congresses; and afterwards a state senator of the
United States. Few men ever enjoyed a more enviable popularity, or preserved
a more voluminous correspondence in every part of the world. In private life
he was distinguished for affability and simplicity of manners, and was always
ready to impart to others of his immense stores of knowledge, which probably
exceeded in value and amount those of any man living. The illustrious Cuvier
always mentioned him in terms of great approbation; and Audubon, the ornitholo-
gist, has bestowed upon him the tribute of his sincere applause. He died, after a
short but severe illness, at his residence in the city of New-York, in the sixty-
seventh year of his age, September 7, 1831. The biography of this illustrious
man, written by his brother-in-law, Dr. Samuel Akerly, is now ready for the
press; and from the importance of the subject as well as the acknowledged ability
of its author, the public may expect a performance of no ordinary excellence.

TOWN OF FLUSHING,

Is bounded north by Long Island Sound, east by North
Hempstead, south by Jamaica, and west by Newtown ; containing an area of sixteen thousand acres, of which about one half
are improved. In consequence of the total destruction of the
records of this town by fire, in the year 1789, it has become
not only difficult, but in a great measure impossible to obtain
much authentic information in relation to its ancient history ;
and we can only give, therefore, such particulars as with much
pains we have been enabled to glean from other resources.

The settlement of this town was commenced in 1644, principally by a company of Englishmen, who, having resided for
a short time in Holland, were induced to attempt a plantation in
some part of the Dutch jurisdiction, by the inducements held
out by the government of the Netherlands, and upon the special understanding that they should here enjoy in the fullest degree the liberty of Englishmen. On the arrival of the immigrants, they concluded to locate upon this part of the island, and

called the place Vlissengen or Flushing, from a town of that name in Holland, where they had previously resided. On the 10th of October of the following year, (1645,) a patent was obtained from Governor Kieft, which was made to Thomas ffarington, John Lawrence, John Hicks, and divers others, as patentees for themselves, their successors, associates and assigns, to be improved, manured, and settled by a competent number of families. A few years after a man of the name of Thorne, with his family, consisting of a wife, three sons and one daughter, arrived from England for the purpose of settling in some part of this island. It so happened that the vessel in which these persons had crossed the ocean came through the Sound, and cast anchor near Throg's Point. Having some curiosity to see the country, and anxious once more to be on shore, they landed on the opposite side of the East River, where they met and conversed with some of the white inhabitants, who, they were happy to find, had come from the same district with themselves; and liking the general appearance of the land, they determined to seek no further for a place of residence. Mr. Thorne accordingly purchased the neck or Point in the eastern part of the town adjoining the East River, called *Thorne's Point*, which continued in his family until near the close of the last century, when it became the property of one *Wilkins*, and has since been known as *Wilkins's Point*. One of the posterity of Mr. Thorne formerly owned the farm of the late John Titus, and was in possession of it some years after the revolution. The only direct communication, which for many years after the first settlement of the town existed with the city of New-York, was by water, there being no mode of getting to the city by land, except by way of Jamaica. An individual keeping a small store near the water, had purchased from the Indians at *Bay-Side* a large canoe, capable of containing a hogshead of molasses, with three or four persons, and was in the habit of carrying passengers to and from the city. There was at that time a *Block-House* near where the town-pond was lately, in which the town records were kept, and where arms and ammunition were deposited, to be not only safe, but ready in case of alarm from the natives or others, for immediate use.

At the time of the revocation of the edict of Nantes, a number of French Protestants fled from their native country into Holland and other places.   Many of these afterwards came to America, and several families to this town, where they settled, most of whose posterity are now extinct.   Fifty years since the old inhabitants of Flushing could point out the places where these Hugonots had resided, the only memorials of them now existing are the famous *Lady Apple* and *Bell-Pear* trees, which they brought with them and planted in different places ; some of which are yet standing, and promise fair to remain another century.   From that time to this the town of Flushing has enjoyed a high reputation for the excellence and variety of its fruit, which, increased by the natural fertility of its soil, has led to the establishment of more extensive nurseries and gardens than can be found in any other part of the United States.   To evince the scarcety of silver coin at this period, it need only be stated that an English shilling being found in the street, excited great public curiosity ;   much inquiry was made for the owner of so rare an article, and it was at length ascertained that the man who kept a store near the water had been seen to have a coin of that description in his possession, and who satisfactorily proved himself the lawful owner.   This place was visited likewise by Quakers a few years after the commencement of the settlement, many of whom became permanent residents of the town.   These persons had, on their first arrival in the country, settled at Gravesend ; but afterwards, probably on account of the persecutions of Governor Stuyvesant, left there, and removed to this and other more eastern towns, where they hoped to remain in the undisturbed enjoyment of their religious freedom. One of the most respectable of this society, a man of very considerable distinction, was John Bowne, who in 1661 erected a dwelling-house, which is still standing, and near which are two large oak trees, under whose shade the celebrated George Fox addressed the assembled inhabitants in 1672.   In the year 1662 Stuyvesant was so much exasperated by the contempt with which his requirements on the subject of religion had been treated by the society of Friends, and particularly by the above-named John Bowne, the most influential individual among them, that he directed him to be put on board of a ship and transported to Holland, to be punished as he deserved for his heretical opinions and practices. The vessel and prisoner arriving in Holland, and the facts charged upon him by the governor being fully considered by the Dutch authorities, he was released, and sent back in triumph to his friends, with the following epistle to his Excellency, bearing date at Amsterdam, April 16, 1663 :

" Sir.—We perceive from your last letter, that you had exiled and transported hither a certain Quaker, named John Bowne. Although it is our anxious desire that similar and other sectarians may not be found among you, yet we *doubt* extremely the policy of adopting rigorous measures against them. In the youth of your existence, you ought rather to encourage than check the population of the colony. The *consciences* of men ought to be *free* and *unshackled* so long as they continue moderate, peaceable, inoffensive, and not hostile to the government. Such have been the maxims of prudence and toleration by which the magistrates of this city (Amsterdam) have been governed; and the consequences have been, that the *oppressed* and *persecuted* from every country have found among us an *asylum* from distress. *Follow in the same steps, and you will be blessed.*"

The case of John Bowne is but one out of many instances in which the same governor presumed to interfere with the free exercise of religion among the people of this colony, and was only prevented from still more unwarrantable aggression by the termination of his authority on the arrival of Colonel Nicolls in 1664.

Two years after the conquest of New-York, and on the 16th of February, 1666, a patent was obtained from Governor Nicolls, confirming to the inhabitants all the purchases of land formerly made. This patent was in the usual form, and made to certain persons named therein, in substance as follows :

" *To John Lawrence, alderman of the city of New-York, Richard Cornell, Charles Bridges, William Lawrence, Robert Terry, William Noble, John Forbush, Elias Doughty, Robert Field, Edward Farrington, John Maston, Anthony Field, Phillip Udall, Thomas Stiles, Benjamin Field, William Fidgeon, John Adams, John Hinchman, Nicolas Parcell, Tobias Feels, and John Bowne,* as patentees for and in behalf of themselves and their associates, the freeholders and inhabitants of the town of Flushing, their heirs, successors, and assigns for ever; All that certain town in the north-riding of Yorkshire upon Long Island, called by the name of *Flushing,* situate and lying and being on the north side of the said island; which said town hath a certain tract of land belonging thereunto, and bounded westward, beginning at the mouth of a creek upon the East River known by the name of Flushing Creek, and from thence including a certain neck of land called *Tews-Neck,* to run eastward as far as Mathew Garretson's Bay, from the head or middle whereof a line is to be run south-east, in length about three miles

and about two miles in breadth, as the land hath been surveyed and laid out by'virtue of an order made at the general meeting held at Hempstead in the month of
March, 1665 ; and that there be the same latitude in breadth on the south side as
on the north, to run in two direct lines southward to the middle of the hills, to
the bounds between the said towns of Flushing and Jamaica."

A further patent of confirmation to the town was issued by
Governor Dongan on the 24th of March, 1685, which was declared to be made for the purpose of strengthening the aforesaid title, the peaceable enjoyment of the premises heretofore
granted, and for preventing all controversy that might at any
time thereafter arise from Tackapausha, Succanemen, Runasuck, or other Indian Sachems, or any other person who might
claim the land belonging to the inhabitants of the said town of
Flushing.   The persons named as patentees therein were *Elias
Doughty, Thomas Willet, John Bowne, Mathias Harvey,
Thomas Hicks, Richard Cornell, John Hinchman, Jonathan
Wright,* and *Samuel Hoyt.*

In the year 1672 the celebrated GEORGE FOX, founder of
the society of Friends, and a man greatly distinguished for his
zeal, intelligence, courage, and perseverance, came to America ;
who in the course of his travels visited this town, where he held
several meetings ; and there being at that time no house sufficiently large to accommodate the people assembled on those occasions, the inhabitants were convened under the shade of two
large white oak trees, which are yet standing in front of the
house of the said John Bowne, which had been built ten years
before. As the visit of this wonderful man is an important
event in the early history of the colony, we will, for the gratification of the reader, make a short extract from his own Journal of so much as relates to Long Island. After remaining
awhile in Philadelphia, and passing into New Jersey :

" At length (says he), we came to Middletown, an English plantation in East
Jersey, where there were some Friends ; but we could not stay to have a meeting,
being earnestly possessed in our spirits to get to the half-yearly meeting of
Friends at Oyster-Bay in Long Island, which was near at hand. We got to
Gravesend, where we tarried all night. Next day got to Flushing. The day
following we reached Oyster-Bay. Several from Flushing and Gravesend accompanied us. Thence to Shelter Island and Fisher's Island ; but could not stay
for the mosquitoes, which abound there and are very troublesome. We returned to Oyster-Bay, where we had a very large meeting. From Oyster-Bay we
went about thirty miles, to Flushing, where we had a meeting of *many hundred*

people. Meantime Christopher Holden and some other Friends went to a town in Long Island, called Jamaica, and had a meeting there. We passed from Flushing to Gravesend, about twenty miles, and had three precious meetings there. While we were at Shrewsbury, John Jay, a Friend of Barbadoes, who came with us from Rhode Island, fell from his horse and *broke his neck*, as the people said. Those near him took him up for dead, carried him a good way, and laid him on a tree. I got to him as soon as I could, and concluded he was dead. Whereupon I took his head in both my hands, and setting my knees against the tree, raised his head two or three times with all my might, and *brought it in*. He soon began to rattle in his throat, and quickly after, to breathe. The people were amazed, but I told them to be of good faith, and carry him into the house. He began to speak, but did not know where he had been. The next day we passed away, and he with us, about sixteen miles, to a meeting at Middletown, through woods and bogs, and over a river where we swam our horses. *Many hundred miles* did he travel with us after this."

A Friends' meeting-house was first erected in this town in 1690, at which time a majority of the inhabitants were attached to that denomination of Christians. An Episcopal society was formed in 1720, under the sanction of the society for propagating the gospel in foreign parts; their meetings were held in the guard-house before mentioned, and continued to be held there till the erection of the first church. In the year 1746 half an acre of land west of the town pond, was given by Ralph Wentworth, for the purpose of having a church erected thereon. The conveyance was made to the Rev. Thomas Colgan, the minister, and his successors in office. Mr. Wentworth gave a considerable sum of money also, to aid in the building of the church. The edifice was soon after erected, and at a subsequent period a charter was bestowed upon it by Governor Colden, by the name of *St. George's Church*. In 1782 a legacy of two hundred pounds was made to the church by the Hon. Samuel Cornell of North Carolina, which was accordingly paid at his decease by his executor. In the year 1762 a Mr. Kneeland was appointed catechist of the church, with a salary of ten pounds a-year. This church was from its origin associated with the churches of Jamaica and Newtown, and all were supplied in rotation by the same clergymen. In 1770 the congregation raised the sum of one hundred and twenty-six pounds for repairing the church, and in 1803 the churches of Flushing and Newtown united in procuring for their joint minister the Rev. Abraham L. Clark, who remained with them in common for six years, after which his services were confined exclu-

sively to the church at Newtown.   In 1809 the Rev. Barzilla
Buckly was chosen pastor of this church, and the corporation
of Trinity Church, in New-York, presented to the congregation
three lots of ground toward the future support of their minister. Mr. Buckly continued here till his death, March 29, 1820.
From which period the Rev. Mr. Muhlenburgh, Mr. Lewis,
Mr. Forbes, Mr. Johnson, and Mr. Van Kleek, officiated successively in the church for the aggregate term of seventeen
years ; when, on the 10th of February, 1837, the Rev. Mr. Good-
win was settled as minister of this church. The present church
edifice was erected in 1812.

In the year 1789 the dwelling-house of John Vanderbilt,
clerk of the town, was burnt, together with a great part of his
furniture and the whole of the town records.   The fire was
designedly communicated by a young negro girl, who is reported to have possessed a very moderate share of intellect.   The
court and jury must have judged her to be of sufficient capacity to be a fit object of criminal punishment, for she was found
guilty of arson, and soon after executed ; being the last instance
of a capital execution in this county.   On the 5th of April,
1791, the town deputed John Vanderbilt, Lewis Cornell, and
Francis Lewis, to obtain from Governor George Clinton a renewal of the patent of the town, which had been destroyed, and
one was accordingly issued the 24th of February, 1792.

One of the most important objects in this town, one which
most attracts the attention of strangers, is the extensive garden
and nursery of the Messrs. Prince, called the *Linnean Botanic
Garden.*   This establishment was commenced as long ago as
the year 1750, by William Prince (deceased), father of the
present senior proprietor.   It is now conducted by William
Prince and Sons.   The quantity of ground occupied by the
gardens previous to 1793 was about eight acres.   In that year
it was increased to twenty-four.   The quantity has been gradually enlarged as the business extended, until at this time more
than sixty acres are covered with an extraordinary variety of
trees and plants.   At the beginning of the revolutionary war
the grounds were full of the finest well-grown fruit trees, among
which were thirty thousand grafted English cherry-trees.   An

end was of course put to the sale of trees, except for hoop-poles ; for which purpose many thousands of the best young trees were disposed of. It may here be mentioned, as a fact honorable to the character of General Howe, that when the British troops entered Flushing on the 29th of August, 1777, he of his own accord ordered a guard to be stationed for the protection of the garden and nurseries, which was continued as long as was required for their safety. The original introduction of some of the most delicious fruits into this town, by the French immigrants in 1685, (among which were some of the finest apples, pears, peaches, plums, and cherries,) gave rise to the cultivation of trees for sale ; and Flushing early became famous for the excellence of its fruit. Many of the trees planted by the persecuted Hugonots are still existing, vigorous and thriving. This splendid establishment now contains more than ten thousand species and varieties of trees and flowering plants ; many the most rare and beautiful, from every part of the world. Much attention has been given to the vine and mulberry. In the green-house alone there are more than twenty thousand flowering plants. Here there may, of course, be procured a vast variety of fruit and ornamental trees, both indigenous and exotic ; herbaceous, flowering, and medicinal plants ; bulbous and tuberous flowers, &c. This immense collection, as well as the grounds occupied by the nurseries, are constantly open to visitors without any charge whatever. The *Morus Multicaulis tree*, now so well known in the culture of silk, was first introduced into this country by the proprietors of the Linnean Garden from France in 1826, where it had been brought, the year before, from the Phillippine Islands ; since when millions have been raised and disposed of.

Flushing Village, which has lately been incorporated, is the largest in the county, and contains a poulation of about two thousand in a square mile. It has long possessed many attractions, which, with its facilities for communication with New-York, have induced many wealthy citizens to locate in its immediate neighborhood. Many of the private residences are among the most sumptuous and elegant in the state, particularly that of the late Hon. Nathan Sandford. the expense of

48

which is said to have been nearly one hundred thousand dollars.   This gentleman was born at Bridgehampton, in Suffolk
County, in 1777, and received his education at Yale College.
Having chosen the profession of the law, he was admitted to
the bar in 1799 ; and was soon after appointed by Mr. Jefferson
attorney of the United States for the southern district of New-
York, which he held for more than twenty years, having, besides, a very extensive and lucrative private practice.   He succeeded the Hon. James Kent as chancellor of this state in 1823,
which he retained till 1825, when he was elected by the New-
York legislature a state senator in the nineteenth congress, as
the colleague of Mr. Van Beuren.   At the end of six years he
returned to private life, and a few years since took up his residence in this town.   For more than twenty years he was afflicted with an affection of the lungs, which terminated his life on
the 17th of October, 1838.

The *Flushing Institute* was incorporated the 16th of April, 1827, and is one of
the most imposing public edifices in the town.   While under the management of
the Rev. Mr. Muhlenburgh, it proved to be one of the most popular and useful
schools in the state, but having been given up by him, it has been transferred
to other hands, and ceased to be used for the purpose originally intended.   This
gentleman has located his seminary at a place called *College Point*, upon the
north-west part of Lawrence's Neck, adjoining the Sound, one of the most beautiful, heathy, and commanding situations which could have been chosen.   The
name given to this new establishment is *St. Paul's College*, the corner-stone of
which was laid by the Right Rev. Bishop Onderdonk, Oct. 15, 1836.   The main
building has not yet been completed, but sufficient erections have been made for the
accommodation of more than one hundred students.   From the high reputation
sustained by the founder, there is no reason to doubt of the prosperity of his undertaking.   It is in all respects an Episcopal Seminary, and the members of the
college constitute an Episcopal congregation.   The course of instruction is nearly
the same as that in other colleges, and conducted by professors of known ability.
The government of this institution is parental, and the students are required to
reside in the college.

A *mineral spring* was discovered, in the year 1816, upon
the land of Mr. Walter Roe in the village of Flushing, which
for a time attracted the attention of scientific men and the public.   The water was examined by Dr. Mitchill and other
chemists, and found to be a chalybeate ; and in its medicinal
properties nearly resembling that of *Schooley's Mountain*.   Its
day of excitement, however, has passed away, and for ma-

ny years nothing more has been heard of this famous sanative.

The surface of this town is for the most part level, and the remainder moderately undulating. The soil is in general of the best quality, and its agriculture probably exceeds that of any other portion of Long Island. The farms in the vicinity of the village, on the road to Whitestone and at Bay-Side, are not excelled for their beauty, fertility, and excellence, by any in the country; and very justly excite the wonder and admiration of strangers. At *Whitestone*, on the Sound, are several dwellings, some of which are extremely elegant. A ferry was formerly kept here to Westchester, and a *distillery* has been in operation also for nearly thirty years. At the head of Little Neck is a place called the *Alley*, where is a mill, several houses, and a public landing. Upon this part of the town, and at the head of Little Neck Bay, is a tract of salt-meadow containing several hundred acres, which is crossed by a turnpike road and bridge leading to Hempstead Harbor. On the western part of the town is a fine tract of land nearly insulated by creeks, known by the name of *Ireland;* which was formerly the residence of Governor Colden, called by him *Spring Hill*, now the property of the Hon. Benjamin W. Strong. Between this tract of land and Newtown is another body of meadow comprising more than one thousand acres. In the lower part of this meadow, adjoining the causeway leading to New-York, is a singular hill, covered with timber, which, when the meadow is overflowed by the tide, is of course an island. It contains seven acres, and has lately been purchased by a wealthy citizen of New-York for the purpose of building thereon a summer residence. *Zion Church*, at the head of Little Neck, was erected by the late Wynant Van Zandt, Esq. in 1830, and of which the Rev. Eli Wheeler was rector for several years. Another has been lately built at Clintonville, between the village of Flushing and Whitestone, by Samuel Leggett, Esq. which is understood to be a free church.

FRANCIS LEWIS. This gentleman was born at Landaff, in South Wales, in 1713, and educated at Westminster. He early concluded to be a merchant, and converting his patrimony into money, sailed for New-York in 1735; from whence he went to Philadelphia, and established himself in business. Two years after he returned to New-York, and engaged extensively in navigation. His commercial transactions induced him to visit Russia and other parts of Europe; and was twice shipwrecked upon the coast of Ireland. As agent for supplying the British troops, he was at Fort Oswego when it surrendered to Montcalm, after Col. Mercer had been killed by his side. He was carried a prisoner to Montreal, and thence to France. After his liberation he returned to New-York, and was first among the sons of Liberty in the revolutionary movements of the country. In 1775 he was unanimously elected a delegate to the continental congress, where his commercial knowledge and habits rendered his services peculiarly important. The next year he affixed his signature, with his fellow patriots, to the declaration of independence. He was afterwards employed by congress in the importation of military stores, and on various secret services. He had, in 1776, removed his family to his farm at Flushing. In the autumn of that year his house was plundered by a party of British light horse, and his extensive library and papers wantonly destroyed. They thirsted for revenge upon a man who had dared to affix his name to a document which proclaimed the independence of America. Unfortunately Mrs. Lewis fell into their power, and was retained a prisoner several months by the brutal foe, without a change of clothes or a bed to lie upon. Through the influence of Washington, she was released, but her health was so injured that she soon sank into the grave. Mr. Lewis continued to reside here about twenty years, when he removed again to New-York. Of his subsequent life little is known, except that his last days were spent in comparative poverty. his large fortune having been sacrificed upon the altar of his country's freedom. The life of this excellent man was, however, protracted to his ninetieth year. He died Dec. 30, 1803.

CADWALLADER COLDEN. former lieutenant-governor of the colony of New-York, was for many years a resident of Flushing. He was the son of the Rev. Alexander Colden of Dunse, in Scotland, where he was born February 17, 1688; graduated at Edinburgh in 1705, and devoted himself to medicine and the mathematics till the year 1708. The fame of Penn's colony allured him to America in 1710, and he practised physic in Philadelphia till 1715, when he returned to England. Here he formed an acquaintance with many eminent men, with whom he maintained a correspondence ever after. From London he went to Scotland, where he married Alice Christie. daughter of a clergyman of Kelso. In 1716 he came back to America, with his wife. and practised medicine in Philadelphia for two years. In 1718 he removed to New-York, where he relinquished his profession, and became a public character. He soon distinguished himself as a philosopher and statesman. His writings in several departments of science attest his extraordinary industry and ability. His correspondence with most of the learned men of the age in which he lived, is an evidence of the estimation in which he was held by them. His character as a statesman will be found in his political writings, and in his correspondence with the ministry of Great Britain at the critical times in which he administered the colonial government. He held successively the offices of surveyor-general of the colony, master in chancery, member of the council under Governor Burnet, and lieutenant-governor at several periods. He purchased a tract of land near Newburgh, which he named Coldenham, and to which he removed in 1756. Here he occupied himself with botanical and mathematical pursuits, carrying on at the same time a correspondence with Collinson, Linneus, Gronovius, and others, in Europe; and with

Franklin, Garden, Bartram, Alexander, and others, in America. He wrote treatises upon Gravitation, on Matter, on Fluxions, and various other subjects of science. While holding the office of lieutenant-governor, he resided most of the time at his farm in Flushing, called Spring-Hill, where he built a spacious and substantial mansion. His death took place here on the 20th of September, 1776, at the age of eighty-eight years; and he was buried in a private cemetery on the farm attached to Spring-Hill. He had five sons and five daughters, a part of whom only survived him. His daughter *Elizabeth* married Peter De Lancy, Esq.; *Jane* married Dr. William Farquhar; and *Alice* married Col. William Willet. Three of Governor Colden's sons, *Alexander*, *Cadwallader*, and *David*, were successively surveyor-generals, and prominent men in the colony. His son David, to whom he devised the farm at Spring-Hill, (now the property of the Hon. Benjamin W. Strong,) becoming a warm and active loyalist in the revolution, lost his estate by forfeiture, and he retired to England in 1784, where he died the 10th of July of the same year. He was bred to the profession of physic, which however he never practised. He was fond of retirement, was much devoted to scientific pursuits; and his correspondence with learned men in Europe and America is to be found in the publications of the time. His wife was Ann, daughter of John Willet, Esq. of Flushing. She died at Coldenham, Orange County, in August, 1785. Mr. Colden had one son and eight daughters. His daughter Mary married the late Josiah Ogden Hoffman, Esq.; Elizabeth married Edward W. Laight, Esq; and Catharine married the late Thomas Cooper, Esq.

CADWALLADER D. COLDEN, the only son of David Colden, was born at Spring-Hill in Flushing, April 4, 1769; and received the first part of his education at a school in the town of Jamaica. In the spring of 1784 he accompanied his father to England, where he attended a classical school near London till the close of 1785, when he returned to New-York, and entered upon the study of the law in the office of the late Richard Harrison, one of the most eminent barristers of New-York. He completed it with Mr. Van Schaick of Kinderhook, and was admitted to the bar in 1791. He practised his profession at Poughkeepsie till 1796, when he removed to New-York, where he was soon after made district attorney, and laid the foundation of his future fame. On the 8th of April, 1793, he married Maria, daughter of the Rev. Samuel Provoost, bishop of the diocese of New-York. In 1803 he visited France and Switzerland for his health, and returned at the end of 1804. For a young man at that time to attain distinction at the bar, with such competitors as the elder *Jones, Harrison, Hamilton,* and *Livingston,* was no easy task. Mr. Colden made the effort, and by dint of talent and discipline succeeded. In a few years he stood as a commercial lawyer at the head of his profession, and in the other branches, among the first. In 1812 he commanded a regiment of volunteers, and was very active in assisting to raise fortifications for the defence of the city. In 1818 he was elected to the assembly, and in the same year was appointed mayor of New-York at a period when the mayor presided in the court of sessions. In 1822 he was chosen a representative in congress, and proved a useful and distinguished member of that body. In 1824 he was elected to the senate of this state, which he held for three years. The most untiring industry and patient research were peculiar traits in his professional character, and marked his proceedings in every thing he undertook. He was among the earliest and most efficient promoters, in connection with De Witt

Clinton, of the system of internal improvement, now the pride and boast of our state. At the completion of that splendid and herculean project, the Erie Canal, he composed and published the well-known memoir upon the subject. He wrote also the life of Robert Fulton, the successful promoter of steam navigation, and one of the greatest benefactors of mankind. Mr. Colden died, universally esteemed and lamented, at his residence in Jersey City, on the 7th of February, 1834. He was, in every sense of the word, a great man, and one of whose nativity the people of Long Island may well be proud.

TOWN OF JAMAICA ;

Is situated in the south-western part of Queen's County, centrally about twelve miles from the city of New-York. It is bounded north by Flushing and Newtown, east by Hempstead, south by the Jamaica Bay, and west by King's County. This town is deprived of any ocean-front in consequence of Hempstead or Rockaway beach extending south-westerly between the bay and ocean, as far as Rockaway Inlet, ten miles beyond the Marine Pavilion. It is generally supposed that in former times a small tribe or family of Indians, subject to some other, dwelt upon the shore of the creek putting up from the bay south of the present village of Jamaica, and called the "*Jameco*" tribe, from whom the name of the town is derived ; and not from an island in the West Indies, to which it has been assimilated in sound by the modern way of spelling the word. At that remote period the *Beaver Pond*, so called, was large and deep, in which the beavers were common; and the way leading to it from the Indian settlement below was called the *Beaver Path*. The first purchases of land in this town were made from the Canarsee Indians, who inhabited the southern part of Queen's County, particularly on the shores of Jamaica Bay. The lands were afterwards procured from the Rockaway tribe also, who claimed jurisdiction over the eastern portion of the town. In the grant of Governor Stuyvesant, hereafter mentioned, the former are denominated the *Canarise* Indians. The first English settlers of the town in 1656 were as follows ·

Daniel Denton,	Henry Townsend,	George Mills,
Richard Chasmore,	Richard Sweet,	Luke Watson, '
John Townsend,	Richard Harker,	Richard Townsend,
John Laran,	Richard Evert,	Roger Lines,
Abraham Smith,	Samuel Mathews,	Nicholas Tanner,
Nathaniel Denton,	Robert Rhodes,	Robert Coe.
Benjamin Coe,	Henry Messenger,	

These individuals, or most of them, came immediately from Milford, and uniting with a few of the inhabitants of Hempstead, requested of Governor Stuyvesant permission to begin a plantation here, well knowing that to attempt a settlement without authority from the Dutch government would but expose them to the certain consequence of being driven off. This request of the settlers has not been discovered, but may be judged of from what is contained in the following grant of the governor, in answer to their application :

" Having seen the request or desire of the inhabitants of the town of Hempstead, and subjects of the province, the governor-general and council have consented and granted unto the aforesaid inhabitants, free leave to erect or build a town according unto their place limited, named *Canarise*, about the midway from Hempstead, upon such privileges and particular ground-briefs, such as the inhabitants of the New Netherlands generally do possess in their lands ; and likewise in the choice of their magistrates, as in the other villages or towns, as Middleborough, Breuklin, Midwout, and Amersfort.

" Done at the fort in New-Netherland, this 21st of March, 1656,

" PETER STUYVESANT.

" By order of the governor-general and council of the New-Netherlands,

" CORNELIUS VAN RUYVEN, Secretary."

A more formal and extensive patent was granted to the town in 1660, in which it was incorporated by the name of *Rusdorpe*, from a town of that name in Holland, and which it retained till the conquest, when the present appellation was adopted. The Dutch governor was characteristically jealous of the exercise of authority by others, and endeavored, as far as possible, to concentrate all power in himself and his council, who were most generally subservient to his wishes. April 12, 1660, he ordered the magistrates of this town to refer a certain cause then pending before them, to the council to be determined, although the magistrates, by the charter, were vested with full power to hold courts, civil and criminal, with a limited jurisdiction, and to make ordinances for the welfare and good government of the town. They were authorized to choose their own magistrates, subject to the approval or otherwise of the governor ; and it was the practice in all the English towns in subordination to the Dutch, to select double the number to which they were entitled, out of which the governor designated those who should serve. The first town meeting of which any record remains, was held the 18th of February, 1656, when it was "voted, among other things, that Daniel Denton should enter all acts and orders of public concernment, *and to have five shillings a-year for his trouble.*" August 16, 1659, the town chose Robert Coe, Richard Everit, Samuel Mathews, Luke Watson, and Nathaniel Denton, to be presented to the governor for the nomination of magistrates. "At a town meeting, March 25, 1659, it was voted that the people mow by *squadrons ;* to wit, John Townsend and his squadron at the East Neck ; Robert Coe and his squadron at the Long Neck ; Nicholas Tanner and his squadron at the Old House ; and Nathaniel Denton and his squadron at the Haw-trees." In many Indian deeds for land in this town, there is a singular exception or reservation, "of the tall trees upon which the *eagles* build their nests." These were probably not what we call eagles, but hawks or cranes, which, it is well known, were deemed sacred birds by some Indian tribes.

"Town meeting, February 18, 1660, it is voted that Daniel Denton make a rate for paying for the bull's hire the last year by the town, and that Luke Watson and John Rhodes gather the same. The town also agreed to cast lots for the south meadows, they being divided into four necks and the inhabitants into four squadrons." It was in the power of any one of the magistrates by warrant to notify a town meeting, and all who neglected to attend after twenty-four hours' notice, forfeited their rates for that year. In 1661, Jan. 15, it was ordered that a rate be made "*to pay for a wolf of Abraham's killing, and one that John Townsend's pit catched.*" On the 30th of April, 1661, it was "voted and agreed to hire a cow-keeper, to keep all the town's cows and calves for the year ; and also to pay to Mr. Coe eleven pounds in good passable wampum, out of money lent to the town by Mr. Tanner. "The town being informed of *one* that milk'd other folk's cows, and having been catched in the act, it was ordered that William Foster should prosecute the offender to the *uttermost,* either here or at the Manhattoes." "January 30, 1662, the town agreed and voted to pay Abraham Smith thirty shillings a-year *for beating the drum on Sunday.*" On the 6th of March, 1662, the town voted a trooper's coat and a kettle to the Indians, in full of the claim due them for land heretofore purchased of them; and also to build a house for the minister, twenty-six feet long, seventeen wide, and ten feet between joint and joint. On the 29th of January, 1663, town voted to pay thirty shillings a-year for beating drum on Sundays and other public meeting days, to be paid in *tobacco payment*, or in wheat at six and eight pence, or Indian corn at four shillings a bushel. "Town agreed, Feb. 6, 1663, that whoever shall kill any wolf, the head being shown to the town or nailed upon a tree, shall have seven bushels of Indian corn; and that Mr. Coe and Ralph Keeler agree with George Norton about building the meeting-house." On the 16th of Feb. 1663, it was ordered by the town that every dwelling-house shall have a sufficient ladder to reach within two feet of the ridge, under penalty of two and sixpence.

"February 19, 1665, the town voted that Richard Everit should go to *Naumitampak*, the Rockaway Sachem, to get him to come to the general court at Hempstead, to maintain the several purchases that have been made of him by the town, and for a recompense for his attendance the town will give him a coat." This request, it seems, was made in pursuance of an order issued by Governor Richard Nicolls, for the deputies of all the towns to meet him in convention at Hempstead, in March, 1665, and to bring with them such evidences as they had for their lands, and such of the Indian chiefs as could be prevailed upon to attend. On the 5th of February, 1665, a patent of confirmation for the lands purchased by the town at various times was granted by Governor Nicolls, to Daniel Denton, Robert Coe, Bryan Newton, William Hallet, Andrew Messenger, Anthony Waters, and Nathaniel Denton, for and on behalf of themselves and their associates, the freeholders and inhabitants of the said town, their heirs, successors, and assigns, as follows, to wit:

"All that certain tract of land, which already hath been, or hereafter shall be purchased for and on behalfe of ye said towne of Jameca, whether from ye native proprietors or others, within the limits and bounds hereafter expiest; that is to say, ye eastern bounds beginning on the east side of ye Little-Plains, to extende south-east to Rockaway Swampe; then north-east from Hempstead bounds, to runne west as ye trees are mark't, on or about ye middle of ye Hills, until it reach to fflushing creeke (which are their north bounds, and divides them from the towne of fflushing) according unto an order made at the Generall meeting at the towne of Hempstead in the month of March, 1665; then to meet Newtown bounds at ye south-west edge of the Hills, ye north-west corner beginning at certaine mark't trees at ye edge of ye said Hills, from whence to runne in a south line to a certaine river, that is, to ye east of Plunder's-Neck, and bounded south by the sea."

On the 5th of November, 1668, the town agreed with John Waget to fence the burying-place, ten rods square, for the sum of £4, in current pay ; and on the 6th of March, 1670, voted to give Mr. Prudden £40 as their minister, with the house and lot in possession of Mr. Walker ; and that a convenient pew be built for him to preach in. The amount ordered by the town, Nov. 7, 1674, to be paid to the Indians for their west purchase, consisted of one trooper's coat, five guns, three blankets, sixteen coats, nine kettles, ten pounds of powder, ten bars of lead, one coat in *liquors*, thirty fathoms of wampum, and a *quart more liquor*. On the 17th of May, 1686, Governor Dongan issued a new patent for the town, to the following persons named therein as patentees on behalf of themselves and their associates:

Nicholas Everit,	Jonas Wood,	Richard Rhodes,
Nathaniel Denton,	William ffoster,	Thomas Lamberson,
Nehemiah Smith,	John Everit,	Joseph Smith,
Daniel Denton,	Edward Higbie,	George Woolsey,
John Oldfields,	Daniel Whitehead,	John Baylis,
William Creed,	John Carpenter,	Thomas Smith,
Bryant Newton,	John ffurman,	Wait Smith,
Benjamin Coe,	Samuel Smith,	Samuel Mills.

The said last-mentioned patent sets forth that an agreement had been entered into the 2d of December, 1684, by which it was concluded and determined that the town of Jamaica should make no claim to Rockaway-Neck; and that by Rockaway river should be understood the river that runs out of Rockaway Swamp, and to be Jamaica's east bounds ; and that the meadows on the west thereof should belong to Jamaica.

" The town being called together in arms on the 8th of October, 1689, John Baylis, Jr., was chosen captain, Jonas Wood, lieutenant, and Hope Carpenter, ensign." On the 6th day of December next following, the town voted and agreed that there should be a meeting-house built sixty feet long, thirty feet wide, and *every way else* that should be convenient and *comely* for a meeting-house. There was no other than a Presbyterian church in this town for more than half a century after the settlement. The first house for religious worship was built in 1662, and the town, by a public vote, agreed to give the *Rev. Zachariah Walker* as their minister, a salary of sixty pounds a-year, payable in wheat and Indian corn at current prices; he was accordingly settled here in 1663, and continued till his removal to Stratford in 1668. From Stratford he went to Woodbury, where he died. He was the son of Robert Walker, who lived in Boston in 1634. He had also a son named Robert, afterwards a judge of the superior court of Connecticut, who died at Stratford in 1772, one of whose daughters was the wife of the Rev. Mr. Wetmore, and another the wife of John M. Reed, mayor of Norwich. His son, Gen. Joseph Walker, a brave and patriotic officer, died at Saratoga, August 11, 1810. The *Rev. John Prudden* succeeded Mr. Walker as the minister of this town. He was son of the Rev. Peter Prudden, who came to New-Haven with the celebrated John Davenport, and settled at Milford in 1639. Mr. Prudden graduated at Harvard College in 1668, and was settled here in 1670, where he remained, respected and useful, till 1692, when he removed to Newark, and continued there till his death, December 11, 1725. The *Rev. George Phillips* of Rowley, Massachusetts, was the next clergyman. He graduated at Harvard College in 1686, and was settled here in 1693. He continued about four years, when he removed to Setauket in the town of Brookhaven in 1697, and died there in 1739. His character and qualifications were of a high order, and his descendants are both numerous and respectable. In 1698 the *Rev. John Hubbard* became the minister of Jamaica, and measures were taken in the year following to erect a new church, and persons were duly appointed to solicit donations for the purpose. A tract of land had been set apart for a parsonage in 1676, together with a piece of meadow, which, it was voted, should continue at the disposal of the town. In 1700 a new stone church was erected, (which stood in the middle of the public street,) but without restricting the use of it to any particular denomination ; and in a short time thereafter the most serious and bitter disputes arose, which kept the people in difficulty and agitation for more than twenty years. The matter was thus : In the year 1702, in consequence of a dangerous sickness. Governor Cornbury removed with the council to the village of Jamaica, and for the special accommodation of his Excellency, as well as from respect to his exalted station, the Rev. Mr. Hubbard cheerfully accorded to him the use of the parsonage-house, which was one of the best in the place, and himself removed into another. It should here be recollected that it was one of the conditions published by authority of the Duke of York in the infancy of the colony administration under him, that every town should elect their own ministers, and compensate them according to such agreement as they should make with them. This was, of course, a great encouragement to new settlers, and for fresh immigrations from Europe ; at which time there was probably not half a dozen professed Episcopalians in the County of Queens, the inhabitants being almost, without exception, Presbyterians or Independents. Therefore there was no reasonable cause why, in the establishment of churches by them, any precautions should have been adopted to prohibit the use of them to other denominations, or prevent other sects from claiming any right to possess them. The Episcopalians had become somewhat numerous about the time the governor took up his residence here, and being countenanced, if not instigated by him, they made a bold attempt to obtain possession of the stone church, with a determination to divest the Presbyterians of the right to occupy it, and convert it entirely to their own use. It so happened that Mr. Hubbard, who had performed religious services in the forenoon, upon returning to the church in the afternoon, to his great surprise, found it occupied by the Episcopalians ; their clergyman, the Rev. Mr. Gordon, in the pulpit, and holding forth to a few auditors who had taken possession of the seats. He thereupon, with true Christian forbearance, invited his people to an orchard near by, where he preached to them under the shade of a large tree. The Presbyterians subsequently obtained the key of the church, regained the possession, and locked it up; but early the next Sunday, some *heroic* individuals of the Episcopal party, with suitable implements, broke open the door, and forcibly maintained possession till their minister arrived and had gone through the service. Having thus again become the occupants of the church, and being countenanced and assisted by the civil authority, with the governor at their head, they kept possession of it for more than twenty-five years; when, after a tedious, expensive, and afflicting litigation, the Presbyterians recovered the possession by due course of law. The Hon. Lewis Morris, afterwards governor of New Jersey, was at this time chief justice of New-York, and presided at the trial, which resulted in favor of the rightful claimants of the church. But such was the indignation of the Episcopal party at their defeat, that even his Honor did not escape their malevolent aspersions; and was compelled, out of respect to public opinion, to repel the charge of judicial partiality, by publishing a vindication of his official conduct in relation to the opinion expressed by him at the trial. Cardwell, the sheriff, under the protection of Lord Cornbury, was an active agent in this nefarious transaction. He seized upon the church glebe, divided it into lots, and leased them out for the benefit of the delinquent party. He sustained a despicable character, and being afterwards imprisoned, hanged himself in despair. This unpleasant contest, so unworthy the Catholic spirit which now characterises most denominations of Christians, may, in a great measure, be ascribed to the peculiar temper of the times, fostered, if not excited, by the odious bigotry of the governor, who did more to disgrace the administration of the colony than all his predecessors. Never was there a governor of New-York so universally detested, or so deserving of abhorrence. His behavior was trifling, mean, and extravagant; while his despotism, bigotry, injustice, and insatiable avarice, aroused the indignation of the people; and at the termination of his administration, he was thrown into jail by his creditors. After his return to England, however, he succeeded his father as Earl of Clarendon.

The *Rev. George Magnis* was the next minister of this church in 1712; but little more is known of him than that,

after remaining here eight years, he removed, in 1720, to Wal-
kill in Orange County, where he received the grant of some
lands from the crown. He was succeeded by the *Rev. Robert
Cross*, an Irish gentleman, in 1723. He had been previously
settled as a minister at Newcastle, New Jersey. He was much
respected for his amiable manners and christian conduct; and
after remaining here till 1730, he was invited to take charge
of the first Presbyterian church in New-York, where he remained till his death at a very advanced age. His immediate
successor in the church here, was the *Rev. George Heathcote*,
an Englishman, much distinguished for his respectability and
learning, and who was followed in 1738 by the *Rev. Walter
Wilmot*. He graduated at Yale College in 1735, and remained the pastor of this church till his decease, Aug. 6, 1744. He
was a native of the town of Southampton, and married Freelove Townsend of Oyster-Bay, of the society of Friends. He
is supposed to be the first minister buried in this town. The
succeeding clergyman was the *Rev. David Bostwick*, of Scotch
extraction. He was born in Connecticut in 1720, and graduated at Yale College in 1741. Upon his settlement here in
1745, a sermon was preached by the Rev. Aaron Burr, then
president of Princeton College. He was of a mild, catholic disposition, of great piety and zeal; confining himself entirely -
to the proper business of his calling, and was respected by
good men of all denominations. He was the author of Memoirs
of President Davies, prefixed to his sermon on the death of
George II. in 1761. In 1756 he removed to New-York, where he
died Nov. 12, 1763. He was suceeded here by the *Rev. Elisha
Spencer*, born, (says the Rev. Dr. Miller, who married his
grand-daughter,) at East Haddam in 1722, and graduated at
Yale College in 1746. He was the brother of Major Gen.
Joseph Spencer of the American Revolutionary army, who
died at East Haddam in 1789. Mr. Spencer settled here May
22, 1748, as the colleague of Mr. Bostwick, but was part of
the time employed as a chaplain of the army during the French
war. He continued here, after the removal of Mr. Bostwick
in 1756, until 1760, when he succeeded the Rev. Dr. Rogers,
at St. George's, Delaware, after the removal of the latter gen-

tleman to New-York in 1765. He removed again, in 1770, to Trenton, where he died in Dec. 1784. The *Rev. Benoni Bradner* graduated at Princeton in 1755, and was settled here in 1760. In two years after he removed to Nine Partners, Dutchess County; and was succeeded by the *Rev. William Mills.* Mr. Mills was born at Smithtown, March 13, 1739; graduated at Yale College in 1756; and settled here in 1762, where he remained till his death in 1774. He was one of the most amiable of men, and faithfully devoted to the duties of his station. The Rev. Nathan Woodhull, minister of Newtown, was his nephew, and came into the possession of his manuscript sermons, which were numerous and well written. The next minister of this church was the *Rev. Mathias Burnet,* born at Bottle Hill, New Jersey, and graduated at Princeton College in 1769. He settled here in 1775, and continued greatly respected and useful till 1785; when he removed to Norwalk, Connecticut, and took charge of an Episcopal church there, where he died in 1806. The *Rev. James Glassbrook* was a native of Scotland, and settled here in 1786, but removed in two or three years, and was succeeded by the *Rev. George Fatoute,* a native of the city of New-York. He graduated at Princeton in 1774, and was settled at Cumberland, New Jersey; whence he removed to this place in Aug. 1789, where he continued until his death, Aug. 21, 1815. He was for a part of the time of his residence here an instructor in Union-Hall academy; and universally esteemed for learning and the excellence of his character. The *Rev. Henry R. Weed,* who graduated at Union College in 1812, was settled here Jan. 4, 1816, and remained till 1822, when he removed to Albany, and afterwards to Wheeling in Virginia. He was succeeded here by the *Rev. Seymour P. Funk,* March 6, 1823. He was dismissed May 9, 1825, and died at Flatlands, King's County, a short time after. The present worthy minister, the *Rev. Elias W. Crane,* is a native of Elizabethtown, New Jersey; and was settled at Springfield in that state, Jan. 5, 1820, from whence he removed to this church Oct. 31, 1826. *The Reformed Dutch Church* in this town was first organized in 1702, by Dutch settlers from the adjoining county of

King's and the city of New-York. The first church was erected in 1715. It was of an octagonal shape, and stood upon the
south side of the present Fulton Street, opposite to the present
Dutch church. Many other churches were constructed of
a similar form, as most agreeable to their notions of architectural elegance, and best calculated to accommodate conveniently the greatest number of persons in the least space. The
first minister of this congregation was the *Rev. Henry Goetschius*, who, when a boy, came with his father from Zurich
in Switzerland, to Philadelphia, having received a call to the
First Reformed German church of that city. Young Goetschius
had previously commenced his education at the university of
Zurich, which he completed with his father upon his arrival
in America. After his ordination he preached for awhile in
the Dutch churches of North and Southampton, in Pennsylvania ; from whence he removed here, and became pastor of the
Reformed Dutch churches in Queen's County, which were associate churches, and constituted one congregation. His residence was in Jamaica. At this period an unhappy division existed in the churches relative to their subordination to the church
of Holland. Most of the Dutch clergy in this country came
from thence, and remained strongly attached to their *father-
land ;* while the churches continued under the supervision and
control of the *Classis* of Amsterdam, which claimed the exclusive right of ordaining all licentiates for the ministry.
This requirement was soon found to be vexatious, expensive,
and dilatory. The necessity of being independent of the mother
church was felt by a portion of the church here, while others
thought best to preserve their connection with the church of
Holland. The claim of independence finally prevailed ; and
in 1771 harmony was restored to the churches in this state.
Mr. Goetschius remained here till 1751, employing much of
his time in preparing young men for the ministry, when he
was called to take charge of the Dutch church at Hackensack,
where he died. The second minister of this church was the
Rev. Thomas Romeyn, brother of the late Rev. Derick
Romeyn of Schenectady, and uncle of the Rev. Dr. John
B. Romeyn of New-York. He was settled here in 1752, and re-

mained about twenty years, when he removed, and was succeeded by the *Rev. Hermanus Boelen.* He came from Holland in 1766, and after remaining a few years, returned again to his native country. The *Rev. Solomon Frælingh* settled here in 1775, but left the island in 1776 on its being taken possession of by the British troops. He afterwards settled at Hackensack as successor to Mr. Goetchius, and was appointed Professor of Divinity by the general synod of the Reformed Dutch Church. He was succeeded here by the *Rev. Rynier Van Nest,* who was settled in 1785, and remained several years. The *Rev. Zachariah Kuypers* was settled in 1794, and labored at stated intervals, as his predecessors had done, in the Dutch churches of Newtown, Success, and Wolver-Hollow. In the year 1802, the churches of Jamaica and Newtown separated from those in North-Hempstead and Oyster-Bay, and in the same year settled, as their joint minister, the *Rev. Jacob Schoonmaker,* who still continues a blessing to the church, and greatly esteemed by all who know him. It is a curious fact, that this gentleman is the great-grandson, in the maternal line, of the Rev. Henry Goetchius, the first minister of this church, and who preached here nearly a century ago. The present Dutch church is a large and handsome edifice, and was dedicated July 4, 1833.

Of the *Episcopal Church* in this town, its history, like those of the other churches, is defective and unsatisfactory. The society for propagating the gospel in foreign parts, chartered in England, June 16, 1701, concluded to send missionaries to this country, to ascertain from personal inspection in what manner the benevolent objects of the society could best be carried into effect. The first person selected for this purpose was the Rev. George Keith, who had once resided in Pennsylvania, and apostatised from the society of Friends. The *Rev. Patrick Gorden,* intended as a missionary for Long Island, accompanied Mr. Keith, and arrived at Boston, June 11, 1702. Mr. Gorden proceeded thence to this town, where he was settled the same year, and was styled, " *Rector of Queen's County.*" His death took place in a short time, and he was succeeded by the *Rev. William Urquhart.* In the report of the British society, published Feb. 16, 1705, it is, among other things, remarked,

" There is a provision in Queen's County for two ministers, of £60 each. In Queen's and Suffolk counties are two church of England congregations, many *Independents* and some *Quakers* and *Libertines*." The death of Mr. Gorden was much regretted, as he was a man of much learning, great moderation, sensible and prudent. A part of his library is still preserved in the vestry-room of Grace Church. In the report of the society in England for 1706, it is related that " Her Majesty, Queen Ann, was pleased to allow the churches of Hempstead, Jamaica, Westchester, Rye, and Staten Island, each a *large church Bible, common-prayer book, book of homilies, a cloth for the pulpit, a communion table, a silver chalice and paten.*" Mr. Urquhart's death occurred in about two years after his settlement here, and was followed by the *Rev. Thomas Poyer,* from England, in 1810. He was shipwrecked in his passage, and was with great difficulty saved from a watery grave. He arrived in this town while the controversy was raging between the Presbyterians and Episcopalians, in reference to the possession and the use of the stone church ; he soon after drew up, and transmitted to the Queen of England, a statement of the existing difficulties ; and in consequence of which, as is supposed through the influence of Governor Hunter, her Majesty ordered " *That in all cases where the church is immediately concerned, as in the case of Jamaica, liberty be given to the clergy to appeal from the inferior courts to the governor and council only, without limitation of any sum ; and that as well in this, as in other like cases, liberty be given to the clergy to appeal from the governor and council to her Majesty and the privy council, without limitation as aforesaid.*" The motive which dictated this extraordinary measure, and the object intended to be subserved by it, are too apparent to require explanation ; and the natural consequence was, to protract the dissentions above mentioned, and to render the minds of the people more obstinate. In 1730 the Rev. Mr. Poyer, on account of his *advanced age and great infirmities,* as he expressed it, requested permission from the society to return to England ; and his death took place the year following. His successor was the Rev. Thomas Colgan, from England also, who was settled here in 1732, and remained till his death in 1755. At the time of his settlement religious services were performed in a building appropriated for the county courts, on the site of the present female academy in the village of Jamaica. In 1734 was erected the first Episcopal church in this town, which was incorporated by a charter from Lieut. Governor Colden in 1761, by the name of *Grace Church.* At the dedication in 1734, Governor Cosby and his lady, together with the council, and other gentlemen and ladies of distinction from the city, honored the occasion with their presence; and a splendid entertainment was given at the house of Samuel Clowes. The wife of his Excellency presented the congregation a large *Bible, Common Prayer-Book,* and a surplice for the minister. The Rev. Mr. Colgan, speaking of this church in his letter to the society in England, says, " *It is thought to be one of the handsomest in North America ;*" and in regard to a religious excitement then existing in the county, says, " *The late predominant enthusiasm is very much declined, several of the teachers, as well as hearers, having been found guilty of the foulest immoralities, and others having wrought themselves into downright madness.*" Mr. Colgan died in 1755, and the governor, Sir Charles Hardy, introduced the *Rev. Samuel Seabury* in 1756. He was born in 1728, and graduated at Yale College in 1748. Going to Scotland, to study medicine, in 1750, he changed his design, gave his attention to theology, and took orders in 1753. On his return to America he settled at New Brunswick, from whence he removed to this parish. John Troup, Esq., a wealthy citizen, contributed liberally to the church, and presented it a *silver collection plate,* a large *Prayer-Book,* and *table for the communion.* Mr. Seabury, in his letter to the society in England, complains much of the influence of *Infidelity* and *Quakerism* upon his people; which, he says, " *have spread their corrupt principles to a surprising degree.*" He mentions the celebrated *Whitfield,* who, about this time visited the island, and says that " *He, with other strolling preachers, represent the Church of England as popish, and teaching people to expect salvation by good works.*" In 1766 Mr. Seabury removed to Westchester, where he remained till

the commencement of the revolution. At the return of peace
he settled in New London: and in 1784 was consecrated, (in
Scotland,) the first bishop in the United States, and presided for
the remainder of his life over the diocess of Connecticut and
Rhode Island. He died Feb. 25. 1796. The *Rev. Joshua
Bloomer* had been an officer in the provincial service, and a
merchant in New-York. He was educated at King's College,
where he graduated in 1761 ; went to England for ordination
in 1765, settled in this town in 1769, where he died June
23, 1790 ; and was succeeded by the *Rev. William Hammel*.
This gentleman having unfortunately become blind, and therefore unable to discharge his pastoral duties acceptably, resigned
in Aug. 1795. These several ministers officiated occasionally
in the churches of Newtown and Flushing, which were associated with Grace Church : but in consequence of some dissatisfaction, Newtown withdrew from the union in 1796 : and on
May 10, 1797, the *Rev. Elijah D. Rattoone* was settled here
in connection with the church of Flushing. This gentleman
graduated at Princeton in 1787, and in 1802 he removed from
this place to Baltimore : he was succeeded by the *Rev. Calvin
White*, who graduated at Yale College in 1786, and settled
here in 1803: but removed the year following, and was succeeded by the *Rev. George Strebeck* in May, 1805. He remained
only a short time, as was the case with the *Rev. Andrew Fow-
ler, Rev. John Ireland, Rev. Edmund D. Barry,* and the *Rev.
Timothy Clowes ;* who were successively ministers of this
church from 1805 to 1810. The Rev. Gilbert Sayer graduated
at Columbia College in 1808, was settled here in 1810, and
continued to discharge his pastoral duties with fidelity and zeal,
till loss of health compelled him to desist ; and was succeeded
by the present worthy clergyman, the Rev. William L. Johnson, in 1830.

The present church was erected about the year 1814, and is
a very handsome edifice : the interior is neat and convenient,
with an organ of the finest tone. The old Presbyterian stone
church was taken down in 1814, and the materials made use
of in inlaying the foundation of the present church, which was
completed in the year following.

Union Hall Academy was founded in 1792, built by subscription in sums of from one to thirty pounds. Among the contributors are the venerable names of George Clinton and John
Jay ; and it was incorporated the same year, upon the application of James Foster and forty-nine other gentlemen. The
names of the first trustees are as follows ·—

John Depeyster,	Abraham Skinner,	Joseph Robinson,
Daniel Minema,	Abraham Ditmars, jr.	Williame Hammell,
Abraham Ditmars,	John Smith,	Daniel Kissam,
George Fatoute,	Eliphalet Wicks,	Jacob Ogden,
John Williamson,	Isaac Lefferts,	Jost. Van Brunt.

The building then erected has, since 1820, been appropriated
for the female department ; and a larger edifice was in that year
completed in another part of the village for the male school.
This latter structure is eighty feet long, forty wide, and two
stories in height; having three rooms upon each floor. Both
schools constitute one institution, and are governed by the same
board of trustees. The real and personal estate are estimated
at ten thousand dollars, including a library of five hundred
volumes, and a small philosophical apparatus. The principals
of this useful institution have been as follows:

Malby Gelston,	Henry Crosswell,	Michael Tracie,
Samuel Crosset,	George Fatoute,	Wm. Ermeupeutch,
John W. Cox,	Albert Oblenas,	John Mulligan,
Wm. Martin Johnson,	Lewis E. A. Eigenbrodt,	Henry Onderdonk, jr.
Henry Liverpool,		

At the opening of this academy in 1792, an excellent oration
was delivered by Abraham Skinner, Esq. one of the trustees, a
resident of the village, and a lawyer distinguished for his talents
and elocution. This gentleman was a zealous and active Whig
in the revolution, and honored with the confidence of the commander-in-chief, by whom he was appointed deputy commis-
sary-general of prisoners. In Sparks's life and writings of
Washington is the copy of a letter addressed to Mr. Skinner, acquainting him of an arrangement made with Sir Henry Clinton,
for the British commissary to meet Mr. Skinner at Elizabethtown on the 19th of September, 1780, to agree upon an exchange
of officers, prisoners of war, upon a footing of equal rank ; and
to include the whole of the officers on parole at New-York or

in Europe. " An exchange," says the General, "of all the officers, prisoners of war in our hands, is earnestly wished ; but if
you cannot make it so as to comprehend the whole, make it
as extensive as you can."   Mr. Skinner met the British commissary at the time and place appointed, but failed to accomplish
a plan of mutual exchange within the range of his instructions.
In 1778 Mr. Skinner was appointed clerk of Queen's County,
and held the office till 1796.   In 1785 he was chosen a member of the state legislature.   A few years after he removed to
the city of New-York, where he enjoyed a lucrative practice
for many years ; from whence he removed to Babylon in
Suffolk County, where he died in 1825, and was interred in
this village.

A press was established in this place in 1819 by Henry C.
Sleight, and a weekly newspaper issued, called the " *Long Island Farmer*." This publication has since been conducted
by several others in succession, and for some time past by Isaac
F. Jones, its present editor and proprietor.   A second newspaper
was commenced in May, 1835, called the " *Long Island Demo-
crat*," and is still continued by James J. Brenton.

The Village of Jamaica is the only one in the town deserving the appellation, and is in all respects a beautiful place.
It is located near the centre of the town, and upon the great
thoroughfare from Brooklyn to the east end of Long Island, enjoying every desirable facility of intercourse with the surrounding country.   Here are concentrated the different roads leading
to Brooklyn, Williamsburgh, Rockaway. Flushing, Jericho, and
Hempstead.   This village was made the seat of justice for the
north-riding of Yorkshire at its organization in 1665 ; and so
continued after the division of Long Island into counties in
1683, until the erection of the court-house on Hempstead
Plains in 1788.   The offices of surrogate and county clerk
are still required to be kept here, and for which a suitable building has been erected.   The village was incorporated April 15,
1814, and has been gradually increasing in buildings and population, till it now contains about two hundred dwellings and
fifteen hundred inhabitants.   It has, besides the academies, five
places for public worship, six hotels and boarding-houses, two

drug-stores, eight .dry-goods and grocery-stores, two book and stationary stores, circulating library, bindery, three carriage-makers, blind and sash manufactory, cabinet-maker, locksmith, pianoforte manufacturer, and many other mechanics and artisans. There are several splendid private residences in the village and its immediate vicinity, erected by gentlemen of the city, who find it both convenient and agreeable. *Beaver-Pond*, once so famous in the sporting world, and around which was formerly a race-course, where thousands of dollars have been lost and won, has within a few years been completely drained, from an opinion generally entertained that its contents were unfavorable to the health of the village. Here is the depot of the Brooklyn and Jamaica Rail-road Company, with their large and commodious car-house, engine-house, and machine-shops. This company was incorporated, April 25, 1832, to continue for fifty years, with a capital of $300,000. In 1836 it was leased for a term of years to the Long Island Rail-road Company at an annual rent, and has since been under the direction of that incorporation. The latter company commenced running cars upon their road as far as Hicksville on the 1st of March, 1837, from which time it has been in constant operation.

Union Course, where thousands congregate at stated periods to witness the sports of the turf, is located upon the western limits of the town, and near the line of King's County; it was established immediately after the passage of the act in 1821, allowing of trials of speed for a term of years, during the months of May and October, in the County of Queens. In 1834 the time was enlarged for fifteen years more, and trials of speed may now be made between the 1st of April and the 15th of June, and from the 1st of September to the 15th of November, in every year during the said term. This beautiful course is a few feet over a mile in length, on a perfectly level surface, with a good track; and is universally considered one of the best in the United States. Better time has been *made* upon it, and more frequently, than on any other course in the country. Connected with it is a Jockey Club of above two hundred and fifty members, who contribute annually twenty dollars each toward the Jockey Club purses. There was run over this

course, the 27th of May, 1823, one of the most remarkable and
best-contested races that ever took place in America; being a
match race of four mile heats, for twenty thousand dollars
aside, between the North and the South, upon their respective
champions, *Eclipse* and *Henry ;* and which was won in three
heats by Eclipse. The time was as follows: first heat, 7' 37 —
second heat, 7' 49 —and the third heat, 8' 24 ; whole time,
twenty-three minutes and fifty seconds. *Eclipse* was bred by
General Nathaniel Coles of Dos-Oris, and was nine years old
when the race was run. *Henry* was bred by Samuel Long,
Esq. near Halifax, North Carolina, and was nearly four years
old. Here, doubtless, have often been assembled more than
twenty thousand spectators, and more than a hundred thousand
dollars have been lost and won on a single race.

It may not be generally known that the first settlement of
Elizabethtown, New Jersey, was commenced by a few individuals
from this place. In the records of that town, it appears, that
on the 26th of September, 1664, John Bailey, Daniel Denton,
Thomas Benedick, Nathaniel Denton. John Foster, and Luke
Watson, of Jamaica, made a written application to Col. Richard
Nicolls for "liberty to settle a plantation upon the river called
Arthur-Cull-Bay in New Jersey." The answer of the governor is in the following words : " *Upon the perusal of this
petition, I do consent unto the proposals, and shall give the
undertakers all due encouragement in so good a work. Given
under my hand in Fort James, this 30th day of September.
1664 Richard Nicolls.*" The place was named Elizabethtown
in honor of the lady of Phillip Carteret, to whom the province of New Jersey was subsequently assigned.

Extracted from the New-York Gazette of July 17, 1780.
"Three days ago Captain William Dickson, commander of one
of the New-York volunteer companies, was unfortunately
drowned while bathing in a pond in the neighborhood of
Jamaica, Long Island, whither the corpse were brought and
interred on Monday evening, attended by Major Small and the
officers of the regiment of Royal Highland Emigrants stationed
there."—"Last Sunday evening was married, at Jamaica, Long
Island, Captain Meredith, of the 70th regiment, to the amiable

and accomplished Miss Gertrude Skinner, third daughter of Brigadier-general Skinner."

Same paper of August 7, 1780. "About five o'clock last Friday morning, an account was brought to Rockaway that two rebel boats were at Hog-Island, and had taken a schooner in Jamaica-Bay; in consequence of which Captain Charles Hicks, of the militia of that place, mustered his company, and with a few volunteers in two boats went in quest of them. At four the next morning he sent a flag of truce, to inform the rebels that if they would surrender prisoners, they should have good quarters, which they refused, and a smart action ensued; but seeing they could not escape, agreed to the terms offered by Captain Hicks. The prisoners amount to twenty-eight, and among them a *clergyman.* Several grape-shot went through Captain Hicks's jacket; but nobody killed."

Same, September 11, 1780. "On Wednesday last departed this life, in the 75th year of his age, Captain Benjamin White-head of Jamaica, Long Island. His attachment to government involved him in many difficulties, which he bore with the greatest fortitude."

In the Presbyterian burial-ground is the following inscription: "Sacred to the memory of the Rev. Abraham Keteltas, obiit 30 September, 1798, aged 65. He possessed unusual talents, which were improved by profound erudition, and a heart firmly attached to the interests of his country. It may not, perhaps, be unworthy of record, that he had frequently officiated in three different languages, having preached in the Dutch and French languages in his native city of New-York."

Mr. Keteltas was the son of Abraham Keteltas, who came to America from Holland about the year 1720. He was born in New-York, December 26, 1732, and graduated at Yale College in 1752; he settled soon after in the borough of Eliza-beth, where he continued till his removal to the village of Jamaica. Here he spent the remainder of his days, (except the period of exile occasioned by the revolution,) which he devoted to the service of several churches on Long Island and in New-England. In 1777 he was chosen a member of the convention that framed the constitution of this state, and was

51

a warm and active supporter of American independence. He married a daughter of the Hon. William Smith of New-York in 1755. She was a sister of William Smith, who, as well as his father, was a judge of the supreme court of this state, and author of a history of New-York from the period of its discovery to the year 1732. Mr. Keteltas had eleven children, only two of whom are now living. He possessed an uncommonly large and excellent private library, and was generally considered a man of good abilities and superior literary attainments. He published many Discourses, and wrote an Eulogy upon Mr. Whitfield, the manuscript of which is preserved in the archives of the New-York Historical Society. *Mr. James H. Hacket*, the popular American comedian, is a grandson of Mr. Keteltas. He was born at Jamaica, March 15, 1800, and received his early education at Union Hall Academy, under Mr. Eigenbrodt. At the age of fifteen he entered Columbia College, which he left at the end of a year from bad health. After his recovery, he entered the office of General Robert Bogardus as a law student; but not relishing the subject, he abandoned it at the end of a year, and turned his attention to mercantile business. In this he experienced some reverses, which forced him upon the stage as a last resort. Here he met with decided success, and has long maintained an elevated rank as an able and amusing actor, both in his own country and in Europe, where he now resides. He has not only acquired a fortune by his profession, but has hitherto sustained a moral character above reproach. None of the vices or frailties which have been thought nearly inseparable from the character of players have ever attached to him; few individuals are more amiable or respectable in private life, and still fewer who have contributed more to the common stock of *harmless pleasure*, or conferred more honor upon the morality of the stage.

WILLIAM MARTIN JOHNSON. In the year 1790, (says John Howard Payne,) there was found at the head of a little school in Bridgehampton, Long Island, a young gentleman of extraordinary genius, calling himself by the above name, appearing to be about nineteen years of age, a stranger in these parts; of unknown parentage, and all that he thought proper to communicate of himself was, that he came from Boston. He was a proficient upon several instruments, particularly the violin, which he played with wonderful accuracy and taste;

and had. moreover, a genius for sketching and drawing. He was also a poet of no mean pretensions. Having a preference for the medical profession, he removed to Easthampton, and placed himself under the instruction of Dr. Sage, an intelligent man and excellent physician. His pecuniary resources being soon exhausted, his worthy preceptor assisted him in procuring employment in a school at Smithtown; and when his funds were, as he thought, sufficiently recruited, he again returned to the Doctor. When his small stock of means was again expended, he made arrangements with a cabinet-maker in the place, to labor for him two days in the week, as a compensation for his board for the remainder of the time. Here he exhibited a fickleness of disposition, pursuing his studies in a very desultory manner; spending a good part of his time visiting about the neighborhood, playing upon his violin, and sometimes upon the hearts of the ladies. Dr. Sage, who felt a deep interest in the stranger, says he was well versed in the most common theories of physic; was a most ready mathematician and natural philosopher, and master of the principles of music. He possessed a critical knowledge of his own language, understood the French, had some knowledge of Italian, and translated with ease any Latin author. He also appeared to have much taste and skill in architecture, could use almost all kinds of tools, and even excelled in many of the mechanic arts. It was surprising to think, that at the age of twenty years, and with such unstable habits, he should possess such variety and degree of knowledge. How and where he could have acquired it all, unless by intuition. could never be imagined. He was a runaway boy, and had been traversing the country, without friends, *poor, dependant*, and *wretched*. In the year 1795 we find him engaged as a teacher in Union-Hall Academy, and highly esteemed for his ability and good conduct. In Feb. 1796, he sailed with Captain Gabriel Havens to the south, and arrived in Savannah, where he spent a year, and returned to New-York in August, 1797. He came shortly after to the village of Jamaica, where he fell sick, and expired the 21st of September, 1797, and was buried at the expense of his friends, in the Episcopal cemetery.

THOMAS TRUXTUN. Of that ardent spirit of enterprize, which, for the most important purposes, *Nature* has implanted in the heart of man, where shall we find stronger instances than in the biography of seamen? Inured to toil and familiar with danger, it is in difficulty and peril that they are seen to advantage; and though their country, unmindful of their services, may have treated them with coldness and neglect, yet, generous to excess and brave to temerity, should the tempest of war lower upon her coast, in them, regardless of the bickerings of party, should we again behold the most zealous of her defenders. Thomas Truxtun, whose achievements shed lustre on the infant navy of this country, was the son of an eminent English lawyer of the (then) colony of New-York, and born at Jamaica (L I) on the 17th of February, 1755; and, in consequence of the death of his father (while yet a child), he was placed under the guardianship of his father's intimate friend, John Troup, Esq., of Jamaica, who bestowed every kind attention on him which his bereaved situation required. At the age of twelve years he made choice of the profession of a sailor, and entered on board a ship bound to Bristol; and the next year, at his own request, was bound apprentice to Captain Chambers, a well-known commander in the London trade. In the dispute relative to the Falkland Islands, he was impressed on board a British sixty-four. In 1775 he commanded a vessel, and brought a considerable quantity of powder into the colony, but his vessel was afterwards taken and condemned.   Having arrived, soon after, at Philadelphia, he sailed early in 1776 as lieutenant in the private armed ship Congress, and captured several valuable Jamaica ships off the Havanna, and taking command of one of them, brought her safe into New Bedford.   In 1777, in conjunction with Isaac Sears, he fitted out a vessel called the Independence, of which he took command ; and off the Azores, besides making several other prizes, he fell in with a part of the Windward-Island convoy, of which he captured three large and valuable ships, one of which was superior to his own in guns and men.   On his return he fitted out the ship Mars, mounting upwards of twenty guns, and sailed on a cruise in the English channel, and took many prizes.   Sailing in the St. James, of twenty guns, he disabled a British ship of thirty-two guns.   He returned from France with a most valuable cargo.   On his return he settled in Philadelphia, was part owner of several armed vessels built there, and brought from France and the West India Islands large cargoes of such articles as were of the first necessity for the army.   After the peace in 1783, he turned his attention to commerce, and was concerned in an extensive trade to Europe, China, and the East Indies, until the commencement of our naval establishment in 1794; when he was one of the first six captains selected by President Washington.   He superintended the building of the Constellation of thirty-six guns, and in her he was the same year appointed, with a squadron under his command, to protect the American commerce in the West Indies ; and such was his vigilance and success, that an enemy's privateer could scarcely look out of port without being captured.   On the 9th of Feb. 1799, he engaged with the Constellation, and captured the French frigate L'Insurgente, of forty guns and four hundred and seventeen men, twenty-nine of whom were killed and forty-four wounded, while on board his own ship he had but one killed and two wounded.   He received congratulatory addresses from all quarters, and the merchants at Lloyd's coffee-house sent him a service of plate valued at six hundred guineas, with the action between the frigates engraved upon it ; and which offering was presented through Mr. King, our minister at London.   Capt. Barreau of the L'Insurgente says, in a letter to Commodore Truxtun, " I am sorry our two nations are at war ; but since I have unfortunately been vanquished, I felicitate myself and crew upon being prisoners to you ; you have united all the qualities which characterize a man of honor, courage, and humanity. Receive from me the most sincere thanks ; and be assured I shall make it a duty to publish to all my fellow-citizens the generous conduct which you have observed toward us '   Hearing that the L'Vengeance, a large French national ship, with fifty-four guns and upwards of five hundred men, including officers, was lying at Guadaloupe, he proceeded, in January, 1800, off that port.   The ships came to action on the 1st of February, which lasted nearly five hours, when the French ship was completely silenced.   But the mainmast of the Constellation going by the board, and a gale coming on, the French ship escaped in the night, and got in Curaçoa, having one hundred and sixty men killed and wounded, and nearly all her masts and rigging shot away.   The Constellation lost fourteen men killed, and had twenty-five wounded.   For the signal gallantry displayed in this action, the congress of the United States voted that a gold medal be presented to Commodore Truxtun.   This was his last cruise.   Having, during the administration of Mr. Jefferson, been appointed to the command of the expedition against Tripoli, and being denied a captain to command his flag-ship, he declined the service ; which the president construing into a re-signation of his rank, he was therefore dismissed. He retired to the country until the citizens of Philadelphia, in 1816, elected him high sheriff. He remained in that office till 1819, and died May 5th, 1822, in his sixty-seventh year. He left two daughters, both of whom are married : and one son by the name of William, who died at Key-West in April, 1830. Commodore Truxtun was a man of whom Long Island may well be proud ; and his excellent example and extraordinary success may serve to stimulate those who are left like-him to struggle, unfriend-ed and alone, against the difficulties of poverty and the allurements of folly.

RUFUS KING. This eminent individual, statesman, and patriot, was the son of Richard King, a merchant of Scarborough in Maine ; and was born in 1755. He began his education at Byfield Academy in the town of Newbury, under the care of the celebrated Samuel Moody. In 1773 he entered Harvard College, soon after which he lost his father ; and in 1775, in consequence of the war, the studies of the college were suspended, and the students dispersed. They, however, assembled again in the fall at Concord, and continued there till the British army evacuated Boston in 1776, when they returned to the college at Cambridge. He graduated in 1777 with a high reputation for scholarship, and immediately entered upon his juridical studies in the office of the late Theophilus Parsons at Newburyport, where he was admitted to the bar in 1780. He had previously, in 1778, joined General Sullivan, to whom he was appointed in his enterprise with Count D'Estaing against the British in Rhode Island. In the first cause in which he was engaged at the bar, he had for his competitor his legal preceptor, Parsons. Soon after he was chosen to represent the town of Newburyport in the state legislature, or the general court as it is called, in which he manifested much ability. In 1784 he was elected a delegate to the *old congress*, which assembled at Trenton, and subsequently adjourned to New-York. In that body he became an active and leading member in all the great measures which led eventually to the establishment of the present national government. In 1787 he was appointed by the legislature of Massachusetts a delegate to the general con-vention held at Philadelphia, which formed the federal constitution. Mr. King now renounced the practice of his profession. In 1786 he married Mary, only child of John Alsop, an opulent merchant of New-York, and a delegate to the first continent-al congress. In 1788 the subject of this notice removed from Massachusetts to the city of New-York, and in 1789 was chosen by the citizens a representative to the state assembly ; the same year, he and General Schuyler were elected the first senators from this state under the constitution of the United States. In 1794 Mr. King, in conjunction with General Hamilton, published a series of papers over the signature of Camillus, on the subject of the British treaty, which helped to reconcile the people to its various provisions. After the expiration of his first term, he was re-elected to the senate ; and in 1796 was appointed by General Washington minister plenipotentiary to Great Britain ; he remained at the court of England during the residue of the administration of Washington, the whole of that of John Adams, and for two years of that of Mr. Jefferson, when he returned home. In the month of May, 1806, he removed permanently with his family to Jamaica, where they continued ever after to reside. In 1813 he was again chosen by the legislature of this state a senator in congress ; and although he was personally opposed to the declaration of war in 1812, as in his opinion both unwise and impolitic, yet no man exhibited a higher degree of patriotism in supporting it, pledging his credit and fortune to the government in its prosecution, rather than yield any of the national rights to the enemy, or submit to an inglorious peace. In 1816 he was the candidate of the anti-administration party for governor of this state, which was done without his knowledge, and failed without his regret. In the summer of 1819 he lost his wife, she having been for several years in feeble health; a loss which he but too deeply felt, for she added to strong affection and humble piety, a gentle temper and a cultivated mind. In 1820 he was re-elected again to the senate, in which he continued till the expiration of his term in 1825. During this period, in 1821, he was chosen a delegate from this county to the state convention for amending the constitution; and was one of the most useful and intelligent, as well as active members of that dignified and enlightened body. Upon his retirement from the senate in 1825, with the intention of closing his political career, he was solicited by President John Quincy Adams again to represent the United States at the court of St. James. But on his passage he was attacked by disease, which prevented him, on his arrival in England, entering upon an active discharge of the duties of his office. After remaining abroad a year, in the hope of being enabled, by returning health, to assume the high functions with which he was charged, he returned to the United States; and here, in the bosom of his family, and with exemplary calmness and resignation, awaited his approaching end. This event took place the 29th of April, 1827, at the age of seventy-two. In person, Mr. King was above the common size, and somewhat athletic; with a countenance manly, dignified, and bespeaking high intelligence. His manners were courteous, his disposition affable, and his conversation and writings remarkable for conciseness and force.

Mr. King left five sons. 1. *John Alsop*, born in 1788, and having read law retired to the country; and since the death of his father has occupied the paternal estate. 2. *Charles*, born in 1789, and has been for many years past, editor and proprietor of the newspaper entitled the New-York American. 3. *James Gore*, born in 1791, and has long been a partner in an extensive banking house in the city of New-York. 4. *Edward*, born in 1795, and settled as a lawyer in Ohio, where he died in 1837. 5. *Frederick Gore*, born in 1802, and educated as a physician and surgeon, in which he gave early promise of eminence, but was cut off at a premature age, April 23, 1829.

John A. King, Esq. accompanied his father to England in 1825, as secretary of legation, and has several times represented the County of Queens in the state legislature with distinguished ability.

LEWIS E. A. EIGENBRODT, so long and advantageously known as an able and efficient instructor of youth, was descended from one of the most respectable families of Hesse-Darmstadt upon the Upper Rhine, Germany; and came to the United States at the age of twenty, in the year 1796. He was destined by his previous education for the ministry; but hearing, soon after his arrival, that a teacher was wanted in the grammar-school at Jamaica, he made a visit to the place, and producing satisfactory credentials of his character and qualifications, was immediately engaged as principal instructor in the classical department of the academy. His reputation as a scholar, and his capacity for imparting instruction, as well as enforcing a correct discipline, increased with his age, and was never more exalted than at the time of his decease. He was united, a short time after his establishment here, with a daughter of Mr. David Lamberson, a highly respected and opulent merchant of the village, by whom he had a number of children. He was, as may well be supposed, an enthusiast in his profession, than which there is none, upon the able and conscious discharge of which, more important results to society depend, and whose moral influence upon the future character of a people is more important and valuable. It is, in truth, one of the most responsible situations in which an individual can be placed, and by him was felt to be so; for he made the station of a teacher of youth, what all reflecting men ever desire to make it, a most honorable one. He was aware of its proper dignity, as well as the obligations it imposed; and aimed to secure the one by an exact and skilful discharge of the other. He was not impelled forward by the mere feeling that so much time and labor were to be bestowed for a certain amount of money, but with the solemn conviction that responsibilities rested upon him, and of his moral accountability for the gradual improvement of those confidentially committed to his charge. By his talents, learning, great method, and untiring industry, he raised *Union Hall Academy*, from the condition of an ordinary *grammar-school*, to a high rank among the incorporated seminaries of the state; and hundreds were educated here, who now hold distinguished stations in every department of society, and who must always entertain the most sincere and profound respect and veneration for the memory of their former instructor and friend.

Mr. Eigenbrodt perished in the ripeness of manhood, and in the midst of his usefulness, in the year 1828, at the age of fifty-four; having presided over the institution more than thirty successive years, and with a character for learning and virtue among his fellow-citizens which only time can diminish. He was eminent as a linguist, and for his attainments in general literature; and had been honored with the title of *doctor of laws*, the highest degree known in the American colleges. In his manners, Dr. Eigenbrodt was modest and unpretending; in his habits, temperate and retiring; and in all the endearing relations of husband, father, citizen, and friend, kind, affectionate, generous, and exemplary. There are those who have enjoyed a more brilliant reputation, and filled a larger space in the public eye; but none in whom the mild and gentle virtues have shone more clearly, or by whom they have been more steadily and effectively inculcated. The influence and glare of exalted station, the splendor of particular feats in arms, the triumph of an hour, are apt to captivate attention, and even obscure or pervert the judgments of men, so that they may have little sympathy with, or admiration for, the ever-enduring, unostentatious exertions which mark the life of such a man as Dr. Eigenbrodt; yet, if measured by their importance, by the self-denial they evince, the fortitude they require, by the daily, hourly abnegation of self which they imply; how vast is the difference between such services, and the public estimate of them—between *common fame* and *real merit?* Such men, beyond all question, deserve infinitely more respect and consideration from their cotemporaries than they generally receive; few are ready to confer honor where none is demanded; experience shows that those most deserving of praise are the least obtrusive, and therefore often superseded and thrown into the shade of neglect by others, who, in reality, have little or no solid claim to public respect and gratitude. The subject of this notice was remarkable for his economy and prudence, while, at the same time, he gave liberally for purposes of charity and benevolence. By his exemplary prudence in pecuniary matters, he left an ample fortune to his children, with the more inestimable inheritance of an unblemished private character, and the animating example of a life spent in doing good, in the practice of virtue, and the diffusion of knowledge and science.

EGBERT BENSON. This eminent jurist resided many years in Jamaica, where he died, the 24th of August, 1833, at the age of eighty-seven years. The following eloquent sketch of his life and services is from the pen of his intimate friend and associate, Chancellor Kent:

Judge Benson was born in the city of New-York, June 22d, 1746, of respectable Dutch parents, and was educated at King's (now Columbia) College, where he graduated in 1765. He was one of those sound classical scholars for the formation of which that learned seminary always has been, and still is, most justly distinguished His taste for classical literature never forsook him, even during the strength and vigor of his age, and amidst the ardor of official duties. His legal education was acquired in the office of John Morin Scott, one of that band of deep-read and thorough lawyers of the old school, who were an ornament to the city at the commencement of the revolution. When he came to the bar, there were very few, if any, better instructed in the ancient and modern learning of the English common law. To great quickness and acuteness of mind, and profound discernment of character, he added much deliberation and candor. He was a master of order and method in business. If he was not the first, he was one of the first proficients in the science of pleading; and his equal does not exist at the present day. But, though a strict technical lawyer, he did not cease to penetrate the depths of the science, and rest himself upon fundamental principles. He was more distinguished than any man among us, Hamilton alone excepted, for going, in all his researches, to the reasons and grounds of the law, and placing his opinion on what he deemed to be solid and elementary principles. His morals and manners were pure and chaste. He was liberal and catholic in his sentiments, without the smallest tincture of fanaticism or affectation of austerity; and nothing could weaken his faith or disturb his tranquillity, though he had to pass through the storms of a tempestuous age, in which the French revolution, and the daring speculations which accompanied it, attacked equally the foundations of religious belief and the best institutions of social life.

Mr. Benson commenced the practice of the law at Red Hook, Dutchess County, in 1772; but before he had time to enter largely into business, or to acquire much more than a scanty temporary provision for his support, the American war broke out, and raised him at once to an elevated scene of action. Here his abilities and spirit were brought to a test, and proved to be of sterling value. He was present at, and guided the earliest meetings in Dutchess County, preparatory to a more organized resistance to the claims of the British Government. He took the lead in all the Whig measures adopted in that county; a more zealous and determined patriot, or one more thoroughly master of the grounds of the great national contest, did not exist. It followed, of course, that his knowledge of law and of the enlightened principles of civil liberty, and his practical and business talents, would carry him forward rapidly to places of high public trust. He was accordingly appointed first attorney-general of this state, by the ordinance of the convention of the 8th of May, 1777; and this painful and most responsible office he discharged with the utmost zeal, ability, and integrity, during the whole period of the American war, and down to the spring of 1787, when he voluntarily resigned it, on assuming other public duties. He was a member of the first legislative assembly of this state elected in 1777. His name in the public opinion seemed to be identified with wisdom, patriotism, and integrity. He drafted almost every important bill that passed the assembly during the war; and it is matter of public notoriety with those persons whose memories can date back to that period, that his name truly merits this transcendant eulogy. During the war he was the most confidential and efficient adviser of the elder Governor Clinton; and it is well known that no governor had greater difficulties to contend with, as such, or surmounted them with better discretion and firmness. He was importuned and taxed with a perplexing variety of public concerns during the most busy and perilous periods of our revolutionary history. He was president of the board of commissioners in Dutchess County for detecting and defeating conspiracies, and it was under this authority that the board, in July, 1778, sent the Hon. William Smith, the historian of New-York, into the British lines; and who did not fail to complain severely of the stern and inflexible manner in which the chairman of the commissioners had executed the power. Amidst the various and important duties of his several trusts, he was brought in contact, and formed friendships with, that host of eminent men that then swayed the councils of the state. A common sympathy, as well as a common interest, is excited and felt at times of public calamity, and leads to generous and disinterested actions. Mutual respect and strong friendships were created and subsisted between Mr. Benson and Governor Clinton, Gen. Schuyler, Chief-Justice Jay, Chancellor Livingston, Judge Hobart, James Duane, Alexander McDougal, Alexander Hamilton, William Duer, and a roll of other distinguished patriots, who adorn the page of revolutionary history; and we need no better evidence of the great and useful talents of Mr. Benson, than to know the fact, that he was admired and beloved, and his counsels and society anxiously sought after, by all the leading men of the state during the best and brightest period of our domestic history. He took a zealous part in the adoption of the constitution of the United States, on which, as he uniformly thought and declared, rested all his hopes of American liberty, safety, and glory. No person could be more devoted to its success. In 1789 he was elected one of the six representatives from this state to the first congress, in which he was continued four years. He drew the bills organizing the executive department of the government, and he labored incessantly to further and sustain the measures that distinguished the glorious and unparalleled administration of Washington. In this situation he had the happiness to add largely to the number of his particular friends, and to associate on cordial and confidential terms with such men as George Cabot, Fisher Ames, Oliver Ellsworth, Rufus King, William Patterson, George Clymer, and others of the same brilliant stamp, with whom there was an equal interchange of respect and esteem. As for Hamilton, he never thought or spoke of him without expressing his highest admiration of his talents, and reverence for his patriotism. Of Fisher Ames he used to say that he thought him the most perfect man he ever knew, and that he had the purity and wisdom of a *seraph*.

In 1794 Mr. Benson was called into judicial life, and appointed a judge of the supreme court of this state; in which situation he remained several years, and fulfilled all its duties with the utmost precision, diligence, and fidelity. He did more to reform the practice of that court than any member of it ever did before, or ever did since. The object of the rules of practice which he drew, was to save useless time and trouble, and facilitate business. He resigned in 1801, on receiving the appointment of chief judge in the second circuit, under a new arrangement of the circuit courts of the United States; but was deprived of the office by a repeal, in the following year, of the statute creating the new courts. During the remainder of his life Judge Benson was principally confined to the occasional calls of professional duty, and with short assumptions of places of public trust. He removed, many years ago, to Jamaica, where he continued during the rest of his life, boarding in the family of Mr. William Puntine. He continued to be blessed with a protracted old age, "exempt from scorn or crime," and that "glided in modest innocence away;" while the circle of his old friends and acquaintances became gradually more and more contracted, as his descending sun was casting its lengthened shadows before him. He used to amuse himself with the publication, now and then, of short tracts on what he deemed the errors and follies of the times; for he had naturally a quick and keen perception of the false and ridiculous, and the flame of genuine patriotism never ceased to live and glow in his bosom, of which his criticism on the "*British Rule of* 1756," and his "*Vindication of the Captors of Andre*," may be cited as examples. His writings never received the attention which the good contained under a forbidding exterior justly demanded; for by his constant efforts to attain sententious brevity he became oftentimes obscure. This great and good man lived to survive all his contemporaries, and seems to have died almost unknown and forgotten by the profession which he once so greatly adorned. He was happy, however, to have preserved his mental faculties, in respect to all ancient recollections and impressions, perfectly unimpaired to the last; and died as he had lived, in the most serene tranquillity, with entire resignation to the will of God, and in humble reliance on those means of salvation upon which he placed his hope from early life.

TOWN OF NEWTOWN.

This town is situated in the north-west part of Queen's, centrally distant from New-York about eight miles. It is bounded north by the East River, east by Flushing, south by Jamaica, and west by King's County, together with the islands called the North and South Brother, and Riker's Island, formerly called Hallet's Island, lying in the East River. The general Indian appellation for the territory was *Wandowenock*, and was within the jurisdiction claimed by the Rockaway tribe. There was a small tribe of Indians at the head of Newtown Creek, known by the name of the *Maspeth tribe*, whose authority did not extend beyond the limits of their settlement. The place has since been called Maspeth, or the English Kill. The first white inhabitants of this town were enterprising English emigrants, who came directly from the colonies of New-England, and settled themselves under the Dutch government of the New Netherlands; although fully recognized as Dutch subjects, yet they were allowed many privileges appertaining to an independent community, being permitted to enjoy their religious freedom, to be governed by ordinances of their own adoption, and to elect their own magistrates, to be approved, however, as in other cases, by the governor. The settlement was commenced in 1651, but no formal purchase was made from the natives till several years after, the reason for which does not appear. It was customary, in the municipal regulations of the early inhabitants, to elect at town meetings certain officers, designated town's-men, whose duty it was to superintend and manage the public interests of the town, and to execute what in their opinion the common good required, except as related to the admission of new inhabitants and the distribution of lands; these matters being considered of more vital importance, were reserved to be acted upon by the whole people assembled in town-meeting. It is probable, as was the case in most of the towns under the Dutch authority, that a general title to the lands had been originally acquired by the governor, as the first charter was obtained from Governor Stuyvesant in the year 1652; and a second, with more liberal provisions, and with more exactness as to the boundaries, was issued in 1655. Both of these documents, as well as a mass of other valuable papers relative to the early history of this town, were destroyed or taken away during the revolution; the commanding officer having fixed his head-quarters here for a part of the time, and the British troops had full possession of the town for many years, committing the most extensive and wanton depredations upon property of every description. It appears, from the few records which have escaped destruction, that the following persons were inhabitants, and probably owners of land in the town, in the years 1655–6

Thomas Stephenson,	William Hallet,	Content Titus,
Gershom Moore,	Samuel Hallet,	Lambert Woodward,
Jonathan Hazzard,	Hendrick Martinson,	Joseph Reeder,
Daniel Bloomfield,	Robert Blackwell,	Jeremiah Reeder,
Caleb Leveridge,	John Pearsall,	Nathaniel Woodward,
Joseph Sacket,	George Stephenson,	John Bull, ————
Robert Field,	Thomas Skillman,	John Wood,
Thomas Pettit,	John Johnson,	Thomas Morrell,
John Gray,	Richard Alsop,	Theophilus Phillips,
Robert Field, jun.,	John Denman,	Ræliff Patterson,

John Smith,	Henry Maybe,	Benjamin Stephens,
Josiah Forman,	John Reed,	Jacob Leonardson,
George Wood,	Joseph Phillips,	Luke Depaw,
Nathan Fish,	Francis Way,	Nathaniel Pettit,
Edward Hunt,	John Wilson,	James Hayes,
Jeremiah Burroughs,	Moses Pettit,	Richard Owen,
Richard Betts,	John Forman,	Peter Burkhead,
Thomas Betts,	Samuel Ketcham,	John Alden,
John Al-Burtis,	John Ramsden,	John Rosell,
James Way,	Rineer Williamson,	Angela Burger,
Cornelius Johnson,	John Harrison,	Stephen Georgeson,
Jacob Reeder,	John Coe,	John Lawrence,
John Morrell,	Joseph Burroughs,	Thomas Wandell,
Elias Doughty,	William Osborn,	John Kirtshaw,
Thomas Lawrence,	Thomas Robertson,	Jonathan Strickland,
William Lawrence,	Benjamin Cornish,	Gershom Hazzard,
William Hallet, jun ,	Francis Combs,	Henry Sawtley.

This town, at the first settlement, and while it remained under the Dutch, was called Middleburgh; but why it was so named, we have at this time no means of ascertaining. A considerable portion of the oldest record is occupied with details of trials before the town court, and among these, actions of slander hold a prominent place. The following is a fair sample of many others which might be quoted from these ancient chronicles: "*Middleburgh, Aug.* 21, 1659. At a cort held by the magestrates of the place aforesaid, *John fforman*, plaintive, enters an action against *ffrancis Doughty*, defen', an action of slander. John fforman declared that ffrancis Doughty charged him, that he had stole his choes, and therefore he was satisfied which way his things went. The cort finds for the defen', too guilders for attendance and the charge of the cort, to be payd by John fforman, because he doth not support his charge that he layd against the defen'."

"At a general town meeting, held October 6, 1665, voted that Thomas Lawrence, Ralph Hunt, and Jo. Burrows shall be employed to get a draft of the bounds of the town, and get a pattin for the same; also the town people to bear the charge according to their several proportions." Upon this application, a patent issued 16th of March, 1666, by which was granted and assured unto "Capt. Richard Betts, Capt. Thomas Lawrence, Capt. John Coe, John Burroughs, Ralph Hunt, Daniel Whitehead, and Joost Burger, as patentees for and on behalf of themselves and their associates, the freeholders and inhabitants of Newtowne, their heirs, successors, and assigns, as follows :

"All that the said tract of land herein menconed to have been purchased from the Indian natives, bounded on the east by Flushing Creek and a line to be drawne from the head thereof due south, extending to the south side of the hills; on the north by the Sound ; on the west by the Maspeth Crecke or Kill, and a line to be drawne from the head thereof due south, extending to the south side of the hills ; on the north by the Sound ; on the west by the said Maspeth Creeke or Kill ; and a line to be drawne from the most westerly branch thereof due south, extending unto the south side of the said hills ; and on the south by a straight line to be drawne from the south points of the said west line, alongst the south side of the said hills, it meets with the said east line soe menconed, to extend from the head of Flushing Creeke as aforesaid ; as also all that one-third part of a certaine neck of meadow called Cellers-Neck, scituate, lying, and being within the bounds of Jamaica, upon the south side of Long Island; as also liberty to cut what timber within the bounds of Jamaica aforesaid they should have occasion for, for the fencing the said neck, and to make and lay out to themselves what highway or highways they should think fit, for their free and convenient egresse and regresse to and from the aforesaid neck or parcell of meadow. And that the said patentees, their associates, heyres, successors, and assigns shall enjoy all the privileges belonging to any town within this government; and that the place of their habitation shall continue and retaine the name of Newtown, and so be distinguished and known in all bargains, sailes, deeds, records, and writings."

December 13, 1670. "At a town meeting, voated, that if Mr. Leverich shall continue in this town to *preach the word of God*, a rate of £40 shall be made for the building of a meeting-house, one-half to be payd in corn and the other half in cattle." —"At a cort, held May 6, 1674, the order of the cort is, that *Thomas Case* shall not entertayne *William Smith's wife*, unknowne to her husband, as he will answer for the contrary at his peril."—"February 28, 1683, voated that *Mr. Morgan Jones* be schoolmaster of our town, and will teach on the Sabbath days those that will come, allowing for *exercising* on that day what any one pleases." Of this person we find the following entry made by himself: "Whereas I, Morgan Jones, have officiated for some time as a *minister* in Newtown without any agreement for a salary, upon the promise of some particular persons of the town to *allow* me some small recompense of their own *accord*, I do hereby acquit and discharge the town of all salary, moneys, goods, or wares, which I might claim, August

28, 1686, *Morgan Jones.*"—" At a cort, held April 4th, 1688, *Ann Cleven* did, in presents of the cort, own that she had spoken several tymes scandalous and reproachful *speaches* against *William Francis,* touching his good name; she doth now confess her fault, and says she had done the said William wrong, and is sorry she spoke such words against him; and hopes, for the time to come, she shall be more careful. She owns that she charged the plaintive with cheating her of a pound of flax, and told the people to take notice he had stole her yarn."—" On the 29th July, 1688, voated that Edward Stephenson and Joseph Sacket shall appear at the supream cort, held at Flatlands, to defend the town's right; and that they have full power to employ an atturney if they shall see fit, and what they do, we will ratify and confirm."—" June 11, 1689, it was voated and agreed that Capt. Richard Betts and Lieut. Samuel Moore go to the county-town to meet the deputys of other towns, to vote for too men out of the county to go to Yorke to act with the rest in counsil as a committe of safety." —" These may certify all whom it may concern, that I, ffrancis Combs, being accused for speaking scandalous words and speeches, tending to the deffamacon of Marget, the wife of John fforman of Newtown; I doe publicly declare that I am hertily sorry that the said Marget is anywise by me defamed, not knowing any thing against her name, fame, or reputacon; but that she lives *honestly and grately* with her neighbors, and all other their Magesty's subjects. As witness my hand, October 2, 1691, ffrancis Combs."—" July 14, 1694, voted at town meeting, that the town will make a rate toward repairing the meeting-house and the town-house; also for paying the messenger's expense, that is sent for a minister and for making a pair of *stocks.*"

On the 25th of November, 1686, a new patent was granted by Governor Dongan, which, after reciting the date of previous patents, and the boundaries of the town as before mentioned, states that the freeholders and inhabitants had made application to him by William Lawrence, Joseph Sacket, John Way, and Content Titus, persons deputed by them, for a more full and ample confirmation of the tract or parcel of land contained in the patent of 1666.from Governor Nicolls ; therefor he, the said Thomas Dongan, doth ratify, confirm, and grant all the said land and premises, with the houses, messuages, tenements, fencings, buildings, gardens, orchards, trees, woods, under-woods, pastures, feedings, common of pastures, meadows, marshes, lakes, ponds, creeks, harbors, rivers, rivulets, brooks, streams, easements, and highways, together with the islands, mines, minerals, (royal mines only excepted), fishing, hawking, hunting, and fowling, in free and common soccage, according to the tenure of East-Greenwich in the county of Kent, in his Majesty's kingdom of England, (yielding and paying on the five and twentieth day of March, yearly for ever, the chiefe or quit-rent of three pounds four shillings,) unto the following-named persons, then being the freeholders and inhabitants of the town, to wit :

Richard Betts,
Thomas Stephenson,
Gershom Moore,
Jonathan Hazzard,
Samuel Moore,
Daniel Bloomfield,
Caleb Leverich,
Edward Stevenson,
Joseph Sacket,
Samuel Scudder,
Robert Field, sen.,
Thomas Wandell,
John Catcham,
Thomas Petet,
John Woulton Crafts,
Johannis Lawresse,
John Rosell,
Joseph Reed,
Roaleffe Peterson,
Jacob Severson Van De Griff,
Stoffell Van Law,
Abraham Ricke,
Francis Comes,
Thomas Etherinson,
Jeremiah Rider,
John Way,
Robert Field, jun.,
Jonathan Stacklin,

Jonathan Stevenson,
Thomas Case,
John Alburtise,
James Way,
John Johnson,
Richard Alsop,
Hendrick B. Smith,
John Reed,
Benjamin Sufferns,
Luke Depaw,
Nathaniel Petet,
Samuel Katcham,
John Harickson,
Isaac Gray,
Content Titus,
John Fish,
Cornelius Johnson,
Abram Yoris,
John Coe,
Samuel Fish,
Joseph Burroughs,
Thomas Robinson,
James Hays,
Jacob Rider,
John Rider,
John Richard,
Woulter Gisbertson,
John Petet,
Thomas Morell,

Garsham Hazard,
Francis Way,
Moses Petet,
John Ramsden,
Philip Katcham,
Josias floreman, jun.,
Lambert Woodward,
John Moore,
Thomas Lawrence,
William Lawrence,
John Lawrence,
William Hallet, sen.,
William Hallet, jun.,
Samuel Hallet,
Hendrick Martinson,
Robert Blackwell,
John Parcell,
William Parcell,
George Stevenson,
Thomas Parcell,
Stephen Georgeson,
John Bockhout,
Anellchie Bower,
Thomas Cillman,
Peter Bockhout,
John Denman,
Henry Mayel, jun.,
Theophilus Phillips,
Anthony Gleen,

John Smyth,   John Roberts,   John Willson,
Josias fforman, sen.,   Isaacke Swinton   John fforeman,
George Wood,   Elias Doughty,   Rinier Williamson,
Nathan'Fish.   Jane Rider,   Benjamin Cornish,
Edward Hunt,   John Allene.   Henry Safly,
Jeremiah Burroughs.   Henry Mayel, sen.,   Joseph Rider,
Thomas Be.ts.   Joseph Phillips,   Thomas Morrell. jun.
John Scudder, jun.,

The first church was erected in the present village of Newtown in the year 1670, on the arrival of the *Rev. William*
Leverich, (sometimes spelled Leveridge.)   He had been the
first Presbyterian minister of Huntington, and was likewise one
of the original purchasers of the town of Oyster-Bay in 1653.
Mr. Leverich remained here till his death in 1692, and was a
highly useful man, being well acquainted with public business,
and distinguished for great industry and enterprise.   The most
ancient volume of records in the clerk's office of this town is
prefaced by about one hundred pages, in the hand-writing of
this gentleman, but in abbreviated characters ; purporting to be
a commentary upon a portion of the Old Testament, affording
conclusive evidence of his learning, patience, and industry.
He is characterized by Hubbard, in his history of New-England,
ae " an able and worthy minister.   Many of his descendants
are at this time residents of the town.   The *Rev. John Morse*
succeeded Mr. Leverich in 1694, and although he is believed
to have continued here several years, very little is known in
relation to his family.   The next minister was the *Rev. Sam-*
uel Pomeroy : he graduated at Princeton College in 1705, and
settled here in 1709, where he continued till his decease in
1744.   His son Benjamin graduated at Yale College in 1733,
and was ordained at Hebron. Connecticut, in 1735, where he
died, Dec. 22, 1784.   The *Rev. Simon Horton* succeeded Mr.
Pomeroy.   He graduated at Princeton in 1731, and settled in
this town in 1746 ; where he died, after a labor of forty years,
in 1786. His immediate successor was the *Rev. Nathan Wood-*
hull.   He was born at Setauket, in the town of Brookhaven,
in 1752 ; graduated at Yale College in 1775 ; and was first settled at Huntington, from whence he removed to this town in
1775, where he died, March 13, 1810.   He was of prepossess-

ing appearance and manners, possessed a fine genius, an amiable disposition, and was considered an eloquent preacher. He was succeeded by the *Rev. William Boardman* in 1811, who deceased in 1818, greatly lamented by all that knew him. His place was supplied in the following year by the present respectable clergyman, the *Rev. John Goldsmith*, a native of Southold, and a graduate of Princeton College in the year 1815. *St. James's Episcopal Church* in this town was erected in 1734, and obtained a charter of incorporation from Governor Colden on the 9th of September, 1761. The persons named in the charter as wardens, are James Hazard and Richard Alsop; and for vestrymen, Samuel Moore, Jacob Blackwell, William Hazard, Jacob Hallet, Richard Alsop the fourth, and William Sacket the third. A site for this church, consisting of twenty square rods of ground, was granted at a town meeting held the 19th of April, 1733, and a deed was thereupon executed for the same by ninety freeholders of the town. The church was originally united with those of Jamaica and Flushing, and enjoyed for many years the services of the same ministers in rotation. The first clergyman employed exclusively in this parish was the *Rev. Mr. Van Dyke*, who commenced his clerical labors in 1797. He removed in 1802, and was succeeded, some years after, by the *Rev. Abraham L. Clark*, who graduated at Yale College in 1785, and had been previously settled in Flushing. His death took place in 1811. The *Rev. William Wyatt*, who graduated at Columbia College in 1809, was settled here in 1812; but was soon after invited to St. Paul's church, Baltimore, where he ranks among the most able and eloquent divines of that city. The *Rev. Evan M. Johnson* is a native of Rhode Island, and graduated at Brown University in 1808. His settlement took place in this parish in 1814, where he remained about ten years, when he removed to St. John's Church in Brooklyn, of which he still continues rector.

A Dutch Reformed Church has been erected in this town for more than a century, and has generally been supplied by the clergymen of the associated Dutch churches in the county. The present church edifice was completed in 1832.

In the year 1822 a large and expensive female seminary was
built here by a few liberal and wealthy individuals, and incorporated on the 15th of March of the same year, by the name of
the "*Newtown Female Academy.*" It in a short time acquired
a high reputation, and was for some years much patronized by
the public; since when it ceased to attract attention, and has
long been relinquished as a place of education.   Besides the
village of Newtown, there are several other small settlements
scattered over the town, none of which, however, except
Hallet's Cove, contain more than some half a dozen dwellings
and a proportionate number of inhabitants.   The population is
generally diffused over the whole surface of the town, upon the
shores of the Bay, the East River, and upon Newtown Creek.
The village of Newtown is conveniently located upon the turn-
pike-road leading from Brooklyn and Williamsburgh to Flushing.   It has the three churches before mentioned, a large town-
house occupied as an hotel, three or four stores, a few mechanic
shops, and about two hundred inhabitants.   *Middle-Village* is
a small hamlet occupying an elevated position upon the turnpike leading from Jamaica to Williamsburgh.   *Middletown* is
situated on the road from the village of Newtown to Hallet's
Cove, and consists of a tavern, a store, and three or four dwellings.   *Maspeth,* sometimes called the English Kills, is at the
head of Newtown Creek, and is supposed to have been the
former residence of a small family or tribe of Indians, which
gave name to the place.   Here is a large hotel, and several
handsome dwellings; one of which was formerly occupied
by Governor De Witt Clinton as a country-seat, and where he
probably composed some of his most valuable literary productions.   His fame and public services are deserving to be held in
long remembrance by the future patriots of America.

Hallet's Cove, so called from the first purchaser, is the most
important place in the town, eligibly situated upon the shore
of the East River, a little above Blackwell's Island, and opposite
to Eighty-Sixth Street, New-York, where there is a convenient
steam-ferry.   The shore in this vicinity being considerably
elevated, offers fine sites for building; and no small degree of
taste and elegance have been displayed in those already erected.

The village itself is compactly built, and well calculated for
commercial and manufacturing purposes.   It is almost in sight
of the spires of the metropolis, and possesses great facilities
of intercourse.   Of this remarkable spot, the tradition is, that
an English adventurer, whose name was Hallet, about the year
1640, for a barrel of beef and a few trinkets, purchased from
the Indians this tract of land ; having taken to himself in marriage an industrious and sturdy Dutch lass, settled down here,
and in the process of some twenty years, by their united exertions became not only independent, but the parents of a numerous race, many of whom are still respectable in character and connections.   How the preliminaries were arranged
between the said couple has never been satisfactorily settled,
seeing the gentleman understood not a word of Dutch, and the
lady was equally unacquainted with English.   In this dilemma
the negotiation was necessarily conducted by those signs and
gestures which are the universal language of mankind.   This
suburban village has, within a few years past, exhibited much
of the spirit of improvement, and has consequently already
become the theatre of activity and enterprise in various
branches of business.

Two handsome churches and several splendid private mansions have been lately erected here, which make an imposing
appearance, especially when seen from the river.   There are.
besides, an extensive manufactory of carpets, chair factory,
wood-card factory, bellows factory, one for chemical preparations, and several gardens and nurseries for the rearing of fruit
and ornamental trees.   A great national improvement has been
proposed, that of opening a passage for ships through Blackwell's-Point, avoiding thereby the delays and dangers attendant upon a navigation through Hell-gate.   This celebrated
strait is in the immediate vicinity, where those, says a certain
writer, who love to witness the impetuous strife of angry
currents, with cragged and zigzag courses among the rocks,
can hardly find a better place for full gratification.   Our esteemed
countryman, Washington Irving, Esq., speaking of this famous *pass*, says, " *Hell-gate is as pacific at low water as any
other stream ; as the tide rises, it begins to fret ; at half*

tide it rages and roars, as if bellowing for more water : but when the tide is full, it relapses again into quiet, and for a time seems almost to sleep as soundly as an alderman after dinner. It may be compared to an inveterate drinker, who is a peaceful fellow enough when he has no liquor at all, or when he is skinfull ; but when half seas over, plays the very devil." Among other persons of taste and opulence, who have chosen this as a place of residence, is the well-known *seedsman and florist,* Mr. Grant Thorburn, an extraordinary example of virtuous industry and perseverance, crowned by great and well-merited success. Here is also the residence of the late General Ebenezer Stevens, a distinguished patriot of the revolution, and highly esteemed for integrity and honor through life. It is now occupied by his son Samuel Stevens, a highly respectable member of the legal profession. The Hallet's Cove Railway Company was incorporated April 15, 1828. with a capital of $50,000, for repairing vessels, &c.

Considerable efforts have been made to build up a beautiful *villa* upon the banks of the East River, a little south of Hallet's Cove ; upon which has been conferred the name of *Ravenswood.* The site is sufficiently elevated to afford the most charming view of the adjacent country, and possessing charms which almost equal some descriptions in eastern romance. The situation will hardly suffer by comparison with the beautiful scenery of the Thames at Windsor. Already several houses have been completed, and others are in the course of erection. In the vicinity are the valuable farms of the corporation of New-York, upon which buildings have been constructed for the accommodation of more than five hundred orphan children, maintained and educated at the public expense.

The surface of this town is generally undulating, in some parts hilly ; the soil of a middling quality ; in the neighborhood of the Sound and the shores of Flushing Bay, it is much superior and better cultivated. There is, however, within its limits a good deal of low, swampy land, not susceptible of profitable culture, some of which yields turf or peat of a kind which has been extensively used for fuel. Upon the south side of the town, adjoining the Jamaica and Williamsburgh road, is one of the most extraórdinary milk establishments in this part of the country. In 1834 Mr. David Mills purchas_ ed, for eight thousand dollars, the farm of the late Dr. Isaac Ledyard, containing two hundred acres. The whole has since been divided into, fields of five and ten acres by substantial stone walls, whereby the land has been cleared of the surface stone. By the course of husbandry pursued, the grounds have been rendered fertile and productive. A two-story stone edifice has been constructed, one hundred and fifty feet long and forty wide, divided into fifty stalls on each side, three feet by twelve, and a way left through the centre, to pass with a loaded wagon. Here are maintained one hundred cows, which consume one ton of English hay, and eight hundred quarts of Indian meal per day. The average quantity of milk obtained being nine hundred quarts daily, and which, at seven cents a quart, amounts to sixty-three dollars a-day, or twenty-two thousand nine hundred and ninety-five dollars per annum. It is much to be lamented that the inhabitants of our cities should not be fully supplied with milk of this description, seeing that no reasonable impediment exists to prevent it.

JONATHAN LAWRENCE. This gentleman, so conspicuous in the most trying pe- riod of American history, was descended from a family who were among the earliest settlers of the English towns within the Dutch jurisdiction upon Long Is- land. *Thomas,* his great grandfather, with two elder brothers, *John* and *William,* left England during the political troubles which preceded the death of Charles I. They landed in Massachusetts, and subsequently proceeded to this province, then called New Netherlands. John Lawrence, the eldest brother, was one of the six persons to whom the patent of Hempstead was granted in 1644. In the next year he and his brother William, with sixteen others, obtained the original pa- tent of Flushing from the same governor. They were also among those to whom the confirmatory patent was issued by Governor Nicolls in 1666. Soon after the two Dutch patents before mentioned were granted, John Lawrence removed from Flushing, where he had established his residence, to the city of New Amsterdam (New-York,) and accumulated a large fortune for those times by mercantile pur- suits. He held important public stations under both the Dutch and English go- vernments. In 1663 he was deputed by Governor Stuyvesant to the general court at Hartford, as a commissioner on the part of the New Netherlands to adjust the boundaries between the Dutch and English colonies, and other disputed matters ; was appointed an alderman of New-York upon the first organization of that city, after its capture by the English in 1664 ; was twice mayor of New-York ; was a member of the council of the province during a great part of the interval between 1675 and 1698 ; and at the time of his death, in 1699, was one of the judges of the supreme court, to which he was appointed in 1692. His will, on file in the office of the surrogate of New-York, neatly written in 1698, in his own hand, states that he was then over eighty years of age ; and he devises his interests in the towns of Hempstead and Flushing, as the survivor of the patentees of both towns.

William Lawrence, the second brother of John, above mentioned, became the proprietor of Lawrence's Neck, (so called,) which stretches into the Sound between Flushing Bay and Whitestone, containing about nine hundred acres, a part of which is the present site of St. Paul's College. He served in the magistracy of Flushing under the Dutch, and afterwards held both civil and military offices in the north-riding of Yorkshire upon Long Island. He died in 1680, leaving numerous descendants and a widow, Elizabeth. (daughter of Richard Smith, the patentee of Smithtown), who was afterwards married to the Hon. Philip Carteret, governor of New Jersey, and from whom Elizabethtown received its name. *Major William Lawrence*, his eldest son by his first wife, married in 1680, *Deborah*, the youngest daughter of the above-named Richard Smith, and had a numerous family. *Adam Lawrence*, one of the descendants of William the first settler, was high-sheriff of Queen's County under the colonial government, and *Joseph Lawrence*, another descendant, represented that county in the assembly in 1785. Some of his descendants, marrying among the numerous followers, in Flushing, of George Fox, became attached to the respectable religious society of Friends, of whom they proved among the most intelligent, enterprising, and exemplary members. Among the owners of land found upon the records of Newtown, in the year 1655, appear the names of the said Thomas Lawrence, and his brothers John and William. To the first-named, with six other persons, the patent for Newtown was issued by Governor Nicolls in 1666. By purchase from the Dutch settlers, Thomas Lawrence became proprietor of the whole of Hell-gate Neck, then divided into a number of cultivated farms, and extending along the East River, from Hell-gate Cove to the Bowery Bay. In the patent for Newtown from Governor Dongan, in 1686, Thomas, William, and John Lawrence, all sons of the above-mentioned Thomas Lawrence, are named as patentees.

On receiving the news of the revolution in England of 1668, and of the removal of Sir Edmund Andros as Governor of Massachusetts, the family of Thomas became decided actors in asserting the principles which had prompted his departure from England. Many persons in Queen's, however, as well as Suffolk County, were not disposed to second the popular feeling which had vacated the offices at the city of New-York, and placed Leisler at the head of affairs Not discouraged at the lukewarmness of his neighbors, Thomas Lawrence, though far advanced in years, accepted the command of the forces of Queen's County. William, one of his sons, was appointed one of the committee of safety, by whom the government of the colony was for a time assumed, and soon after one of the council of the province; an office which he subsequently held from 1702 to 1706, under a commission from Queen Anne. John Lawrence, another of the sons of Thomas, had the command of the troop of horse of the county assigned to him, with his brother Daniel as cornet. John was soon afterwards appointed high-sheriff of the county, to which place he was also chosen in 1698. Among the meagre records which are left of Leisler's times, is the entry of an order to Major Thomas Lawrence, dated 29th July, 1690, *"to press seventy men, horse and foot, as he shall think fit; and horses and provisions; and despatch them to Southold for*

the defence and protection of their Majestie's subjects there." The misconception
or obstinacy, whichever it was, that influenced Leisler in delaying to surrender the
fort at New-York to Governor Slaughter on his arrival, involved all the members
of his council in the consequences of this omission; and William Lawrence, with
the rest of them, were seized and committed on a charge of high treason. John
Lawrence, his uncle, who, from the caution of age or a disapprobation of the violence of some of Leisler's proceedings, had never countenanced his elevation, was
appointed on the commission with Sir Thomas Robinson, Col. William Smith,
and others, to try these political offenders. These proceedings do not appear,
however, to have interrupted the mutual confidence and affection of the uncle and
nephew.

Thomas Lawrence died at Newtown in July, 1703, leaving five sons—Thomas, William, John, Daniel, and Jonathan; of whom John alone permanently remained at Newtown. He was the grandfather of Jonathan Lawrence,
the subject of this notice; and married Deborah, the daughter of Richard Woodhull, one of the patentees of Brookhaven; and died at Newtown, December 17,
1729. He left three sons—Thomas, John, and Nathaniel. Of these, JOHN was
born at Newtown, September 9th, 1695, and intermarried, on the 8th December, 1720, with Patience, daughter of Joseph Sacket, Esq. He was a very
wealthy farmer, possessing great perseverance and intelligence, and served in
the magistracy of the county for many years. He died May 7, 1765, leaving
seven sons and one daughter; two sons and one daughter having died in his life-
time. *Jonathan Lawrence,* his eighth son, named at the head of this article, was
born at Newtown, October 4, 1737, and was early engaged in mercantile pursuits,
visiting Europe and the West Indies under the direction and in the employ of his
eldest brother John, an eminent merchant of New-York, and connecting himself
afterwards in commercial affairs as a partner of the house of *Watson, Murray,
and Lawrence.* His own gains, the property left him by his said brother John,
his portion of the estate of his brother Nathaniel, who died unmarried in the West
Indies, and the patrimony derived from his parent, enabled him to retire from
business when about thirty-four years of age. He purchased a residence at
Hell-gate, which had belonged to his great-grandfather, Thomas Lawrence
(one of the three emigrating brothers,) intending to enjoy the ease which his
pecuniary circumstances seemed to secure to him. The agitating questions
between the mother country and her colonies, soon, however, forbade him to be
inactive. In 1774 we find him a leading member of the political committees
of Newtown; his efforts and the influence of his brothers and relatives there,
contributed to redeem the town from the ill-timed loyalty which distinguished
most of the other portions of the county. In 1775 he was appointed a member
of the provincial congress that met at New-York. In 1776 he was again deputed
to that body, and was afterwards elected to the convention of 1776–7, which
formed the first constitution of this state. He had previously, in 1772, received
the commission of captain in the provincial militia from the royal government;
and on the organization of the militia by the provincial congress in 1775, he was
appointed major of the brigade, composed of the militia of Queen's and
Suffolk, of which Nathaniel Woodhull, Esq. was at the same time appointed
general. He accompanied that brave officer in the expedition ordered by the
convention in 1776, to prevent the supplies of Long Island falling into the hands
of the invaders, and was probably saved from participating the sad fate of his

gallant commander, by having been dispatched by him to the convention at
Harlaem for further orders; and having been thereupon sent by that body to
General Washington to endeavor to obtain the additional force that had
been promised from the army at Brooklyn. During the time spent in these
military operations, the battle of Long Island had been fought, much of the island
had fallen under the control of the enemy, and stragglers from their ranks had
spread over it in search of booty. All personal communication with his family
being cut off, he could only trust to sending a letter secretly to advise them of his
situation and to direct their future course. The convention had adjourned from
Harlaem, and sought a place of more safety for their deliberations at Fishkill.
His anxiety for his family was soon relieved by their arrival at Harlaem.
Having embarked at the river side in the night, on board a small boat, under the
guidance of a faithful slave, they crossed over amid the darkness, unobserved, to
Great Barn Island, leaving the house and the rest of the property, (except a few
articles of clothing, and a small chest containing some money, plate, and other
valuables,) to the mercy of the invaders, who had already taken possession thereof.
From this time Mr. Lawrence was the only attending member of the convention from the county of Queens. On the 9th of May, 1777, he, William
Harper, and Matthew Cantine, were appointed commissioners to superintend
the manufacture of gun-flints, sulphur, lead, and salt; the want of which was
severely felt, and which could not then be obtained from abroad. In the course
of his duties, he visited the Oneida Indians, procured the holding of a council
of their chiefs, made satisfactory experiments on the waters of some of the salt
springs in the western part of the state, and contracted with the Indians for
such salt as they might be able to produce. Some veins of excellent lead-ore
were also discovered, but not in sufficient quantity to justify the working of them.
The supplies afterwards obtained from France and elsewhere superseded the
necessity of further efforts on the part of the commissioners. On the adoption of
the state constitution in 1777, and the organization of the government, it became
impracticable for those parts of the southern district possessed by the enemy to
elect representatives to the legislature, and the convention deemed it their duty
to appoint members of assembly for those counties; they also chose *Lewis
Morris, Pierre Van Cortlandt, John Morin Scott, Jonathan Lawrence, William
Floyd, William Smith, Isaac Roosevelt, John Jones, and Philip Livingston*, to
be senators of the district, till others could be elected in their places as prescribed
by the ordinance of the convention. Mr. Lawrence served under this appointment during the residue of the war. In 1778 he was appointed a commissioner
to execute a law for completing the five continental battalions raised under the
directions of this state, the duties of which office he successfully performed. On
the arrival of Count d' Estaing's squadron off Sandy-Hook, and in the hope of
aiding an enterprise that might hasten the termination of the contest, Mr.
Lawrence, with other volunteers, joined the fleet in the expedition against
Rhode Island, embarking on the 20th of July from Black-Point in New Jersey.
He was assigned to the man-of-war L'Hector, of seventy-four guns, Captain
Mories. The wind was unfavorable; and on their arrival off Newport, much
delay ensued from the state of the weather and other circumstances; and it was
not till the 6th of August, 1778, that they were enabled to get into the harbor,
which was effected under an incessant fire from Brenton's Point, Fort Island, and
other places. Most of the troops had been landed on the 9th, when the fleet of

Lord Howe, anchoring off the harbor, a re-embarkation was ordered; and the next day, the wind favoring, the French fleet cut their cables and stood out of port, exposed to an increased fire from the forts guarding the passage. Howe cut his cables also, and proceeded to sea; but by the time the fleets had obtained position, which rendered an engagement apparently inevitable, a storm ensued, which dispersed the hostile ships, and made it necessary they should seek places of repair at New-York and Boston. In the October following, Mr. Lawrence was chosen a member of the council of appointment for the southern district. In February, 1780, he was appointed, with Isaac Stoutenburgh and Stephen Ward, commissioners of forfeitures for the said district; and on the 15th of August was made one of the commissioners of sequestration for Dutchess County. In October of the same year he was placed at the head of the commission of the southern district, under acts previous passed for raising a sum in specie, the better to secure the redemption of a new emission of bills contemplated by the continental congress, and was actively engaged in that office in 1781. He was again a member of the council of appointment in 1782. In 1783 he resisted, though unsuccessfully, the passage of a bill declaring those described therein, who had adhered to the enemy, to have been aliens from the date of the declaration of independence; and which, if carried into effect, must have produced the most deplorable consequences. The council of revision, in the exercise of their prerogative, retained the bill till the ensuing session, when the objections made by them were acquiesced in by the senate, and the bill of course rejected.

Peace being concluded in September, 1783, Mr. Lawrence was enabled to visit his long-deserted home. He found his land stripped of its timber and fences, his stock and furniture destroyed or removed, and his house, having been occupied by British officers, greatly injured. During his long exile, he had not only exhausted those means which had been saved from the enemy, the gains which he had occasionally been enabled to make during its continuance, and numerous sums owing to him; but had also contracted debts, which the sale of his lands and other resources would little more than repay. Having now, at the age of forty-seven, a large family to support and educate, he resolved to recommence business in the city of New-York, and endeavor to repair his ruined fortune. Though nearly destitute of pecuniary means, he found himself in good credit; yet his mercantile pursuits were not productive of all the benefit he had anticipated. The lands belonging to the state being offered for sale, he embarked somewhat largely in the purchase of them, and by resale from time to time, not only avoided the bankruptcy which befell other purchasers, but found himself in comfortable circumstances, with a considerable surplus of land unsold. His fortunes gradually improving until the time of his death, he was enabled to distribute a very considerable estate among his family. This result was aided by a well-regulated economy, equally removed from wastefulness and parsimony. Although he declined again to be returned to the legislature, he was not an indifferent spectator of passing events. He took an active part in the re-election of Governor George Clinton; and when the constitution had been ratified by the requisite number of states, he was anxious for the concurrence of this state; from which period he acted uniformly with the republican party of the Union. His death occurred in the city of New-York, at the age of seventy-five, on the 4th of September, 1812. He was twice married; *first*, to Judith, daughter of Nathaniel

Fish, who died at the age of eighteen years, and by whom he had one son ;
secondly, to Ruth, daughter of Andrew Riker of Newtown, who survived him,
and by whom he had seven sons and two daughters. One of these, Samuel
Lawrence, lately deceased, has been both a representative in the assembly of this
state and the congress of the United States ; and was one of the electors of president and vice-president in 1816.

The brothers of Major Jonathan Lawrence were all born at Newtown, and
those who survived till the period of the revolution were zealous Whigs. His only
younger brother, *Col. Daniel Lawrence*, was, like himself, an exile from his home
from 1776 to 1783 ; and served as a member of assembly from Queens, under the
ordinance of the convention of 1777, from that year till the termination of the war.
He married Miss Van Horn, a lady of highly respectable family in the city of
New-York ; and died, leaving numerous descendants, in 1807, at the age of
sixty-eight years. *Samuel Lawrence*, the brother next older than Jonathan, was
a man of great probity and imperturbable courage, united with great goodness of
heart. He died in 1810, at the age of seventy-five, leaving no issue. *Thomas
Lawrence*, the next eldest brother, was born in 1733, and died in his eighty-fourth
year in 1816. About the age of twenty-five he was appointed to the command of
the ship Tartar of eighteen guns, and made several cruises in her from New-York
during the old French war. His wife was Elizabeth, daughter of Nathaniel Fish,
Esq of Newtown. Possessed of wealth, he settled on a farm on the shore of
Flushing-Bay. He was appointed, in 1784, one of the judges of Queen's County ;
and was distinguished for great decision of character, and by all the punctilious
observances which characterise the *eleves* of the old school. He had a numerous
family, most of whom he survived. His son, Nathaniel, born in 1761, entered the
North Carolina line of the regular American army as a lieutenant, after he had
left Princeton College, and while under lawful age. He was made prisoner by
the enemy, after behaving with great gallantry. In 1788 he was chosen from
Queens to the convention which ratified the constitution of the United States.
He also held the office of attorney-general of this state from December 24, 1792,
to November 30, 1795 ; and represented Queen's County in the assembly in 1791,
2, 5 and 6 ; in which latter year he died, at the age of thirty-five. His wife was
Elizabeth, daughter of Judge Berrien, and aunt of John McPherson Berrien, late
attorney-general of the United States. His only child, Margaret, is the wife of
President Lindsley of the college at Nashville in Tennessee.

William Lawrence, the next eldest brother, was, for many years a magistrate
of Queen's County, and filled the station with usefulness. On the capture of
Long Island in 1776, part of his house at Newtown was made the head-quarters
of the British General Robertson, and himself and family were subjected to many
of the exactions and vexations which others who had rebel predelictions, experienced from the invaders. He died in his sixty-fifth year, in 1794. His eldest son,
John, served as an officer on board the American frigate Confederacy, Capt.
Harding, and died in 1816 at New-York. His son, Richard, was an eminent
merchant in New-York, who, becoming blind, retired to Newtown, where he
died. His son William died on his plantation in Demarara ; and Isaac, another
son, was the late President of the United States bank in New-York. The
Hon. James Lent, who died during his attendance in congress in 1833, was a
grandson of the said William Lawrence. *Richard Lawrence*, the next eldest
brother, born in 1725, died in 1781. He was a captain of horse in the militia of

Queen's County. Falling into the hands of the loyalists during the revolution, he was confined in the Provost at New-York, and while there contracted an illness which terminated his life. The news of the capture of Cornwallis being communicated to him in his last moments, he declared his readiness to die, now that the ultimate triumph of his country was secured. This gentleman left no issue. *Nathaniel Lawrence,* the next eldest brother, died at St. Eustatia in the West Indies, unmarried, in 1761, aged thirty-four years. *Joseph Lawrence,* the next eldest brother, married Patience Moore, aunt of the late Bishop Moore of New-York, and died at Newtown, aged seventy years, in 1793. One of his daughters, Anna, married Samuel Riker, Esq. (father of the Hon. Richard Riker, late recorder of the city of New-York,) who was for several years a representative from this state in congress. *John Lawrence,* the eldest brother of Jonathan Lawrence, settled in New-York at an early age, and became a distinguished merchant in that city. In 1759 he married Catherine, daughter of Phillip Livingston and sister of Governor William Livingston of New Jersey. Having no issue, after making ample provision for his widow, he distributed the residue of his property among his brothers and sisters. The celebrated Whitfield, then in this country, pronounced his funeral sermon. His death took place in 1764, in his forty-third year; and his body was deposited in the family vault of the right Honorable the Earl of Stirling, in the yard of Trinity Church.

JOHN BERRIEN RIKER. Generally speaking, there are few men who stand in such bold relief among the mass of mankind as to be peculiarly distinguished by great and noble deeds, and to be worthy also of having their names enchased among the biographical memoirs of their distinguished cotemporaries. Yet some such men there are, so peculiarly fortunate, who, with only good talents, virtue, and honor for their portion, are so intimately associated with the times and events in which they lived, as to become an essential and interesting portion of their history. Of this class of men was Dr. John B. Riker.

He was born at Newtown, Long Island, in the year 1738, and was descended from a worthy and highly respectable family of the same name, settled there about two hundred years ago. This family originally emigrated from the town of Lintz in Lower Rhine, and, driven by Catholic persecution from their native country, fled into Holland, where they were finally induced by the flattering representations of the Dutch government, to embark for America. *Guisbert Riker,* the common ancestor, arrived at New Amsterdam, (now New-York,) about the year 1640 ; and soon after became the owner of a considerable tract of land in the town of Newtown, adjoining the Sound, and also the island which has for many years borne the name of Riker's Island, situate in the Sound, opposite the mouth of Flushing Bay, and containing about fifty acres of excellent land. This property has descended in a direct line in the family for many generations to the present time. Indeed, few families have been more conspicuous for their amiable qualities and usefulness than the descendants of Guisbert Riker.

Dr. Riker was a gentleman of talents and high professional attainments ; he engaged as a surgeon in the American army in 1775, was with the troops under General Washington at Trenton, in 1777, and proved of the most essential service, as well for his perfect knowledge of the country, as for his excellent advice on several important occasions. He continued with the army from the commencement of the war till the establishment of peace in 1783 ; after which he settled as a physician in his native town, where he lived universally respected and beloved till his death, at the age of fifty-seven. His brother, Abraham Riker, was a captain in the American army that captured Burgoyne on the plains of Saratoga. He died at Valley Forge in 1778, occasioned in a great measure from severe exposure, having, as he expressed it, " *a rock for his pillow and the heavens for his canopy.*" His brother, Samuel Riker, was a farmer, and lived at Newtown, where he died, at the age of fourscore years. He was also engaged in the service of his country in the revolution. He was a member of assembly from Queen's County in 1784, and the last act of his public life was to represent his district in Congress in 1708-9. The Hon. Richard Riker and John L. Riker, Esq., are sons of the said Samuel Riker, and his daughter is the wife of Dr. James NcNeven.

Of the eminent talents and profound judicial knowledge of the late Recorder, little need be said; they are both extensively known and universally acknowledged. The able manner with which he presided for so long a period in the court of sessions in New-York, and the extraordinary qualities he displayed in the discharge of his onerous and important duties, are conclusive evidence of his great attainments and high moral worth. Perhaps by no individual, at any time or in any country, have the principles of criminal law been more firmly yet temperately administered, and where the rigid rules of law have been more happily blended with the benign precepts of moral justice and equity.

DE WITT CLINTON. This great and good man, though not a native of Newtown, yet spent so considerable a portion of his valuable life here, as to render it highly appropriate to give a brief detail of his private and public character, in connection with the history of the town. It has been doubted, (says Dr. Mitchill,) whether it is more desirable to be descended from an illustrious ancestry, or to rise in the world, and be the maker of one's own fortune. The former appears to be the preferable case; though even here, where titles, estates, and honors have been won, they not unfrequently descend to some unworthy or unqualified individual, or, for lack of heirs, the family becomes extinct. Generally, it is harder work to establish a name than to inherit it; still it strikes many, that on that very account the achievement is more glorious and honorable.

As far back as the reign of Charles I. the family from whom Mr. Clinton was lineally descended, were possessed of such character and influence as to invoke the displeasure of the ruling powers for their attachment to that ill-fated monarch. On which account, during the usurpation of Cromwell, they were obliged to expatriate themselves, and finally settled at Longford in Ireland, where Col. Charles Clinton, the grandfather of Mr. Clinton, was born. He emigrated to this country in 1729, and was soon after appointed surveyor-general. His intimacy with George Clinton, who was governor of the colony of New-York from 1743 to 1753, doubtless contributed to give him greater influence. He settled in Ulster County, New-York. His sons, Alexander and Charles, were bred to the profession of medicine; James and George distinguished themselves in the French war, and in the war of the revolution, holding the office of majors-general in the American army. James died in 1812, and George on the 20th of April of the same year, having been governor of this state for twenty-one years, and was vice-president of the United States at the period of his death. The truly illustrious subject of this memoir was the son of Gen. James Clinton, was born at his father's residence, Little Britain, Orange County, March 2d, 1769; and received his early education at a grammar-school in the neighboring village of

Stonefield, under the care of the Rev. John Moffat, from which, at the age of thirteen, he was sent to an academy at Kingston, taught by Mr. John Addison, where he remained till prepared to enter the junior class of Columbia College in 1784, and graduated at the first public commencement of that institution after the revolution in 1786. He was acknowledged to be the best scholar in his class, manifesting at an early age a remarkable quickness of perception and a vigorous power of intellect, which he ever after exhibited, added to a fine talent for composition and extemporaneous debate. On his leaving college he entered upon the study of the law, in the office of the late Samuel Jones, a gentleman deservedly eminent in his profession, formerly recorder of the city, and subsequently comptroller of the state. Under such tuition, with a mind well disciplined to habits of study, and richly stored with all the elementary knowledge of his profession, he soon accomplished his judicial studies; and accordingly, in 1790 we find him practising at the bar with a success that gave promise of high legal reputation, when he was invited to be secretary to his uncle, Governor Clinton, which he retained till the close of his administration in 1795. In the mean time he had been chosen secretary to the board of regents of the university. In 1797 he was elected a member of assembly for the city of New-York, in 1800 a member of the senate, and in 1810 was chosen by the legislature a senator of the United States, as the colleague of Governeur Morris. He was appointed, in 1799, first judge of Queen's County, where he occasionally resided ; but circumstances induced him to decline the appointment. In 1803 he resigned his seat in the senate of the United States, on being made mayor of New-York, which office he retained till March, 1807. He continued in this situation, by successive re-appointments, till 1815, when, from violent party opposition, he was compelled to retire; and during the years 1815, '16, and '17, was but a private citizen. In 1817 he was elected, almost unanimously, to succeed Daniel D. Tompkins as governor of the state. He was re-elected again in 1820, although opposed by Mr. Tompkins, then vice-president of the United States, who had once more become a candidate. In 1823 he voluntarily declined the office, and once more retired to private life, devoting himself to the pursuits of science and literature, holding only the unprofitable office of canal commissioner, but from which he was removed, in 1824, by the shameless malignity of political opponents. This extraordinary act of party meanness and puny persecution was thoroughly rebuked by the majesty of public opinion, and resulted in his elevation to the gubernatorial office by a larger majority than had ever been known in this state at a contested election. He was re-elected in 1826, and retained the office till his death, which occurred suddenly at his house in Albany, on the 11th of February, 1828. This great calamity was universally felt ; and the public testimonials of respect and veneration for his memory in every part of the state and Union, were alike honorable to the people, and a due appreciation of the character, talents, and services of the deceased. As a philosopher, a statesman, a writer, a scholar, an orator, a delightful companion, a correct citizen, and a pure and honest man, his name, (says Dr. Hosack,) will go down to posterity divested of every reproach. His reputation was not confined to the country he immediately benefited by his services. In the literary circles, and in the scientific institutions of Europe, his name was familiarly known as among the most eminent men of his day. It is evidence of the high estimation in which he was held, that he was honored by being made a member of many learned societies in Great Britain, and held also an extensive correspondence with some of the most distinguished men of the age. He was an honorary member of the Linnean, the Horticultural Societies of London, and of the Wernerian Society of Edinburgh; was in habits of intercourse with the late Sir James Edward Smith, the learned president of the first, and with Mr. Knight and Mr. Sabine, the able officers of the latter. The acknowledged reputation which Mr. Clinton attained in his literary character, taken in connection with his extensive public services, is to be ascribed, not only to his native taste and ardent love of knowledge, but to the wonderful industry and order with which he performed his many and various duties. He was an early riser, and devoted every moment that could be spared from official and necessary calls to the cultivation of his mind. No one was more ambitious of a reputation for science and literature, and few ever made a more successful progress in the acquisition of useful knowledge. In some of the physical sciences he was especially well versed; and as a classical and belles-lettres scholar, his proficiency was very considerable. He observed the utmost punctuality in all his engagements; his regard for truth and honor being one of the cardinal principles of his mind and character. When released from the severer labors which employed his attention, a volume of the classics or a work on science occupied his moments of relaxation; and his large and well-stored library constantly afforded him ample sources of study and entertainment. The ordinary amusements of fashionable life presented no attractions for him, but were avoided, as not only involving the loss of time, money, and reputation, but as incompatible with those pursuits and views, belonging to him who has at heart the dignity of his own character, the higher interests of science, and the welfare of his country. In his person Mr. Clinton was tall, finely proportioned, and of commanding aspect. His physiognomy pointed out great mental activity and power, and the phrenological developments of his head were of the most remarkable character, uniting great benevolence with the highest degree of integrity and moral courage. The superior dignity of his person indicated a bold and haughty temper; yet nothing was further from the truth, for he was constitutionally timid, and only an exalted sense of public duty caused him to exercise on any occasion his ability for public speaking. His untiring industry and perseverance in various public stations were distinguishing attributes, and exercised, to their fullest extent, amidst the abuse, calumny, and ridicule, which he was compelled to encounter from the vampires of reputation, while prosecuting his great projects of internal improvement. Indeed, few men were ever assailed by a more determined opposition, and no man ever triumphed more completely over every obstacle which came in his way. The task was truly herculian, and the issue most honorable and glorious for his future fame.

In his domestic and social relations he was cheerful and kind; in his friendships warm and sincere; and in his moral character most unexceptionabe. As a speaker, he was slow, cautious and deliberate, manifesting the constant exercise of his understanding. He never indulged in rant or vehemence, either of voice or gesture; yet his clear and logical method, force and perspicuity of style, and dignity of manner, gave, whether in the judgment seat or in a deliberate assembly, an effect and influence which few others ever exercised in this state. If, indeed, the possession of strong native powers of mind, aided by extensive attainments; if an innate spirit of patriotism, quickened and directed by a knowledge of the interests of his country; if a life devoted to the unceasing performance of public duty and ex-

pended in the service of his native state, entitle the possessor to respect and gratitude, Mr. Clinton presents the strongest claims, not only to the affections of his
countrymen, but to a distinguished place among the sages, statesmen, and benefactors of America.

Two of the most important objects of his heart he lived to see accomplished—
the establishment of a better system of common schools, and the Erie Canal, the
last of which should be called by his name, as the most appropriate and durable
monument of his fame and services. Whatever claims may be asserted by others
in this stupendous project, all impartial and intelligent men are now convinced
that the glory of its execution of right belongs to him. From its commencement,
through all its subsequent embarrassments, he stood forward, through good and evil
report, as its fearless and unwavering advocate, staked his character upon its success and tendered his reputation as its surety. He lived to see the consummation of
the work, desiring no other recompense for his time and services than a conscious-
ness of the incalculable importance of the project to present and future generations.
In the performance of his judicial duties, his learning, firmness, and integrity have
received an unqualified encomium from all. As a magistrate, he was enlightened
and dignified; in all the relations of life public, and private, he had few equals and
no superior; and his death was truly a subject of regret, not only to his friends but
to the nation. As yet no monument has by the public been raised to his memory;
but, to the honor of the present executive of the state of New-York, the subject has
been brought before the legislature, and will, it is presumed, result in the adoption of
some measure creditable alike to all. For, in the words of Governor Seward, " *the
custom of honoring the dead commends itself to the natural sentiments of mankind ;
and although, in ignorant and depraved countries, it has been abused by the erection
of pyramids, and temples, and tombs, to preserve the ashes of tyrants, it cannot,
among an enlightened people, be otherwise than right and expedient to perpetuate
the memory of public benefactors, and thus stimulate and encourage emulation of
their deeds.*"

TOWN OF BUSHWICK.

This town, situated in the north-east extremity of King's
County, is bounded westerly by the East River, northerly by
Maspeth or Newtown Creek, easterly by Newtown, and
southerly by Brooklyn, and that part of Flatbush called *New-
Lotts*. Its area is 3,860 acres, of which a greater portion
is under cultivation; its proximity to the cities of Brooklyn
and New-York rendering it valuable in a high degree. The
precise period of its settlement is not satisfactorily ascertained,
but is believed to have been some years later than Brooklyn and
the more southern towns. It was commenced by the Dutch,
who were joined, many years after, by a number of Hugonot
families, whose descendants are numerous and respectable in

this and the neighboring towns. The name is of Dutch origin, indicating that the territory was remarkable for the woods which covered its surface in early times. There are some families here, who can trace their ancestry back nearly two hundred years, and, as possessing at that period, the identical lands now in the occupation of their descendants. The increase of population in this part of the country, was so small as not to acquire its municipal character before the year 1648, at which time application was made to the governor for a patent or ground-brief. One was accordingly issued, and under which the inhabitants remained till the conquest of New Netherlands in 1664. The government having now fallen into other hands, and many considerable defects existing in the chárter granted by Governor Stuyvesant, the people of Bushwick, in 1666, at a town meeting assembled for the purpose, appointed a committee to wait upon Governor Nicolls, " to solicit him for a new patent, and to request that therein the boundaries of their plantation might be more expressly defined and set forth."

This patent was obtained on the 25th of October, 1667, wherein, among other things, the limits and bounds of the town are set forth in the words following

" Bounded with the mouth of a certain creeke or kill, called Maspeth-Kill, right over against Dominic-Hook, soe their bounds goe to David Jocham's Hook; then stretching upon a south-east line along the said Kill, they come to Smith's Island, including the same, together with all the meadow-ground or valley thereunto belonging ; and continuing the same course, they pass along by the ffence at the wood-side, soe to Thomas Wandall's meadow, from whence, stretching upon a south-east by south line, along the woodland to the Kills, taking in the meadow or valley there ; then pass along near upon a south-east by south line six hundred rod into the woods ; then running behind the lots as the woodland lyes, south-west by south ; and out of the said woods they goe again north-west, to a certain small swamp; from thence they run behind the New Lotts, to John, the Sweede's-meadow; then over the Norman's-Kill, to the west end of his old house, from whence they goe alongst the river, till you come to the mouth of Maspeth-Kill and David Jocham's Hook, whence they first began."

From the organization of the town till the year 1690, it was for certain civil purposes associated with the other towns in the county, except Gravesend, constituting a separate district under the appellation of the " *Five Dutch Towns ;*" and for which a secretary or register was specially commissioned by the governor, whose duty it was to take the proof of wills, of marriage settlements, also the acknowledgment of "*Transcripts*," or conveyances, and many of the more important contracts and agreements ; all which were required to be recorded. This office was, in 1674, held by Nicasius de Sille, who had once held the office of attorney-general under the administration of Stuyvesant. These five towns likewise formed but one ecclesiastical congregation, and joined in the support of their ministers in common. The inhabitants, with few exceptions, professed the doctrines promulgated at the synod of Dort in 1618, most of whose resolutions are still adhered to in the Reformed Dutch churches. The churches were at that period, and for a long time after, governed by the classis of Amsterdam, and so continued till about the year 1772, when the American churches repudiated any dependence upon the mother church, and established classes and synods of their own, on the model of the church of Holland. In the year 1662, according to one authority the dwellings in this town did not exceed twenty-five, and were located on the site of the village of Bushwick, which, with the Octagon church, built in 1720, were enclosed by palisades, as most of the other settlements were. In the minutes of the court of sessions is the following entry :

"At a Court of Sessions, held at Flatbush for King's County, May 10, 1699. Uppon the desire of the inhabitants of Breucklyn, that according to use and order every three yeare the limmitts betweene towne and towne must be runn, that a warrant or order may be given, that upon the 17th day off May, the line and bounds betwixt said townes of Breucklyn and Boswyck shall be run according to their pattents or agrements. Ordered, That an order should be past according to theire request."

The population of this town was very inconsiderable at the time of the revolution compared with other parts of the county ; yet they suffered greatly from the depredations of the enemy. They were particularly exposed to the invaders, who made, of course, an indiscriminate destruction of whatever their caprice or revenge dictated. The nearness of its forests to the garrisons and barracks of New-York and Brooklyn led to the entire waste of the valuable timber which abounded at the commencement of the contest. On the return of the owners to their homes at the close of the war, they found not only the woods and fences destroyed, but their dwellings, in many instances, greatly deteriorated in value.

On the 12th of May, 1664, the magistrates of this town sentenced one John Van Lyden, convicted of publishing a libel, to be fastened to a stake, with a bridle in his mouth, eight rods under his arm, and a label on his breast with the words, "*writer of lampoons, false accuser, and defamer of magistrates,*" upon it, and then to be banished from the colony. An instance also occurred, of a clergyman, who had improperly married a couple, being sentenced to "*flogging and banishment,*" but which, on account of the *advanced age* of the delinquent, was mitigated by the governor to *banishment* only. Another person, convicted of theft, was compelled to stand for the space of three hours under a gallows, with a rope around his neck and an empty scabbard in his hands. In 1664 permission was given by the town to Abraham Janson to erect a mill on Maspeth Kill, which was probably the first water-mill built within the town, and for grinding of the *town's grain* he was to receive the "*customary duties.*" November 12, 1695, the court of sessions of King's County made an order "That *Mad James* should be kept at the expense of the county, and that the deacons of each towne within the same doe forthwith meet together, and consider about their *propercons* for maintainence of said James."

The Village of Williamsburgh is not only the principal settlement, but contains within its corporate limits more than two thirds of the whole population of the town. This flourishing village was, till within a few years, an inconsiderable place, although it was commenced, by a few spirited individuals, nearly thirty years ago, by erecting a few houses and establishing a ferry between it and the foot of Grand Street. At which period the houses on the New-York side, in the vicinity of the ferry, were scattering; and where extensive blocks of buildings and a large population now exist, was then, in a great measure, an open field of broken ground ; and a general want of confidence in the project of making this a place of business, retarded its operations and prevented its growth. In the year 1817 a ferry-boat, impelled by horse power, gave a new impulse to Williamsburgh, and it began, to assume an importance before unknown. Still, the main current of travel was by way of Brooklyn, and the progress of improvement here was slow and gradual. At that time the road leading to the ferry was the principal thoroughfare of the village, and where there are now wide and handsome streets partially built upon, were then cultivated fields, orchards, &c. Such was the state of things, in a great degree, when the first act of incorporation was obtained, April 14, 1827, which proved, in fact a new and important era in the increase and prosperity of the village. The territory embraced in the act is as follows : " Beginning at the bay or river opposite the town of Brooklyn, and running thence easterly along the division line between the towns of Bushwick and Brooklyn to the land of Abraham A. Remsen ; thence northerly by the same to a road or highway at a place called Sweed's Fly ; thence by the said highway to the dwelling-house late of John Vandervoort, deceased ; thence in a straight line northerly, to a small ditch or creek, against the meadow of John Skillman ; thence by said creek to Norman's Kill ; thence by the middle or centre of Norman's Kill to the East River ; thence by the same to the place of beginning." The first trustees appointed in this act were Noah Waterbury, John Miller, Abraham Meserole, Lewis Sandford, and Thomas T. Morrill ; of whom the first-named, a well-known and spirited individual, was chosen president. The board, under the extensive and liberal provisions of this charter, applied themselves immediately and vigorously to the laying out of streets and building-lots as the basis for future improvements ; and every thing was done by them which the state of things at that time seemed to authorize or require. Nevertheless the increase of business and population was not equal to the public expectations until another portion of territory was included in the incorporated part of the village, and additional powers conferred upon the trustees by the act of April 18, 1835. This additional legislative provision vested the pub-

lic concerns of the village in the hands of nine trustees, o f
which new board Edmund Frost was chosen president; and
by whose zeal, industry, and perseverance, much has, within a
short time, been accomplished for the increase and welfare of
the place. Such has been the progress of improvement, that
the ancient village of Bushwick can scarcely be identified, having
become amalgamated with the village of Williamsburgh. Indeed, it now seems both a matter of surprise and deep regret
that public attention should not have been sooner and more
efficiently attracted towards a place possessing so many and
superior natural advantages for the successful prosecution of
every species of manufacture and commerce, and for the erection of pleasant and convenient private residences. Situated
opposite the very heart of the city of New-York, it has a
bold water-front upon the East River of a mile and a half,
with a sufficient depth for all commercial purposes; and has this
advantage over Brooklyn, that its entire shore is under the control of its own local authorities. There has already been constructed, under the act of the 22d of April, 1835, and the statutes before mentioned, several large and substantial wharves
and docks, affording safe and convenient mooring for vessels,
even of the largest class. Its ferry is, by two or three miles,
the nearest approximation to the upper parts of the city from
the eastern towns, and is connected with the upper and lower
parts of the city by double lines of steam ferry boats of the best
kind, and remarkable for their accommodations and speed.
The ferry to Peck Slip may be said to unite the village with
the Fulton and Catharine markets, while another is in contemplation to the foot of Houston Street, leading to the upper wards
and Harlaem. Williamsburgh now contains seventy-three streets
permanently laid out, of which twenty-seven have been opened
and regulated, including one McAdamised and seven paved
streets. The number of dwellings is five hundred and eighty,
and the inhabitants about three thousand five hundred. There
are one Dutch Reformed and two Methodist churches, ten fire
companies, one hook and ladder company, two distilleries,
which consume annually more than two hundred thousand
bushels of grain, one steam spice mill, five rope-walks, an ex-

tensive glue factory, two hat manufactories, one iron foundry, two lumber-yards, two lime and brick yards, one coal yard, six hotels, one drug store, and a due proportion of other mechanics and tradesmen. A considerable number of elegant dwellings have lately been erected in the southern part of the village, owned and occupied by persons doing business in New-York. Many other inducements exist, besides an easy and speedy communication with the city, that will insure a rapid influx of inhabitants, and an expansion of business in every department. The improvements in contemplation, and partially in progress, along the shore south of the present ferries, will in time unite with those in the vicinity of the navy-yard at Brooklyn ; and in half a century perhaps form a continuous city from the mouth of Newtown Creek to Red-Hook, a distance of four miles.

TOWN OF GRAVESEND.

This town occupies the most southerly part of King's County, including also Coney Island, which is washed by the Atlantic Ocean. It is centrally distant from New-York city about ten miles ; bounded east by Flatlands, south by the sea, and west by New Utrecht, of a triangular shape with its base upon the ocean, and terminating northerly in a point adjoining Flatbush. Much of the territory consists of salt-marsh, not more than one third being returned as improved land ; the surface generally level, but near the sea-shore are some ridges of sand-hills. This town, unlike the rest of the county, was settled by English people, mostly from Massachusetts, as early as 1640, who gave it the name of Gravesend, they having sailed from a place of that name in England on their departure for America. They were joined soon after by a small colony of English Quakers, accompanied by Lady Deborah Moody, a woman of rank, education, and wealth, who, with several others residing at Lynn, Sandwich, and other towns in New England, had imbibed the religious sentiments of George Fox, and being objects of jealousy and persecution with the Puritans there, determined to settle elsewhere. Considering the situation of this town calculated for the site of a commercial village, they proceeded almost immediately to lay out ten acres of ground near the centre into streets and squares, which they enclosed with a palisado defence.   The plan of the village is still preserved in the clerk's office of the town, and is worthy admiration for its simplicity and beauty.   It seems the project was soon after abandoned on discovering the insufficient depth of the water for the approach of large vessels.   One of the original squares of the contemplated city was occupied by the court-house of the county so long as the courts continued to be held here; another contained the first Dutch church; and a third has long been used for a public cemetery.   On the same plot are a considerable number of graves of the first Quakers, the whole of which have been levelled by the plough, except that of Peter Sullivan and his wife, at the head of which is a large granite slab, containing only the names of the deceased.   As this particular sect make no use of such memorials, it was probably placed here by some friend or relative who was not a Quaker.

The first patent or ground-brief was granted by Governor Kieft in 1643 to Antonie Jansen Van Sale (or Anthony Johnson) for one hundred morgen of land, which was afterwards known as the Old Bowery.   A morgen was a Dutch measure of little less than two acres, consisting of six hundred square Dutch rods.   On the 24th of May, 1644, a patent was also granted to Guisbert Op-Dyck for Coney Island, called in the patent Cunny Island, and by the Dutch Conynen-Eylandt, probably from the name of an individual who had possessed some part of it. *Pine Island*, then called *Conyne-Hook*, was at that time separated from the former by a creek, which has since disappeared. The latter was doubtless the spot upon which the discoverer Hudson and his crew landed in 1609 before entering the bay of New-York.   A general patent for this town, written both in Dutch and English, was obtained from Governor William Kieft on the 19th of December, 1645.   The patentees named therein are the Lady Deborah Moody, Sir Henry Moody, Baonet, Ensign George Baxter, and Sergeant James Hubbard, with their associates; and is for "*A certain quantity of land lying or being upon or about the westernmost part of Long Island, beginning at the north of a creek adjacent to Conyne-Island,*

*and bounded on the west part thereof with the lands belonging
to Anthony Johnson and Robert Pennoyre ; and to run as far
as the westernmost part of a certain pond in an old Indian
field on the north side of the plantation of the said Robert
Pennoyre ; and from thence to run directly east as far as a
valley, being at the head of a fly or marsh some time belonging
to the land of Hugh Garretson ; and being bounded on the
south with the main Ocean, with liberty to put what cattle
they shall see fitting to feed or graze upon the aforesaid
Conyne-Island, and with liberty to build a town, with such
necessary fortifications as to them shall seem expedient ; and
to have and enjoy the free liberty of conscience according to
the customs and manners of Holland without molestation, and
to establish courts, and elect magistrates, to try all causes not
exceeding fifty Holland guilders."*

The circumstance of this patent being granted to a female,
and her being also first-named, is a matter of some curiosity ; and, in connection with events hereinafter mentioned,
exhibits the Lady Moody in a conspicuous light. She being a
considerable personage in the early history of the town, it is
important to ascertain, as far as possible, the particulars
of her history. We find it mentioned in the very interesting
publication by Mr. Alonzo Lewis, entitled " *History of Lynn,*"
that the Lady Deborah Moody came to that town in the year
1640. That in 1635 she went from one of the remote counties
in England to London, where she remained in opposition to a
statute which directed that no person should reside beyond a
limited time from their own homes. On the 21st of April of
that year, the court of Star-Chamber ordered that "*Dame Deborah Mowdie*" and others, should return to their hereditaments
in forty days, in the good example necessary for the poorer
class. That soon after her arrival at Lynn, on the 5th of
April, 1640, she united with the church of Salem ; and on the
13th of May the court granted her four hundred acres of land.
In 1641 she purchased the farm of the deputy-governor, John
Humfrey, called Swamscut, for which she paid £1100. That
some time afterwards she became imbued with the erroneous
doctrine that the baptism of infants was a sinful ordinance,

and was thereupon excommunicated; and that in 1643 she removed to Long Island.   Governor Winthrop, in his journal, says, that " in 1613 Lady Moody was in the colony of Massachusetts, a wise and anciently religious woman ; and being taken with the error of denying baptism to infants, was dealt withal by many of the elders and others, and admonished by the church of Salem, whereof she was a member; but persisting still, and to avoid further trouble, &c. she removed to the Dutch, against the advice of her friends."   "After her arrival at Long Island, (says Mr. Lewis,) she experienced much trouble from the Indians, her house being assaulted by them many times.   Her wealth enabled her to render assistance to Governor Stuyvesant in some trouble with the neighboring settlers in 1654 ; and so great was her influence over him, that he conceded in part the nomination of the magistrates to her. In the quarterly court records her son is styled *Sir* Henry Moody."   "At the same court, December 14, 1642, the Lady Deborah Moodie, Mrs. King, and the wife of John Tilton, were presented, for holding that the baptism of infants is no ordinance of God."   From these historical relations we learn the reason why the Lady Moody, her son *Sir* Henry Moody, Ensign Baxter, Sergeant Hubbard, John Tilton, and many others of her associates and friends, left New England, and planted themselves at Gravesend, where they hoped to enjoy the most perfect freedom of opinion, unawed by the civil power, and he allowed unmolested to propagate those religious principles which to them seemed most agreeable to their principles of reason and justice.   All this, it would seem, was intended to be secured by the patent above-mentioned; how far it was realized under the governor's successor will appear hereafter, when we view the persecutions practised upon the Quakers of this and other towns under the Dutch jurisdiction.   Lady Moody probably retained a portion of her large real estate in New England ; for Governor Winthrop says, that in 1646 the house of Lady Moody at Salem was injured by a tempest, the roof being torn off; which fact he likewise mentions in a letter to his son John, then living at Fisher's Island.   A release or conveyance from the Canarsee Indians was obtained for Gravesend-Neck and Conyne Island, on the 7th of May, 1654. Other conveyances in different parts of the town were procured at different times, both by the town and by individuals, which in the end occasioned no small difficulty, in consequence of the clashing of boundaries, the description of which, in deeds, were frequently inconsistent and obscure.

On the 1st of January, 1643, a soldier was convicted before the court of sessions at Gravesend of having left his station while on guard, and was punished by being compelled to sit upon a wooden horse during the parade, with a pitcher in one hand and a drawn sword in the other ; to show that he loved beer more than his duty, and that his courage was always to be determined by the quantity consumed. " *At a town meeting, September* 27, 1644, it was *voted* that those as should have Boweries, (farms,) should have fifty morgen of upland, with meadow proportionable to their stock ; and it was further *ordered,* that if any did not build a habitable house by the last of May next, should be defaulted, and forfeit their land to the town." The records of this town, which were kept uniformly in the English language, are still preserved almost entire. They commence with the year 1645, and for a series of years are chiefly occupied with records of wills, inventories, letters of administration, and a variety of private contracts, bargains, sales, &c. In January, 1648, the town elected Sergeant James Hubbard, a man of respectability and influence, to execute the office of a scout or constable, which was considered of much importance. On the 14th of April, 1649, John Furman agreed with the town to keep their calves three months for twenty guilders a month, to be paid in *money, tobacco,* or *corn,* and *some bitters,* if desired. In March, 1650, it was required of every owner of a lot of ground to pay one guilder toward the common charges of the town, to be collected and paid by Mr. Stillwell and Jos. Tilton. In December of the same year it was ordered that every man should fence the head of his lot upon the town square, with a sufficiency of palisades, by the middle of April next. Within this palisade enclosure, which included the original town-plot of ten acres,

56

the inhabitants secured their cattle during the night, and themselves also, when apprehensive of danger from the natives; in
which case an armed guard was employed.   That wolves
were both plentiful and mischievous at that time, appears from
the fact, that on the 8th of August, 1650, three guilders were
offered for each wolf killed in the town, and two guilders for
a fox.   It was ordered also that every man be provided with
a gun, a pound of powder, and two pounds of lead or bullets.
Every owner of a house was likewise required to provide himself a ladder of twenty feet or more in length.   It was also voted
and agreed in town meeting, that whoever should transgress,
in word or deed, in defaming, scandalizing, slandering, or
falsely accusing any, *to the breach of the peace* and the reproach of the place, should suffer condign punishment according to his demerit, as should be thought meet by the magistrates, by fine, imprisonment, *stocking*, or *standing at a
public post.*

In the year 1650 the following persons are ascertained to
have been inhabitants and freeholders of the town :

William Goulding,	John Van Cleef,	William Nicolls,
Jacob Swart,	Thomas Spicer,	Edward Brown,
Walter Wall,	Ralph Cardell,	John Thomas,
Charles Morgan,	James Grover,	Lady Deborah Moody,
Peter Simson,	Carson Johnson,	Elizabeth Applegate,
John Cock,	Thomas Baxter,	John Bowne,
John Laus,	William Bowne,	John Peters,
Lawrence Johnson,	Thomas Whitlock,	John Applegate,
John Broughman,	Richard Gibson,	Lyman Law,
William Wilkins,	Richard Stout,	Thomas Morrell,
John Tilton,	James Hubbard,	James Curlear.

In 1654 Governor Stuyvesant rejected certain persons who
had been nominated by the town for magistrates, and submitted
for his approbation ; these were Baxter and Hubbard, who had
rendered themselves obnoxious to his displeasure by their
fidelity to the people, and their opposition to the arbitrary
measures of his administration.   This produced great offence,
and the popular indignation rose to so high a pitch, that his
Excellency found it expedient to go in person to Gravesend.
In order to allay the general excitement, he was induced to
avail himself of the popularity and influence of the Lady

Moody, and even committed the appointment of the magistrates to her discretion. Whether this remarkable woman continued here till her death, or returned again to New England, is not certainly known. It is supposed, that while she remained here, she occupied the farm of the late Van Brunt Magaw, now owned by Samuel Smith, Esq., and one of the best in the county. It appears that the neighboring Indians were some-times troublesome to the white settlers; and on one occasion a considerable body of Indians from the Main attacked the place, assaulting the house of the Lady Moody, and would have destroyed her and her family, (as they did Lady Ann Hutchinson and her party a short time before at Throg's Point,) had they not been overpowered by the number and courage of the inhabitants. Upon the Dutch records in the office of the secretary of the state, is the following entry, bearing date March 25, 1643:

"Whereas, in some time past, several misunderstandings have taken place between the savages of Long Island and our nation, by which, from both sides, the blood has streamed upon the land, the houses have been robbed and turned, with the killing of the stock and carrying off the corn by the Indians, so it is, that between us and them, who already follow the banner of their great chief, *Pennowits*, a solid peace has been established, so that all injuries, from whatever side, are hereby forgiven and forgotten."

A confirmation patent for this town was obtained from Governor Nicolls on the 13th of August, 1668, in which the boundaries do not vary from those described in the patent of Governor Kieft in 1644. An additional patent was issued on the 1st of July, 1670, by Governor Francis Lovelace; which, after reciting the most material parts of the original Dutch patent, and the bounds therein-mentioned, proceeds as follows:

"Know ye, that by virtue of the commission and authority unto me given by his Royal Highness, I have ratified, confirmed, and granted, and by these presents do ratify, confirm, and grant unto Thomas Delavall, Esq. Mr. James Hubbard, Ralph Cardall, William Bowne, John Tilton, William Goulding, and Samuel Spicer, as patentees, for and on behalf of themselves and their associates the freeholders and inhabitants of the said town, their heirs, successors, and assigns, all the fore-mentioned quantity, tract, and parcel of land, together with the inheritance of all Coney Island, (reserving only the privilege of erecting huts for fishing and drying of nets there upon occasion for all persons who shall undertake that design for the public good.) Including all the land within a line stretching from the uttermost part of the said Island, unto the southernmost part of Antony Jansen's Old Bowry; their east bounds being the Strome Kill, which comes to the marsh or Fly of Mathew Gerritsen's land aforementioned. As also the meadow-ground and upland not specified in their former patent; concerning which there have been several disputes and differences between the inhabitants of the said town and their neighbor Francis Brown, the which in part were issued both by my predecessors and myself, but since fully concluded and determined between them by articles of agreement; the which articles I do hereby confirm and allow, with all havens, quarries, rivers, &c. Given under my hand, and seal of the Province at Fort James in New-York, this first day of July, in the 22d year of his Majesties Reign, Anno Domini, 1670.

"FRANCIS LOVELACE.

" Mathias Nicolls, Sec."

On the 26th of March, 1777, an agreement was entered into between the towns of Gravesend and New Utrecht in relation to their boundaries, which was confirmed in the patent granted by Governor Dongan on the 10th of September, 1686. The boundaries mentioned in this instrument are as follows :

" Beginning at the westernmost part of a certain place called Coney Island, and from thence to the westernmost part of Anthony Jansen and Robert Pennoyer's land ; and so from thence by New Utrecht fence, according to agreement, to the bounds of Flatbush, and from thence along John Ditmas his land unto the bounds of Flatlands, upon a line agreed upon between Flatlands and Gravesend, which from John Ditmas his land, runs to a certain bound stake, and from thence to a white-oak tree marked and standing near New-Utrecht wagon path, and so to the north-west corner of Albert the weaver's field, and so going to a certain marked white-oak tree that stands by the highway side in the Hollow, and from thence running along the Hollow to the head of a certain creek commonly called and known by the name of the Strome Kill, and along the said creek to the main Ocean, and so along the sea-side to the westernmost part of Coney Island."

The patentees in this instrument are James Hubbard, John Tilton, jun., William Goulder, Nicholas Stillwell, and Jocham Guilock; and the quit-rent reserved was six bushels of *good winter merchantable wheat,* to be paid on the 20th day of March annually, for his Majesty's use, at the city of New-York, for ever.

"*At a court of Sessions held at Gravesend,* June 21, 1676, John Cooke and John Tilton, being Quakers, and refusing to take the oath, were ordered to give their engagement to Mr. Justice Hubbard to perform their office as overseers, under the penalty of perjury." "At the same court, holden Dec. 17, 1679. Mr. Jos. Lee, deputy-sheriff, presented Ferdinandus Van Strickland for refusing to give entertainment to a stranger who came from Huntington about business at this court ; upon which the court do order, that if the said Ferdinandus does not make his submission to the sheriff and the justices to-morrow, that he be dismissed from *tapping*. It is believed that many of the Friends who settled in this town removed to New Jersey at or about the time of the visit of George Fox to Long Island in the year 1672.

Coney Island, on the sea-board, is a place of great resort for strangers in the summer season, is constantly fanned by cool sea breezes, and affords an unlimited view of the ocean. It is separated from Long Island by a narrow creek or inlet, over which a handsome bridge has been erected. A large and spacious hotel is established here, called, the *Ocean House*, and hitherto conducted in a superior manner. A rail-road is attached to the establishment, with cars leaving the hotel for the beach, a distance of eighty rods, at particular intervals during the day. The bathing at this place is not surpassed by any in the United States. The beach is a beautiful white sand. The island is about five miles long and one wide, and is entirely of alluvial formation. The effect of severe ocean storms has long been visible here, and much of what was once Coney Island has disappeared. It has been conjectured by some persons that Coney Island proper, two hundred years ago, lay at the entrance of Sandy Hook, and separated from the present Coney Island by a channel of considerable width, which is supposed to have been entirely demolished by a storm about the year 1715. It is well ascertained, that in 1643 there was a convenient harbor for vessels of a large size, which is now in a great measure filled up. The exposed situation of this island subjects it to the encroachments of the sea, and to be entirely destroyed at some future period. In the terrible gale which occurred upon the coast on the 26th of January, 1839, the whole of this island, with the exception of a few sand-hills, was completely inundated by the sea; the basement story of the Ocean House was filled with water; the bridge was carried away, several small vessels cast upon the shore, and in one instance carried to a considerable distance toward Flatlands.

The first church built here was by the Dutch in 1655. It

was rebuilt in 1770, and stood till 1833, when the present church was erected. It is located in the village of Gravesend, upon one of the original squares of the town-plot made by the first settlers, and near the place where the court-house formerly stood. Here the court of sessions was held till the Ridings were abolished in 1685, after which it was removed to Flatbush. All the lands in this town were laid out in reference to the village plan, the exterior lines of most of the farms converging towards this centre like the radii of a circle. The soil of this town is light and sandy, yet it is generally well cultivated; and the surplus produce of the farms is supposed to exceed forty thousand bushels of different kinds of grain annually, which is a permanent mine of wealth and independence to its inhabitants, their number being seven hundred.

In many Dutch patents there was a clause requiring the patentees and their associates, after the expiration of ten years from the date thereof, to pay, by way of quit-rent, to the governor, or his agent lawfully authorized to receive the same, one tenth part of all the produce of the lands cultivated by them; and as difficulties and disputes sometimes occurred in reference thereto, Governor Stuyvesant issued a preremptory order, on the 6th of June, 1656, prohibiting the inhabitants of Flatlands, Flatbush, and Brooklyn from removing their crops of grain from the fields until the tythes reserved by their patents had either been taken or commuted for.

The following is a true copy of the commission issued by the governor to the magistrates of the several Dutch towns:

"Fort Amsterdam, April 24, 1660.

" Loving Friendes.

" Out of the nomination presented unto us we have maade choice, as you may knowe bee theese presents off Tunis Guisbert, the which wee for the yeare followinge doe confirme and establish ffor magistraate off the towne called New-Amersforte, requrringe all and every one whome these may concerne to esteeme them as our elected and confirmed magestraate ffor the towne, so after mee respects, I rest, your lovinge friende and Governor.

" P. Stuyvesant."

Form of a Commission from Lieut. Governor Liesler.

" *By the Lieut. Gov. and commander in chieffe, &c. By virtue off the authoritie unto mee, I doe hereby authorise and empower you Jacobus Van De Water to be Clark and Register ffor Kings County, giving you ffull power and authoritie to acte and officiate therein as a Clark may and ought to doe, and this commission to continue till I receive further orders from his Magesty King William. Given under my hand and seal 20 off Dec. 1689.*

" *Jacob Liesler.*"

TOWN OF FLATLANDS.

This town, called by the Dutch New Amersfort, is bounded northerly by Flatbush, southerly by Jamaica Bay, and westerly by Gravesend. Barren Island, situated upon the west side of Rockaway Inlet, and at the mouth of Jamaica Bay, is attached to this town, and the south part of the town is indented by numerous small bays. Along the shore of Jamaica Bay is an extensive salt-marsh, which yields abundance of hay of an inferior quality. With the exception of this marsh, there are no waste lands, the whole being divided into farms well cultivated and productive. The settlement was commenced in 1636, cotemporaneously with Gravesend ; and one of the first grants for land was that for Barren Island, which was at that time a great deal larger than at present, and was also covered with cedar and other timber. The woods have long since disappeared, and much of the island is composed of sand-hills, affording but a scanty subsistence to a few cattle. Ex Governor Van Twiller had a farm in this town at the time of the first settlement, and called Van Twiller's Bowery for a long time after. The village of Flatlands is a very pretty spot, in the centre of which is the Dutch church, originally erected in 1661, and has since been twice rebuilt.

By the Duke's laws. passed in 1665 in relation to public officers, it was declared that the " Overseers shall be eight in number, men of good fame and life, chosen by the plurality of voyces of the freeholders in each town, whereof foure shall remain in

their office two years successively, and foure shall be changed
for new ones every yeare; which election shall preceed the
election of constables, in point of time, in regard the constable
for the yeare ensuing is to bee chosen out of that number which
are dismist from their office of Overseer."—The following
is a copy of the oath, administered to the overseers elect:
" Whereas you are chosen and appointed an Overseer for the
towne of fflatlands, you doe sweare by the Ever-Living-God, that
you will ffaithfully and diligently discharge the trust reposed
in you, in relation to the publique and towne affaires, accordinge
to the present lawes established, without favoure, affection, or
partiality to any person or cause which shall fall under your
cognizance ; and at times, when you shall bee required by your
superiors to attend the private differences of neighbors, you
will endeavor to reconcile them : and in all causes conscien-
tiously, and according to the best of your judgment, deliver your
voyce in the towne meetings of constable and overseers.   So
help you God."   It was the duty of the overseers, together with
the constable, to hold *Town Courts*, for the trial of causes under
five pounds.   They, with the constable, were frequently to admonish the inhabitants " *to instruct their children and servants
in matters of religion and the lawes of the country ;* to appoint an officer to record every man's particular marke, and
see each man's horse and colt branded."   The constable and
two overseers were to pay the value of an Indian coat for each
wolf killed ; and " cause the wolf's head to be nayled over the
door of the constable, there to remaine ; as also to cut off both the
ears, in token that the head is brought in and payd for."

The custom of putting Dutch inscriptions upon tombstones,
which was the general practice in former times, was continued
as late as 1770 ; and some may be seen even of a much later
date in many of the burying-grounds in this county.   For
the last fifty years the English language has been generally
adopted in epitaphs and inscriptions.   Many individuals, and
even families, employ the Dutch language in their ordinary
intercourse with each other at this day.

An extraordinary interview took place on the 2d of April,
1691, between the Governor of New-York and a Sachem of

Long Island, attended by his two sons and twenty other In.
dians. The Sachem, on being introduced, congratulated Governor Slaughter, in an eloquent manner, upon his arrival, and
claimed his friendship and protection for himself and his people;
observing also that he had, in his own mind, fancied his Excellency as a *mighty tall tree*, with wide, *spreading branches;*
and therefore prayed leave to *stoop* under the *shadow* thereof.
Of old (said he) the Indians were a *great and mighty people,*
but now they are reduced to a mere *handful.* He concluded
his visit by presenting the governor with thirty fathoms of wam-
púm, which he graciously accepted, and ordered the Sachem to
attend him again in the afternoon. On taking leave, the youngest son of the Sachem handed to the officer in attendance a bun-
dle of brooms, saying at the same time, " that as Leisler and his
party had left the house very foul, he had been advised to bring
the brooms with him for the purpose of making it clean again."
In the afternoon the Sachem and his party again attended the
governor, who made a speech to them, and on receiving a few
presents, they departed. To exhibit the relative value of some
kinds of property, the following is extracted from an in-
ventory of the effects of a deceased person, which was taken
December 16, 1719: A negro wench and child, valued at £60;
while five milch cows, five calves, three young bulls, and two
heifers, were valued together at £20 only.

From the New-York Gazette of August 13, 1781. "On
the night of the 4th inst. the crew of a rebel whale-boat from
New Jersey landed near Flatlands on Long Island, and robbed
the house of Col. Lott of about six hundred pounds, and carried off with them two of his slaves. They also robbed the
house of Captain Lott of a considerable amount of specie."

The surface of this town is, as its name indicates, a perfect
level; the soil, a light sandy loam, warm and pleasant to till;
and from the skill and industry of its farming population,
yields a large amount over and above the wants of the inhabitants. The people, generally, are conspicuous for habits of
economy; and modern fashions have not yet extinguished their
love of simplicity and substantial comfort. The character of
the inhabitants is tolerably well portrayed by the traveller,

James Stewart, when he says that "some of the farmers of
Long Island are wealthy, but are, in general, contented to live
comfortably and hospitably, with all the ordinary necessaries
and conveniences of life, without ostentation or parade, and
without seeming to care so much, as other classes of people in
this country do, about money." To satisfy any doubts that
may be entertained in regard to the prevalence of good order
and morality in this and the adjoining towns, the compiler
considers the following facts as affording pretty satisfactory
evidence.   Elias Hubbard, Esq. a respectable magistrate of this
town, states that he has held the office of justice of the peace
therein for more than twelve years, and in that period transacted most of the judicial business for Flatlands, Flatbush,
New Utrecht, and Gravesend; and during the whole time had
scarcely a dozen trials, and only two suits in which a jury
was demanded; that another gentleman held the office of justice in the town of Gravesend for eight years, who had, during
that period, but one jury trial; and even in that one case the
difference was compromised by the parties before the jury had
delivered their verdict into court.   Such a pacific temper is
honorable to the people, and creditable to the government under
which they live.

It was upon Barren Island that the notorious pirate,
Gibbs, and his associates in crime, secreted a portion of the
money which they had plundered upon the high seas, part of
which only was recovered.   The names of the pirates were
Charles Gibbs, Thomas Wansley, Robert Dawes, and John
Brownrig.   The last of whom saved his life by becoming a
witness against his companions, who were convicted and executed upon Gibbet Island in the harbor of New-York, in the fall
of 1830.

TOWN OF NEW UTRECHT.

This town is bounded north by Brooklyn and Flatbush, east
by Gravesend, and west and south by Gravesend Bay and the
Narrows opposite Staten Island.   It was settled in 1654 by
about twenty families from Holland, and a few Palatines; who

at first erected a block-house, as well for security against the
natives as from the hordes of wandering savages, robbers, and
pirates, which at that time, and for several years after, infested
the country and adjacent coast to such a degree that the inter-
position of the government became necessary for the more
complete protection of the inhabitants, who, from their position,
were peculiarly exposed to their predatory excursions. The
population of this part of the country increased in a very
moderate degree compared with other places in the vicinity,
in consequence of the constant danger apprehended from the
attacks of enemies; and the first steps taken to organize a separate community was in 1660, when, on application to the
governor, he appointed a scout or constable for the town, together with a secretary or clerk, and an assessor, with power to
make a division among the inhabitants of the land held in
common; to cause the same to be enclosed and cultivated; to
lay out a street or highway through the village; to make
arrangements for the erection of a place of defence, with a mill
in it, and a well by it, at the common charge of the people; to
decide differences among individuals, and do as other subaltern
village courts were accustomed to do. In 1662 a patent was
obtained from Governor Stuyvesant, by which the inhabitants
were not only confirmed in the several purchases and divisions
of land already made, but were vested with the right of pre-
emption of all the remaining lands not included in the patents
previously granted to the adjoining towns. By this patent they
were partially incorporated, with power to build a town, to
elect magistrates subject to the approval of the governor, and to
hold town courts for the trial of causes not exceeding in value
five pounds. On the 15th of August, 1666, two years after
the conquest of New-York, another patent or grant of confirmation was issued by Governor Richard Nicolls, in which the
boundaries of the town are described as follows:

"All that tract of land, together with the several parcels of land which
already have been or hereafter shall be purchased or procured for or on behalf of
the said town, whether from the native Indian proprietors or others, within the
bounds and limits hereinafter set forth and exprest; that is to say, the bounds of
the said town begins from Nayack-Point, stretching alongst the Bay to the land
belonging to ffrancis Bruyin, and from thence run into the woods along the said

ffrancis Bruyin's land to the land heretofore belonging to Robert Pennoyer, near upon a north-east line, twelve hundred Dutch rods; from which they goe again in a direct line to the North River, running three hundred rod, to the north of the whole Hook or Neck of land; and then again alongst the North River to Nay-ack-Point, comprehending within the said bounds or limits twenty lotts as they are now layd out."

The paucity of the records of this town, as well as the great difficulty of decyphering those that remain, render it impossible to obtain from them much information in relation to the early history of its inhabitants; and the little we have been enabled to procure, has been derived from extraneous sources.

It was off the shores of this town that the squadron under the command of Colonel Richard Nicolls, destined as the future English governor of New-York, anchored in 1664; and the first communication addressed to the Dutch governor bears date on board the ship Guyney, riding before Nayack, on the 20th of August of that year. The place at that time known by this name, is near the present site of *Fort Hamilton*, and is a delightful place of residence; being in sight of the ocean, it commands a full view of all the shipping leaving and entering the harbor of New-York, and steam-boats passing down the Bay. It has now become an important military station by the construction of a fort and batteries, and the maintenance of a considerable garrison for the defence of the harbor. Several handsome buildings have likewise been erected, and few situations can boast of a more sublime and beautiful prospect. A handsome Episcopal church, called St. John's, was built a few years since, and adds much to the appearance of the place. In 1836 a company was incorpo-rated for the purpose of making a rail-road from Brooklyn to Fort Hamilton, Bath, and Coney Island, which has not yet been undertaken, but which, if accomplished, would make each of them places of more extensive resort than heretofore. The village of *New Utrecht* is pleasantly situated on a fine plain, nine miles south of Brooklyn, containing a Dutch Reformed Church, and about fifteen dwellings. This church was ori-ginally built in 1700, and was occupied during the revolution, as most of the other Dutch churches were, for a store, hospital, or prison, as suited the convenience of the enemy. The present church was erected nearly upon the site of the old one in 1820. It is a substantial stone edifice, and an important feature in the general aspect of this delightful spot. *Bath House* and village is upon the margin of the Bay, a mile or two south-east from the Narrows or entrance of the harbor, in full view of the military works and the commerce of the Bay. It has for many years been a favorite place of resort for sea-bathing. Here is a large and well-kept public-house, with a lawn in front, beautifully shaded by trees, where the luxury of the ocean breezes may be enjoyed in their fullest extent during the heat of summer. It is the nearest watering-place to New-York, and new accommodations have recently been erected within a short distance of the beach, which commands a most charming prospect of the ocean. It was near this delightful spot that the British army, commanded by Sir William Howe, protected by the guns of their fleet, landed on the 22d of August, 1776, and followed, a few days after, by the disastrous battle of Long Island. South of the hills the surface of the town is perfectly smooth and level; but along the shore of the Narrows it is rough and uneven. The woody ridge that borders the town is the western termination of the range which extends to the eastern part of Southold, and is denominated the ridge of a spine of Long Island. The shad-fishery of the town is one of the most important and valuable in this part of the country, in which many of the inhabitants engage at the proper season, and find it a profitable employment. It is affirmed that ten thousand of these fish have been caught here at a single draught. On digging a few feet below the surface, some years ago, at the Narrows, more than a wagon load of Indian stone arrow-heads were discovered lying together, under circumstances calculated to induce a belief that a large manufactory of that indispensable article of Indian warfare must once have existed at that place. They were of all sizes, and from one to six inches in length; some perfect, others partly finished; together with blocks of the like kind of stone in the same condition as when brought from the quarry. They had the appearance of, and were nearly as hard as ordinary flint; from which not only arrow heads were formed, but axes and other articles of domestic utility. It must ever remain a matter of astonishment how these native artificers, destitute, as . they were, of the knowledge or possession of tools of iron, could form and polish with such exquisite art so many various instruments from so hard a material.

. In the year 1663 one of the clergy of this town was accused before the court of sessions, of having performed the ceremony of his *own marriage*, and that, too, while he had *another wife* living. The reverend gentleman pleaded his own cause, and alleged, by way of excuse for so novel a procedure, that his first wife had eloped from him without cause ; and being minded to take another, he conceived he had as good a right to execute the ceremony for himself as for any other person. This mode of reasoning did not, it seems, satisfy the court. The marriage was declared void, and the delinquent was fined in two hundred guilders, forty beaver-skins ; and also forty guilders more for his insolence and impertinence to the court In addition to the patents before-mentioned, another was granted by Governor Dongan on the 13th of May, 1686, of which the following is an extract :

" THOMAS DONGAN, Lieut. Governor and Vice Admirall of New-Yorke and its dependencies under his Majesty James the II, by the Grace of God of England, Scotland, France and Ireland, King, Defender of the faith, &c. Supreame Lord and proprieter of the Colony and Province of New-Yorke and its Dependencies in America, &c. To all whome this shall come, sendeth greeting. Whereas there is a certain Towne in King's County on Long-Island, commonly called and knowne by the name of New-Utrecht, Beginning at the North-East corner of the Land appurtaining to Mr. Paulus Vanderbeeck called Goanus to the Bounds of Flattbush Pattent, and soe along the said bounds of the said Pattent, and stretching from thence South-East and by South till they meete the Limitts of Flattlands, Gravesend, and the said Utrecht, and from thence along Gravesend Bounds to the Bay of the North River, and soe along the said Bay and River till it meets the Land of the said Paulus Vanderbeeke as according to severall agreements and writeings and the pattent from Governor Richard Nicholls, dated in the year 1666. And whereas applicacon hath to mee been made by persons deputed from the aforesaid Towne of New-Utrecht for- a confirmation of the aforesaid Tract of Land and premises ; now Knowe Yee, that by Virtue of, &c. I have Given, Graned, Ratified and Confirmed, and by these presents doe Give, Grant, Ratify and Confirme unto Jackues Coiteljour, Ruth Joosten, John Verkerke, Hendrick Mathyse, Jolm Kiersen, John Vandyck, Guisbert Thyson, Carel Van Dyck, Jan Van Cleef, Cryn Jansen, Meyndert Coerten, John Hansen, Barent Joosten, Teunis Van Pelt, Hendrick Van Pelt, Lawrence Janse, Gerrit Cornelisson, Dirk Van Stutphen, Thomas Tierkson, Gerrit Stoffelson, Peter Thyson, Anthony Van

Pelt, Anthony Duchaine, Jan Vandeventer, and Cornelis Wynhart, on Behalf of of themselves and their associates, the present Freeholders and Inhabitants of the said Towne of New Utrecht, their Heirs, Successors and Assigns; All and singular, &c. To *have and to hold* the said Tract and parcell of Land with their and every of their appurtenances to them the said Jackues Corteljour, &c.—To bee holden of his said Majesty, his Heires and Successors in free and common Soccage, according to the Tenure of East Greenwich in the County of Kent in his Majestyes Kingdome of England; Yeilding, Rendering, and paying therefor, Yearly and every year, on every five and twentyeth Day of March, foreever, six bushels of good Winter merchantable Wheate att thee Citty of New-Yorke, &c. Given under my hand, and sealed with the scale of the Province att Fortt,James, in New-Yorke, the 13th day of May,'1686, and in the 2nd yeare of his Majestyes Reigne.

"THOMAS DONGAN."

* * * * * * *
* L. S. *
* * * * * * *

" *May it please your Honor.*

"The Atturny Generall hath perused this Pattent, and finds nothing con. tained therein prejudiciall to his Majestyes Interest.

"JA. GRAHAM"

In 1706 the negroes, who had become numerous both in the city of New-York and the adjoining country, were at times so disorderly and dangerous to the peace and safety of the people, that the government was compelled to take measures for restraining their depredations upon the community. A proclamation was issued by the governor for this purpose in the words following

"Whereas I am informed that several negroes in King's County have assembled themselves in a riotous manner, which, if not prevented, may prove of ill con sequence; You, the Justices of the peace in the said county, are hereby required and commanded to take all proper methods for the seizing and apprehending all such negroes as shall be found to be assembled in such manner as aforesaid, or have run away or absconded from their masters or owners, whereby there may be reason to suspect them of ill practices or designs ; and to secure them in safe custody ; and if any of them refuse to submit, then to *fire* upon them, *kill* or *destroy* them, if they *cannot* otherwise be taken ; and for so doing this shall be your sufficient warrant. Given under my hand, at Fort Anne, the 22nd day of July, 1706.

" CORNBURY."

In the clerk's office is the copy of a proclamation issued on the 16th of June, 1780, by James Robinson, a British officer, styling himself captain-general and governor-in-chief in and over the province of New-York ; by which the inhabitants of Long Island are peremptorily required to furnish a sufficiency

of wood for the barrack-yard in New-York ; that King's County shall get *fifteen hundred cords ;* Queen's County *four thousand five hundred;* and the western part of Suffolk County, including Huntington, Islip, Smithtown, and Brookhaven, *three
thousand cords ;* all to be cut and carted to the landing by the
15th of August next ensuing. And the inhabitants of Southold,
Southampton, and Easthampton, were specially required to cut
upon the wood-lands of *William Smith* and *William Floyd,*
(notorious rebels,) in those parts nearest to the landing by Mas-
tic-Neck, *three thousand cords,* to be ready by the 1st of September ; and for which they were to receive at the rate of ten
shillings per cord.   This requisition it was made highly penal
to neglect, and those who did so were severely punished ; instances of which were not uncommon.

On the 26th of May, 1836, an act of the legislature was passed to incorporate the New Utrecht Dock and Steam-Boat Company, but as yet, it is believed, nothing has been done to carry
this very desirable measure into operation.

TOWN OF FLATBUSH.

This town, called by the Dutch Midwout, or Middle Woods,
is bounded north by Brooklyn and Bushwick, and a small part
of Queen's County ; east by Jamaica ; south by Jamaica-Bay,
Flatlands, and Gravesend ; and west by Gravesend ; being of
an irregular shape, containing an area of about seven thousand acres, most of which is under cultivation.   The settlement
of this town was begun in 1651, and the next year a patent or
ground-brief was obtained from Governor Stuyvesant, authorizing the inhabitants to erect a town or plantation, with the usual
privileges of other towns under the Dutch jurisdiction ; and under which the settlers managed their public concerns during the
remainder of his administration. In October, 1667, application
was made to Governor Nicolls for a patent of confirmation and
assurance of their lands and boundaries ; and on the 11th day of
the same month one was issued unto Mr. Joaannes Megapalen-
sis, one of the ministers of the city of New-York, Mr. Cornelius Van Ruyven one of the justices of the peace, Adrian Hege-

man, Jan Snedeger, Jan Stryker, Frans Barents, (Pastor,) Jacob
Stryker, and Cornelius Jause Bougaert, as patentees for and
on behalf of themselves and associates, the freeholders and inhabitants of the said town, their heirs, successors, and assigns,
for the premises described therein, as follows :

" All yt tract wt ye severall parcells of land wh already have or hereafter shall
be purchased or procured for and on ye behalf of ye sd town; whether from ye
native Indian proprietors or others, wt in the bounds and limits hereafter set
forth and expresst ; That is to say, bounded to ye south by ye hills, and to the
north by ye fence lately sett between them and the town of Amsfort, alias Flatlands, beginning at a certain tree standing upon ye Little-Flats, marked by ye
order and determination of severall arbitrators appointed by me, to view and
issue ye difference between ye two towns concerning the same, wh accordingly
they did upon the 17th of October, 1666, and to ye east and west by the common
woodlands, including two tracts heretofore called by ye names of Curler's and
Twillers flatts wh lye to ye East of ye town ; As also a parcell of meadow
ground or valley on ye East-north-east side of Canaresse planting land, and having to ye South ye meadow ground belonging to Amsfort als Flatbush, according
to ye division made by an East line running half a point northerly between them
without variation of ye Compass, and so to go to ye mouth of ye creek or Kill,
which said meadows were on ye 20th of April last by common consent staked
out and by my approbation allowed of."

On the 12th of November, 1685, a further confirmatory patent was executed by Governor Thomas Dongan to the following persons named therein as patentees:

Corneleus Vanderwick,	John Stryker,	John Johnson,
John Okie.	John Ramsden,	Petimus Lewis,
Joseph Hegeman,	Jacob Hendricks,	Okie Johnson,
Art Jansen Vanderbilt,	Direck Vanderfleet,	Jan. Jansen,
Lafford Peterson,	Hendrick Rick,	William Jacobs,
William Guiliamson,	Peter Lott,	Hendrick Hegeman,
Hendrick Williams,	Daniel Polhemus,	Jan Stryker,
Peter Guilliams,	Cornelius Vanderveere,	Garret Lubberts,
Arien Ryers,	Direck Johnson,	Hans Bogaert.
Peter Stryker,	Hooglant Denise,	

The premises are in this patent described, as "A certain town in King's County
known by the name of Middwout, alias Flatbush, the bounds whereof begin att
the mouth of ye fress Kill, and soe along by a certain ditch which lyes betwixt
Armsford and Flatbush meadows, and soe running alongst the ditch and fence
to a certain white oake markt tree ; and from thence uppon a straight line to the
westernmost point of a small island of woodland lying before John Striker's
bridge ; and from thence with a straight line to the north-west hooke or corner
of the ditch of John Okie's meadow ; and from thence alongst the said ditch and
fence to the swamp of the Fresh-Kill, and soe alongst the swamp and hollow of
the aforesaid Kill to the land of Krewler's hooke; then alongst the same to a

marked white oak tree; from thence with a straight line to a black-oake markt tree standing uppon the north-east side of Twilder's Flatts, having a small snip of flatts upon the south-east side of the line, and soe from thence to a white-oak tree standing to the west side of Mustahole upon a small island, leaving a snip of flatts in the Flattlands bounds; and from thence to a certain markt tree or stump standing by the highway which goes to Flattlands upon the Little Flatts, about twenty rod from Flattbush Lotts, and soe alongst the fence six hundred Dutch rodd to the corner of Flattbush fence, and soe alongst by the rear of the Lotts to a sassafras stump standing in Cornelius Jansen's Bowery lott of land; and from thence with straight line to a certain old marked tree or stump standing by the rush-pond under the hills, and so along upon the south side of the hill till it comes to the west end of the long hill, and soe along upon the south side of the said hill till itt comes to the east end of the long hill; and then with a straight line from the east end of the said long hill to a mark'd white-oake tree standing to the west side of the roade near the place called the gale or porte of hills, and so from the east side of the porte or gale along upon the south side of the maine hills as far as Browklin pattent doth extend, and soe along the said hills to the bounds of Jamaica pattent; and from thence with a southerly line to the Kill or crecke by the east of the Plunder's Neck, and soe alongst the said Kill to the sea, as according to the several deeds or purchases from the Indian owners, the patent from Governor Nicolls, and the award between Browkline and the town of Flattbush, as by reference thereto will fully and at large appear."

On the 17th of December, 1654, Governor Stuyvesant, who seems to have exercised entire authority as well in ecclesiastical as in civil and military affairs, gave orders that a house of public worship should be erected in this town, "sixty feet long, thirty-eight wide, and fourteen feet in height below the beams." And on the 9th of February, 1655, he issued his commands that the people of Brooklyn and Amersfort should assist the people of Midwout or Flatbush in getting timber for the house. In September, 1660, those who had the charge of the building reported that it had cost four thousand six hundred and thirty-seven guilders; of which sum three thousand four hundred and thirty-seven had been collected in New Amsterdam, Fort Orange, and on Long Island. Upon which the governor contributed out of the public funds four hundred guilders, leaving a balance of eight hundred against the church. In June, 1656, the governor directed the inhabitants of Brooklyn, Flatbush, and Flatlands, to enclose a place in each of them with palisades for their common defence. In 1660 the Rev. Mr. Polhemus petitioned the governor to have a window placed in the church, which request was granted; and it being reported that the church was indebted to the amount of six hundred and twenty-four guilders, it was ordered to be satisfied out of the treasury as soon as funds should be received. Complaint being made that the minister was inattentive to his calling, attending only once a *fortnight*, and then only for a *quarter of an hour*, giving the people a *prayer* instead of a *sermon*, the governor gave orders *"that he should attend more diligently to his work."* October 1, 1673, an ordinance of the governor and council was published, enjoining it upon the sheriff and constables to take care that the reformed religion be maintained, to the exclusion of all other sects. It is supposed that the first Dutch church erected in this country was one built in the city of New Amsterdam in 1642, although a society had been organized as early as 1629. And the inhabitants of King's County attended religious worship in the city until the church was built in Flatbush as above-mentioned. The Rev. Everardus Bogardus was the first minister, and officiated in the city from 1638 to 1647; and was succeeded by the Rev. Johannis Megapolensis, who continued till the conquest in 1664. The latter gentleman, with John Snedicor and John Stryker, were the persons appointed to superintend the erection of the church here, which stood nearly on the site of the present Dutch church. It was directed to be in the form of a cross; and the rear part of the building was reserved and fitted up for the accommodation of the minister and his family. The original subscription list of this church is still preserved among its records, and shows the names of the inhabitants of the Dutch towns at that time. A church was ordered to be built at Flatlands in 1662, and completed the next year; another was erected in Brooklyn in 1666, which, with the one in Flatbush, being associate churches, constituted but a single congregation, and were under the pastoral care of the same minister. The *Rev. Johannis Polhemus* was employed to preach soon after the erection of the church at Flatbush, with a salary of one thousand and forty guilders, (about four hundred and sixteen dollars,) a-year, raised by assessment upon the towns in which he officiated. He was required by the governor, in March, 1656, to preach every Sunday morning at Midwout; and in the afternoon, alternately at Amersfort and

Brooklyn.   In 1660 the *Rev. Henericus Selwyn* was installed
at Brooklyn by order of the governor, at a salary of six hundred guilders a-year, one-half to be paid by the people, and the
other half by Father-land or Holland.   He resided in New
Amsterdam; and in 1662 the inhabitants of Brooklyn petitioned
the governor that he should be required to reside among them.
The governor agreed to pay a part of his salary, provided he
should preach at the Bowery every Sunday evening.   At the
conquest he returned to Holland.   Mr. Polhemus died June 9,
1666.   In 1667 the churches engaged the *Rev. Casperus Van
Zuren*, who remained about the period of ten years, when he
returned again to Europe.   The *Rev. James Clark* was the
next minister, who remained till 1695; and was followed by
the *Rev. William Lupardus*, who died in 1702.   The *Rev.
Vicentius Antonides* was settled in 1706, and continued till
his death in 1714.   His successor was the *Rev. Bernardus
Freeman*, who remained till the close of life in 1741.   In 1742
the church engaged the services of the *Rev. Johannes Arondius*,
but who, in 1747, removed to New Jersey.   The *Rev. Anthony
Curtenius* was settled as an associate minister in 1730, and
remained till his death in 1750.   The *Rev. Ulpianus Van
Sinderen* was employed in 1747, about which period much
controversy arose in the churches touching the necessity of
foreign ordination; the opinion being entertained by great
numbers, both clergy and laity, that ministers should be ordained in Holland.   This unhappy schism continued for several
years to agitate the churches, to interrupt their peace, and
retard their prosperity.   These dissentions having much
abated, the *Rev. John Caspar Rubel* was in 1760 employed
as a colleague of Mr. Van Sinderen, but was, for some reason,
deposed from the ministry in 1784.   The death of Mr. Van
Sinderen took place in 1796.   The *Rev. Martinus Schoonmaker* was settled in 1785, and continued till his death at an
advanced age in 1824, and with him terminated the practice of
preaching occasionally in the Dutch language.   The Rev.
Peter Lowe became an associate minister of the churches in
1787, where he remained to the end of his life in 1718.
   The church built here in 1663 stood, with occasional repairs,

till 1717, when it was succeeded by another, built of stone. This building fronting the east, had a large double-arched door-way in the centre ; a steep quadrangular roof, with a small steeple rising from the middle. It was sixty-five by fifty feet, the pulpit being in the west side. It was repaired and altered in 1775, at an expense of more than seven hundred dollars ; but in 1794 it was taken down, and the present large and commodious edifice erected, which cost about twelve thousand dollars. It was completed in December, 1796, with a fine bell, imported from Holland, and presented to the church by John Vanderbilt, Esq. In 1818 the churches of Flatbush and Flatlands united in settling the *Rev. Walter Monteith*, who removed in a short time thereafter; and in 1822 was settled their present highly respected clergyman, the Rev. Thomas M. Strong. In 1824 a new congregation was organized, and a church erected in the eastern part of the town, called New-Lotts, from the circumstance of the land having been divided or allotted among the inhabitants at a later period than some other sections of the town. The soil is generally of a good quality, and by careful cultivation is made highly productive. The village of Flatbush, situated about four miles from the City Hall of New-York, is hardly excelled by any other as a place of residence. The spirit of improvement has reached this delightful spot, and several splendid private edifices have been erected, bearing all the insignia of taste and opulence. A softer or more agreeable landscape than is here presented, is seldom met with. Its surface is an inclined plane, elevated about fifty feet above the ocean, toward which the descent is regular and gradual. The *court-house* of the county was erected here in 1685, and the courts continued to be held therein till it was destroyed by fire in 1832. *St. Paul's Episcopal Church* in the village was built in 1836, mainly by the liberality and munificence of one of its citizens, Matthew Clarkson, Esq., and is a neat and handsome edifice. *Erasmus-Hall*, a noble accademical institution here, was incorporated November 20, 1787, being the second in point of time upon Long Island. It has always maintained a high reputation as a place of education, and its pupils are diffused over almost

every part of the United States. The building is not only
spacious and airy, but replete with every convenience, having sufficient grounds about it, filled with ornamental trees
and shrubbery. A little north of the village is an elevation,
called Prospect-Hill, which is estimated to be one hundred feet
above the surrounding country, and from whose summit the
view is sublime and beautiful beyond description.

The *Poor-House* of the County of Kings is located a short
distance from the village. The farm contains sixty acres of
excellent land, which cost three thousand dollars. The main
building is forty-four feet square, with two wings, each sixty
by thirty-five feet. The whole is two stories in height. There
is also a building detached from these, appropriated for patients
laboring under infectious diseases; and likewise another for de-
ranged persons, where these unfortunate individuals are treated with the attention which humanity requires. Surely this
benign establishment does honor to the county, and deserves
the imitation of every other in the state. The soil of this town
is inferior to none other, and improved in the highest degree,
furnishing to the markets of Brooklyn and New-York a
large quantity of produce. Many of the farmers are wealthy,
and there is an appearance of independence and opulence
seldom witnessed in many other places.

TOWN OF RROOKLYN.

This town, the whole of which is now included within the
corporation of the city of Brooklyn, lies upon the extreme western part of Long Island, opposite the southern portion of the
city of New-York, and separated therefrom by the East River,
which is here about three quarters of a mile in width. The
length from north-east to south-west is six miles, and its greatest breadth four miles; giving an area of nine thousand two
hundred acres, most of which has been apportioned into city
lots. The surface is high, broken and stony; and the more
elevated points afford beautiful and romantic sites, many of
which have been built upon, and are not excelled in elegance
by any others in the country. The soil, in common with the whole

county, was originally claimed by the Canarsee Indians, a numerous tribe, inhabiting chiefly the more southern parts of the county, and from whom the title to the lands was procured by the Dutch government. The situation of this tribe rendered them peculiarly obnoxious to invasion from their savage neighbors of the north, and it has been supposed that they were once tributary to the Mohawks, and obliged to conciliate their forbearance by yearly contributions of dried clams and wampum. At the first settlement of the white people, the Indians were persuaded to withhold the accustomed tribute, being promised protection from these unjust exactions of their enemies ; in consequence of which they were unexpectedly assailed by a hostile force, and numbers of them destroyed or taken captive.

The name conferred upon this town by the Dutch was Breucklen, (or broken land ;) and in the act for dividing the province into counties and towns, passed November 1, 1685, it is called *Breucklyn ;* nor does the present appellation appear to have been generally adopted until after the Revolution. Many changes have doubtless taken place upon the shore, and it is believed that Governor's Island was formerly connected with Red Hook Point. It is well known that a short period previous to the war of independence, cattle were driven across what is called Buttermilk Channel, now sufficiently deep to afford passage to vessels of the largest class. The alteration is no doubt in great measure attributable to the vast extension of the wharves on both sides of the river, thereby diverting the course, and increasing the force of the currents. The first European settler in this town is supposed to have been George Jansen de Rapelje, at the Waalboght, or Waaloons Bay, during the Directorship of Peter Minuit, under the charter of the West India Company. In a family record in the possession of Jeremiah Johnson, Esq., it is stated that the first child of Rapelje was Sarah, born in 1625, unquestionably the first white child born upon Long Island. Watson says she was born on the 9th of June, and honored as the first-born child of the Dutch settlers ; also that, in consideration of such distinction, and of her widowhood, she was afterwards presented with a tract of land at the Wallabout. She was twice married ; first

to *Hans Hanse-Bergen,* by whom she had six children, namely, *Michael Hanse, Joris Hanse, Jan Hanse, Jacob Hanse,
Breckje Hanse, and Marytje Hanse.* Her second husband
was *Teunis Guisbertse Bogart,* by whom also she had six children, namely, *Aurtie, Antje, Neelje, Aultje, Catalyntje,* and
Guysbert. The account of this remarkable woman in the
archives of the New-York Historical Society contains the
names of the persons to whom eleven of her children were
married, and the places where they settled. The twelfth,
Breckje Hanse, went to Holland. In the journal of the Dutch
Council in 1656, it is related that "the widow Hans Hanson,
the first-born Christian daughter in New Netherlands, burdened with seven children, petitions for a grant of a piece of meadow, in addition to the twenty morgen granted to her at the
Waale-Boght." There is a tradition in the family, that the Indians, induced by the circumstance of her being the first white
child born here, gave to her father and his brethren, the other
French who followed them, the lands adjacent to the bay;
hence called (says Judge Benson) *Het· Waalé-Boght,* corrupted
to *Wallabout Bay.* A few of the other associates of De Rapelje were *Le Escuyer, Duryee, La Sillier, Cershow, Con-
scillaer. Musserol;* these, with some changes in the mode of
spelling, are still found among us. It appears by the Dutch
records, that in 1634 a part of the land at Red-Hook was the
property of Wouter Van Twiller, being one of the oldest titles
in the town. The earliest deed for land was from Governor
Kieft to Abraham Rycken, in 1638. The oldest grant recorded is to Thomas Besker in 1639. This must be considered as
the commencement of permanent Dutch settlements on Long
Island, and there is no evidence of any direct and systematic
efforts being made for the purpose till this period. In 1641
the governor and council, in order to strengthen their claim to
the island, consented that the English should settle under their
jurisdiction on taking the oath of allegiance to the States-General and the Dutch West India Company. The following
grant for land in 1642 is given as a specimen of conveyances
at that remote period:

"By William Kieft, Director General and Counsellor, about the high and mighty Lords, the States General of the United Low Country, and his highness of Orange, and the Lords Commanders of the privileged West India Company, residing in the New-Netherland, do ratify and declare by these presents, that we, upon the date hereinafter written, did give and grant to Jan Manje, a piece of land, greatly twenty morgan stretching about south-east one hundred and ninety rods inward the woods towards to Sassians maise land—long is the limits of the said maise land fifty rod, and then again to the water side, two hundred and twenty rod, about north north-west, well so northerly and along the strand or water side, seventy rod. Which above-said land is lying upon Long Island, between Andries Hudde and Claes Janse Ruyter. With express conditions, &c. Dated at Fort Amsterdam, in the New-Netherland, the 11th day of September, 1642.

"WILLIAM KIEFT.

"By order of the Lord the Director General, and Counsellor of New-Netherland.

"CORNELIUS VANTIENHOVEN, Sec'ry."

Between the years 1642 and 1647 grants were made by his Excellency Governor Kieft, to different individuals for all the lands on the Brooklyn shore, from Red-Hook Point to the Wallabout Bay, which were generally in the above form. It is believed that a general patent of the town was granted by Governor Stuyvesant in 1657, the same being frequently referred to in conveyances between individuals at an after-period, and is evident from the following extract from the records : "*August 10th*, 1695. *The patentees and freeholders of the town sold unto Stephanus Van Cortlandt the neck of land called Red-Hook, containing, by estimation, fifty acres ; which they state in their deed was formerly given and granted to the town of Broocklyn in the year 1657, by Governor Stuyvesant, the Dutch governor, then, at that time, and since confirmed by the English governors, Nicolls and Dongan.*" On the 18th of October, 1667, a full and ample patent was granted by Governor Richard Nicolls to Jan Everts, Jan Damen, Albert Cornelisson, Paulus Veerbeeck, Michael Eneyl, Thomas Lamberts, Teunis Guisbert Bogart, and Joris Jacobson, as patentees for and on behalf of themselves and their associates, the freeholders and inhabitants of the town of Breucklen, their heirs, successors and assigns, for "all that tract, together with the several parcels of land which already have been or hereafter shall be purchased procured for and on behalf of the said town, whether

59

from the native Indian proprietors, or others, within the bounds and limits hereafter set forth and expressed; that is to say:

" The town is bounded westward on the farther side of the land of Mr. Paulus Veerbeck, from whence stretching south-east, they go over the hills, and so eastward along the said hills to a south-east point which takes in all the lotts behind the swamp; from which said lotts they run north-west to the river and extend to the farm on the t'other side of the hill heretofore belonging to Hans Hansen, over against the Kicke or Looke-out, including within the said bounds and limitts all the lotts and plantations lying and being at the Gowanis, Bedford, Wallaboucht, and the Ferry. All which said parcels and tracts of land and premises within the bounds and limitts aforementioned, described, and all or any plantation or plantations thereupon, from henceforth are to bee, appertaine and belong to the said town of Breucklen ; together with all havens, harbors, creeks, quarryes, wood-land, meadow-ground, reed-laud, or valley of all sorts, pastures, marshes, runs, rivers, lakes, hunting, fishing, hawking, and fowling, and all other profitts, commodities, emoluments, and hereditaments, to the said lands and premises within the bounds and limitts aforesaid belonging, or in any wise appertaining. And withal to have freedome of commonage for range and feed of cattle and horse into the woods, as well without as within these bounds and limitts, with the rest of their neighbors ; as also one-thud part of a certain neck of meadow-ground or valley called Seller's Neck, lying and being within the limitts of the town of Jamaica, purchased by the said town of Jamaica from the Indians, and sold by them unto the inhabitants of Breucklen aforesaid, as it has lately been laid out and divided by their mutual consent and my order, whereunto and from which they are likewise to have free egress and regress as their occasions may require. And that the place of their present habitation shall continue and retain the name of Breucklen, by which name and stile it shall be distinguished and known in all bargains and sales made by them, the said patentees, and their associates, their heirs, successors, and assigns, rendering and paying such duties and acknowledgments as now are or hereafter shall be constituted and established by the laws of this government, under the obedience of his Royal Highness, his heirs and successors. Given under my hand and seal at Fort James, in New-York, on the Island of Manhattat, the 18th of October, 1667.

" RICHARD NICOLLS." L. S.

In 1670 the inhabitants, being desirous of enlarging the bounds of their common lands by extinguishing the Indian claim, applied to Governor Lovelace, and obtained from him the following license:

L. S " Whereas, the inhabitants of Breucklyn, in the West Riding of Yorkshire, upon Long Island, who were seated there in a township by the authority then in being ; and having bin at considerable charges in clearing, ffencing, and manuring their land, as well as building ffor their conveniency ; have requested my lycense for their further security, to make purchase of the said land of some Indians, who lay claim and interest therein. These are to certify all whom it may concerne, that I have and doe hereby give the said inhabitants lycense to purchase their land according to their request, the said Indians concerned appearing before me, as in the law is required, and making their acknowledgments as to fully satisfyed and payed for the same. Given under my hand and seal at ffort James, in New-Yorke, this ffirst of May, in the 22d yeare of his Majestyies reigne, Anno Dom. 1670.

"FRANCIS LOVELACE."

This purchase had been agreed upon the 14th of May, 1670, between the town and five Indian chiefs, and is described in the conveyance as "*all that parcell of land in and about Bedford, within the jurisdiction of Breucklyn, beginning ffrom Hendrick Van Aarnhem's land by a swampe of water, and stretching to the hills; then going along the hills to the port or entrance thereof, and so to Rockaway foot-path, as their purchase is more particularly sett fforth. To have and to hold all the said parcell and tract of land unto Monsieur Machiell Haimelle, Thomas Lambertse, John Lewis, and Peter Darmantier, ffor and on behalfe of the inhabitants aforesaid, their heyres and successors for ever.*" The port or entrance mentioned in this instrument is the valley upon the Flatbush Turnpike, a short distance beyond the three-mile post from Brooklyn Ferry, where a freestone monument has been placed to designate the line between this town and Flatbush. The price paid for the land in and about Bedford was one hundred guilders seawant, half a ton of strong beer, two tons of good beer, three guns, long barrels, with each a pound of powder, and lead proportionable, two bars to a gun, and four match coats.

Notwithstanding the early inhabitants of this town had previously obtained patents for their lands both from the Dutch and English governors, yet Col. Thomas Dongan, who succeeded to that office in 1683, had the address to make them believe that a new patent was necessary to confirm and assure their lands. Accordingly, on the 13th of May, 1686, a new patent was issued, which, after reciting the boundaries of the town as described in former grants, with reference to the charter of Governor Nicolls in 1667, the powers and privileges of which are recognized to the fullest extent, concludes in the following words:

" Now know ye, that I, the said Thomas Dongan, by virtue of the commission and authority derived from me, and power in me residing, have granted, ratified and confirmed, and by these presents do grant, ratifie and confirm, unto Teunis Gysberts, Thomas Lamberts, Peter Jansen, Jacobus Vander Water, Jan Dame, Joris Jacobs, Jeronimus Rapalle, Daniel Rapalle, Jan Jansen, Adrian Bennet, and Michael Hanse, for and on the behalf of themselves and the rest of the present freeholders and inhabitants of the said town of Breucklen, their heirs and assigns for ever, all and singular the afore-recited tract and parcels of land set forth, limited and bounded as aforesaid ; together with all and singular the houses, messuages, tenements, fencings, buildings, gardens, orchards, trees, woods, underwoods, pastures, feedings, common of pasture, meadows, marshes, lakes, ponds, creeks, harbors, rivers, rivulets, brooks, streams, highways and easements whatsoever, belonging or in any wise appertaining to any of the afore-recited tract or parcells of land and divisions, allotments, settlements made and appropriated before the day and date hereof. To Have and To Hold, all and singular, the said tract or parcels of land and premises, with their, and every of their appurtenances, unto the said Teunis Gysberts, Thomas Lamberts, Peter Jansen, Jacobus Vander Water, Joris Jacobs, Jeronimus Rappalle, Daniel Rappalle, Jan Jansen, Adrian Bennet, and Michael Hanse, for and on behalf of themselves and the present freeholders and inhabitants of the town of Breucklen, their and every of their heirs and assigns for ever, as tenants in common without any let, hindrance, molestation, right of survivorship or otherwise, to be holden in free and common socage according to the tenure of East Greenwich, in the county of Kent, in his Majesty's kingdom of England.   Yielding, rendering, and paying therefor yearly, and every year, on the five and twentyeth day of March, for ever, in lieu of all services and demands whatsoever, as a quit rent to his most sacred Majesty aforesaid, his heirs and successors, at the city of New-York, twenty bushels of good merchantable wheat. In testimony whereof, I have caused these presents to be entered and recorded in the Secretary's office, and the seal of the Province to be hereunto affixed this thirteenth day of May, Anno Domini, one thousand six hundred and eighty-six, and in the second year of his Majesty's reign.

" THOMAS DONGAN."

Under this and other patents considerable sums have been paid at different times for quit-rents, for which receipts have been preserved.   June 8, 1713, there was paid to Benjamin Vandewater, treasurer, the sum of £96 7s 1d, for upwards of sixteen years quit-rent.   April 6, 1775, Charles Debevoice, collector of the town, paid to the receiver-general of the colony, twenty bushels of wheat for one year's quit-rent ; and, November 9, 1786, Fernandus Suydam and Charles C. Doughty, two of the trustees, paid to the treasurer of the state, £105 10s. in full for arrears of quit-rent due from the town.   During the early years of the colony, the old ferry was from near the foot of Jerolemon Street to the Breede-Graft, now Broad Street, in the city of New-York; but it is difficult to ascertain the exact period when the old ferry was first established at its pre_sent situation on the Brooklyn side. It appears that, in 1693 John Areson, the lessee of the ferry, complained of his inability to pay the rent of £147, and it was reduced to £140. At this time the ferriage for every *single* person was eight stivers in wampum, or a silver two-pence; each person in company half the above; and if after sunset, double price; each horse or beast one shilling if single, or nine pence in company. In 1698 Rip Van Dam was lessee of the ferry for seven years at £165 per annum. During the Revolution the old ferry was kept by Van Winkle and Bukett, when the usual charge for crossing was sixpence. The corporation of the city of New-York has long claimed and exercised the control of the ferry, which has produced a considerable revenue. August 1, 1795, the ferry from the foot of Main Street was established by William Furman and Theodosius Hunt, on a lease from the cor_poration of New-York. In May, 1814, the first steam-boat com_menced running upon the Fulton Ferry, and at a later period upon the other ferries also.

The town having acquired so great an extent of common land by the purchase of 1670 from the Indians, the inhabitants thought proper to take some order for the division and defending thereof, together with their other lands; accordingly, "At a town meeting held on the 25th day of February, 169⅔ at Breuklyn, in King's County. They Resolved to divide their common lands and woods into three parts, in manner follow_ing, to witt:

"1. All the lands and woods after Bedford and Cripplebush, over the hills to the path of Newlotts, shall belong to the inha_bitants and freeholders of the town of Gowanis, beginning from Jacob Brewer and soe to the uttermost bounds of the limits of New-Utrectht.

"2. And all the lands and woods that lyes betwixt the above-said path and the highway from the ferry towards Flattbush, shall belong to the freeholders and inhabitants of Bedford and Cripplebush.

"3. And all the lands that lyes in common after the Gowanis, betwixt the limits and bounds of Flattbush and New-Utrecht, shall belong to the freeholders and inhabitants of Brooklyn, fred. neck, the ferry and the Wallabout." This proceeding of the town meeting was allowed of by the court of sessions, held at Flatbush on the 10th day of May, 1693.

The following will serve to show the manner in which the inhabitants of this town elected the trustees of their common lands, and the duties of those trustees. " Att a towne meeting held this 29th day off Aprill, 1699, at Breucklyn, by order off Justice Machiel Haussen, ffor to chose townsmen ffor to order all townes busines and to deffend theire limitts and bounds, and to dispose and lay out sum part thereoff in lotts, to make lawes and orders ffor the best off the inhabitants, and to raise a small tax ffor to defray the towne charges, now being or hereaffter to come, to receive townes revenues, and to pay townes debts; and that with the advice off the Justices off this said towne standing the space and time off two years. Chosen ffor that purpose by pluralitie off votes. Benjamin Van de Water, Joores Hanssen, Jan Garretse Dorlant. By order of the inhabitants afforesaid. 1. Vande Water, Clarke."

Although it may not be generally known, yet it is true that the records of this town, from its first settlement to the end of Revolutionary war, were either destroyed during the contest between Britain and her colonies, or carried off at its close by some evil-disposed individual. The person suspected is John Rapalje, Esq., who was in authority here during that period, and against whom an act of attainder was passed in Octotober, 1777, by which his large real estate was confiscated, and himself forced to depart from the country. The necessary consequence is, that we have been deprived of many valuable materials toward a history of the town. It might be expected, that in a state of hostility, every measure would be adopted to afflict an enemy; yet it may be questioned whether abstracting the records of a country is strictly justifiable by the customs and usages of civilized warfare.

The hope is still entertained that these important documents are still in existence, and that by proper exertions they may yet be found in some of the public offices in England.

Some facts of recent occurrence corroborate this opinion, and a correspondence was set on foot a few years since, between General Jeremiah Johnson, supervisor of the town, and Governor De Witt Clinton, which led to examinations in one or more places in London, where it was supposed they might chance to be deposited; but nothing satisfactory was elicited. The subject matter of this correspondence is thought sufficiently important to justify its insertion in this place.

General Johnson to Governor Clinton.

Albany, April 11, 1827.

Sir:

I visited this city, in December last, for the purpose of examining the Dutch records and public papers in the secretary's office, particularly the Dutch patents of the towns of Brooklyn, Flatbush, Flatlands, and Jamaica; and not finding them, the search was continued among the English records to the year 1684, wherein I found that in that year the governor and council of the colony issued an order commanding all the inhabitants of the Dutch towns in the provinces of New-York and New Jersey to bring their Dutch patents and Indian deeds into the Secretary's office in New-York. This measure, in my opinion, accounts for the absence of many papers supposed to be lost. Subsequent to my search in the office in 1826, I had been informed that many old papers relating to this state are in the colonial office in London. And, as the records of the town of Brooklyn were removed during the revolutionary war, I entertain a hope that we may regain them. This information is presented to your Excellency in the expectation that inquiry may be made in London whether the papers alluded to, or authenticated copies, cannot be obtained. The recovery of the records of the town would be of great importance, and the patents and Indian deeds serve to improve the history of the town.

Yours, respectfully,

Jeremiah Johnson, *Supervisor.*

His Excellency, Governor Clinton.

Governor Clinton to Albert Gallatin, Esq.

Albany, 12th May, 1827.

Sir:

I take the liberty of transmitting to you a letter from General Johnson, a respectable citizen of this state, and of requesting your attention to it. According to a report made at the last session of congress, there will be no difficulty on the part of the British government. The papers wanted may be found in the former plantation office. Yours, &c.

De Witt Clinton.

Albert Gallatin, Esq.

Mr. Gallatin to Governor Clinton.

London, 25th August, 1827.

Sir:

I had the honor to receive your Excellency's letter of the 12th May last, enclosing one from General Johnson, and requesting that application might be made to this government for certain town records, and other papers therein-mentioned as having been carried away, and being now either in the colonial office, or that of trade and plantations in London. I regret to say, that after diligent inquiry, and although the various departments here were anxious for the restoration of the papers if they could be found, there is no trace of them whatever. There are two deposites for records and documents connected with the colonies; the office of the Board of Trade and Plantations, and the State Paper office, where the records and papers of the colonial, as well as the home and foreign departments, are kept. There is nothing in the colonial office; and you will perceive by the enclosed letters, that nothing was found in the others; and that it is believed the papers in question were carried away by individuals who never deposited them in any office. Mr. Charles Grant, the writer of two of the notes, is the vice-president of the board of trade, one of the commissioners appointed to treat with me, a gentleman of distinguished merit and obliging disposition. Another search may nevertheless be made, if Gen. Johnson will state the time when the records were carried away, and other circumstances, which may afford a cue to the inquiry.

I have the honor to be, &c.

Albert Gallatin.

His Excellency, De Witt Clinton.

Charles Grant, Esq. to Mr. Gallatin.

London, August 14, 1827.

DEAR SIR:

I have only this morning received the enclosed from Mr. Rice, whose absence from town prevented his sooner transmitting it to me. I regret much the result. As a last hope, I have sent Governor Clinton's letter to the colonial office, that inquiries may be made; but I fear there is little probability of success.

I am, Sir, &c.

C. Grant.

A. Gallatin, Esq.

Spring Rice, Esq. to Charles Grant, Esq.]

MY DEAR GRANT:

On coming down to the office this morning, I found the enclosed, which relates to your communication with me. I enclose it as the best means of answering Mr. Gallatin's request, regretting that we cannot do more to furnish you with the information requested.

Ever and most truly yours,

Spring Rice.

Judge Furman, in speaking of the history of this town, observes, " that its great antiquity is apparent from the fact that the English colonists, who came out from Holland for professed purposes of settlement, were those brought out in 1623, only two years before the settlement of Brooklyn, in the ship of Capt.

Kornelis Jacobse Mey; and that soon after two ships of the West India company brought, as agriculturists, the Walloons, who settled in Brooklyn." In 1646 the town was permitted to choose two magistrates, who were authorized "*to give judgment in all events as they should deem proper, not contrary to the charter of New-Netherlands ;*" and, to give complete effect to their authority, the governor ordered that if any one disobeyed the decision of the magistrates, he should forfeit his right to the lands within the village. This privilege seems not to have been extended to any other town, probably because no other was at that time so populous as to require it.

The first public officer appointed by the Dutch government for this town after its settlement in 1625, was a "*superintendant*," whose duties were to preserve the peace and regulate the police of the town. A few years after the office of superintendant was abolished, and the offices of schout, secretary, and assessor, created. These were, like others, appointed by the governor.

The-inhabitants suffering very much under the arbitrary exercise of power on the part of the government, frequently remonstrated against the same. Finally, a convention of delegates from this, and the other towns under the Dutch government, assembled at New Amsterdam, November 26th, 1663, on an invitation from the governor; where they, on the 11th of December following, entered into a remonstrance against the exclusion of the people from any share in legislation, and generally against their mode of government. The governor and his council sent them no answer, but entered one on the minutes, in which they denied the right of this town, Flatbush, and Flatlands, to send deputies; and protested against the meeting, notwithstanding the same was held at the governor's request. Entertaining a just sense of the responsibility attached to them, the deputies made another, but ineffectual attempt, to obtain a recognition of their rights; and on the 13th of the aforesaid month presented another remonstrance, in which they declared, "that if they could not obtain them from the governor and council, they would be under the necessity of appealing to their superiors, the States-general." The gover-

60

nor, in a fit of anger, dissolved their meeting, and sent them home.

In order to secure the settlement against the depredations of the Indians. the governor, in 1660, required the inhabitants to fortify the town, and remove their families within the enclosure, constructed of palisadoes, set close together and made sharp at the top. This order was probably in consequence of threatened hostility from the northern Indians, who had in 1655 made a descent upon Staten Island, and massacred sixty-seven persons; and the settlement of Gravesend was only saved by the timely arrival of soldiers from New Amsterdam.

It seems to have been enjoined upon the overseers and constables to admonish the inhabitants to instruct their children and servants in matters of religion and the laws of the country. They likewise appointed an officer to record every man's particular mark, and see each man's horse and colt branded. They were to pay the value of an Indian coat for killing a wolf, whose head was to be nailed over the door of the constable. In October, 1675, an order was passed by the court of assize that a fair or market should be yearly kept near the ferry, for the sale of grain, cattle, or other produce of the country; to be held the first Monday, Tuesday, and Wednesday in November; and in the city of New-York the Thursday, Friday, and Saturday following. Although the population of this town has augmented every year since its settlement, yet, previous to the incorporation of the village in 1816, the increase was far from what it has been since; and within the last fifteen years the accession in number and wealth has been greater than for the preceding hundred years. In 1706 the real and personal estate in the town was valued only at £3,112, the tax thereon £41. In 1824 the valuation was over two million six hundred thousand dollars, and the taxes between six and seven thousand. In 1834 the valuation in the city of Brooklyn alone was $7,257,473.

The controversies which have heretofore existed between this town and the corporation of the city of New-York in relation to the ferry across the East River, and the claim of the latter to the soil below high water-mark along the Brooklyn

shore ; and also concerning the title of the United States to a
valuable tract of land at the Wallabout, are of the highest importance to the inhabitants ; but their merits would require
more space for examination than could be afforded in this work.
For an exposition of the legal principles involved in the discussion, the reader · is referred to Judge Furman's notes, and
other productions of the same author.

The history of the Dutch church in this county has been
so fully detailed in our account of Flatbush, that little more is
necessary on that head.

In the year 1659 the inhabitants of the town applied to
Governor Stuyvesant for permission to call a minister for their
congregation, assigning, as a reason for their application, the
badness of the road to Flatbush, the difficulty of attending
divine service at New-York, and the extreme old age and
inability of the Rev. Mr. Polhemus to perform ministerial services at Brooklyn.

The governor deemed this request reasonable, and sent
Nicasius de Sille, Fiscal of New-Netherland, and Martin Kregier, Burgomaster of New-Amsterdam, to this town, as a committee of inquiry, who reported in favor of the application ;
whereupon the request of the inhabitants was granted. They
accordingly prepared a call for the Rev. Henry Solinus, alias
Henricus Selwyn, from Holland ; who was approved of by the
classis of Amsterdam, on the 16th of February, 1660, when the
classis also gave the Rev. Mr. Solinus a dismission, wishing
him a safe and prosperous journey by land and by water to
his congregation in the New-Netherland. The time of the
arrival of this minister is not known. He was installed in the
church on the 3d of September, 1660, in the presence of the
Fiscal and Burgomaster Kregier, by the order of Governor
Stuyvesant, who appears to have been at the head of the ecclesiastical as well as the civil and military government of the
colony. The salary of Mr. Selwyn was fixed at six hundred
guilders ; and the marriage fees, instead of being a perquisite of
his office, were to be accounted for to the church. On the 29th
of October, 1662, it appears that he paid over to the consistory
seventy-eight guilders and ten stivers, for fourteen marriages

performed by him during the year. On the 23d of July, 1664, he returned to Holland; and after his departure, Charles Debevoice, schoolmaster and sexton, was directed to read the prayers in the church, and a sermon from an approved author, every Sabbath, till another should be called. The first Dutch church was built here in 1666, and stood about forty years; when another was erected on the same spot, which was taken down in 1810, and a new and substantial one built in Jerolemon Street. This last, not being found sufficiently large, has lately given place to a more splendid edifice, on nearly the same site.

An Episcopal society existed in this town as early as 1766. It was incorporated in 1787; and in 1795 St. Ann's church was occupied for the first time. This building was of stone, and was superseded by the present elegant edifice in 1824. The first Methodist church was incorporated in 1794; the first Presbyterian church in 1822; the first Baptist church in 1823; the first Roman Catholic church in 1822; and the first Congregational church in 1839.

The first printing-press established in this town was by Thomas Kirk in 1799, from which was issued a weekly newspaper, entitled *"The Courier, and New-York and Long Island Advertiser,"* and was continued for about four years. The first number of the "Long Island Star," by the same gentleman, was issued on the first of June, 1809, and transferred to Alden Spooner in the year 1811.

The most compact part of this town was incorporated into a village on the 12th of April, 1816, which, although violently opposed by a portion of the population, gave a new impulse to the spirit of improvement, and has resulted in raising it to the third rank among the cities of the State of New-York. The village charter authorized the election of five trustees, and those named in the act were Andrew Mercein, John Garrison, John Doughty, John Seaman, and John Dean. This charter was several times amended and enlarged as the increase of population required, until it became indispensable to endow the place with the name and privileges of a city. On the 8th of April, 1834, the whole territory of the town was incorporated under the name of the " *City of Brooklyn*," and its inhabitants a body corporate and politic, by the style of " *The Mayor and Common Council of the City of Brooklyn.*" It is divided into nine wards; the powers of the corporation are vested in a mayor, and a board of aldermen composed of two, elected annually from each ward. These have the appointing of most of the subordinate officers of the city. *Bedford*, upon the eastern part of the town, was formerly a separate hamlet; but is now so far swallowed up by the progress of improvement, as to have nearly lost its identity. *Gowanus* is that part of Brooklyn which joins Flatbush and the waters of the bay, consisting principally of a low tract of salt marsh, ponds, and creeks, over which a highway and bridge have been constructed, and is fast becoming more valuable as the city advances in that direction.

The *Wallabout* is a part of Brooklyn north-east from the ferry, and rendered famous in the revolution from having been the scene of the most heart-rending sufferings of many thousand American citizens, confined on board the prison-ships stationed in the bay. The United States possess about forty acres, including the site of the old mill-pond. Here have been erected a spacious navy-yard, public store-houses, machine-shops, and two immense edifices, in which the largest ships are protected from the weather, while building. On the opposite side of the bay has lately been constructed the *Naval Hospital*, which is not only splendid, but magnificent. The " *Apprentices' Library Association* " was formed in 1824, the corner-stone of which was laid by the Marquis La Fayette during his last visit to America in that year. The library is now in the Brooklyn Lyceum; and the building having become the property of the city, is appropriated for public offices, and the holding of courts, being denominated the " *City Buildings.*" The *Brooklyn Lyceum* was instituted October 10, 1833. The edifice is a beautiful specimen of architecture, composed of granite, and every way adapted to the purpose of its projection. The objects of this institution are intellectual and moral improvement, by means of certain specified committees, and by gratuitous public lectures. A course of lectures by gentlemen of the city of New-York was commenced the 7th of November, 1833;

and has been varied occasionally by essays, principally from the pens of ladies. The Brooklyn Collegiate Institute for young ladies was incorporated in 1829. The building is large and beautifully located near the East River. It flourished for a few years, and gave promise of permanent utility; but from want of sufficient patronage, the school has been given up. The " *City-Hall*," which was commenced a few years since upon a magnificent scale, has been interrupted in its progress, and doubts are entertained of its completion, at least upon the plan and to the extent originally contemplated.

This town had a full share of the military operations during the Revolutionary war; and was for a long time in the possession of the British army. It is covered with the remains of fortifications, which were thrown up by the Americans and English for their defence against each other. In this town was fought the most sanguinary part of the battle of Long Island, August 27, 1776; which took place on the retreat of the American army within their lines, and the attempt of a portion of them to ford the mill-pond at Gowanus; in which attempt nearly the whole of a regiment of young men from Maryland were cut off.

Many of the minor events connected with this battle and the Revolutionary contest are fast sinking into the shades of oblivion; the compiler has therefore thought proper to give place to the following piece of history, not with an idea that he can immortalize any event which he relates; but with a hope that his efforts will call forth some nobler pen to do justice to the memories of many of the almost forgotten heroes of those hard-fought battles and arduous contests. In the battle above-mentioned part of the British army marched down a lane, or road, leading from the Brush tavern to Gowanus, pursuing the Americans. Several of the American riflemen, in order to be more secure, and at the same time more effectually to succeed in their designs, had posted themselves in the high trees near the road. One of them, whose name is not now known, shot the English Major Grant; in this he passed unobserved. Again he loaded his deadly rifle, and fired; another English officer fell. He was then discovered, and a platoon ordered to advance, and fire into the tree; which order was immediately carried into execution, and the rifleman fell to the ground, dead. After the battle was over the two British officers were buried in a field near the place, and their graves fenced in with some posts and rails, where their remains still rest. But, for "an example to the rebels," they refused to the American rifleman the rites of sepulture, and his body lay exposed on the ground till the flesh was rotten, and torn off the bones by the fowls of the air. After a considerable length of time, in a heavy gale of wind a large tree was uprooted; in the cavity formed by which some friend to the Americans, notwithstanding the prohibition of the English, deposited the soldier's skeleton to mingle in peace with its kindred earth.

In the year 1776 and the subsequent years, there was stationed at the Wallabout several ships for the reception and confinement of American seamen taken prisoners by the enemy. The circumstances in relation to this event are so interesting, and are so intimately connected with the Revolutionary history of the town, that we cannot omit giving a brief account of some of the more prominent ones, which have been derived from the pen of Jeremiah Johnson, Esq., mayor of the city of Brooklyn, a gentleman of great intelligence and research, and whose memory extends back to the period to which the facts themselves relate. The qualifications of this respectable individual, and the large share of public confidence enjoyed by him, are evinced by the fact of his having held the office of supervisor of tho town for more than forty years in succession. He has, moreover, represented the county in the legislature, and risen from a private in the militia to the rank of major-general. He has also been a judge of the common pleas; and on the 3d of April, 1814, was appointed to the command of the 22d brigade of New-York infantry, consisting of one thousand seven hundred and fifty men, who were stationed at Fort-Green during the late war.

The following particulars were communicated by him to the editor of the "Naval Magazine," for September, 1836:

" The subject of the naval prisoners, and of the British prison-ships stationed at the Wallabout during the revolution, is one which cannot be passed by in silence. From printed journals published in New-York at the close of the war, it appears that eleven thousand five hundred American prisoners had died on board the prison ships. Although the number is very great, still if the number who perished had been less, the commissary of naval prisoners, David Sprout, Esq , and his deputy, had it in their power, by an official return, to give the true number exchanged, escaped, and dead. Such a return has never appeared in the United States. This man returned to America after the war, and resided in Philadelphia, where he died. He could not have been ignorant of the statement published here on this interesting subject. We may therefore infer, that about that number perished in the prison ships. A large transport, named the *Whitby*, was the first prison ship anchored in the Wallabout. She was moored near " Remsen's Mill," about the 20th of October, 1776, and was crowded with prisoners. Many landsmen were prisoners on board this vessel; she was said to be the most sickly of *all* the prison ships. Bad provisions, bad water, and scanted rations were dealt to the prisoners. No medical men attended the sick. Disease reigned unrelieved, and hundreds died from pestilence, or were starved, on board this floating prison. I saw the sand-beach between a ravine in the hill and Mr. Remsen's dock become filled with graves in the course of two months; and before the 1st of May, 1777, the ravine alluded to was itself occupied in the same way. In the month of May of that year two large ships were anchored in the Wallabout, when the prisoners were transferred from the Whitby to them. These vessels were also very sickly, from the causes before stated. Although many prisoners were sent on board of them, and were exchanged, death made room for all. On a Sunday afternoon, about the middle of October, 1777, one of the prison ships was burnt; the prisoners, except a few, who, it was said, were burnt in the vessel, were removed to the remaining ship. It was reported at the time that the prisoners had fired their prison'; which, if true, proves that they preferred death, even by fire, to the lingering sufferings of pestilence and starvation. In the month of February, 1778, the remaining prison ship was burnt at night; when the prisoners were removed from her to the ships then wintering in the Wallabout. In the month of April, 1778, the Old Jersey was moored in the Wallabout, and all the prisoners (except the sick) were transferred to her. The sick were carried to two hospital ships, named the Hope and Falmouth, anchored near each other about two hundred yards east from the Jersey. These ships remained in the Wallabout until New-York was evacuated by the British. The Jersey was the receiving-ship—the others, truly, the ships of Death! It has been generally thought that all the prisoners died on board of the Jersey. This is not true ; many may have died on board of her who were not reported as sick : but all the men who were placed on the sick-list were removed to the hospital ships, from which they were usually taken, sewed up in a blanket, to their *long home*.

After the hospital ships were brought into the Wallabout, it was reported that the sick were attended by physicians; few, very few, however, recovered. It was no uncommon thing to see five or six dead bodies brought on shore in a single morning ; when a small excavation would be made at the foot of the hill, the bodies be cast in, and a man with a shovel would cover them by shovelling sand down the hill upon them. Many were buried in a ravine on the hill; some on the farm. The whole shore from Rennie's Point to Mr. Remsen's dock-yard was a place of graves ; as were also the slope of the hill near the house, the shore

from Mr. Remsen's barn along the mill-pond to Rapelje's farm and the s
island, between the flood-gates and the mill-dam; while a few were burie
the shore, the east side of the Wallabout. Thus did *Death* reign *here*, from
until the peace. The whole Wallabout was a sickly place during the war.
atmosphere seemed to be charged with foul air from the prison ships, and
the effluvia of the dead bodies washed out of their graves by the tides. We
ourselves examined many of the *skulls* lying on the shore; from the teeth,
appear to be the remains of men in the prime of-life. A singularly darin
successful escape was effected from the Jersey about 4 o'clock one afternoc
December, 1780. The best boat of the ship had returned from New-York,
left fastened at the gangway, with the oars on board. It was stormy
wind blew from the north-east, and the tide ran flood. A watch-word, was g
and a number of prisoners placed themselves between the ship's waist anc
sentinel; at this juncture four eastern captains got on board the boat, which
cast off by their friends. The boat passed close under the bows of the ship
was a considerable distance from her before the sentinel on the forecastle
the alarm, and fired 'at her. The boat passed Hell-Gate, and arrived sa
Connecticut next morning.

Suffice it to say, in conclusion, that here more than eleven thousand Ame
citizens and soldiers perished, many of whose names are unknown, and w
sufferings are buried in oblivion! They lingered where no eye of pity wit
ed their agony; no voice administered consolation'; no tongue could praise
patriotic devotion, or friendly hand be stretched out for their relief. He
pass the weary day and night, unvaried, except by new scenes of painful e
rance, and new inflictions of hopeless misery. The hope of death was to
the only consolation which their situation afforded.

----

close of the war,
prisoners had died on
real, still if the number
..., David Sprout,
return to give the true
} never appeared in
war, and resided in
aint of the statement
re infer, that about
" named the *Whitby*.
She was moored near
as crowded with prison-
, she was said to be
bad water, and scanted
added the sick. Disease
r were starved, on board
vine in the hill and Mr.
two months; and be-
self occupied in the same
ps were anchored in the
the *Whitby* to them.
fore stated Although
xchanged, death made
on October, 1777, one of
who, it was said, were
. l was reported at the
if t be proves that they
o pestilence and starva-
rison ship was burnt at
sh ps then wintering in
Jersey was moored in the
....sf rred to her. The
nd Falmouth, anchor
e Jersey. These ships
el by the British. The
ps of Death! It has
ol the Jersey. This is
no reported as sick
moved to the hospital
a blanket, to their long

at it was reported that
wever, recovered. It
ught on shore in a sin
the foot of the hill, the
r them by shovelling
rine on the hill; some
l Remsen's dock yard

APPENDIX.

APPENDIX

No. I.

Capitulation by the Dutch to the English.   Referred to at page 96.

THESE Articles following were consented to by the Persons here under subscribed, at the Governour's Bowery, August the 27th, Old Style, 1664.

I. WE consent That the States-General, or the West India Company, shall freely injoy all Farms and Houses, (except such as are in the Forts,) and that within six months they shall have free Liberty to transport all such Arms and Ammunition as now does belong to them, or else they shall be paid for them.

II. All Publique Houses shall continue for the Uses which they are for.

III. All people shall continue free Denizens, 'and shall injoy their Lands, Houses, Goods, wheresover they are within this Country, and dispose of them as they please.

IV. If any Inhabitant have a Mind to remove himself, he shall have a Year and six Weeks from this day, to remove himself, Wife, Children, Servants, Goods, and to dispose of his lands here.

V. If any Officer of State, or Publique Minister of State, have a Mind to go for England, they shall be transported Fraught free, in his Majesty's Frigotts, when these Frigotts shall return thither.

VI. It is consented to, that any People may freely come from the Netherlands, and plant in this Colony; and that Dutch Vessels may freely come hither, and any of the Dutch may freely return home, or send any Sort of Merchandize home in Vessels of their own Country.

VII. All Ships from the Netherlands, or any other Place, and Goods therein, shall be received here, and sent hence, after the manner which formerly they were, before our coming hither, for six Months next ensuing.

VIII. The Dutch here shall injoy the Liberty of their Consciences in divine Worship and Church Discipline.

IX. No Dutchman here, or Dutch Ship here, shall upon any occasion be pressed to serve in War against any Nation whatsoever.

X: That the Townsmen of the Manhattans shall not have any Soldiers quartered upon them, without being satisfied and paid for them by the Officers; and that at this present, if the Fort be not capable of lodging all the Soldiers, then the Burgomasters, by his Officers, shall appoint some Houses capable to receive them.

XI. The Dutch here shall injoy their own Customs concerning their Inheritanecs.

XII. All Publique Writings and Records, which concern the Inheritances of any People, or the Reglement of the Church or Poor, or Orphans, shall be carefully kept by those in whose Hands now they are, and such Writings as particularly concern the States-General, may at any Time be sent to them.

XIII. No Judgment that has passed any Judicature here, shall be called in Question; but if any conceive that he hath not had Justice done him, if he apply himself to the States-General, the other Party shall be bound to answer for the supposed Injury.

XIV. If any Dutch, living here, shall at any Time desire to travaile or traffique into England, or any Place, or Plantation, in obedience to his Majesty of England, or with the Indians, he shall have (upon his Request to the Governor,) a Certificate that he is a free Denizen of this Place, and Liberty to do so.

XV. If it do appeare that there is a publique Engagement of Debt by the Town of the Manhattoes, and a Way agreed on for the satisfying of that Engagement, it is agreed that the same Way proposed shall go on, and that the Engagement shall be satisfied.

XVI. All inferior Civil Officers and Magistrates shall continue as now they are, (if they please,) till the customary Time of new Elections, and then new ones to be chosen by themselves ; provided that such new chosen Magistrates shall take the Oath of Allegiance to his Majesty of England before they enter upon their Office.

XVII. All Differences of Contracts and Bargains made before this Day, by any in this Country, shall be determined according to the Manner of the Dutch.

XVIII. If it do appeare that the West India Company of Amsterdam do really owe any Sums of Money to any Person here, it is agreed that Recognition and other Duties payable by Ships going for the Netherlands, be continued for 6 Months longer.

XIX. The Officers Military, and Soldiers, shall march out with their Arms, Drums beating, and Colors flying, and lighted Matches; and if any of them will plant, they shall have fifty Acres of Land set out for them ; if any of them will serve as Servants, they shall continue with all Safety, and become free Denizens afterwards.

XX. If at any Time hereafter the King of Great Britain, and the States of the Netherland, do agree that this Place and Country be re delivered into the Hands of the said States, whensoever his Majestie will send his Commands to re-deliver it, it shall immediately be done.

XXI. That the Town of Manhattans shall choose Deputyes, and those Deputyes shall have free Voyces in all publique Affairs, as much as any other Deputyes.

XXII. Those who have any Property in any Houses in the Fort of Aurania, shall (if they please) slight the Fortifications there, and then enjoy all their Houses, as all People do where there is no Fort.

XXIII. If there be any Soldiers that will go into Holland, and if the Company of West India in Amsterdam, or any private Persons here, will transport them into Holland, then they shall have a safe Passport from Colonel Richard Nicolls, Deputy-Governor under his Royal Highness; and the other Commissioners, to defend the Ships that shall transport such Soldiers, and all the Goods in them, from any Surprizal or Acts of Hostility, to be done by any of his Majestie's Ships or Subjects. That the Copies of the King's Grant to his Royal Highness and the Copy of his Royal Highness's Commission to Colonel Richard Nicolls, testified by two Commissioners more, and Mr. Winthrop, to be true Copies, shall be delivered to the Hon. Mr. Stuyvesant, the present Governor, on Munday next by Eight of the Clock in the Morning, at the Old Miln; and these Articles consented to, and signed by Colonel Richard Nicolls, Deputy-Governor to his Royal Highness; and that within two Hours after the Fort and Town called New Amsterdam, upon the Isle of Manhatoes, shall be delivered into the Hands of the said Colonel Richard Nicolls, by the Service of such as shall be by him thereunto deputed, by his Hand and Seal.

John De Decker,	Robert Carr,
Nich. Verleet,	Geo. Cartwright,
Sam. Megapolensis,	John Winthrop,
Cornelius Steenwick,	Sam. Willys,
Oloffe Stevens Van Kortlant,	Thomas Clarke,
James Cousseau,	John Pinchon.

I do consent to these articles,

RICHARD NICOLLS.

No. II.

List of Governors, Lieutenant-Governors, and Presidents of the Council, who have administered the Government of the Colony and State of New-York from its settlement to the present time.

DUTCH.

Peter Minuet, Director-General,	1625 to 1629
Wauter Van Twiller,	1629 to 1638
William Keift,	1638 to 1647
Peter Stuyvesant,	1647 to 1664
Anthony Colve,	from October 14, 1673, to February 9, 1674

ENGLISH.

Richard Nicolls,	from September 7, 1664 to 1667
Francis Lovelace,	1667 to 1673
Edmund Andross,	1674 to 1681
Anthony Brockholst,	1681 to 1683
Thomas Dongan,	1683 to 1688
Francis Nicholson,	1688 to 1689
Jacob Liesler, (Lieutenant-Governor,)	1689 to 1691
Henry Slaughter, a few months in	1691
Richard Ingolsby, (Lieutenant-Governor,)	1691 to 1692
Benjamin Fletcher,	1692 to 1698
Richard, Earl of Bellamont,	1698 to 1701
John Nanfan, (Lieutenant-Governor,)	1701 to 1702
Edward Hyde, (Lord Cornbury,)	1702 to 1708
Lord Lovelace, (Baron of Hurley,)	1708 to 1709
Richard Ingolsby, (Lieutenant-Governor,)	few months in 1709
Gerardus Beekman, (President,)	1709 to 1710
Robert Hunter,	1710 to 1718
Peter Schuyler, (President,)	1718 to 1720

William Burnet, - - - - - - -	1720 to 1728
John Montgomerie, - - - - - -	1728 to 1731
Rip Van Dam, (President,) - - - - -	1731 to 1732
William Cosby, - - - - - -	1732 to 1736
George Clarke, - - - - - - -	1736 to 1743
George Clinton, - - - - - - -	1743 to 1753
James De Lancey, (Lieutenant-Governor,) in	1753
Danvers Osborn, a few days in - - -	1753
James De Lancey, (Lieutenant-Governor,)	1753 to 1755
Charles Hardy, - - - - - -	1755 to 1757
James De Lancey, (Lieutenant-Governor,)	1757 to 1760
Calwallader Colden, (Lieutenant-Governor,)	1760 to 1762
Robert Monkton, - - - - - -	1762 to 1763
Cadwalader Colden, (Lieutenant-Governor,)	1763 to 1765
Henry Moore, - - - - - - -	1765 to 1769
Cadwalader Colden, (Lieutenant-Governor,) till	1770
John Murray, Earl of Dunmore, - - -	1770 to 1771
William Tryon, - - - - - -	1771 to 1775

(The colonial government was suspended in May, 1775; from which time, till April, 1777, New-York was governed by the provincial congress; Nathaniel Woodhull, president of the congress in August, 1775. The state-government went into operation after the adoption of the constitution, the 20th of April, 1777.)

State Governors.

George Clinton, from - - - - - -	1777 to 1795
John Jay, - - - - - - - -	1795 to 1801
George Clinton, - - - - - - -	1801 to 1804
Morgan Lewis, - - - - - - -	1804 to 1807
Daniel D. Tompkins, - - - - - -	1807 to 1817
John Taylor, (Lieutenant-Governor,) in	1717
De Witt Clinton, - - - •	1817 to 1822
Joseph C. Yates, - - - - - - -	1822 to 1824
De Witt Clinton, - - - - - - -	1824 to 1828
Nathaniel Pitcher, (Lieutenant-Governor,) - -	1828 to 1829
Martin Van Beuren, three months in -	1829
Enos T. Throop, (Lieutenant-Governor,)	1829 to 1830
Elected Governor, - - - - - - -	1830 to 1832
William L. Marcy, - - - - -	1832 to 1839
William H. Seward, - - - - -	1839

The Terms of the Courts of Common Pleas.

IN SUFFOLK. { First Tuesday in January, last Tuesday in } at River-Head.
{ May, first Tuesday in October. }

IN QUEENS. { First Tuesday in June, last Tuesday in Oc- } at N. Hempstead
{ tober, third Tuesday in February. }

IN KINGS. { Third Tuesday in January, third Tuesday in April, third Tues-
{ day in July, third Tuesday in October. At Brooklyn.

CITY OF BROOKLYN. { First Tuesday of every month at the Exchange Build-
{ ings.

Brooklyn Municipal Court, at the City Buildings, every day, except Sundays.

No. III.

Treaty of Hartford, 1650 ; mentioned at pages 87 and 322.

Articles of agreement made and conluded at Hartford, upon Conecticut, September 19, 1650, between delegates of the Commissioners of the United English colonies, and the delegates of Peter Stuyvesant, governor-general of New Netherlands—concerning the bounds and limits between the English United Colonies and the Dutch province of New Netherlands.

We agree and determine as follows :

That upon Long Island, a line run from the westernmost part of Oysterbay, and so in a straight and direct line to the sea, shall be the bounds between the English and the Dutch there, the easterly part to belong to the English, and the westernmost part to the Dutch.

The bounds upon the main to begin upon the west side of Greenwich Bay, being about four miles from Stamford, and so to run a westerly line twenty miles up into the country, and after, as it shall be agreed by the two governments of the Dutch and New-Haven, provided that said line run not within ten miles of Hudson's River, and it is agreed that the Dutch shall not, at any time hereafter, build any house or habitation within six miles of the said line. The inhabitants of Greenwich to remain (till further consideration thereof be had,) under the government of the Dutch.

That the Dutch shall hold and enjoy all the lands in Hartford that they are actually in possession of, known or set out by certain marks and bounds, and all the remainder of the said lands, on both sides of Connecticut River, to be and remain to the English there.

And it is agreed, that the aforesaid bounds and limits, both upon the island and main, shall be observed and kept inviolable, both by the English of the united Colonies and all the Dutch nation, without any encroachment or molestation, until a full determination be agreed upon in Europe, by mutual consent of the two States of England and Holland. And in testimony of our joint consent to the several foregoing conditions, we have hereunto set our hands this 19th day of September, 1650.

SIMON BRADSTREET,   THOMAS WILLET,
THOMAS PRINCE,   GEORGE BAXTER.

No. IV.

Remonstrance of the several towns in the Dutch territory, to the Governor and council, in 1653, a part of which is quoted at pages 80, 81 and 82; the remainder is as follows :

" Wherefore, although with all humility, we will declare freely our anxious fears by which we some time since have been alarmed and discouraged in our labors and callings, so that it is not in our power to act with that rigor and affection in promoting the welfare of our country as well as before, although in a wilderness, for the following reasons :

1. Our apprehension to see an arbitrary government established among us, which is contrary to the first intention and genuine principles of every well-regulated government, to wit : that one or more should arrogate the exclusive power

to dispose arbitrarily of the life and property of any individual, and this in virtue or under pretext of a law or order which he might fabricate, without the consent, knowledge, or approbation of the whole body, their agents or representatives.

Thus new laws relative to the lives and property of the inhabitants, contrary to the privileges of the Netherlands, and odious to every free-born man, and principally so to those whom God had placed under a free government on new settled lands, who are entitled to claim laws which are as near resembling those of Netherland as possible.

It is our humble opinion that it is one of our privileges, that in making new laws, our explicit consent, or that of our representatives, is unavoidably required for their adoption.

2. Casually we are every year full of apprehension that the natives of the land may commence a new war against us, by the murders they commit under the pretext that they have not been paid for their land, which creates many calamities and discourages settlers, and even contributes to lessening the number and industry of the remainder.

It has, thus far, not been in our power to discover the truth hereof, or ascertain to what tribe these murderers belong. It is too often disregarded as committed by savages who reside at a considerable distance. But, be that as it may, it fills us with daily anxiety, so that we are compelled to look out for own defence, as we cannot discover in what manner our lives and property shall be protected, except by our own means.

3. That officers and magistrates, although personally, from their qualifications, deserving similar offices, are appointed contrary to the laws of the Netherlands, to many offices, without consent or nomination of the people, which nevertheless are the most concerned in the choice.

4. That many orders and proclamations made before, without approbation of the country in the days of yore, by the authority of the Director-General and council, either of former days or actually ruling, which remain obligatory, although we are ignorant of their force, and become transgressors from ignorance without knowing it, by which we are exposed to many dangers and troubles, and may occasion our own ruin without knowing it.

5. On the promises of grants and general letters of privileges and exemptions, various plantations have been made at a great expense of the inhabitants in building their houses, making fences, &c., the cultivation of the land, and principally so by those of Middleburgh, and Middlewout, with their neighborhoods and other places.

Many single farms were taken up by persons who solicited a deed of such a grant, but were always delayed and disappointed, to their great loss, which creates a suspicion that some innovations are in contemplation, or that there is a lurking intention to alter former stipulations.

6. That to some individuals, large quantities of land are granted for their private profit, on which a large village of 20 or 30 families might have been established, which, in the end, must effect an immense loss to the Patroons, with regard to their revenues, as well now as in future, and which must weaken the strength of the Province, and disable that part of the country to provide in or contribute to its defence, and that of its inhabitants, except we or our commonalty are enabled to effect it.

7. As we exert ourselves to reduce all our griefs within six points, which we

confidentially explained, as we renew our allegiance, in the hope that these will soon be redressed, agreeably to the privileges of our country, when all discontents shall cease, a mutual harmony be restored, and our anxiety relieved.

We apply therefore to your wisdom to heal our sicknesses and pains. We shall remain thankful, and consider any further application needless, as we otherwise should be compelled to do.

Upon which, humbly soliciting your honors' answer on every point or article in such a manner that we may remain satisfied, or proceed further, &c., as God shall direct our steps.

Your Honors' suppliant Servants."

Done December 11, 1653.

No. V.

Narrative and remonstrance of the Deputies previously assembled at Hempstead, in March, 1665, as mentioned at page 108, relating to the different apprehension of some matters then and there transacted.

" His Majesty having employed his ships of war, and sent a considerable number of soldiers to reduce these parts of America to his obedience, the present government was readily received, and peaceably settled on Long Island, by virtue of his Majesty's letters patent, made and granted by his Royal Highness James, Duke of York and Albany, bearing date the twelfth day of March, in the sixteenth of the reign of our sovereign Lord King Charles the II, published a Gravesend, on Long Island, aforesaid, about the middle of August following, in the audience of a great number of the inhabitants thereof, by the Right Honorable Col. Richard Nicolls, deputy governor under his royal highness. At which time and place Governor Winthrop, being then present, openly declared that their colonies claimed no jurisdiction de jure over Long Island; but what they had done was for the welfare, peace, and quiet settlement of his Majesty's subjects, as they were the nearest court of record to them under his Majesty; but now his Majesty's pleasure was fully signified by his letters patent, as above said, their jurisdiction over them ceased and became null; whereupon our honorable Governor then replied also, that he would not put out any of the officers which Connecticut had set up in the civil state, but confirm them under his power to act in every town, until a convenient season served to convene deputies from all the towns on the island, when and where laws were to be enacted and civil officers established.

Shortly after, at another meeting of our honorable governor and Connecticut Commissioners, several persons were there confirmed by him in civil authority, by his writing under his hand, which they published in several towns where they were to collect rates and former dues for Connecticut, unto which power these eastern towns readily and willingly obeyed and submitted for the space of six months at least.

In March following, we were convened, being deputies chosen by the several towns in a general assembly held at Hempstead, where his Majesty's aforesaid patent was first read, and a commission from his royal highness the Duke of York, empowering and investing the aforesaid Col. Richard Nicolls, with authority to put the contents of the said patent into practice and execution, who declared unto us that our first business should be to decide some, and to compose

other differences which were on float before he came to the government, according to the manner and form in practice since our late acknowledgment of the Connecticut authority ; but that he had prepared a body of general laws hereafter to
be observed; the which were delivered to us, and upon perusal we found them to
be a collection of the laws now in practice in his Majesty's other colonies in
New England, with abatement of the severity against such as differ in matters
of conscience and religion.

We proceeded to object against some and propose other clauses in the laws ;
whereupon several amendments were made with further assurance from the governor, that when any reasonable alteration should be offered from any town to
the sessions, the Justices should tender the same at the assizes, and receive satisfaction therein, the truth and effects whereof we have since found.

The Governor further declared that for his own part he expected no benefit for
his labors out of the purses of the inhabitants, not so much as to defray his charge
and expenses at the courts ; but that it was absolutely necessary for him to establish a form and rule of county rates, to support the public charge; whereupon
we pitched upon the form and rule at this day observed in Connecticut, which
was known to some of those present.

In the next place we conceived that two hundred pounds yearly might defray
the public charge; to which the Governor replied that he would touch none of the
public money, but that the high sheriff from year to year should cause the same
to be collected, and give, at the expiration of his office, in open court at the general assizes, an account of his receipts and disbursements.

If it should happen the rate was more than the charge of his year, the overplus
should remain to the use of the country the next year ; if the charge was greater
than the rate, the country was obliged to bear it with an additional rate ; in all
which transactions we acted with sincerity of heart, according to the best of our
understanding, and in obedience to his Majesty's authority established by his letters patent over us.

Moreover we appointed a committee to attend the governor for his resolution,
whether we might not, according to the custom of the other colonies, choose our
magistrates: We received answer by our deputies, that they had seen the instruction of his Royal Highness, wherein the choice of all the offices of Justice
was solely to be made by the Governor, and some of us do know that a parliament of England can neither make a judge nor justice of the peace.

In conclusion the Governor told us that we had seen and read his Majesty's
letters patent, the commission and instructions from his Royal Highness the
Duke of York, and if we would have a greater share in the government than he
could allow, we must go to the king for it.

Nevertheless some malicious men have aspersed us as betrayers of their liberties and privileges, in subscribing to an address to his Royal Highness, full of
duty and gratitude, whereby his Royal Highness may be encouraged the more to
take us and the welfare of our posterity into his most princely care and consideration.

Neither can any clause in that address bear any other natural sense and construction than our obedience and submission to his Majesty's letters patent, according to our duty and allegiance.

However, that our neighbors and fellow-subjects may be undeceived of the
false aspersions thrown upon us, and the impostures of men disaffected to go-

vernment manifested, lest they should further prevail upon the weakness of others; we, the then deputies and subscribers of the said address, conceive our_ selves obliged to publish this narrative and remonstrance of the several pas_ sages and steps conducting to the present government under which we now live, and we desire that a record hereof may be kept in each town, that future ages may not be seasoned with the sour malice of such unreasonable and groundless aspersions.

Signed by the Deputies.

Dated the 21st day of June, 1666.

No. VI.

Remonstrance of Southampton against the order requiring them to take out a new patent.

Southampton, February 15, 1670.

To the Governor:

Honorable Sir.—We, the inhabitants of this town, do hereby present unto you our humble service, &c. to show our respect to your honor's pleasure, and our obedience to the order of the honorable court of assize—we are bold to manifest herein unto you some reasons why we are unwilling to receive any further patent for our lands, as followeth:

1st, Because, as we have honestly purchased them of the natives, (the proper and natural owners of them,) so also we have already the patent right, lawfully obtained and derived from the honorable Earl of Stirling, we being to pay one fifth part of gold and silver ore, and four bushels of Indian corn yearly.

2dly, Because the injunction laid on persons and plantations by the laws in 1666, to take forth patents for their lands from our then governor, we grounded- ly conceive intended not the plantations on this east end of the island, but only those at the west end who were reduced from a foreign government, even as here· tofore. Those English that came to dwell within the precincts which the Dutch claimed took out land briefs from the Dutch governor.

3dly, Because those of us, who were first beginners of this plantation, put none but ourselves to the vast charge in our transport hither, we greatly hazard- ed our lives (as some lost theirs) here amongst and by the then numerous and barbarously cruel natives; yet through divine Providence we have possessed these our lands above thirty years without interruption or molestation by any claiming them from us, and therefore we cannot, see why we should lose any of our rightful privileges, so dearly and honestly purchased, or how our lands can be better assured to us by taking out another patent from any one.

4thly, And materially because by our said patent we had licence (we being but few) to put ourselves under any of his Majesty's colonies for government, whereupon accordingly, by willing consent on all sides, we adjoined ourselves to Hartford jurisdiction, and divers of us became members of the king's court there, and when the worthy Mr. Winthrop obtained a patent from his Majesty our present lord, King Charles II., for the said colony of Hartford, our town is included, and some of the then chief members of our town expressly nominated in the patent; so that this place became undeniably an absolute limb or part of the said colony; and moreover, since that and after his Majesty's commis- sioners came into these parts, his Majesty of grace and free motion was pleased so far to encourage his people of the said colony, as by his letter to assure them that their ecclesiastical and civil privileges which he had granted them, should not be infringed or diminished by his said commissioners, or any others whatsoever.

5ly, It is not only in all our experience beyond all parallel that each town should be constrained to take forth a patent, but also the patents here imposed and those given forth, which yet we have seen, seem to bind persons and towns in matter of payment to the will and mercy of their lord and his successors, or lieutenants ; and who can tell but in time to come those may succeed who, through an avaricious distemper, may come upon us with such heavy taxes and intolerable burdens, as may make us, or our poor posterity, to groan like Israel in Egypt.

6ly, Because people are enjoined to acknowledge in the said patent (if we mistake not greatly) that his royal highness the Duke of York is sole proprietor of the whole island ; which we cannot consent unto, because we know ourselves to be the true proprietors of the land we here possess, with the appurtenances thereunto belonging, and also because men are enjoined by the said patent to pay not only all just dues, but also all demands that may be made by his royal highness or his authorised agent.

7ly, Because we are more than confident his Majesty will desire no more of us than already we are, even his faithful liege people, who have many of us already taken, and the rest of us are ready to take, the oath of allegiance unto him. Willing we are to pay our just dues in town and to the country, and ready to serve his Majesty with our lives and fortunes ; we are his subjects, and we know that he will not make us slaves to any.

. 8ly, Because General Nichols gave it under his hand that we at this end should have as great privileges as any colony in New-England, and yet we are denied our deputies at the courts ; we are forced to pay customs for goods imported, for which custom hath before been paid to his Majesty's use in England.

9ly, and lastly.—The king's commissioners, in the year 1664, by their proclamation, seemed to demand only the government, with exact and full promise that the people should enjoy whatsoever God's blessing and their own industry had furnished them withal ; and we see not what more a patent can assure us, especially considering that the patents here taken forth by places, or particular persons, secure them not absolutely ; for it seems to us by the order of the court of assizes, even from them who have received a patent, wood and timber may be taken away without leave and without pay ; in all which respects, and some other, we cannot be willing to take forth more patent than we have. And if we do succeed otherwise than we expect, we hope we shall, like good christians, patiently bear the pressure that may be permitted to fall upon us, yet never fail to be fervent votaries for your honor's real happiness.

[Signed by Thomas Halsey, jun. and 49 other inhabitants of the town.]

No. VII.

Of the Quaker Persecutions.

Whether the persecutions formerly practised toward the respectable sect of Christians, called *Quakers*, ought to be ascribed to the peculiar temper and disposition of the age in which they were perpetrated, or to the bigotry of particular sects or individuals, it is not our province to determine ; yet at the same time some account of those unjustifiable outrages upon the rights of conscience and the liberty of speech, seems a necessary part of the duty of the historian. These acts of violence were more particularly frequent and notorious from the year 1647 to 1664, during the administration of Peter Stuyvesant, who appears to have been a zealous and intolerant member of the Dutch Calvinistic church, and disposed to execute the instructions accompanying his commission with the most extravagant rigor. The official oath required by those instructions was, "*the maintenance of the Reformed Religion in conformity to the word and the decrees of the synod of Dordrecht, and not to tolerate in public any other sect.*" By an ordinance of 1656, any one preaching doctrines other than those authorized by the Synod, was finable one hundred, and every one attending thereon, twenty-five guilders. In the spirit of this provision, the governor, in 1656, imprisoned some Lutherans, and in 1658 banished a clergyman of that church. He was reproved for the former by the Dutch West India Company, who directed him to permit the free exercise of their religion to all persons within their own houses; and though commended for the latter, was instructed to use moderate measures in future. Against the Quakers, who had, by their peaceful and prudent conduct, made many converts in some of the western towns on the island, particularly at Jamaica and Flushing, the temper of the governor was violent and revengeful. Orders in writing, or placards, were issued to the town authorities not to entertain members of this *odious sect ;* and the ordinance of 1662 provided, that besides the Reformed religion, no *conventicles* should be holden in *houses, barns, ships, woods,* or *fields*, under the penalty of fifty guilders for each person, man, woman, or child, attending for the first offence ; double for the second ; quadruple for the third ; and arbitrary correction for every other. The importation of *seditious and seducing books*, and the *lodging* of persons arriving in the Province without reporting themselves and taking the oath of allegiance, subjected the offenders to severe penalties. These, with some other causes of discontent, rendered the government very unpopular; and it is probable, that, had not the Province been conquered in 1664 by a foreign power, a revolution would have, in a very short time, been effected by the inhabitants themselves, either with or without the aid of the other colonies.

Materials upon the subject of these Quaker persecutions are both abundant and authentic; yet want of space will necessarily restrict our inquiries within narrow limits, and confine our attention to a few cases of more than ordinary severity. The most prominent individuals against whom these atrocities were committed were—Robert Hodgson, Edward Farrington, William Bowne, William Noble, Edward Peake, Henry Townsend, John Townsend, Edward Hart, John Bowne, Samuel Spicer, and John Tilton. Of Hodgson little more is known than that he was a worthy man, and highly esteemed by the Friends for his intelligence and zeal in defence of civil and religious liberty. The cruel treatment he received from the government drove him from the Province after the termination of his sufferings and imprisonment. Spicer and Tilton, and probably Farrington, came with Baxter and Hubbard to Gravesend in 1643, accompanied by the Lady Moody, from Massachusetts. William Bowne came about the same time to Gravesend, and was a magistrate there in 1657. He afterwards removed with his family, and a few other Quakers, from that town to New Jersey, where they made a purchase, embracing the present county of Middlesex and part of Monmouth. John and Henry Townsend, with their brother Richard, emigrated, it is believed, from Lynn Regis in Norfolkshire, England, to Saugus, (now Lynn,) Massachusetts, a little previous to 1640, and soon after arrived in the New Netherlands. John first located at New Amsterdam, and afterwards with Henry at Flushing; from whence they, with Richard, went to Jamaica, and eventually to Oyster-Bay, where they became large proprietors of land, and the progenitors of a numerous offspring. Their posterity, by repeated intermarriages with the families of that and the neighboring towns, have become very extensively connected, and rank among the most respectable citizens. John Bowne, and his father Thomas Bowne, were among the earliest and most venerable inhabitants of Flushing. They embraced with zeal the opinions and principles of George Fox, and were, with others, on this account, marked out by the minions of arbitrary power, as fit subjects of rigorous and unceasing persecution. It has been mentioned in a former part of this work, that John Bowne was, in 1663, transported to Holland for his supposed heretical opinions, and for which act the Governor was severely reprimanded by the West India Company, whose servant he was. The communication made by the governor and council at the time, and addressed to the directors, was as follows:

"*Honorable, right respectable gentlemen* We omitted in our general letter, the troubles and difficulties which we, and many of our good inhabitants, have since some time met with, and which daily are renewed by the sect called Quakers; chiefly in the country, and principally in the English villages; establishing forbidden *conventicles*, and frequenting those against our published *placards*, and disturbing in this manner the public peace; in so far that several of our magistrates and well-affectioned subjects remonstrated, and complained to us from time to time of their insufferable obstinacy; unwilling to obey our orders or judgments. Among others, has one of their principal leaders, named John Bowne, who, for his transgressions was in conformity to the placards, condemned in an amende of 150 guilders, in *seawant*, who has been under arrest more than three months for his unwillingness to pay, obstinately persisting, in his refusal in which he still continues; so that we at last resolved, or were rather compelled, to transport him in this ship from this province, in the hope that others might, by it, be discouraged. If, nevertheless, by these means no more salutary impression is made upon others, we shall, though against our inclinations, be compelled to prosecute such persons in a more severe manner; on which we previously solicit to be favored with your Honors' wise and foreseeing judgment. With which, after our cordial salutations, we recommend your Honors to God's protection, and remain, Honorable and Right Respectable gentlemen,

"Your Honors' faithful Servants."

"Fort Amsterdam in New Netherlands,
        9th January, 1663."

This man had been arrested, September 1, 1662, charged with harboring Quakers, permitting them to hold their meetings at his house, attending them himself, and suffering his family to attend them. After remaining in prison for some time for the non-payment of his fine, he was offered his liberty on condition of leaving the province, which, refusing to do, he was transported as aforesaid. His father, Thomas Bowne, died at an advanced age, September 18, 1677.

From the first appearance of the Quakers in the jurisdiction, it seems to have been the determination of Governor Stuyvesant to prevent, by every possible means, the dissemination of opinions, which he was pleased to denominate " *sedi_ tious, heretical, and abominable* ;" and the whole sect was always spoken of with the utmost contempt and with the most opprobrious epithets. Among the first that fell under his displeasure was Hodgson. He was accused of holding *conventicles*, and, proceeding toward Hempstead, he was seized by order of Richard Gildersleeve, a magistrate there, and committed to prison. Information being sent to the city, a guard was ordered to bring him before the governor and council. Two women, who had entertained him, were also taken ; one of whom had a young child. These were put into a cart ; and Hodgson being fastened behind it, was dragged through woods by night to the city, and thrust into the dungeon of Fort Amsterdam. On being brought out next day, he was examined, condemned, and sentenced to two years' hard labor, or to pay a fine of 600 guilders. With the latter alternative he was either unable or unwilling to comply, and was again confined, without permission to see or converse with any one. Being afterwards chained to a wheel-barrow and commanded to work, he refused to do so, and was, by order of the court, beaten by a negro with a tarred rope till he fainted : the punishment was continued at intervals to one hundred lashes with the same results. After having been for some months confined, and frequently scourged as before, he was liberated at the solicitations of the governor's sister, and banished from the province. Upon the Dutch records, the case of Henry Townsend is alluded to, who, on the 15th of September, 1657, was condemned in an *amende* of £8 *Flanders*, or else to depart the province within six weeks, upon the penalty of corporal punishment, for having called together *conventicles*. Being a person of great worth and consideration with the people of Flushing, where he had previously resided, they assembled, and addressed a remonstrance to the governor, dated December 27, 1657, in which they acknowledge the receipt of a prohibition to retain or entertain any of the people called Quakers, and say that they cannot *condemn*, nor *stretch out* their hands against them, to *punish, banish,* or *persecute* them, considering it a case of conscience between *God and their own souls.* That the love of peace and liberty extends to *Jews, Turks,* and *Egyptians,* as the *sons of Adam,* condemning *hatred, war,* and *bondage ;* all which they said was according to the patent of their town, which they were unwilling to infringe or violate. This document was subscribed by Edward Hart, as town clerk, and thirty others ; together with John and Henry Townsend of Jamaica, then called Rustdorp. It was presented next day in person by Tobias Feaks, sheriff, one of the signers. The governor was highly incensed, and ordered his attorney-general, Nicasius De Sille, immediately to arrest him. Farrington and Noble, two of the magistrates, signers also, were taken and imprisoned. Hart admitted writing the paper, saying he was requested to do so as containing the sentiments of the village meeting at the house of Michael Milnor. He was therefore imprisoned. On the 8th of January, 1658, the magistrates of Rustdorp informed the governor that the Quakers and their adherents were lodged, and entertained, and *unrelentingly corresponded* in said village, at the house of Henry Townsend ; who, they say, formerly convocated a conventicle of the Quakers, and assisted in it, for which he had been condemned on the 15th of September, 1657, in an amende of £8 Flanders, that had not as yet been paid. He was thereupon cited to appear. John Townsend, who had also been summoned, January 10, on being asked if he had gone with

Hart to persuade Farrington to sign the remonstrance, answered that he had been at Flushing, and visited Farrington as an old acquaintance; and that he had also been at Gravesend, but not in company with the banished female Quaker. The court having suspicions of his favoring the Quakers, he was ordered to find bail for £12, to appear when summoned. On the 15th of January, Henry Townsend attended, and was told by the attorney-general, "*that as he had treated the placards of the director-general and council with contempt, and persisted in lodging Quakers, he should be condemned in an amende of £100 Flanders, to be an example for other transgressors and contumelious offenders of the good order and placards of the director-general and council in New Netherlands, and so to remain arrested till the said amende be paid, besides the costs and mises of justice.*" On the 28th, Sheriff Feaks was brought from prison, and "though (says the record) he confessed that he had received an order of the director-general not to admit in the aforesaid village any of that *heretical and abominable sect* called Quakers, or procure them lodgings, yet did so in the face of the placards; and, what was worse, was a leader in composing a *seditious and detestable chartabel*, delivered by him and signed by himself and his accomplices, wherein they justify the *abominable sect* of the Quakers, *who treat with contempt all political and ecclesiastical authority, and undermine the foundations of all government and religion.*" He was therefore degraded from his office, and sentenced to be banished or pay an *amende* of 200 guilders. On the 26th March, 1658, the governor, in order to prevent as much as possible the consequences of Quaker influence among the people, resolved to change the municipal government of the town of Flushing; and therefore, after formally *pardoning* the town for its *mutinous orders* and resolutions, says, "in future I shall appoint a sheriff, acquainted not only with the English and Dutch language, but with *Dutch practical law;* and that in future there shall be chosen seven of the most reasonable and respectable of the inhabitants, to be called *Tribunes* or *Townsmen;* and whom the sheriff and magistrates shall consult in all cases; and that a tax of twelve stivers per morgen is laid on the inhabitants for the support of an *Orthodox minister;* and such as do not sign a written submission to the same in six weeks, may dispose of their property at their pleasure, and leave the soil of this government."

On the council records of January 8, 1661, it is stated that the governor addressed the people of Jamaica, informing them that he had received their petition for a minister to *baptize* some of their children; and their *information* that the *Quakers and other sects* held private conventicles. He tells them that he had despatched his deputy-sheriff, Resolve Waldron, and one of his clerks, Nicholas Bayard, to take notice thereof, and requiring the inhabitants to give exact information where and in what house such unlawful *conventicles* were kept; what persons had *exercised* therein; what men or women had been present; who called the meeting, and of all the circumstances appertaining thereunto. In consequence of this inquisitorial espionage of the governor's deputy, Henry Townsend was a third time dragged to the city, and again incarcerated in the dungeons at Fort Amsterdam. On the day following, he and Samuel Spicer, who had also given entertainment to a Quaker at his mother's house in Gravesend, were brought from their loathsome prison. It was proved by witnesses procured for the occasion, that Townsend had given lodging to a Quaker, and besides notifying his neighbors, had even allowed him to preach at *his* house and in *his* presence; also, that Spicer was present, both at the meeting at Jamaica and Gravesend, and procured lodging for the Quaker at his mother's house. They were accordingly condemned in an *amende* of 600 guilders each, in conformity to the placard respecting conventicles, and to be imprisoned until the said *amende* be paid ; and further, that the said Henry Townsend be banished out of the province, *for an example to others*. The widow Spicer, mother of Samuel, was also arrested, accused, and condemned in an *amende* of £15 Flanders. The said Henry Townsend having ingenuously acknowledged that he lodged in his house some other friends who are called Quakers, and had a meeting of friends at his house, at which one of them spoke, he was thereupon again sentenced as follows : " *Whereas, Henry Townsend, now a prisoner residing at Rustdorp, was heretofore imprisoned and punished for lodging and retaining some of the sect of Quakers, has done the same de novo, whereby this abominable sect, who vilify both the political magistrates and the ministers of God's holy word, are confirmed and encouraged in their errors, and others are lured and seduced, and led astray from the right road ; all which are cases of the most pernicious consequence, from which nothing can arise but calamities and divisions, directly contrary to the orders of the director-general, and therefore he deserves to be further punished as an example for others. The council having heard the prisoner's confession, condemn him in an amende of £25 Flanders, with an express warning to abstain in future from all such conventicles, on the penalty of being banished from the province.*"

On the 5th of October, 1662, John Tilton and Mary his wife, having been accused and committed before the governor and council of New Amsterdam, of having entertained Quakers and frequented their *conventicles*, were condemned, and ordered to depart from the province before the 20th of November following, upon pain of corporal puishment. It is presumed, that through the influence of Lady Moody, the last sentence was either reversed or commuted for the payment of a fine, as they continued to reside at Gravesend for the remainder of their lives.

Many more instances, with almost equally aggravated circumstances, might be mentioned, showing that the severe reprimand which the governor received from the authorities of Holland was well merited, and ought to have been followed by his expulsion from an office he so unworthily filled. But his power was soon after terminated by the conquest of New-York ; yet his Excellency, though deprived of the government, was nevertheless permitted to retain his large possessions upon Manhattan Island, a good portion of which is still enjoyed by his descendants.

Before closing this interesting article, we will cite an example of Quaker persecution, which took place during the administration of Lord Cornbury, a man of most detestable character, and fully equal to the Dutch Governor for religious intolerance. He in his turn persecuted other sects as well as Quakers, instances of which are adverted to in other parts of this work. The case we now allude to is that of *Samuel Bownas*, a Quaker preacher, who came to America at the beginning of the 18th century. The facts are stated in the journal of his travels afterwards published. He left England on the 24th of March, 1702, and landed in Maryland, where he received a challenge from George Keith, an Episcopal missionary, who had once been a Quaker. He was followed by Keith through Pennsylvania and New Jersey to Long Island, and a meeting being appointed at Hempstead, he preached November 21, 1702, at the house of one Thomas Pearsall. As Keith could not, by other means, silence his adversary, he procured Richard Smith and William Bradford of Hempstead to make an affidavit, charging him with heresy, and for which a warrant was issued by Joseph Smith and Edward Burroughs, justices, for his apprehension. On the 29th, while attending a meeting of friends at Flushing, Cardell the high sheriff, with a posse armed with guns, pitchforks, swords, and clubs, entered the house, and took him prisoner. He appeared before the court at Jamaica, consisting of four justices, Joseph Smith, Edward Burroughs, John Smith, and Jonathan Whitehead, the last of whom, says the prisoner, was a very moderate man, and did much to set him at liberty; but they had a priest with them, who put the worst construction upon every thing he said, and had also a man secreted in a closet to note down what he should say; but the man was so drunk, that in going home he lost his papers, for which great inquiry was made. The justices ordered the prisoner to give bail in £2000, with sureties to appear and answer an indictment, which the prisoner said he would not give, "*were it only three half-pence.*" Justice Whitehead offered himself as bail, and took the prisoner home till next day, when he was committed to gaol in Jamaica for the term of three months. At the end of which, a special commission of oyer and terminer was granted to Chief Justice Bridges, and Robert Miller, Thomas Willet, John Jackson and Edward Burroughs, associates, who met at the county hall in Jamaica. The names of the grand jury were Richard Cornell, Ephraim Goulding, John Clayer, Isaac Hicks, Robert Hubbs, Reginald Mott, Theodore Vanderwick, Samuel Denton, Joseph Mott, Richard Valentine, Nathaniel Coles, Joseph Dickerson, Isaac Doughty, Samuel Emery, John Smith, John Sering, John Oakley, Samuel Hallet, Richard Alsop, John Hunt, James Clement, and William Bloodgood. The jury presented the bill to the court, endorsed "*Ignoramus;*" upon which the judge was very angry, and told the jury that surely they had *forgot their oaths,* and for so doing he could give them some *hard names,* but for the present should forbear. " Is this your verdict (said the judge) touching the quaker?" " It is," said the forman; at which the judge raged, and threatened to "*lay the jury by the heels,* and to impose a fine upon them;" to which one of them replied, if he did, " the matter should soon be exposed in *Westminster-Hall.*" The judge now ordered the prisoner to be kept more close than before, and threatened to send him to London, chained to the deck of a man-of-war, then ready to said for England. " Thomas Hicks, an honest old man, who had been a justice of the province, and was well versed in the law, came to visit me, (says he,) and consoled me with many kind words, saying that they dare not send me out of the country." His old enemy, Keith, published a pamphlet against him, which rather increased the number of his friends. During his imprisonment he learned to make shoes, by which he earned fifteen shillings a week, refusing at the same time all pecuniary aid from his friends. While here, he was visited, he says, by an Indian sachem, who asked him if *he was a Christian;* and being told *yea,* and are *they* not Christians who *keep* you here?" Being told they *called* themselves so, he expressed much surprise, and said, " the *Mang Manetou* (meaning God) looked at the heart." Then the Indian took a piece of coal, and drawing a circle, said, " *they believed the Great Spirit to be all eye, that he saw every thing; all ear, that he heard every thing; and all mind, that he knew every thing.*" At the sitting of the court in October, 1703, the bill was again returned, " *Ignoramus,*" and he was discharged. He visited America again in 1727, and died in England on the 2d of April, 1753.

No. IX.

Of Colonel Smith and his descendants, or the Tangier Smiths.

' COLONEL WILLIAM SMITH was born at Newton near Higham Ferrers, in Northamptonshire in England, February 2d, 1665. It seems that in his youth he was destined for the active scenes of life, and it is not probable that he receiv_ ed either a classical or legal education. He, however, possessed a vigorous mind, with a versatility of genius capable of attaining distinction in any employment to which it was applied. The family probably were attached to the royal cause, as he seems to have been in great favor with Charles II, which was continued during the reigns of James II, William and Mary, and while he continued under Queen Anne.

Charles II, in 1675, appointed him governor of Tangiers, which place, as well as Bombay, was given to him by the king of Portugal as a part of the marriage portion of his wife, Queen Catharine, the daughter of that king; and he proba-bly at the same time gave him the commission of colonel, and the command of the troops necessary to protect an establishment on that barbarous coast. It was intended to make Tangiers a place of trade, and to establish a colony there. The project, however, did not succeed; and in 1683 the place was abandoned, and Col. Smith returned to England. He married Martha, daughter of Henry Tunstall, Esq., of Putney, in the County of Surrey, November 6, 1675.

After his return, he embarked in trade in London, and continued in business until he left he country in July, 1686.

It would also seem that he was for a short time concerned in trade after his ar-rival here, and may have come over for that purpose. There is an entry of a note on the records of Brookhaven, bearing date April 23, 1690, given by Col. Thomas Dongan, the late governor of the province, to Col. Smith, for £993, purporting to be for goods, in which the colonel is styled a-merchant.

Col. Smith arrived with his family at New-York August 6th, 1686. He very early visited Brookhaven, and seems to have taken a fancy to a valuable neck of land there, called Little Neck, which was held in shares by various proprietors, who were in some dispute about the premises. Governor Dongan aided him in effecting the purchase. He wrote to the proprietors, and recommended it to them to sell out to Colonel Smith, as the best mode of terminating the contro-versy, to which a considerable portion of them agreed; and on the 22d of Octo-ber, 1687, Colonel Smith made his first purchase in Brookhaven, of Little Neck, now owned by S. B. Strong Esq., one of his descendants.

In 1689, it is supposed he removed to Brookhaven with his family, and took up his permanent residence there. After his settlement at Brookhaven, he made a purchase of a large tract of country, extending from the country road to the South Bay, and from the Fireplace River to Mastic River, to which the town assented, and which, with his former purchases, was erected into a manor, by the name St. George's manor, by patent of Colonel Fletcher in 1693; and sub-sequent to this he purchased all the lands unpurchased, lying between his for-mer purchase and the bounds of Southampton, which were annexed to his manor by another patent of Col. Fletcher in 1697, whose grants to individuals were so extravagant, that several of them were annulled by an act of the colony legis-ture under the succeeding administration.

Governor Slaughter arrived at New-York March 19th, 1691, and on the 25th he appointed Col. Smith one of the members of the council: he also appointed him one of the commissioners of oyer and terminer, which tried and convicted Leisler and his associates.

The supreme court was established by an act of the legislature, May 6th, 1691; consisting of a chief justice, with a salary of £130; a second judge, with a salary of £100; and three other judges, without a salary. On the 15th, the governor and council appointed Joseph Dudley chief justice, Thomas Johnson the second judge, and Col. Smith, Stephen Van Cortland, and William Pinhorne, the other judges. Col. Smith was at the same time appointed a judge or delegate of the prerogative court for the county of Suffolk.

Col. Fletcher arrived, and took upon him the government, August 29th, 1692. November 11th. 1692, the seat of Joseph Dudley was vacated for non-residence, and Col. Smith was appointed chief justice in his room. On the 8th of June, 1693, he was commissioned to succeed Col. Youngs in the command of the militia of Suffolk county. During the time he held the office of chief justice, the colony was divided into rancorous parties, and the public measures were of course influenced by party spirit; yet he seems to have discharged the duties of his office with great dignity and impartiality. Governor Bellamont, on his arrival, April 2d, 1698, took part with the friends of Leisler, and, as might be expected, removed Col. Smith from the office of chief justice, and on the 30th of October, 1700, appointed Mr. Van Cortland in his stead. He was, however, allowed to retain his place at the council board, as his loyalty was so well known in England, and such his popularity with the ministry, that his Excellency dare not carry his resentment so far as to remove him. The governor died 5th of March, 1701, and John Nanfan, the lieut. governor, being absent from the colony, Col. Smith, president of the council, claimed and exercised the authority of government. This claim was opposed by the adherents of Leisler, and denied by a majority of the assembly, who were of the same party. The minutes of the supreme court, while Col. Smith presided, from Oct. 4, 1693, to Oct. 5, 1700, are preserved in the collections of the New-York Historical Society. In 1702 Lord Cornbury re-appointed him chief justice, which office he held till April, 1703. He continued a member of the council till his death, which took place at his residence upon Little Neck, Setauket, Feb. 18, 1705. The inscription upon his tomb in the family cemetary, is as follows:

" Here lyes intered ye body of ye Honb. Coll. William Smith, Chiefe Justice and President of ye Councill of ye Province of New-Yorke. Born in England at Higham-Ferrers in Northamptonshire Feb. ye 2d. 165⅘, and died at the mansion of St. George, Feb. 18, 170⅘, in ye 51st yeare of his age."

The wife of Col. Smith is said to have been a remarkably intelligent and well bred lady, and eminently skilled in domestic economy. They had three sons, *Henry, William,* and *Charles Jeffery;* the last-named died young and without issue. Henry Smith, like his father, was a gentleman of talents and information, and filled the office of clerk of Suffolk County from 1710 to 1716; was for many years one of the judges of the county and a delegate of the prerogative court, for taking the proof of wills, &c. for the said county. William Smith, the second son of Col. Smith, commonly called Major Smith, settled on a part of his father's purchase at Mastic. *His* son William, who also lived at the same place, was for many years a judge of the court of common pleas of the county, and a member of the first provincial congress: In 1777 he was elected a senator under the state constitution, which office he retained till peace in 1783. His sons were John and William. The former was the late General Smith, a man of good abilities, well acquainted with public business, and greatly respect- ed by the community. He was in office from early life till his death. He was a member of the state legislature for most of the time from 1784 to 1800. In 1788 he was in the convention that adopted the constitution of the United States. In 1799 he was elected a representative in congress, and was continu- ed for four years, from which station he was appointed by the legislatuie of this state a senator in the congress of the United States. In 1814 he was made marshal of the southern district of New-York, which he held till his decease June 25, 1816. His wife, whom he left a widow, was the daughter of the la- mented General Woodhull, and who yet survives. The only daughter of Gen. Smith is the wife of John L. Lawrence, Esq., of New-York. William Smith, brother of General Smith, was a iespectable farmer of Brookhaven, and lived and died upon that part of St. George's manor, since called Longwood, now in possession of his son, William Sidney Smith, Esq.

Col. William Smith, son of Henry and giandson of the chief justice, was likewise a gentleman of consideration and ability. He was cleik of the coun- ty of Suffolk fiom 1730 to 1750, and was also judge of the common pleas for several years before the Revolution. He married Margaret, daughter of Hen- ry Lloyd, Esq, of Lloyd Neck, and had several children. His daughter, Anna, a lady of much amiability and worth, became the wife of the late Judge Selah Strong of Sctauket.

No. X.

Of General Nathaniel Woodhull.

This gentleman was the son of Nathaniel Woodhull, of Brookhaven, a descendant of Richard Woodhull, one of the first settlers of that town, and who is supposed to have left England in consequence of having taken an active pait in favor of liberty a short time before the restoration of Charles II. in 1660. He is named in the original deeds for Jamaica as one of the first proprietors of that town, but settled in Brookhaven soon after. An original letter of Lord Crew to him, dated in 1687, in answer to one of his, is among the papeis of the late Abraham Woodhull, Esq., of Brookhaven, in which he styles him cousin, and speaks of his relations, among whom he enumerates a bishop, and a number of families of the first rank in society. General Woodhull had three brothers younger than himself, Richard, Jesse, and Ebenezer. The first-named graduated at Yale College in 1752, was a tutor there some years, where he died. Jesse and Ebenezer removed to Orange county, where many of their posteiity still ieside.

General Woodhull, the eldest son, was born at Mastic, Long Island, Decem- ber 30, 1722. His early life was passed in assisting his father to cultivate the possession which he afterwards inherited, and his education was such as calcu- lated to fit him for the duties of active life. He was endowed by nature with a strong, discriminating mind and a sound judgment, which soon attracted the notice of his fellow-citizens, and pointed him out as peculiaily qualified for pub- lic usefulness. In 1761 he married Ruth, daughter of Nicoll Floyd, and sister

of General William Floyd. His first public employment was in a military capacity in the war between Great Britain and France, which commenced in
1754 and terminated in 1760. But it is not known that he entered the army before 1758. Previously to that year, the war had been conducted without much
system or vigor, and the French had the superiority in every campaign. Being
appointed a major in the provincial forces of New-York, Mr. Woodhull in 1758
served in that capacity in the army under General Abercrombie, intended for
the reduction of Ticonderoga and Crown Point. He was engaged in the daring, or rather rash assault, ordered by the English General, before the arrival of
the artillery, upon the former place, which, strongly fortified, was defended by a
garrison of more than five thousand, and protected on its only assailable side
by fallen trees, with their branches projecting outward, so cut as to answer the
purpose of a chevaux-de-frize. After an exposed fire of four hours from the
French, during which time every effort of heroic perseverance proved ineffectual in making an impression on the enemy's works, the assailing force was obliged to retire to the southern side of Lake George, with the loss of about two
thousand killed and wounded. Desirous of wiping off the stain of this repulse, General Abercrombie detatched a portion of his army against Cadaraqui,
or Fort Frontinac, (now Kingston,) an important fortress at the communication
of Lake Ontario with the St. Lawrence. Lieut. Col. Bradstreet, with whom
the design originated, commanded the enterprise, having a train of eight cannon and three mortars, and a body of three thousand men, of whom one hundred and fifty were regulars. The rest of the detachment was composed of
Provincials from different places. On the 27th of August, 1758, a combined
operation was made against the fort by land and water. The conduct of the
forces in the boats being committed to Corse and Woodhull, the latter with orders to receive the fire of the fort without returning it, until their troops had
loaded and fired. The resolution with which the operations were conducted dispirited the enemy, whose forces were insufficient to the defence of their works,
and, after a feeble resistance, the garrison struck their colors, and capitulated.
Immense stores of provisions and merchandise, intended for the French forces
in America, sixty pieces of cannon, sixteen mortars, and nine armed vessels,
some carrying eighteen guns, were the fruits of this surrender. Whether Mr.
Woodhull was employed in the campaign of the following year is not ascertained, most of his papers having been destroyed by a fire a few years after his
death. It is believed, however, that he either marched with the force which
General Prideux conducted in 1759, against Niagara, or that led by General
Amherst against Ticonderoga and Crown Point, which last enterprise had a
successful issue. In 1760 he served as colonel of the third regiment of New-
York Provincials, under General Amherst, which marched against Montreal,
and effected the final reduction of Canada. Upon the capitulation of the Marquis De Vaudreul, on the 8th of September, Col. Woodhull, with his troops, returned to New-York, and retired to private life. The removal of French
power from their neighborhood, so dangerous to the colonists, and their con-
sciousness of having efficiently contributed to its achievement, produced, naturally, a more free inquiry into the relative rights of the provinces and the mother
country. The spirit to which this inquiry gave rise was stimulated by the pre-
tentions of Britain that Americans were to be taxed by parliament for the expenses of whatever attacks might be made upon them, occasioned by any wars

of interest or ambition, in which the parent state might engage; and which grew into assertions of a right to tax them in all cases whatsoever. Acts of parliament rashly passed, and sometimes timidly repealed, only served to in. crease the existing discontent, and hasten the impending crisis. Participating, in the general feeling, the Assembly of New-York, at the close of December, 1768, unanimously resolved that no tax *could*, or *ought to be*, imposed on the persons or estates of his majesty's subjects within the colony, but by their *own free gift*, and by their *representatives* in general assembly ; that the rights and privileges of the legislatures could not be abridged, superseded, abrogated or an. nulled ; and that they had a right to consult with the other colonies in matters wherein their liberties might be affected. In consequence of these resolutions, the Governor, Sir Henry Moore, dissolved the assembly on the 2d of January, 1769. The languages and proceedings of the assembly were highly approved by the people of Suffolk, and at the election in the spring of 1769, they return- ed to the assembly Col. Woodhull and William Nicoll, Esq. In their in- structions, drawn for their representatives, the county emphatically express- ed their reliance on the exertions of their members *to preserve their freedom, and the command over their own purses.* The injunction was faithfully observed by Col. Woodhull, who, during the six years that followed, of the continuance of the royal government, was constant in his devotion to the rights of his coun- trymen and his opposition to the court party. In the convention which met in the city of New-York, April 10, 1775, to choose delegates to the continental congress, Col. Woodhull appeared from the county of Suffolk. Pursuant to a recommendation from the New-York local committee, a provincial congress was deputed by the several counties, which met in the city, May 22d, 1775. This body practically asserted its right to entire sovereignty, suspending, in effect, from the time of its organization, and ultimately dissolving and expelling, the royal authority. Col. Woodhull was placed at the head of the delegation from Suffolk. On the 22d of August, 1775, the provincial congress re-organized the militia of this colony into brigades, directing that a brigadier-general, with a major of brigade, be commissioned to the command of each. The militia of Suffolk and Queens constituted one brigade, of which Col. Woodhull was sub- sequently appointed general, and Jonathan Lawrence, Esquire, a member of the provincial congress from Queens, major of brigade. On the 28th of August, 1775, General Woodhull was elected president of the provincial congress, which office he held in the body that succeeded it in 1776. The provincial congress, doubting its powers to conform to the recommendation of the continental con- gress, by erecting a new form of government, to the exclusion of all foreign con- trol, on the 31st of May, 1776, recommended to the electors of the several coun- ties to vest the necessary powers either in their present delegates, or in others to be chosen in their stead. The British army having, on the 30th of June, ap- peared off the harbor of New-York, the provincial congress, on its adjournment that day, directed that the congress in which those new powers were vested, should immediately assemble at White Plains. They did not, in fact, assemble till the 9th of July, 1776, when General Woodhull was chosen president. The declaration of independence, passed on the 4th, had not yet received the unani- mous approbation of the colonies in continental congress, the delegates from the colony of New-York having declined to vote, (although they were personal- ly in favor of the measure, and believed their constituents to be so,) because they were fettered by instructions drawn nearly twelve months before, when the hope of reconciliation was yet cherished. Immediately on this meeting, the new provincial congress unanimously adopted the declaration, (General Woodhull presiding,) on the part of the people of New-York; thus filling the void occasioned by the want of the necessary powers in their delegates at Philadelphia. On the next day they assumed the title of the *representatives of the State of New-York*. The invading army under Lord Howe had landed on Staten Island, and by the command which their naval force secured over the adjacent waters, they were enabled to threaten an attack from this point either upon Long Island or the Island of New-York. General Washington was therefore obliged to divide the force collected to oppose them, a portion of which entrenched themselves at Brooklyn, when the residue was stationed at different places on York Island. The New-York convention had, on the 20th of July, ordered one fourth of the militia of Queens and Suffolk to be drafted; and the second regiment thus obtained, had marched under command of Col. Josiah Smith of Brookhaven, and Col. Jeromus Remsen of Newtown, within the lines at Brooklyn, then commanded by General Sullivan. On the 10th of August General Woodhull's affairs requiring his return home, he obtained leave of temporary absence from the convention, whose sittings had been transferred to Harlaem; and proceeded to his residence at Mastic, seventy-five miles from New-York. On the 22d of August, the uncertainty that had prevailed as to the first point of attack on the part of the invaders, was dispelled by the landing of a portion of their forces at New Utrecht, at the place now called Bath. Aware of the increasing want of provisions among the enemy, and the American army being confined to the lines, the whole stock and produce of Long Island would be in the power of the hostile troops, unless means were promptly used to prevent it. The convention adopted a policy since successfully pursued by the Russians on a larger scale. This was, to deprive the invading foe of supplies, and thus compel their abandonment of the island, by removing the stock and other provisions in the vicinity; and if that could not be effected, by destroying them. Resolutions were accordingly passed on the 24th of August, ordering General Woodhull, or, in his absence, Col. Potter, (Doctor Potter, of Huntington, who had served against the French in 1758-9,) to march, without delay, one half of the western regiment of militia of Suffolk County, with five days' provisions, into the western parts of Queen's County; and that the officers of the militia of Queen's County should immediately order out the whole militia of that county, to effect the desired object. An express being sent with these directions to Major Lawrence, Colonel Potter, and General Woodhull, the latter reached Jamaica on the next day, (Sunday,) and immediately took measures to apprise the convention of his arrival there, and awaited the approach of the forces intended to act under his command. He was, however, doomed to experience not only delay, but disappointment, and his feelings may be more easily imagined than described. The convention were fully aware that the militia to be collected on this emergency would be wholly insufficient to effect the desired object, and more particularly to enable the General to station a force, agreeably to their wishes, on the high grounds in the western part of Queen's County, to repel the ravaging parties of the enemy. In the preceding year it had been found necessary to dispatch some of the troops under the command of General Wooster to Suffolk County, to prevent depredations along its exposed coast, and its armed inhabitants were not now more than competent to the same purpose. In Queen's a majority of the inhabitants were disaffected to the patriotic cause, and rendered the defence of the county much more difficult. The Tories there had, in the preceding month of December, obtained a quantity of arms from the Asia man-of-war; and had even prevented, by their superior numbers at the polls, an election, then attempted, of delegates to the provincial congress; insomuch that a military intervention, under the direction of the continental congress, had become necessary to deprive the Tories of offensive weapons, and to secure to the Whigs the freedom of election. A large body of the Whigs of that county were already embodied in the regiment of Colonel Remsen, and many of those at home were overawed by the neighborhood of the British force, or were employed in preparations for the flight of their families, if fortune should favor the British arms. The convention accordingly deputed a committee to General Washington, advising him of their object; of their apprehension of the insufficiency of the force they had ordered to join General Woodhull; and of their conviction that it would be most conducive to the public welfare that the regiments of Colonels Smith and Remsen should be added. The committe reported on the 26th, that at the conference with General Washington he seemed well pleased, but said he was afraid it was too late. He, however, expressed his willingness to afford every assistance to the convention consistent with the public good; and stated that he would immediately give orders that Smith's and Remsen's regiments should march into Queen's County and join General Woodhull. Notice of this was forwarded to General Woodhull; as well as of the expectation that by the time he received their letter the promised reinforcement would have joined him. On the same day the whole militia that had been collected was assembled at Jamaica, and was found to consist only of about one hundred men, led by Colonel Potter of Suffolk, about forty militia from Queens, and fifty horsemen belonging to the troop of King's and Queen's Counties. With this handful of men, General Woodhull advanced to the westward of Queen's County, agreeably to his orders. Owing, probably, to the receipt of information that increased numbers of the British had disembarked on the preceding day at New Utrecht, the commanding officer at Brooklyn did not detach the second Long Island regiment to join General Woodhull; and by some fatality, the omission was neither communicated to the convention, nor to the expecting General. Disappointed at not meeting the additional troops, without whom he could not post any force on the heights to repel depredations of the enemy, he nevertheless commenced with vigor the execution of the rest of his orders. He placed guards and sentries to prevent communication between the Tories and the enemy; and scouring this and the succeeding day the country southward of the hills in King's, and a considerable part of Newtown and Jamaica, he sent off an immense quantity of stock, collected them toward the great plains, and ordered off a further quantity from near Hempstead. In the mean time his numbers had dwindled (by the anxiety of the militia to reach their homes, and protect or remove their families) to less than a hundred men, who, as well as their horses, were worn down. What they had effected, demonstrated that with the force the convention had expected to place under his command, the object to which they attached so much importance could have been accomplished. The subsequent disasters to the American arms would, however, have rendered its accomplishment useless. Early on the 27th of August, a pass through the hills in King's County, which had been left unguarded by the American troops, was taken possession of by the enemy. The American outposts were surprised, and the army driven, after a sanguinary engagement, within their entrenchments at Brooklyn. Numbers of the British troops during the same day posted themselves on the hills between New-York and Jamaica, and parties of the enemy's horse made incursions into the country within a short distance of the General's force. In this state of things he retired to Jamaica, sending, at different times, two messages to the convention, apprising them of his situation; of the absolute necessity of reinforcements, and of his conviction that the two Long Island regiments could not join him in consequence of the interruption of the communication. Unfortunately, the convention did not sit on that day, and the General receiving no answer, dispatched his brigade-major, who was also a member of that body, to repeat his representation and obtain their orders. The convention, at their meeting on the 28th, still adhered to their former project; believing that by crossing the East River to York Island, and making a detour to Flushing, the two regiments might still reach Jamaica. They accordingly sent Major Lawrence to Gen. Washington with a letter expressing that opinion, and referring him to the brigade-major for explanations as to the means, at the same time they directed the necessary preparations for the transportation and landing of the troops, and receiving soon after a reiteration of the call for an immediate reinforcement, they deputed two of their body, John Sloss Hobart and James Townsend, Esquires, to repair to General Woodhull with instructions and advice. Owing, probably, to the intermediate roads being in possession of the enemy, these gentlemen, it is believed, never reached him.

Whether the express dispatched by Maj. Lawrence, as soon as ordered, on the mission to Gen. Washington, was more successful, is not known. On the same morning the convention forwarded a circular to the committees of the different towns of Connecticut lying upon the Sound, requesting their co-operation in removing the stock from Long Island to that State, and an application to the governor for such force as could be speedily obtained. An application to him had been intermediately made by General Washington to throw over one thousand men upon the island. In the afternoon Maj. Lawrence returned from the American camp, bringing a letter from the commander-in-chief declining the request of the convention for the desired reinforcement; because, in the opinion of himself and his general officers, the men they had were not more than competent to the defence of their lines. The retreat across the river, which was effected on that night, might have been suspected and thwarted if the passage of the second regiment had been attempted in open day. This, no doubt, formed an additional reason for non-compliance. In the mean time Gen. Woodhull, whose notions of military obedience had been formed in the strictest school, was awaiting the expected orders and reinforcements. At this time the situation of Gen. Woodhull was peculiarly embarrassing If he had not received encouragement that he should be relieved, the smallness of his force would have justified an immediate retreat. Every communication from the convention, from whom he received his orders, imported it to be their wish he should retain his station in the western part of Queen's County, and encouraged him to expect a reinforcement. The omission of any intelligence to the contrary, with the delay of the return of his brigade-major, who was detained by the convention, was calculated to strengthen that expectation. To have retreated under these circumstances, would have been a violation of military rules, and in case of relief being sent, would have been deemed highly dishonorable. In this emergency, the General had no counsel but his own honorable feelings to consult, and he adopted the course which they dictated. He resolved not to make a final retreat until he heard from the convention. On the morning of the 28th, he ordered his troops to fall back, and take a station about four miles east of Jamaica, and there to remain until further orders. The General remained at Jamaica till afternoon, in momentary expectation of a message from the convention. He then retired slowly with one or two companions, still indulging the hope of intelligence from the convention, until he fell a sacrifice to his reliance on their vigilance and his own high sense of military honor, which forbid his abandoning the station assigned him, however perilous, before he was assured that relief was hopeless, or he had orders to that effect. A severe thunder-shower, as is supposed, obliged him to take refuge in a public-house about two miles east of Jamaica; he was there overtaken by a detachment of the 17th regiment of British dragoons, and the 71st regiment of British infantry, accompanied by some of the disaffected inhabitants as pilots.

The General immediately, on being discovered, gave up his sword in token of surrender. The ruffian who first approached him, (said to be a Major Baird, of the 71st.) as reported, ordered him to say, *God save the King;* the General replied, "God save us all ;" on which he most cowardly and cruelly assailed the defenceless General with his broad sword, and would have killed him upon the spot if he had not been prevented by the interference of an officer of more honor and humanity, (said to be Major Delancey of the dragoons,) who arrested his savage violence.

The General was badly wounded in the head, and one of his arms was mangled from the shoulder to the wrist. He was taken to Jamaica, where his wounds were dressed, and, with other prisoners, was confined there till the next day. He was then conveyed to Gravesend, and with about eighty other prisoners, (of which number Col. Robert Troup, of New-York, was one,) was confined on board a vessel which had been employed to transport live stock for the use of the army, and was without accommodations for health or comfort. The General was released from the vessel on the remonstrance of an officer who had more humanity than his superiors, and removed to a house near the church in New Utrecht, where he was permitted to receive some attendance and medical assistance. A cut in the joint of the elbow rendered an amputation of the arm necessary. As soon as this was resolved on, the General sent for his wife, with a request that she should bring with her all the money she had in her possession, and all she could procure ; which being complied with, he had it distributed among the American prisoners, to alleviate their sufferings—thus furnishing a lesson of humanity to his enemies, and closing a useful life by an act of charity. He then suffered the amputation, which soon issued in a mortification, which terminated his life September 20th, 1776, in the fifty-fourth year of his age. He left only one child, who is now living on her paternal estate at Mastic, in Brookhaven, and is the widow of the late General John Smith, deceased.

It is said that one of the battalions employed in this inglorious warfare against an unresisting individual was commanded by a Major Crew, a distant kinsman of the General ; and that when he came to be apprized of that fact, and of the circumstances of the case, he was so disgusted, that he either resigned his commission and quit the service, or obtained permission to leave the army and return to England. All the transactions of that period bear the marks of inexperience and improvidence, of precipitation and alarm.   The talents of General Woodhull were peculiarly adapted to a military station.   With personal courage, he possessed judgment, decision, and firmness of character, tempered with conciliating manners, which commanded the respect and obedience of his troops, and at the same time secured their confidence and esteem.

His excellent wife, who had barely arrived soon enough to attend him in his last moments, was permitted to remove his dead body, which was prepared for the purpose by the British surgeons.   Painful as her feelings must have been while attending the mangled corse of her deceased husband and dearest friend, in its slow progress over a distance of seventy miles, she had the satisfaction of reflecting that it was out of the possession of the enemy, and the consolation of depositing it on his own farm, amid the graves of his ancestors.   The cruel treatment of this gallant officer and eminent citizen aroused in every patriotic bosom feelings of indignation.   Nor can the circumstances ever be recollected without admiring the lofty spirit which no extremity could bend to dishonor, nor without disdain and abhorrence of a coward brutality, which vainly seeks for extenuation in the bitter animosities of the times.

It is proper here to state, that the late Chief Justice Marshall, in the Biography of Washington, while narrating the disposition of the American forces immediately prior to the battle of Long Island, fought on the morning of the 27th of August, 1776, makes the following remark : " *The convention of New-York had ordered General Woodhull, with the militia of Long Island, to take post on the high ground as near the enemy as possible ; but he remained at Jamaica, and seemed scarcely to suppose himself under the control of the regular officer commanding on the Island.*"

The unjust imputation contained in this short sentence, upon the well-known character and principles of General Woodhull, and its total variance from facts, make it obvious to every well-informed person that the learned historian was entirely unacquainted with what transpired on the occasion referred to, and had mistaken the circumstances attending the conduct and fate of the unfortunate General.   To remedy, as far as possible, the consequences of this erroneous statement, and rescue the memory of the noble martyr from the grave charge above mentioned. a communication was addressed to Judge Marshall, on the 13th of Feb 1834, by John L. Lawrence, Esq. containing a plain and candid relation of facts relative to the matter above mentioned ; and to which his Honor responded in a manner which was to be expected from a great and generous mind, when convinced of an important error, unconsciously committed.   The letter is as follows :

" Washington, Feb. 21st, 1834.

" Sir :

       " Judge Edwards did me the favor to deliver yesterday evening your letter of the 13th, with the documents to which it refers.   It is to me matter for deep concern and self-reproach that the Biographer of Washington should, from whatever cause, have mis-stated the part performed by any individual in the war of our revolution.   Accuracy of detail ought to have been, and was, among my primary objects.   If in any instance I have failed to attain this object, the failure is the more lamented, if its consequence be the imputation of blame where praise was merited.

" The evidence with which you have furnished me, demonstrate that the small body of militia assembled near Jamaica, Long Island, in August, 1776, was not called out for the purpose of direct co-operation with the troops in Brooklyn, and was not placed by the convention under the officer commanding at that post. It is apparent that their particular object, after the British had landed on Long Island, was, to intercept the supplies they might draw from the country. It is apparent, also, that General Woodhull joined them only a day or two before the battle; and there is every reason to believe that he executed with intelligence and vigor the duty confided to him. I had supposed that the order to march to the western part of Queen's County directed an approach to the enemy, and that the heights alluded to, were between Jamaica and Brooklyn. But I have not the papers which I read at the time from the publications then in my possession. I only recollect the impression they made, that General Woodhull was called into the field for the purpose of aiding the operations from Brooklyn; and that General Washington, knowing the existence of this corps, had a right to count upon it in some slight degree, as guarding the road leading from Jamaica. In this I was mistaken; and in this the mistake of which you complain originated.

" I think, however, you misconstrue it; no allusion is made to the number of the militia under his command, nor to any jealousy of the military officer commanding at Brooklyn; nor is it hinted that the convention had placed him under that officer. I rather infer that it appeared to me to be an additional example of the many inconveniences arising, in the early part of the war, from the disposition of the civil authorities to manage affairs belonging to the military department.

" I wish much that I had possessed the information you have now given me. The whole statement would most probably have been omitted, the fact not being connected with the battle; or, if introduced, have been essentially varied.

"I am, with great respect, your obed't

" John L. Lawrence, Esq.   " J. MARSHALL."
New-York."

Correspondence between General Woodhull and the Convention.

The capture of General Woodhull was one of the most calamitous events of the revolution. It deprived the country of the talents, the experience, and counsels of one of the ablest and most patriotic of her citizens. The cruel and dastardly treatment of a prisoner, especially of his rank and character, after a peaceable surrender, roused a spirit of indignation in the breast of every honest and disinterested man. It contributed to alienate the affections of the people from a country whose officers were capable of such unprincipled barbarity, and to strengthen the determination of all ranks to adhere to the resolution then recently adopted by the continental congress and the convention of this state, to render the United States independent of her control. General Woodhull was as much distinguished for his private and domestic virtues as for his zeal for the rights of his country, and was held in the highest estimation by all those who enjoyed his society, or had he pleasure of an intimate acquaintance with him. His death spread a gloom over Long Island—was universally lamented by the friends of freedom, to whom he was known, as well as by all those to whom he was endeared by social relations; and while the revolution continues to be a subject of gratitude with the people of Long Island, his memory will be cherished among their fondest recollections.

August 25th, 1776, General Woodhull wrote to the convention. His letter cannot be found, but the contents may be inferred from the following answer:

August 26th, 1776.

Sir—Your's of yesterday is just come to hand, in answer to which we would inform you that Robert Townsend, the son of Samuel Townsend, Esq., is appointed commissary for the troops under your command, of which we hope you will give him the earliest notice; and that we have made application to General Washington for the regiments under the command of Cols. Smith and Remsen to join you. He assured our committee that he would issue out orders immediately for that purpose, and we expect that they are upon the spot by this time.

Confiding in your known prudence and zeal in the common cause, and wishing you the protection and blessing of heaven,

We are, with respect, your very
humble servants,
By order, &c.   ABRAHAM YATES, Jun.

To Gen. NATHANIEL WOODHULL.

Jamaica, August 27th, 1776.

Gentlemen—I am now at Jamaica, with less than 100 men, having brought all the cattle from the westward and southward of the hills, and have sent them off with the troops of horse, with orders to take all the rest eastward of this place, to the eastward of Hempstead Plains, to put them into fields, and to set a guard over them. The enemy, I am informed, are entrenching southward, and from the heights near Howard's. I have now received yours, with several resolutions, which I wish it was in my power to put in execution; but, unless Cols. Smith and Remsen, mentioned in yours, join me with their regiments, or some other assistance immediately, I shall not be able; for the people are all moving east, and I cannot get any assistance from them. I shall continue here as long as I can, in hopes of a reinforcement; but if none comes soon, I shall retreat, and drive the stock before me into the woods.

Cols. Smith and Remsen, I think, cannot join me. Unless you can send me some other assistance, I fear I shall soon be obliged to quit this place. I hope soon to hear from you.

I am, gentlemen, your most humble serv't.
NATHANIEL WOODHULL.

To the Hon. Convention of
the State of New-York.

Westward of Queen's County, August 27th, 1776.

Gentlemen—Inclosed I send you a letter from Col. Potter, who left me yesterday at 11 o'clock, after bringing about 100 men to me at Jamaica. Major Smith, I expect, has all the rest that were to come from Suffolk County. There have about 40 of the militia joined me from the regiments in Queen's County, and about 50 of the troop belonging to King's and Queen's counties, which is nearly all I expect. I have got all the cattle southward of the hills in King's County, to the eastward of the cross-road between the two counties, and have placed guards and sentinels from the north road to the south side of the island, in order to prevent the cattle's going back, and to prevent the communication of the Tories with the enemy. I am within about six miles of the enemy's camp: their light horse have been within about two miles, and, unless I have more men, our stay here will answer no purpose. We shall soon want to be supplied with provisions, if we tarry here.

I am, gentlemen, your most ob'dt. humble serv't.

NATHANIEL WOODHULL.

The Hon. Convention of New-
    York, at Harlaem.

Jamaica, August 28th, 1776.

Gentlemen—I wrote two letters to you yesterday, one by express and another by Mr. Harper, and also sent my brigade-major to you, to let you know my situation, and I expected an answer to one of them last night; but my express informed me that he was detained till last night for an answer.

I have now received yours of the 26th, which is only a copy of the last, without a single word of answer to my letter, or the message by my brigade-major. I must again let you know my situation. I have about 70 men and about 20 of the troop, which is all the force I have or can expect, and I am daily growing less in number. The people are so alarmed in Suffolk, that they will not any more of them march; and as to Cols. Smith and Remsen, they cannot join me, for the communication is cut off between us. I have sent about 1100 cattle to the great fields on the plains yesterday. About 300 more have gone off this morning to the same place, and I have ordered a guard of an officer and seven privates. They can get no water in those fields. My men and horses are worn out with fatigue. The cattle are not all gone off towards Hempstead. I ordered them off yesterday; but they were not able to take them along. I yesterday brought about 300 from Newtown. I think the cattle are in as much danger on the north side as on the south side; and have ordered the inhabitants to remove them, if you cannot send me an immediate reinforcement.

I am, &c.

NATHANIEL WOODHULL.

The Hon. Convention of
    New-York.

Correspondence between the Convention and General Washington.

Wednesday morning, Aug. 28th, 1776.

Sir—I am commanded by the convention to enclose to your Excellency the copy of a letter they received last evening from General Woodhull. The convention are of opinion that the enemy may be prevented from getting the stock and grain on Long Island if the regiments under the command of Col. Smith and Col. Remsen be sent to join Gen. Woodhull. That this junction may effected, and how, Major Lawrence, who is a member of this convention and the bearer hereof, will inform your Excellency.

I have the honor to be, with great respect,

Your Excellency's most obedient servant,

By order, ABRAHAM YATES.

His Excellency Gen. WASHINGTON.

Long Island, Aug. 28th, 1776.

Sir—I was just now honored with your favor of this date, with General Woodhull's letter, and should esteem myself happy, were it in my power to afford the assistance required ; but the enemy having landed a considerable part of their force here, and at the same time may have reserved some to attack New-York, it is the opinion, not only of myself, but of all my general officers I have had an opportunity of consulting with, that the men we have are not more than competent to the defence of those lines, and the several posts which must be defended. This reason, and this alone, prevents my complying with your request. I shall beg leave to mention, in confidence, that a few days ago, upon the enemy's first landing here, I wrote to Governor Trumbull, recommending him to throw over a body of 1000 men on the island to annoy the enemy in their rear, if the state of the colony would admit of it. Whether it will be done I cannot determine. That colony having furnished a large proportion of men, I was, and still am, doubtful whether it could be done. If it could, I am satisfied it will, from the zeal and readiness they have ever shown to give every possible succor. I am hopeful they will be in a condition to do it; and if they are, those troops, I doubt not, will be ready and willing to give General Woodhull any assistance he may want. But cannot the militia effect what he wishes to do? They, I believe, must be depended on in the present instance for relief.

I have the honor to be, in great haste,

Sir, your most obedient servant,

GEORGE WASHINGTON.

The Hon. ABRAHAM YATES.

Continuation of the correspondence by the Committee of Safety.

King's Bridge, Aug. 30th, 1776.

Sir—In our way to Fishkill, agreeable to an adjournment of the convention, we are informed that the army on Long Island is removed to the city of New-York; and anxiety to know the fact, as well as to be informed whether you think any measures necessary for us to take, induces us to trouble your Excellency at this time for an answer hereto. We have ordered, last night, all the militia of the counties of Ulster, Dutchess, Orange, and Westchester, to be ready, on a minute's warning, with five days' provisions. We shall wait the return of our messenger at this place, and are,

Sir, your most obed't and very humble serv't.

By order. ABRAHAM YATES, Jun.

His Excellency Gen. WASHINGTON.

August 30th, 1776.

Sir—Your favor of this date is just come to hand. Circumstanced as this army was, in respect to situation, strength, &c. it was the unanimous advice of a council of general officers to give up Long Island, and not, by dividing our force, be unable to resist the enemy in any one point of attack. This reason, added to some others, particularly the fear of having our communication cut off from the main, of which there seemed no small probability, and the extreme fatigue our troops were laid under in guarding such extensive lines without proper shelter from the weather, induced the above resolution. It is the most intricate thing in the world, Sir, to know in what manner to conduct one's self with respect to the militia. If you do not begin many days before they are wanted to raise them, you cannot have them in time. If you do, they get tired and return, besides being under very little order or government, whilst in the service. However, if the enemy have a design of serving us at this place, as we apprehend they meant to do on Long Island, it might not be improper to have a body in readiness, to prevent or retard a landing of them east of Harlaem river, if need be.   In haste, and not a little fatigued,

I remain, with great respect and esteem,

Sir, your most obedient humble servant,

GEORGE WASHINGTON.

The Hon. ABRAHAM YATES, Esq.

No. XI.

Of the Battle of Long Island.

After the commencement of hostilities in 1776, New-York being situated near the centre of the colonial sea-board, and readily accessible from the sea, was selected by the enemy as a principal point for their future operations. With this view, a first division of their army arrived at Staten Island in the latter part of June of that year, followed, about the middle of July, by the grand armament under Lord Howe, consisting of six ships of the line, thirty frigates, with smaller armed vessels, and a great number of transports, victuallers, and ships with ordinance.

The Americans anticipating the invasion of Long Island, had fortified Brooklyn before the arrival of the British at Staten Island. A line of intrenchment was formed from a ditch near the late Toll-House of the Bridge Company at the Navy-yard to Fort Green, then called Fort Putnam, and from thence to Freek's mill-pond. A strong work was erected on the lands of Johannis Debevoice and of Van Brunt; a redoubt was thrown up on Bæmus' Hill opposite Brown's mill, and another on the land of John Johnson, west of Fort Green. Ponkiesberg, now Fort Swift, was fortified, and a fort built on the land of Mr. Hicks on Brooklyn Heights. Such were the defences of Brooklyn in 1776, while a *chevaux de frise* was sunk in the main channel of the river below New-York. The troops of both divisions of the British army were landed on Staten Island after their arrival in the bay, to recruit their strength and prepare for the coming conflict. It was not till the middle of August, that a first landing on Long Island was made by them at New Utrecht. Here they were joined by many royalists from the neighborhood, who probably acted the infamous part of informers and guides to the enemy. General Sir Henry Clinton arrived about the same time, with the troops re-conducted from the expedition to Charleston."

Commodore Hotham already appeared there with the reinforcements under his escort; so that in a short time the hostile army amounted to about twenty-four thousand men; English, Hessians, and Waldeckers. Several regiments of Hessian infantry were expected to arrive shortly, when the army would be swelled to the number of thirty-five thousand combatants, of the best troops of Europe, all abundantly supplied with arms and ammunition, and manifesting an extreme ardor for the service of their king. The plan was, first to get possession of New-York, which was deemed of most essential importance. Then, if General Carleton, after having passed, as was hoped, the lakes of Canada, could penetrate to the banks of the Hudson, and descend this river at the same time that General Howe should ascend it, their junction would have the immediate effect of interrupting all communication between the provinces of New-England, on the left bank, and those of the middle and south upon the right. While General Howe was seconded in his invasion of New-York by the twelve or thirteen thousand men coming from Canada under Governor Carleton, General Clinton was to operate in the provinces of the south, and to attack Charleston. The American troops being thus divided, and their generals surprised and pressed on so many sides at once, it was not doubted but that the British arms would soon obtain a complete triumph. But, in executing this design, they had counted too much on an admirable concurrence of a great number of parts, and had not taken into account the difficulties of the winds and seasons. Admiral Howe did not arrive until after Clinton's expedition of Charleston had totally miscarried. The army at Canada was entirely interrupted at the lakes. It was still, however, confidently expected that General Howe would be able alone to make a decisive campaign.

To resist this impending storm, Congress had ordained the construction of rafts, gun-boats, galleys, and floating batteries, for the defence of the port of New-York and the mouth of the Hudson. They had also decreed that thirteen thousand of the provincial militia should join the army of Washington, who, being seasonably apprized of the danger of New-York, had made a movement into that quarter; they also directed the organization of a corps of ten thousand men, destined to serve as a reserve in the provinces of the centre. All the weakest posts had been carefully intrenched, and furnished with artillery. A strong detachment occupied Long Island, to prevent the English from landing there, or to repulse them if they should effect a debarkation. But the army of Congress was very far from having all the necessary means to support the burden of so terrible a war. It wanted arms, and it was wasted by diseases. The reiterated instances of the commander-in-chief had drawn into his camp the militia of the neighboring provinces, and some regular regiments from Maryland, from Pennsylvania, and from New-England, which had swelled his army to the number of twenty-seven thousand men; but a fourth of these troops were composed of invalids, and scarcely was another fourth furnished with arms.

The American army, such as it was, occupied the positions most suitable to cover the menaced points. The corps which had been stationed on Long Island, was commanded by Major-General Greene, who, on account of sickness, was afterwards succeeded by General Sullivan. The main body of the army encamped on the island of New-York, which, it appeared, was destined to receive the first blows of the English.

Two feeble detachments guarded Governor's Island and the point of Paulus' Hook. The militia of the province, commanded by the American General Clinton, were posted upon the banks of the Sound, where they occupied the two Chesters, East and West, and New Rochelle. For it was to be feared that the enemy, landing in force upon the north shore of the Sound, might penetrate to Kingsbridge, and thus entirely lock up all the American troops on the island of New-York. Lord Howe made some overtures of peace upon terms of submission to the royal clemency, which, resulting in nothing, decided the British General to attack Long Island. " Accordingly," says Botta, " on the twenty second of August, the fleet approached the *Narrows* ; all the troops found an easy and secure landing-place between the villages of Gravesend and New-Utrecht, where they debarked without meeting any resistance on the part of the Americans. A great part of the American army, under the command of General Putnam, encamped at Brooklyn in a part of the island itself which forms a sort of peninsula. He had strongly fortified the entrance of it with moats and intrenchments; his left wing rested upon the *Wallabout* Bay, and his right was covered by a marsh contiguous to *Gowanus' Cove*. Behind him he had Governor's Island, and the arm of the sea which separates Long Island from the Island of New-York, and which gave him a direct communication with the city, where the other part of the army was stationed under Washington himself. The commander-in-chief, perceiving the battle was approaching, continually exhorted his men to keep their ranks, and summon all their courage: he reminded them that in their valor rested the only hope that remained to American liberty; that upon their resistance depended the preservation or the pillage of their property by barbarians; that they were about to combat in defence of their parents, their wives, and their children, from the outrages of a licentious soldiery; that the eyes of America were fixed upon her champions, and expected from their success on this day either safety or total destruction."

The English having effected their landing, marched rapidly forward. The two armies were separated by a chain of hills, covered with woods, called the heights, and which, running from west to east, divide the island into two parts. They are only practicable upon three points; one of which is near the Narrows, the road leading to that of the centre passes the village of *Flatbush*, and the third is approached, far to the right, by the route of another village called *Flatlands*. Upon the summit of the hills is found a road, which follows the length of the range, and leads from *Bedford* to *Jamaica*, which is intersected by the two roads last described : these ways are all interrupted by precipices, and by excessively difficult and narrow defiles.

The American general, wishing to arrest the enemy upon these heights, had carefully furnished them with troops ; so that, if all had done their duty, the English would not have been able to force the passages without extreme difficulty and danger. The posts were so frequent upon the road from Bedford to Jamaica, that it was easy to transmit, from one of these points to the other, the most prompt intelligence of what passed upon the three routes. Colonel Miles, with his battalion, was to guard the road of Flatland, and to scour it continually with his scouts, as well as that of Jamaica, in order to reconnoitre the movements of the enemy. Meanwhile the British army pressed forward, its left wing being to

the north and its right to the south; the village of Flatbush was found in its
centre. The Hessians, commanded by General Heister, formed the main body;
the English, under Major-general Grant, the left; and other corps, conducted by
General Clinton, and the two lords, Percy and Cornwallis, composed the right.
In this wing the British generals had placed their principal hope of success;
they directed it upon Flatland. Their plan was, that while the corps of General
Grant, and the Hessians of General Heister, should disquiet the enemy upon the
two first defiles, the left wing, taking a circuit, should march through Flatland,
and endeavor to seize the point of intersection of this road with that of Jamaica;
and then rapidly descending into the plain which extends at the foot of the heights
upon the other side, should fall upon the Americans in flank and rear. The English hoped, that as this post was the most distant from the centre of the army,
the advanced guards would be found more feeble there. and perhaps more negli-
gent: finally, they calculated that, in all events, the Americans would not be
able to defend it against a force so superior. This right wing of the English
was the most numerous. and entirely composed of select troops.

The evening of the twenty-sixth of August, General Clinton commanded the
vanguard, which consisted in light infantry: Lord Percy the centre, where were
found the grenadiers, the artillery, and the cavalry; and Cornwallis, the rear-
guard, followed by the baggage, some regiments of infantry and of heavy artillery; all this part of the English army put itself in motion with admirable order
and silence, and leaving Flatland, traversed the country called New Lots. Colonel Miles, who this night perfomed his service with little exactness, did not perceive the approach of the enemy; so that two hours before day the English were
already arrived within a half mile of the road to Jamaica. upon the heights.
Then General Clinton halted, and prepared himself for the attack. He had met
one of the enemy's patrols, and made him prisoner. General Sullivan, who commanded all the troops in advance of the camp of Brooklyn, had no advice of what
passed in this quarter. He neglected to send out fresh scouts; perhaps he supposed the English would direct their principal efforts against his right wing, as
being the nearest to them.

General Clinton, learning from his prisoners that the road to Jamaica was not
guarded, hastened to avail himself of the circumstance, and occupied it by a rapid
movement. Without loss of time he immediately bore to his left towards Bedford, and seized an important defile, which the American generals had left unguarded. From this moment the success of the day was decided in favor of the
English. Lord Percy came up with his corps; and the entire column descended
by the village of Bedford from the heights into the plain which lay between the
hills and the camp of the Americans. During this time General Grant, in order
to amuse the enemy, and divert his attention from the events which took place
upon the route of Flatland, endeavored to disquiet him upon his right: accord-
dingly, as if he intended to force the defile which led to it, he had put himself in
motion about midnight. and had attacked the militia of New-York and of Pennsylvania, who guarded it. They at first gave ground; but General Parsons being arrived, and having occupied an eminence, he renewed the combat, and maintained his position till Brigadier-general Lord Stirling came to his assistance
with fifteen hundred men. The action became extremely animated, and fortune
favored neither the one side nor the other. The Hessians, on their part, had attacked the centre at break of day; and the Americans, commanded by General

Sullivan in person, valiantly sustained their efforts. At the same time the English ships, after having made several movements, opened a very brisk cannonade against a battery established in the little island of Red Hook, upon the right flank of the Americans, who combated against General Grant. This also was a diversion, the object of which was to prevent them from attending to what passed in the centre and on the left. The Americans defended themselves, however, with extreme gallantry, ignorant that so much valor was exerted in vain, since victory was already in the hands of the enemy. General Clinton being descended into the plain, fell upon the left flank of the centre, which was engaged with the Hessians. He had previously detached a small corps, in order to intercept the Americans.

As soon as the appearance of the English light infantry apprized them of their danger, they sounded the retreat, and retired in good order towards their camp, bringing off their artillery. But they soon fell in with the party of royal troops which had occupied the ground on their rear, and who now charged them with fury; they were compelled to throw themselves into the neighboring woods, where they met again with the Hessians, who repulsed them upon the English; and thus the Americans were driven several times by the one against the other with great loss. They continued for some time in this desperate situation, till at length several regiments, animated by an heroic valor, opened their way through the midst of the enemy, and gained the camp of General Putnam; others escaped through the woods. The inequality of the ground, the great numbers of positions which it offered, and the disorder which prevailed throughout the line, were the cause that for several hours divers partial combats were maintained, in which many of the Americans fell.

Their left wing and centre being discomfited, the English, desirous of a complete victory, made a rapid movement against the rear of the right wing, which, in ignorance of the misfortune which had befallen the other corps, was engaged with General Grant. Finally, having received the intelligence, they retired. But, encountering the English, who cut off their retreat, a part of the soldiers took shelter in the woods; others endeavored to make their way through the marshes of Gowan's Cove; but here many were drowned in the waters or perished in the mud; a very small number only escaped the hot pursuit of the victors, and reached the camp in safety. The total loss of the Americans, in this battle, was estimated at more than three thousand men in killed, wounded, and prisoners. Among the last were found General Sullivan, and Brigadier-general Lord Stirling. Almost the entire regiment of Maryland, consisting of young men of the best families in that province, was cut to pieces. Six pieces of cannon fell into the power of the victors. The loss of the English was very inconsiderable; in killed, wounded, and prisoners, it did not amount to four hundred men.

The enemy encamped in front of the American lines; and on the succeeding night broke ground within six hundred yards of a redoubt on the left, and threw up a breast-work on the Wallabout heights, upon the Debevoice farm, commenced firing on Fort Putnam, and reconnoitred the American forces. The Americans were here prepared to receive them; and orders issued to the men to reserve their fire till they could see the eyes of the enemy. A few of the British officers reconnoitred the position, and one, on coming near, was shot by William Van Cotts, of Bushwick. The same afternoon Captain Rutgers, brother of the late Colonel Rutgers, also fell. Several other British troops were killed, and the column which had incautiously advanced, fell back beyond the range of the American fire. In this critical state of the American army on Long Island ; in front a numerous and victorious enemy with a formidable train of artillery, the fleet indicating an intention of forcing a passage up the East River; the troops lying without shelter from heavy rains, fatigued and dispirited, General Washington determined to withdraw the army from the island; and this difficult movement was effected with great skill and judgment, and with complete success. The retreat was to have commenced at eight o'clock in the evening of the 29th, but a strong north-east wind and a rapid tide caused a delay of several hours; a south-west wind springing up at eleven, essentially facilitated it passage from the island to the city ; and a thick fog hanging over Long Island toward morning, concealed its movements from the enemy, who were so near that the sound of their pick-axes and shovels were distinctly heard by the Americans. General Washington, as far as possible, inspected every thing from the commencement of the action on the morning of the 27th; till the troops were safely across the river, he never closed his eyes, and was almost constantly on horseback. After this the British and their allies, the Tories and refugees, had possession of Long Island; and many distressing scenes occurred, which were never made public, and can therefore never be known. The Whigs, who had been at all active in behalf of independence, were exiled from their homes, and their dwellings were objects of indiscriminate plunder. Such as could be taken, were incarcerated in the church of New Utrecht and Flatlands ; while royalists, by wearing a red badge in their hats, were protected and encouraged. It is believed that had Lord Howe availed himself of the advantages he possessed by passing his ships up the river between Brooklyn and New-York, the whole American army must have been almost inevitably captured or annihilated. General Washington saw but too plainly the policy which might have been pursued, and wisely resolved rather to abandon the island than attempt to retain it at the risk of sacrificing his army.

The unfortunate issue of the battle of Long Island was doubtless to be ascribed, in part, to the illness of General Greene. He had superintended the erection of the works, and become thoroughly acquainted with the ground. In the hope of his recovery, Washington deferred sending over a successor till the urgency of affairs made it absolutely necessary : and then General Putnam took the command, without any previous knowledge of the posts which had been fortified beyond the lines, or of the places by which the enemy could make their approach ; nor had he time to acquire this knowledge before the action. The consequence was, that, although he was the commander on the day of the battle, he never went beyond the lines at Brooklyn; and could give no other orders than for sending out troops to meet the enemy at different points. The following is a letter to congress, describing the events of the day, by Colonel Harrison, secretary to the commander-in-chief.

New-York, 8 o'clock P. M:
27 Aug. 1776.

Sir:

I this minute returned from our lines on Long Island, where I left his Excellency the General. From him I have it in command to inform congress, that yesterday he went there, and continued till evening, when, from the enemy's having landed a considerable part of their forces, and from many of their movements, there was reason to apprehend they would make in a little time a general attack. As they would have a wood to pass through before they could approach the lines, it was thought expedient to place a number of men there on the differ- ent roads leading from where they were stationed, in order to harass and an- noy them in their march.. This being done, early this morning a smart engage- ment ensued between the enemy and our detachments, which, being unequal to the force they had to contend with, have sustained a considerable loss; at least many of our men are missing. Among those that have not returned are Ge- neral Sullivan and Lord Stirling. The enemy's loss is not known certainly; but we are told by such of our troops as were in the engagement, and have come in, that they had many killed and wounded. Our party brought off a lieute- nant, sergeant, and corporal, with twenty privates, prisoners.

While these detachments were engaged, a column of the enemy descended from the woods, and marched towards the centre of our lines with a design to make an impression, but were repulsed. This evening they appeared very nu- merous about the skirts of the woods, where they have pitched several tents; and his Excellency inclines to think they mean to attack and force us from our lines by way of regular approaches, rather than in any other manner. To-day five ships of the line came up towards the town, where they seemed desirous of getting, as they turned a long time against an unfavorable wind; and, on my return this evening, I found a deserter from the twenty-third regiment, who in- formed me that they design, as soon as the wind will permit them to come up, to give us a severe cannonade, and to silence our batteries if possible. I have the honor to be, in great haste, Sir, your most obedient.

ROBERT H. HARRISON.

As the two Generals, who commanded in the engagement, were taken prison- ers, no detailed official account of the action was ever reported to the Command- er-in-chief. The following letter from Lord Stirling, and extracts from Ge- neral Sullivan's, contain a few particulars not hitherto published. Lord Stirling was a prisoner on board Lord Howe's ship when he wrote.

Lord Stirling to General Washington.

Eagle, 29 August, 1776.

My Dear General,

I have now an opportunity of informing you of what has happened to me since I had the pleasure of seeing you. About three o'clock in the morning of the 27th, I was called up, and informed by General Putnam that the enemy were advancing by the road from Flatbush to the Red Lion, and he ordered me to march with the two regiments nearest at hand to meet them. These happen- ed to be Haslet's and Smallwood's, with which I accordingly marched, and was on the road to the Narrows just as the daylight began to appear. We pro- ceeded to within about half a mile of the Red Lion, and there met Colonel At- lee with his regiment, who informed me that the enemy were in sight; indeed, I then saw their front between us and the Red Lion. I desired Colonel Atlee to place his regiment on the left of the road, and to wait their coming up; while I went to form the two regiments I had brought with me along a ridge from the road up to a piece of wood on the top of the hill. This was done instantly on very advantageous ground.

66

to send some one competent to the task into the heart of the enemy's camp, and
Colonel Knowlton was charged with the selection of an individual to perform
the delicate and hazardous service. On being informed of the views and wishes
of Washington, Hale, without hesitation, volunteered his services, saying that he
did not accept a commission for fame alone; that he had been some time in the
army without being able thus far to render any signal aid to his country ; and
that he now felt impelled, by high considerations of duty, to peril his life in a
cause of so vital importance when an opportunity presented itself of being useful.   The arguments of his friends were unavailing to dissuade him from
the undertaking; and having disguised himself as well as he could, he left
his quarters at Harlaem Heights, and having an order from the commander-in-
chief to all the American armed vessels to convey him to any point which he
should designate, he was enabled to cross the Sound from Fairfield to Long
Island, and arrived at Huntington about the middle of September, 1776. When he
reached Brooklyn, the British army had taken possession of New-York. He
examined with the utmost caution the fortifications of the enemy, and ascertained
as far as possible their number, position, and future intentions ; and having satisfactorily accomplished the objects of his mission, he again reached Huntington
for the purpose of re-crossing the Sound. While waiting for a passage, a boat
came on shore, which he at first supposed to be from Connecticut, but proved to
be from a British vessel, the Cerberus, lying in the Sound; and on board this
boat, it is said, was a relative of Capt. Hale, a Tory refugee, who recognized and
betrayed him. He had assumed a character which did belong to him, that of
pretending to be what he was not. That he was a *spy*, could no longer be concealed, and he was immediately sent to General Howe at New-York. Here the
parallel between *his* case and that of *Andre* ceases. The latter was allowed
time and an impartial trial before officers of honorable rank and character, and
his last moments were soothed by tenderness and sympathy. Not so with the
former; he was delivered into the possession of the infamous provost-martial,
Cunningham, and ordered immediately for execution, without even the formality
of a trial. The order was performed in a brutal manner on the twenty-first of
September, 1776, and his body was buried on the spot where he breathed his last.
He was, indeed, permitted to consecrate a few previous moments in writing to his
family; but as soon as the work of death was done, even this testimony of affection and patriotism was destroyed, assigning as the cause, " *that the rebels should
never know they had a man in their army who could die with such firmness.*" In
this trying hour the use of a bible and the attendance of a minister, which he desired, were also denied him.   Thus unknown to those around him, with no eye
to pity, or a voice to administer consolation, fell one of the most noble and amiable
youths which America could boast; with this his dying observation, " *that he
only lamented he had but one life to lose for his country.*" Though the manner of
his execution will be abhorred by every friend of humanity, yet there cannot be
a question but that the sentence of death was conformable to the practice of all
civilized nations. It is, however, but common justice to the character of Captain
Hale to state, that his motives for engaging in this service were entirely different
from those which sometimes influence others in like cases. Neither expectation
of promotion or pecuniary reward induced the attempt. A high sense of public
duty, and a hope of being in this way useful to his country, and the opinion
which he had adopted, that every kind of service became honorable by being ne-

cessary, were the motives which prompted him to this hazardous, and, to him, fatal enterprise. To see such an one, in the bloom of youth, influenced by the purest intentions, and emulous of doing good to his beloved country, fall a victim to the policy of nations, must have been wounding even to the feelings of his enemies.

Among other causes of distress in 1776, the want of provisions and clothing was severely felt by the American army. Just previous to the battle of Long Island it was ascertained that an *English sloop*, with supplies of these essential articles, had arrived in the East River, and lay there under the protection of the ship Asia, of ninety guns. Captain Hale conceived the bold project of capturing this sloop, and bringing her into the port of New-York, and found a sufficient number of bold hearts and stout hands to make the attempt. At an hour concerted they passed in a boat to a point of land nearest the sloop, where they lay till the moon was down; and when all was quiet, except the voice of the watchman on the quarter-deck of the Asia, they pulled for the sloop, and in a few minutes were on board. She became their prize, and the goods were distributed to those who needed them in our army.

The father of Captain Hale was born September 28, 1717, and died June 1, 1802; having been a magistrate many years, and several times a representative from Coventry to the state legislature. He had twelve children. John Hale, one of his sons, held the commission of major in the militia of Connecticut, and was frequently a representative in the assembly. He died December 18, 1802. David Hale, another son, was for some years a judge of the county court; and the Rev. Enoch Hale of Westhampton Massachusetts, another son, was a person of extraordinary abilities, and held in high estimation by the clergymen of New England.

A meeting of the citizens of Coventry and the neighboring towns was held on the 25th of November, 1836, at which a society was formed called the HALE MONUMENT ASSOCIATION; for the purpose of taking measures to erect a suitable memorial to the memory of the subject of this notice. An eloquent address was delivered on the occasion, by Andrew T. Judson, Esq., to whom we are indebted for much of the information contained in this brief memoir.

The following poetical tribute to the lamented Hale is from the pen of the late President Dwight:

> "Thus, while fond virtue wished in vain to save,,
> HALE, bright and generous, found a hapless grave;
> With *genius'* living flame his bosom glow'd,
> And *science* charmed him to her sweet abode;
> In *worth's* fair path, adventured far,
> The *pride* of peace, and rising *grace* of war."

As yet no monument has been erected, nor have his ashes ever been recovered. A select committee of congress, on the 19th of January, 1836, recommended an appropriation of one thousand dollars from the treasury of the United States towards carrying the object into effect; but no action was ever had upon it afterwards, and it is much to be feared so praiseworthy a design will be suffered to sleep, perhaps for ever.

No. XII.

Recollections of Brooklyn and New-York in 1776.
(*Communicated to the Editor of the Naval Magazine, by General Jeremiah Johnson.*)

THE enterprising whale-boat privateers-men of our country deserve our notice, although their acts of robbery are censurable. Captains Hyler and Marriner of New Brunswick annoyed the British troops so much, that an armed force was sent to that place to destroy their boats. The object was effected, but the cost was more than it was worth. New boats were immediately built.

Hyler and Marriner cruised between Egg-Harbor and Staten Island. Hyler took several ships, and levied contributions on the New-York fishermen on the fishing-banks. He frequently visited Long Island. He took a Hessian major at night from the house of Michael Bergen, at Gowanus, when his soldiers were encamped near the house. He surprised and took a sergeant's guard at Canausie, from the house of their captain, Schenck. The guards were at supper, and their muskets standing in the hall, when Hyler entered with his men. He seized the arms, and, after jesting with the guard, he borrowed the *silver spoons* for his family ; took a few other articles with all the muskets, and made one prisoner. He sent the guard to report themselves to Colonel Axtell, and returned to New Jersey.

Capt. Hyler also paid a visit to Colonel Lott at Flatlands. The colonel was known to be rich; his money and his person were the objects desired. He was surprised in his house at night, and taken. His cupboard was searched for money, and some silver found ; and, on further search, two bags supposed to contain guineas, were discoveed. These, with the silver, the colonel and two of his negroes, were embarked, and taken to New Brunswick. In the morning, on the passage up the Raritan, the captain and crew agreed to count and divide the guineas. The bags were opened, when, to the mortification of the crew, they found the bags contained only half-pennies belonging to the church of Flatlands ; and the colonel also discovered that his guineas were safe at home. The crew were disappointed in their Scotch prize. They, however, determined to make the most of the adventure ; they took the colonel and his negroes to New Brunswick, where they compelled him to ransom his negroes, and then permitted him to return home on parole.

Captain Hyler also, with two boats, took a corvette of twenty guns, about nine o'clock at night in Coney Island Bay. The ship lay at anchor, bound for Halifax, to complete her crew. The night was dark ; one of the boats, with muffled oars, was rowed up close under the stern of the ship, when the officers were to be seen at a game of cards in the cabin, and no watch on deck. The spy-boat then fell astern to her consort, and reported ; when orders were passed to board. The boats were rowed up silently—the ship boarded instantly on both sides—and not a man was injured. The officers were confined in the cabin, and the crew below. The captain ordered the officers and crew to be taken out the ship, well fettered, and placed in the whale-boats. Afterwards a few articles were taken from the ship, and she was set on fire ; when Captain Hyler left her, with his prisoners, for New Brunswck. My informant, one of the men who took the ship, stated that the captain of the corvette wept as they were crossing the Bay, and reproached himself for permitting one of his Majesty's ships to be surprised and taken " by two d——d egg-shells ;" and he added, that there were $40,000 on board the burning vessel, which Captain Hyler and his crew deserved for their gallant enterprise. The booty, however, was lost.

After the notorious refugee, *Lippencott*, had barbarously murdered Captain Huddy at Sandy-Hook, General Washington was very anxious to have the murderer secured. He had been demanded from the British general, and his surrender refused. Retaliation was decided upon by General Washington. Young Argill was to be the innocent victim to atone for the death of Captain Huddy. He was saved by the mediation of the Queen of France. Captain Hyler determined to take Lippencott. On inquiry, he found that he resided in a well-known house in Broad Street, New-York. Dressed and equipped like a man-of-war press-gang, he left the Kilns with one boat after dark, and arrived at Whitehall about nine o'clock. Here he left his boat in charge of three men, and then passed to the residence of Lippencott, where he inquired for him, and found he was absent, and gone to a cock-pit. Captain Hyler thus failed in the object of his pursuit and visit to the city. He returned to his boat with his *press-gang*, and left Whitehall; but finding a sloop laying at anchor off the Battery, from the West Indies, laden with rum, he took the vessel, cut her cable, set her sails, and with a north-east wind sailed to Elizabethtown Point, and before daylight had landed from her, and secured forty hogsheads of rum. He then burnt the sloop to prevent her re-capture.

Captain Marriner resided many years at Harlaem, and on Ward's Island, after the war. He was a man of eccentric character, witty and ingenious, and abounding in anecdotes; but he had his faults. He had been taken by the British, was on parole in King's County, and quartered with Rem Van Pelt of New-Utrecht. The prisoners among the officers had the liberty of the four southern towns of the county. Many of them frequented Dr. Van Buren's tavern in Flatbush. Here our captain's sarcastic wit, in conversation with Major Sherbrook of the British army, led to abusive language from the Major to the prisoner. After some time Marriner was exchanged, when he determined to capture Major Sherbrook, Colonel Matthews, (the mayor of New-York,) Colonel Axtell, and a Major Bache, who all resided in Flatbush— were noted and abusive Tories, and obnoxious to the American officers. For the purpose of carrying his design into execution, he repaired to New-Brunswick, and procured a whale-boat. This he manned with a crew of well-armed volunteers, with whom he proceeded to New-Utrecht, and landed on the beach at Bath about half past nine o'clock in the evening. Leaving two men in charge of the boat, with the rest of the crew he marched unmolested to Flatbush church, where he divided his men into four squads, assigning a house to each; each party or squad was provided with a heavy post, to break in the doors. All was silent in the village. Captain Marriner selected the house of George Martence, where his friend, the Major, quartered, for himself; the other parties proceeded to their assigned houses. Time was given to each to arrive at its destination; and it was agreed that when Marriner struck his door, the others were to break in theirs, and repair to the church with their prisoners. The doors were broken at the same time. Marriner found the Major behind a large chimney in the garret, where he had hidden himself; and where he surrendered, in presence of his landlady, who lit the way for Marriner. The Major was permitted to take his small clothes in his hand, and thus was marched to the church, where the parties assembled. Mr. Bache was taken. Cols. Axtell and Matthews being at New-

York, escaped capture. The parties marched, with their prisoners, unmolested to their boat, and returned safe to New Brunswick. This event took place about midsummer, on a fine moonlight night.

Captain Marriner also paid Simon Cortelyou of New Utrecht, a visit; and took him to New Brunswick as a return for his uncivil conduct to the American prisoners. He took his tankard, and several articles also, which he neglected to *return*. After Captain Marriner's visit to Flatbush, four inhabitants of New Utrecht were taken separately, and separately imprisoned in the Provost in New-York, on suspicion of having been connected with Marriner in his enterprise; viz: Col. Van Brunt, his brother Adrian Van Brunt, Rem Vanpelt, and his brother Art Vanpelt.

The Connecticut whale-boats rendered Long Island Sound very unsafe to the British, except to strong-armed vessels. The whale-boats visited certain positions along the Sound whenever they pleased; and carried on a trade with New-York in dry goods, &c. to a great amount. The enterprizing and predatory warfare of the American whale-boat-men alarmed the Royalists greatly, and they considered themselves unsafe unless surrounded by an armed force; and many British officers, residing on Long Island, repaired to Brooklyn or New-York. Col. Robertson, who commanded Queen's County, resided at Jamaica. He considered himself safe under the protection of two dragoons, and of the troops usually stationed there.

A Major Stockton, who murdered a miller named Amerman, at Flushing, without justifiable cause or provocation, was tried for the crime at *Bedford*, before a court-martial. The culprit was acquitted for want of surgical evidence that Amerman died of the wound inflicted by him. James Hedges, of Flushing, was murdered in his house by six soldiers of the 54th regiment, who also plundered the house. Five of them were subsequently tried, and two of them, Teach and Porter, were hanged upon land late of Francis Skillman. Some soldiers had killed one of Captain Suydam's cattle of Bedford, three of whom were shot by him while in the act of skinning it. Two other persons were killed in Bushwick, three in Newtown; one at the Half-way House, and others at Jamaica and Flushing.

In the year 1777, two police courts were established—one in the city of New-York, under Mayor Matthews, and another for Long Island, under Judge Ludlow at Jamaica.

In 1777, the continental paper money had depreciated so much, that it was of little value, and it was contrived to borrow money for the use of the army from the Whigs of Long Island. Perfect secrecy was preserved in these transactions; and before the year 1782, loans to a large amount were obtained. Major Hendrick Wyckoff crossed the Sound frequently, and was concealed at the house of Peter Onderdonk at Cow Neck; from thence he came to the house of his father at New-Lots, and by his means a large amount of money was procured, and safely conveyed to head-quarters at Poughkeepsie.

Within the American lines at Brooklyn, during the Revolution, lived a Mr. Rapelje; who being suspected of disaffection to the American cause had been sent by the Whigs to the interior of New Jersey. His wife remained in possession of the house, and probably felt more hostile to the party who had deprived her of her husband than she would have done had he been permitted to remain at home. The house was near the shore, whence General Washington embarked in his memorable retreat from Long Island in August, 1776. She obtained early knowledge of this movement the night it took place, and herself saw the first detachment push off. Thinking it a good opportunity to be revenged upon those who, she believed, had deeply injured her family, she resolved to inform the British of what was taking place among their enemies. She had no one to send, however, with the information, but a black servant; and accordingly dispatched him, with orders to communicate the intelligence to the first British officer he could find. The black succeeded in passing the American sentinels, and made his way to the neighboring camp; but, unluckily for the success of his mission, came to a part of the encampment where the Germans were stationed, and was stopped by a soldier who could not understand English, and to whom consequently, he could not communicate the message. He was committed, therefore, to the guard, as a suspicious person, and kept until morning; when an officer visiting the post examined him, and was informed of what had taken place during the night. The alarm was immediately given, but it was too late—Washington and his troops were all safely landed on the opposite shore.

No. XIII.

Members of Congress from Long Island.

THE following persons were members of the Old Congress, first from the Province, and then from the State of New-York, from 1774 to 1789 ; with the time of taking their seats, viz:

1774, September 5, William Floyd.
1775, May 10, same.
1778, October 15, same.
1779, December 2, same, and Ezra L'Hommedieu.
November 23, William Floyd.
1782, August 28, Ezra L'Hommedieu.
November 27, William Floyd.
1783, August 7, Ezra L'Hommedieu.
1785, January 11, Zepheniah Flatt.
•March 29, Melancton Smith.
1787, January 16, same.

The following named individuals have been elected to congress since the adoption of the constitution of the United States, with the time for which they respectively served, viz:

1789 to 1791, William Floyd.
1791 to 1795, Thomas Tredwell.
1795 to 1799, Jonathan N. Havens.
1799 to 1804, John Smith.
1804 to 1805, Samuel Riker.
1805 to 1807, Eliphalet Wickes.
1807 to 1809, Samuel Riker.
1809 to 1813, Ebenezer Sage.
1813 to 1815, John Lefferts.
1815 to 1817, George Townsend.

1517 to 1829, Silas Wood.
1829 to 1833, James Lent.
1833 to 1837, Abel Huntington.
1837 to the present time, Thomas B. Jackson.

INDEX.

S

T

U

V

W

536   INDEX.

ERRATA.

The reader is requested to correct with his pen the following errors in the text of this work, viz

Page 11, line 6, for 90° read 69°.——13, line 4 from foot, for *east* read west —— 97, line 12 from foot, for 1614 read 1664.——109, line 9 from foot, for *county* read country.——119, line 6, for 1773, read 1673.——130, line 2 from foot, for 1589 read 1689.——133, line 7, for 1679 read 1699.——155, in title, for *Queens* read Suffolk.——158, line 6, for 1778 read 1788.——171, line 13, after *immediately,* insert and.——200, second paragraph, for *Daniel* read David.——261, in title, for *Riverhead* read Brookhaven.——251, line 2 from foot, for *Huntington* read Hunting.——253, lines 11 and 12 from foot, for 1734 and 1737, read 1834 and 1837.——363, line 20, for *north* read south.——394, line 15, for 1810 read 1710. ——405, line 21, after *appointed* insert aid.——416, last line, for 1775 read 1789. ——419, line 26, for wood read wool.——440, line 11, for *principles* read views.

THE END.

CPSIA information can be obtained
at www.ICGtesting.com
Printed in the USA
LVOW01s1610090616

491939LV00027B/593/P